Django 4 By Example
Fourth Edition

Build powerful and reliable Python web applications
from scratch

Antonio Melé

BIRMINGHAM—MUMBAI

Django 4 By Example

Fourth Edition

Copyright © 2022 Packt Publishing

Senior Publishing Product Manager: Manish Nainani
Acquisition Editor – Peer Reviews: Suresh Jain
Project Editor: Amisha Vathare
Content Development Editor: Bhavesh Amin
Copy Editor: Safis Editing
Technical Editor: Aditya Sawant
Proofreader: Safis Editing
Indexer: Sejal Dsilva
Presentation Designer: Pranit Padwal

First published: November 2015
Second edition: May 2018
Third edition: March 2020
Fourth edition: August 2022

Production reference: 2230822

Published by Packt Publishing Ltd.
Livery Place
35 Livery Street
Birmingham
B3 2PB, UK.

ISBN 978-1-80181-305-1

www.packt.com

To my sister Paloma.

Foreword

Django: The web framework for perfectionists with deadlines.

I like this tagline because it can be easy for developers to fall prey to perfectionism when having to deliver workable code on time.

There are many great web frameworks out there, but sometimes they assume too much of the developer, for example, how to properly structure a project, find the right plugins and elegantly use existing abstractions.

Django takes most of that decision fatigue away and provides you with so much more. But it's also a big framework, so learning it from scratch can be overwhelming.

I learned Django in 2017, head-on, out of necessity, when we decided it would be our core technology for our Python coding platform (CodeChalleng.es). I forced myself to learn the ins and outs by building a major real-world solution that has served thousands of aspiring and experienced Python developers since its inception.

Somewhere in this journey, I picked up an early edition of this book. It turned out to be a treasure trove. Very close to our hearts at Pybites, it teaches you Django by **building** interesting, real-world applications. Not only that, Antonio brings a lot of real-world experience and knowledge to the table, which shows in how he implements those projects.

And Antonio never misses an opportunity to introduce lesser-known features, for example, optimizing database queries with Postgres, useful packages like django-taggit, social auth using various platforms, (model) managers, inclusion template tags, and much more.

In this new edition, he even added additional schemas, images, and notes in several chapters and moved from jQuery to vanilla JavaScript (nice!)

This book not only covers Django thoroughly, using clean code examples that are well explained, it also explains related technologies which are a must for any Django developer: Django REST Framework, django-debug-toolbar, frontend / JS, and, last but not least, Docker.

More importantly, you'll find many nuances that you'll encounter and best practices you'll need to be an effective Django developer in a professional setting.

Finding a multifaceted resource like this is hard, and I want to thank Antonio for all the hard work he consistently puts into keeping it up to date.

As a Python developer that uses Django a lot, Django by Example has become my **GO TO** guide, an unmissable resource I want to have close by my desk. Every time I come back to this book, I learn new things, even after having read it multiple times and having used Django for a solid five years now.

If you embark on this journey, be prepared to get your hands dirty. It's a practical guide, so brew yourself a good coffee and expect to sink your teeth into a lot of Django code! But that's how we best learn, right? :)

- Bob Belderbos
Co-Founder of Pybites

Contributors

About the author

Antonio Melé is the co-founder and chief technology officer of Nucoro, the fintech platform that allows financial institutions to build, automate, and scale digital wealth management products. Antonio is also CTO of Exo Investing, an AI-driven digital investment platform for the UK market.

Antonio has been developing Django projects since 2006 for clients across several industries. In 2009 Antonio founded Zenx IT, a development company specialized in building digital products. He has been working as a CTO and technology consultant for multiple technology-based startups and he has managed development teams building projects for large digital businesses. Antonio holds an MSc. in Computer Science from ICAI - Universidad Pontificia Comillas, where he mentors early-stage startups. His father inspired his passion for computers and programming.

About the reviewer

Asif Saif Uddin is a software craftsman from Bangladesh. He has a decade-long professional experience working with Python and Django. Besides working for different start-ups and clients, Asif also contributes to some frequently used Python and Django packages. For his open-source contributions, he is now a core maintainer of Celery, oAuthLib, PyJWT, and auditwheel. He is also co-maintainer of several Django and Django REST framework extension packages. He is a voting member of the Django **Software Foundation** (**DSF**) and a contributing/managing member of the **Python Software Foundation** (**PSF**). He has been mentoring many young people to learn Python and Django, both professionally and personally.

*A special thanks to **Karen Stingel** and **Ismir Kullolli** for reading and providing feedback on the book to enhance the content further. Your help is much appreciated!*

Table of Contents

Chapter 6: Sharing Content on Your Website   239

Chapter 7: Tracking User Actions   287

Chapter 13: Creating a Content Management System   541

Chapter 14: Rendering and Caching Content   579

Preface

Django is an open-source Python web framework that encourages rapid development and clean, pragmatic design. It takes care of much of the hassle of web development and presents a relatively shallow learning curve for beginner programmers. Django follows Python's "batteries included" philosophy, shipping with a rich and versatile set of modules that solve common web-development problems. The simplicity of Django, together with its powerful features, makes it attractive to both novice and expert programmers. Django has been designed for simplicity, flexibility, reliability, and scalability.

Nowadays, Django is used by countless start-ups and large organizations such as Instagram, Spotify, Pinterest, Udemy, Robinhood, and Coursera. It is not by coincidence that, over the last few years, Django has consistently been chosen by developers worldwide as one of the most loved web frameworks in Stack Overflow's annual developer survey.

This book will guide you through the entire process of developing professional web applications with Django. The book focuses on explaining how the Django web framework works by building multiple projects from the ground up. This book not only covers the most relevant aspects of the framework but also explains how to apply Django to very diverse real-world situations.

This book not only teaches Django but also presents other popular technologies like PostgreSQL, Redis, Celery, RabbitMQ, and Memcached. You will learn how to integrate these technologies into your Django projects throughout the book to create advanced functionalities and build complex web applications.

Django 4 By Example will walk you through the creation of real-world applications, solving common problems, and implementing best practices, using a step-by-step approach that is easy to follow.

After reading this book, you will have a good understanding of how Django works and how to build full-fledged Python web applications.

Who this book is for

This book should serve as a primer for programmers newly initiated to Django. The book is intended for developers with Python knowledge who wish to learn Django in a pragmatic manner. Perhaps you are completely new to Django, or you already know a little but you want to get the most out of it. This book will help you to master the most relevant areas of the framework by building practical projects from scratch. You need to have familiarity with programming concepts in order to read this book. In addition to basic Python knowledge, some previous knowledge of HTML and JavaScript is assumed.

What this book covers

This book encompasses a range of topics of web application development with Django. The book will guide you through building four different fully-featured web applications, built over the course of 17 chapters:

- A blog application (chapters 1 to 3)
- An image bookmarking website (chapters 4 to 7)
- An online shop (chapters 8 to 11)
- An e-learning platform (chapters 12 to 17)

Each chapter covers several Django features:

Chapter 1, Building a Blog Application, will introduce you to the framework through a blog application. You will create the basic blog models, views, templates, and URLs to display blog posts. You will learn how to build QuerySets with the Django **object-relational mapper** (**ORM**), and you will configure the Django administration site.

Chapter 2, Enhancing Your Blog with Advanced Features, will teach you how to add pagination to your blog, and how to implement Django class-based views. You will learn to send emails with Django, and handle forms and model forms. You will also implement a comment system for blog posts.

Chapter 3, Extending Your Blog Application, explores how to integrate third-party applications. This chapter will guide you through the process of creating a tagging system, and you will learn how to build complex QuerySets to recommend similar posts. The chapter will teach you how to create custom template tags and filters. You will also learn how to use the sitemap framework and create an RSS feed for your posts. You will complete your blog application by building a search engine using PostgreSQL's full-text search capabilities.

Chapter 4, Building a Social Website, explains how to build a social website. You will learn how to use the Django authentication framework, and you will extend the user model with a custom profile model. The chapter will teach you how to use the messages framework and you will build a custom authentication backend.

Chapter 5, Implementing Social Authentication, covers implementing social authentication with Google, Facebook, and Twitter using OAuth 2 with Python Social Auth. You will learn how to use Django Extensions to run the development server through HTTPS and customize the social authentication pipeline to automate the user profile creation.

Chapter 6, Sharing Content on Your Website, will teach you how to transform your social application into an image bookmarking website. You will define many-to-many relationships for models, and you will create a JavaScript bookmarklet that integrates into your project. The chapter will show you how to generate image thumbnails. You will also learn how to implement asynchronous HTTP requests using JavaScript and Django and you will implement infinite scroll pagination.

Chapter 7, Tracking User Actions, will show you how to build a follower system for users. You will complete your image bookmarking website by creating a user activity stream application. You will learn how to create generic relations between models and optimize QuerySets. You will work with signals and implement denormalization. You will use Django Debug Toolbar to obtain relevant debug information. Finally, you will integrate Redis into your project to count image views and you will create a ranking of the most viewed images with Redis.

Chapter 8, Building an Online Shop, explores how to create an online shop. You will build models for a product catalog, and you will create a shopping cart using Django sessions. You will build a context processor for the shopping cart and will learn how to manage customer orders. The chapter will teach you how to send asynchronous notifications using Celery and RabbitMQ. You will also learn to monitor Celery using Flower.

Chapter 9, Managing Payments and Orders, explains how to integrate a payment gateway into your shop. You will integrate Stripe Checkout and receive asynchronous payment notifications in your application. You will implement custom views in the administration site and you will also customize the administration site to export orders to CSV files. You will also learn how to generate PDF invoices dynamically.

Chapter 10, Extending Your Shop, will teach you how to create a coupon system to apply discounts to the shopping cart. You will update the Stripe Checkout integration to implement coupon discounts and you will apply coupons to orders. You will use Redis to store products that are usually bought together, and use this information to build a product recommendation engine.

Chapter 11, Adding Internationalization to Your Shop, will show you how to add internationalization to your project. You will learn how to generate and manage translation files and translate strings in Python code and Django templates. You will use Rosetta to manage translations and implement per-language URLs. You will learn how to translate model fields using django-parler and how to use translations with the ORM. Finally, you will create a localized form field using django-localflavor.

Chapter 12, Building an E-Learning Platform, will guide you through creating an e-learning platform. You will add fixtures to your project, and create initial models for the content management system. You will use model inheritance to create data models for polymorphic content. You will learn how to create custom model fields by building a field to order objects. You will also implement authentication views for the CMS.

Chapter 13, Creating a Content Management System, will teach you how to create a CMS using class-based views and mixins. You will use the Django groups and permissions system to restrict access to views and implement formsets to edit the content of courses. You will also create a drag-and-drop functionality to reorder course modules and their content using JavaScript and Django.

Chapter 14, Rendering and Caching Content, will show you how to implement the public views for the course catalog. You will create a student registration system and manage student enrollment on courses. You will create the functionality to render different types of content for the course modules. You will learn how to cache content using the Django cache framework and configure the Memcached and Redis cache backends for your project. Finally, you will learn how to monitor Redis using the administration site.

Chapter 15, Building an API, explores building a RESTful API for your project using Django REST framework. You will learn how to create serializers for your models and create custom API views. You will handle API authentication and implement permissions for API views. You will learn how to build API viewsets and routers. The chapter will also teach you how to consume your API using the Requests library.

Chapter 16, Building a Chat Server, explains how to use Django Channels to create a real-time chat server for students. You will learn how to implement functionalities that rely on asynchronous communication through WebSockets. You will create a WebSocket consumer with Python and implement a WebSocket client with JavaScript. You will use Redis to set up a channel layer and you will learn how to make your WebSocket consumer fully asynchronous.

Chapter 17, Going Live, will show you how to create settings for multiple environments and how to set up a production environment using PostgreSQL, Redis, uWSGI, NGINX, and Daphne with Docker Compose. You will learn how to serve your project securely through HTTPS and use the Django system check framework. The chapter will also teach you how to build a custom middleware and create custom management commands.

To get the most out of this book

- · The reader must possess a good working knowledge of Python.
- · The reader should be comfortable with HTML and JavaScript.
- · It is recommended that the reader goes through parts 1 to 3 of the tutorial in the official Django documentation at `https://docs.djangoproject.com/en/4.1/intro/tutorial01/`.

Download the example code files

The code bundle for the book is hosted on GitHub at `https://github.com/PacktPublishing/Django-4-by-example`. We also have other code bundles from our rich catalog of books and videos available at `https://github.com/PacktPublishing/`. Check them out!

Download the color images

We also provide a PDF file that has color images of the screenshots/diagrams used in this book. You can download it here: `https://static.packt-cdn.com/downloads/9781801813051_ColorImages.pdf`.

Conventions used

There are a number of text conventions used throughout this book.

`CodeInText`: Indicates code words in text, database table names, folder names, filenames, file extensions, pathnames, dummy URLs, user input, and Twitter handles. For example: "Edit the `models.py` file of the `shop` application."

A block of code is set as follows:

```
from django.contrib import admin
from .models import Post


admin.site.register(Post)
```

When we wish to draw your attention to a particular part of a code block, the relevant lines or items are set in bold:

```
INSTALLED_APPS = [
    'django.contrib.admin',
    'django.contrib.auth',
    'django.contrib.contenttypes',
    'django.contrib.sessions',
    'django.contrib.messages',
    'django.contrib.staticfiles',
    'blog.apps.BlogConfig',
]
```

Any command-line input or output is written as follows:

```
python manage.py runserver
```

Bold: Indicates a new term, an important word, or words that you see on the screen. For instance, words in menus or dialog boxes appear in the text like this. For example: "Fill in the form and click the **Save** button."

Warnings or important notes appear like this.

Tips and tricks appear like this.

Get in touch

Feedback from our readers is always welcome.

General feedback: Email feedback@packtpub.com and mention the book's title in the subject of your message. If you have questions about any aspect of this book, please email us at questions@packtpub.com.

Errata: Although we have taken every care to ensure the accuracy of our content, mistakes do happen. If you have found a mistake in this book, we would be grateful if you reported this to us. Please visit http://www.packtpub.com/submit-errata, click **Submit Errata**, and fill in the form.

Piracy: If you come across any illegal copies of our works in any form on the internet, we would be grateful if you would provide us with the location address or website name. Please contact us at copyright@packtpub.com with a link to the material.

If you are interested in becoming an author: If there is a topic that you have expertise in and you are interested in either writing or contributing to a book, please visit http://authors.packtpub.com.

Share your thoughts

Once you've read *Django 4 By Example, Fourth Edition*, we'd love to hear your thoughts! Scan the QR code below to go straight to the Amazon review page for this book and share your feedback.

https://packt.link/r/1801813051

Your review is important to us and the tech community and will help us make sure we're delivering excellent quality content.

1

Building a Blog Application

In this book, you will learn how to build professional Django projects. This chapter will teach you how to build a Django application using the main components of the framework. If you haven't installed Django yet, you will discover how to do so in the first part of this chapter.

Before starting our first Django project, let's take a moment to see what you will learn. This chapter will give you a general overview of the framework. The chapter will guide you through the different major components to create a fully functional web application: models, templates, views, and URLs. After reading it, you will have a good understanding of how Django works and how the different framework components interact.

In this chapter, you will learn the difference between Django projects and applications, and you will learn the most important Django settings. You will build a simple blog application that allows users to navigate through all published posts and read single posts. You will also create a simple administration interface to manage and publish posts. In the next two chapters, you will extend the blog application with more advanced functionalities.

This chapter should serve as a guide to build a complete Django application and shall provide an insight into how the framework works. Don't be concerned if you don't understand all the aspects of the framework. The different framework components will be explored in detail throughout this book.

This chapter will cover the following topics:

- Installing Python
- Creating a Python virtual environment
- Installing Django
- Creating and configuring a Django project
- Building a Django application
- Designing data models
- Creating and applying model migrations
- Creating an administration site for your models

- Working with QuerySets and model managers
- Building views, templates, and URLs
- Understanding the Django request/response cycle

Installing Python

Django 4.1 supports Python 3.8, 3.9, and 3.10. In the examples in this book, we will use Python 3.10.6.

If you're using Linux or macOS, you probably have Python installed. If you're using Windows, you can download a Python installer from `https://www.python.org/downloads/windows/`.

Open the command-line shell prompt of your machine. If you are using macOS, open the `/Applications/Utilities` directory in the **Finder**, then double-click **Terminal**. If you are using Windows, open the **Start** menu and type `cmd` into the search box. Then click on the **Command Prompt** application to open it.

Verify that Python is installed on your machine by typing the following command in the shell prompt:

```
python
```

If you see something like the following, then Python is installed on your computer:

```
Python 3.10.6 (v3.10.6:9c7b4bd164, Aug  1 2022, 17:13:48) [Clang 13.0.0
(clang-1300.0.29.30)] on darwin
Type "help", "copyright", "credits" or "license" for more information.
```

If your installed Python version is lower than 3.10, or if Python is not installed on your computer, download Python 3.10.6 from `https://www.python.org/downloads/` and follow the instructions to install it. On the download site, you can find Python installers for Windows, macOS, and Linux.

Throughout this book, when Python is referenced in the shell prompt, we will be using `python`, though some systems may require using `python3`. If you are using Linux or macOS and your system's Python is Python 2 you will need to use `python3` to use the Python 3 version you installed.

In Windows, `python` is the Python executable of your default Python installation, whereas `py` is the Python launcher. The Python launcher for Windows was introduced in Python 3.3. It detects what Python versions are installed on your machine and it automatically delegates to the latest version. If you use Windows, it's recommended that you replace `python` with the `py` command. You can read more about the Windows Python launcher at `https://docs.python.org/3/using/windows.html#launcher`.

Creating a Python virtual environment

When you write Python applications, you will usually use packages and modules that are not included in the standard Python library. You may have Python applications that require a different version of the same module. However, only a specific version of a module can be installed system-wide. If you upgrade a module version for an application, you might end up breaking other applications that require an older version of that module.

To address this issue, you can use Python virtual environments. With virtual environments, you can install Python modules in an isolated location rather than installing them globally. Each virtual environment has its own Python binary and can have its own independent set of installed Python packages in its site directories.

Since version 3.3, Python comes with the venv library, which provides support for creating lightweight virtual environments. By using the Python venv module to create isolated Python environments, you can use different package versions for different projects. Another advantage of using venv is that you won't need any administration privileges to install Python packages.

If you are using Linux or macOS, create an isolated environment with the following command:

```
python -m venv my_env
```

Remember to use python3 instead of python if your system comes with Python 2 and you installed Python 3.

If you are using Windows, use the following command instead:

```
py -m venv my_env
```

This will use the Python launcher in Windows.

The previous command will create a Python environment in a new directory named my_env/. Any Python libraries you install while your virtual environment is active will go into the my_env/lib/python3.10/site-packages directory.

If you are using Linux or macOS, run the following command to activate your virtual environment:

```
source my_env/bin/activate
```

If you are using Windows, use the following command instead:

```
.\my_env\Scripts\activate
```

The shell prompt will include the name of the active virtual environment enclosed in parentheses like this:

```
(my_env) zenx@pc:~ zenx$
```

You can deactivate your environment at any time with the deactivate command. You can find more information about venv at https://docs.python.org/3/library/venv.html.

Installing Django

If you have already installed Django 4.1, you can skip this section and jump directly to the *Creating your first project* section.

Django comes as a Python module and thus can be installed in any Python environment. If you haven't installed Django yet, the following is a quick guide to installing it on your machine.

Installing Django with pip

The `pip` package management system is the preferred method of installing Django. Python 3.10 comes with `pip` preinstalled, but you can find `pip` installation instructions at `https://pip.pypa.io/en/stable/installing/`.

Run the following command at the shell prompt to install Django with `pip`:

```
pip install Django~=4.1.0
```

This will install Django's latest 4.1 version in the Python `site-packages/` directory of your virtual environment.

Now we will check whether Django has been successfully installed. Run the following command in a shell prompt:

```
python -m django --version
```

If you get the output `4.1.X`, Django has been successfully installed on your machine. If you get the message `No module named Django`, Django is not installed on your machine. If you have issues installing Django, you can review the different installation options described in `https://docs.djangoproject.com/en/4.1/intro/install/`.

 Django can be installed in different ways. You can find the different installation options at `https://docs.djangoproject.com/en/4.1/topics/install/`.

All Python packages used in this chapter are included in the `requirements.txt` file in the source code for the chapter. You can follow the instructions to install each Python package in the following sections, or you can install all requirements at once with the command `pip install -r requirements.txt`.

New features in Django 4

Django 4 introduces a collection of new features, including some backward-incompatible changes, while deprecating other features and eliminating old functionalities. Being a time-based release, there is no drastic change in Django 4, and it is easy to migrate Django 3 applications to the 4.1 release. While Django 3 included for the first time **Asynchronous Server Gateway Interface (ASGI)** support, Django 4.0 adds several features such as functional unique constraints for Django models, built-in support for caching data with Redis, a new default timezone implementation using the standard Python package `zoneinfo`, a new `scrypt` password hasher, template-based rendering for forms, as well as other new minor features. Django 4.0 drops support for Python 3.6 and 3.7. It also drops support for PostgreSQL 9.6, Oracle 12.2, and Oracle 18c. Django 4.1 introduces asynchronous handlers for class-based views, an asynchronous ORM interface, new validation of model constraints and new templates for rendering forms. The 4.1 version drops support for PostgreSQL 10 and MariaDB 10.2.

You can read the complete list of changes in the Django 4.0 release notes at `https://docs.djangoproject.com/en/dev/releases/4.0/` and the Django 4.1 release notes at `https://docs.djangoproject.com/en/4.1/releases/4.1/`.

Django overview

Django is a framework consisting of a set of components that solve common web development problems. Django components are loosely coupled, which means they can be managed independently. This helps separate the responsibilities of the different layers of the framework; the database layer knows nothing about how the data is displayed, the template system knows nothing about web requests, and so on.

Django offers maximum code reusability by following the **DRY (don't repeat yourself)** principle. Django also fosters rapid development and allows you to use less code by taking advantage of Python's dynamic capabilities, such as introspection.

You can read more about Django's design philosophies at `https://docs.djangoproject.com/en/4.1/misc/design-philosophies/`.

Main framework components

Django follows the **MTV (Model-Template-View)** pattern. It is a slightly similar pattern to the well-known **MVC (Model-View-Controller)** pattern, where the Template acts as View and the framework itself acts as the Controller.

The responsibilities in the Django MTV pattern are divided as follows:

- **Model** – Defines the logical data structure and is the data handler between the database and the View.
- **Template** – Is the presentation layer. Django uses a plain-text template system that keeps everything that the browser renders.
- **View** – Communicates with the database via the Model and transfers the data to the Template for viewing.

The framework itself acts as the Controller. It sends a request to the appropriate view, according to the Django **URL** configuration.

When developing any Django project, you will always work with models, views, templates, and URLs. In this chapter, you will learn how they fit together.

The Django architecture

Figure 1.1 shows how Django processes requests and how the request/response cycle is managed with the different main Django components: URLs, views, models, and templates:

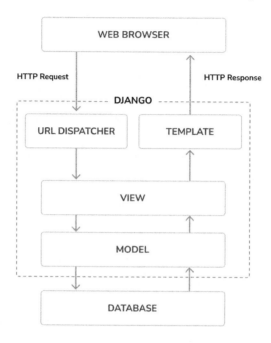

Figure 1.1: The Django architecture

This is how Django handles HTTP requests and generates responses:

1. A web browser requests a page by its URL and the web server passes the HTTP request to Django.
2. Django runs through its configured URL patterns and stops at the first one that matches the requested URL.
3. Django executes the view that corresponds to the matched URL pattern.
4. The view potentially uses data models to retrieve information from the database.
5. Data models provide the data definition and behaviors. They are used to query the database.
6. The view renders a template (usually HTML) to display the data and returns it with an HTTP response.

We will get back to the Django request/response cycle at the end of this chapter in the *The request/response cycle* section.

Django also includes hooks in the request/response process, which are called middleware. Middleware has been intentionally left out of this diagram for the sake of simplicity. You will use middleware in different examples of this book, and you will learn how to create custom middleware in *Chapter 17, Going Live*.

Creating your first project

Your first Django project will consist of a blog application. We will start by creating the Django project and a Django application for the blog. We will then create our data models and synchronize them to the database.

Django provides a command that allows you to create an initial project file structure. Run the following command in your shell prompt:

```
django-admin startproject mysite
```

This will create a Django project with the name mysite.

 Avoid naming projects after built-in Python or Django modules in order to avoid conflicts.

Let's take a look at the generated project structure:

```
mysite/
    manage.py
    mysite/
        __init__.py
        asgi.py
        settings.py
        urls.py
        wsgi.py
```

The outer mysite/ directory is the container for our project. It contains the following files:

- manage.py: This is a command-line utility used to interact with your project. You don't need to edit this file.
- mysite/: This is the Python package for your project, which consists of the following files:
  - __init__.py: An empty file that tells Python to treat the mysite directory as a Python module.
  - asgi.py: This is the configuration to run your project as an **Asynchronous Server Gateway Interface (ASGI)** application with ASGI-compatible web servers. ASGI is the emerging Python standard for asynchronous web servers and applications.
  - settings.py: This indicates settings and configuration for your project and contains initial default settings.
  - urls.py: This is the place where your URL patterns live. Each URL defined here is mapped to a view.
  - wsgi.py: This is the configuration to run your project as a **Web Server Gateway Interface (WSGI)** application with WSGI-compatible web servers.

Applying initial database migrations

Django applications require a database to store data. The `settings.py` file contains the database configuration for your project in the `DATABASES` setting. The default configuration is an SQLite3 database. SQLite comes bundled with Python 3 and can be used in any of your Python applications. SQLite is a lightweight database that you can use with Django for development. If you plan to deploy your application in a production environment, you should use a full-featured database, such as PostgreSQL, MySQL, or Oracle. You can find more information about how to get your database running with Django at `https://docs.djangoproject.com/en/4.1/topics/install/#database-installation`.

Your `settings.py` file also includes a list named `INSTALLED_APPS` that contains common Django applications that are added to your project by default. We will go through these applications later in the *Project settings* section.

Django applications contain data models that are mapped to database tables. You will create your own models in the *Creating the blog data models* section. To complete the project setup, you need to create the tables associated with the models of the default Django applications included in the `INSTALLED_APPS` setting. Django comes with a system that helps you manage database migrations.

Open the shell prompt and run the following commands:

```
cd mysite
python manage.py migrate
```

You will see an output that ends with the following lines:

```
Applying contenttypes.0001_initial... OK
Applying auth.0001_initial... OK
Applying admin.0001_initial... OK
Applying admin.0002_logentry_remove_auto_add... OK
Applying admin.0003_logentry_add_action_flag_choices... OK
Applying contenttypes.0002_remove_content_type_name... OK
Applying auth.0002_alter_permission_name_max_length... OK
Applying auth.0003_alter_user_email_max_length... OK
Applying auth.0004_alter_user_username_opts... OK
Applying auth.0005_alter_user_last_login_null... OK
Applying auth.0006_require_contenttypes_0002... OK
Applying auth.0007_alter_validators_add_error_messages... OK
Applying auth.0008_alter_user_username_max_length... OK
Applying auth.0009_alter_user_last_name_max_length... OK
Applying auth.0010_alter_group_name_max_length... OK
Applying auth.0011_update_proxy_permissions... OK
Applying auth.0012_alter_user_first_name_max_length... OK
Applying sessions.0001_initial... OK
```

The preceding lines are the database migrations that are applied by Django. By applying the initial migrations, the tables for the applications listed in the INSTALLED_APPS setting are created in the database.

You will learn more about the migrate management command in the *Creating and applying migrations* section of this chapter.

Running the development server

Django comes with a lightweight web server to run your code quickly, without needing to spend time configuring a production server. When you run the Django development server, it keeps checking for changes in your code. It reloads automatically, freeing you from manually reloading it after code changes. However, it might not notice some actions, such as adding new files to your project, so you will have to restart the server manually in these cases.

Start the development server by typing the following command in the shell prompt:

```
python manage.py runserver
```

You should see something like this:

```
Watching for file changes with StatReloader
Performing system checks...

System check identified no issues (0 silenced).
January 01, 2022 - 10:00:00
Django version 4.0, using settings 'mysite.settings'
Starting development server at http://127.0.0.1:8000/
Quit the server with CONTROL-C.
```

Now open http://127.0.0.1:8000/ in your browser. You should see a page stating that the project is successfully running, as shown in the *Figure 1.2*:

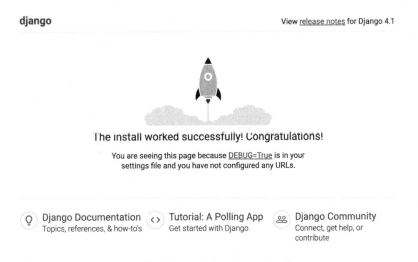

Figure 1.2: The default page of the Django development server

The preceding screenshot indicates that Django is running. If you take a look at your console, you will see the GET request performed by your browser:

```
[01/Jan/2022 17:20:30] "GET / HTTP/1.1" 200 16351
```

Each HTTP request is logged in the console by the development server. Any error that occurs while running the development server will also appear in the console.

You can run the Django development server on a custom host and port or tell Django to load a specific settings file, as follows:

```
python manage.py runserver 127.0.0.1:8001 --settings=mysite.settings
```

 When you have to deal with multiple environments that require different configurations, you can create a different settings file for each environment.

This server is only intended for development and is not suitable for production use. To deploy Django in a production environment, you should run it as a WSGI application using a web server, such as Apache, Gunicorn, or uWSGI, or as an ASGI application using a server such as Daphne or Uvicorn. You can find more information on how to deploy Django with different web servers at https://docs.djangoproject.com/en/4.1/howto/deployment/wsgi/.

Chapter 17, *Going Live*, explains how to set up a production environment for your Django projects.

Project settings

Let's open the settings.py file and take a look at the configuration of the project. There are several settings that Django includes in this file, but these are only part of all the available Django settings. You can see all the settings and their default values at https://docs.djangoproject.com/en/4.1/ref/settings/.

Let's review some of the project settings:

- DEBUG is a Boolean that turns the debug mode of the project on and off. If it is set to True, Django will display detailed error pages when an uncaught exception is thrown by your application. When you move to a production environment, remember that you have to set it to False. Never deploy a site into production with DEBUG turned on because you will expose sensitive project-related data.

- ALLOWED_HOSTS is not applied while debug mode is on or when the tests are run. Once you move your site to production and set DEBUG to False, you will have to add your domain/host to this setting to allow it to serve your Django site.

- INSTALLED_APPS is a setting you will have to edit for all projects. This setting tells Django which applications are active for this site. By default, Django includes the following applications:

    - django.contrib.admin: An administration site
    - django.contrib.auth: An authentication framework

- django.contrib.contenttypes: A framework for handling content types
- django.contrib.sessions: A session framework
- django.contrib.messages: A messaging framework
- django.contrib.staticfiles: A framework for managing static files

- MIDDLEWARE is a list that contains middleware to be executed.
- ROOT_URLCONF indicates the Python module where the root URL patterns of your application are defined.
- DATABASES is a dictionary that contains the settings for all the databases to be used in the project. There must always be a default database. The default configuration uses an SQLite3 database.
- LANGUAGE_CODE defines the default language code for this Django site.
- USE_TZ tells Django to activate/deactivate timezone support. Django comes with support for timezone-aware datetimes. This setting is set to True when you create a new project using the startproject management command.

Don't worry if you don't understand much about what you're seeing here. You will learn more about the different Django settings in the following chapters.

Projects and applications

Throughout this book, you will encounter the terms **project** and **application** over and over. In Django, a project is considered a Django installation with some settings. An application is a group of models, views, templates, and URLs. Applications interact with the framework to provide specific functionalities and may be reused in various projects. You can think of a project as your website, which contains several applications, such as a blog, wiki, or forum, that can also be used by other Django projects.

Figure 1.3 shows the structure of a Django project:

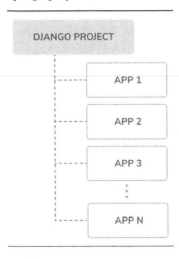

Figure 1.3: The Django project/application structure

Creating an application

Let's create our first Django application. We will build a blog application from scratch.

Run the following command in the shell prompt from the project's root directory:

```
python manage.py startapp blog
```

This will create the basic structure of the application, which will look like this:

```
blog/
    __init__.py
    admin.py
    apps.py
    migrations/
        __init__.py
    models.py
    tests.py
    views.py
```

These files are as follows:

- `__init__.py`: An empty file that tells Python to treat the `blog` directory as a Python module.
- `admin.py`: This is where you register models to include them in the Django administration site—using this site is optional.
- `apps.py`: This includes the main configuration of the `blog` application.
- `migrations`: This directory will contain database migrations of the application. Migrations allow Django to track your model changes and synchronize the database accordingly. This directory contains an empty `__init__.py` file.
- `models.py`: This includes the data models of your application; all Django applications need to have a `models.py` file but it can be left empty.
- `tests.py`: This is where you can add tests for your application.
- `views.py`: The logic of your application goes here; each view receives an HTTP request, processes it, and returns a response.

With the application structure ready, we can start building the data models for the blog.

Creating the blog data models

Remember that a Python object is a collection of data and methods. Classes are the blueprint for bundling data and functionality together. Creating a new class creates a new type of object, allowing you to create instances of that type.

A Django model is a source of information and behaviors of your data. It consists of a Python class that subclasses `django.db.models.Model`. Each model maps to a single database table, where each attribute of the class represents a database field. When you create a model, Django will provide you with a practical API to query objects in the database easily.

We will define the database models for our blog application. Then, we will generate the database migrations for the models to create the corresponding database tables. When applying the migrations, Django will create a table for each model defined in the models.py file of the application.

Creating the Post model

First, we will define a Post model that will allow us to store blog posts in the database.

Add the following lines to the models.py file of the blog application. The new lines are highlighted in bold:

```python
from django.db import models

class Post(models.Model):
    title = models.CharField(max_length=250)
    slug = models.SlugField(max_length=250)
    body = models.TextField()

    def __str__(self):
        return self.title
```

This is the data model for blog posts. Posts will have a title, a short label called slug, and a body. Let's take a look at the fields of this model:

- title: This is the field for the post title. This is a CharField field that translates into a VARCHAR column in the SQL database.
- slug: This is a SlugField field that translates into a VARCHAR column in the SQL database. A slug is a short label that contains only letters, numbers, underscores, or hyphens. A post with the title *Django Reinhardt: A legend of Jazz* could have a slug like *django-reinhardt-legend-jazz*. We will use the slug field to build beautiful, SEO-friendly URLs for blog posts in *Chapter 2, Enhancing Your Blog with Advanced Features*.
- body: This is the field for storing the body of the post. This is a TextField field that translates into a TEXT column in the SQL database.

We have also added a __str__() method to the model class. This is the default Python method to return a string with the human-readable representation of the object. Django will use this method to display the name of the object in many places, such as the Django administration site.

 If you have been using Python 2.x, note that in Python 3, all strings are natively considered Unicode; therefore, we only use the __str__() method. The __unicode__() method from Python 2.x is obsolete.

Let's take a look at how the model and its fields will be translated into a database table and columns. The following diagram shows the Post model and the corresponding database table that Django will create when we synchronize the model to the database:

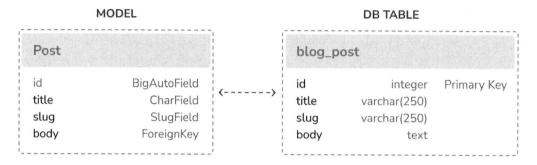

Figure 1.4: Initial Post model and database table correspondence

Django will create a database column for each of the model fields: title, slug, and body. You can see how each field type corresponds to a database data type.

By default, Django adds an auto-incrementing primary key field to each model. The field type for this field is specified in each application configuration or globally in the DEFAULT_AUTO_FIELD setting. When creating an application with the startapp command, the default value for DEFAULT_AUTO_FIELD is BigAutoField. This is a 64-bit integer that automatically increments according to available IDs. If you don't specify a primary key for your model, Django adds this field automatically. You can also define one of the model fields to be the primary key by setting primary_key=True on it.

We will expand the Post model with additional fields and behaviors. Once complete, we will synchronize it to the database by creating a database migration and applying it.

Adding datetime fields

We will continue by adding different datetime fields to the Post model. Each post will be published at a specific date and time. Therefore, we need a field to store the publication date and time. We also want to store the date and time when the Post object was created, and when it was last modified.

Edit the models.py file of the blog application to make it look like this. The new lines are highlighted in bold:

```
from django.db import models
from django.utils import timezone


class Post(models.Model):
    title = models.CharField(max_length=250)
    slug = models.SlugField(max_length=250)
    body = models.TextField()
    publish = models.DateTimeField(default=timezone.now)
    created = models.DateTimeField(auto_now_add=True)
```

```
    updated = models.DateTimeField(auto_now=True)

    def __str__(self):
        return self.title
```

We have added the following fields to the `Post` model:

- `publish`: This is a `DateTimeField` field that translates into a `DATETIME` column in the SQL database. We will use it to store the date and time when the post was published. We use Django's `timezone.now` method as the default value for the field. Note that we imported the `timezone` module to use this method. `timezone.now` returns the current datetime in a timezone-aware format. You can think of it as a timezone-aware version of the standard Python `datetime.now` method.

- `created`: This is a `DateTimeField` field. We will use it to store the date and time when the post was created. By using `auto_now_add`, the date will be saved automatically when creating an object.

- `updated`: This is a `DateTimeField` field. We will use it to store the last date and time when the post was updated. By using `auto_now`, the date will be updated automatically when saving an object.

Defining a default sort order

Blog posts are usually displayed in reverse chronological order (from newest to oldest). We will define a default ordering for our model. The default order will apply when obtaining objects from the database when no order is specified in the query.

Edit the `models.py` file of the `blog` application to make it look like this. The new lines are highlighted in bold:

```
from django.db import models
from django.utils import timezone

class Post(models.Model):
    title = models.CharField(max_length=250)
    slug = models.SlugField(max_length=250)
    body = models.TextField()
    publish = models.DateTimeField(default=timezone.now)
    created = models.DateTimeField(auto_now_add=True)
    updated = models.DateTimeField(auto_now=True)

    class Meta:
        ordering = ['-publish']

    def __str__(self):
        return self.title
```

We have added a Meta class inside the model. This class defines metadata for the model. We use the ordering attribute to tell Django that it should sort results by the publish field. This ordering will apply by default for database queries when no specific order is provided in the query. We indicate descending order by using a hyphen before the field name, -publish. Posts will be returned in reverse chronological order by default.

Adding a database index

Let's define a database index for the publish field. This will improve performance for queries filtering or ordering results by this field. We expect many queries to take advantage of this index since we are using the publish field to order results by default.

Edit the models.py file of the blog application and make it look like this. The new lines are highlighted in bold:

```python
from django.db import models
from django.utils import timezone


class Post(models.Model):
    title = models.CharField(max_length=250)
    slug = models.SlugField(max_length=250)
    body = models.TextField()
    publish = models.DateTimeField(default=timezone.now)
    created = models.DateTimeField(auto_now_add=True)
    updated = models.DateTimeField(auto_now=True)

    class Meta:
        ordering = ['-publish']
        indexes = [
            models.Index(fields=['-publish']),
        ]

    def __str__(self):
        return self.title
```

We have added the indexes option to the model's Meta class. This option allows you to define database indexes for your model, which could comprise one or multiple fields, in ascending or descending order, or functional expressions and database functions. We have added an index for the publish field. We use a hyphen before the field name to define the index in descending order. The creation of this index will be included in the database migrations that we will generate later for our blog models.

   Index ordering is not supported on MySQL. If you use MySQL for the database, a descending index will be created as a normal index.

You can read more information about how to define indexes for models at `https://docs.djangoproject.com/en/4.1/ref/models/indexes/`.

Activating the application

We need to activate the `blog` application in the project, for Django to keep track of the application and be able to create database tables for its models.

Edit the `settings.py` file and add `blog.apps.BlogConfig` to the `INSTALLED_APPS` setting. It should look like this. The new lines are highlighted in bold:

```
INSTALLED_APPS = [
    'django.contrib.admin',
    'django.contrib.auth',
    'django.contrib.contenttypes',
    'django.contrib.sessions',
    'django.contrib.messages',
    'django.contrib.staticfiles',
    'blog.apps.BlogConfig',
]
```

The `BlogConfig` class is the application configuration. Now Django knows that the application is active for this project and will be able to load the application models.

Adding a status field

A common functionality for blogs is to save posts as a draft until ready for publication. We will add a status field to our model that will allow us to manage the status of blog posts. We will be using *Draft* and *Published* statuses for posts.

Edit the `models.py` file of the `blog` application to make it look as follows. The new lines are highlighted in bold:

```
from django.db import models
from django.utils import timezone


class Post(models.Model):

    class Status(models.TextChoices):
        DRAFT = 'DF', 'Draft'
        PUBLISHED = 'PB', 'Published'


    title = models.CharField(max_length=250)
    slug = models.SlugField(max_length=250)
    body = models.TextField()
```

```
publish = models.DateTimeField(default=timezone.now)
created = models.DateTimeField(auto_now_add=True)
updated = models.DateTimeField(auto_now=True)
status = models.CharField(max_length=2,
                          choices=Status.choices,
                          default=Status.DRAFT)


class Meta:
    ordering = ['-publish']
    indexes = [
        models.Index(fields=['-publish']),
    ]


def __str__(self):
    return self.title
```

We have defined the enumeration class Status by subclassing models.TextChoices. The available choices for the post status are DRAFT and PUBLISHED. Their respective values are DF and PB, and their labels or readable names are *Draft* and *Published*.

Django provides enumeration types that you can subclass to define choices simply. These are based on the enum object of Python's standard library. You can read more about enum at https://docs.python.org/3/library/enum.html.

Django enumeration types present some modifications over enum. You can learn about those differences at https://docs.djangoproject.com/en/4.1/ref/models/fields/#enumeration-types.

We can access Post.Status.choices to obtain the available choices, Post.Status.labels to obtain the human-readable names, and Post.Status.values to obtain the actual values of the choices.

We have also added a new status field to the model that is an instance of CharField. It includes a choices parameter to limit the value of the field to the choices in Status.choices. We have also set a default value for the field using the default parameter. We use DRAFT as the default choice for this field.

 It's a good practice to define choices inside the model class and use the enumeration types. This will allow you to easily reference choice labels, values, or names from anywhere in your code. You can import the Post model and use Post.Status.DRAFT as a reference for the *Draft* status anywhere in your code.

Let's take a look at how to interact with the status choices.

Run the following command in the shell prompt to open the Python shell:

```
python manage.py shell
```

Then, type the following lines:

```
>>> from blog.models import Post
>>> Post.Status.choices
```

You will obtain the enum choices with value-label pairs like this:

```
[('DF', 'Draft'), ('PB', 'Published')]
```

Type the following line:

```
>>> Post.Status.labels
```

You will get the human-readable names of the enum members as follows:

```
['Draft', 'Published']
```

Type the following line:

```
>>> Post.Status.values
```

You will get the values of the enum members as follows. These are the values that can be stored in the database for the status field:

```
['DF', 'PB']
```

Type the following line:

```
>>> Post.Status.names
```

You will get the names of the choices like this:

```
['DRAFT', 'PUBLISHED']
```

You can access a specific lookup enumeration member with `Post.Status.PUBLISHED` and you can access its `.name` and `.value` properties as well.

Adding a many-to-one relationship

Posts are always written by an author. We will create a relationship between users and posts that will indicate which user wrote which posts. Django comes with an authentication framework that handles user accounts. The Django authentication framework comes in the `django.contrib.auth` package and contains a `User` model. We will use the `User` model from the Django authentication framework to create a relationship between users and posts.

Edit the `models.py` file of the `blog` application to make it look like this. The new lines are highlighted in bold:

```
from django.db import models
from django.utils import timezone
from django.contrib.auth.models import User
```

```python
class Post(models.Model):

    class Status(models.TextChoices):
        DRAFT = 'DF', 'Draft'
        PUBLISHED = 'PB', 'Published'

    title = models.CharField(max_length=250)
    slug = models.SlugField(max_length=250)
    author = models.ForeignKey(User,
                               on_delete=models.CASCADE,
                               related_name='blog_posts')
    body = models.TextField()
    publish = models.DateTimeField(default=timezone.now)
    created = models.DateTimeField(auto_now_add=True)
    updated = models.DateTimeField(auto_now=True)
    status = models.CharField(max_length=2,
                              choices=Status.choices,
                              default=Status.DRAFT)
    class Meta:
        ordering = ['-publish']
        indexes = [
            models.Index(fields=['-publish']),
        ]

    def __str__(self):
        return self.title
```

We have imported the User model from the django.contrib.auth.models module and we have added an author field to the Post model. This field defines a many-to-one relationship, meaning that each post is written by a user, and a user can write any number of posts. For this field, Django will create a foreign key in the database using the primary key of the related model.

The on_delete parameter specifies the behavior to adopt when the referenced object is deleted. This is not specific to Django; it is an SQL standard. Using CASCADE, you specify that when the referenced user is deleted, the database will also delete all related blog posts. You can take a look at all the possible options at https://docs.djangoproject.com/en/4.1/ref/models/fields/#django.db.models. ForeignKey.on_delete.

We use related_name to specify the name of the reverse relationship, from User to Post. This will allow us to access related objects easily from a user object by using the user.blog_posts notation. We will learn more about this later.

Django comes with different types of fields that you can use to define your models. You can find all field types at https://docs.djangoproject.com/en/4.1/ref/models/fields/.

The Post model is now complete, and we can now synchronize it to the database. But before that, we need to activate the blog application in our Django project.

Creating and applying migrations

Now that we have a data model for blog posts, we need to create the corresponding database table. Django comes with a migration system that tracks the changes made to models and enables them to propagate into the database.

The migrate command applies migrations for all applications listed in INSTALLED_APPS. It synchronizes the database with the current models and existing migrations.

First, we will need to create an initial migration for our Post model.

Run the following command in the shell prompt from the root directory of your project:

```
python manage.py makemigrations blog
```

You should get an output similar to the following one:

```
Migrations for 'blog':
    blog/migrations/0001_initial.py
        - Create model Post
        - Create index blog_post_publish_bb7600_idx on field(s)
        -publish of model post
```

Django just created the 0001_initial.py file inside the migrations directory of the blog application. This migration contains the SQL statements to create the database table for the Post model and the definition of the database index for the publish field.

You can take a look at the file contents to see how the migration is defined. A migration specifies dependencies on other migrations and operations to perform in the database to synchronize it with model changes.

Let's take a look at the SQL code that Django will execute in the database to create the table for your model. The sqlmigrate command takes the migration names and returns their SQL without executing it.

Run the following command from the shell prompt to inspect the SQL output of your first migration:

```
python manage.py sqlmigrate blog 0001
```

The output should look as follows:

```
BEGIN;
--
-- Create model Post
--
```

```
CREATE TABLE "blog_post" (
  "id" integer NOT NULL PRIMARY KEY AUTOINCREMENT,
  "title" varchar(250) NOT NULL,
  "slug" varchar(250) NOT NULL,
  "body" text NOT NULL,
  "publish" datetime NOT NULL,
  "created" datetime NOT NULL,
  "updated" datetime NOT NULL,
  "status" varchar(10) NOT NULL,
  "author_id" integer NOT NULL REFERENCES "auth_user" ("id") DEFERRABLE
INITIALLY DEFERRED);
--
-- Create blog_post_publish_bb7600_idx on field(s) -publish of model post
--
CREATE INDEX "blog_post_publish_bb7600_idx" ON "blog_post" ("publish" DESC);
CREATE INDEX "blog_post_slug_b95473f2" ON "blog_post" ("slug");
CREATE INDEX "blog_post_author_id_dd7a8485" ON "blog_post" ("author_id");
COMMIT;
```

The exact output depends on the database you are using. The preceding output is generated for SQLite. As you can see in the output, Django generates the table names by combining the application name and the lowercase name of the model (blog_post), but you can also specify a custom database name for your model in the Meta class of the model using the db_table attribute.

Django creates an auto-incremental id column used as the primary key for each model, but you can also override this by specifying primary_key=True on one of your model fields. The default id column consists of an integer that is incremented automatically. This column corresponds to the id field that is automatically added to your model.

The following three database indexes are created:

- An index with descending order on the publish column. This is the index we explicitly defined with the indexes option of the model's Meta class.
- An index on the slug column because SlugField fields imply an index by default.
- An index on the author_id column because ForeignKey fields imply an index by default.

Let's compare the Post model with its corresponding database blog_post table:

MODEL	DB TABLE

Post			**blog_post**		
id	BigAutoField		id	integer	Primary Key
title	CharField		title	varchar(250)	
slug	SlugField		slug	varchar(250)	
author	ForeignKey	<------>	author_id	integer	Foreign Key
body	TextField		body	text	
publish	DateTimeField		publish	datetime	
created	DateTimeField		created	datetime	
updated	DateTimeField		updated	datetime	
status	CharField		status	varchar(10)	

Figure 1.5: Complete Post model and database table correspondence

Figure 1.5 shows how the model fields correspond to database table columns.

Let's sync the database with the new model.

Execute the following command in the shell prompt to apply existing migrations:

```
python manage.py migrate
```

You will get an output that ends with the following line:

```
Applying blog.0001_initial... OK
```

We just applied migrations for the applications listed in INSTALLED_APPS, including the blog application. After applying the migrations, the database reflects the current status of the models.

If you edit the models.py file in order to add, remove, or change the fields of existing models, or if you add new models, you will have to create a new migration using the makemigrations command. Each migration allows Django to keep track of model changes. Then, you will have to apply the migration using the migrate command to keep the database in sync with your models.

Creating an administration site for models

Now that the Post model is in sync with the database, we can create a simple administration site to manage blog posts.

Django comes with a built-in administration interface that is very useful for editing content. The Django site is built dynamically by reading the model metadata and providing a production-ready interface for editing content. You can use it out of the box, configuring how you want your models to be displayed in it.

The `django.contrib.admin` application is already included in the `INSTALLED_APPS` setting, so you don't need to add it.

Creating a superuser

First, you will need to create a user to manage the administration site. Run the following command:

```
python manage.py createsuperuser
```

You will see the following output. Enter your desired username, email, and password, as follows:

```
Username (leave blank to use 'admin'): admin
Email address: admin@admin.com
Password: ********
Password (again): ********
```

Then you will see the following success message:

```
Superuser created successfully.
```

We just created an administrator user with the highest permissions.

The Django administration site

Start the development server with the following command:

```
python manage.py runserver
```

Open `http://127.0.0.1:8000/admin/` in your browser. You should see the administration login page, as shown in *Figure 1.6*:

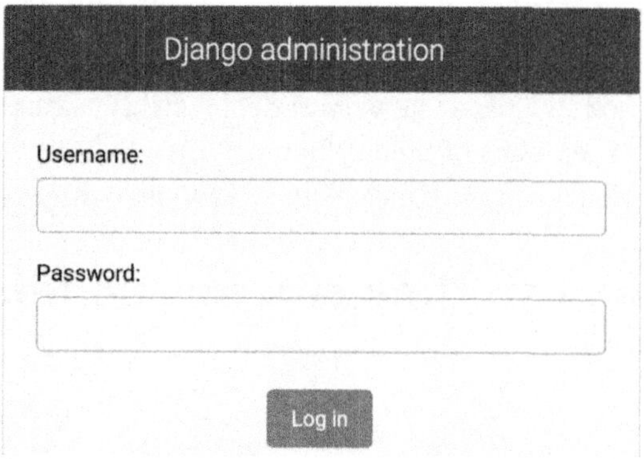

Figure 1.6: The Django administration site login screen

Log in using the credentials of the user you created in the preceding step. You will see the administration site index page, as shown in *Figure 1.7*:

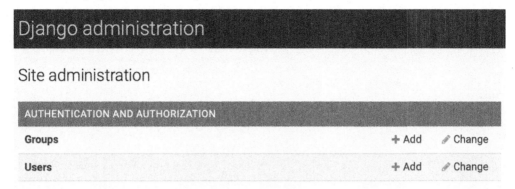

Figure 1.7: The Django administration site index page

The Group and User models that you can see in the preceding screenshot are part of the Django authentication framework located in django.contrib.auth. If you click on **Users**, you will see the user you created previously.

Adding models to the administration site

Let's add your blog models to the administration site. Edit the admin.py file of the blog application and make it look like this. The new lines are highlighted in bold:

```
from django.contrib import admin
from .models import Post

admin.site.register(Post)
```

Now reload the administration site in your browser. You should see your Post model on the site, as follows:

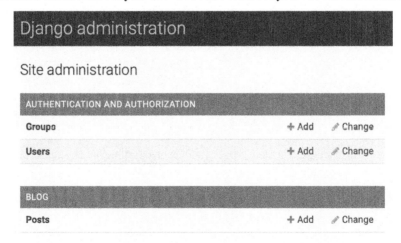

Figure 1.8: The Post model of the blog application included in the Django administration site index page

That was easy, right? When you register a model in the Django administration site, you get a us-er-friendly interface generated by introspecting your models that allows you to list, edit, create, and delete objects in a simple way.

Click on the **Add** link beside **Posts** to add a new post. You will note the form that Django has generated dynamically for your model, as shown in *Figure 1.9*:

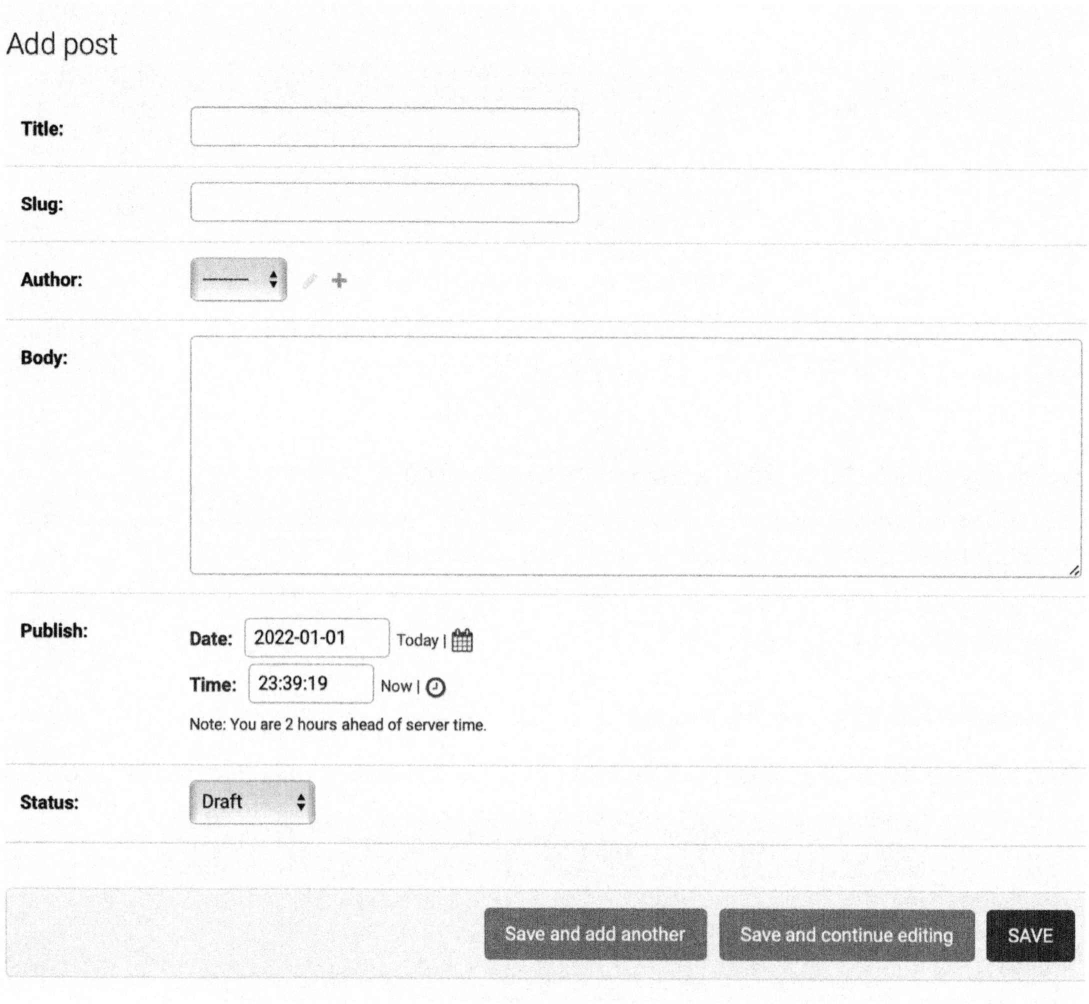

Add post

Title:

Slug:

Author:

Body:

Publish: Date: `2022-01-01`   Today | 📅

Time: `23:39:19`   Now | ⏱

Note: You are 2 hours ahead of server time.

Status: Draft

[Save and add another]   [Save and continue editing]   [SAVE]

Figure 1.9: The Django administration site edit form for the Post model

Django uses different form widgets for each type of field. Even complex fields, such as the `DateTimeField`, are displayed with an easy interface, such as a JavaScript date picker.

Fill in the form and click on the **SAVE** button. You should be redirected to the post list page with a success message and the post you just created, as shown in *Figure 1.10*:

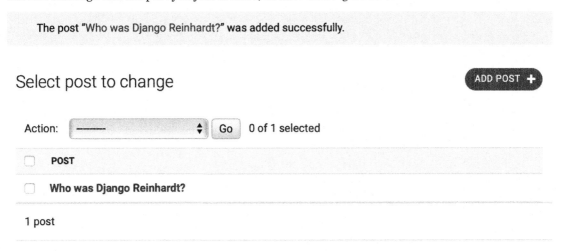

Figure 1.10: The Django administration site list view for the Post model with an added successfully message

Customizing how models are displayed

Now, we will take a look at how to customize the administration site.

Edit the admin.py file of your blog application and change it, as follows. The new lines are highlighted in bold:

```
from django.contrib import admin
from .models import Post

@admin.register(Post)
class PostAdmin(admin.ModelAdmin):
    list_display = ['title', 'slug', 'author', 'publish', 'status']
```

We are telling the Django administration site that the model is registered in the site using a custom class that inherits from ModelAdmin. In this class, we can include information about how to display the model on the site and how to interact with it.

The list_display attribute allows you to set the fields of your model that you want to display on the administration object list page. The @admin.register() decorator performs the same function as the admin.site.register() function that you replaced, registering the ModelAdmin class that it decorates.

Let's customize the admin model with some more options.

Edit the admin.py file of your blog application and change it, as follows. The new lines are highlighted in bold:

```
from django.contrib import admin
from .models import Post


@admin.register(Post)
class PostAdmin(admin.ModelAdmin):
    list_display = ['title', 'slug', 'author', 'publish', 'status']
    list_filter = ['status', 'created', 'publish', 'author']
    search_fields = ['title', 'body']
    prepopulated_fields = {'slug': ('title',)}
    raw_id_fields = ['author']
    date_hierarchy = 'publish'
    ordering = ['status', 'publish']
```

Return to your browser and reload the post list page. Now, it will look like this:

Figure 1.11: The Django administration site custom list view for the Post model

You can see that the fields displayed on the post list page are the ones we specified in the list_display attribute. The list page now includes a right sidebar that allows you to filter the results by the fields included in the list_filter attribute.

A search bar has appeared on the page. This is because we have defined a list of searchable fields using the search_fields attribute. Just below the search bar, there are navigation links to navigate through a date hierarchy; this has been defined by the date_hierarchy attribute. You can also see that the posts are ordered by **STATUS** and **PUBLISH** columns by default. We have specified the default sorting criteria using the ordering attribute.

Next, click on the **ADD POST** link. You will also note some changes here. As you type the title of a new post, the slug field is filled in automatically. You have told Django to prepopulate the slug field with the input of the title field using the prepopulated_fields attribute:

Figure 1.12: The slug model is now automatically prepopulated as you type in the title

Also, the author field is now displayed with a lookup widget, which can be much better than a drop-down select input when you have thousands of users. This is achieved with the raw_id_fields attribute and it looks like this:

Figure 1.13: The widget to select related objects for the author field of the Post model

With a few lines of code, we have customized the way the model is displayed on the administration site. There are plenty of ways to customize and extend the Django administration site; you will learn more about this later in this book.

You can find more information about the Django administration site at https://docs.djangoproject.com/en/4.1/ref/contrib/admin/.

Working with QuerySets and managers

Now that we have a fully functional administration site to manage blog posts, it is a good time to learn how to read and write content to the database programmatically.

The Django **object-relational mapper** (**ORM**) is a powerful database abstraction API that lets you create, retrieve, update, and delete objects easily. An ORM allows you to generate SQL queries using the object-oriented paradigm of Python. You can think of it as a way to interact with your database in pythonic fashion instead of writing raw SQL queries.

The ORM maps your models to database tables and provides you with a simple pythonic interface to interact with your database. The ORM generates SQL queries and maps the results to model objects. The Django ORM is compatible with MySQL, PostgreSQL, SQLite, Oracle, and MariaDB.

Remember that you can define the database of your project in the DATABASES setting of your project's settings.py file. Django can work with multiple databases at a time, and you can program database routers to create custom data routing schemes.

Once you have created your data models, Django gives you a free API to interact with them. You can find the data model reference of the official documentation at `https://docs.djangoproject.com/en/4.1/ref/models/`.

The Django ORM is based on QuerySets. A QuerySet is a collection of database queries to retrieve objects from your database. You can apply filters to QuerySets to narrow down the query results based on given parameters.

Creating objects

Run the following command in the shell prompt to open the Python shell:

```
python manage.py shell
```

Then, type the following lines:

```
>>> from django.contrib.auth.models import User
>>> from blog.models import Post
>>> user = User.objects.get(username='admin')
>>> post = Post(title='Another post',
...             slug='another-post',
...             body='Post body.',
...             author=user)
>>> post.save()
```

Let's analyze what this code does.

First, we are retrieving the user object with the username `admin`:

```
user = User.objects.get(username='admin')
```

The `get()` method allows you to retrieve a single object from the database. Note that this method expects a result that matches the query. If no results are returned by the database, this method will raise a `DoesNotExist` exception, and if the database returns more than one result, it will raise a `MultipleObjectsReturned` exception. Both exceptions are attributes of the model class that the query is being performed on.

Then, we are creating a `Post` instance with a custom title, slug, and body, and set the user that we previously retrieved as the author of the post:

```
post = Post(title='Another post', slug='another-post', body='Post body.',
author=user)
```

This object is in memory and not persisted to the database; we created a Python object that can be used during runtime but that is not saved into the database.

Finally, we are saving the `Post` object to the database using the `save()` method:

```
post.save()
```

The preceding action performs an INSERT SQL statement behind the scenes.

We created an object in memory first and then persisted it to the database. You can also create the object and persist it into the database in a single operation using the create() method, as follows:

```
Post.objects.create(title='One more post',
                    slug='one-more-post',
                    body='Post body.',
                    author=user)
```

Updating objects

Now, change the title of the post to something different and save the object again:

```
>>> post.title = 'New title'
>>> post.save()
```

This time, the save() method performs an UPDATE SQL statement.

> The changes you make to a model object are not persisted to the database until you call the save() method.

Retrieving objects

You already know how to retrieve a single object from the database using the get() method. We accessed this method using Post.objects.get(). Each Django model has at least one manager, and the default manager is called objects. You get a QuerySet object using your model manager.

To retrieve all objects from a table, we use the all() method on the default objects manager, like this:

```
>>> all_posts = Post.objects.all()
```

This is how we create a QuerySet that returns all objects in the database. Note that this QuerySet has not been executed yet. Django QuerySets are *lazy*, which means they are only evaluated when they are forced to. This behavior makes QuerySets very efficient. If you don't assign the QuerySet to a variable but instead write it directly on the Python shell, the SQL statement of the QuerySet is executed because you are forcing it to generate output:

```
>>> Post.objects.all()
<QuerySet [<Post: Who was Django Reinhardt?>, <Post: New title>]>
```

Using the filter() method

To filter a QuerySet, you can use the filter() method of the manager. For example, you can retrieve all posts published in the year 2022 using the following QuerySet:

```
>>> Post.objects.filter(publish__year=2022)
```

You can also filter by multiple fields. For example, you can retrieve all posts published in 2022 by the author with the username `admin`:

```
>>> Post.objects.filter(publish__year=2022, author__username='admin')
```

This equates to building the same `QuerySet` chaining multiple filters:

```
>>> Post.objects.filter(publish__year=2022) \
>>>             .filter(author__username='admin')
```

 Queries with field lookup methods are built using two underscores, for example, `publish__year`, but the same notation is also used for accessing fields of related models, such as `author__username`.

Using exclude()

You can exclude certain results from your `QuerySet` using the `exclude()` method of the manager. For example, you can retrieve all posts published in 2022 whose titles don't start with `Why`:

```
>>> Post.objects.filter(publish__year=2022) \
>>>             .exclude(title__startswith='Why')
```

Using order_by()

You can order results by different fields using the `order_by()` method of the manager. For example, you can retrieve all objects ordered by their `title`, as follows:

```
>>> Post.objects.order_by('title')
```

Ascending order is implied. You can indicate descending order with a negative sign prefix, like this:

```
>>> Post.objects.order_by('-title')
```

Deleting objects

If you want to delete an object, you can do it from the object instance using the `delete()` method:

```
>>> post = Post.objects.get(id=1)
>>> post.delete()
```

Note that deleting objects will also delete any dependent relationships for `ForeignKey` objects defined with `on_delete` set to `CASCADE`.

When QuerySets are evaluated

Creating a QuerySet doesn't involve any database activity until it is evaluated. QuerySets usually return another unevaluated QuerySet. You can concatenate as many filters as you like to a QuerySet, and you will not hit the database until the QuerySet is evaluated. When a QuerySet is evaluated, it translates into an SQL query to the database.

QuerySets are only evaluated in the following cases:

- The first time you iterate over them
- When you slice them, for instance, `Post.objects.all()[:3]`
- When you pickle or cache them
- When you call `repr()` or `len()` on them
- When you explicitly call `list()` on them
- When you test them in a statement, such as `bool()`, `or`, `and`, or `if`

Creating model managers

The default manager for every model is the `objects` manager. This manager retrieves all the objects in the database. However, we can define custom managers for models.

Let's create a custom manager to retrieve all posts that have a `PUBLISHED` status.

There are two ways to add or customize managers for your models: you can add extra manager methods to an existing manager or create a new manager by modifying the initial `QuerySet` that the manager returns. The first method provides you with a `QuerySet` notation like `Post.objects.my_manager()`, and the latter provides you with a `QuerySet` notation like `Post.my_manager.all()`.

We will choose the second method to implement a manager that will allow us to retrieve posts using the notation `Post.published.all()`.

Edit the `models.py` file of your `blog` application to add the custom manager as follows. The new lines are highlighted in bold:

```python
class PublishedManager(models.Manager):
    def get_queryset(self):
        return super().get_queryset()\
                      .filter(status=Post.Status.PUBLISHED)


class Post(models.Model):

    # model fields
    # ...

    objects = models.Manager() # The default manager.
    published = PublishedManager() # Our custom manager.

    class Meta:
        ordering = ['-publish']

    def __str__(self):
        return self.title
```

The first manager declared in a model becomes the default manager. You can use the Meta attribute default_manager_name to specify a different default manager. If no manager is defined in the model, Django automatically creates the objects default manager for it. If you declare any managers for your model, but you want to keep the objects manager as well, you have to add it explicitly to your model. In the preceding code, we have added the default objects manager and the published custom manager to the Post model.

The get_queryset() method of a manager returns the QuerySet that will be executed. We have over-ridden this method to build a custom QuerySet that filters posts by their status and returns a successive QuerySet that only includes posts with the PUBLISHED status.

We have now defined a custom manager for the Post model. Let's test it!

Start the development server again with the following command in the shell prompt:

```
python manage.py shell
```

Now, you can import the Post model and retrieve all published posts whose title starts with Who, executing the following QuerySet:

```
>>> from blog.models import Post
>>> Post.published.filter(title__startswith='Who')
```

To obtain results for this QuerySet, make sure to set the status field to PUBLISHED in the Post object whose title starts with the string *Who*.

Building list and detail views

Now that you understand how to use the ORM, you are ready to build the views of the blog application. A Django view is just a Python function that receives a web request and returns a web response. All the logic to return the desired response goes inside the view.

First, you will create your application views, then you will define a URL pattern for each view, and finally, you will create HTML templates to render the data generated by the views. Each view will render a template, passing variables to it, and will return an HTTP response with the rendered output.

Creating list and detail views

Let's start by creating a view to display the list of posts.

Edit the views.py file of the blog application and make it look like this. The new lines are highlighted in bold:

```
from django.shortcuts import render
from .models import Post


def post_list(request):
```

```
posts = Post.published.all()
return render(request,
              'blog/post/list.html',
              {'posts': posts})
```

This is our very first Django view. The post_list view takes the request object as the only parameter. This parameter is required by all views.

In this view, we retrieve all the posts with the PUBLISHED status using the published manager that we created previously.

Finally, we use the render() shortcut provided by Django to render the list of posts with the given template. This function takes the request object, the template path, and the context variables to render the given template. It returns an HttpResponse object with the rendered text (normally HTML code).

The render() shortcut takes the request context into account, so any variable set by the template context processors is accessible by the given template. Template context processors are just callables that set variables into the context. You will learn how to use context processors in *Chapter 4, Building a Social Website*.

Let's create a second view to display a single post. Add the following function to the views.py file:

```
from django.http import Http404

def post_detail(request, id):
    try:
        post = Post.published.get(id=id)
    except Post.DoesNotExist:
        raise Http404("No Post found.")

    return render(request,
                  'blog/post/detail.html',
                  {'post': post})
```

This is the post detail view. This view takes the id argument of a post. In the view, we try to retrieve the Post object with the given id by calling the get() method on the default objects manager. We raise an Http404 exception to return an HTTP 404 error if the model DoesNotExist exception is raised, because no result is found.

Finally, we use the render() shortcut to render the retrieved post using a template.

Using the get_object_or_404 shortcut

Django provides a shortcut to call get() on a given model manager and raises an Http404 exception instead of a DoesNotExist exception when no object is found.

Edit the `views.py` file to import the `get_object_or_404` shortcut and change the `post_detail` view as follows. The new code is highlighted in bold:

```
from django.shortcuts import render, get_object_or_404


# ...


def post_detail(request, id):
    post = get_object_or_404(Post,
                             id=id,
                             status=Post.Status.PUBLISHED)
    return render(request,
                  'blog/post/detail.html',
                  {'post': post})
```

In the detail view, we now use the `get_object_or_404()` shortcut to retrieve the desired post. This function retrieves the object that matches the given parameters or an HTTP 404 (not found) exception if no object is found.

Adding URL patterns for your views

URL patterns allow you to map URLs to views. A URL pattern is composed of a string pattern, a view, and, optionally, a name that allows you to name the URL project-wide. Django runs through each URL pattern and stops at the first one that matches the requested URL. Then, Django imports the view of the matching URL pattern and executes it, passing an instance of the `HttpRequest` class and the keyword or positional arguments.

Create a `urls.py` file in the directory of the `blog` application and add the following lines to it:

```
from django.urls import path
from . import views


app_name = 'blog'


urlpatterns = [
    # post views
    path('', views.post_list, name='post_list'),
    path('<int:id>/', views.post_detail, name='post_detail'),
]
```

In the preceding code, you define an application namespace with the `app_name` variable. This allows you to organize URLs by application and use the name when referring to them. You define two different patterns using the `path()` function. The first URL pattern doesn't take any arguments and is mapped to the `post_list` view. The second pattern is mapped to the `post_detail` view and takes only one argument `id`, which matches an integer, set by the path converter `int`.

You use angle brackets to capture the values from the URL. Any value specified in the URL pattern as `<parameter>` is captured as a string. You use path converters, such as `<int:year>`, to specifically match and return an integer. For example `<slug:post>` would specifically match a slug (a string that can only contain letters, numbers, underscores, or hyphens). You can see all path converters provided by Django at `https://docs.djangoproject.com/en/4.1/topics/http/urls/#path-converters`.

If using `path()` and converters isn't sufficient for you, you can use `re_path()` instead to define complex URL patterns with Python regular expressions. You can learn more about defining URL patterns with regular expressions at `https://docs.djangoproject.com/en/4.1/ref/urls/#django.urls.re_path`. If you haven't worked with regular expressions before, you might want to take a look at the *Regular Expression HOWTO* located at `https://docs.python.org/3/howto/regex.html` first.

 Creating a `urls.py` file for each application is the best way to make your applications reusable by other projects.

Next, you have to include the URL patterns of the `blog` application in the main URL patterns of the project.

Edit the `urls.py` file located in the `mysite` directory of your project and make it look like the following. The new code is highlighted in bold:

```
from django.contrib import admin
from django.urls import path, include


urlpatterns = [
    path('admin/', admin.site.urls),
    path('blog/', include('blog.urls', namespace='blog')),
]
```

The new URL pattern defined with `include` refers to the URL patterns defined in the `blog` application so that they are included under the `blog/` path. You include these patterns under the namespace `blog`. Namespaces have to be unique across your entire project. Later, you will refer to your blog URLs easily by using the namespace followed by a colon and the URL name, for example, `blog:post_list` and `blog:post_detail`. You can learn more about URL namespaces at `https://docs.djangoproject.com/en/4.1/topics/http/urls/#url-namespaces`.

Creating templates for your views

You have created views and URL patterns for the `blog` application. URL patterns map URLs to views, and views decide which data gets returned to the user. Templates define how the data is displayed; they are usually written in HTML in combination with the Django template language. You can find more information about the Django template language at `https://docs.djangoproject.com/en/4.1/ref/templates/language/`.

Let's add templates to your application to display posts in a user-friendly manner.

Create the following directories and files inside your `blog` application directory:

```
templates/
    blog/
        base.html
        post/
            list.html
            detail.html
```

The preceding structure will be the file structure for your templates. The `base.html` file will include the main HTML structure of the website and divide the content into the main content area and a sidebar. The `list.html` and `detail.html` files will inherit from the `base.html` file to render the blog post list and detail views, respectively.

Django has a powerful template language that allows you to specify how data is displayed. It is based on *template tags*, *template variables*, and *template filters*:

- Template tags control the rendering of the template and look like `{% tag %}`
- Template variables get replaced with values when the template is rendered and look like `{{ variable }}`
- Template filters allow you to modify variables for display and look like `{{ variable|filter }}`

You can see all built-in template tags and filters at `https://docs.djangoproject.com/en/4.1/ref/templates/builtins/`.

Creating a base template

Edit the `base.html` file and add the following code:

```
{% load static %}
<!DOCTYPE html>
<html>
<head>
  <title>{% block title %}{% endblock %}</title>
  <link href="{% static "css/blog.css" %}" rel="stylesheet">
</head>
<body>
  <div id="content">
    {% block content %}
    {% endblock %}
  </div>
  <div id="sidebar">
    <h2>My blog</h2>
```

```
      <p>This is my blog.</p>
    </div>
  </body>
</html>
```

`{% load static %}` tells Django to load the `static` template tags that are provided by the `django.contrib.staticfiles` application, which is contained in the `INSTALLED_APPS` setting. After loading them, you can use the `{% static %}` template tag throughout this template. With this template tag, you can include the static files, such as the `blog.css` file, which you will find in the code of this example under the `static/` directory of the `blog` application. Copy the `static/` directory from the code that comes along with this chapter into the same location as your project to apply the CSS styles to the templates. You can find the directory's contents at `https://github.com/PacktPublishing/Django-4-by-Example/tree/master/Chapter01/mysite/blog/static`.

You can see that there are two `{% block %}` tags. These tell Django that you want to define a block in that area. Templates that inherit from this template can fill in the blocks with content. You have defined a block called `title` and a block called `content`.

Creating the post list template

Let's edit the `post/list.html` file and make it look like the following:

```
{% extends "blog/base.html" %}

{% block title %}My Blog{% endblock %}

{% block content %}
  <h1>My Blog</h1>
  {% for post in posts %}
    <h2>
      <a href="{% url 'blog:post_detail' post.id %}">
        {{ post.title }}
      </a>
    </h2>
    <p class="date">
      Published {{ post.publish }} by {{ post.author }}
    </p>
    {{ post.body|truncatewords:30|linebreaks }}
  {% endfor %}
{% endblock %}
```

With the `{% extends %}` template tag, you tell Django to inherit from the `blog/base.html` template. Then, you fill the `title` and `content` blocks of the base template with content. You iterate through the posts and display their title, date, author, and body, including a link in the title to the detail URL of the post. We build the URL using the `{% url %}` template tag provided by Django.

This template tag allows you to build URLs dynamically by their name. We use `blog:post_detail` to refer to the `post_detail` URL in the `blog` namespace. We pass the required `post.id` parameter to build the URL for each post.

 Always use the `{% url %}` template tag to build URLs in your templates instead of writing hardcoded URLs. This will make your URLs more maintainable.

In the body of the post, we apply two template filters: `truncatewords` truncates the value to the number of words specified, and `linebreaks` converts the output into HTML line breaks. You can concatenate as many template filters as you wish; each one will be applied to the output generated by the preceding one.

Accessing our application

Open the shell and execute the following command to start the development server:

```
python manage.py runserver
```

Open `http://127.0.0.1:8000/blog/` in your browser; you will see everything running. Note that you need to have some posts with the PUBLISHED status to show them here. You should see something like this:

My Blog	**My blog**
	This is my blog.
Who was Django Reinhardt?	
Published Jan. 1, 2022, 11:59 p.m. by admin	
Jean Reinhardt, known to all by his Romani nickname Django, was a Belgian-born Romani-French jazz guitarist and composer. He was the first major jazz talent to emerge from Europe and …	
Another post	
Published Jan. 1, 2022, 11:57 p.m. by admin	
Post body.	

Figure 1.14: The page for the post list view

Creating the post detail template

Next, edit the post/detail.html file:

```
{% extends "blog/base.html" %}

{% block title %}{{ post.title }}{% endblock %}

{% block content %}
  <h1>{{ post.title }}</h1>
  <p class="date">
    Published {{ post.publish }} by {{ post.author }}
  </p>
  {{ post.body|linebreaks }}
{% endblock %}
```

Next, you can return to your browser and click on one of the post titles to take a look at the detail view of the post. You should see something like this:

Figure 1.15: The page for the post's detail view

Take a look at the URL—it should include the auto-generated post ID like /blog/1/.

The request/response cycle

Let's review the request/response cycle of Django with the application we built. The following schema shows a simplified example of how Django processes HTTP requests and generates HTTP responses:

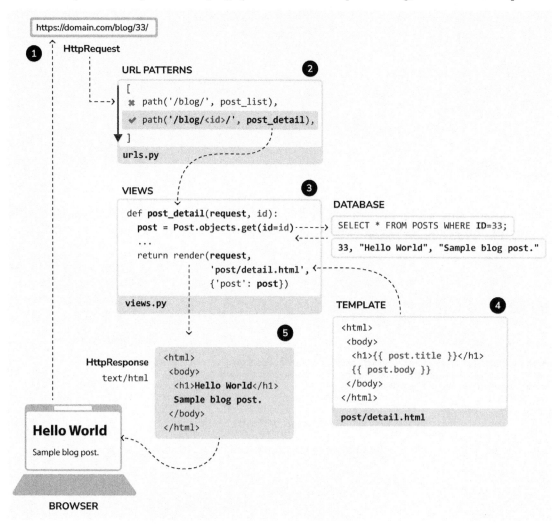

Figure 1.16: The Django request/response cycle

Let's review the Django request/response process:

1.   A web browser requests a page by its URL, for example, `https://domain.com/blog/33/`. The web server receives the HTTP request and passes it over to Django.

2.   Django runs through each URL pattern defined in the URL patterns configuration. The framework checks each pattern against the given URL path, in order of appearance, and stops at the first one that matches the requested URL. In this case, the pattern `/blog/<id>/` matches the path `/blog/33/`.

3. Django imports the view of the matching URL pattern and executes it, passing an instance of the `HttpRequest` class and the keyword or positional arguments. The view uses the models to retrieve information from the database. Using the Django ORM QuerySets are translated into SQL and executed in the database.

4. The view uses the `render()` function to render an HTML template passing the `Post` object as a context variable.

5. The rendered content is returned as a `HttpResponse` object by the view with the `text/html` content type by default.

You can always use this schema as the basic reference for how Django processes requests. This schema doesn't include Django middleware for the sake of simplicity. You will use middleware in different examples of this book, and you will learn how to create custom middleware in *Chapter 17, Going Live*.

Additional resources

The following resources provide additional information related to the topics covered in this chapter:

- Source code for this chapter – `https://github.com/PacktPublishing/Django-4-by-example/tree/main/Chapter01`
- Python venv library for virtual environments – `https://docs.python.org/3/library/venv.html`
- Django installation options – `https://docs.djangoproject.com/en/4.1/topics/install/`
- Django 4.0 release notes – `https://docs.djangoproject.com/en/dev/releases/4.0/`
- Django 4.1 release notes – `https://docs.djangoproject.com/en/4.1/releases/4.1/`
- Django's design philosophies – `https://docs.djangoproject.com/en/dev/misc/design-philosophies/`
- Django model field reference – `https://docs.djangoproject.com/en/4.1/ref/models/fields/`
- Model index reference – `https://docs.djangoproject.com/en/4.1/ref/models/indexes/`
- Python support for enumerations – `https://docs.python.org/3/library/enum.html`
- Django model enumeration types – `https://docs.djangoproject.com/en/4.1/ref/models/fields/#enumeration-types`
- Django settings reference – `https://docs.djangoproject.com/en/4.1/ref/settings/`
- Django administration site – `https://docs.djangoproject.com/en/4.1/ref/contrib/admin/`
- Making queries with the Django ORM – `https://docs.djangoproject.com/en/4.1/topics/db/queries/`
- Django URL dispatcher – `https://docs.djangoproject.com/en/4.1/topics/http/urls/`
- Django URL resolver utilities – `https://docs.djangoproject.com/en/4.1/ref/urlresolvers/`
- Django template language – `https://docs.djangoproject.com/en/4.1/ref/templates/language/`

- Built-in template tags and filters – `https://docs.djangoproject.com/en/4.1/ref/templates/builtins/`
- Static files for the code in this chapter – `https://github.com/PacktPublishing/Django-4-by-Example/tree/master/Chapter01/mysite/blog/static`

Summary

In this chapter, you learned the basics of the Django web framework by creating a simple blog application. You designed the data models and applied migrations to the database. You also created the views, templates, and URLs for your blog.

In the next chapter, you will learn how to create canonical URLs for models and how to build SEO-friendly URLs for blog posts. You will also learn how to implement object pagination and how to build class-based views. You will also implement Django forms to let your users recommend posts by email and comment on posts.

Join us on Discord

Read this book alongside other users and the author.

Ask questions, provide solutions to other readers, chat with the author via *Ask Me Anything* sessions, and much more. Scan the QR code or visit the link to join the book community.

`https://packt.link/django`

2

Enhancing Your Blog with Advanced Features

In the preceding chapter, we learned the main components of Django by developing a simple blog application. We created a simple blog application using views, templates, and URLs. In this chapter, we will extend the functionalities of the blog application with features that can be found in many blogging platforms nowadays. In this chapter, you will learn the following topics:

- Using canonical URLs for models
- Creating SEO-friendly URLs for posts
- Adding pagination to the post list view
- Building class-based views
- Sending emails with Django
- Using Django forms to share posts via email
- Adding comments to posts using forms from models

The source code for this chapter can be found at `https://github.com/PacktPublishing/Django-4-by-example/tree/main/Chapter02`.

All Python packages used in this chapter are included in the `requirements.txt` file in the source code for the chapter. You can follow the instructions to install each Python package in the following sections, or you can install all the requirements at once with the command `pip install -r requirements.txt`.

Using canonical URLs for models

A website might have different pages that display the same content. In our application, the initial part of the content for each post is displayed both on the post list page and the post detail page. A canonical URL is the preferred URL for a resource. You can think of it as the URL of the most representative page for specific content. There might be different pages on your site that display posts, but there is a single URL that you use as the main URL for a post. Canonical URLs allow you to specify the URL for the master copy of a page. Django allows you to implement the `get_absolute_url()` method in your models to return the canonical URL for the object.

We will use the `post_detail` URL defined in the URL patterns of the application to build the canonical URL for `Post` objects. Django provides different URL resolver functions that allow you to build URLs dynamically using their name and any required parameters. We will use the `reverse()` utility function of the `django.urls` module.

Edit the `models.py` file of the `blog` application to import the `reverse()` function and add the `get_absolute_url()` method to the `Post` model as follows. New code is highlighted in bold:

```python
from django.db import models
from django.utils import timezone
from django.contrib.auth.models import User
from django.urls import reverse


class PublishedManager(models.Manager):
    def get_queryset(self):
        return super().get_queryset()\
                    .filter(status=Post.Status.PUBLISHED)


class Post(models.Model):

    class Status(models.TextChoices):
        DRAFT = 'DF', 'Draft'
        PUBLISHED = 'PB', 'Published'

    title = models.CharField(max_length=250)
    slug = models.SlugField(max_length=250)
    author = models.ForeignKey(User,
                               on_delete=models.CASCADE,
                               related_name='blog_posts')
    body = models.TextField()
    publish = models.DateTimeField(default=timezone.now)
    created = models.DateTimeField(auto_now_add=True)
    updated = models.DateTimeField(auto_now=True)
    status = models.CharField(max_length=2,
                              choices=Status.choices,
                              default=Status.DRAFT)

    class Meta:
        ordering = ['-publish']
        indexes = [
            models.Index(fields=['-publish']),
        ]
```

```
    def __str__(self):
        return self.title

    def get_absolute_url(self):
        return reverse('blog:post_detail',
                       args=[self.id])
```

The reverse() function will build the URL dynamically using the URL name defined in the URL patterns. We have used the blog namespace followed by a colon and the URL name post_detail. Remember that the blog namespace is defined in the main urls.py file of the project when including the URL patterns from blog.urls. The post_detail URL is defined in the urls.py file of the blog application. The resulting string, blog:post_detail, can be used globally in your project to refer to the post detail URL. This URL has a required parameter that is the id of the blog post to retrieve. We have included the id of the Post object as a positional argument by using args=[self.id].

You can learn more about the URL's utility functions at https://docs.djangoproject.com/en/4.1/ref/urlresolvers/.

Let's replace the post detail URLs in the templates with the new get_absolute_url() method.

Edit the blog/post/list.html file and replace the line:

```
<a href="{% url 'blog:post_detail' post.id %}">
```

With the line:

```
<a href="{{ post.get_absolute_url }}">
```

The blog/post/list.html file should now look as follows:

```
{% extends "blog/base.html" %}

{% block title %}My Blog{% endblock %}

{% block content %}
  <h1>My Blog</h1>
  {% for post in posts %}
    <h2>
      <a href="{{ post.get_absolute_url }}">
        {{ post.title }}
      </a>
    </h2>
    <p class="date">
      Published {{ post.publish }} by {{ post.author }}
    </p>
```

```
        {{ post.body|truncatewords:30|linebreaks }}
    {% endfor %}
{% endblock %}
```

Open the shell prompt and execute the following command to start the development server:

```
python manage.py runserver
```

Open `http://127.0.0.1:8000/blog/` in your browser. Links to individual blog posts should still work. Django is now building them using the `get_absolute_url()` method of the `Post` model.

Creating SEO-friendly URLs for posts

The canonical URL for a blog post detail view currently looks like `/blog/1/`. We will change the URL pattern to create SEO-friendly URLs for posts. We will be using both the `publish` date and `slug` values to build the URLs for single posts. By combining dates, we will make a post detail URL to look like `/blog/2022/1/1/who-was-django-reinhardt/`. We will provide search engines with friendly URLs to index, containing both the title and date of the post.

To retrieve single posts with the combination of publication date and slug, we need to ensure that no post can be stored in the database with the same `slug` and `publish` date as an existing post. We will prevent the `Post` model from storing duplicated posts by defining slugs to be unique for the publication date of the post.

Edit the `models.py` file and add the following `unique_for_date` parameter to the `slug` field of the `Post` model:

```
class Post(models.Model):
    # ...
    slug = models.SlugField(max_length=250,
                            unique_for_date='publish')
    # ...
```

By using `unique_for_date`, the `slug` field is now required to be unique for the date stored in the `publish` field. Note that the `publish` field is an instance of `DateTimeField`, but the check for unique values will be done only against the date (not the time). Django will prevent from saving a new post with the same slug as an existing post for a given publication date. We have now ensured that slugs are unique for the publication date, so we can now retrieve single posts by the `publish` and `slug` fields.

We have changed our models, so let's create migrations. Note that `unique_for_date` is not enforced at the database level, so no database migration is required. However, Django uses migrations to keep track of all model changes. We will create a migration just to keep migrations aligned with the current state of the model.

Run the following command in the shell prompt:

```
python manage.py makemigrations blog
```

You should get the following output:

```
Migrations for 'blog':
    blog/migrations/0002_alter_post_slug.py
    - Alter field slug on post
```

Django just created the 0002_alter_post_slug.py file inside the migrations directory of the blog application.

Execute the following command in the shell prompt to apply existing migrations:

```
python manage.py migrate
```

You will get an output that ends with the following line:

```
Applying blog.0002_alter_post_slug... OK
```

Django will consider that all migrations have been applied and the models are in sync. No action will be done in the database because unique_for_date is not enforced at the database level.

Modifying the URL patterns

Let's modify the URL patterns to use the publication date and slug for the post detail URL.

Edit the urls.py file of the blog application and replace the line:

```
path('<int:id>/', views.post_detail, name='post_detail'),
```

With the lines:

```
path('<int:year>/<int:month>/<int:day>/<slug:post>/',
        views.post_detail,
        name='post_detail'),
```

The urls.py file should now look like this:

```
from django.urls import path
from . import views

app_name = 'blog'

urlpatterns = [
    # Post views
    path('', views.post_list, name='post_list'),
    path('<int:year>/<int:month>/<int:day>/<slug:post>/',
        views.post_detail,
        name='post_detail'),
]
```

The URL pattern for the `post_detail` view takes the following arguments:

- `year`: Requires an integer
- `month`: Requires an integer
- `day`: Requires an integer
- `post`: Requires a slug (a string that contains only letters, numbers, underscores, or hyphens)

The `int` path converter is used for the year, month, and day parameters, whereas the `slug` path converter is used for the post parameter. You learned about path converters in the previous chapter. You can see all path converters provided by Django at https://docs.djangoproject.com/en/4.1/topics/http/urls/#path-converters.

Modifying the views

Now we have to change the parameters of the `post_detail` view to match the new URL parameters and use them to retrieve the corresponding `Post` object.

Edit the `views.py` file and edit the `post_detail` view like this:

```
def post_detail(request, year, month, day, post):
    post = get_object_or_404(Post,
                             status=Post.Status.PUBLISHED,
                             slug=post,
                             publish__year=year,
                             publish__month=month,
                             publish__day=day)
    return render(request,
                  'blog/post/detail.html',
                  {'post': post})
```

We have modified the `post_detail` view to take the year, month, day, and post arguments and retrieve a published post with the given slug and publication date. By adding `unique_for_date='publish'` to the `slug` field of the `Post` model before, we ensured that there will be only one post with a slug for a given date. Thus, you can retrieve single posts using the date and slug.

Modifying the canonical URL for posts

We also have to modify the parameters of the canonical URL for blog posts to match the new URL parameters.

Edit the `models.py` file of the `blog` application and edit the `get_absolute_url()` method as follows:

```
class Post(models.Model):
    # ...
    def get_absolute_url(self):
        return reverse('blog:post_detail',
```

```
                 args=[self.publish.year,
                       self.publish.month,
                       self.publish.day,
                       self.slug])
```

Start the development server by typing the following command in the shell prompt:

```
python manage.py runserver
```

Next, you can return to your browser and click on one of the post titles to take a look at the detail view of the post. You should see something like this:

Figure 2.1: The page for the post's detail view

Take a look at the URL—it should look like /blog/2022/1/1/who-was-django-reinhardt/. You have designed SEO-friendly URLs for the blog posts.

Adding pagination

When you start adding content to your blog, you can easily store tens or hundreds of posts in your database. Instead of displaying all the posts on a single page, you may want to split the list of posts across several pages and include navigation links to the different pages. This functionality is called pagination, and you can find it in almost every web application that displays long lists of items.

For example, Google uses pagination to divide search results across multiple pages. *Figure 2.2* shows Google's pagination links for search result pages:

Figure 2.2: Google pagination links for search result pages

Django has a built-in pagination class that allows you to manage paginated data easily. You can define the number of objects you want to be returned per page and you can retrieve the posts that correspond to the page requested by the user.

Adding pagination to the post list view

Edit the `views.py` file of the `blog` application to import the Django `Paginator` class and modify the `post_list` view as follows:

```python
from django.shortcuts import render, get_object_or_404
from .models import Post
from django.core.paginator import Paginator

def post_list(request):
    post_list = Post.published.all()
    # Pagination with 3 posts per page
    paginator = Paginator(post_list, 3)
    page_number = request.GET.get('page', 1)
    posts = paginator.page(page_number)

    return render(request,
                  'blog/post/list.html',
                  {'posts': posts})
```

Let's review the new code we have added to the view:

1. We instantiate the `Paginator` class with the number of objects to return per page. We will display three posts per page.

2. We retrieve the page GET HTTP parameter and store it in the `page_number` variable. This parameter contains the requested page number. If the page parameter is not in the GET parameters of the request, we use the default value 1 to load the first page of results.

3. We obtain the objects for the desired page by calling the `page()` method of `Paginator`. This method returns a `Page` object that we store in the `posts` variable.

4. We pass the page number and the `posts` object to the template.

Creating a pagination template

We need to create a page navigation for users to browse through the different pages. We will create a template to display the pagination links. We will make it generic so that we can reuse the template for any object pagination on our website.

In the `templates/` directory, create a new file and name it `pagination.html`. Add the following HTML code to the file:

```html
<div class="pagination">
  <span class="step-links">
    {% if page.has_previous %}
      <a href="?page={{ page.previous_page_number }}">Previous</a>
    {% endif %}
```

```
    <span class="current">
      Page {{ page.number }} of {{ page.paginator.num_pages }}.
    </span>
    {% if page.has_next %}
      <a href="?page={{ page.next_page_number }}">Next</a>
    {% endif %}
  </span>
</div>
```

This is the generic pagination template. The template expects to have a `Page` object in the context to render the previous and next links, and to display the current page and total pages of results.

Let's return to the `blog/post/list.html` template and include the `pagination.html` template at the bottom of the `{% content %}` block, as follows:

```
{% extends "blog/base.html" %}

{% block title %}My Blog{% endblock %}

{% block content %}
  <h1>My Blog</h1>
  {% for post in posts %}
    <h2>
      <a href="{{ post.get_absolute_url }}">
        {{ post.title }}
      </a>
    </h2>
    <p class="date">
      Published {{ post.publish }} by {{ post.author }}
    </p>
    {{ post.body|truncatewords:30|linebreaks }}
  {% endfor %}
  {% include "pagination.html" with page=posts %}
{% endblock %}
```

The `{% include %}` template tag loads the given template and renders it using the current template context. We use `with` to pass additional context variables to the template. The pagination template uses the `page` variable to render, while the `Page` object that we pass from our view to the template is called `posts`. We use `with page=posts` to pass the variable expected by the pagination template. You can follow this method to use the pagination template for any type of object.

Start the development server by typing the following command in the shell prompt:

```
python manage.py runserver
```

Open `http://127.0.0.1:8000/admin/blog/post/` in your browser and use the administration site to create a total of four different posts. Make sure to set the status to **Published** for all of them.

Now, open `http://127.0.0.1:8000/blog/` in your browser. You should see the first three posts in reverse chronological order, and then the navigation links at the bottom of the post list like this:

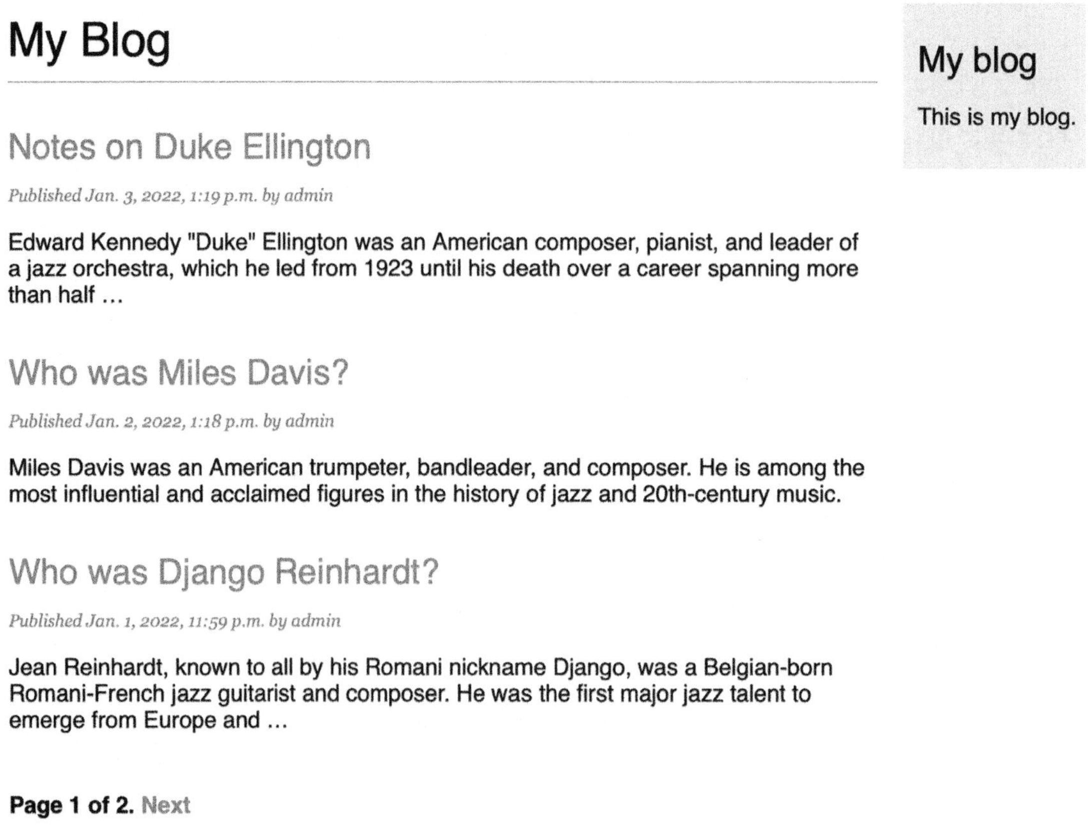

My Blog

Notes on Duke Ellington

Published Jan. 3, 2022, 1:19 p.m. by admin

Edward Kennedy "Duke" Ellington was an American composer, pianist, and leader of a jazz orchestra, which he led from 1923 until his death over a career spanning more than half …

Who was Miles Davis?

Published Jan. 2, 2022, 1:18 p.m. by admin

Miles Davis was an American trumpeter, bandleader, and composer. He is among the most influential and acclaimed figures in the history of jazz and 20th-century music.

Who was Django Reinhardt?

Published Jan. 1, 2022, 11:59 p.m. by admin

Jean Reinhardt, known to all by his Romani nickname Django, was a Belgian-born Romani-French jazz guitarist and composer. He was the first major jazz talent to emerge from Europe and …

Page 1 of 2. Next

My blog

This is my blog.

Figure 2.3: The post list page including pagination

If you click on **Next**, you will see the last post. The URL for the second page contains the `?page=2 GET` parameter. This parameter is used by the view to load the requested page of results using the paginator.

Figure 2.4: The second page of results

Great! The pagination links are working as expected.

Handling pagination errors

Now that the pagination is working, we can add exception handling for pagination errors in the view. The page parameter used by the view to retrieve the given page could potentially be used with wrong values, such as non-existing page numbers or a string value that cannot be used as a page number. We will implement appropriate error handling for those cases.

Open http://127.0.0.1:8000/blog/?page=3 in your browser. You should see the following error page:

EmptyPage at /blog/

That page contains no results

Request Method:	GET
Request URL:	http://127.0.0.1:8000/blog/?page=3
Django Version:	4.1
Exception Type:	EmptyPage
Exception Value:	That page contains no results
Exception Location:	/Users/amele/Documents/env/dbe4/lib/python3.10/site-packages/django/core/paginator.py, line 57, in validate_number
Raised during:	blog.views.post_list
Python Executable:	/Users/amele/Documents/env/dbe4/bin/python
Python Version:	3.10.6

Figure 2.5: The EmptyPage error page

The `Paginator` object throws an `EmptyPage` exception when retrieving page 3 because it's out of range. There are no results to display. Let's handle this error in our view.

Edit the `views.py` file of the `blog` application to add the necessary imports and modify the `post_list` view as follows:

```python
from django.shortcuts import render, get_object_or_404
from .models import Post
from django.core.paginator import Paginator, EmptyPage


def post_list(request):
    post_list = Post.published.all()
    # Pagination with 3 posts per page
    paginator = Paginator(post_list, 3)
    page_number = request.GET.get('page', 1)
    try:
        posts = paginator.page(page_number)
    except EmptyPage:
        # If page_number is out of range deliver last page of results
        posts = paginator.page(paginator.num_pages)
    return render(request,
                  'blog/post/list.html',
                  {'posts': posts})
```

We have added a try and except block to manage the `EmptyPage` exception when retrieving a page. If the page requested is out of range, we return the last page of results. We get the total number of pages with `paginator.num_pages`. The total number of pages is the same as the last page number.

Open `http://127.0.0.1:8000/blog/?page=3` in your browser again. Now, the exception is managed by the view and the last page of results is returned as follows:

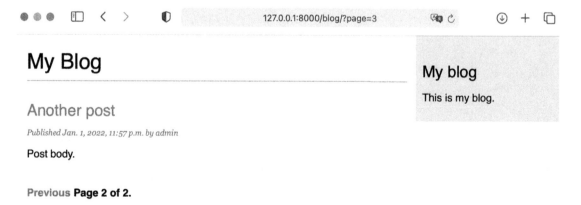

Figure 2.6: The last page of results

Our view should also handle the case when something different than an integer is passed in the page parameter.

Open http://127.0.0.1:8000/blog/?page=asdf in your browser. You should see the following error page:

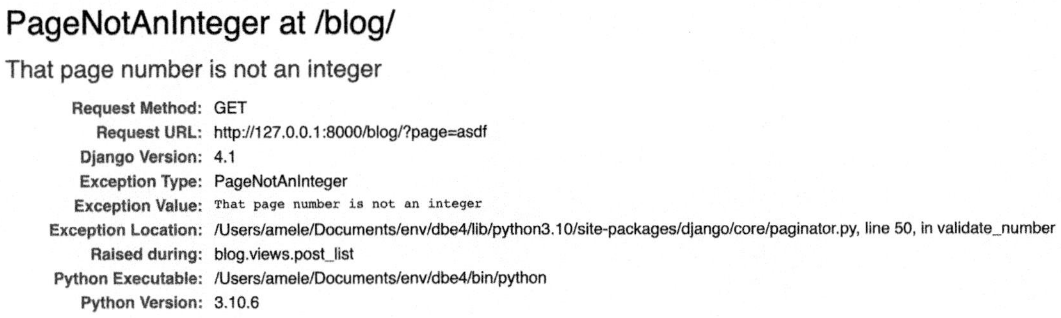

PageNotAnInteger at /blog/

That page number is not an integer

Request Method: GET
Request URL: http://127.0.0.1:8000/blog/?page=asdf
Django Version: 4.1
Exception Type: PageNotAnInteger
Exception Value: That page number is not an integer
Exception Location: /Users/amele/Documents/env/dbe4/lib/python3.10/site-packages/django/core/paginator.py, line 50, in validate_number
Raised during: blog.views.post_list
Python Executable: /Users/amele/Documents/env/dbe4/bin/python
Python Version: 3.10.6

Figure 2.7: The PageNotAnInteger error page

In this case, the Paginator object throws a PageNotAnInteger exception when retrieving the page asdf because page numbers can only be an integer. Let's handle this error in our view.

Edit the views.py file of the blog application to add the necessary imports and modify the post_list view as follows:

```
from django.shortcuts import render, get_object_or_404
from .models import Post
from django.core.paginator import Paginator, EmptyPage,\
                                  PageNotAnInteger


def post_list(request):
    post_list = Post.published.all()
    # Pagination with 3 posts per page
    paginator = Paginator(post_list, 3)
    page_number = request.GET.get('page')
    try:
        posts = paginator.page(page_number)
    except PageNotAnInteger:
        # If page_number is not an integer deliver the first page
        posts = paginator.page(1)
    except EmptyPage:
```

```
        # If page_number is out of range deliver last page of results
        posts = paginator.page(paginator.num_pages)
    return render(request,
                  'blog/post/list.html',
                  {'posts': posts})
```

We have added a new except block to manage the `PageNotAnInteger` exception when retrieving a page. If the page requested is not an integer, we return the first page of results.

Open `http://127.0.0.1:8000/blog/?page=asdf` in your browser again. Now the exception is managed by the view and the first page of results is returned as follows:

My Blog

Notes on Duke Ellington

Published Jan. 3, 2022, 1:19 p.m. by admin

Edward Kennedy "Duke" Ellington was an American composer, pianist, and leader of a jazz orchestra, which he led from 1923 until his death over a career spanning more than half …

Who was Miles Davis?

Published Jan. 2, 2022, 1:18 p.m. by admin

Miles Davis was an American trumpeter, bandleader, and composer. He is among the most influential and acclaimed figures in the history of jazz and 20th-century music.

Who was Django Reinhardt?

Published Jan. 1, 2022, 11:59 p.m. by admin

Jean Reinhardt, known to all by his Romani nickname Django, was a Belgian-born Romani-French jazz guitarist and composer. He was the first major jazz talent to emerge from Europe and …

Page 1 of 2. Next

My blog

This is my blog.

Figure 2.8: The first page of results

The pagination for blog posts is now fully implemented.

You can learn more about the `Paginator` class at `https://docs.djangoproject.com/en/4.1/ref/paginator/`.

Building class-based views

We have built the blog application using function-based views. Function-based views are simple and powerful, but Django also allows you to build views using classes.

Class-based views are an alternative way to implement views as Python objects instead of functions. Since a view is a function that takes a web request and returns a web response, you can also define your views as class methods. Django provides base view classes that you can use to implement your own views. All of them inherit from the `View` class, which handles HTTP method dispatching and other common functionalities.

Why use class-based views

Class-based views offer some advantages over function-based views that are useful for specific use cases. Class-based views allow you to:

- Organize code related to HTTP methods, such as `GET`, `POST`, or `PUT`, in separate methods, instead of using conditional branching
- Use multiple inheritance to create reusable view classes (also known as *mixins*)

Using a class-based view to list posts

To understand how to write class-based views, we will create a new class-based view that is equivalent to the `post_list` view. We will create a class that will inherit from the generic `ListView` view offered by Django. `ListView` allows you to list any type of object.

Edit the `views.py` file of the `blog` application and add the following code to it:

```python
from django.views.generic import ListView


class PostListView(ListView):
    """
    Alternative post list view
    """
    queryset = Post.published.all()
    context_object_name = 'posts'
    paginate_by = 3
    template_name = 'blog/post/list.html'
```

The `PostListView` view is analogous to the `post_list` view we built previously. We have implemented a class-based view that inherits from the `ListView` class. We have defined a view with the following attributes:

- We use `queryset` to use a custom QuerySet instead of retrieving all objects. Instead of defining a `queryset` attribute, we could have specified `model = Post` and Django would have built the generic `Post.objects.all()` QuerySet for us.

- We use the context variable posts for the query results. The default variable is object_list if you don't specify any context_object_name.
- We define the pagination of results with paginate_by, returning three objects per page.
- We use a custom template to render the page with template_name. If you don't set a default template, ListView will use blog/post_list.html by default.

Now, edit the urls.py file of the blog application, comment the preceding post_list URL pattern, and add a new URL pattern using the PostListView class, as follows:

```
urlpatterns = [
    # Post views
    # path('', views.post_list, name='post_list'),
    path('', views.PostListView.as_view(), name='post_list'),
    path('<int:year>/<int:month>/<int:day>/<slug:post>/',
        views.post_detail,
        name='post_detail'),
]
```

In order to keep pagination working, we have to use the right page object that is passed to the template. Django's ListView generic view passes the page requested in a variable called page_obj. We have to edit the post/list.html template accordingly to include the paginator using the right variable, as follows:

```
{% extends "blog/base.html" %}

{% block title %}My Blog{% endblock %}

{% block content %}
  <h1>My Blog</h1>
  {% for post in posts %}
    <h2>
      <a href="{{ post.get_absolute_url }}">
        {{ post.title }}
      </a>
    </h2>
    <p class="date">
      Published {{ post.publish }} by {{ post.author }}
    </p>
    {{ post.body|truncatewords:30|linebreaks }}
  {% endfor %}
  {% include "pagination.html" with page=page_obj %}
{% endblock %}
```

Open `http://127.0.0.1:8000/blog/` in your browser and verify that the pagination links work as expected. The behavior of the pagination links should be the same as with the previous `post_list` view.

The exception handling in this case is a bit different. If you try to load a page out of range or pass a non-integer value in the `page` parameter, the view will return an HTTP response with the status code 404 (page not found) like this:

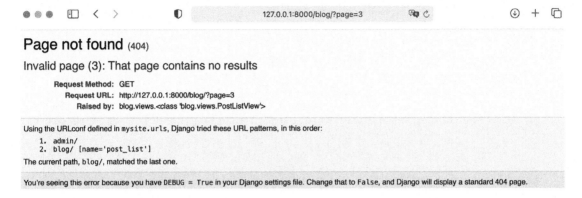

Figure 2.9: HTTP 404 Page not found response

The exception handling that returns the HTTP 404 status code is provided by the `ListView` view.

This is a simple example of how to write class-based views. You will learn more about class-based views in *Chapter 13, Creating a Content Management System*, and successive chapters.

You can read an introduction to class-based views at `https://docs.djangoproject.com/en/4.1/topics/class-based-views/intro/`.

Recommending posts by email

Now, we will learn how to create forms and how to send emails with Django. We will allow users to share blog posts with others by sending post recommendations via email.

Take a minute to think about how you could use *views*, *URLs*, and *templates* to create this functionality using what you learned in the preceding chapter.

To allow users to share posts via email, we will need to:

- Create a form for users to fill in their name, their email address, the recipient email address, and optional comments
- Create a view in the `views.py` file that handles the posted data and sends the email
- Add a URL pattern for the new view in the `urls.py` file of the blog application
- Create a template to display the form

Creating forms with Django

Let's start by building the form to share posts. Django has a built-in forms framework that allows you to create forms easily. The forms framework makes it simple to define the fields of the form, specify how they have to be displayed, and indicate how they have to validate input data. The Django forms framework offers a flexible way to render forms in HTML and handle data.

Django comes with two base classes to build forms:

- Form: Allows you to build standard forms by defining fields and validations.
- ModelForm: Allows you to build forms tied to model instances. It provides all the functionalities of the base Form class, but form fields can be explicitly declared, or automatically generated, from model fields. The form can be used to create or edit model instances.

First, create a forms.py file inside the directory of your blog application and add the following code to it:

```
from django import forms


class EmailPostForm(forms.Form):
    name = forms.CharField(max_length=25)
    email = forms.EmailField()
    to = forms.EmailField()
    comments = forms.CharField(required=False,
                               widget=forms.Textarea)
```

We have defined our first Django form. The EmailPostForm form inherits from the base Form class. We use different field types to validate data accordingly.

 Forms can reside anywhere in your Django project. The convention is to place them inside a forms.py file for each application.

The form contains the following fields:

- name: An instance of CharField with a maximum length of 25 characters. We will use it for the name of the person sending the post.
- email: An instance of EmailField. We will use the email of the person sending the post recommendation.
- to: An instance of EmailField. We will use the email of the recipient, who will receive the email recommending the post recommendation.
- comments: An instance of CharField. We will use it for comments to include in the post recommendation email. We have made this field optional by setting required to False, and we have specified a custom widget to render the field.

Each field type has a default widget that determines how the field is rendered in HTML. The name field is an instance of CharField. This type of field is rendered as an <input type="text"> HTML element. The default widget can be overridden with the widget attribute. In the comments field, we use the Textarea widget to display it as a <textarea> HTML element instead of the default <input> element.

Field validation also depends on the field type. For example, the email and to fields are EmailField fields. Both fields require a valid email address; the field validation will otherwise raise a forms. ValidationError exception and the form will not validate. Other parameters are also taken into account for the form field validation, such as the name field having a maximum length of 25 or the comments field being optional.

These are only some of the field types that Django provides for forms. You can find a list of all field types available at https://docs.djangoproject.com/en/4.1/ref/forms/fields/.

Handling forms in views

We have defined the form to recommend posts via email. Now we need a view to create an instance of the form and handle the form submission.

Edit the views.py file of the blog application and add the following code to it:

```python
from .forms import EmailPostForm

def post_share(request, post_id):
    # Retrieve post by id
    post = get_object_or_404(Post, id=post_id, status=Post.Status.PUBLISHED)
    if request.method == 'POST':
        # Form was submitted
        form = EmailPostForm(request.POST)
        if form.is_valid():
            # Form fields passed validation
            cd = form.cleaned_data
            # ... send email
    else:
        form = EmailPostForm()
    return render(request, 'blog/post/share.html', {'post': post,
                                                      'form': form})
```

We have defined the post_share view that takes the request object and the post_id variable as parameters. We use the get_object_or_404() shortcut to retrieve a published post by its id.

We use the same view both for displaying the initial form and processing the submitted data. The HTTP request method allows us to differentiate whether the form is being submitted. A GET request will indicate that an empty form has to be displayed to the user and a POST request will indicate the form is being submitted. We use request.method == 'POST' to differentiate between the two scenarios.

This is the process to display the form and handle the form submission:

1. When the page is loaded for the first time, the view receives a GET request. In this case, a new EmailPostForm instance is created and stored in the form variable. This form instance will be used to display the empty form in the template:

    ```
    form = EmailPostForm()
    ```

2. When the user fills in the form and submits it via POST, a form instance is created using the submitted data contained in request.POST:

    ```
    if request.method == 'POST':
        # Form was submitted
        form = EmailPostForm(request.POST)
    ```

3. After this, the data submitted is validated using the form's is_valid() method. This method validates the data introduced in the form and returns True if all fields contain valid data. If any field contains invalid data, then is_valid() returns False. The list of validation errors can be obtained with form.errors.

4. If the form is not valid, the form is rendered in the template again, including the data submitted. Validation errors will be displayed in the template.

5. If the form is valid, the validated data is retrieved with form.cleaned_data. This attribute is a dictionary of form fields and their values.

 If your form data does not validate, cleaned_data will contain only the valid fields.

We have implemented the view to display the form and handle the form submission. We will now learn how to send emails using Django and then we will add that functionality to the post_share view.

Sending emails with Django

Sending emails with Django is very straightforward. To send emails with Django, you need to have a local **Simple Mail Transfer Protocol (SMTP)** server, or you need to access an external SMTP server, like your email service provider.

The following settings allow you to define the SMTP configuration to send emails with Django:

*   EMAIL_HOST: The SMTP server host; the default is localhost
*   EMAIL_PORT: The SMTP port; the default is 25
*   EMAIL_HOST_USER: The username for the SMTP server
*   EMAIL_HOST_PASSWORD: The password for the SMTP server

- EMAIL_USE_TLS: Whether to use a **Transport Layer Security** (**TLS**) secure connection
- EMAIL_USE_SSL: Whether to use an implicit TLS secure connection

For this example, we will use Google's SMTP server with a standard Gmail account.

If you have a Gmail account, edit the settings.py file of your project and add the following code to it:

```
# Email server configuration
EMAIL_HOST = 'smtp.gmail.com'
EMAIL_HOST_USER = 'your_account@gmail.com'
EMAIL_HOST_PASSWORD = ''
EMAIL_PORT = 587
EMAIL_USE_TLS = True
```

Replace your_account@gmail.com with your actual Gmail account. If you don't have a Gmail account, you can use the SMTP server configuration of your email service provider.

Instead of Gmail, you can also use a professional, scalable email service that allows you to send emails via SMTP using your own domain, such as SendGrid (https://sendgrid.com/) or Amazon Simple Email Service (https://aws.amazon.com/ses/). Both services will require you to verify your domain and sender email accounts and will provide you with SMTP credentials to send emails. The Django applications django-sengrid and django-ses simplify the task of adding SendGrid or Amazon SES to your project. You can find installation instructions for django-sengrid at https://github.com/sklarsa/django-sendgrid-v5, and installation instructions for django-ses at https://github.com/django-ses/django-ses.

If you can't use an SMTP server, you can tell Django to write emails to the console by adding the following setting to the settings.py file:

```
EMAIL_BACKEND = 'django.core.mail.backends.console.EmailBackend'
```

By using this setting, Django will output all emails to the shell instead of sending them. This is very useful for testing your application without an SMTP server.

To complete the Gmail configuration, we need to enter a password for the SMTP server. Since Google uses a two-step verification process and additional security measures, you cannot use your Google account password directly. Instead, Google allows you to create app-specific passwords for your account. An app password is a 16-digit passcode that gives a less secure app or device permission to access your Google account.

Open `https://myaccount.google.com/` in your browser. On the left menu, click on **Security**. You will see the following screen:

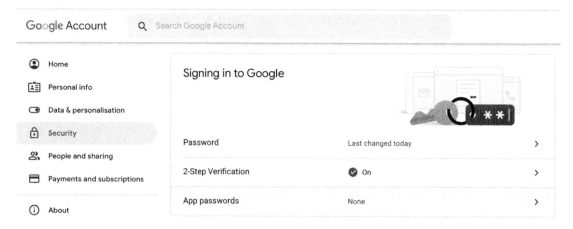

Figure 2.10: The Signing in to Google page for Google accounts

Under the **Signing in to Google** block, click on **App passwords**. If you cannot see **App passwords**, it might be that 2-step verification is not set for your account, your account is an organization account instead of a standard Gmail account, or you turned on Google's advanced protection. Make sure to use a standard Gmail account and to activate 2-step verification for your Google account. You can find more information at `https://support.google.com/accounts/answer/185833`.

When you click on **App passwords**, you will see the following screen:

← **App passwords**

App passwords let you sign in to your Google Account from apps on devices that don't support 2-Step Verification. You'll only need to enter it once so you don't need to remember it. Learn more

> You don't have any app passwords.
>
> **Select the app and device for which you want to generate the app password.**
>
> Select app   Select device   ▼
>
> Mail
>   GENERATE
> Calendar
>
> Contacts
>
> YouTube
>
> Other *(Custom name)*

Figure 2.11: Form to generate a new Google app password

In the **Select app** dropdown, select **Other.**

Then, enter the name Blog and click the **GENERATE** button, as follows:

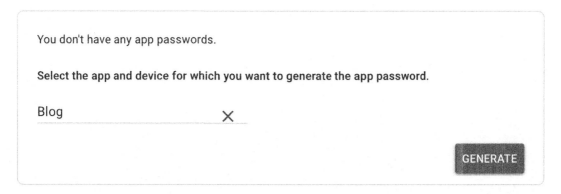

Figure 2.12: Form to generate a new Google app password

A new password will be generated and displayed to you like this:

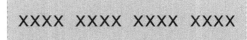

Figure 2.13: Generated Google app password

Copy the generated app password.

Edit the settings.py file of your project and add the app password to the EMAIL_HOST_PASSWORD setting, as follows:

```
# Email server configuration
EMAIL_HOST = 'smtp.gmail.com'
EMAIL_HOST_USER = 'your_account@gmail.com'
EMAIL_HOST_PASSWORD = 'xxxxxxxxxxxxxxxx'
EMAIL_PORT = 587
EMAIL_USE_TLS = True
```

Open the Python shell by running the following command in the system shell prompt:

```
python manage.py shell
```

Execute the following code in the Python shell:

```
>>> from django.core.mail import send_mail
>>> send_mail('Django mail',
...           'This e-mail was sent with Django.',
...           'your_account@gmail.com',
...           ['your_account@gmail.com'],
...           fail_silently=False)
```

The send_mail() function takes the subject, message, sender, and list of recipients as required arguments. By setting the optional argument fail_silently=False, we are telling it to raise an exception if the email cannot be sent. If the output you see is 1, then your email was successfully sent.

Check your inbox. You should have received the email:

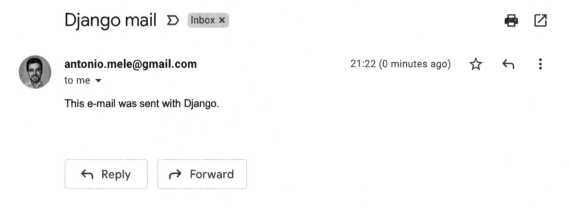

Figure 2.14: Test email sent displayed in Gmail

You just sent your first email with Django! You can find more information about sending emails with Django at https://docs.djangoproject.com/en/4.1/topics/email/.

Let's add this functionality to the post_share view.

Sending emails in views

Edit the post_share view in the views.py file of the blog application, as follows:

```python
from django.core.mail import send_mail

def post_share(request, post_id):
    # Retrieve post by id
    post = get_object_or_404(Post, id=post_id, status=Post.Status.PUBLISHED)
    sent = False

    if request.method == 'POST':
        # Form was submitted
        form = EmailPostForm(request.POST)
        if form.is_valid():
            # Form fields passed validation
            cd = form.cleaned_data
            post_url = request.build_absolute_uri(
                post.get_absolute_url())
            subject = f"{cd['name']} recommends you read " \
                      f"{post.title}"
            message = f"Read {post.title} at {post_url}\n\n" \
                      f"{cd['name']}\'s comments: {cd['comments']}"
            send_mail(subject, message, 'your_account@gmail.com',
                      [cd['to']])
            sent = True
    else:
        form = EmailPostForm()
    return render(request, 'blog/post/share.html', {'post': post,
                                                    'form': form,
                                                    'sent': sent})
```

Replace your_account@gmail.com with your real email account if you are using an SMTP server instead of console.EmailBackend.

In the preceding code, we have declared a sent variable with the initial value True. We set this variable to True after the email is sent. We will use the sent variable later in the template to display a success message when the form is successfully submitted.

Since we have to include a link to the post in the email, we retrieve the absolute path of the post using its get_absolute_url() method. We use this path as an input for request.build_absolute_uri() to build a complete URL, including the HTTP schema and hostname.

We create the subject and the message body of the email using the cleaned data of the validated form. Finally, we send the email to the email address contained in the to field of the form.

Now that the view is complete, we have to add a new URL pattern for it.

Open the urls.py file of your blog application and add the post_share URL pattern, as follows:

```python
from django.urls import path
from . import views

app_name = 'blog'

urlpatterns = [
    # Post views
    # path('', views.post_list, name='post_list'),
    path('', views.PostListView.as_view(), name='post_list'),
    path('<int:year>/<int:month>/<int:day>/<slug:post>/',
        views.post_detail,
        name='post_detail'),
    path('<int:post_id>/share/',
        views.post_share, name='post_share'),
]
```

Rendering forms in templates

After creating the form, programming the view, and adding the URL pattern, the only thing missing is the template for the view.

Create a new file in the blog/templates/blog/post/ directory and name it share.html.

Add the following code to the new share.html template:

```html
{% extends "blog/base.html" %}

{% block title %}Share a post{% endblock %}

{% block content %}
  {% if sent %}
    <h1>E-mail successfully sent</h1>
    <p>
      "{{ post.title }}" was successfully sent to {{ form.cleaned_data.to }}.
    </p>
  {% else %}
    <h1>Share "{{ post.title }}" by e-mail</h1>
    <form method="post">
```

```
        {{ form.as_p }}
        {% csrf_token %}
        <input type="submit" value="Send e-mail">
      </form>
    {% endif %}
{% endblock %}
```

This is the template that is used to both display the form to share a post via email, and to display a success message when the email has been sent. We differentiate between both cases with {% if sent %}.

To display the form, we have defined an HTML form element, indicating that it has to be submitted by the POST method:

```
<form method="post">
```

We have included the form instance with {{ form.as_p }}. We tell Django to render the form fields using HTML paragraph <p> elements by using the as_p method. We could also render the form as an unordered list with as_ul or as an HTML table with as_table. Another option is to render each field by iterating through the form fields, as in the following example:

```
{% for field in form %}
  <div>
    {{ field.errors }}
    {{ field.label_tag }} {{ field }}
  </div>
{% endfor %}
```

We have added a {% csrf_token %} template tag. This tag introduces a hidden field with an autogenerated token to avoid **cross-site request forgery** (CSRF) attacks. These attacks consist of a malicious website or program performing an unwanted action for a user on the site. You can find more information about CSRF at https://owasp.org/www-community/attacks/csrf.

The {% csrf_token %} template tag generates a hidden field that is rendered like this:

```
<input type='hidden' name='csrfmiddlewaretoken'
value='26JjKo2lcEtYkGoV9z4XmJIEHLXN5LDR' />
```

 By default, Django checks for the CSRF token in all POST requests. Remember to include the csrf_token tag in all forms that are submitted via POST.

Edit the blog/post/detail.html template and make it look like this:

```
{% extends "blog/base.html" %}

{% block title %}{{ post.title }}{% endblock %}
```

```
{% block content %}
  <h1>{{ post.title }}</h1>
  <p class="date">
    Published {{ post.publish }} by {{ post.author }}
  </p>
  {{ post.body|linebreaks }}
  <p>
    <a href="{% url "blog:post_share" post.id %}">
      Share this post
    </a>
  </p>
{% endblock %}
```

We have added a link to the post_share URL. The URL is built dynamically with the {% url %} template tag provided by Django. We use the namespace called blog and the URL named post_share. We pass the post id as a parameter to build the URL.

Open the shell prompt and execute the following command to start the development server:

```
python manage.py runserver
```

Open http://127.0.0.1:8000/blog/ in your browser and click on any post title to view the post detail page.

Under the post body, you should see the link that you just added, as shown in *Figure 2.15*:

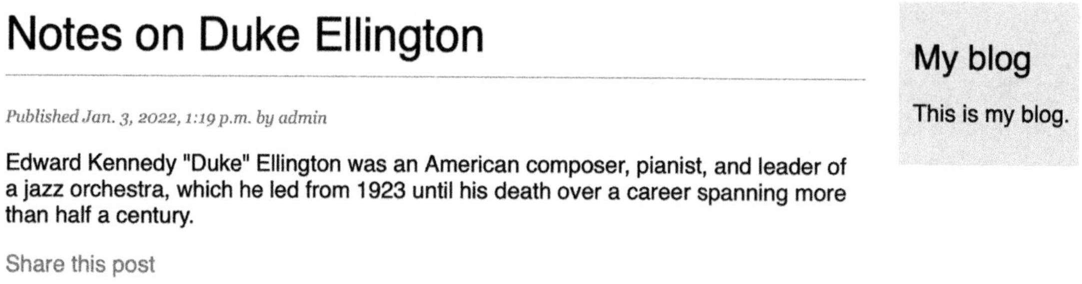

Notes on Duke Ellington

My blog

Published Jan. 3, 2022, 1:19 p.m. by admin

This is my blog.

Edward Kennedy "Duke" Ellington was an American composer, pianist, and leader of a jazz orchestra, which he led from 1923 until his death over a career spanning more than half a century.

Share this post

Figure 2.15: The post detail page, including a link to share the post

Click on **Share this post,** and you should see the page, including the form to share this post by email, as follows:

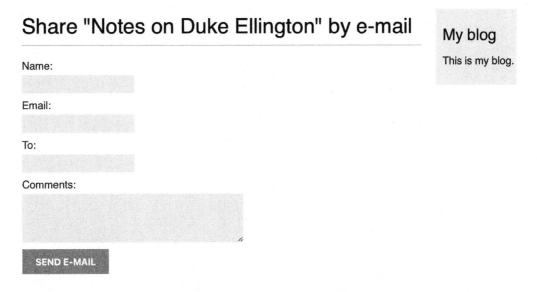

Figure 2.16: The page to share a post via email

CSS styles for the form are included in the example code in the `static/css/blog.css` file. When you click on the **SEND E-MAIL** button, the form is submitted and validated. If all fields contain valid data, you get a success message, as follows:

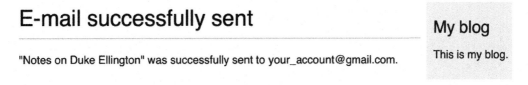

Figure 2.17: A success message for a post shared via email

Send a post to your own email address and check your inbox. The email you receive should look like this:

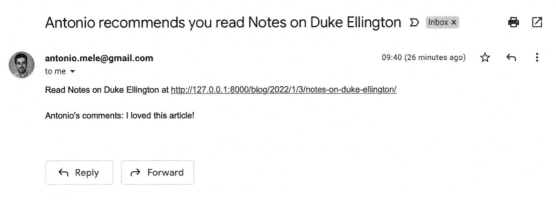

Figure 2.18: Test email sent displayed in Gmail

If you submit the form with invalid data, the form will be rendered again, including all validation errors:

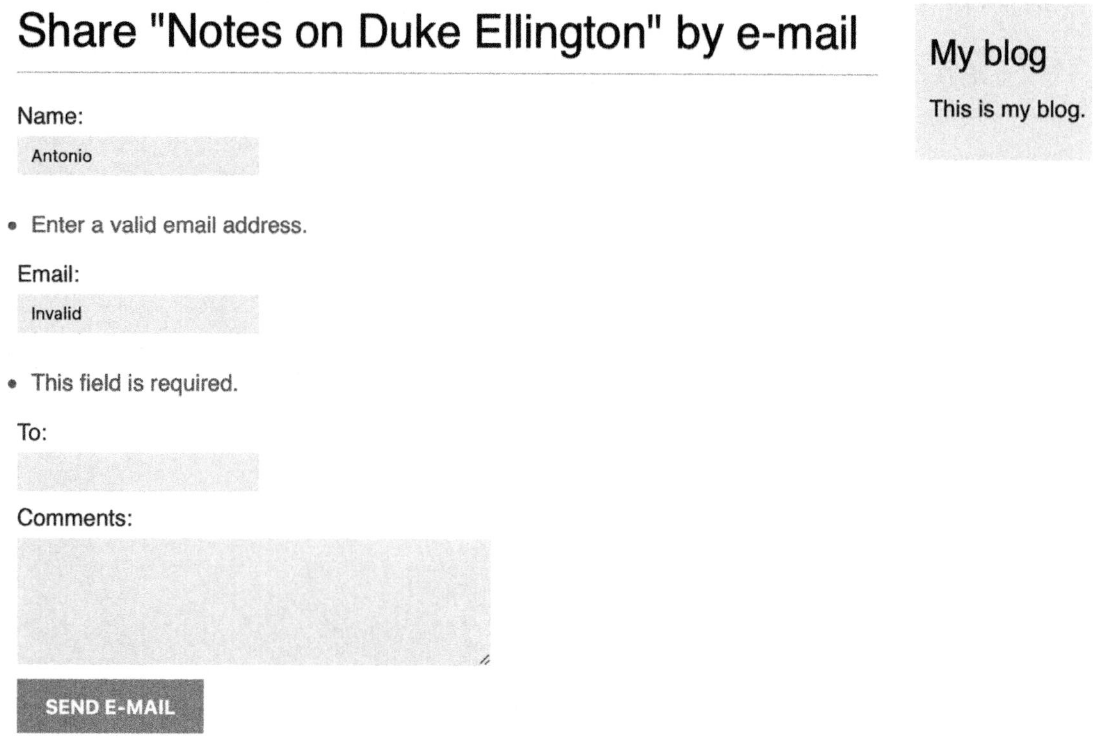

Share "Notes on Duke Ellington" by e-mail

My blog

This is my blog.

Name:

Antonio

- Enter a valid email address.

Email:

Invalid

- This field is required.

To:

Comments:

SEND E-MAIL

Figure 2.19: The share post form displaying invalid data errors

Most modern browsers will prevent you from submitting a form with empty or erroneous fields. This is because the browser validates the fields based on their attributes before submitting the form. In this case, the form won't be submitted, and the browser will display an error message for the fields that are wrong. To test the Django form validation using a modern browser, you can skip the browser form validation by adding the `novalidate` attribute to the HTML `<form>` element, like `<form method="post" novalidate>`. You can add this attribute to prevent the browser from validating fields and test your own form validation. After you are done testing, remove the `novalidate` attribute to keep the browser form validation.

The functionality for sharing posts by email is now complete. You can find more information about working with forms at `https://docs.djangoproject.com/en/4.1/topics/forms/`.

Creating a comment system

We will continue extending our blog application with a comment system that will allow users to comment on posts. To build the comment system, we will need the following:

- A comment model to store user comments on posts
- A form that allows users to submit comments and manages the data validation

- A view that processes the form and saves a new comment to the database
- A list of comments and a form to add a new comment that can be included in the post detail template

Creating a model for comments

Let's start by building a model to store user comments on posts.

Open the `models.py` file of your `blog` application and add the following code:

```
class Comment(models.Model):
    post = models.ForeignKey(Post,
                             on_delete=models.CASCADE,
                             related_name='comments')
    name = models.CharField(max_length=80)
    email = models.EmailField()
    body = models.TextField()
    created = models.DateTimeField(auto_now_add=True)
    updated = models.DateTimeField(auto_now=True)
    active = models.BooleanField(default=True)

    class Meta:
        ordering = ['created']
        indexes = [
            models.Index(fields=['created']),
        ]

    def __str__(self):
        return f'Comment by {self.name} on {self.post}'
```

This is the `Comment` model. We have added a `ForeignKey` field to associate each comment with a single post. This many-to-one relationship is defined in the `Comment` model because each comment will be made on one post, and each post may have multiple comments.

The `related_name` attribute allows you to name the attribute that you use for the relationship from the related object back to this one. We can retrieve the post of a comment object using `comment.post` and retrieve all comments associated with a post object using `post.comments.all()`. If you don't define the `related_name` attribute, Django will use the name of the model in lowercase, followed by `_set` (that is, `comment_set`) to name the relationship of the related object to the object of the model, where this relationship has been defined.

You can learn more about many-to-one relationships at https://docs.djangoproject.com/en/4.1/topics/db/examples/many_to_one/.

We have defined the `active` Boolean field to control the status of the comments. This field will allow us to manually deactivate inappropriate comments using the administration site. We use `default=True` to indicate that all comments are active by default.

We have defined the `created` field to store the date and time when the comment was created. By using `auto_now_add`, the date will be saved automatically when creating an object. In the `Meta` class of the model, we have added `ordering = ['created']` to sort comments in chronological order by default, and we have added an index for the `created` field in ascending order. This will improve the performance of database lookups or ordering results using the `created` field.

The `Comment` model that we have built is not synchronized into the database. We need to generate a new database migration to create the corresponding database table.

Run the following command from the shell prompt:

```
python manage.py makemigrations blog
```

You should see the following output:

```
Migrations for 'blog':
  blog/migrations/0003_comment.py
    - Create model Comment
```

Django has generated a `0003_comment.py` file inside the `migrations/` directory of the `blog` application. We need to create the related database schema and apply the changes to the database.

Run the following command to apply existing migrations:

```
python manage.py migrate
```

You will get an output that includes the following line:

```
Applying blog.0003_comment... OK
```

The migration has been applied and the `blog_comment` table has been created in the database.

Adding comments to the administration site

Next, we will add the new model to the administration site to manage comments through a simple interface.

Open the `admin.py` file of the `blog` application, import the `Comment` model, and add the following `ModelAdmin` class:

```
from .models import Post, Comment


@admin.register(Comment)
class CommentAdmin(admin.ModelAdmin):
    list_display = ['name', 'email', 'post', 'created', 'active']
    list_filter = ['active', 'created', 'updated']
    search_fields = ['name', 'email', 'body']
```

Open the shell prompt and execute the following command to start the development server:

```
python manage.py runserver
```

Open `http://127.0.0.1:8000/admin/` in your browser. You should see the new model included in the **BLOG** section, as shown in *Figure 2.20*:

BLOG
Comments
+ Add
Change
Posts
+ Add
Change

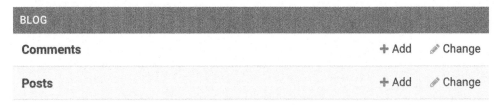

Figure 2.20: Blog application models on the Django administration index page

The model is now registered on the administration site.

In the **Comments** row, click on **Add**. You will see the form to add a new comment:

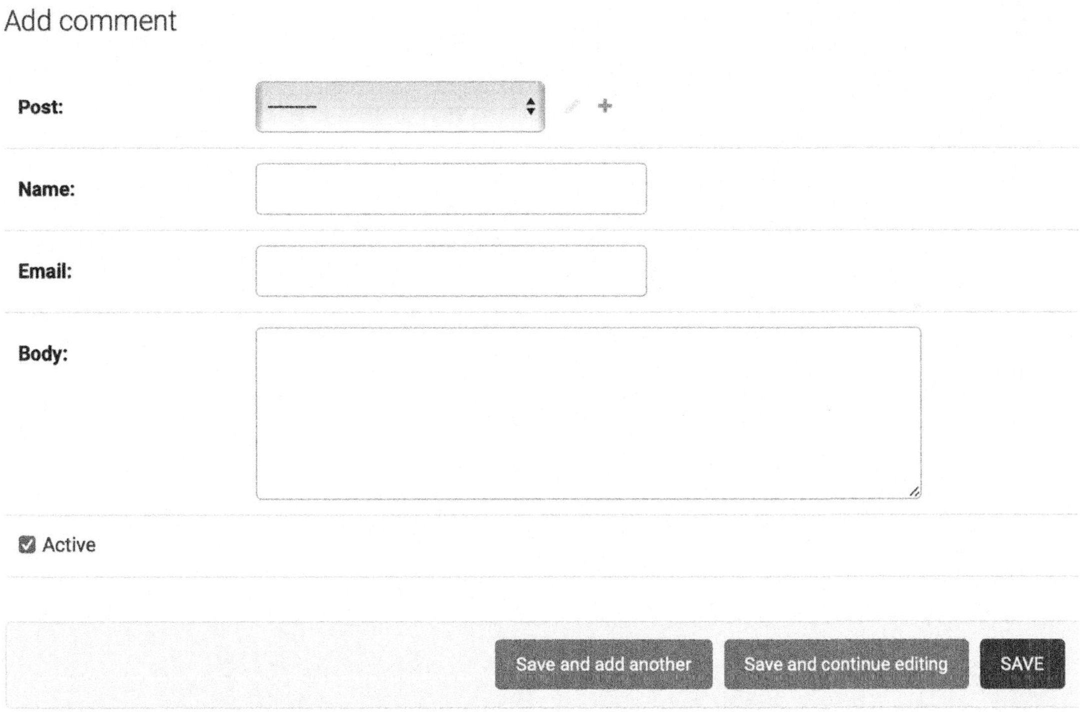

Add comment
Post:
Name:
Email:
Body:
Active
Save and add another
Save and continue editing
SAVE

Figure 2.21: Blog application models on the Django administration index page

Now we can manage `Comment` instances using the administration site.

Creating forms from models

We need to build a form to let users comment on blog posts. Remember that Django has two base classes that can be used to create forms: Form and ModelForm. We used the Form class to allow users to share posts by email. Now we will use ModelForm to take advantage of the existing Comment model and build a form dynamically for it.

Edit the forms.py file of your blog application and add the following lines:

```
from .models import Comment


class CommentForm(forms.ModelForm):
    class Meta:
        model = Comment
        fields = ['name', 'email', 'body']
```

To create a form from a model, we just indicate which model to build the form for in the Meta class of the form. Django will introspect the model and build the corresponding form dynamically.

Each model field type has a corresponding default form field type. The attributes of model fields are taken into account for form validation. By default, Django creates a form field for each field contained in the model. However, we can explicitly tell Django which fields to include in the form using the fields attribute or define which fields to exclude using the exclude attribute. In the CommentForm form, we have explicitly included the name, email, and body fields. These are the only fields that will be included in the form.

You can find more information about creating forms from models at https://docs.djangoproject.com/en/4.1/topics/forms/modelforms/.

Handling ModelForms in views

For sharing posts by email, we used the same view to display the form and manage its submission. We used the HTTP method to differentiate between both cases; GET to display the form and POST to submit it. In this case, we will add the comment form to the post detail page, and we will build a separate view to handle the form submission. The new view that processes the form will allow the user to return to the post detail view once the comment has been stored in the database.

Edit the views.py file of the blog application and add the following code:

```
from django.shortcuts import render, get_object_or_404, redirect
from .models import Post, Comment
from django.core.paginator import Paginator, EmptyPage,\
                                  PageNotAnInteger
from django.views.generic import ListView
from .forms import EmailPostForm, CommentForm
from django.core.mail import send_mail
```

```python
from django.views.decorators.http import require_POST

# ...

@require_POST
def post_comment(request, post_id):
    post = get_object_or_404(Post, id=post_id, status=Post.Status.PUBLISHED)
    comment = None
    # A comment was posted
    form = CommentForm(data=request.POST)
    if form.is_valid():
        # Create a Comment object without saving it to the database
        comment = form.save(commit=False)
        # Assign the post to the comment
        comment.post = post
        # Save the comment to the database
        comment.save()
    return render(request, 'blog/post/comment.html',
                          {'post': post,
                           'form': form,
                           'comment': comment})
```

We have defined the post_comment view that takes the request object and the post_id variable as parameters. We will be using this view to manage the post submission. We expect the form to be submitted using the HTTP POST method. We use the require_POST decorator provided by Django to only allow POST requests for this view. Django allows you to restrict the HTTP methods allowed for views. Django will throw an HTTP 405 (method not allowed) error if you try to access the view with any other HTTP method.

In this view, we have implemented the following actions:

1. We retrieve a published post by its id using the get_object_or_404() shortcut.

2. We define a comment variable with the initial value None. This variable will be used to store the comment object when it gets created.

3. We instantiate the form using the submitted POST data and validate it using the is_valid() method. If the form is invalid, the template is rendered with the validation errors.

4. If the form is valid, we create a new Comment object by calling the form's save() method and assign it to the new_comment variable, as follows:

    ```python
    comment = form.save(commit=False)
    ```

5. The save() method creates an instance of the model that the form is linked to and saves it to the database. If you call it using commit=False, the model instance is created but not saved to the database. This allows us to modify the object before finally saving it.

The `save()` method is available for `ModelForm` but not for `Form` instances since they are not linked to any model.

6. We assign the post to the comment we created:

    ```
    comment.post = post
    ```

7. We save the new comment to the database by calling its `save()` method:

    ```
    comment.save()
    ```

8. We render the template `blog/post/comment.html`, passing the post, `form`, and `comment` objects in the template context. This template doesn't exist yet; we will create it later.

Let's create a URL pattern for this view.

Edit the `urls.py` file of the `blog` application and add the following URL pattern to it:

```
from django.urls import path
from . import views

app_name = 'blog'

urlpatterns = [
    # Post views
    # path('', views.post_list, name='post_list'),
    path('', views.PostListView.as_view(), name='post_list'),
    path('<int:year>/<int:month>/<int:day>/<slug:post>/',
        views.post_detail,
        name='post_detail'),
    path('<int:post_id>/share/',
        views.post_share, name='post_share'),
    path('<int:post_id>/comment/',
        views.post_comment, name='post_comment'),
]
```

We have implemented the view to manage the submission of comments and their corresponding URL. Let's create the necessary templates.

Creating templates for the comment form

We will create a template for the comment form that we will use in two places:

*   In the post detail template associated with the `post_detail` view to let users publish comments
*   In the post comment template associated with the `post_comment` view to display the form again if there are any form errors.

We will create the form template and use the {% include %} template tag to include it in the two other templates.

In the templates/blog/post/ directory, create a new includes/ directory. Add a new file inside this directory and name it comment_form.html.

The file structure should look as follows:

```
templates/
  blog/
    post/
      includes/
        comment_form.html
      detail.html
      list.html
      share.html
```

Edit the new blog/post/includes/comment_form.html template and add the following code:

```html
<h2>Add a new comment</h2>
<form action="{% url "blog:post_comment" post.id %}" method="post">
  {{ form.as_p }}
  {% csrf_token %}
  <p><input type="submit" value="Add comment"></p>
</form>
```

In this template, we build the action URL of the HTML <form> element dynamically using the {% url %} template tag. We build the URL of the post_comment view that will process the form. We display the form rendered in paragraphs and we include {% csrf_token %} for CSRF protection because this form will be submitted with the POST method.

Create a new file in the templates/blog/post/ directory of the blog application and name it comment.html.

The file structure should now look as follows:

```
templates/
  blog/
    post/
      includes/
        comment_form.html
      comment.html
      detail.html
      list.html
      share.html
```

Edit the new blog/post/comment.html template and add the following code:

```
{% extends "blog/base.html" %}

{% block title %}Add a comment{% endblock %}

{% block content %}
  {% if comment %}
    <h2>Your comment has been added.</h2>
    <p><a href="{{ post.get_absolute_url }}">Back to the post</a></p>
  {% else %}
    {% include "blog/post/includes/comment_form.html" %}
  {% endif %}
{% endblock %}
```

This is the template for the post comment view. In this view, we expect the form to be submitted via the POST method. The template covers two different scenarios:

- If the form data submitted is valid, the comment variable will contain the comment object that was created, and a success message will be displayed.
- If the form data submitted is not valid, the comment variable will be None. In this case, we will display the comment form. We use the {% include %} template tag to include the comment_form. html template that we have previously created.

Adding comments to the post detail view

Edit the views.py file of the blog application and edit the post_detail view as follows:

```
def post_detail(request, year, month, day, post):
    post = get_object_or_404(Post,
                             status=Post.Status.PUBLISHED,
                             slug=post,
                             publish__year=year,
                             publish__month=month,
                             publish__day=day)
    # List of active comments for this post
    comments = post.comments.filter(active=True)
    # Form for users to comment
    form = CommentForm()
    return render(request,
                  'blog/post/detail.html',
                  {'post': post,
                   'comments': comments,
                   'form': form})
```

Let's review the code we have added to the post_detail view:

- We have added a QuerySet to retrieve all active comments for the post, as follows:

  ```
  comments = post.comments.filter(active=True)
  ```

- This QuerySet is built using the post object. Instead of building a QuerySet for the Comment model directly, we leverage the post object to retrieve the related Comment objects. We use the comments manager for the related Comment objects that we previously defined in the Comment model, using the related_name attribute of the ForeignKey field to the Post model.

- We have also created an instance of the comment form with form = CommentForm().

Adding comments to the post detail template

We need to edit the blog/post/detail.html template to implement the following:

- Display the total number of comments for a post
- Display the list of comments
- Display the form for users to add a new comment

We will start by adding the total number of comments for a post.

Edit the blog/post/detail.html template and change it as follows:

```
{% extends "blog/base.html" %}

{% block title %}{{ post.title }}{% endblock %}

{% block content %}
  <h1>{{ post.title }}</h1>
  <p class="date">
    Published {{ post.publish }} by {{ post.author }}
  </p>
  {{ post.body|linebreaks }}
  <p>
    <a href="{% url "blog:post_share" post.id %}">
      Share this post
    </a>
  </p>
  {% with comments.count as total_comments %}
    <h2>
      {{ total_comments }} comment{{ total_comments|pluralize }}
    </h2>
  {% endwith %}
{% endblock %}
```

We use the Django ORM in the template, executing the `comments.count()` QuerySet. Note that the Django template language doesn't use parentheses for calling methods. The {% with %} tag allows you to assign a value to a new variable that will be available in the template until the {% endwith %} tag.

 The {% with %} template tag is useful for avoiding hitting the database or accessing expensive methods multiple times.

We use the `pluralize` template filter to display a plural suffix for the word "comment," depending on the `total_comments` value. Template filters take the value of the variable they are applied to as their input and return a computed value. We will learn more about template filters in *Chapter 3, Extending Your Blog Application*.

The `pluralize` template filter returns a string with the letter "s" if the value is different from 1. The preceding text will be rendered as *0 comments*, *1 comment*, or *N comments*, depending on the number of active comments for the post.

Now, let's add the list of active comments to the post detail template.

Edit the `blog/post/detail.html` template and implement the following changes:

```
{% extends "blog/base.html" %}

{% block title %}{{ post.title }}{% endblock %}

{% block content %}
  <h1>{{ post.title }}</h1>
  <p class="date">
    Published {{ post.publish }} by {{ post.author }}
  </p>
  {{ post.body|linebreaks }}
  <p>
    <a href="{% url "blog:post_share" post.id %}">
      Share this post
    </a>
  </p>
  {% with comments.count as total_comments %}
    <h2>
      {{ total_comments }} comment{{ total_comments|pluralize }}
    </h2>
  {% endwith %}
  {% for comment in comments %}
    <div class="comment">
```

```
      <p class="info">
        Comment {{ forloop.counter }} by {{ comment.name }}
        {{ comment.created }}
      </p>
      {{ comment.body|linebreaks }}
    </div>
  {% empty %}
    <p>There are no comments.</p>
  {% endfor %}
{% endblock %}
```

We have added a `{% for %}` template tag to loop through the post comments. If the `comments` list is empty, we display a message that informs users that there are no comments for this post. We enumerate comments with the `{{ forloop.counter }}` variable, which contains the loop counter in each iteration. For each post, we display the name of the user who posted it, the date, and the body of the comment.

Finally, let's add the comment form to the template.

Edit the `blog/post/detail.html` template and include the comment form template as follows:

```
{% extends "blog/base.html" %}

{% block title %}{{ post.title }}{% endblock %}

{% block content %}
  <h1>{{ post.title }}</h1>
  <p class="date">
    Published {{ post.publish }} by {{ post.author }}
  </p>
  {{ post.body|linebreaks }}
  <p>
    <a href="{% url "blog:post_share" post.id %}">
      Share this post
    </a>
  </p>
  {% with comments.count as total_comments %}
    <h2>
      {{ total_comments }} comment{{ total_comments|pluralize }}
    </h2>
  {% endwith %}
  {% for comment in comments %}
```

```
    <div class="comment">
      <p class="info">
        Comment {{ forloop.counter }} by {{ comment.name }}
        {{ comment.created }}
      </p>
      {{ comment.body|linebreaks }}
    </div>
  {% empty %}
    <p>There are no comments.</p>
  {% endfor %}
  {% include "blog/post/includes/comment_form.html" %}
{% endblock %}
```

Open `http://127.0.0.1:8000/blog/` in your browser and click on a post title to take a look at the post detail page. You will see something like *Figure 2.22*:

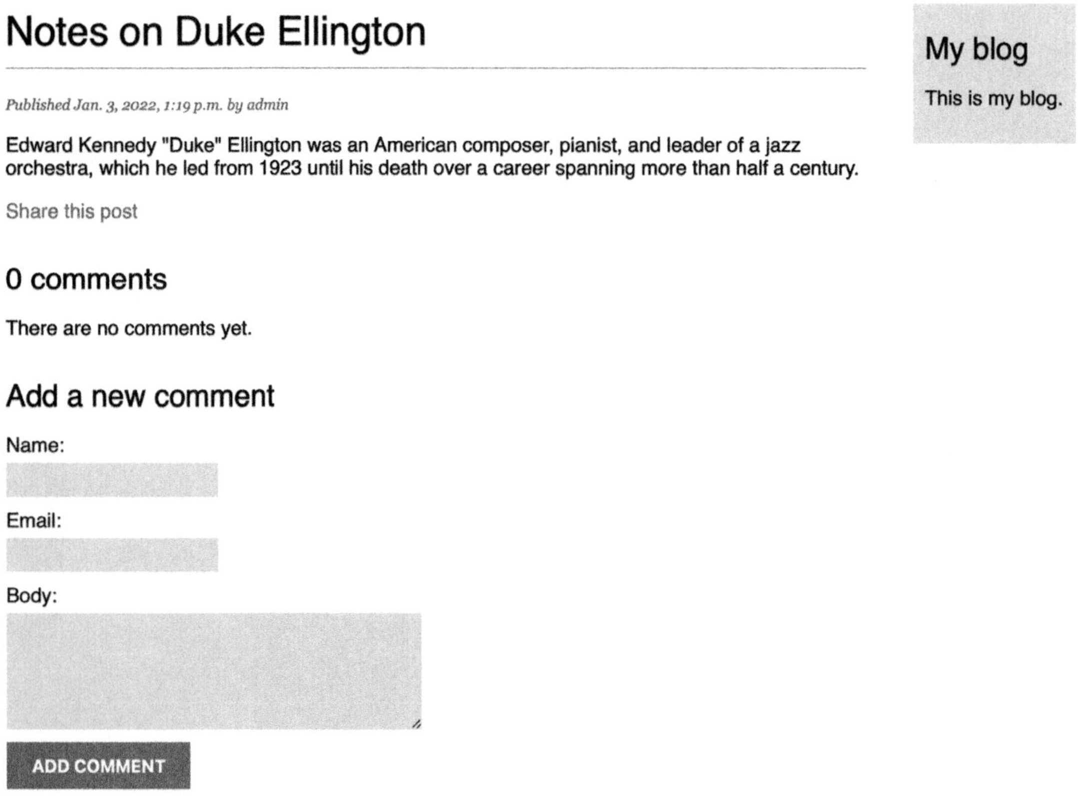

Notes on Duke Ellington

Published Jan. 3, 2022, 1:19 p.m. by admin

Edward Kennedy "Duke" Ellington was an American composer, pianist, and leader of a jazz orchestra, which he led from 1923 until his death over a career spanning more than half a century.

Share this post

My blog

This is my blog.

0 comments

There are no comments yet.

Add a new comment

Name:

Email:

Body:

ADD COMMENT

Figure 2.22: The post detail page, including the form to add a comment

Fill in the comment form with valid data and click on **Add comment.** You should see the following page:

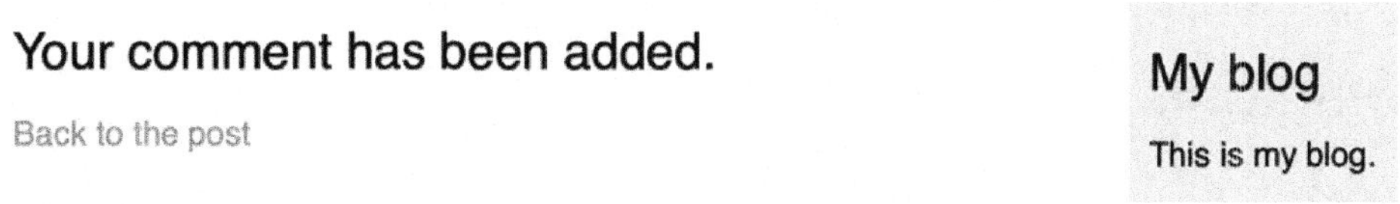

Your comment has been added.

Back to the post

My blog

This is my blog.

Figure 2.23: The comment added success page

Click on the **Back to the post** link. You should be redirected back to the post detail page, and you should be able to see the comment that you just added, as follows:

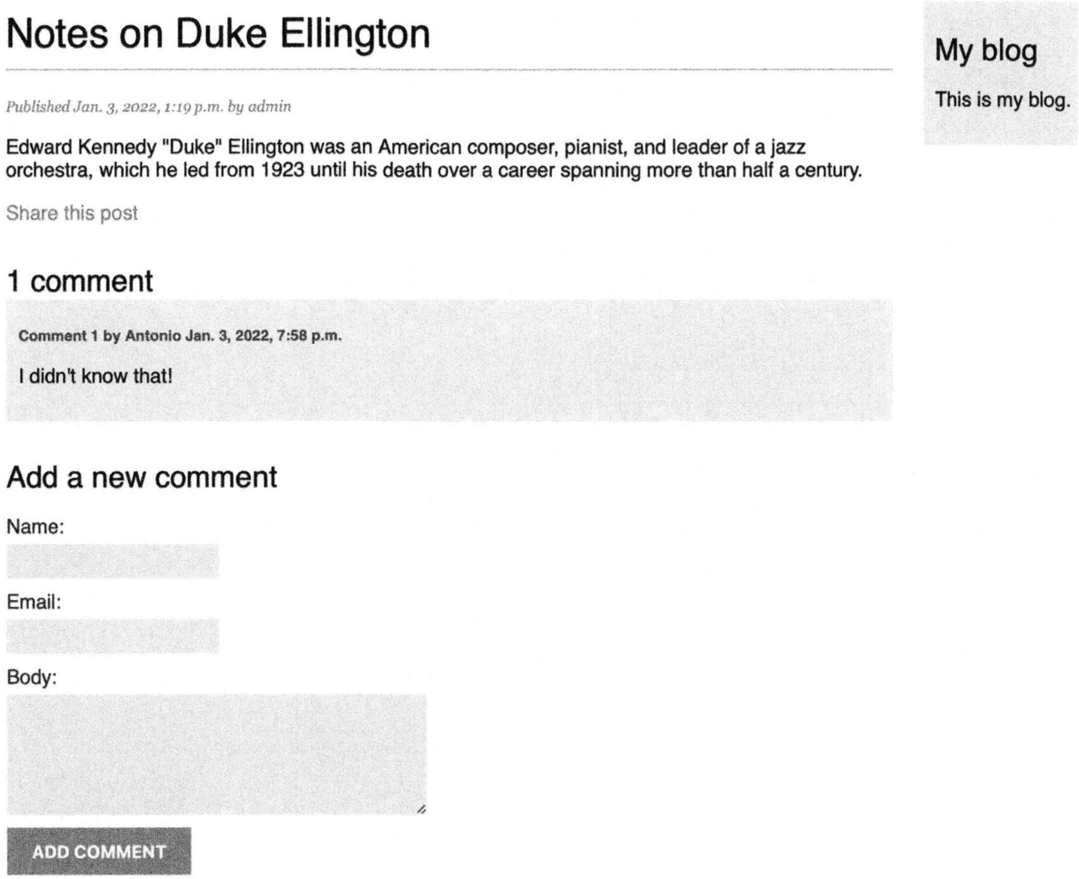

Notes on Duke Ellington

My blog

This is my blog.

Published Jan. 3, 2022, 1:19 p.m. by admin

Edward Kennedy "Duke" Ellington was an American composer, pianist, and leader of a jazz orchestra, which he led from 1923 until his death over a career spanning more than half a century.

Share this post

1 comment

Comment 1 by Antonio Jan. 3, 2022, 7:58 p.m.

I didn't know that!

Add a new comment

Name:

Email:

Body:

ADD COMMENT

Figure 2.24: The post detail page, including a comment

Add one more comment to the post. The comments should appear below the post contents in chronological order, as follows:

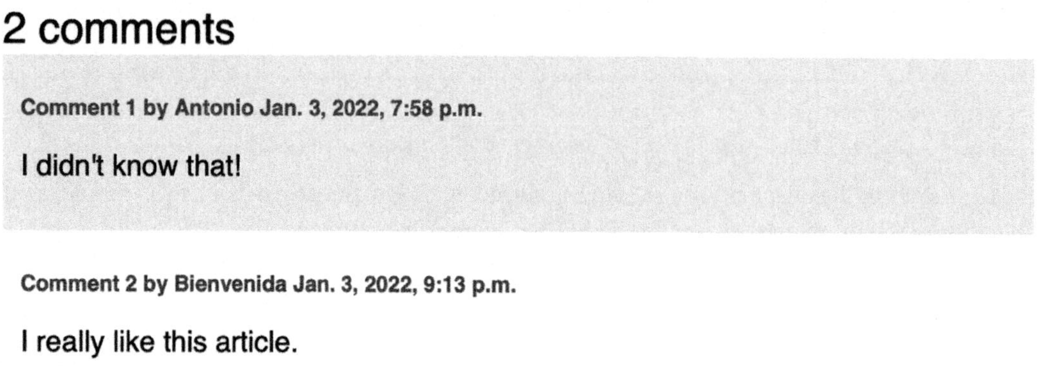

2 comments

Comment 1 by Antonio Jan. 3, 2022, 7:58 p.m.

I didn't know that!

Comment 2 by Bienvenida Jan. 3, 2022, 9:13 p.m.

I really like this article.

Figure 2.25: The comment list on the post detail page

Open `http://127.0.0.1:8000/admin/blog/comment/` in your browser. You will see the administration page with the list of comments you created, like this:

Select comment to change

	NAME	EMAIL	POST	CREATED	ACTIVE
☐	**Antonio**	test_account@gmail.com	Notes on Duke Ellington	Jan. 3, 2022, 7:58 p.m.	✓
☐	**Bienvenida**	test_account2@gmail.com	Notes on Duke Ellington	Jan. 3, 2022, 9:13 p.m.	✓

2 comments

Figure 2.26: List of comments on the administration site

Click on the name of one of the posts to edit it. Uncheck the **Active** checkbox as follows and click on the **Save** button:

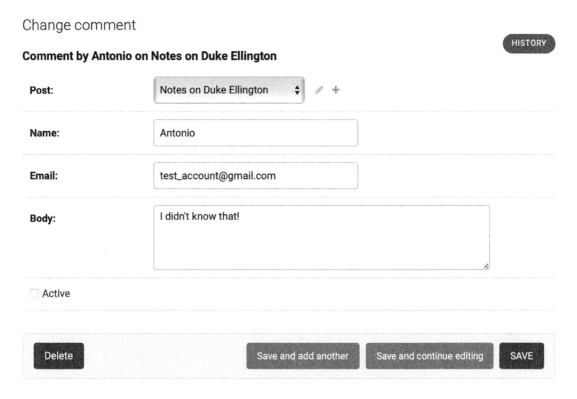

Figure 2.27: Editing a comment on the administration site

You will be redirected to the list of comments. The **Active** column will display an inactive icon for the comment, as shown in *Figure 2.28*:

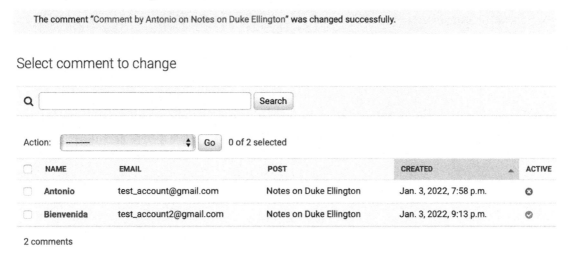

Figure 2.28: Active/inactive comments on the administration site

If you return to the post detail view, you will note that the inactive comment is no longer displayed, neither is it counted for the total number of active comments for the post:

1 comment

Comment 1 by Bienvenida Jan. 3, 2022, 9:13 p.m.

I really like this article.

Figure 2.29: A single active comment displayed on the post detail page

Thanks to the `active` field, you can deactivate inappropriate comments and avoid showing them on your posts.

Additional resources

The following resources provide additional information related to the topics covered in this chapter:

- Source code for this chapter – `https://github.com/PacktPublishing/Django-4-by-example/tree/main/Chapter02`
- URLs utility functions – `https://docs.djangoproject.com/en/4.1/ref/urlresolvers/`
- URL path converters – `https://docs.djangoproject.com/en/4.1/topics/http/urls/#path-converters`
- Django paginator class – `https://docs.djangoproject.com/en/4.1/ref/paginator/`
- Introduction to class-based views – `https://docs.djangoproject.com/en/4.1/topics/class-based-views/intro/`
- Sending emails with Django – `https://docs.djangoproject.com/en/4.1/topics/email/`
- Django form field types – `https://docs.djangoproject.com/en/4.1/ref/forms/fields/`
- Working with forms – `https://docs.djangoproject.com/en/4.1/topics/forms/`
- Creating forms from models – `https://docs.djangoproject.com/en/4.1/topics/forms/modelforms/`
- Many-to-one model relationships – `https://docs.djangoproject.com/en/4.1/topics/db/examples/many_to_one/`

Summary

In this chapter, you learned how to define canonical URLs for models. You created SEO-friendly URLs for blog posts, and you implemented object pagination for your post list. You also learned how to work with Django forms and model forms. You created a system to recommend posts by email and created a comment system for your blog.

In the next chapter, you will create a tagging system for the blog. You will learn how to build complex QuerySets to retrieve objects by similarity. You will learn how to create custom template tags and filters. You will also build a custom sitemap and feed for your blog posts and implement a full-text search functionality for your posts.

3

Extending Your Blog Application

The previous chapter went through the basics of forms and the creation of a comment system. You also learned how to send emails with Django. In this chapter, you will extend your blog application with other popular features used on blogging platforms, such as tagging, recommending similar posts, providing an RSS feed to readers, and allowing them to search posts. You will learn about new components and functionalities with Django by building these functionalities.

The chapter will cover the following topics:

- Integrating third-party applications
- Using `django-taggit` to implement a tagging system
- Building complex QuerySets to recommend similar posts
- Creating custom template tags and filters to show a list of the latest posts and most commented posts in the sidebar
- Creating a sitemap using the sitemap framework
- Building an RSS feed using the syndication framework
- Installing PostgreSQL
- Implementing a full-text search engine with Django and PostgreSQL

The source code for this chapter can be found at `https://github.com/PacktPublishing/Django-4-by-example/tree/main/Chapter03`.

All Python packages used in this chapter are included in the `requirements.txt` file in the source code for the chapter. You can follow the instructions to install each Python package in the following sections, or you can install all the requirements at once with the command `pip install -r requirements.txt`.

Adding the tagging functionality

A very common functionality in blogs is to categorize posts using tags. Tags allow you to categorize content in a non-hierarchical manner, using simple keywords. A tag is simply a label or keyword that can be assigned to posts. We will create a tagging system by integrating a third-party Django tagging application into the project.

django-taggit is a reusable application that primarily offers you a Tag model and a manager to easily add tags to any model. You can take a look at its source code at https://github.com/jazzband/django-taggit.

First, you need to install django-taggit via pip by running the following command:

```
pip install django-taggit==3.0.0
```

Then, open the settings.py file of the mysite project and add taggit to your INSTALLED_APPS setting, as follows:

```
INSTALLED_APPS = [
    'django.contrib.admin',
    'django.contrib.auth',
    'django.contrib.contenttypes',
    'django.contrib.sessions',
    'django.contrib.messages',
    'django.contrib.staticfiles',
    'blog.apps.BlogConfig',
    'taggit',
]
```

Open the models.py file of your blog application and add the TaggableManager manager provided by django-taggit to the Post model using the following code:

```
from taggit.managers import TaggableManager

class Post(models.Model):
    # ...
    tags = TaggableManager()
```

The tags manager will allow you to add, retrieve, and remove tags from Post objects.

The following schema shows the data models defined by django-taggit to create tags and store related tagged objects:

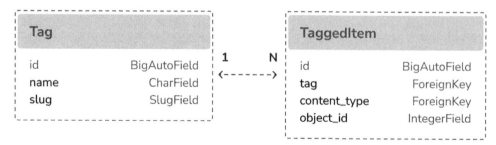

Figure 3.1: Tag models of django-taggit

The Tag model is used to store tags. It contains a name and a slug field.

The TaggedItem model is used to store the related tagged objects. It has a ForeignKey field for the related Tag object. It contains a ForeignKey to a ContentType object and an IntegerField to store the related id of the tagged object. The content_type and object_id fields combined form a generic relationship with any model in your project. This allows you to create relationships between a Tag instance and any other model instance of your applications. You will learn about generic relations in *Chapter 7, Tracking User Actions*.

Run the following command in the shell prompt to create a migration for your model changes:

```
python manage.py makemigrations blog
```

You should get the following output:

```
Migrations for 'blog':
  blog/migrations/0004_post_tags.py
    - Add field tags to post
```

Now, run the following command to create the required database tables for django-taggit models and to synchronize your model changes:

```
python manage.py migrate
```

You will see an output indicating that migrations have been applied, as follows:

```
Applying taggit.0001_initial... OK
Applying taggit.0002_auto_20150616_2121... OK
Applying taggit.0003_taggeditem_add_unique_index... OK
Applying taggit.0004_alter_taggeditem_content_type_alter_taggeditem_tag... OK
Applying taggit.0005_auto_20220424_2025... OK
Applying blog.0004_post_tags... OK
```

The database is now in sync with the taggit models and we can start using the functionalities of django-taggit.

Let's now explore how to use the tags manager.

Open the Django shell by running the following command in the system shell prompt:

```
python manage.py shell
```

Run the following code to retrieve one of the posts (the one with the 1 ID):

```
>>> from blog.models import Post
>>> post = Post.objects.get(id=1)
```

Then, add some tags to it and retrieve its tags to check whether they were successfully added:

```
>>> post.tags.add('music', 'jazz', 'django')
>>> post.tags.all()
<QuerySet [<Tag: jazz>, <Tag: music>, <Tag: django>]>
```

Finally, remove a tag and check the list of tags again:

```
>>> post.tags.remove('django')
>>> post.tags.all()
<QuerySet [<Tag: jazz>, <Tag: music>]>
```

It's really easy to add, retrieve, or remove tags from a model using the manager we have defined.

Start the development server from the shell prompt with the following command:

```
python manage.py runserver
```

Open http://127.0.0.1:8000/admin/taggit/tag/ in your browser.

You will see the administration page with the list of Tag objects of the taggit application:

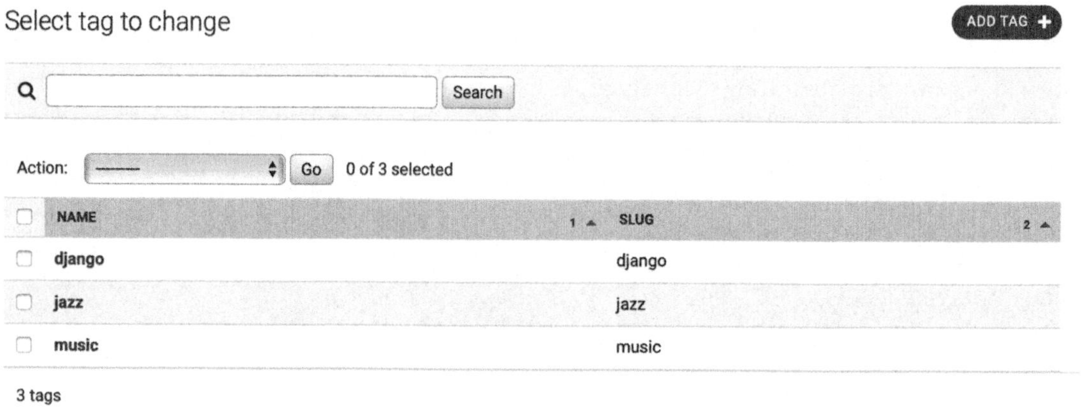

Select tag to change

ADD TAG +

	NAME	1 ▲	SLUG	2 ▲
☐	django		django	
☐	jazz		jazz	
☐	music		music	

Action: [———] [Go] 0 of 3 selected

3 tags

Figure 3.2: The tag change list view on the Django administration site

Click on the jazz tag. You will see the following:

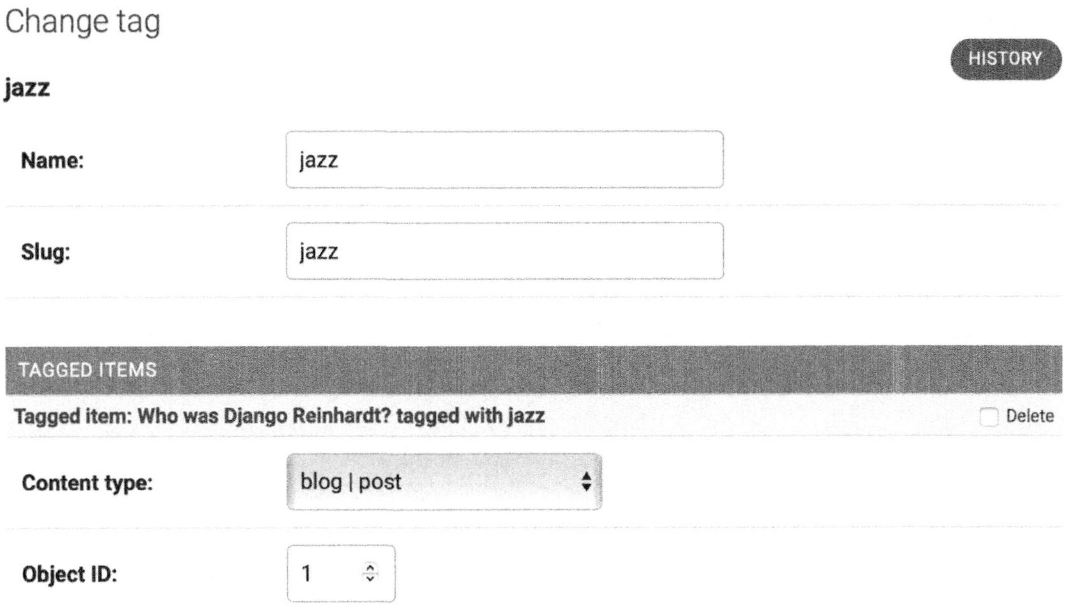

Change tag

jazz

HISTORY

Name: jazz

Slug: jazz

TAGGED ITEMS

Tagged item: Who was Django Reinhardt? tagged with jazz ☐ Delete

Content type: blog | post

Object ID: 1

Figure 3.3: The related tags field of a Post object

Navigate to `http://127.0.0.1:8000/admin/blog/post/1/change/` to edit the post with ID 1.

You will see that posts now include a new **Tags** field, as follows, where you can easily edit tags:

Tags: jazz, music

A comma-separated list of tags.

Figure 3.4: The related tags field of a Post object

Now, you need to edit your blog posts to display tags.

Open the blog/post/list.html template and add the following HTML code highlighted in bold:

```
{% extends "blog/base.html" %}

{% block title %}My Blog{% endblock %}

{% block content %}
  <h1>My Blog</h1>
  {% for post in posts %}
    <h2>
      <a href="{{ post.get_absolute_url }}">
        {{ post.title }}
      </a>
    </h2>
    <p class="tags">Tags: {{ post.tags.all|join:", " }}</p>
    <p class="date">
      Published {{ post.publish }} by {{ post.author }}
    </p>
    {{ post.body|truncatewords:30|linebreaks }}
  {% endfor %}
  {% include "pagination.html" with page=page_obj %}
{% endblock %}
```

The join template filter works the same as the Python string join() method to concatenate elements with the given string.

Open http://127.0.0.1:8000/blog/ in your browser. You should be able to see the list of tags under each post title:

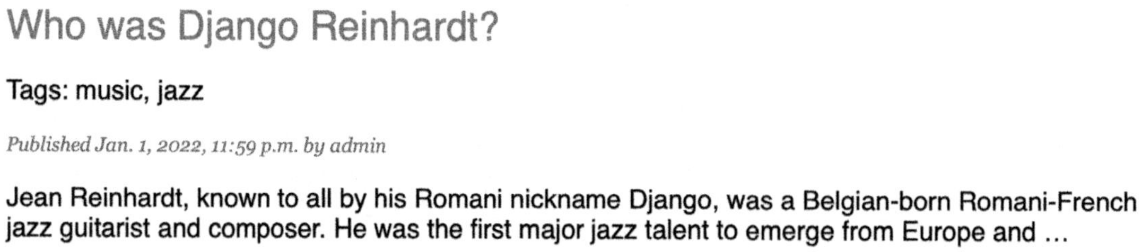

Who was Django Reinhardt?

Tags: music, jazz

Published Jan. 1, 2022, 11:59 p.m. by admin

Jean Reinhardt, known to all by his Romani nickname Django, was a Belgian-born Romani-French jazz guitarist and composer. He was the first major jazz talent to emerge from Europe and …

Figure 3.5: The Post list item, including related tags

Next, we will edit the post_list view to let users list all posts tagged with a specific tag.

Open the `views.py` file of your `blog` application, import the `Tag` model from `django-taggit`, and change the `post_list` view to optionally filter posts by a tag, as follows. New code is highlighted in bold:

```python
from taggit.models import Tag


def post_list(request, tag_slug=None):
    post_list = Post.published.all()
    tag = None
    if tag_slug:
        tag = get_object_or_404(Tag, slug=tag_slug)
        post_list = post_list.filter(tags__in=[tag])
    # Pagination with 3 posts per page
    paginator = Paginator(post_list, 3)
    page_number = request.GET.get('page', 1)
    try:
        posts = paginator.page(page_number)
    except PageNotAnInteger:
        # If page_number is not an integer deliver the first page
        posts = paginator.page(1)
    except EmptyPage:
        # If page_number is out of range deliver last page of results
        posts = paginator.page(paginator.num_pages)
    return render(request,
                  'blog/post/list.html',
                  {'posts': posts,
                   'tag': tag})
```

The `post_list` view now works as follows:

1. It takes an optional `tag_slug` parameter that has a `None` default value. This parameter will be passed in the URL.

2. Inside the view, we build the initial QuerySet, retrieving all published posts, and if there is a given tag slug, we get the `Tag` object with the given slug using the `get_object_or_404()` shortcut.

3. Then, we filter the list of posts by the ones that contain the given tag. Since this is a many-to-many relationship, we have to filter posts by tags contained in a given list, which, in this case, contains only one element. We use the `__in` field lookup. Many-to-many relationships occur when multiple objects of a model are associated with multiple objects of another model. In our application, a post can have multiple tags and a tag can be related to multiple posts. You will learn how to create many-to-many relationships in *Chapter 6, Sharing Content on Your Website*. You can discover more about many-to-many relationships at `https://docs.djangoproject.com/en/4.1/topics/db/examples/many_to_many/`.

4. Finally, the `render()` function now passes the new `tag` variable to the template.

Remember that QuerySets are lazy. The QuerySets to retrieve posts will only be evaluated when you loop over the post list when rendering the template.

Open the urls.py file of your blog application, comment out the class-based PostListView URL pattern, and uncomment the post_list view, like this:

```
path('', views.post_list, name='post_list'),
# path('', views.PostListView.as_view(), name='post_list'),
```

Add the following additional URL pattern to list posts by tag:

```
path('tag/<slug:tag_slug>/',
     views.post_list, name='post_list_by_tag'),
```

As you can see, both patterns point to the same view, but they have different names. The first pattern will call the post_list view without any optional parameters, whereas the second pattern will call the view with the tag_slug parameter. You use a slug path converter to match the parameter as a lowercase string with ASCII letters or numbers, plus the hyphen and underscore characters.

The urls.py file of the blog application should now look like this:

```
from django.urls import path
from . import views


app_name = 'blog'


urlpatterns = [
    # Post views
    path('', views.post_list, name='post_list'),
    # path('', views.PostListView.as_view(), name='post_list'),
    path('tag/<slug:tag_slug>/',
         views.post_list, name='post_list_by_tag'),
    path('<int:year>/<int:month>/<int:day>/<slug:post>/',
         views.post_detail,
         name='post_detail'),
    path('<int:post_id>/share/',
         views.post_share, name='post_share'),
    path('<int:post_id>/comment/',
         views.post_comment, name='post_comment'),
]
```

Since you are using the post_list view, edit the blog/post/list.html template and modify the pagination to use the posts object:

```
{% include "pagination.html" with page=posts %}
```

Add the following lines highlighted in bold to the `blog/post/list.html` template:

```
{% extends "blog/base.html" %}

{% block title %}My Blog{% endblock %}

{% block content %}
  <h1>My Blog</h1>
  {% if tag %}
    <h2>Posts tagged with "{{ tag.name }}"</h2>
  {% endif %}
  {% for post in posts %}
    <h2>
      <a href="{{ post.get_absolute_url }}">
        {{ post.title }}
      </a>
    </h2>
    <p class="tags">Tags: {{ post.tags.all|join:", " }}</p>
    <p class="date">
      Published {{ post.publish }} by {{ post.author }}
    </p>
    {{ post.body|truncatewords:30|linebreaks }}
  {% endfor %}
  {% include "pagination.html" with page=posts %}
{% endblock %}
```

If a user is accessing the blog, they will see the list of all posts. If they filter by posts tagged with a specific tag, they will see the tag that they are filtering by.

Now, edit the `blog/post/list.html` template and change the way tags are displayed, as follows. New lines are highlighted in bold:

```
{% extends "blog/base.html" %}

{% block title %}My Blog{% endblock %}

{% block content %}
  <h1>My Blog</h1>
  {% if tag %}
    <h2>Posts tagged with "{{ tag.name }}"</h2>
  {% endif %}
  {% for post in posts %}
    <h2>
      <a href="{{ post.get_absolute_url }}">
        {{ post.title }}
```

```
      </a>
    </h2>
    <p class="tags">
      Tags:
      {% for tag in post.tags.all %}
        <a href="{% url "blog:post_list_by_tag" tag.slug %}">
          {{ tag.name }}
        </a>
        {% if not forloop.last %}, {% endif %}
      {% endfor %}
    </p>
    <p class="date">
      Published {{ post.publish }} by {{ post.author }}
    </p>
    {{ post.body|truncatewords:30|linebreaks }}
  {% endfor %}
  {% include "pagination.html" with page=posts %}
{% endblock %}
```

In the preceding code, we loop through all the tags of a post displaying a custom link to the URL to filter posts by that tag. We build the URL with {% url "blog:post_list_by_tag" tag.slug %}, using the name of the URL and the slug tag as its parameter. You separate the tags by commas.

Open http://127.0.0.1:8000/blog/tag/jazz/ in your browser. You will see the list of posts filtered by that tag, like this:

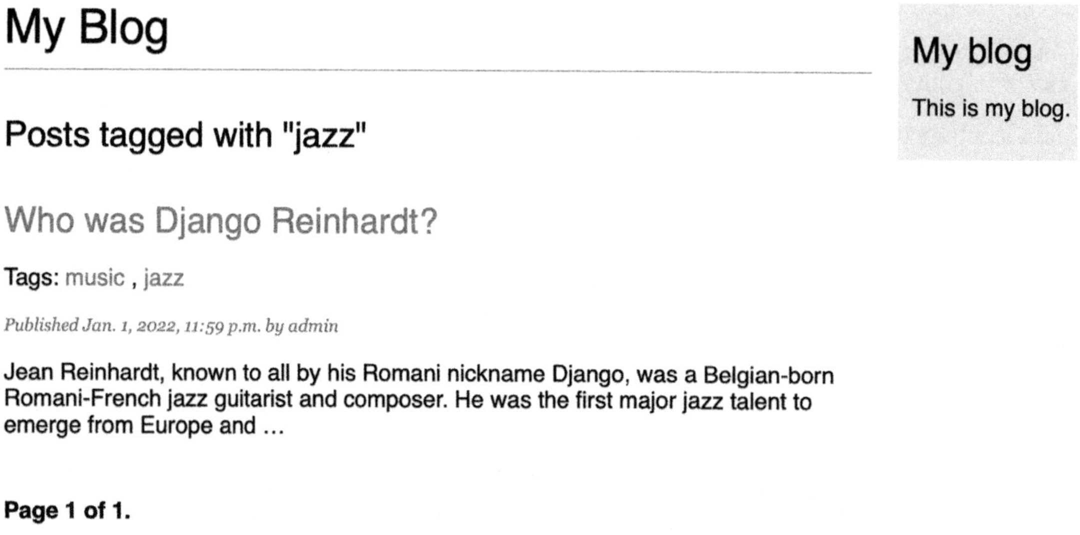

My Blog

My blog

This is my blog.

Posts tagged with "jazz"

Who was Django Reinhardt?

Tags: music , jazz

Published Jan. 1, 2022, 11:59 p.m. by admin

Jean Reinhardt, known to all by his Romani nickname Django, was a Belgian-born Romani-French jazz guitarist and composer. He was the first major jazz talent to emerge from Europe and …

Page 1 of 1.

Figure 3.6: A post filtered by the tag "jazz"

Retrieving posts by similarity

Now that we have implemented tagging for blog posts, you can do many interesting things with tags. Tags allow you to categorize posts in a non-hierarchical manner. Posts about similar topics will have several tags in common. We will build a functionality to display similar posts by the number of tags they share. In this way, when a user reads a post, we can suggest to them that they read other related posts.

In order to retrieve similar posts for a specific post, you need to perform the following steps:

1. Retrieve all tags for the current post
2. Get all posts that are tagged with any of those tags
3. Exclude the current post from that list to avoid recommending the same post
4. Order the results by the number of tags shared with the current post
5. In the case of two or more posts with the same number of tags, recommend the most recent post
6. Limit the query to the number of posts you want to recommend

These steps are translated into a complex QuerySet that you will include in your `post_detail` view.

Open the `views.py` file of your `blog` application and add the following import at the top of it:

```
from django.db.models import Count
```

This is the `Count` aggregation function of the Django ORM. This function will allow you to perform aggregated counts of tags. `django.db.models` includes the following aggregation functions:

- `Avg`: The mean value
- `Max`: The maximum value
- `Min`: The minimum value
- `Count`: The total number of objects

You can learn about aggregation at `https://docs.djangoproject.com/en/4.1/topics/db/aggregation/`.

Open the `views.py` file of your `blog` application and add the following lines to the `post_detail` view. New lines are highlighted in bold:

```
def post_detail(request, year, month, day, post):
    post = get_object_or_404(Post,
                             status=Post.Status.PUBLISHED,
                             slug=post,
                             publish__year=year,
                             publish__month=month,
                             publish__day=day)

    # List of active comments for this post
    comments = post.comments.filter(active=True)
```

```python
    # Form for users to comment
    form = CommentForm()

    # List of similar posts
    post_tags_ids = post.tags.values_list('id', flat=True)
    similar_posts = Post.published.filter(tags__in=post_tags_ids)\
                                  .exclude(id=post.id)
    similar_posts = similar_posts.annotate(same_tags=Count('tags'))\
                                  .order_by('-same_tags','-publish')[:4]

    return render(request,
                  'blog/post/detail.html',
                  {'post': post,
                   'comments': comments,
                   'form': form,
                   'similar_posts': similar_posts})
```

The preceding code is as follows:

1. You retrieve a Python list of IDs for the tags of the current post. The `values_list()` QuerySet returns tuples with the values for the given fields. You pass `flat=True` to it to get single values such as `[1, 2, 3, ...]` instead of one-tuples such as `[(1,), (2,), (3,) ...]`.
2. You get all posts that contain any of these tags, excluding the current post itself.
3. You use the `Count` aggregation function to generate a calculated field—`same_tags`—that contains the number of tags shared with all the tags queried.
4. You order the result by the number of shared tags (descending order) and by `publish` to display recent posts first for the posts with the same number of shared tags. You slice the result to retrieve only the first four posts.
5. We pass the `similar_posts` object to the context dictionary for the `render()` function.

Now, edit the `blog/post/detail.html` template and add the following code highlighted in bold:

```html
{% extends "blog/base.html" %}

{% block title %}{{ post.title }}{% endblock %}

{% block content %}
  <h1>{{ post.title }}</h1>
  <p class="date">
```

```
        Published {{ post.publish }} by {{ post.author }}
    </p>
    {{ post.body|linebreaks }}
    <p>
        <a href="{% url "blog:post_share" post.id %}">
            Share this post
        </a>
    </p>

    <h2>Similar posts</h2>
    {% for post in similar_posts %}
        <p>
            <a href="{{ post.get_absolute_url }}">{{ post.title }}</a>
        </p>
    {% empty %}
        There are no similar posts yet.
    {% endfor %}

    {% with comments.count as total_comments %}
        <h2>
            {{ total_comments }} comment{{ total_comments|pluralize }}
        </h2>
    {% endwith %}
    {% for comment in comments %}
        <div class="comment">
            <p class="info">
                Comment {{ forloop.counter }} by {{ comment.name }}
                {{ comment.created }}
            </p>
            {{ comment.body|linebreaks }}
        </div>
    {% empty %}
        <p>There are no comments yet.</p>
    {% endfor %}
    {% include "blog/post/includes/comment_form.html" %}
{% endblock %}
```

The post detail page should look like this:

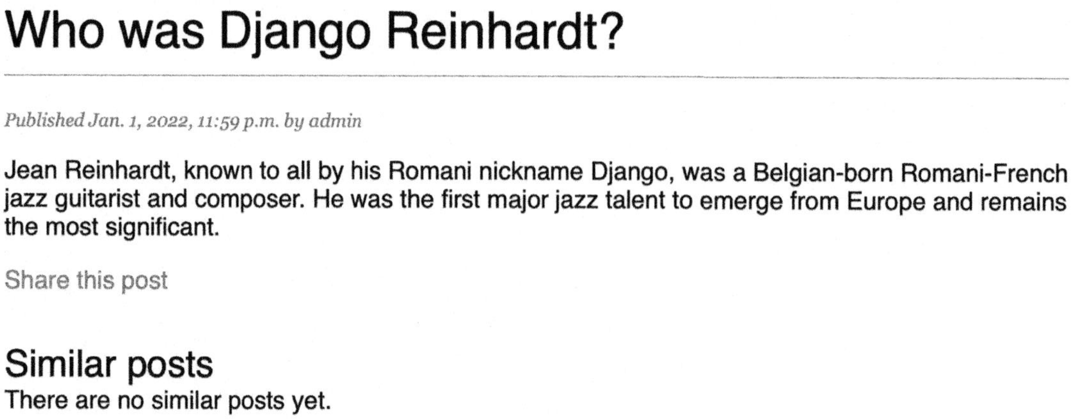

Who was Django Reinhardt?

Published Jan. 1, 2022, 11:59 p.m. by admin

Jean Reinhardt, known to all by his Romani nickname Django, was a Belgian-born Romani-French jazz guitarist and composer. He was the first major jazz talent to emerge from Europe and remains the most significant.

Share this post

Similar posts
There are no similar posts yet.

Figure 3.7: The post detail page, including a list of similar posts

Open `http://127.0.0.1:8000/admin/blog/post/` in your browser, edit a post that has no tags, and add the `music` and `jazz` tags as follows:

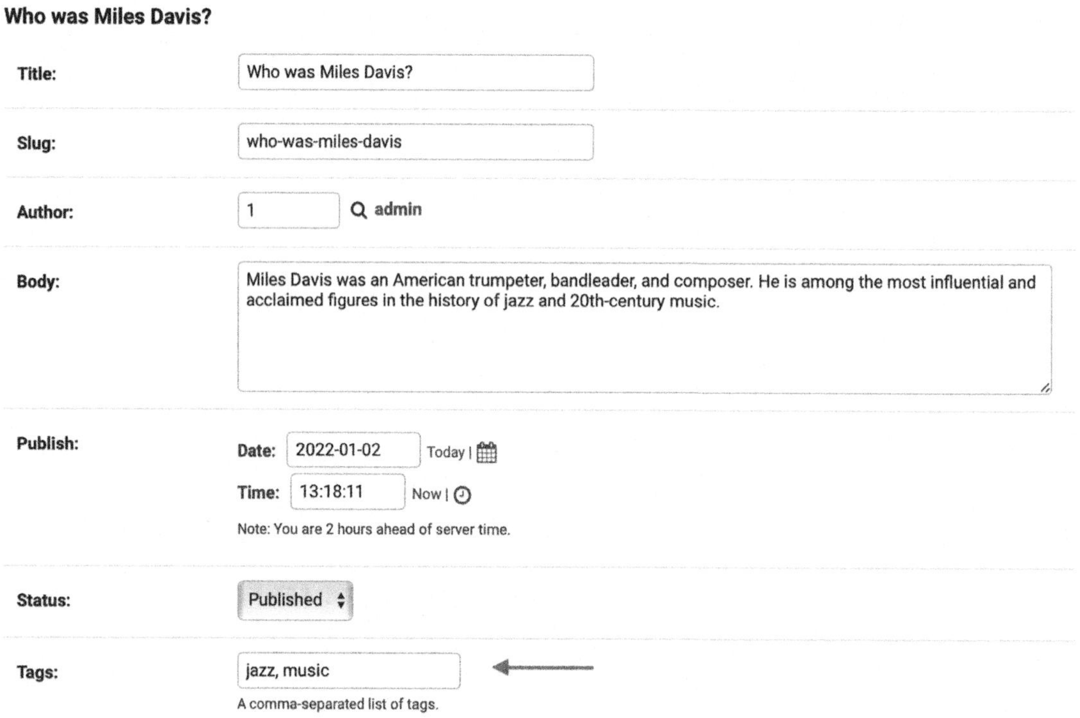

Who was Miles Davis?

Title:	Who was Miles Davis?
Slug:	who-was-miles-davis
Author:	1 Q admin
Body:	Miles Davis was an American trumpeter, bandleader, and composer. He is among the most influential and acclaimed figures in the history of jazz and 20th-century music.
Publish:	Date: 2022-01-02 Today | 🗓 Time: 13:18:11 Now | 🕐 Note: You are 2 hours ahead of server time.
Status:	Published ♦
Tags:	jazz, music ⟵ A comma-separated list of tags.

Figure 3.8: Adding the "jazz" and "music" tags to a post

Edit another post and add the `jazz` tag as follows:

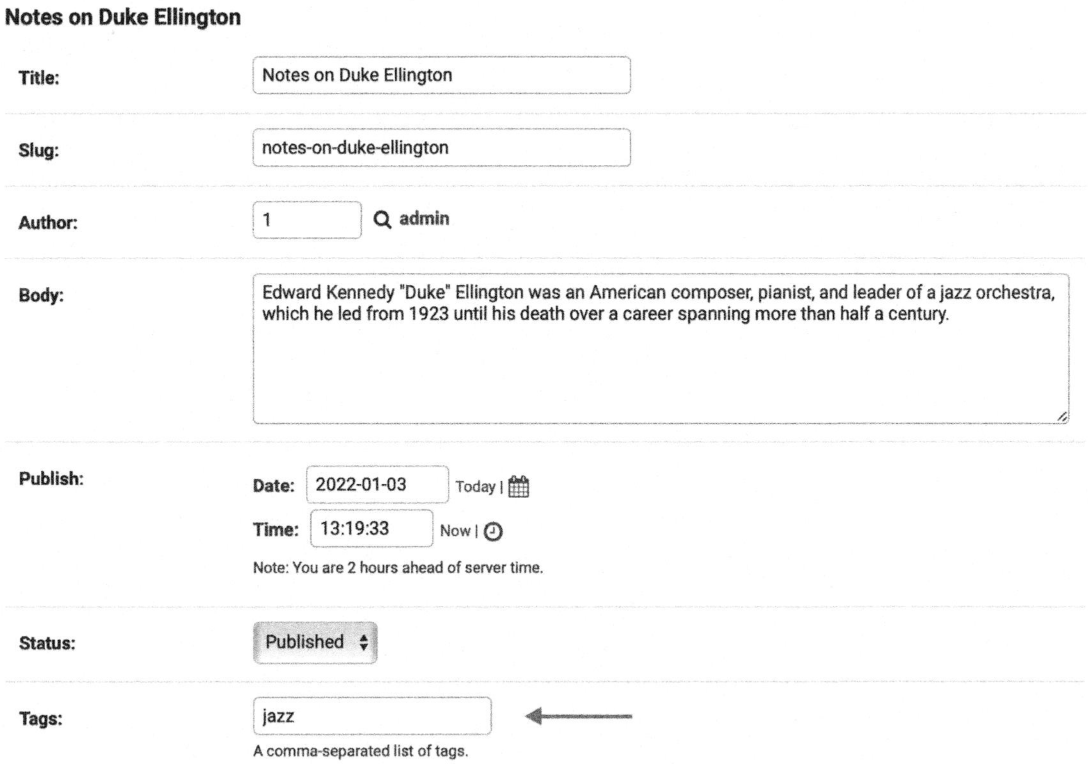

Notes on Duke Ellington

Title:	Notes on Duke Ellington
Slug:	notes-on-duke-ellington
Author:	1　　🔍 admin
Body:	Edward Kennedy "Duke" Ellington was an American composer, pianist, and leader of a jazz orchestra, which he led from 1923 until his death over a career spanning more than half a century.
Publish:	Date: 2022-01-03　Today | 📅 Time: 13:19:33　Now | 🕐 Note: You are 2 hours ahead of server time.
Status:	Published ⬍
Tags:	jazz　　⬅ A comma-separated list of tags.

Figure 3.9: Adding the "jazz" tag to a post

The post detail page for the first post should now look like this:

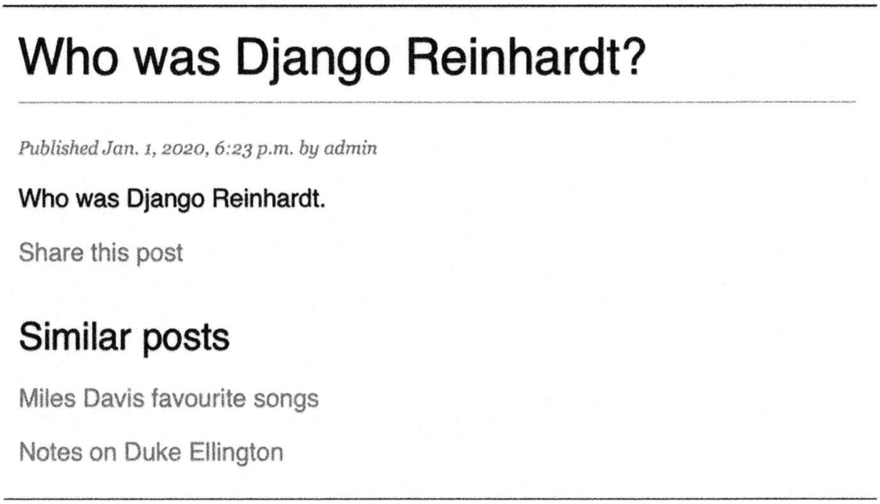

Who was Django Reinhardt?

Published Jan. 1, 2020, 6:23 p.m. by admin

Who was Django Reinhardt.

Share this post

Similar posts

Miles Davis favourite songs

Notes on Duke Ellington

Figure 3.10: The post detail page, including a list of similar posts

The posts recommended in the **Similar posts** section of the page appear in descending order based on the number of shared tags with the original post.

We are now able to successfully recommend similar posts to the readers. `django-taggit` also includes a `similar_objects()` manager that you can use to retrieve objects by shared tags. You can take a look at all `django-taggit` managers at `https://django-taggit.readthedocs.io/en/latest/api.html`.

You can also add the list of tags to your post detail template in the same way as you did in the `blog/post/list.html` template.

Creating custom template tags and filters

Django offers a variety of built-in template tags, such as `{% if %}` or `{% block %}`. You used different template tags in *Chapter 1, Building a Blog Application*, and *Chapter 2, Enhancing Your Blog with Advanced Features*. You can find a complete reference of built-in template tags and filters at `https://docs.djangoproject.com/en/4.1/ref/templates/builtins/`.

Django also allows you to create your own template tags to perform custom actions. Custom template tags come in very handy when you need to add a functionality to your templates that is not covered by the core set of Django template tags. This can be a tag to execute a QuerySet or any server-side processing that you want to reuse across templates. For example, we could build a template tag to display the list of latest posts published on the blog. We could include this list in the sidebar, so that it is always visible, regardless of the view that processes the request.

Implementing custom template tags

Django provides the following helper functions that allow you to easily create template tags:

- `simple_tag`: Processes the given data and returns a string
- `inclusion_tag`: Processes the given data and returns a rendered template

Template tags must live inside Django applications.

Inside your `blog` application directory, create a new directory, name it `templatetags`, and add an empty `__init__.py` file to it. Create another file in the same folder and name it `blog_tags.py`. The file structure of the blog application should look like the following:

```
blog/
    __init__.py
    models.py
    ...
    templatetags/
        __init__.py
        blog_tags.py
```

The way you name the file is important. You will use the name of this module to load tags in templates.

Creating a simple template tag

Let's start by creating a simple tag to retrieve the total posts that have been published on the blog.

Edit the `templatetags/blog_tags.py` file you just created and add the following code:

```
from django import template
from ..models import Post

register = template.Library()

@register.simple_tag
def total_posts():
    return Post.published.count()
```

We have created a simple template tag that returns the number of posts published in the blog.

Each module that contains template tags needs to define a variable called `register` to be a valid tag library. This variable is an instance of `template.Library`, and it's used to register the template tags and filters of the application.

In the preceding code, we have defined a tag called `total_posts` with a simple Python function. We have added the `@register.simple_tag` decorator to the function, to register it as a simple tag. Django will use the function's name as the tag name. If you want to register it using a different name, you can do so by specifying a `name` attribute, such as `@register.simple_tag(name='my_tag')`.

 After adding a new template tags module, you will need to restart the Django development server in order to use the new tags and filters in templates.

Before using custom template tags, we have to make them available for the template using the `{% load %}` tag. As mentioned before, we need to use the name of the Python module containing your template tags and filters.

Edit the `blog/templates/base.html` template and add `{% load blog_tags %}` at the top of it to load your template tags module. Then, use the tag you created to display your total posts, as follows. The new lines are highlighted in bold:

```
{% load blog_tags %}
{% load static %}
<!DOCTYPE html>
<html>
<head>
  <title>{% block title %}{% endblock %}</title>
```

```
    <link href="{% static "css/blog.css" %}" rel="stylesheet">
  </head>
  <body>
    <div id="content">
      {% block content %}
      {% endblock %}
    </div>
    <div id="sidebar">
      <h2>My blog</h2>
      <p>
        This is my blog.
        I've written {% total_posts %} posts so far.
      </p>
    </div>
  </body>
</html>
```

You will need to restart the server to keep track of the new files added to the project. Stop the development server with *Ctrl + C* and run it again using the following command:

```
python manage.py runserver
```

Open http://127.0.0.1:8000/blog/ in your browser. You should see the total number of posts in the sidebar of the site, as follows:

My blog

This is my blog. I've written 4 posts so far.

Figure 3.11: The total posts published included in the sidebar

If you see the following error message, it's very likely you didn't restart the development server:

TemplateSyntaxError at /blog/2022/1/1/who-was-django-reinhardt/

'blog_tags' is not a registered tag library. Must be one of:
admin_list
admin_modify
admin_urls
cache
i18n
l10n
log
static
tz

Figure 3.12: The error message when a template tag library is not registered

Template tags allow you to process any data and add it to any template regardless of the view executed. You can perform QuerySets or process any data to display results in your templates.

Creating an inclusion template tag

We will create another tag to display the latest posts in the sidebar of the blog. This time, we will implement an inclusion tag. Using an inclusion tag, you can render a template with context variables returned by your template tag.

Edit the `templatetags/blog_tags.py` file and add the following code:

```
@register.inclusion_tag('blog/post/latest_posts.html')
def show_latest_posts(count=5):
    latest_posts = Post.published.order_by('-publish')[:count]
    return {'latest_posts': latest_posts}
```

In the preceding code, we have registered the template tag using the `@register.inclusion_tag` decorator. We have specified the template that will be rendered with the returned values using `blog/post/latest_posts.html`. The template tag will accept an optional count parameter that defaults to 5. This parameter will allow us to specify the number of posts to display. We use this variable to limit the results of the query `Post.published.order_by('-publish')[:count]`.

Note that the function returns a dictionary of variables instead of a simple value. Inclusion tags have to return a dictionary of values, which is used as the context to render the specified template. The template tag we just created allows us to specify the optional number of posts to display as `{% show_latest_posts 3 %}`.

Now, create a new template file under `blog/post/` and name it `latest_posts.html`.

Edit the new `blog/post/latest_posts.html` template and add the following code to it:

```
<ul>
  {% for post in latest_posts %}
    <li>
      <a href="{{ post.get_absolute_url }}">{{ post.title }}</a>
    </li>
  {% endfor %}
</ul>
```

In the preceding code, you display an unordered list of posts using the `latest_posts` variable returned by your template tag. Now, edit the `blog/base.html` template and add the new template tag to display the last three posts, as follows. The new lines are highlighted in bold:

```
{% load blog_tags %}
{% load static %}
<!DOCTYPE html>
```

```
<html>
<head>
  <title>{% block title %}{% endblock %}</title>
  <link href="{% static "css/blog.css" %}" rel="stylesheet">
</head>
<body>
  <div id="content">
    {% block content %}
    {% endblock %}
  </div>
  <div id="sidebar">
    <h2>My blog</h2>
    <p>
      This is my blog.
      I've written {% total_posts %} posts so far.
    </p>
    <h3>Latest posts</h3>
    {% show_latest_posts 3 %}
  </div>
</body>
</html>
```

The template tag is called, passing the number of posts to display, and the template is rendered in place with the given context.

Next, return to your browser and refresh the page. The sidebar should now look like this:

Figure 3.13: The blog sidebar, including the latest published posts

Creating a template tag that returns a QuerySet

Finally, we will create a simple template tag that returns a value. We will store the result in a variable that can be reused, rather than outputting it directly. We will create a tag to display the most commented posts.

Edit the `templatetags/blog_tags.py` file and add the following import and template tag to it:

```
from django.db.models import Count


@register.simple_tag
def get_most_commented_posts(count=5):
    return Post.published.annotate(
            total_comments=Count('comments')
        ).order_by('-total_comments')[:count]
```

In the preceding template tag, you build a QuerySet using the `annotate()` function to aggregate the total number of comments for each post. You use the `Count` aggregation function to store the number of comments in the computed `total_comments` field for each `Post` object. You order the QuerySet by the computed field in descending order. You also provide an optional count variable to limit the total number of objects returned.

In addition to `Count`, Django offers the aggregation functions `Avg`, `Max`, `Min`, and `Sum`. You can read more about aggregation functions at `https://docs.djangoproject.com/en/4.1/topics/db/aggregation/`.

Next, edit the `blog/base.html` template and add the following code highlighted in bold:

```
{% load blog_tags %}
{% load static %}
<!DOCTYPE html>
<html>
<head>
  <title>{% block title %}{% endblock %}</title>
  <link href="{% static "css/blog.css" %}" rel="stylesheet">
</head>
<body>
  <div id="content">
    {% block content %}
    {% endblock %}
  </div>
  <div id="sidebar">
    <h2>My blog</h2>
    <p>
      This is my blog.
      I've written {% total_posts %} posts so far.
    </p>
    <h3>Latest posts</h3>
    {% show_latest_posts 3 %}
    <h3>Most commented posts</h3>
```

```
    {% get_most_commented_posts as most_commented_posts %}
    <ul>
        {% for post in most_commented_posts %}
        <li>
            <a href="{{ post.get_absolute_url }}">{{ post.title }}</a>
        </li>
        {% endfor %}
    </ul>
  </div>
</body>
</html>
```

In the preceding code, we store the result in a custom variable using the as argument followed by the variable name. For the template tag, we use {% get_most_commented_posts as most_commented_posts %} to store the result of the template tag in a new variable named most_commented_posts. Then, we display the returned posts using an HTML unordered list element.

Now open your browser and refresh the page to see the final result. It should look like the following:

My Blog

Notes on Duke Ellington

Tags: jazz

Published Jan. 3, 2022, 1:19 p.m. by admin

Edward Kennedy "Duke" Ellington was an American composer, pianist, and leader of a jazz orchestra, which he led from 1923 until his death over a career spanning more than half …

Who was Miles Davis?

Tags: music , jazz

Published Jan. 2, 2022, 1:18 p.m. by admin

Miles Davis was an American trumpeter, bandleader, and composer. He is among the most influential and acclaimed figures in the history of jazz and 20th-century music.

Who was Django Reinhardt?

Tags: music , jazz

Published Jan. 1, 2022, 11:59 p.m. by admin

Jean Reinhardt, known to all by his Romani nickname Django, was a Belgian-born Romani-French jazz guitarist and composer. He was the first major jazz talent to emerge from Europe and …

Page 1 of 2. Next

My blog

This is my blog. I've written 4 posts so far.

Latest posts

- Notes on Duke Ellington
- Who was Miles Davis?
- Who was Django Reinhardt?

Most commented posts

- Notes on Duke Ellington
- Who was Django Reinhardt?
- Another post
- Who was Miles Davis?

Figure 3.14: The post list view, including the complete sidebar with the latest and most commented posts

You have now a clear idea about how to build custom template tags. You can read more about them at `https://docs.djangoproject.com/en/4.1/howto/custom-template-tags/`.

Implementing custom template filters

Django has a variety of built-in template filters that allow you to alter variables in templates. These are Python functions that take one or two parameters, the value of the variable that the filter is applied to, and an optional argument. They return a value that can be displayed or treated by another filter.

A filter is written like `{{ variable|my_filter }}`. Filters with an argument are written like `{{ variable|my_filter:"foo" }}`. For example, you can use the `capfirst` filter to capitalize the first character of the value, like `{{ value|capfirst }}`. If `value` is `django`, the output will be `Django`. You can apply as many filters as you like to a variable, for example, `{{ variable|filter1|filter2 }}`, and each filter will be applied to the output generated by the preceding filter.

You can find the list of Django's built-in template filters at `https://docs.djangoproject.com/en/4.1/ref/templates/builtins/#built-in-filter-reference`.

Creating a template filter to support Markdown syntax

We will create a custom filter to enable you to use Markdown syntax in your blog posts and then convert the post body to HTML in the templates.

Markdown is a plain text formatting syntax that is very simple to use, and it's intended to be converted into HTML. You can write posts using simple Markdown syntax and get the content automatically converted into HTML code. Learning Markdown syntax is much easier than learning HTML. By using Markdown, you can get other non-tech savvy contributors to easily write posts for your blog. You can learn the basics of the Markdown format at `https://daringfireball.net/projects/markdown/basics`.

First, install the Python `markdown` module via `pip` using the following command in the shell prompt:

```
pip install markdown==3.4.1
```

Then, edit the `templatetags/blog_tags.py` file and include the following code:

```
from django.utils.safestring import mark_safe
import markdown


@register.filter(name='markdown')
def markdown_format(text):
    return mark_safe(markdown.markdown(text))
```

We register template filters in the same way as template tags. To prevent a name clash between the function name and the `markdown` module, we have named the function `markdown_format` and we have named the filter `markdown` for use in templates, such as `{{ variable|markdown }}`.

Django escapes the HTML code generated by filters; characters of HTML entities are replaced with their HTML encoded characters. For example, `<p>` is converted to `&lt;p&gt;` (*less than* symbol, *p* character, *greater than* symbol).

We use the `mark_safe` function provided by Django to mark the result as safe HTML to be rendered in the template. By default, Django will not trust any HTML code and will escape it before placing it in the output. The only exceptions are variables that are marked as safe from escaping. This behavior prevents Django from outputting potentially dangerous HTML and allows you to create exceptions for returning safe HTML.

Edit the `blog/post/detail.html` template and add the following new code highlighted in bold:

```
{% extends "blog/base.html" %}
{% load blog_tags %}

{% block title %}{{ post.title }}{% endblock %}

{% block content %}
  <h1>{{ post.title }}</h1>
  <p class="date">
    Published {{ post.publish }} by {{ post.author }}
  </p>
  {{ post.body|markdown }}
  <p>
    <a href="{% url "blog:post_share" post.id %}">
      Share this post
    </a>
  </p>

  <h2>Similar posts</h2>
  {% for post in similar_posts %}
    <p>
      <a href="{{ post.get_absolute_url }}">{{ post.title }}</a>
    </p>
  {% empty %}
    There are no similar posts yet.
  {% endfor %}

  {% with comments.count as total_comments %}
    <h2>
      {{ total_comments }} comment{{ total_comments|pluralize }}
    </h2>
  {% endwith %}
  {% for comment in comments %}
    <div class="comment">
      <p class="info">
```

```
          Comment {{ forloop.counter }} by {{ comment.name }}
          {{ comment.created }}
        </p>
        {{ comment.body|linebreaks }}
      </div>
    {% empty %}
      <p>There are no comments yet.</p>
    {% endfor %}


    {% include "blog/post/includes/comment_form.html" %}
  {% endblock %}
```

We have replaced the `linebreaks` filter of the `{{ post.body }}` template variable with the `markdown` filter. This filter will not only transform line breaks into `<p>` tags; it will also transform Markdown formatting into HTML.

Edit the `blog/post/list.html` template and add the following new code highlighted in bold:

```
{% extends "blog/base.html" %}
{% load blog_tags %}


{% block title %}My Blog{% endblock %}


{% block content %}
  <h1>My Blog</h1>
  {% if tag %}
    <h2>Posts tagged with "{{ tag.name }}"</h2>
  {% endif %}
  {% for post in posts %}
    <h2>
      <a href="{{ post.get_absolute_url }}">
        {{ post.title }}
      </a>
    </h2>
    <p class="tags">
      Tags:
      {% for tag in post.tags.all %}
        <a href="{% url "blog:post_list_by_tag" tag.slug %}">
          {{ tag.name }}
        </a>
        {% if not forloop.last %}, {% endif %}
      {% endfor %}
```

```
    </p>
    <p class="date">
      Published {{ post.publish }} by {{ post.author }}
    </p>
    {{ post.body|markdown|truncatewords_html:30 }}
  {% endfor %}
  {% include "pagination.html" with page=posts %}
{% endblock %}
```

We have added the new markdown filter to the {{ post.body }} template variable. This filter will transform the Markdown content into HTML. Therefore, we have replaced the previous truncatewords filter with the truncatewords_html filter. This filter truncates a string after a certain number of words avoiding unclosed HTML tags.

Now open http://127.0.0.1:8000/admin/blog/post/add/ in your browser and create a new post with the following body:

```
This is a post formatted with markdown
--------------------------------------


*This is emphasized* and **this is more emphasized**.


Here is a list:

* One
* Two
* Three


And a [link to the Django website](https://www.djangoproject.com/).
```

The form should look like this:

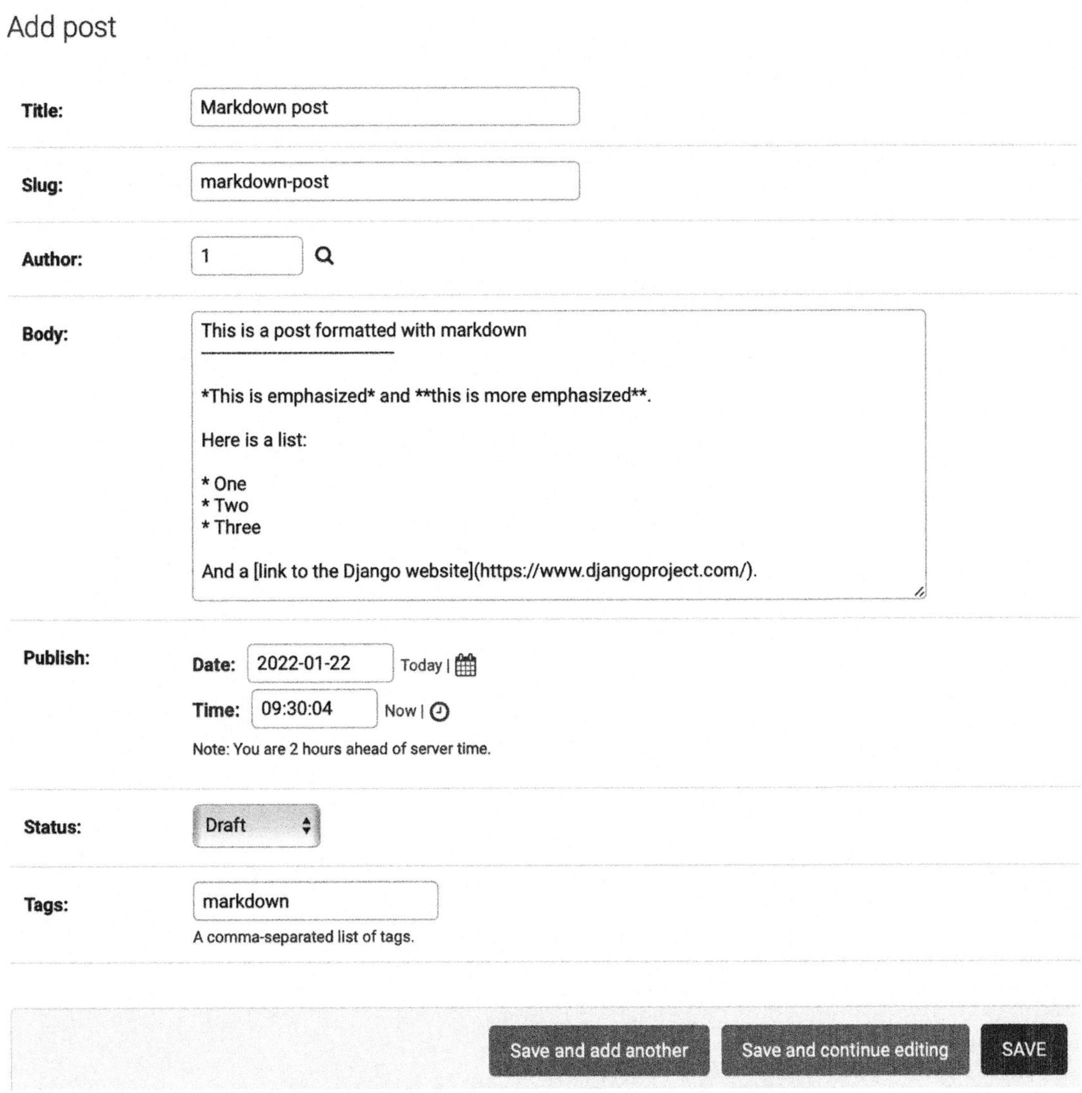

Add post

Title: Markdown post

Slug: markdown-post

Author: 1   Q

Body: This is a post formatted with markdown
                    ─────────────────────────────

                    This is emphasized and **this is more emphasized**.

                    Here is a list:

                    * One
                    * Two
                    * Three

                    And a [link to the Django website](https://www.djangoproject.com/).

Publish: **Date:** 2022-01-22   Today | 🗓

                    Time: 09:30:04   Now | 🕐

                    Note: You are 2 hours ahead of server time.

Status: Draft ⬍

Tags: markdown

                    A comma-separated list of tags.

[Save and add another]   [Save and continue editing]   [SAVE]

Figure 3.15: The post with Markdown content rendered as HTML

Open `http://127.0.0.1:8000/blog/` in your browser and take a look at how the new post is rendered. You should see the following output:

My Blog

Markdown post

Tags: markdown

Published Jan. 22, 2022, 9:30 a.m. by admin

This is a post formatted with markdown

This is emphasized and **this is more emphasized**.

Here is a list:

- One
- Two
- Three

And a link to the Django website …

Figure 3.16: The post with Markdown content rendered as HTML

As you can see in *Figure 3.16*, custom template filters are very useful for customizing formatting. You can find more information about custom filters at `https://docs.djangoproject.com/en/4.1/howto/custom-template-tags/#writing-custom-template-filters`.

Adding a sitemap to the site

Django comes with a sitemap framework, which allows you to generate sitemaps for your site dynamically. A sitemap is an XML file that tells search engines the pages of your website, their relevance, and how frequently they are updated. Using a sitemap will make your site more visible in search engine rankings because it helps crawlers to index your website's content.

The Django sitemap framework depends on `django.contrib.sites`, which allows you to associate objects to particular websites that are running with your project. This comes in handy when you want to run multiple sites using a single Django project. To install the sitemap framework, we will need to activate both the `sites` and the `sitemap` applications in your project.

Edit the settings.py file of the project and add django.contrib.sites and django.contrib.sitemaps to the INSTALLED_APPS setting. Also, define a new setting for the site ID, as follows. New code is highlighted in bold:

```
# ...

SITE_ID = 1

# Application definition

INSTALLED_APPS = [
    'django.contrib.admin',
    'django.contrib.auth',
    'django.contrib.contenttypes',
    'django.contrib.sessions',
    'django.contrib.messages',
    'django.contrib.staticfiles',
    'blog.apps.BlogConfig',
    'taggit',
    'django.contrib.sites',
    'django.contrib.sitemaps',
]
```

Now, run the following command from the shell prompt to create the tables of the Django site application in the database:

```
python manage.py migrate
```

You should see an output that contains the following lines:

```
Applying sites.0001_initial... OK
Applying sites.0002_alter_domain_unique... OK
```

The sites application is now synced with the database.

Next, create a new file inside your blog application directory and name it sitemaps.py. Open the file and add the following code to it:

```
from django.contrib.sitemaps import Sitemap
from .models import Post

class PostSitemap(Sitemap):
    changefreq = 'weekly'
    priority = 0.9
```

```
    def items(self):
        return Post.published.all()

    def lastmod(self, obj):
        return obj.updated
```

We have defined a custom sitemap by inheriting the `Sitemap` class of the `sitemaps` module. The `changefreq` and `priority` attributes indicate the change frequency of your post pages and their relevance in your website (the maximum value is 1).

The `items()` method returns the QuerySet of objects to include in this sitemap. By default, Django calls the `get_absolute_url()` method on each object to retrieve its URL. Remember that we implemented this method in *Chapter 2, Enhancing Your Blog with Advanced Features*, to define the canonical URL for posts. If you want to specify the URL for each object, you can add a `location` method to your sitemap class.

The `lastmod` method receives each object returned by `items()` and returns the last time the object was modified.

Both the `changefreq` and `priority` attributes can be either methods or attributes. You can take a look at the complete sitemap reference in the official Django documentation located at `https://docs.djangoproject.com/en/4.1/ref/contrib/sitemaps/`.

We have created the sitemap. Now we just need to create an URL for it.

Edit the main `urls.py` file of the `mysite` project and add the sitemap, as follows. New lines are highlighted in bold:

```
from django.urls import path, include
from django.contrib import admin
from django.contrib.sitemaps.views import sitemap
from blog.sitemaps import PostSitemap

sitemaps = {
    'posts': PostSitemap,
}

urlpatterns = [
    path('admin/', admin.site.urls),
    path('blog/', include('blog.urls', namespace='blog')),
    path('sitemap.xml', sitemap, {'sitemaps': sitemaps},
        name='django.contrib.sitemaps.views.sitemap')
]
```

In the preceding code, we have included the required imports and have defined a `sitemaps` dictionary. Multiple sitemaps can be defined for the site. We have defined a URL pattern that matches with the `sitemap.xml` pattern and uses the `sitemap` view provided by Django. The `sitemaps` dictionary is passed to the `sitemap` view.

Start the development from the shell prompt with the following command:

```
python manage.py runserver
```

Open `http://127.0.0.1:8000/sitemap.xml` in your browser. You will see an XML output including all of the published posts like this:

```
<urlset xmlns="http://www.sitemaps.org/schemas/sitemap/0.9"
xmlns:xhtml="http://www.w3.org/1999/xhtml">
  <url>
    <loc>http://example.com/blog/2022/1/22/markdown-post/</loc>
    <lastmod>2022-01-22</lastmod>
    <changefreq>weekly</changefreq>
    <priority>0.9</priority>
  </url>
  <url>
    <loc>http://example.com/blog/2022/1/3/notes-on-duke-ellington/</loc>
    <lastmod>2022-01-03</lastmod>
    <changefreq>weekly</changefreqa>
    <priority>0.9</priority>
  </url>
  <url>
    <loc>http://example.com/blog/2022/1/2/who-was-miles-davis/</loc>
    <lastmod>2022-01-03</lastmod>
    <changefreq>weekly</changefreq>
    <priority>0.9</priority>
  </url>
  <url>
    <loc>http://example.com/blog/2022/1/1/who-was-django-reinhardt/</loc>
    <lastmod>2022-01-03</lastmod>
    <changefreq>weekly</changefreq>
    <priority>0.9</priority>
  </url>
  <url>
    <loc>http://example.com/blog/2022/1/1/another-post/</loc>
    <lastmod>2022-01-03</lastmod>
    <changefreq>weekly</changefreq>
    <priority>0.9</priority>
  </url>
</urlset>
```

The URL for each Post object is built by calling its get_absolute_url() method.

The lastmod attribute corresponds to the post updated date field, as you specified in your sitemap, and the changefreq and priority attributes are also taken from the PostSitemap class.

The domain used to build the URLs is example.com. This domain comes from a Site object stored in the database. This default object was created when you synced the site's framework with your database. You can read more about the sites framework at https://docs.djangoproject.com/en/4.1/ref/contrib/sites/.

Open http://127.0.0.1:8000/admin/sites/site/ in your browser. You should see something like this:

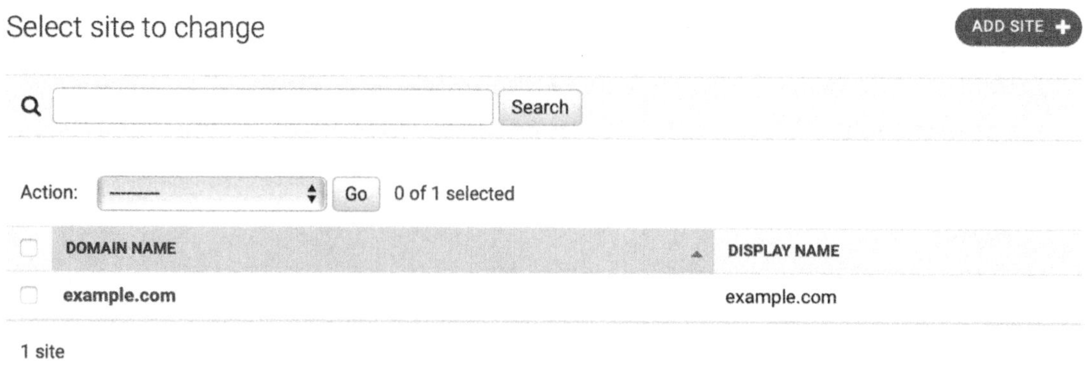

Select site to change

ADD SITE +

	DOMAIN NAME	DISPLAY NAME
	example.com	example.com

Action: ———— Go   0 of 1 selected

1 site

Figure 3.17: The Django administration list view for the Site model of the site's framework

Figure 3.17 contains the list display administration view for the site's framework. Here, you can set the domain or host to be used by the site's framework and the applications that depend on it. To generate URLs that exist in your local environment, change the domain name to localhost:8000, as shown in *Figure 3.18*, and save it:

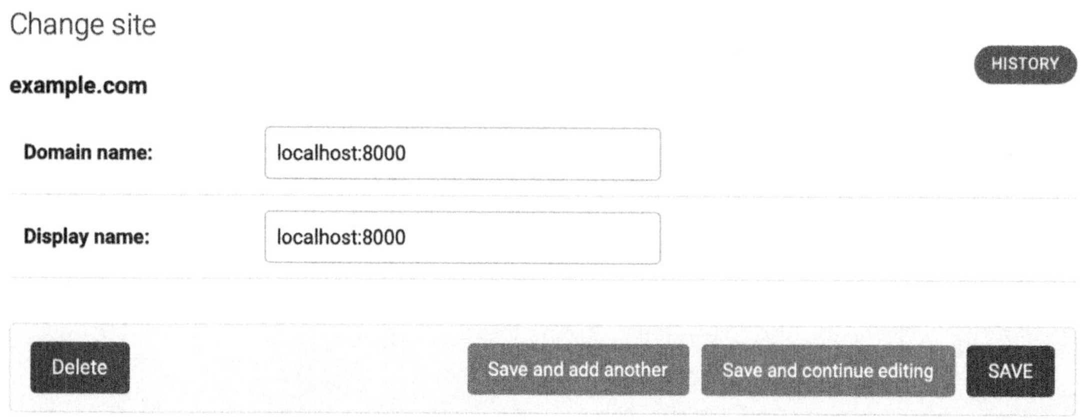

Change site

HISTORY

example.com

Domain name: localhost:8000

Display name: localhost:8000

Delete   Save and add another   Save and continue editing   SAVE

Figure 3.18: The Django administration edit view for the Site model of the site's framework

Open `http://127.0.0.1:8000/sitemap.xml` in your browser again. The URLs displayed in your feed will now use the new hostname and look like `http://localhost:8000/blog/2022/1/22/markdown-post/`. Links are now accessible in your local environment. In a production environment, you will have to use your website's domain to generate absolute URLs.

Creating feeds for blog posts

Django has a built-in syndication feed framework that you can use to dynamically generate RSS or Atom feeds in a similar manner to creating sitemaps using the site's framework. A web feed is a data format (usually XML) that provides users with the most recently updated content. Users can subscribe to the feed using a feed aggregator, a software that is used to read feeds and get new content notifications.

Create a new file in your `blog` application directory and name it `feeds.py`. Add the following lines to it:

```python
import markdown
from django.contrib.syndication.views import Feed
from django.template.defaultfilters import truncatewords_html
from django.urls import reverse_lazy
from .models import Post

class LatestPostsFeed(Feed):
    title = 'My blog'
    link = reverse_lazy('blog:post_list')
    description = 'New posts of my blog.'

    def items(self):
        return Post.published.all()[:5]

    def item_title(self, item):
        return item.title

    def item_description(self, item):
        return truncatewords_html(markdown.markdown(item.body), 30)

    def item_pubdate(self, item):
        return item.publish
```

In the preceding code, we have defined a feed by subclassing the `Feed` class of the syndication framework. The `title`, `link`, and `description` attributes correspond to the `<title>`, `<link>`, and `<description>` RSS elements, respectively.

We use `reverse_lazy()` to generate the URL for the `link` attribute. The `reverse()` method allows you to build URLs by their name and pass optional parameters. We used `reverse()` in *Chapter 2, Enhancing Your Blog with Advanced Features*.

The reverse_lazy() utility function is a lazily evaluated version of reverse(). It allows you to use a URL reversal before the project's URL configuration is loaded.

The items() method retrieves the objects to be included in the feed. We retrieve the last five published posts to include them in the feed.

The item_title(), item_description(), and item_pubdate() methods will receive each object returned by items() and return the title, description and publication date for each item.

In the item_description() method, we use the markdown() function to convert Markdown content to HTML and the truncatewords_html() template filter function to cut the description of posts after 30 words, avoiding unclosed HTML tags.

Now, edit the blog/urls.py file, import the LatestPostsFeed class, and instantiate the feed in a new URL pattern, as follows. New lines are highlighted in bold:

```python
from django.urls import path
from . import views
from .feeds import LatestPostsFeed

app_name = 'blog'

urlpatterns = [
    # Post views
    path('', views.post_list, name='post_list'),
    # path('', views.PostListView.as_view(), name='post_list'),
    path('tag/<slug:tag_slug>/',
        views.post_list, name='post_list_by_tag'),
    path('<int:year>/<int:month>/<int:day>/<slug:post>/',
        views.post_detail,
        name='post_detail'),
    path('<int:post_id>/share/',
        views.post_share, name='post_share'),
    path('<int:post_id>/comment/',
        views.post_comment, name='post_comment'),
    path('feed/', LatestPostsFeed(), name='post_feed'),
]
```

Navigate to http://127.0.0.1:8000/blog/feed/ in your browser. You should now see the RSS feed, including the last five blog posts:

```xml
<?xml version="1.0" encoding="utf-8"?>
<rss xmlns:atom="http://www.w3.org/2005/Atom" version="2.0">
  <channel>
    <title>My blog</title>
```

```
      <link>http://localhost:8000/blog/</link>
      <description>New posts of my blog.</description>
      <atom:link href="http://localhost:8000/blog/feed/" rel="self"/>
      <language>en-us</language>
      <lastBuildDate>Fri, 2 Jan 2020 09:56:40 +0000</lastBuildDate>
      <item>
        <title>Who was Django Reinhardt?</title>
        <link>http://localhost:8000/blog/2020/1/2/who-was-django-
        reinhardt/</link>
        <description>Who was Django Reinhardt.</description>
        <guid>http://localhost:8000/blog/2020/1/2/who-was-django-
        reinhardt/</guid>
      </item>
      ...
    </channel>
  </rss>
```

If you use Chrome, you will see the XML code. If you use Safari, it will ask you to install an RSS feed reader.

Let's install an RSS desktop client to view the RSS feed with a user-friendly interface. We will use Fluent Reader, which is a multi-platform RSS reader.

Download Fluent Reader for Linux, macOS, or Windows from `https://github.com/yang991178/fluent-reader/releases`.

Install Fluent Reader and open it. You will see the following screen:

Figure 3.19: Fluent Reader with no RSS feed sources

Click on the settings icon on the top right of the window. You will see a screen to add RSS feed sources like the following one:

Sources
Groups
Rules
Service
Preferences
About
OPML File
Import
Export
Add source
http://127.0.0.1:8000/blog/feed/
Add

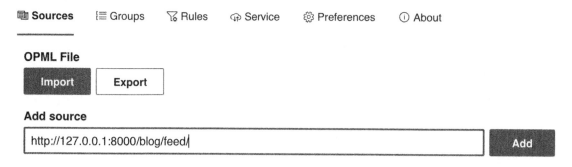

Figure 3.20: Adding an RSS feed in Fluent Reader

Enter `http://127.0.0.1:8000/blog/feed/` in the **Add source** field and click on the **Add** button.

You will see a new entry with the RSS feed of the blog in the table below the form, like this:

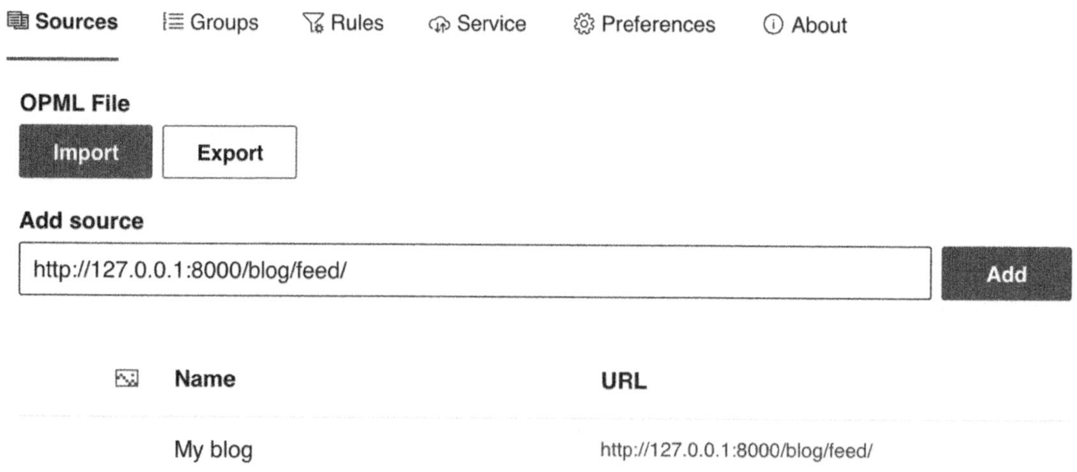

Sources
Groups
Rules
Service
Preferences
About
OPML File
Import
Export
Add source
http://127.0.0.1:8000/blog/feed/
Add
Name
URL
My blog
http://127.0.0.1:8000/blog/feed/

Figure 3.21: RSS feed sources in Fluent Reader

Now, go back to the main screen of Fluent Reader. You should be able to see the posts included in the blog RSS feed, as follows:

All articles
My blog
now
Markdown post
This is a post formatted with markdown This is emphasized and this is more emphasized. Here is a list: One Two Three And a link to the Django website ...
My blog
now
Notes on Duke Ellington
Edward Kennedy "Duke" Ellington was an American composer, pianist, and leader of a jazz orchestra, which he led from 1923 until his death over a career spanning more than half ...
My blog
now
Who was Miles Davis?
Miles Davis was an American trumpeter, bandleader, and composer. He is among the most influential and acclaimed figures in the history of jazz and 20th-century music.
My blog
now
Who was Django Reinhardt?
Jean Reinhardt, known to all by his Romani nickname Django, was a Belgian-born Romani-French jazz guitarist and composer. He was the first major jazz talent to emerge from Europe and ...
My blog
now
Another post
Post body.

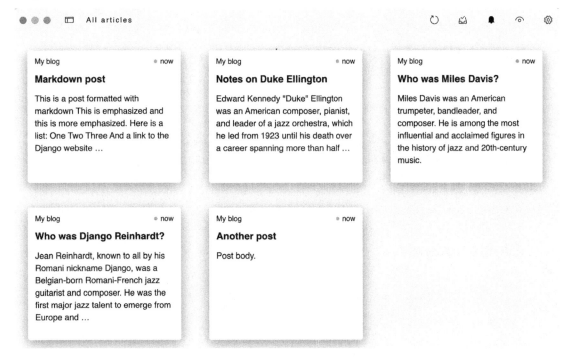

Figure 3.22: RSS feed of the blog in Fluent Reader

Click on a post to see a description:

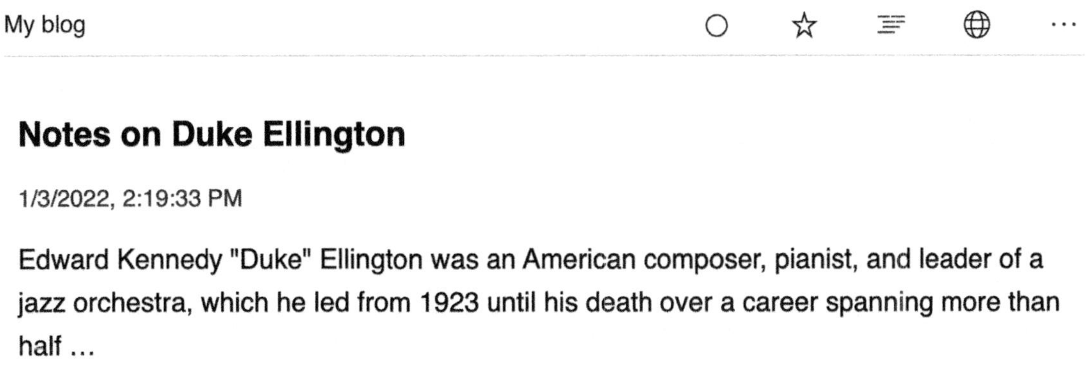

My blog
Notes on Duke Ellington
1/3/2022, 2:19:33 PM
Edward Kennedy "Duke" Ellington was an American composer, pianist, and leader of a jazz orchestra, which he led from 1923 until his death over a career spanning more than half ...

Figure 3.23: The post description in Fluent Reader

Click on the third icon at the top right of the window to load the full content of the post page:

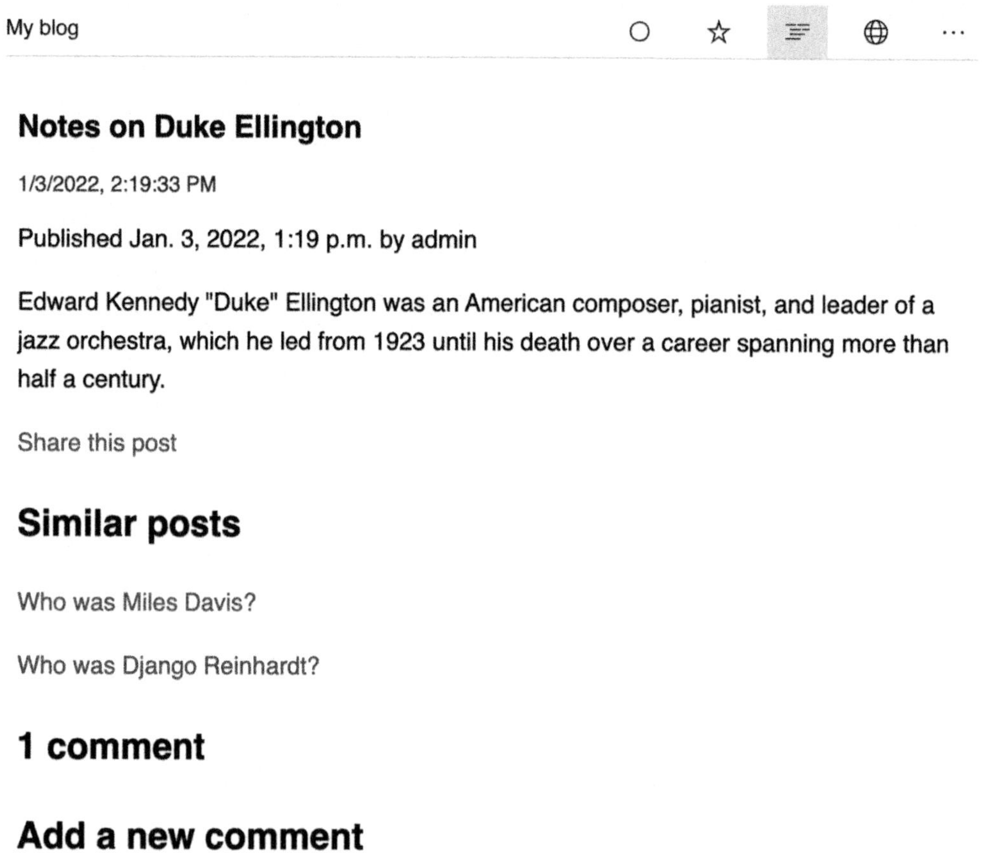

My blog   ○   ☆   ☰   ⊕   · · ·

Notes on Duke Ellington

1/3/2022, 2:19:33 PM

Published Jan. 3, 2022, 1:19 p.m. by admin

Edward Kennedy "Duke" Ellington was an American composer, pianist, and leader of a jazz orchestra, which he led from 1923 until his death over a career spanning more than half a century.

Share this post

Similar posts

Who was Miles Davis?

Who was Django Reinhardt?

1 comment

Add a new comment

Figure 3.24: The full content of a post in Fluent Reader

The final step is to add an RSS feed subscription link to the blog's sidebar.

Open the `blog/base.html` template and add the following code highlighted in bold:

```
{% load blog_tags %}
{% load static %}
<!DOCTYPE html>
<html>
<head>
  <title>{% block title %}{% endblock %}</title>
  <link href="{% static "css/blog.css" %}" rel="stylesheet">
</head>
```

```html
<body>
  <div id="content">
    {% block content %}
    {% endblock %}
  </div>
  <div id="sidebar">
    <h2>My blog</h2>
    <p>
      This is my blog.
      I've written {% total_posts %} posts so far.
    </p>
    <p>
      <a href="{% url "blog:post_feed" %}">
        Subscribe to my RSS feed
      </a>
    </p>
    <h3>Latest posts</h3>
    {% show_latest_posts 3 %}
    <h3>Most commented posts</h3>
    {% get_most_commented_posts as most_commented_posts %}
    <ul>
      {% for post in most_commented_posts %}
        <li>
          <a href="{{ post.get_absolute_url }}">{{ post.title }}</a>
        </li>
      {% endfor %}
    </ul>
  </div>
</body>
</html>
```

Now open `http://127.0.0.1:8000/blog/` in your browser and take a look at the sidebar. The new link will take users to the blog's feed:

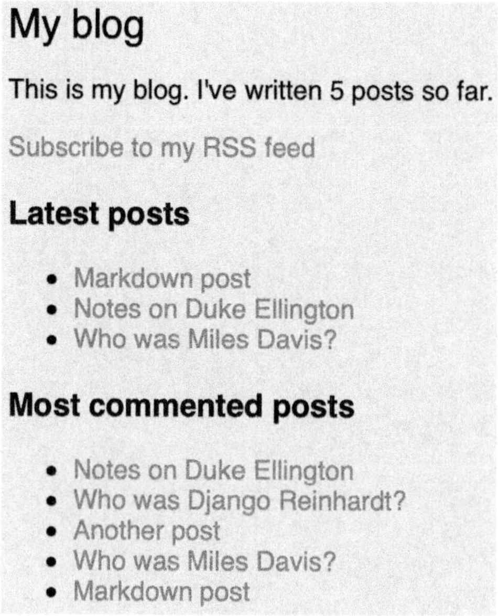

My blog

This is my blog. I've written 5 posts so far.

Subscribe to my RSS feed

Latest posts

- Markdown post
- Notes on Duke Ellington
- Who was Miles Davis?

Most commented posts

- Notes on Duke Ellington
- Who was Django Reinhardt?
- Another post
- Who was Miles Davis?
- Markdown post

Figure 3.25: The RSS feed subscription link added to the sidebar

You can read more about the Django syndication feed framework at `https://docs.djangoproject.com/en/4.1/ref/contrib/syndication/`.

Adding full-text search to the blog

Next, we will add search capabilities to the blog. Searching for data in the database with user input is a common task for web applications. The Django ORM allows you to perform simple matching operations using, for example, the `contains` filter (or its case-insensitive version, `icontains`). You can use the following query to find posts that contain the word `framework` in their body:

```
from blog.models import Post
Post.objects.filter(body__contains='framework')
```

However, if you want to perform complex search lookups, retrieving results by similarity, or by weighting terms based on how frequently they appear in the text or by how important different fields are (for example, relevancy of the term appearing in the title versus in the body), you will need to use a full-text search engine. When you consider large blocks of text, building queries with operations on a string of characters is not enough. A full-text search examines the actual words against stored content as it tries to match search criteria.

Django provides a powerful search functionality built on top of PostgreSQL's full-text search features. The `django.contrib.postgres` module provides functionalities offered by PostgreSQL that are not shared by the other databases that Django supports. You can learn about PostgreSQL's full-text search support at `https://www.postgresql.org/docs/14/textsearch.html`.

Although Django is a database-agnostic web framework, it provides a module that supports part of the rich feature set offered by PostgreSQL, which is not offered by other databases that Django supports.

Installing PostgreSQL

We are currently using an SQLite database for the mysite project. SQLite support for full-text search is limited and Django doesn't support it out of the box. However, PostgreSQL is much better suited for full-text search and we can use the django.contrib.postgres module to use PostgreSQL's full-text search capabilities. We will migrate our data from SQLite to PostgreSQL to benefit from its full-text search features.

 SQLite is sufficient for development purposes. However, for a production environment, you will need a more powerful database, such as PostgreSQL, MariaDB, MySQL, or Oracle.

Download the PostgreSQL installer for macOS or Windows at https://www.postgresql.org/download/. On the same page, you can find instructions to install PostgreSQL on different Linux distributions. Follow the instructions on the website to install and run PostgreSQL.

If you are using macOS and you choose to install PostgreSQL using Postgres.app, you will need to configure the $PATH variable to use the command line tools, as explained in https://postgresapp.com/documentation/cli-tools.html.

You also need to install the psycopg2 PostgreSQL adapter for Python. Run the following command in the shell prompt to install it:

```
pip install psycopg2-binary==2.9.3
```

Creating a PostgreSQL database

Let's create a user for the PostgreSQL database. We will use psql, which is a terminal-based frontend to PostgreSQL. Enter the PostgreSQL terminal by running the following command in the shell prompt:

```
psql
```

You will see the following output:

```
psql (14.2)
Type "help" for help.
```

Enter the following command to create a user that can create databases:

```
CREATE USER blog WITH PASSWORD 'xxxxxx';
```

Replace xxxxxx with your desired password and execute the command. You will see the following output:

```
CREATE ROLE
```

The user has been created. Let's now create a blog database and give ownership to the blog user you just created.

Execute the following command:

```
CREATE DATABASE blog OWNER blog ENCODING 'UTF8';
```

With this command we tell PostgreSQL to create a database named blog, we give the ownership of the database to the blog user we created before, and we indicate that the UTF8 encoding has to be used for the new database. You will see the following output:

```
CREATE DATABASE
```

We have successfully created the PostgreSQL user and database.

Dumping the existing data

Before switching the database in the Django project, we need to dump the existing data from the SQLite database. We will export the data, switch the project's database to PostgreSQL, and import the data into the new database.

Django comes with a simple way to load and dump data from the database into files that are called **fixtures**. Django supports fixtures in JSON, XML, or YAML formats. We are going to create a fixture with all data contained in the database.

The dumpdata command dumps data from the database into the standard output, serialized in JSON format by default. The resulting data structure includes information about the model and its fields for Django to be able to load it into the database.

You can limit the output to the models of an application by providing the application names to the command, or specifying single models for outputting data using the app.Model format. You can also specify the format using the --format flag. By default, dumpdata outputs the serialized data to the standard output. However, you can indicate an output file using the --output flag. The --indent flag allows you to specify indentation. For more information on dumpdata parameters, run python manage.py dumpdata --help.

Execute the following command from the shell prompt:

```
python manage.py dumpdata --indent=2 --output=mysite_data.json
```

You will see an output similar to the following:

```
[...................................................]
```

All existing data has been exported in JSON format to a new file named `mysite_data.json`. You can view the file contents to see the JSON structure that includes all the different data objects for the different models of your installed applications. If you get an encoding error when running the command, include the `-Xutf8` flag as follows to activate Python UTF-8 mode:

```
python -Xutf8 manage.py dumpdata --indent=2 --output=mysite_data.json
```

We will now switch the database in the Django project and then we will import the data into the new database.

Switching the database in the project

Edit the `settings.py` file of your project and modify the `DATABASES` setting to make it look as follows. New code is highlighted in bold:

```
DATABASES = {
    'default': {
        'ENGINE': 'django.db.backends.postgresql',
        'NAME': 'blog',
        'USER': 'blog',
        'PASSWORD': 'xxxxxx',
    }
}
```

Replace xxxxxx with the password you used when creating the PostgreSQL user. The new database is empty.

Run the following command to apply all database migrations to the new PostgreSQL database:

```
python manage.py migrate
```

You will see an output, including all the migrations that have been applied, like this:

```
Operations to perform:
  Apply all migrations: admin, auth, blog, contenttypes, sessions, sites,
  taggit
Running migrations:
  Applying contenttypes.0001_initial... OK
  Applying auth.0001_initial... OK
  Applying admin.0001_initial... OK
  Applying admin.0002_logentry_remove_auto_add... OK
  Applying admin.0003_logentry_add_action_flag_choices... OK
  Applying contenttypes.0002_remove_content_type_name... OK
  Applying auth.0002_alter_permission_name_max_length... OK
  Applying auth.0003_alter_user_email_max_length... OK
  Applying auth.0004_alter_user_username_opts... OK
```

```
Applying auth.0005_alter_user_last_login_null... OK
Applying auth.0006_require_contenttypes_0002... OK
Applying auth.0007_alter_validators_add_error_messages... OK
Applying auth.0008_alter_user_username_max_length... OK
Applying auth.0009_alter_user_last_name_max_length... OK
Applying auth.0010_alter_group_name_max_length... OK
Applying auth.0011_update_proxy_permissions... OK
Applying auth.0012_alter_user_first_name_max_length... OK
Applying taggit.0001_initial... OK
Applying taggit.0002_auto_20150616_2121... OK
Applying taggit.0003_taggeditem_add_unique_index... OK
Applying blog.0001_initial... OK
Applying blog.0002_alter_post_slug... OK
Applying blog.0003_comment... OK
Applying blog.0004_post_tags... OK
Applying sessions.0001_initial... OK
Applying sites.0001_initial... OK
Applying sites.0002_alter_domain_unique... OK
Applying taggit.0004_alter_taggeditem_content_type_alter_taggeditem_tag... OK
Applying taggit.0005_auto_20220424_2025... OK
```

Loading the data into the new database

Run the following command to load the data into the PostgreSQL database:

```
python manage.py loaddata mysite_data.json
```

You will see the following output:

```
Installed 104 object(s) from 1 fixture(s)
```

The number of objects might differ, depending on the users, posts, comments, and other objects that have been created in the database.

Start the development server from the shell prompt with the following command:

```
python manage.py runserver
```

Open http://127.0.0.1:8000/admin/blog/post/ in your browser to verify that all posts have been loaded into the new database. You should see all the posts, as follows:

Select post to change

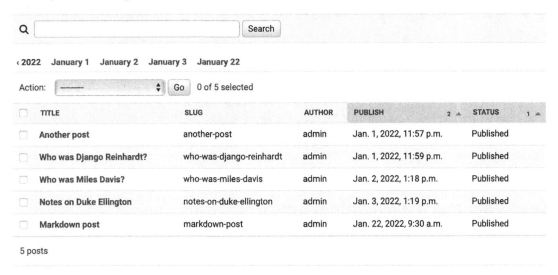

Figure 3.26: The list of posts on the administration site

Simple search lookups

Edit the settings.py file of your project and add django.contrib.postgres to the INSTALLED_APPS setting, as follows:

```
INSTALLED_APPS = [
    'django.contrib.admin',
    'django.contrib.auth',
    'django.contrib.contenttypes',
    'django.contrib.sessions',
    'django.contrib.messages',
    'django.contrib.staticfiles',
    'blog.apps.BlogConfig',
    'taggit',
    'django.contrib.sites',
    'django.contrib.sitemaps',
    'django.contrib.postgres',
]
```

Open the Django shell by running the following command in the system shell prompt:

```
python manage.py shell
```

Now you can search against a single field using the `search` QuerySet lookup.

Run the following code in the Python shell:

```
>>> from blog.models import Post
>>> Post.objects.filter(title__search='django')
<QuerySet [<Post: Who was Django Reinhardt?>]>
```

This query uses PostgreSQL to create a search vector for the body field and a search query from the term `django`. Results are obtained by matching the query with the vector.

Searching against multiple fields

You might want to search against multiple fields. In this case, you will need to define a `SearchVector` object. Let's build a vector that allows you to search against the `title` and body fields of the `Post` model.

Run the following code in the Python shell:

```
>>> from django.contrib.postgres.search import SearchVector
>>> from blog.models import Post
>>>
>>> Post.objects.annotate(
...     search=SearchVector('title', 'body'),
... ).filter(search='django')
<QuerySet [<Post: Markdown post>, <Post: Who was Django Reinhardt?>]>
```

Using `annotate` and defining `SearchVector` with both fields, you provide a functionality to match the query against both the `title` and body of the posts.

 Full-text search is an intensive process. If you are searching for more than a few hundred rows, you should define a functional index that matches the search vector you are using. Django provides a `SearchVectorField` field for your models. You can read more about this at `https://docs.djangoproject.com/en/4.1/ref/contrib/postgres/search/#performance`.

Building a search view

Now, you will create a custom view to allow your users to search posts. First, you will need a search form. Edit the `forms.py` file of the `blog` application and add the following form:

```
class SearchForm(forms.Form):
    query = forms.CharField()
```

You will use the query field to let users introduce search terms. Edit the views.py file of the blog application and add the following code to it:

```python
# ...
from django.contrib.postgres.search import SearchVector
from .forms import EmailPostForm, CommentForm, SearchForm

# ...

def post_search(request):
    form = SearchForm()
    query = None
    results = []

    if 'query' in request.GET:
        form = SearchForm(request.GET)
        if form.is_valid():
            query = form.cleaned_data['query']
            results = Post.published.annotate(
                search=SearchVector('title', 'body'),
            ).filter(search=query)

    return render(request,
                  'blog/post/search.html',
                  {'form': form,
                   'query': query,
                   'results': results})
```

In the preceding view, first, we instantiate the SearchForm form. To check whether the form is submitted, we look for the query parameter in the request.GET dictionary. We send the form using the GET method instead of POST so that the resulting URL includes the query parameter and is easy to share. When the form is submitted, we instantiate it with the submitted GET data, and verify that the form data is valid. If the form is valid, we search for published posts with a custom SearchVector instance built with the title and body fields.

The search view is now ready. We need to create a template to display the form and the results when the user performs a search.

Create a new file inside the templates/blog/post/ directory, name it search.html, and add the following code to it:

```
{% extends "blog/base.html" %}
{% load blog_tags %}
```

```
{% block title %}Search{% endblock %}

{% block content %}
  {% if query %}
    <h1>Posts containing "{{ query }}"</h1>
    <h3>
      {% with results.count as total_results %}
        Found {{ total_results }} result{{ total_results|pluralize }}
      {% endwith %}
    </h3>
    {% for post in results %}
      <h4>
        <a href="{{ post.get_absolute_url }}">
          {{ post.title }}
        </a>
      </h4>
      {{ post.body|markdown|truncatewords_html:12 }}
    {% empty %}
      <p>There are no results for your query.</p>
    {% endfor %}
    <p><a href="{% url "blog:post_search" %}">Search again</a></p>
  {% else %}
    <h1>Search for posts</h1>
    <form method="get">
      {{ form.as_p }}
      <input type="submit" value="Search">
    </form>
  {% endif %}
{% endblock %}
```

As in the search view, we distinguish whether the form has been submitted by the presence of the query parameter. Before the query is submitted, we display the form and a submit button. When the search form is submitted, we display the query performed, the total number of results, and the list of posts that match the search query.

Finally, edit the `urls.py` file of the `blog` application and add the following URL pattern highlighted in bold:

```
urlpatterns = [
    # Post views
    path('', views.post_list, name='post_list'),
    # path('', views.PostListView.as_view(), name='post_list'),
```

```
        path('tag/<slug:tag_slug>/',
            views.post_list, name='post_list_by_tag'),
        path('<int:year>/<int:month>/<int:day>/<slug:post>/',
            views.post_detail,
            name='post_detail'),
        path('<int:post_id>/share/',
            views.post_share, name='post_share'),
        path('<int:post_id>/comment/',
            views.post_comment, name='post_comment'),
        path('feed/', LatestPostsFeed(), name='post_feed'),
        path('search/', views.post_search, name='post_search'),
]
```

Next, open `http://127.0.0.1:8000/blog/search/` in your browser. You should see the following search form:

Search for posts

Query:

SEARCH

My blog

This is my blog. I've written 5 posts so far.

Subscribe to my RSS feed

Latest posts

- Markdown post
- Notes on Duke Ellington
- Who was Miles Davis?

Most commented posts

- Notes on Duke Ellington
- Who was Django Reinhardt?
- Another post
- Who was Miles Davis?
- Markdown post

Figure 3.27: The form with the query field to search for posts

Enter a query and click on the **SEARCH** button. You will see the results of the search query, as follows:

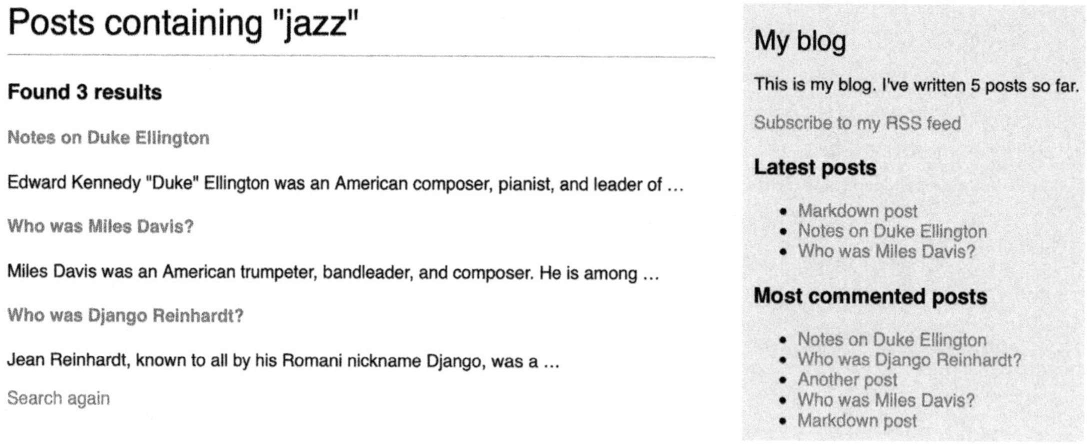

Posts containing "jazz"

Found 3 results

Notes on Duke Ellington

Edward Kennedy "Duke" Ellington was an American composer, pianist, and leader of ...

Who was Miles Davis?

Miles Davis was an American trumpeter, bandleader, and composer. He is among ...

Who was Django Reinhardt?

Jean Reinhardt, known to all by his Romani nickname Django, was a ...

Search again

My blog

This is my blog. I've written 5 posts so far.

Subscribe to my RSS feed

Latest posts

- Markdown post
- Notes on Duke Ellington
- Who was Miles Davis?

Most commented posts

- Notes on Duke Ellington
- Who was Django Reinhardt?
- Another post
- Who was Miles Davis?
- Markdown post

Figure 3.28: Search results for the term "jazz"

Congratulations! You have created a basic search engine for your blog.

Stemming and ranking results

Stemming is the process of reducing words to their word stem, base, or root form. Stemming is used by search engines to reduce indexed words to their stem, and to be able to match inflected or derived words. For example, the words "music", "musical" and "musicality" can be considered similar words by a search engine. The stemming process normalizes each search token into a lexeme, a unit of lexical meaning that underlies a set of words that are related through inflection. The words "music", "musical" and "musicality" would convert to "music" when creating a search query.

Django provides a SearchQuery class to translate terms into a search query object. By default, the terms are passed through stemming algorithms, which helps you to obtain better matches.

The PostgreSQL search engine also removes stop words, such as "a", "the", "on", and "of". Stop words are a set of commonly used words in a language. They are removed when creating a search query because they appear too frequently to be relevant to searches. You can find the list of stop words used by PostgreSQL for the English language at https://github.com/postgres/postgres/blob/master/src/backend/snowball/stopwords/english.stop.

We also want to order results by relevancy. PostgreSQL provides a ranking function that orders results based on how often the query terms appear and how close together they are.

Edit the views.py file of the blog application and add the following imports:

```
from django.contrib.postgres.search import SearchVector, \
                            SearchQuery, SearchRank
```

Then, edit the post_search view, as follows. New code is highlighted in bold:

```
def post_search(request):
    form = SearchForm()
    query = None
    results = []

    if 'query' in request.GET:
        form = SearchForm(request.GET)
        if form.is_valid():
            query = form.cleaned_data['query']
            search_vector = SearchVector('title', 'body')
            search_query = SearchQuery(query)
            results = Post.published.annotate(
                search=search_vector,
                rank=SearchRank(search_vector, search_query)
            ).filter(search=search_query).order_by('-rank')

    return render(request,
                  'blog/post/search.html',
                  {'form': form,
                   'query': query,
                   'results': results})
```

In the preceding code, we create a SearchQuery object, filter results by it, and use SearchRank to order the results by relevancy.

You can open http://127.0.0.1:8000/blog/search/ in your browser and test different searches to test stemming and ranking. The following is an example of ranking by the number of occurrences of the word django in the title and body of the posts:

Posts containing "django"

Found 2 results

Who was Django Reinhardt?

Jean Reinhardt, known to all by his Romani nickname Django, was a ...

Markdown post

This is a post formatted with markdown

This is emphasized and **this** ...

Search again

My blog

This is my blog. I've written 5 posts so far.

Subscribe to my RSS feed

Latest posts

- Markdown post
- Notes on Duke Ellington
- Who was Miles Davis?

Most commented posts

- Notes on Duke Ellington
- Who was Django Reinhardt?
- Another post
- Who was Miles Davis?
- Markdown post

Figure 3.29: Search results for the term "django"

Stemming and removing stop words in different languages

We can set up SearchVector and SearchQuery to execute stemming and remove stop words in any language. We can pass a config attribute to SearchVector and SearchQuery to use a different search configuration. This allows us to use different language parsers and dictionaries. The following example executes stemming and removes stops in Spanish:

```python
search_vector = SearchVector('title', 'body', config='spanish')
search_query = SearchQuery(query, config='spanish')
results = Post.published.annotate(
    search=search_vector,
    rank=SearchRank(search_vector, search_query)
).filter(search=search_query).order_by('-rank')
```

You can find the Spanish stop words dictionary used by PostgreSQL at https://github.com/postgres/postgres/blob/master/src/backend/snowball/stopwords/spanish.stop.

Weighting queries

We can boost specific vectors so that more weight is attributed to them when ordering results by relevancy. For example, we can use this to give more relevance to posts that are matched by title rather than by content.

Edit the views.py file of the blog application and modify the post_search view as follows. New code is highlighted in bold:

```python
def post_search(request):
    form = SearchForm()
    query = None
    results = []

    if 'query' in request.GET:
        form = SearchForm(request.GET)
        if form.is_valid():
            query = form.cleaned_data['query']
            search_vector = SearchVector('title', weight='A') + \
                            SearchVector('body', weight='B')
            search_query = SearchQuery(query)
            results = Post.published.annotate(
                search=search_vector,
                rank=SearchRank(search_vector, search_query)
            ).filter(rank__gte=0.3).order_by('-rank')
```

```
return render(request,
              'blog/post/search.html',
              {'form': form,
               'query': query,
               'results': results})
```

In the preceding code, we apply different weights to the search vectors built using the title and body fields. The default weights are D, C, B, and A, and they refer to the numbers 0.1, 0.2, 0.4, and 1.0, respectively. We apply a weight of 1.0 to the title search vector (A) and a weight of 0.4 to the body vector (B). Title matches will prevail over body content matches. We filter the results to display only the ones with a rank higher than 0.3.

Searching with trigram similarity

Another search approach is trigram similarity. A trigram is a group of three consecutive characters. You can measure the similarity of two strings by counting the number of trigrams that they share. This approach turns out to be very effective for measuring the similarity of words in many languages.

To use trigrams in PostgreSQL, you will need to install the pg_trgm extension first. Execute the following command in the shell prompt to connect to your database:

```
psql blog
```

Then, execute the following command to install the pg_trgm extension:

```
CREATE EXTENSION pg_trgm;
```

You will get the following output:

```
CREATE EXTENSION
```

Let's edit the view and modify it to search for trigrams.

Edit the views.py file of your blog application and add the following import:

```
from django.contrib.postgres.search import TrigramSimilarity
```

Then, modify the post_search view as follows. New code is highlighted in bold:

```
def post_search(request):
    form = SearchForm()
    query = None
    results = []

    if 'query' in request.GET:
        form = SearchForm(request.GET)
        if form.is_valid():
```

```
            query = form.cleaned_data['query']
            results = Post.published.annotate(
                similarity=TrigramSimilarity('title', query),
            ).filter(similarity__gt=0.1).order_by('-similarity')

    return render(request,
                    'blog/post/search.html',
                    {'form': form,
                     'query': query,
                     'results': results})
```

Open http://127.0.0.1:8000/blog/search/ in your browser and test different searches for trigrams. The following example displays a hypothetical typo in the django term, showing search results for yango:

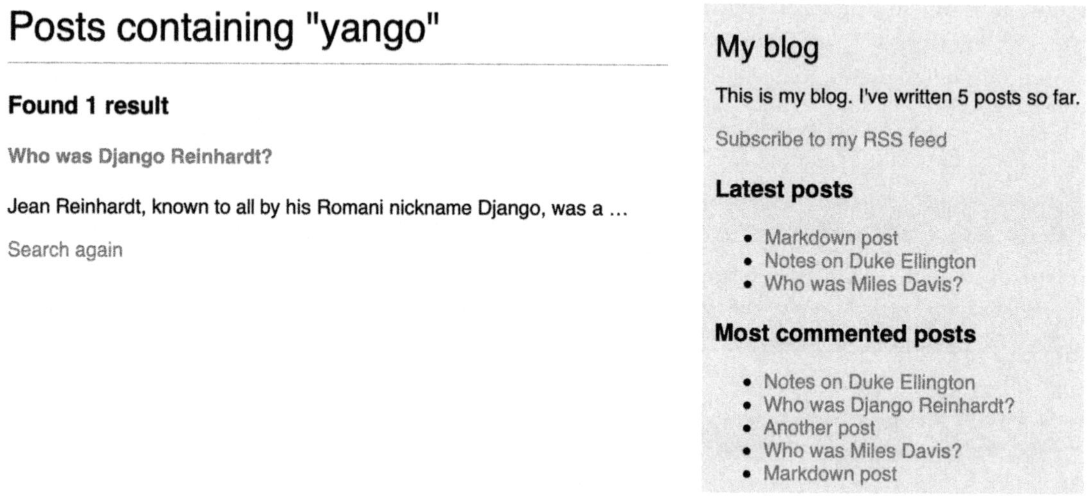

Posts containing "yango"

Found 1 result

Who was Django Reinhardt?

Jean Reinhardt, known to all by his Romani nickname Django, was a ...

Search again

My blog

This is my blog. I've written 5 posts so far.

Subscribe to my RSS feed

Latest posts

- Markdown post
- Notes on Duke Ellington
- Who was Miles Davis?

Most commented posts

- Notes on Duke Ellington
- Who was Django Reinhardt?
- Another post
- Who was Miles Davis?
- Markdown post

Figure 3.30: Search results for the term "yango"

We have added a powerful search engine to the blog application.

You can find more information about full-text search at https://docs.djangoproject.com/en/4.1/ref/contrib/postgres/search/.

Additional resources

The following resources provide additional information related to the topics covered in this chapter:

- Source code for this chapter – https://github.com/PacktPublishing/Django-4-by-example/tree/main/Chapter03

- Django-taggit – https://github.com/jazzband/django-taggit

- Django-taggit ORM managers – `https://django-taggit.readthedocs.io/en/latest/api.html`
- Many-to-many relationships – `https://docs.djangoproject.com/en/4.1/topics/db/examples/many_to_many/`
- Django aggregation functions – `https://docs.djangoproject.com/en/4.1/topics/db/aggregation/`
- Built-in template tags and filters – `https://docs.djangoproject.com/en/4.1/ref/templates/builtins/`
- Writing custom template tags – `https://docs.djangoproject.com/en/4.1/howto/custom-template-tags/`
- Markdown format reference – `https://daringfireball.net/projects/markdown/basics`
- Django Sitemap framework – `https://docs.djangoproject.com/en/4.1/ref/contrib/sitemaps/`
- Django Sites framework – `https://docs.djangoproject.com/en/4.1/ref/contrib/sites/`
- Django syndication feed framework – `https://docs.djangoproject.com/en/4.1/ref/contrib/syndication/`
- PostgreSQL downloads – `https://www.postgresql.org/download/`
- PostgreSQL full-text search capabilities – `https://www.postgresql.org/docs/14/textsearch.html`
- Django support for PostgreSQL full-text search – `https://docs.djangoproject.com/en/4.1/ref/contrib/postgres/search/`

Summary

In this chapter, you implemented a tagging system by integrating a third-party application with your project. You generated post recommendations using complex QuerySets. You also learned how to create custom Django template tags and filters to provide templates with custom functionalities. You also created a sitemap for search engines to crawl your site and an RSS feed for users to subscribe to your blog. You then built a search engine for your blog using the full-text search engine of PostgreSQL.

In the next chapter, you will learn how to build a social website using the Django authentication framework and how to implement user account functionalities and custom user profiles.

4

Building a Social Website

In the preceding chapter, you learned how to implement a tagging system and how to recommend similar posts. You implemented custom template tags and filters. You also learned how to create sitemaps and feeds for your site, and you built a full-text search engine using PostgreSQL.

In this chapter, you will learn how to develop user account functionalities to create a social website, including user registration, password management, profile editing, and authentication. We will implement social features into this site in the next few chapters, to let users share images and interact with each other. Users will be able to bookmark any image on the internet and share it with other users. They will also be able to see activity on the platform from the users they follow and like/unlike the images shared by them.

This chapter will cover the following topics:

- Creating a login view
- Using the Django authentication framework
- Creating templates for Django login, logout, password change, and password reset views
- Extending the user model with a custom profile model
- Creating user registration views
- Configuring the project for media file uploads
- Using the messages framework
- Building a custom authentication backend
- Preventing users from using an existing email

Let's start by creating a new project.

The source code for this chapter can be found at `https://github.com/PacktPublishing/Django-4-by-example/tree/main/Chapter04`.

All Python packages used in this chapter are included in the `requirements.txt` file in the source code for the chapter. You can follow the instructions to install each Python package in the following sections, or you can install all requirements at once with the command `pip install -r requirements.txt`.

Creating a social website project

We are going to create a social application that will allow users to share images that they find on the internet. We will need to build the following elements for this project:

- An authentication system for users to register, log in, edit their profile, and change or reset their password
- A follow system to allow users to follow each other on the website
- Functionality to display shared images and a system for users to share images from any website
- An activity stream that allows users to see the content uploaded by the people that they follow

This chapter will address the first point on the list.

Starting the social website project

Open the terminal and use the following commands to create a virtual environment for your project:

```
mkdir env
python -m venv env/bookmarks
```

If you are using Linux or macOS, run the following command to activate your virtual environment:

```
source env/bookmarks/bin/activate
```

If you are using Windows, use the following command instead:

```
.\env\bookmarks\Scripts\activate
```

The shell prompt will display your active virtual environment, as follows:

```
(bookmarks)laptop:~ zenx$
```

Install Django in your virtual environment with the following command:

```
pip install Django~=4.1.0
```

Run the following command to create a new project:

```
django-admin startproject bookmarks
```

The initial project structure has been created. Use the following commands to get into your project directory and create a new application named account:

```
cd bookmarks/
django-admin startapp account
```

Remember that you should add the new application to your project by adding the application's name to the INSTALLED_APPS setting in the settings.py file.

Edit settings.py and add the following line highlighted in bold to the INSTALLED_APPS list before any of the other installed apps:

```
INSTALLED_APPS = [
    'account.apps.AccountConfig',
    'django.contrib.admin',
    'django.contrib.auth',
    'django.contrib.contenttypes',
    'django.contrib.sessions',
    'django.contrib.messages',
    'django.contrib.staticfiles',
]
```

Django looks for templates in the application template directories by order of appearance in the INSTALLED_APPS setting. The django.contrib.admin app includes standard authentication templates that we will override in the account application. By placing the application first in the INSTALLED_APPS setting, we ensure that the custom authentication templates will be used by default instead of the authentication templates contained in django.contrib.admin.

Run the following command to sync the database with the models of the default applications included in the INSTALLED_APPS setting:

```
python manage.py migrate
```

You will see that all initial Django database migrations get applied. Next, we will build an authentication system into our project using the Django authentication framework.

Using the Django authentication framework

Django comes with a built-in authentication framework that can handle user authentication, sessions, permissions, and user groups. The authentication system includes views for common user actions such as logging in, logging out, password change, and password reset.

The authentication framework is located at django.contrib.auth and is used by other Django contrib packages. Remember that we already used the authentication framework in *Chapter 1*, *Building a Blog Application*, to create a superuser for the blog application to access the administration site.

When we create a new Django project using the startproject command, the authentication framework is included in the default settings of our project. It consists of the django.contrib.auth application and the following two middleware classes found in the MIDDLEWARE setting of our project:

- AuthenticationMiddleware: Associates users with requests using sessions
- SessionMiddleware: Handles the current session across requests

Middleware is classes with methods that are globally executed during the request or response phase. You will use middleware classes on several occasions throughout this book, and you will learn how to create custom middleware in *Chapter 17*, *Going Live*.

The authentication framework also includes the following models that are defined in `django.contrib.auth.models`:

- **User**: A user model with basic fields; the main fields of this model are `username`, `password`, `email`, `first_name`, `last_name`, and `is_active`
- **Group**: A group model to categorize users
- **Permission**: Flags for users or groups to perform certain actions

The framework also includes default authentication views and forms, which you will use later.

Creating a login view

We will start this section by using the Django authentication framework to allow users to log into the website. We will create a view that will perform the following actions to log in a user:

- Present the user with a login form
- Get the username and password provided by the user when they submit the form
- Authenticate the user against the data stored in the database
- Check whether the user is active
- Log the user into the website and start an authenticated session

We will start by creating the login form.

Create a new `forms.py` file in the `account` application directory and add the following lines to it:

```python
from django import forms


class LoginForm(forms.Form):
    username = forms.CharField()
    password = forms.CharField(widget=forms.PasswordInput)
```

This form will be used to authenticate users against the database. Note that you use the `PasswordInput` widget to render the `password` HTML element. This will include `type="password"` in the HTML so that the browser treats it as a password input.

Edit the `views.py` file of the `account` application and add the following code to it:

```python
from django.http import HttpResponse
from django.shortcuts import render
from django.contrib.auth import authenticate, login
from .forms import LoginForm


def user_login(request):
    if request.method == 'POST':
        form = LoginForm(request.POST)
        if form.is_valid():
```

```
                cd = form.cleaned_data
            user = authenticate(request,
                                username=cd['username'],
                                password=cd['password'])
            if user is not None:
                if user.is_active:
                    login(request, user)
                    return HttpResponse('Authenticated successfully')
                else:
                    return HttpResponse('Disabled account')
            else:
                return HttpResponse('Invalid login')
    else:
        form = LoginForm()
    return render(request, 'account/login.html', {'form': form})
```

This is what the basic login view does:

When the user_login view is called with a GET request, a new login form is instantiated with form = LoginForm(). The form is then passed to the template.

When the user submits the form via POST, the following actions are performed:

- The form is instantiated with the submitted data with form = LoginForm(request.POST).
- The form is validated with form.is_valid(). If it is not valid, the form errors will be displayed later in the template (for example, if the user didn't fill in one of the fields).
- If the submitted data is valid, the user gets authenticated against the database using the authenticate() method. This method takes the request object, the username, and the password parameters and returns the User object if the user has been successfully authenticated, or None otherwise. If the user has not been successfully authenticated, a raw HttpResponse is returned with an **Invalid login** message.
- If the user is successfully authenticated, the user status is checked by accessing the is_active attribute. This is an attribute of Django's User model. If the user is not active, an HttpResponse is returned with a **Disabled account** message.
- If the user is active, the user is logged into the site. The user is set in the session by calling the login() method. An **Authenticated successfully** message is returned.

 Note the difference between authenticate() and login(): authenticate() checks user credentials and returns a User object if they are correct; login() sets the user in the current session.

Now we will create a URL pattern for this view.

Create a new `urls.py` file in the account application directory and add the following code to it:

```python
from django.urls import path
from . import views

urlpatterns = [
    path('login/', views.user_login, name='login'),
]
```

Edit the main `urls.py` file located in your bookmarks project directory, import `include`, and add the URL patterns of the account application, as follows. New code is highlighted in bold:

```python
from django.contrib import admin
from django.urls import path, include

urlpatterns = [
    path('admin/', admin.site.urls),
    path('account/', include('account.urls')),
]
```

The login view can now be accessed by a URL.

Let's create a template for this view. Since there are no templates in the project yet, we will start by creating a base template that will be extended by the login template.

Create the following files and directories inside the account application directory:

```
templates/
    account/
        login.html
    base.html
```

Edit the `base.html` template and add the following code to it:

```html
{% load static %}
<!DOCTYPE html>
<html>
<head>
  <title>{% block title %}{% endblock %}</title>
  <link href="{% static "css/base.css" %}" rel="stylesheet">
</head>
<body>
  <div id="header">
    <span class="logo">Bookmarks</span>
  </div>
```

```
    <div id="content">
      {% block content %}
      {% endblock %}
    </div>
  </body>
</html>
```

This will be the base template for the website. As you did in your previous project, include the CSS styles in the main template. You can find these static files in the code that comes with this chapter. Copy the `static/` directory of the `account` application from the chapter's source code to the same location in your project so that you can use the static files. You can find the directory's contents at `https://github.com/PacktPublishing/Django-4-by-Example/tree/master/Chapter04/bookmarks/account/static`.

The base template defines a `title` block and a `content` block that can be filled with content by the templates that extend from it.

Let's fill in the template for your login form.

Open the `account/login.html` template and add the following code to it:

```
{% extends "base.html" %}

{% block title %}Log-in{% endblock %}

{% block content %}
  <h1>Log-in</h1>
  <p>Please, use the following form to log-in:</p>
  <form method="post">
    {{ form.as_p }}
    {% csrf_token %}
    <p><input type="submit" value="Log in"></p>
  </form>
{% endblock %}
```

This template includes the form that is instantiated in the view. Since your form will be submitted via POST, you will include the `{% csrf_token %}` template tag for **cross-site request forgery** (CSRF) protection. You learned about CSRF protection in *Chapter 2, Enhancing Your Blog with Advanced Features*.

There are no users in the database yet. You will need to create a superuser first to access the administration site to manage other users.

Execute the following command in the shell prompt:

```
python manage.py createsuperuser
```

You will see the following output. Enter your desired username, email, and password, as follows:

```
Username (leave blank to use 'admin'): admin
Email address: admin@admin.com
Password: ********
Password (again): ********
```

Then you will see the following success message:

```
Superuser created successfully.
```

Run the development server using the following command:

```
python manage.py runserver
```

Open http://127.0.0.1:8000/admin/ in your browser. Access the administration site using the credentials of the user you just created. You will see the Django administration site, including the User and Group models of the Django authentication framework.

It will look as follows:

Figure 4.1: The Django administration site index page including Users and Groups

In the **Users** row, click on the **Add** link.

Create a new user using the administration site as follows:

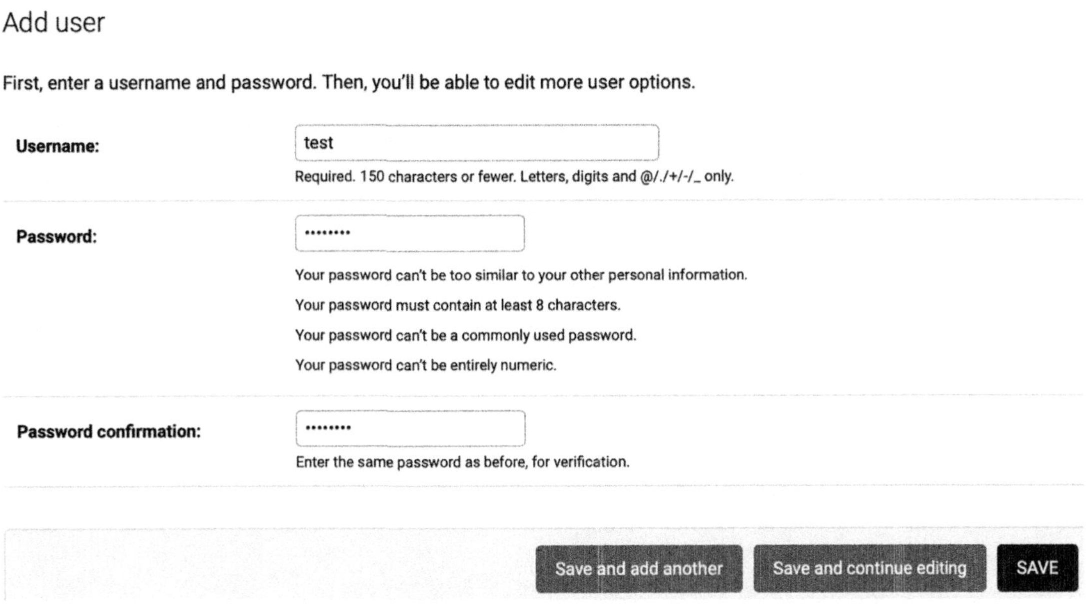

Add user

First, enter a username and password. Then, you'll be able to edit more user options.

Username:
```
test
```
Required. 150 characters or fewer. Letters, digits and @/./+/-/_ only.

Password:
```
••••••••
```
Your password can't be too similar to your other personal information.

Your password must contain at least 8 characters.

Your password can't be a commonly used password.

Your password can't be entirely numeric.

Password confirmation:
```
••••••••
```
Enter the same password as before, for verification.

> Save and add another   Save and continue editing   SAVE

Figure 4.2: The Add user form on the Django administration site

Enter the user details and click on the **SAVE** button to save the new user in the database.

Then, in **Personal info**, fill in the **First name**, **Last name**, and **Email address** fields as follows and click on the **Save** button to save the changes:

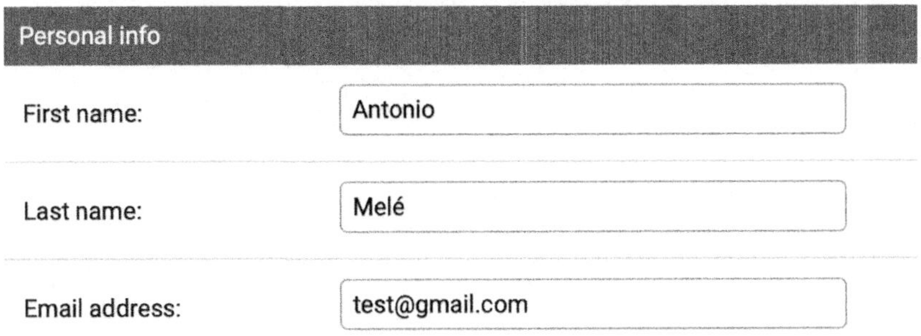

Personal info

First name:	Antonio
Last name:	Melé
Email address:	test@gmail.com

Figure 4.3: The user editing form in the Django administration site

Open `http://127.0.0.1:8000/account/login/` in your browser. You should see the rendered template, including the login form:

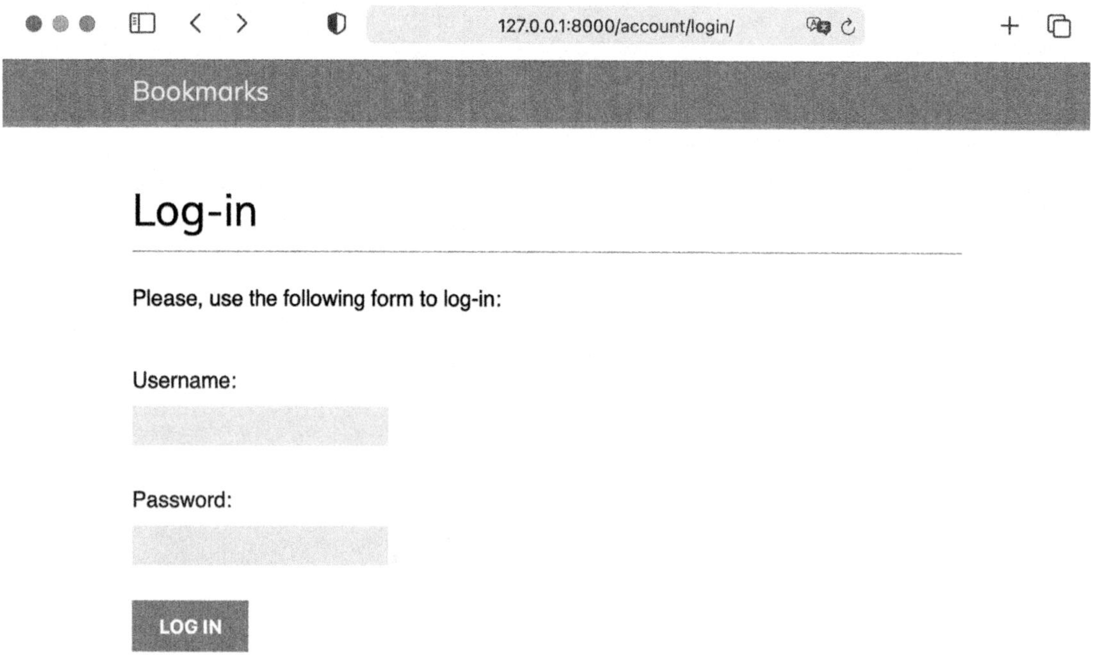

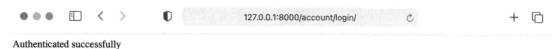

Figure 4.4: The user Log-in page

Enter invalid credentials and submit the form. You should get the following **Invalid login** response:

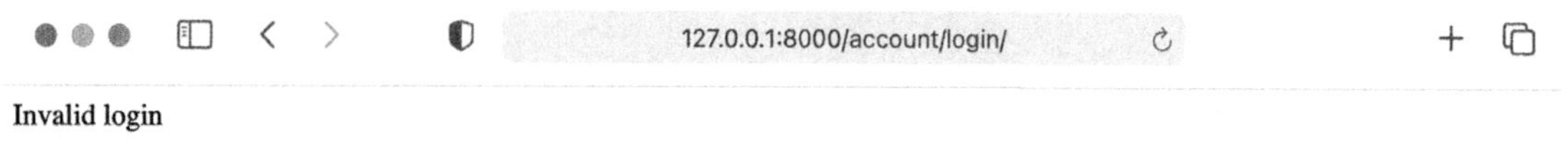

Figure 4.5: The invalid login plain text response

Enter valid credentials; you will get the following **Authenticated successfully** response:

Figure 4.6: The successful authentication plain text response

You have learned how to authenticate users and create your own authentication view. You can build your own auth views but Django ships with ready-to-use authentication views that you can leverage.

Using Django authentication views

Django includes several forms and views in the authentication framework that you can use right away. The login view we have created is a good exercise to understand the process of user authentication in Django. However, you can use the default Django authentication views in most cases.

Django provides the following class-based views to deal with authentication. All of them are located in django.contrib.auth.views:

- LoginView: Handles a login form and logs in a user
- LogoutView: Logs out a user

Django provides the following views to handle password changes:

- PasswordChangeView: Handles a form to change the user's password
- PasswordChangeDoneView: The success view that the user is redirected to after a successful password change

Django also includes the following views to allow users to reset their password:

- PasswordResetView: Allows users to reset their password. It generates a one-time-use link with a token and sends it to a user's email account
- PasswordResetDoneView: Tells users that an email—including a link to reset their password—has been sent to them
- PasswordResetConfirmView: Allows users to set a new password
- PasswordResetCompleteView: The success view that the user is redirected to after successfully resetting their password

These views can save you a lot of time when building any web application with user accounts. The views use default values that can be overridden, such as the location of the template to be rendered, or the form to be used by the view.

You can get more information about the built-in authentication views at https://docs.djangoproject.com/en/4.1/topics/auth/default/#all-authentication-views.

Login and logout views

Edit the urls.py file of the account application and add the code highlighted in bold:

```
from django.urls import path
from django.contrib.auth import views as auth_views
from . import views

urlpatterns = [
    # previous login url
    # path('login/', views.user_login, name='login'),
```

```
# login / logout urls
path('login/', auth_views.LoginView.as_view(), name='login'),
path('logout/', auth_views.LogoutView.as_view(), name='logout'),
]
```

In the preceding code, we have commented out the URL pattern for the `user_login` view that we created previously. We'll now use the `LoginView` view of Django's authentication framework. We have also added a URL pattern for the `LogoutView` view.

Create a new directory inside the `templates/` directory of the `account` application and name it `registration`. This is the default path where the Django authentication views expect your authentication templates to be.

The `django.contrib.admin` module includes authentication templates that are used for the administration site, like the login template. By placing the `account` application at the top of the `INSTALLED_APPS` setting when configuring the project, we ensured that Django would use our authentication templates instead of the ones defined in any other application.

Create a new file inside the `templates/registration/` directory, name it `login.html`, and add the following code to it:

```
{% extends "base.html" %}

{% block title %}Log-in{% endblock %}

{% block content %}
  <h1>Log-in</h1>
  {% if form.errors %}
    <p>
      Your username and password didn't match.
      Please try again.
    </p>
  {% else %}
    <p>Please, use the following form to log-in:</p>
  {% endif %}
  <div class="login-form">
    <form action="{% url 'login' %}" method="post">
      {{ form.as_p }}
      {% csrf_token %}
      <input type="hidden" name="next" value="{{ next }}" />
      <p><input type="submit" value="Log-in"></p>
    </form>
  </div>
{% endblock %}
```

This login template is quite similar to the one we created before. Django uses the `AuthenticationForm` form located at `django.contrib.auth.forms` by default. This form tries to authenticate the user and raises a validation error if the login is unsuccessful. We use `{% if form.errors %}` in the template to check whether the credentials provided are wrong.

We have added a hidden HTML `<input>` element to submit the value of a variable called next. This variable is provided to the login view if you pass a parameter named next to the request, for example, by accessing `http://127.0.0.1:8000/account/login/?next=/account/`.

The next parameter has to be a URL. If this parameter is given, the Django login view will redirect the user to the given URL after a successful login.

Now, create a `logged_out.html` template inside the `templates/registration/` directory and make it look like this:

```
{% extends "base.html" %}

{% block title %}Logged out{% endblock %}

{% block content %}
  <h1>Logged out</h1>
  <p>
    You have been successfully logged out.
    You can <a href="{% url "login" %}">log-in again</a>.
  </p>
{% endblock %}
```

This is the template that Django will display after the user logs out.

We have added the URL patterns and templates for the login and logout views. Users can now log in and out using Django's authentication views.

Now, we will create a new view to display a dashboard when users log into their accounts.

Edit the `views.py` file of the `account` application and add the following code to it:

```
from django.contrib.auth.decorators import login_required

@login_required
def dashboard(request):
    return render(request,
                  'account/dashboard.html',
                  {'section': 'dashboard'})
```

We have created the `dashboard` view, and we have applied to it the `login_required` decorator of the authentication framework. The `login_required` decorator checks whether the current user is authenticated.

If the user is authenticated, it executes the decorated view; if the user is not authenticated, it redirects the user to the login URL with the originally requested URL as a GET parameter named next.

By doing this, the login view redirects users to the URL that they were trying to access after they successfully log in. Remember that we added a hidden <input> HTML element named next in the login template for this purpose.

We have also defined a section variable. We will use this variable to highlight the current section in the main menu of the site.

Next, we need to create a template for the dashboard view.

Create a new file inside the templates/account/ directory and name it dashboard.html. Add the following code to it:

```
{% extends "base.html" %}

{% block title %}Dashboard{% endblock %}

{% block content %}
  <h1>Dashboard</h1>
  <p>Welcome to your dashboard.</p>
{% endblock %}
```

Edit the urls.py file of the account application and add the following URL pattern for the view. The new code is highlighted in bold:

```
urlpatterns = [
    # previous login url
    # path('login/', views.user_login, name='login'),

    # login / logout urls
    path('login/', auth_views.LoginView.as_view(), name='login'),
    path('logout/', auth_views.LogoutView.as_view(), name='logout'),

    path('', views.dashboard, name='dashboard'),
]
```

Edit the settings.py file of the project and add the following code to it:

```
LOGIN_REDIRECT_URL = 'dashboard'
LOGIN_URL = 'login'
LOGOUT_URL = 'logout'
```

We have defined the following settings:

- `LOGIN_REDIRECT_URL`: Tells Django which URL to redirect the user to after a successful login if no `next` parameter is present in the request
- `LOGIN_URL`: The URL to redirect the user to log in (for example, views using the `login_required` decorator)
- `LOGOUT_URL`: The URL to redirect the user to log out

We have used the names of the URLs that we previously defined with the `name` attribute of the `path()` function in the URL patterns. Hardcoded URLs instead of URL names can also be used for these settings.

Let's summarize what we have done so far:

- We have added the built-in Django authentication login and logout views to the project.
- We have created custom templates for both views and defined a simple dashboard view to redirect users after they log in.
- Finally, we have added settings for Django to use these URLs by default.

Now, we will add login and logout links to the base template. In order to do this, we have to determine whether the current user is logged in or not in order to display the appropriate link for each case. The current user is set in the `HttpRequest` object by the authentication middleware. You can access it with `request.user`. You will find a `User` object in the request even if the user is not authenticated. A non-authenticated user is set in the request as an instance of `AnonymousUser`. The best way to check whether the current user is authenticated is by accessing the read-only attribute `is_authenticated`.

Edit the `templates/base.html` template by adding the following lines highlighted in bold:

```
{% load static %}
<!DOCTYPE html>
<html>
<head>
  <title>{% block title %}{% endblock %}</title>
  <link href="{% static "css/base.css" %}" rel="stylesheet">
</head>
<body>
  <div id="header">
    <span class="logo">Bookmarks</span>
    {% if request.user.is_authenticated %}
      <ul class="menu">
        <li {% if section == "dashboard" %}class="selected"{% endif %}>
          <a href="{% url "dashboard" %}">My dashboard</a>
        </li>
        <li {% if section == "images" %}class="selected"{% endif %}>
          <a href="#">Images</a>
        </li>
```

```
                <li {% if section == "people" %}class="selected"{% endif %}>
                    <a href="#">People</a>
                </li>
            </ul>
        {% endif %}
        <span class="user">
            {% if request.user.is_authenticated %}
                Hello {{ request.user.first_name|default:request.user.username }},
                <a href="{% url "logout" %}">Logout</a>
            {% else %}
                <a href="{% url "login" %}">Log-in</a>
            {% endif %}
        </span>
    </div>
    <div id="content">
        {% block content %}
        {% endblock %}
    </div>
</body>
</html>
```

The site's menu is only displayed to authenticated users. The `section` variable is checked to add a `selected` class attribute to the menu `<li>` list item of the current section. By doing so, the menu item that corresponds to the current section will be highlighted using CSS. The user's first name and a link to log out are displayed if the user is authenticated; a link to log in is displayed otherwise. If the user's name is empty, the username is displayed instead by using `request.user.first_name|default:request.user.username`.

Open `http://127.0.0.1:8000/account/login/` in your browser. You should see the **Log-in** page. Enter a valid username and password and click on the **Log-in** button. You should see the following screen:

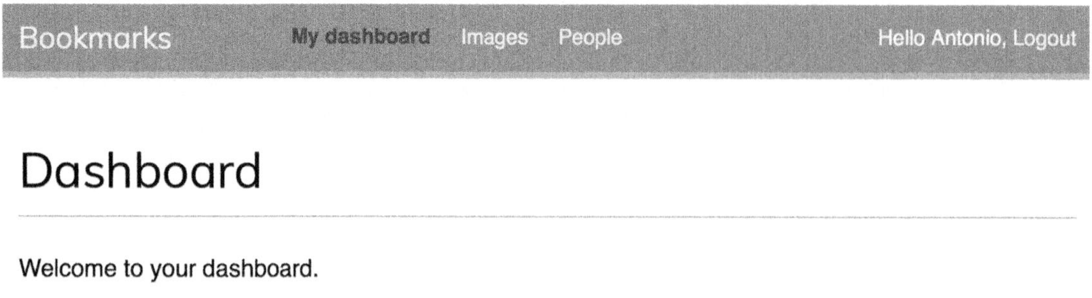

Dashboard

Welcome to your dashboard.

Figure 4.7: The Dashboard page

The **My dashboard** menu item is highlighted with CSS because it has a `selected` class. Since the user is authenticated, the first name of the user is displayed on the right side of the header. Click on the **Logout** link. You should see the following page:

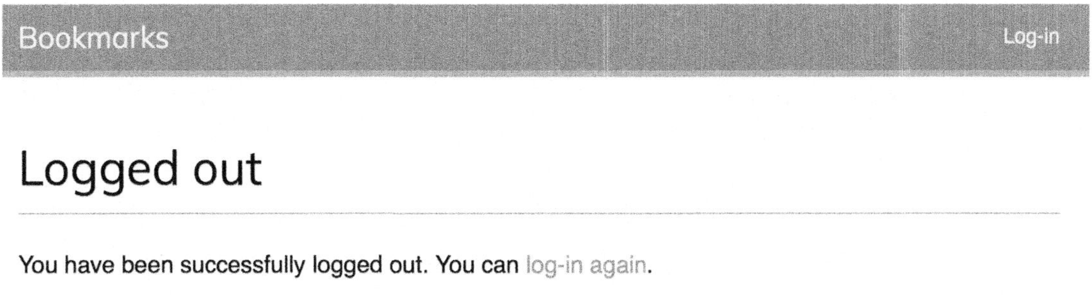

Bookmarks   Log-in

Logged out

You have been successfully logged out. You can log-in again.

Figure 4.8: The Logged out page

On this page, you can see that the user is logged out, and, therefore, the menu of the website is not displayed. The link displayed on the right side of the header is now **Log-in**.

 If you see the **Logged out** page of the Django administration site instead of your own **Logged out** page, check the `INSTALLED_APPS` setting of your project and make sure that `django.contrib.admin` comes after the `account` application. Both applications contain logged-out templates located in the same relative path. The Django template loader will go through the different applications in the `INSTALLED_APPS` list and use the first template it finds.

Change password views

We need users to be able to change their password after they log into the site. We will integrate the Django authentication views for changing passwords.

Open the `urls.py` file of the `account` application and add the following URL patterns highlighted in bold:

```python
urlpatterns = [
    # previous login url
    # path('login/', views.user_login, name='login'),

    # login / logout urls
    path('login/', auth_views.LoginView.as_view(), name='login'),
    path('logout/', auth_views.LogoutView.as_view(), name='logout'),

    # change password urls
    path('password-change/',
        auth_views.PasswordChangeView.as_view(),
        name='password_change'),
    path('password-change/done/',
```

```
            auth_views.PasswordChangeDoneView.as_view(),
         name='password_change_done'),

    path('', views.dashboard, name='dashboard'),
]
```

The `PasswordChangeView` view will handle the form to change the password, and the `PasswordChangeDoneView` view will display a success message after the user has successfully changed their password. Let's create a template for each view.

Add a new file inside the `templates/registration/` directory of the account application and name it `password_change_form.html`. Add the following code to it:

```
{% extends "base.html" %}

{% block title %}Change your password{% endblock %}

{% block content %}
  <h1>Change your password</h1>
  <p>Use the form below to change your password.</p>
  <form method="post">
    {{ form.as_p }}
    <p><input type="submit" value="Change"></p>
    {% csrf_token %}
  </form>
{% endblock %}
```

The `password_change_form.html` template includes the form to change the password.

Now create another file in the same directory and name it `password_change_done.html`. Add the following code to it:

```
{% extends "base.html" %}

{% block title %}Password changed{% endblock %}

{% block content %}
  <h1>Password changed</h1>
  <p>Your password has been successfully changed.</p>
{% endblock %}
```

The `password_change_done.html` template only contains the success message to be displayed when the user has successfully changed their password.

Open `http://127.0.0.1:8000/account/password-change/` in your browser. If you are not logged in, the browser will redirect you to the **Log-in** page. After you are successfully authenticated, you will see the following change password page:

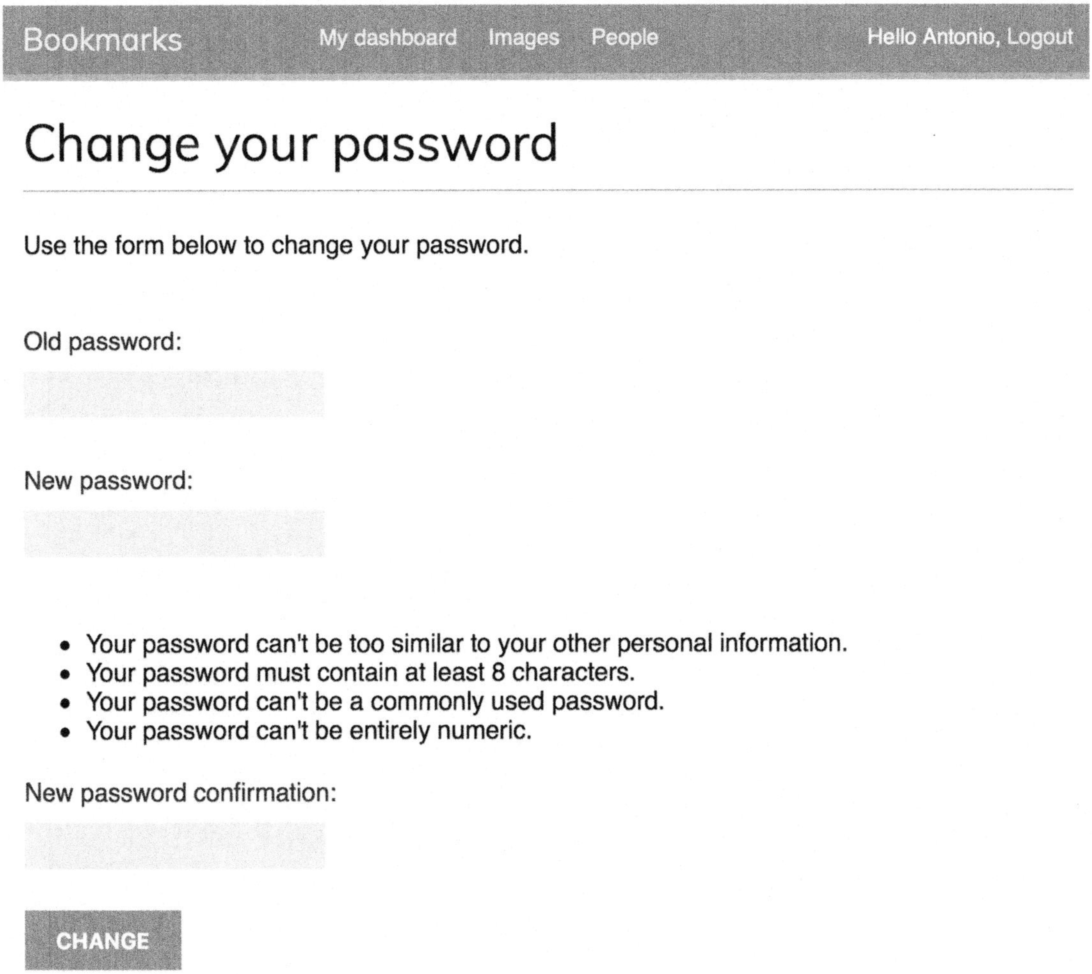

| Bookmarks | My dashboard   Images   People | Hello Antonio, Logout |

Change your password

Use the form below to change your password.

Old password:

New password:

- Your password can't be too similar to your other personal information.
- Your password must contain at least 8 characters.
- Your password can't be a commonly used password.
- Your password can't be entirely numeric.

New password confirmation:

CHANGE

Figure 4.9: The change password form

Fill in the form with your current password and your new password and click on the **CHANGE** button. You will see the following success page:

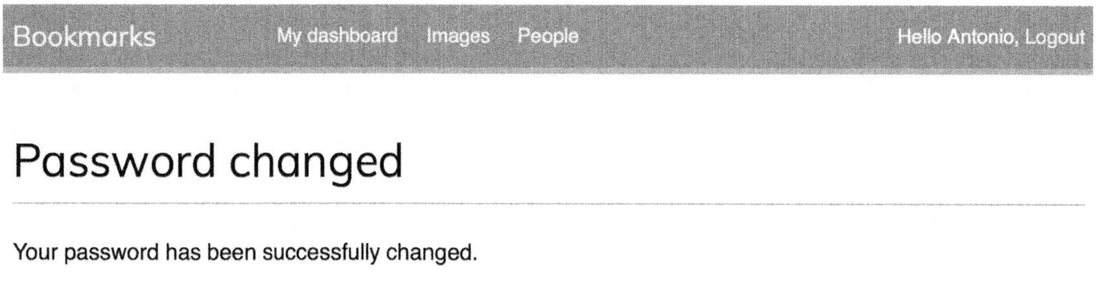

Bookmarks   My dashboard   Images   People   Hello Antonio, Logout

Password changed

Your password has been successfully changed.

Figure 4.10: The successful password change page

Log out and log in again using your new password to verify that everything works as expected.

Reset password views

Edit the urls.py file of the account application and add the following URL patterns highlighted in bold:

```python
urlpatterns = [
    # previous login url
    # path('login/', views.user_login, name='login'),

    # login / logout urls
    path('login/', auth_views.LoginView.as_view(), name='login'),
    path('logout/', auth_views.LogoutView.as_view(), name='logout'),

    # change password urls
    path('password-change/',
        auth_views.PasswordChangeView.as_view(),
        name='password_change'),
    path('password-change/done/',
        auth_views.PasswordChangeDoneView.as_view(),
        name='password_change_done'),

    # reset password urls
    path('password-reset/',
        auth_views.PasswordResetView.as_view(),
        name='password_reset'),
    path('password-reset/done/',
        auth_views.PasswordResetDoneView.as_view(),
        name='password_reset_done'),
    path('password-reset/<uidb64>/<token>/',
```

```
            auth_views.PasswordResetConfirmView.as_view(),
            name='password_reset_confirm'),
    path('password-reset/complete/',
            auth_views.PasswordResetCompleteView.as_view(),
            name='password_reset_complete'),

    path('', views.dashboard, name='dashboard'),
]
```

Add a new file in the `templates/registration/` directory of the account application and name it `password_reset_form.html`. Add the following code to it:

```
{% extends "base.html" %}

{% block title %}Reset your password{% endblock %}

{% block content %}
  <h1>Forgotten your password?</h1>
  <p>Enter your e-mail address to obtain a new password.</p>
  <form method="post">
    {{ form.as_p }}
    <p><input type="submit" value="Send e-mail"></p>
    {% csrf_token %}
  </form>
{% endblock %}
```

Now create another file in the same directory and name it `password_reset_email.html`. Add the following code to it:

```
Someone asked for password reset for email {{ email }}. Follow the link below:
{{ protocol }}://{{ domain }}{% url "password_reset_confirm" uidb64=uid
token=token %}
Your username, in case you've forgotten: {{ user.get_username }}
```

The `password_reset_email.html` template will be used to render the email sent to users to reset their password. It includes a reset token that is generated by the view.

Create another file in the same directory and name it `password_reset_done.html`. Add the following code to it:

```
{% extends "base.html" %}

{% block title %}Reset your password{% endblock %}

{% block content %}
```

```
<h1>Reset your password</h1>
<p>We've emailed you instructions for setting your password.</p>
<p>If you don't receive an email, please make sure you've entered the address
you registered with.</p>
{% endblock %}
```

Create another template in the same directory and name it `password_reset_confirm.html`. Add the following code to it:

```
{% extends "base.html" %}

{% block title %}Reset your password{% endblock %}

{% block content %}
  <h1>Reset your password</h1>
  {% if validlink %}
    <p>Please enter your new password twice:</p>
    <form method="post">
      {{ form.as_p }}
      {% csrf_token %}
      <p><input type="submit" value="Change my password" /></p>
    </form>
  {% else %}
    <p>The password reset link was invalid, possibly because it has already
been used. Please request a new password reset.</p>
  {% endif %}
{% endblock %}
```

In this template, we confirm whether the link for resetting the password is valid by checking the `validlink` variable. The view `PasswordResetConfirmView` checks the validity of the token provided in the URL and passes the `validlink` variable to the template. If the link is valid, the user password reset form is displayed. Users can only set a new password if they have a valid reset password link.

Create another template and name it `password_reset_complete.html`. Enter the following code into it:

```
{% extends "base.html" %}

{% block title %}Password reset{% endblock %}

{% block content %}
  <h1>Password set</h1>
  <p>Your password has been set. You can <a href="{% url "login" %}">log in
now</a></p>
{% endblock %}
```

Finally, edit the `registration/login.html` template of the `account` application, and add the following lines highlighted in bold:

```
{% extends "base.html" %}

{% block title %}Log-in{% endblock %}

{% block content %}
  <h1>Log-in</h1>
  {% if form.errors %}
    <p>
      Your username and password didn't match.
      Please try again.
    </p>
  {% else %}
    <p>Please, use the following form to log-in:</p>
  {% endif %}
  <div class="login-form">
    <form action="{% url 'login' %}" method="post">
      {{ form.as_p }}
      {% csrf_token %}
      <input type="hidden" name="next" value="{{ next }}" />
      <p><input type="submit" value="Log-in"></p>
    </form>
    <p>
      <a href="{% url "password_reset" %}">
        Forgotten your password?
      </a>
    </p>
  </div>
{% endblock %}
```

Now, open `http://127.0.0.1:8000/account/login/` in your browser. The **Log-in page** should now include a link to the reset password page, as follows:

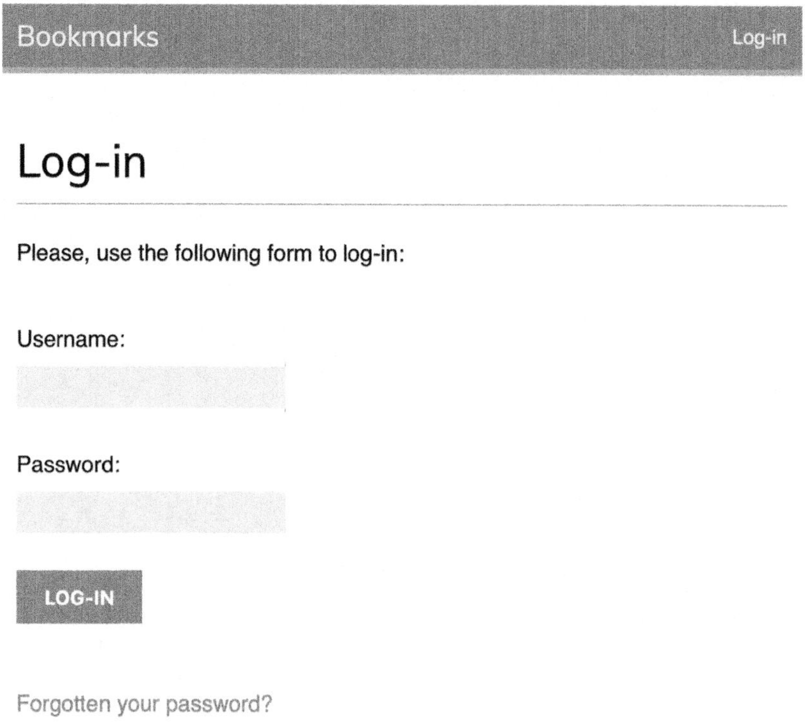

Bookmarks   Log-in

Log-in

Please, use the following form to log-in:

Username:

Password:

LOG-IN

Forgotten your password?

Figure 4.11: The Log-in page including a link to the reset password page

Click on the **Forgotten your password?** link. You should see the following page:

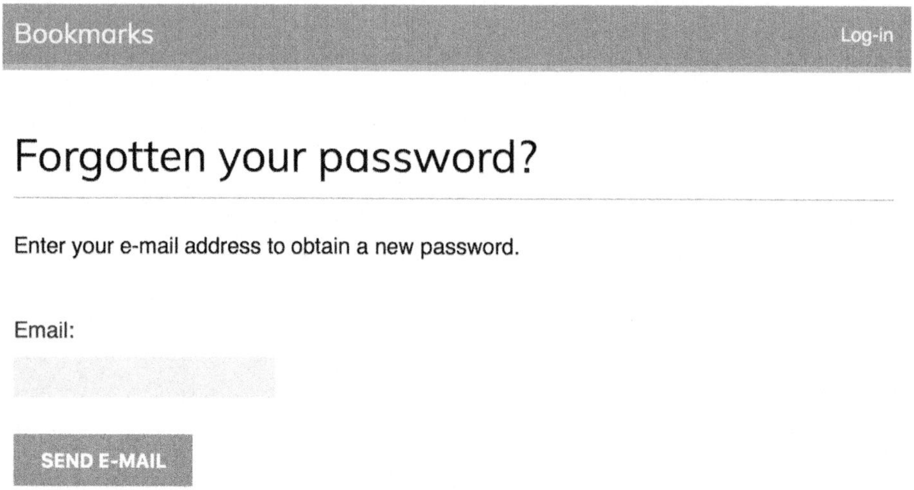

Bookmarks   Log-in

Forgotten your password?

Enter your e-mail address to obtain a new password.

Email:

SEND E-MAIL

Figure 4.12: The restore password form

At this point, we need to add a **Simple Mail Transfer Protocol (SMTP)** configuration to the settings.py file of your project so that Django is able to send emails. You learned how to add email settings to your project in *Chapter 2, Enhancing Your Blog with Advanced Features*. However, during development, you can configure Django to write emails to the standard output instead of sending them through an SMTP server. Django provides an email backend to write emails to the console.

Edit the settings.py file of your project, and add the following line to it:

```
EMAIL_BACKEND = 'django.core.mail.backends.console.EmailBackend'
```

The EMAIL_BACKEND setting indicates the class that will be used to send emails.

Return to your browser, enter the email address of an existing user, and click on the **SEND E-MAIL** button. You should see the following page:

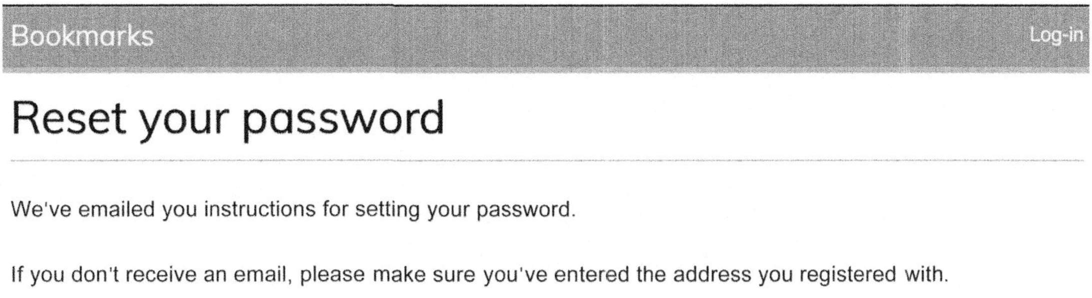

Bookmarks   Log-in

Reset your password

We've emailed you instructions for setting your password.

If you don't receive an email, please make sure you've entered the address you registered with.

Figure 4.13: The reset password email sent page

Take a look at the shell prompt, where you are running the development server. You will see the generated email, as follows:

```
Content-Type: text/plain; charset="utf-8"
MIME-Version: 1.0
Content-Transfer-Encoding: 7bit
Subject: Password reset on 127.0.0.1:8000
From: webmaster@localhost
To: test@gmail.com
Date: Mon, 10 Jan 2022 19:05:18 -0000
Message-ID: <162896791878.58862.14771487060402279558@MBP-amele.local>

Someone asked for password reset for email test@gmail.com. Follow the link
below:
http://127.0.0.1:8000/account/password-reset/MQ/ardx0u-
b4973cfa2c70d652a190e79054bc479a/
Your username, in case you've forgotten: test
```

The email is rendered using the password_reset_email.html template that you created earlier. The URL to reset the password includes a token that was generated dynamically by Django.

Copy the URL from the email, which should look similar to `http://127.0.0.1:8000/account/` `password-reset/MQ/ardx0u-b4973cfa2c70d652a190e79054bc479a/`, and open it in your browser. You should see the following page:

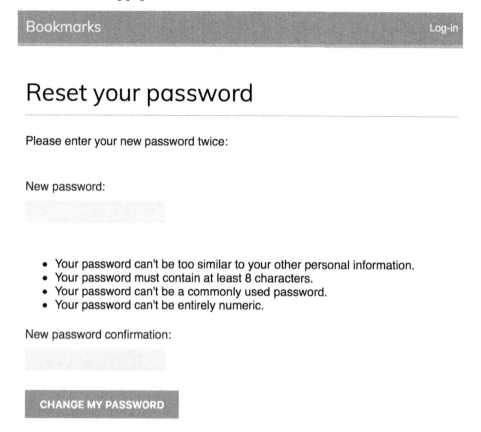

Figure 4.14: The reset password form

The page to set a new password uses the `password_reset_confirm.html` template. Fill in a new password and click on the **CHANGE MY PASSWORD** button. Django will create a new hashed password and save it into the database. You will see the following success page:

Figure 4.15: The successful password reset page

Now you can log back into the user account using the new password.

Each token to set a new password can be used only once. If you open the link you received again, you will get a message stating that the token is invalid.

We have now integrated the views of the Django authentication framework into the project. These views are suitable for most cases. However, you can create your own views if you need different behavior.

Django provides URL patterns for the authentication views that are equivalent to the ones we just created. We will replace the authentication URL patterns with the ones provided by Django.

Comment out the authentication URL patterns that you added to the urls.py file of the account application and include django.contrib.auth.urls instead, as follows. New code is highlighted in bold:

```python
from django.urls import path, include
from django.contrib.auth import views as auth_views
from . import views

urlpatterns = [
    # previous login view
    # path('login/', views.user_login, name='login'),

    # path('login/', auth_views.LoginView.as_view(), name='login'),
    # path('logout/', auth_views.LogoutView.as_view(), name='logout'),

    # change password urls
    # path('password-change/',
    #       auth_views.PasswordChangeView.as_view(),
    #       name='password_change'),
    # path('password-change/done/',
    #        auth_views.PasswordChangeDoneView.as_view(),
    #        name='password_change_done'),

    # reset password urls
    # path('password-reset/',
    #       auth_views.PasswordResetView.as_view(),
    #       name='password_reset'),
    # path('password-reset/done/',
    #       auth_views.PasswordResetDoneView.as_view(),
    #       name='password_reset_done'),
    # path('password-reset/<uidb64>/<token>/',
    #       auth_views.PasswordResetConfirmView.as_view(),
    #       name='password_reset_confirm'),
    # path('password-reset/complete/',
```

```
    #        auth_views.PasswordResetCompleteView.as_view(),
    #        name='password_reset_complete'),

    path('', include('django.contrib.auth.urls')),
    path('', views.dashboard, name='dashboard'),
]
```

You can see the authentication URL patterns included at https://github.com/django/django/blob/
stable/4.0.x/django/contrib/auth/urls.py.

We have now added all the necessary authentication views to our project. Next, we will implement
user registration.

User registration and user profiles

Site users can now log in, log out, change their password, and reset their password. However, we need
to build a view to allow visitors to create a user account.

User registration

Let's create a simple view to allow user registration on your website. Initially, you have to create a
form to let the user enter a username, their real name, and a password.

Edit the forms.py file located inside the account application directory and add the following lines
highlighted in bold:

```
from django import forms
from django.contrib.auth.models import User


class LoginForm(forms.Form):
    username = forms.CharField()
    password = forms.CharField(widget=forms.PasswordInput)


class UserRegistrationForm(forms.ModelForm):
    password = forms.CharField(label='Password',
                               widget=forms.PasswordInput)
    password2 = forms.CharField(label='Repeat password',
                                widget=forms.PasswordInput)

    class Meta:
        model = User
        fields = ['username', 'first_name', 'email']
```

We have created a model form for the user model. This form includes the fields username, first_name, and email of the User model. These fields will be validated according to the validations of their corresponding model fields. For example, if the user chooses a username that already exists, they will get a validation error because username is a field defined with unique=True.

We have added two additional fields—password and password2—for users to set a password and to repeat it. Let's add the field validation to check both passwords are the same.

Edit the forms.py file in the account application and add the following clean_password2() method to the UserRegistrationForm class. New code is highlighted in bold:

```python
class UserRegistrationForm(forms.ModelForm):
    password = forms.CharField(label='Password',
                               widget=forms.PasswordInput)
    password2 = forms.CharField(label='Repeat password',
                                widget=forms.PasswordInput)

    class Meta:
        model = User
        fields = ['username', 'first_name', 'email']

    def clean_password2(self):
        cd = self.cleaned_data
        if cd['password'] != cd['password2']:
            raise forms.ValidationError('Passwords don\'t match.')
        return cd['password2']
```

We have defined a clean_password2() method to compare the second password against the first one and raise a validation error if the passwords don't match. This method is executed when the form is validated by calling its is_valid() method. You can provide a clean_<fieldname>() method to any of your form fields in order to clean the value or raise form validation errors for a specific field. Forms also include a general clean() method to validate the entire form, which is useful to validate fields that depend on each other. In this case, we use the field-specific clean_password2() validation instead of overriding the clean() method of the form. This avoids overriding other field-specific checks that the ModelForm gets from the restrictions set in the model (for example, validating that the username is unique).

Django also provides a UserCreationForm form that resides in django.contrib.auth.forms and is very similar to the one we have created.

Edit the views.py file of the account application and add the following code highlighted in bold:

```python
from django.http import HttpResponse
from django.shortcuts import render
from django.contrib.auth import authenticate, login
```

```python
from django.contrib.auth.decorators import login_required
from .forms import LoginForm, UserRegistrationForm


# ...


def register(request):
    if request.method == 'POST':
        user_form = UserRegistrationForm(request.POST)
        if user_form.is_valid():
            # Create a new user object but avoid saving it yet
            new_user = user_form.save(commit=False)
            # Set the chosen password
            new_user.set_password(
                user_form.cleaned_data['password'])
            # Save the User object
            new_user.save()
            return render(request,
                          'account/register_done.html',
                          {'new_user': new_user})
    else:
        user_form = UserRegistrationForm()
    return render(request,
                  'account/register.html',
                  {'user_form': user_form})
```

The view for creating user accounts is quite simple. For security reasons, instead of saving the raw password entered by the user, we use the set_password() method of the User model. This method handles password hashing before storing the password in the database.

Django doesn't store clear text passwords; it stores hashed passwords instead. Hashing is the process of transforming a given key into another value. A hash function is used to generate a fixed-length value according to a mathematical algorithm. By hashing passwords with secure algorithms, Django ensures that user passwords stored in the database require massive amounts of computing time to break.

By default, Django uses the PBKDF2 hashing algorithm with a SHA256 hash to store all passwords. However, Django not only supports checking existing passwords hashed with PBKDF2, but also supports checking stored passwords hashed with other algorithms such as PBKDF2SHA1, argon2, bcrypt, and scrypt.

The PASSWORD_HASHERS setting defines the password hashers that the Django project supports. The following is the default PASSWORD_HASHERS list:

```
PASSWORD_HASHERS = [
    'django.contrib.auth.hashers.PBKDF2PasswordHasher',
    'django.contrib.auth.hashers.PBKDF2SHA1PasswordHasher',
    'django.contrib.auth.hashers.Argon2PasswordHasher',
    'django.contrib.auth.hashers.BCryptSHA256PasswordHasher',
    'django.contrib.auth.hashers.ScryptPasswordHasher',
]
```

Django uses the first entry of the list, in this case PBKDF2PasswordHasher, to hash all passwords. The rest of the hashers can be used by Django to check existing passwords.

 The scrypt hasher has been introduced in Django 4.0. It is more secure and recommended over PBKDF2. However, PBKDF2 is still the default hasher, as scrypt requires OpenSSL 1.1+ and more memory.

You can learn more about how Django stores passwords and about the password hashers included at https://docs.djangoproject.com/en/4.1/topics/auth/passwords/.

Now, edit the urls.py file of the account application and add the following URL pattern highlighted in bold:

```
urlpatterns = [

    # ...

    path('', include('django.contrib.auth.urls')),
    path('', views.dashboard, name='dashboard'),
    path('register/', views.register, name='register'),
]
```

Finally, create a new template in the `templates/account/` template directory of the account application, name it `register.html`, and make it look as follows:

```
{% extends "base.html" %}

{% block title %}Create an account{% endblock %}

{% block content %}
  <h1>Create an account</h1>
  <p>Please, sign up using the following form:</p>
  <form method="post">
    {{ user_form.as_p }}
    {% csrf_token %}
    <p><input type="submit" value="Create my account"></p>
  </form>
{% endblock %}
```

Create an additional template file in the same directory and name it `register_done.html`. Add the following code to it:

```
{% extends "base.html" %}

{% block title %}Welcome{% endblock %}

{% block content %}
  <h1>Welcome {{ new_user.first_name }}!</h1>
  <p>
    Your account has been successfully created.
    Now you can <a href="{% url "login" %}">log in</a>.
  </p>
{% endblock %}
```

Open `http://127.0.0.1:8000/account/register/` in your browser. You will see the registration page you have created:

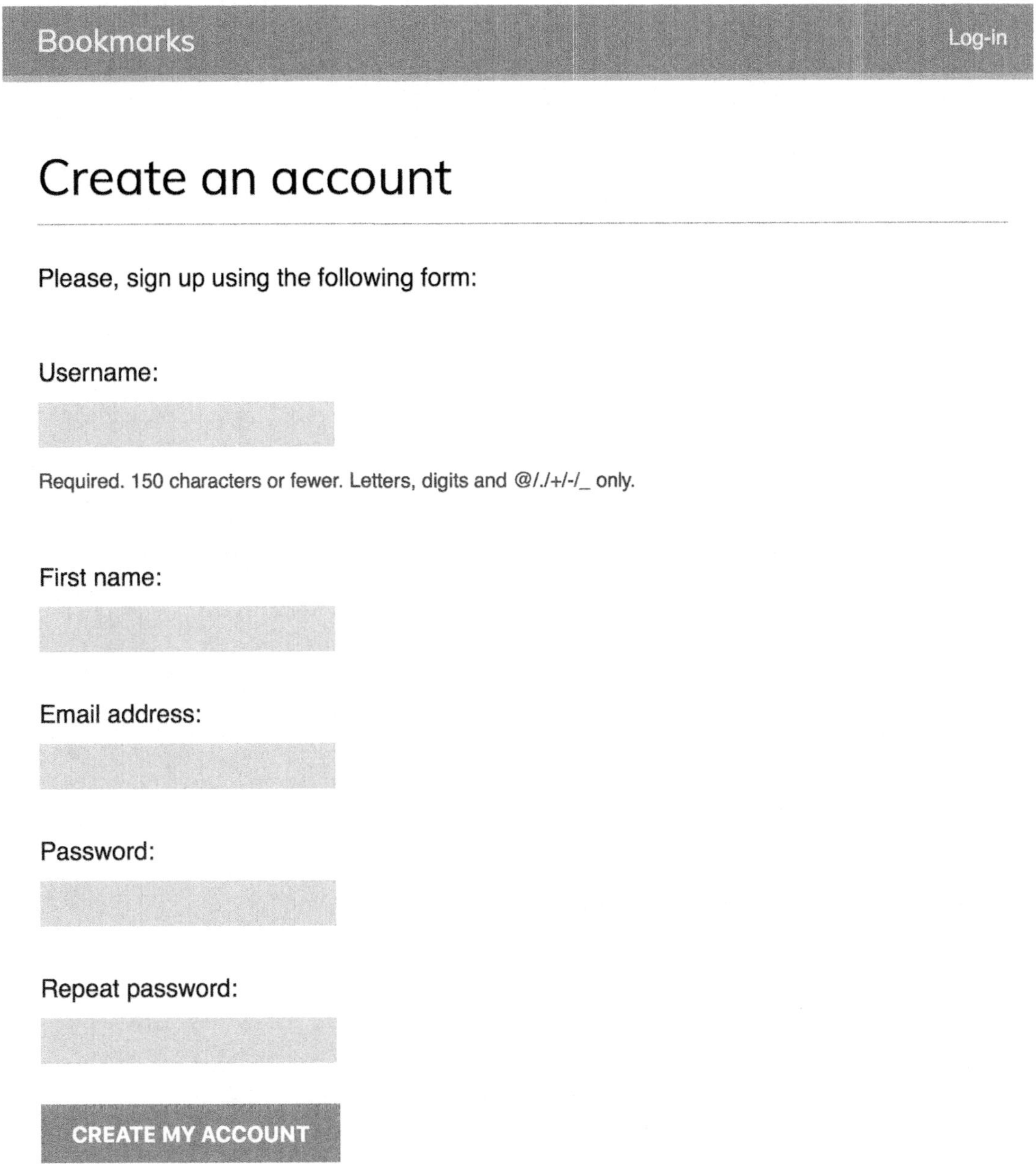

Bookmarks   Log-in

Create an account

Please, sign up using the following form:

Username:

Required. 150 characters or fewer. Letters, digits and @/./+/-/_ only.

First name:

Email address:

Password:

Repeat password:

CREATE MY ACCOUNT

Figure 4.16: The account creation form

Fill in the details for a new user and click on the **CREATE MY ACCOUNT** button.

If all fields are valid, the user will be created, and you will see the following success message:

Bookmarks	Log-in

Welcome Paloma!

Your account has been successfully created. Now you can log in.

Figure 4.17: The account is successfully created page

Click on the **log in** link and enter your username and password to verify that you can access your newly created account.

Let's add a link to register on the login template. Edit the `registration/login.html` template and find the following line:

```
<p>Please, use the following form to log-in:</p>
```

Replace it with the following lines:

```
<p>
  Please, use the following form to log-in.
  If you don't have an account <a href="{% url "register" %}">register here</a>.
</p>
```

Open `http://127.0.0.1:8000/account/login/` in your browser. The page should now look as follows:

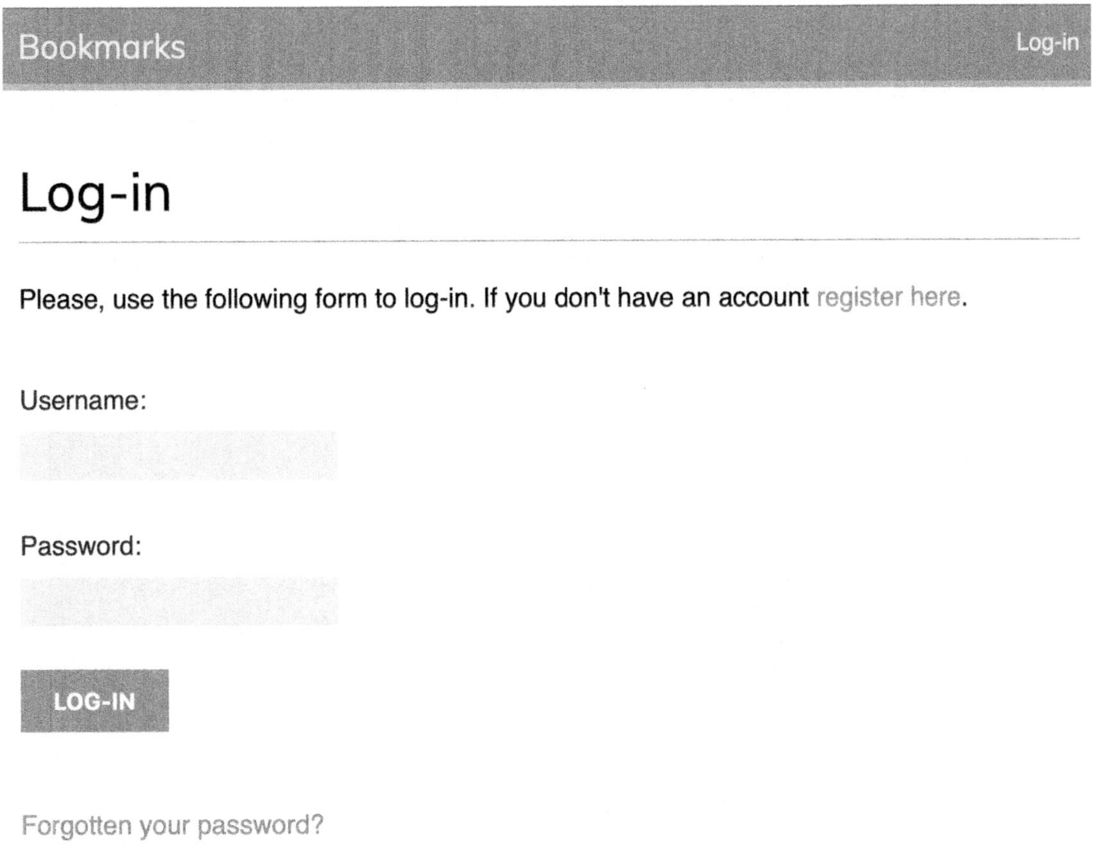

Bookmarks Log-in

Log-in

Please, use the following form to log-in. If you don't have an account register here.

Username:

Password:

LOG-IN

Forgotten your password?

Figure 4.18: The Log-in page including a link to register

We have made the registration page accessible from the **Log-in** page.

Extending the user model

When dealing with user accounts, you will find that the User model of the Django authentication framework is suitable for most common cases. However, the standard User model comes with a limited set of fields. You may want to extend it with additional information that is relevant to your application.

A simple way to extend the User model is by creating a profile model that contains a one-to-one relationship with the Django User model, and any additional fields. A one-to-one relationship is similar to a ForeignKey field with the parameter unique=True. The reverse side of the relationship is an implicit one-to-one relationship with the related model instead of a manager for multiple elements. From each side of the relationship, you access a single related object.

Edit the models.py file of your account application and add the following code highlighted in bold:

```python
from django.db import models
from django.conf import settings


class Profile(models.Model):
    user = models.OneToOneField(settings.AUTH_USER_MODEL,
                                on_delete=models.CASCADE)
    date_of_birth = models.DateField(blank=True, null=True)
    photo = models.ImageField(upload_to='users/%Y/%m/%d/',
                              blank=True)


    def __str__(self):
        return f'Profile of {self.user.username}'
```

 In order to keep your code generic, use the get_user_model() method to retrieve the user model and the AUTH_USER_MODEL setting to refer to it when defining a model's relationship with the user model, instead of referring to the auth user model directly. You can read more information about this at https://docs.djangoproject.com/en/4.1/topics/auth/customizing/#django.contrib.auth.get_user_model.

Our user profile will include the user's date of birth and an image of the user.

The one-to-one field user will be used to associate profiles with users. With on_delete=models.CASCADE, we force the deletion of the related Profile object when a User object gets deleted.

The date_of_birth field is a DateField. We have made this field optional with blank=True, and we allow null values with null=True.

The photo field is an ImageField. We have made this field optional with blank=True. An ImageField field manages the storage of image files. It validates the file provided is a valid image, stores the image file in the directory indicated with the upload_to parameter, and stores the relative path to the file in the related database field. An ImageField field is translated to a VARHAR(100) column in the database by default. A blank string will be stored if the value is left empty.

Installing Pillow and serving media files

We need to install the Pillow library to manage images. Pillow is the de facto standard library for image processing in Python. It supports multiple image formats and provides powerful image processing functions. Pillow is required by Django to handle images with `ImageField`.

Install Pillow by running the following command from the shell prompt:

```
pip install Pillow==9.2.0
```

Edit the `settings.py` file of the project and add the following lines:

```
MEDIA_URL = 'media/'
MEDIA_ROOT = BASE_DIR / 'media'
```

This will enable Django to manage file uploads and serve media files. `MEDIA_URL` is the base URL used to serve the media files uploaded by users. `MEDIA_ROOT` is the local path where they reside. Paths and URLs for files are built dynamically by prepending the project path or the media URL to them for portability.

Now, edit the main `urls.py` file of the `bookmarks` project and modify the code, as follows. New lines are highlighted in bold:

```
from django.contrib import admin
from django.urls import path, include
from django.conf import settings
from django.conf.urls.static import static

urlpatterns = [
    path('admin/', admin.site.urls),
    path('account/', include('account.urls')),
]

if settings.DEBUG:
    urlpatterns += static(settings.MEDIA_URL,
                          document_root=settings.MEDIA_ROOT)
```

We have added the `static()` helper function to serve media files with the Django development server during development (that is when the `DEBUG` setting is set to `True`).

 The `static()` helper function is suitable for development but not for production use. Django is very inefficient at serving static files. Never serve your static files with Django in a production environment. You will learn how to serve static files in a production environment in *Chapter 17, Going Live*.

Creating migrations for the profile model

Open the shell and run the following command to create the database migration for the new model:

```
python manage.py makemigrations
```

You will get the following output:

```
Migrations for 'account':
    account/migrations/0001_initial.py
        - Create model Profile
```

Next, sync the database with the following command in the shell prompt:

```
python manage.py migrate
```

You will see an output that includes the following line:

```
Applying account.0001_initial... OK
```

Edit the `admin.py` file of the account application and register the `Profile` model in the administration site by adding the code in bold:

```
from django.contrib import admin
from .models import Profile


@admin.register(Profile)
class ProfileAdmin(admin.ModelAdmin):
    list_display = ['user', 'date_of_birth', 'photo']
    raw_id_fields = ['user']
```

Run the development server using the following command from the shell prompt:

```
python manage.py runserver
```

Open `http://127.0.0.1:8000/admin/` in your browser. Now you should be able to see the `Profile` model on the administration site of your project, as follows:

ACCOUNT		
Profiles	+ Add	✎ Change

Figure 4.19: The ACCOUNT block on the administration site index page

Click on the **Add** link of the **Profiles** row. You will see the following form to add a new profile:

Add profile

User:	[ ] 🔍
Date of birth:	[ ] Today | 📅 Note: You are 2 hours ahead of server time.
Photo:	Choose File no file selected

Figure 4.20: The Add profile form

Create a Profile object manually for each of the existing users in the database.

Next, we will let users edit their profiles on the website.

Edit the forms.py file of the account application and add the following lines highlighted in bold:

```python
# ...
from .models import Profile


# ...


class UserEditForm(forms.ModelForm):
    class Meta:
        model = User
        fields = ['first_name', 'last_name', 'email']

class ProfileEditForm(forms.ModelForm):
    class Meta:
        model = Profile
        fields = ['date_of_birth', 'photo']
```

These forms are as follows:

- UserEditForm: This will allow users to edit their first name, last name, and email, which are attributes of the built-in Django User model.
- ProfileEditForm: This will allow users to edit the profile data that is saved in the custom Profile model. Users will be able to edit their date of birth and upload an image for their profile picture.

Edit the `views.py` file of the `account` application and add the following lines highlighted in bold:

```python
# ...
from .models import Profile

# ...

def register(request):
    if request.method == 'POST':
        user_form = UserRegistrationForm(request.POST)
        if user_form.is_valid():
            # Create a new user object but avoid saving it yet
            new_user = user_form.save(commit=False)
            # Set the chosen password
            new_user.set_password(
                user_form.cleaned_data['password'])
            # Save the User object
            new_user.save()
            # Create the user profile
            Profile.objects.create(user=new_user)
            return render(request,
                          'account/register_done.html',
                          {'new_user': new_user})
    else:
        user_form = UserRegistrationForm()
    return render(request,
                  'account/register.html',
                  {'user_form': user_form})
```

When users register on the site, a `Profile` object will be created and associated with the `User` object created.

Now, we will let users edit their profiles.

Edit the `views.py` file of the `account` application and add the following code highlighted in bold:

```python
from django.http import HttpResponse
from django.shortcuts import render
from django.contrib.auth import authenticate, login
```

```python
from django.contrib.auth.decorators import login_required
from .forms import LoginForm, UserRegistrationForm, \
                    UserEditForm, ProfileEditForm
from .models import Profile


# ...


@login_required
def edit(request):
    if request.method == 'POST':
        user_form = UserEditForm(instance=request.user,
                                 data=request.POST)
        profile_form = ProfileEditForm(
                                    instance=request.user.profile,
                                    data=request.POST,
                                    files=request.FILES)
        if user_form.is_valid() and profile_form.is_valid():
            user_form.save()
            profile_form.save()
    else:
        user_form = UserEditForm(instance=request.user)
        profile_form = ProfileEditForm(
                                    instance=request.user.profile)
    return render(request,
                  'account/edit.html',
                  {'user_form': user_form,
                   'profile_form': profile_form})
```

We have added the new edit view to allow users to edit their personal information. We have added the login_required decorator to the view because only authenticated users will be able to edit their profiles. For this view, we use two model forms: UserEditForm to store the data of the built-in User model and ProfileEditForm to store the additional personal data in the custom Profile model. To validate the data submitted, we call the is_valid() method of both forms. If both forms contain valid data, we save both forms by calling the save() method to update the corresponding objects in the database.

Add the following URL pattern to the `urls.py` file of the account application:

```
urlpatterns = [
    #...
    path('', include('django.contrib.auth.urls')),
    path('', views.dashboard, name='dashboard'),
    path('register/', views.register, name='register'),
    path('edit/', views.edit, name='edit'),
]
```

Finally, create a template for this view in the `templates/account/` directory and name it `edit.html`. Add the following code to it:

```
{% extends "base.html" %}

{% block title %}Edit your account{% endblock %}

{% block content %}
  <h1>Edit your account</h1>
  <p>You can edit your account using the following form:</p>
  <form method="post" enctype="multipart/form-data">
    {{ user_form.as_p }}
    {{ profile_form.as_p }}
    {% csrf_token %}
    <p><input type="submit" value="Save changes"></p>
  </form>
{% endblock %}
```

In the preceding code, we have added `enctype="multipart/form-data"` to the `<form>` HTML element to enable file uploads. We use an HTML form to submit both the `user_form` and `profile_form` forms.

Open the URL `http://127.0.0.1:8000/account/register/` and register a new user. Then, log in with the new user and open the URL `http://127.0.0.1:8000/account/edit/`. You should see the following page:

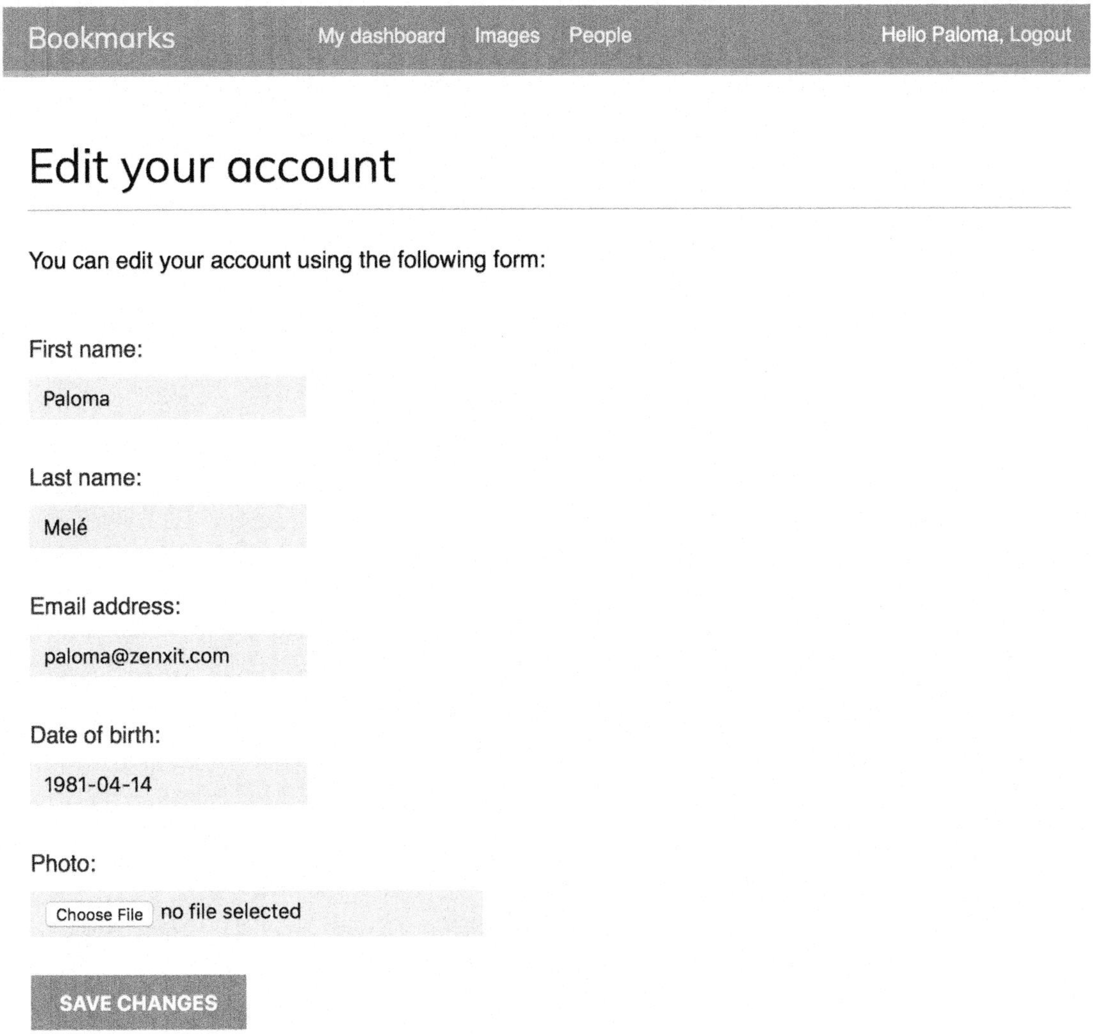

Bookmarks   My dashboard   Images   People   Hello Paloma, Logout

Edit your account

You can edit your account using the following form:

First name:

Paloma

Last name:

Melé

Email address:

paloma@zenxit.com

Date of birth:

1981-04-14

Photo:

Choose File   no file selected

SAVE CHANGES

Figure 4.21: The profile edit form

You can now add the profile information and save the changes.

We will edit the dashboard template to include links to the edit profile and change password pages.

Open the `templates/account/dashboard.html` template and add the following lines highlighted in bold:

```
{% extends "base.html" %}

{% block title %}Dashboard{% endblock %}

{% block content %}
  <h1>Dashboard</h1>
  <p>
    Welcome to your dashboard. You can <a href="{% url "edit" %}">edit your
profile</a> or <a href="{% url "password_change" %}">change your password</a>.
  </p>
{% endblock %}
```

Users can now access the form to edit their profile from the dashboard. Open `http://127.0.0.1:8000/account/` in your browser and test the new link to edit a user's profile. The dashboard should now look like this:

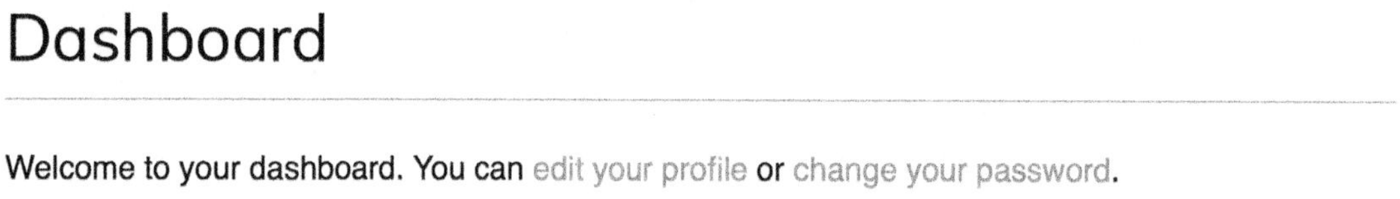

Dashboard

Welcome to your dashboard. You can edit your profile or change your password.

Figure 4.22: Dashboard page content, including links to edit a profile and change a password

Using a custom user model

Django also offers a way to substitute the `User` model with a custom model. The `User` class should inherit from Django's `AbstractUser` class, which provides the full implementation of the default user as an abstract model. You can read more about this method at `https://docs.djangoproject.com/en/4.1/topics/auth/customizing/#substituting-a-custom-user-model`.

Using a custom user model will give you more flexibility, but it might also result in more difficult integration with pluggable applications that interact directly with Django's `auth` user model.

Using the messages framework

When users are interacting with the platform, there are many cases where you might want to inform them about the result of specific actions. Django has a built-in messages framework that allows you to display one-time notifications to your users.

The messages framework is located at django.contrib.messages and is included in the default INSTALLED_APPS list of the settings.py file when you create new projects using python manage.py startproject. The settings file also contains the middleware django.contrib.messages.middleware. MessageMiddleware in the MIDDLEWARE setting.

The messages framework provides a simple way to add messages to users. Messages are stored in a cookie by default (falling back to session storage), and they are displayed and cleared in the next request from the user. You can use the messages framework in your views by importing the messages module and adding new messages with simple shortcuts, as follows:

```
from django.contrib import messages
messages.error(request, 'Something went wrong')
```

You can create new messages using the add_message() method or any of the following shortcut methods:

- success(): Success messages to display when an action was successful
- info(): Informational messages
- warning(): A failure has not yet occurred but it may be imminent
- error(): An action was not successful or a failure occurred
- debug(): Debug messages that will be removed or ignored in a production environment

Let's add messages to the project. The messages framework applies globally to the project. We will use the base template to display any available messages to the client. This will allow us to notify the client with the results of any action on any page.

Open the templates/base.html template of the account application and add the following code highlighted in bold:

```
{% load static %}
<!DOCTYPE html>
<html>
<head>
  <title>{% block title %}{% endblock %}</title>
  <link href="{% static "css/base.css" %}" rel="stylesheet">
</head>
<body>
  <div id="header">
    ...
  </div>
  {% if messages %}
    <ul class="messages">
      {% for message in messages %}
        <li class="{{ message.tags }}">
          {{ message|safe }}
```

```
                    <a href="#" class="close">x</a>
                </li>
            {% endfor %}
        </ul>
    {% endif %}
    <div id="content">
      {% block content %}
      {% endblock %}
    </div>
  </body>
</html>
```

The messages framework includes the context processor django.contrib.messages.context_ processors.messages, which adds a messages variable to the request context. You can find it in the context_processors list in the TEMPLATES setting of your project. You can use the messages variable in templates to display all existing messages to the user.

 A context processor is a Python function that takes the request object as an argument and returns a dictionary that gets added to the request context. You will learn how to create your own context processors in *Chapter 8, Building an Online Shop*.

Let's modify the edit view to use the messages framework.

Edit the views.py file of the account application and add the following lines highlighted in bold:

```
# ...
from django.contrib import messages

# ...

@login_required
def edit(request):
    if request.method == 'POST':
        user_form = UserEditForm(instance=request.user,
                                 data=request.POST)
        profile_form = ProfileEditForm(
                                    instance=request.user.profile,
                                    data=request.POST,
                                    files=request.FILES)
        if user_form.is_valid() and profile_form.is_valid():
            user_form.save()
```

```
            profile_form.save()
            messages.success(request, 'Profile updated '\
                                      'successfully')
        else:
            messages.error(request, 'Error updating your profile')
    else:
        user_form = UserEditForm(instance=request.user)
        profile_form = ProfileEditForm(
                                instance=request.user.profile)
    return render(request,
                  'account/edit.html',
                  {'user_form': user_form,
                   'profile_form': profile_form})
```

A success message is generated when users successfully update their profile. If any of the forms contain invalid data, an error message is generated instead.

Open http://127.0.0.1:8000/account/edit/ in your browser and edit the profile of the user. You should see the following message when the profile is successfully updated:

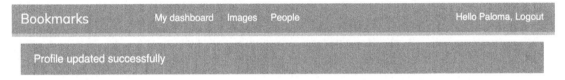

Figure 4.23: The successfully edited profile message

Enter an invalid date in the **Date of birth** field and submit the form again. You should see the following message:

Figure 4.24: The error updating profile message

Generating messages to inform your users about the results of their actions is really straightforward. You can easily add messages to other views as well.

You can learn more about the messages framework at https://docs.djangoproject.com/en/4.1/ref/contrib/messages/.

Now that we've built all the functionality related to user authentication and profile editing, we will dig deeper into customizing authentication. We will learn how to build custom backend authentication so that users can log into the site using their email address.

Building a custom authentication backend

Django allows you to authenticate users against different sources. The AUTHENTICATION_BACKENDS setting includes a list of authentication backends available in the project. The default value of this setting is the following:

```
['django.contrib.auth.backends.ModelBackend']
```

The default ModelBackend authenticates users against the database using the User model of django. contrib.auth. This is suitable for most web projects. However, you can create custom backends to authenticate your users against other sources, such as a **Lightweight Directory Access Protocol (LDAP)** directory or any other system.

You can read more information about customizing authentication at https://docs.djangoproject. com/en/4.1/topics/auth/customizing/#other-authentication-sources.

Whenever the authenticate() function of django.contrib.auth is used, Django tries to authenticate the user against each of the backends defined in AUTHENTICATION_BACKENDS one by one, until one of them successfully authenticates the user. Only if all of the backends fail to authenticate will the user not be authenticated.

Django provides a simple way to define your own authentication backends. An authentication backend is a class that provides the following two methods:

* authenticate(): It takes the request object and user credentials as parameters. It has to return a user object that matches those credentials if the credentials are valid, or None otherwise. The request parameter is an HttpRequest object, or None if it's not provided to the authenticate() function.
* get_user(): It takes a user ID parameter and has to return a user object.

Creating a custom authentication backend is as simple as writing a Python class that implements both methods. Let's create an authentication backend to allow users to authenticate on the site using their email address instead of their username.

Create a new file inside the account application directory and name it authentication.py. Add the following code to it:

```python
from django.contrib.auth.models import User

class EmailAuthBackend:
    """
    Authenticate using an e-mail address.
    """
    def authenticate(self, request, username=None, password=None):
        try:
            user = User.objects.get(email=username)
            if user.check_password(password):
```

```
                return user
            return None
        except (User.DoesNotExist, User.MultipleObjectsReturned):
            return None

    def get_user(self, user_id):
        try:
            return User.objects.get(pk=user_id)
        except User.DoesNotExist:
            return None
```

The preceding code is a simple authentication backend. The `authenticate()` method receives a request object and the `username` and `password` optional parameters. We could use different parameters, but we use `username` and `password` to make our backend work with the authentication framework views right away. The preceding code works as follows:

- `authenticate()`: The user with the given email address is retrieved, and the password is checked using the built-in `check_password()` method of the user model. This method handles the password hashing to compare the given password with the password stored in the database. Two different QuerySet exceptions are captured: `DoesNotExist` and `MultipleObjectsReturned`. The `DoesNotExist` exception is raised if no user is found with the given email address. The `MultipleObjectsReturned` exception is raised if multiple users are found with the same email address. We will modify the registration and edit views later to prevent users from using an existing email address.

- `get_user()`: You get a user through the ID provided in the `user_id` parameter. Django uses the backend that authenticated the user to retrieve the `User` object for the duration of the user session. **pk** is a short for **primary key**, which is a unique identifier for each record in the database. Every Django model has a field that serves as its primary key. By default, the primary key is the automatically generated id field. The primary key can be also referred to as pk in the Django ORM. You can find more information about automatic primary key fields at `https://docs.djangoproject.com/en/4.1/topics/db/models/#automatic-primary-key-fields`.

Edit the `settings.py` file of your project and add the following code:

```
AUTHENTICATION_BACKENDS = [
    'django.contrib.auth.backends.ModelBackend',
    'account.authentication.EmailAuthBackend',
]
```

In the preceding setting, we keep the default `ModelBackend` that is used to authenticate with the username and password and include our own email-based authentication backend `EmailAuthBackend`.

Open `http://127.0.0.1:8000/account/login/` in your browser. Remember that Django will try to authenticate the user against each of the backends, so now you should be able to log in seamlessly using your username or email account.

The user credentials will be checked using `ModelBackend`, and if no user is returned, the credentials will be checked using `EmailAuthBackend`.

 The order of the backends listed in the `AUTHENTICATION_BACKENDS` setting matters. If the same credentials are valid for multiple backends, Django will stop at the first backend that successfully authenticates the user.

Preventing users from using an existing email

The `User` model of the authentication framework does not prevent creating users with the same email address. If two or more user accounts share the same email address, we won't be able to discern which user is authenticating. Now that users can log in using their email address, we have to prevent users from registering with an existing email address.

We will now change the user registration form, to prevent multiple users from registering with the same email address.

Edit the `forms.py` file of the account application and add the following lines highlighted in bold to the `UserRegistrationForm` class:

```python
class UserRegistrationForm(forms.ModelForm):
    password = forms.CharField(label='Password',
                               widget=forms.PasswordInput)
    password2 = forms.CharField(label='Repeat password',
                                widget=forms.PasswordInput)

    class Meta:
        model = User
        fields = ['username', 'first_name', 'email']

    def clean_password2(self):
        cd = self.cleaned_data
        if cd['password'] != cd['password2']:
            raise forms.ValidationError('Passwords don\'t match.')
        return cd['password2']

    def clean_email(self):
        data = self.cleaned_data['email']
        if User.objects.filter(email=data).exists():
            raise forms.ValidationError('Email already in use.')
        return data
```

We have added validation for the email field that prevents users from registering with an existing email address. We build a QuerySet to look up existing users with the same email address. We check whether there are any results with the exists() method. The exists() method returns True if the QuerySet contains any results, and False otherwise.

Now, add the following lines highlighted in bold to the UserEditForm class:

```
class UserEditForm(forms.ModelForm):
    class Meta:
        model = User
        fields = ['first_name', 'last_name', 'email']

    def clean_email(self):
        data = self.cleaned_data['email']
        qs = User.objects.exclude(id=self.instance.id)\
                         .filter(email=data)
        if qs.exists():
            raise forms.ValidationError(' Email already in use.')
        return data
```

In this case, we have added validation for the email field that prevents users from changing their existing email address to an existing email address of another user. We exclude the current user from the QuerySet. Otherwise, the current email address of the user would be considered an existing email address, and the form won't validate.

Additional resources

The following resources provide additional information related to the topics covered in this chapter:

- Source code for this chapter – https://github.com/PacktPublishing/Django-4-by-example/tree/main/Chapter04
- Built-in authentication views – https://docs.djangoproject.com/en/4.1/topics/auth/default/#all-authentication-views
- Authentication URL patterns – https://github.com/django/django/blob/stable/3.0.x/django/contrib/auth/urls.py
- How Django manages passwords and available password hashers – https://docs.djangoproject.com/en/4.1/topics/auth/passwords/
- Generic user model and the get_user_model() method – https://docs.djangoproject.com/en/4.1/topics/auth/customizing/#django.contrib.auth.get_user_model
- Using a custom user model – https://docs.djangoproject.com/en/4.1/topics/auth/customizing/#substituting-a-custom-user-model
- The Django messages framework – https://docs.djangoproject.com/en/4.1/ref/contrib/messages/

- Custom authentication sources – `https://docs.djangoproject.com/en/4.1/topics/auth/customizing/#other-authentication-sources`
- Automatic primary key fields – `https://docs.djangoproject.com/en/4.1/topics/db/models/#automatic-primary-key-fields`

Summary

In this chapter, you learned how to build an authentication system for your site. You implemented all the necessary views for users to register, log in, log out, edit their password, and reset their password. You built a model for custom user profiles, and you created a custom authentication backend to let users log into your site using their email address.

In the next chapter, you will learn how to implement social authentication on your site using Python Social Auth. Users will be able to authenticate with their Google, Facebook, or Twitter accounts. You will also learn how to serve the development server over HTTPS using Django Extensions. You will customize the authentication pipeline to create user profiles automatically.

Join us on Discord

Read this book alongside other users and the author.

Ask questions, provide solutions to other readers, chat with the author via *Ask Me Anything* sessions, and much more. Scan the QR code or visit the link to join the book community.

`https://packt.link/django`

5

Implementing Social Authentication

In the previous chapter, you built user registration and authentication into your website. You implemented password change, reset, and recovery functionalities, and you learned how to create a custom profile model for your users.

In this chapter, you will add social authentication to your site using Facebook, Google, and Twitter. You will use Django Social Auth to implement social authentication using OAuth 2.0, the industry-standard protocol for authorization. You will also modify the social authentication pipeline to create a user profile for new users automatically.

This chapter will cover the following points:

- Adding social authentication with Python Social Auth
- Installing Django Extensions
- Running the development server through HTTPS
- Adding authentication using Facebook
- Adding authentication using Twitter
- Adding authentication using Google
- Creating a profile for users that register with social authentication

The source code for this chapter can be found at `https://github.com/PacktPublishing/Django-4-by-example/tree/main/Chapter05`.

All Python packages used in this chapter are included in the `requirements.txt` file in the source code for the chapter. You can follow the instructions to install each Python package in the following sections, or you can install all requirements at once with the command `pip install -r requirements.txt`.

Adding social authentication to your site

Social authentication is a widely used feature that allows users to authenticate using their existing account of a service provider using **Single Sign-on (SSO)**. The authentication process allows users to authenticate into the site using their existing account from social services like Google. In this section, we will add social authentication to the site using Facebook, Twitter, and Google.

To implement social authentication, we will use the **OAuth 2.0** industry-standard protocol for authorization. **OAuth** stands for *Open Authorization*. OAuth 2.0 is a standard designed to allow a website or application to access resources hosted by other web apps on behalf of a user. Facebook, Twitter, and Google use the OAuth 2.0 protocol for authentication and authorization.

Python Social Auth is a Python module that simplifies the process of adding social authentication to your website. Using this module, you can let your users log in to your website using their accounts from other services. You can find the code for this module at `https://github.com/python-social-auth/social-app-django`.

This module comes with authentication backends for different Python frameworks, including Django. To install the Django package from the Git repository of the project, open the console and run the following command:

```
git+https://github.com/python-social-auth/social-app-django.
git@20fabcd7bd9a8a41910bc5c8ed1bd6ef2263b328
```

This will install Python Social Auth from a GitHub commit that works with Django 4.1. At the writing of this book the latest Python Social Auth release is not compatible with Django 4.1 but a newer compatible release might have been published.

Then add `social_django` to the `INSTALLED_APPS` setting in the `settings.py` file of the project as follows:

```
INSTALLED_APPS = [
    # ...
    'social_django',
]
```

This is the default application to add Python Social Auth to Django projects. Now run the following command to sync Python Social Auth models with your database:

```
python manage.py migrate
```

You should see that the migrations for the default application are applied as follows:

```
Applying social_django.0001_initial... OK
Applying social_django.0002_add_related_name... OK
...
Applying social_django.0011_alter_id_fields... OK
```

Python Social Auth includes authentication backends for multiple services. You can find the list with all available backends at https://python-social-auth.readthedocs.io/en/latest/backends/index. html#supported-backends.

We will add social authentication to our project, allowing our users to authenticate with the Facebook, Twitter, and Google backends.

First, we need to add the social login URL patterns to the project.

Open the main urls.py file of the bookmarks project and include the social_django URL patterns as follows. New lines are highlighted in bold:

```python
urlpatterns = [
    path('admin/', admin.site.urls),
    path('account/', include('account.urls')),
    path('social-auth/',
        include('social_django.urls', namespace='social')),
]
```

Our web application is currently accessible via the localhost IP to 127.0.0.1 or using the localhost hostname. Several social services will not allow redirecting users to 127.0.0.1 or localhost after successful authentication; they expect a domain name for the URL redirect. First, we need to use a domain name to make social authentication work. Fortunately, we can simulate serving our site under a domain name in our local machine.

Locate the hosts file of your machine. If you are using Linux or macOS, the hosts file is located at /etc/hosts. If you are using Windows, the hosts file is located at C:\Windows\System32\Drivers\ etc\hosts.

Edit the hosts file of your machine and add the following line to it:

```
127.0.0.1 mysite.com
```

This will tell your computer to point the mysite.com hostname to your own machine.

Let's verify that the hostname association worked. Run the development server using the following command from the shell prompt:

```
python manage.py runserver
```

Open http://mysite.com:8000/account/login/ in your browser. You will see the following error:

DisallowedHost at /account/login/

Invalid HTTP_HOST header: 'mysite.com:8000'. You may need to add 'mysite.com' to ALLOWED_HOSTS.

Figure 5.1: The invalid host header message

Django controls the hosts that can serve the application using the ALLOWED_HOSTS setting. This is a security measure to prevent HTTP host header attacks. Django will only allow the hosts included in this list to serve the application.

You can learn more about the ALLOWED_HOSTS setting at https://docs.djangoproject.com/en/4.1/ref/settings/#allowed-hosts.

Edit the settings.py file of the project and modify the ALLOWED_HOSTS setting as follows. New code is highlighted in bold:

```
ALLOWED_HOSTS = ['mysite.com', 'localhost', '127.0.0.1']
```

Besides the mysite.com host, we have explicitly included localhost and 127.0.0.1. This allows access to the site through localhost and 127.0.0.1, which is the default Django behavior when DEBUG is True and ALLOWED_HOSTS is empty.

Open http://mysite.com:8000/account/login/ again in your browser. Now, you should see the login page of the site instead of an error.

Running the development server through HTTPS

Some of the social authentication methods we are going to use require an HTTPS connection. The **Transport Layer Security (TLS)** protocol is the standard for serving websites through a secure connection. The TLS predecessor is the **Secure Sockets Layer (SSL)**.

Although SSL is now deprecated, in multiple libraries and online documentation you will find references to both the terms TLS and SSL. The Django development server is not able to serve your site through HTTPS, since that is not its intended use. To test the social authentication functionality serving the site through HTTPS, we are going to use the RunServerPlus extension of the package Django Extensions. Django Extensions is a third-party collection of custom extensions for Django. Please note that you should never use this to serve your site in a real environment; this is only a development server.

Use the following command to install Django Extensions:

```
pip install git+https://github.com/django-extensions/django-extensions.
git@25a41d8a3ecb24c009c5f4cac6010a091a3c91c8
```

This will install Django Extensions from a GitHub commit that includes support for Django 4.1. At the writing of this book the latest Django Extensions release is not compatible with Django 4.1 but a newer compatible release might have been published.

You will need to install Werkzeug, which contains a debugger layer required by the RunServerPlus extension of Django Extensions. Use the following command to install Werkzeug:

```
pip install werkzeug==2.2.2
```

Finally, use the following command to install pyOpenSSL, which is required to use the SSL/TLS functionality of RunServerPlus:

```
pip install pyOpenSSL==22.0.0
```

Edit the settings.py file of your project and add Django Extensions to the INSTALLED_APPS setting, as follows:

```
INSTALLED_APPS = [
    # ...
    'django_extensions',
]
```

Now, use the management command `runserver_plus` provided by Django Extensions to run the development server, as follows:

```
python manage.py runserver_plus --cert-file cert.crt
```

We have provided a file name to the `runserver_plus` command for the SSL/TLS certificate. Django Extensions will generate a key and certificate automatically.

Open `https://mysite.com:8000/account/login/` in your browser. Now you are accessing your site through HTTPS. Note we are now using `https://` instead of `http://`.

Your browser will show a security warning because you are using a self-generated certificate instead of a certificate trusted by a **Certification Authority (CA)**.

If you are using Google Chrome, you will see the following screen:

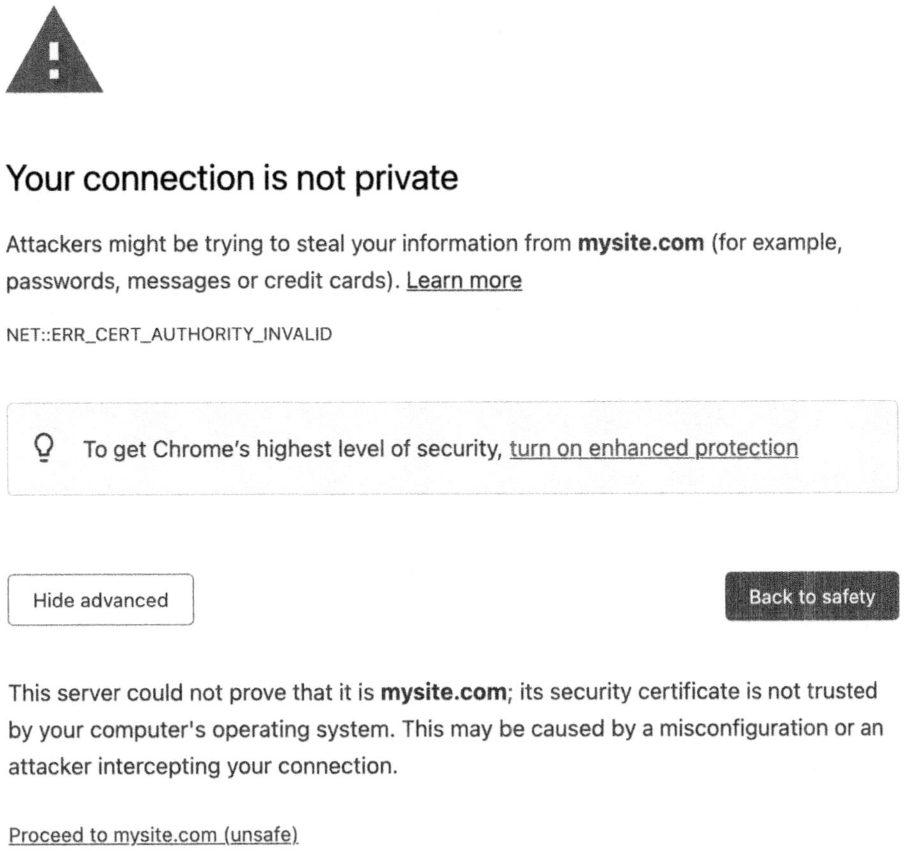

Your connection is not private

Attackers might be trying to steal your information from **mysite.com** (for example, passwords, messages or credit cards). Learn more

NET::ERR_CERT_AUTHORITY_INVALID

   To get Chrome's highest level of security, turn on enhanced protection

Hide advanced   Back to safety

This server could not prove that it is **mysite.com**; its security certificate is not trusted by your computer's operating system. This may be caused by a misconfiguration or an attacker intercepting your connection.

Proceed to mysite.com (unsafe)

Figure 5.2: The safety error in Google Chrome

In this case, click on **Advanced** and then click on **Proceed to 127.0.0.1 (unsafe)**.

If you are using Safari, you will see the following screen:

 # This Connection Is Not Private

This website may be impersonating "mysite.com" to steal your personal or financial information. You should go back to the previous page.

Go Back

Safari warns you when a website has a certificate that is invalid. This may happen if the website is misconfigured or an attacker has compromised your connection.

To learn more, you can view the certificate. If you understand the risks involved, you can visit this website.

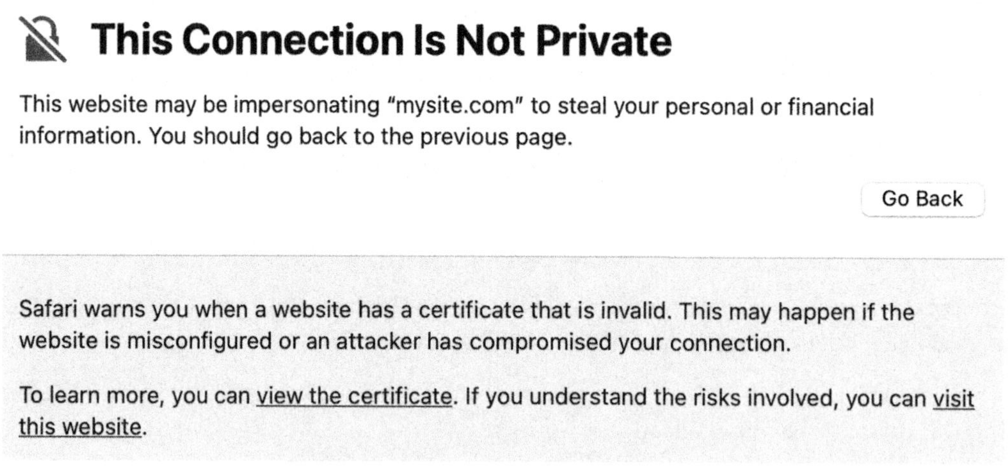

Figure 5.3: The safety error in Safari

In this case, click on **Show details** and then click on **visit this website**.

If you are using Microsoft Edge, you will see the following screen:

Your connection isn't private

Attackers might be trying to steal your information from **mysite.com** (for example, passwords, messages or credit cards).

NET::ERR_CERT_AUTHORITY_INVALID

Hide Advanced   Go Back

This server couldn't prove that it's **mysite.com**; its security certificate is not trusted by your computer's operating system. This may be caused by a misconfiguration or an attacker intercepting your connection.

Continue to mysite.com (unsafe)

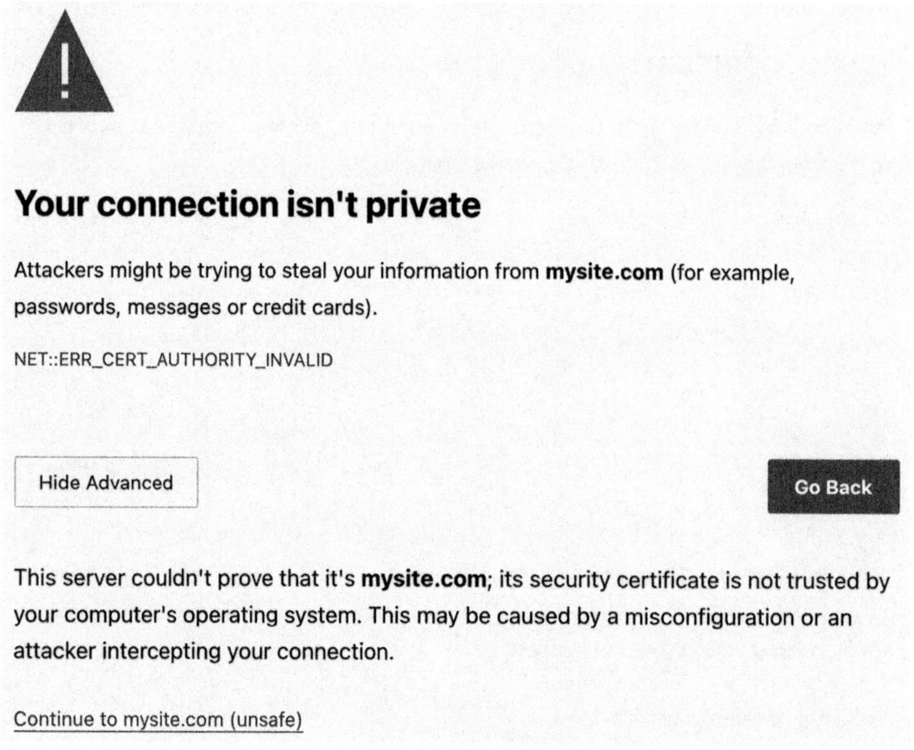

Figure 5.4: The safety error in Microsoft Edge

In this case, click on **Advanced** and then on **Continue to mysite.com (unsafe)**.

If you are using any other browser, access the advanced information displayed by your browser and accept the self-signed certificate so that your browser trusts the certificate.

You will see that the URL starts with `https://` and in some cases a lock icon that indicates that the connection is secure. Some browsers might display a broken lock icon because you are using a self-signed certificate instead of a trusted one. That won't be a problem for our tests:

🔒 127.0.0.1:8000/account/login/

Figure 5.5: The URL with the secured connection icon

 Django Extensions includes many other interesting tools and features. You can find more information about this package at `https://django-extensions.readthedocs.io/en/latest/`.

You can now serve your site through HTTPS during development to test social authentication with Facebook, Twitter, and Google.

Authentication using Facebook

To use Facebook authentication to log in to your site, add the following line highlighted in bold to the `AUTHENTICATION_BACKENDS` setting in the `settings.py` file of your project:

```
AUTHENTICATION_BACKENDS = [
    'django.contrib.auth.backends.ModelBackend',
    'account.authentication.EmailAuthBackend',
    'social_core.backends.facebook.FacebookOAuth2',
]
```

You will need a Facebook developer account and you will need to create a new Facebook application.

Open `https://developers.facebook.com/apps/` in your browser. After creating a Facebook developer account, you will see a site with the following header:

Figure 5.6: The Facebook developer portal header

Click on **Create App**.

You will see the following form to choose an application type:

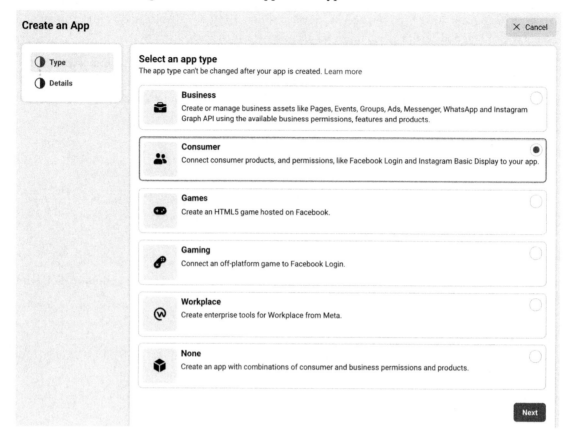

Figure 5.7: The Facebook create app form to select an application type

Under **Select an app type,** choose **Consumer** and click on **Next.**

You will see the following form to create a new application:

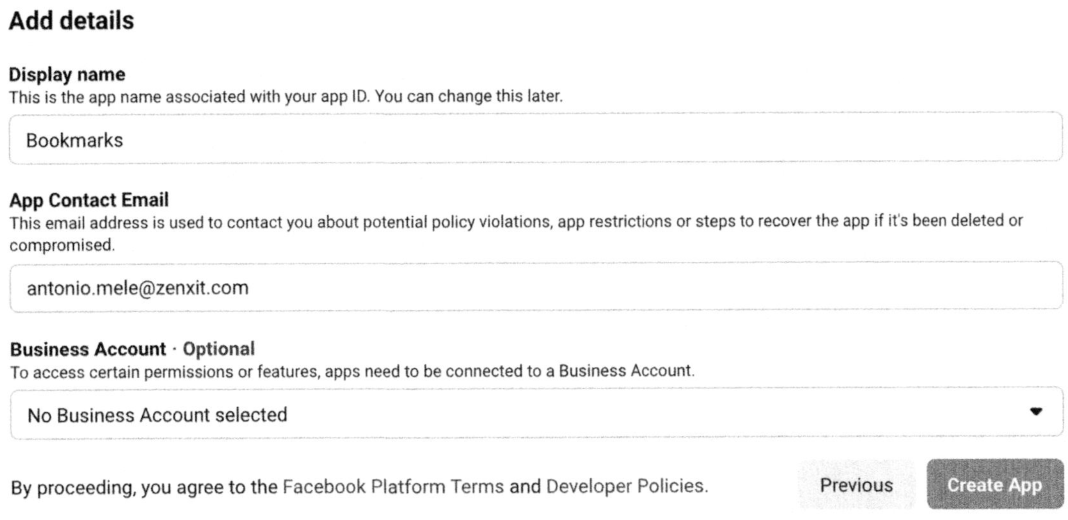

Add details
Display name
This is the app name associated with your app ID. You can change this later.
Bookmarks
App Contact Email
This email address is used to contact you about potential policy violations, app restrictions or steps to recover the app if it's been deleted or compromised.
antonio.mele@zenxit.com
Business Account · Optional
To access certain permissions or features, apps need to be connected to a Business Account.
No Business Account selected
By proceeding, you agree to the Facebook Platform Terms and Developer Policies.
Previous
Create App

Figure 5.8: The Facebook form for application details

Enter `Bookmarks` as the **Display name**, add a contact email address, and click on **Create App**.

You will see the dashboard for your new application that displays different services that you can configure for the app. Look for the following **Facebook Login** box and click on **Set Up**:

Facebook Login
The world's number one social login product.
Read Docs
Set Up

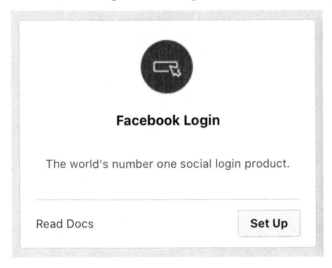

Figure 5.9: The Facebook login product block

You will be asked to choose the platform, as follows:

Use the Quickstart to add Facebook Login to your app. To get started, select the platform for this app.
WWW
iOS
Android
Web
Other

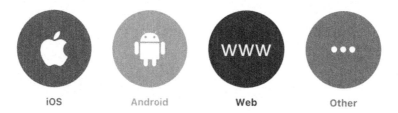

Figure 5.10: Platform selection for Facebook login

Select the **Web** platform. You will see the following form:

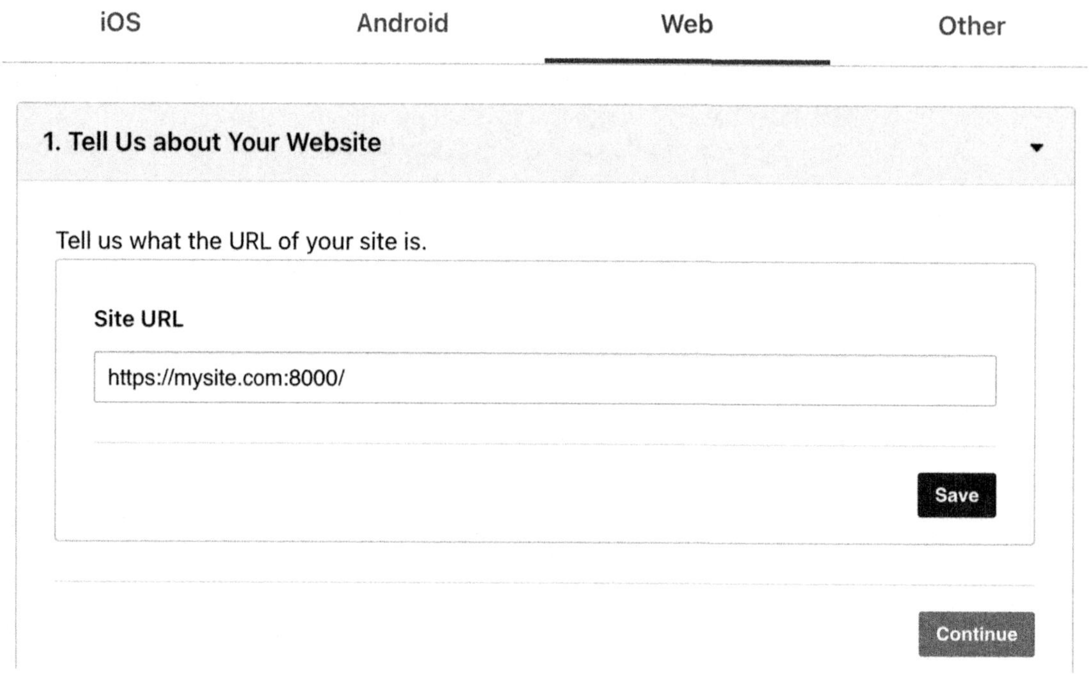
iOS
Android
Web
Other
1. Tell Us about Your Website
Tell us what the URL of your site is.
Site URL
https://mysite.com:8000/
Save
Continue

Figure 5.11: Web platform configuration for Facebook login

Enter `https://mysite.com:8000/` under **Site URL** and click the **Save** button. Then click **Continue**. You can skip the rest of the quick start process.

In the left-hand menu, click on **Settings** and then on **Basic**, as follows:

Figure 5.12: Facebook developer portal sidebar menu

You will see a form with data similar to the following one:

Figure 5.13: Application details for the Facebook application

Copy the **App ID** and **App Secret** keys and add them to the settings.py file of your project, as follows:

```
SOCIAL_AUTH_FACEBOOK_KEY = 'XXX' # Facebook App ID
SOCIAL_AUTH_FACEBOOK_SECRET = 'XXX' # Facebook App Secret
```

Optionally, you can define a SOCIAL_AUTH_FACEBOOK_SCOPE setting with the extra permissions you want to ask Facebook users for:

```
SOCIAL_AUTH_FACEBOOK_SCOPE = ['email']
```

Now, go back to the Facebook developer portal and click on **Settings**. Add mysite.com under **App Domains**, as follows:

Figure 5.14: Allowed domains for the Facebook application

You have to enter a public URL for the **Privacy Policy URL** and another one for the **User Data Deletion Instructions URL**. The following is an example using the Wikipedia page URL for *Privacy Policy*. Please note that you should use a valid URL:

Privacy Policy URL

> https://en.wikipedia.org/wiki/Privacy_policy

User Data Deletion ❶

> Data Deletion Instructions URL   ▾

> https://en.wikipedia.org/wiki/Privacy_policy

Figure 5.15: Privacy policy and user data deletion instructions URLs for the Facebook application

Click on **Save Changes**. Then, in the left-hand menu under **Products**, click on **Facebook Login** and then **Settings**, as shown here:

Facebook Login   ⌃

Settings

Quickstart

Figure 5.16: The Facebook login menu

Ensure that only the following settings are active:

- **Client OAuth Login**
- **Web OAuth Login**
- **Enforce HTTPS**
- **Embedded Browser OAuth Login**
- **Used Strict Mode for Redirect URIs**

Enter `https://mysite.com:8000/social-auth/complete/facebook/` under **Valid OAuth Redirect URIs**. The selection should look like this:

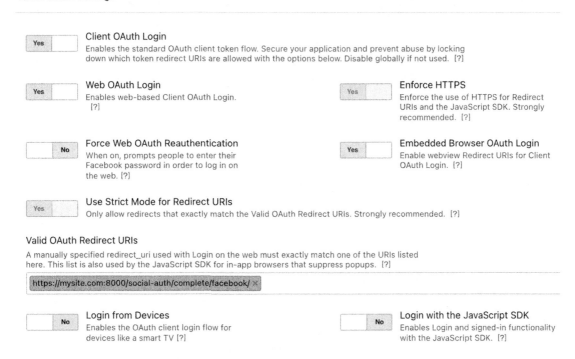

Figure 5.17: Client OAuth settings for Facebook login

Open the `registration/login.html` template of the `account` application and append the following code highlighted in bold at the bottom of the `content` block:

```
{% block content %}
  ...
  <div class="social">
    <ul>
      <li class="facebook">
        <a href="{% url "social:begin" "facebook" %}">
          Sign in with Facebook
        </a>
      </li>
    </ul>
  </div>
{% endblock %}
```

Use the management command `runserver_plus` provided by Django Extensions to run the development server, as follows:

```
python manage.py runserver_plus --cert-file cert.crt
```

Open `https://mysite.com:8000/account/login/` in your browser. The login page will look now as follows:

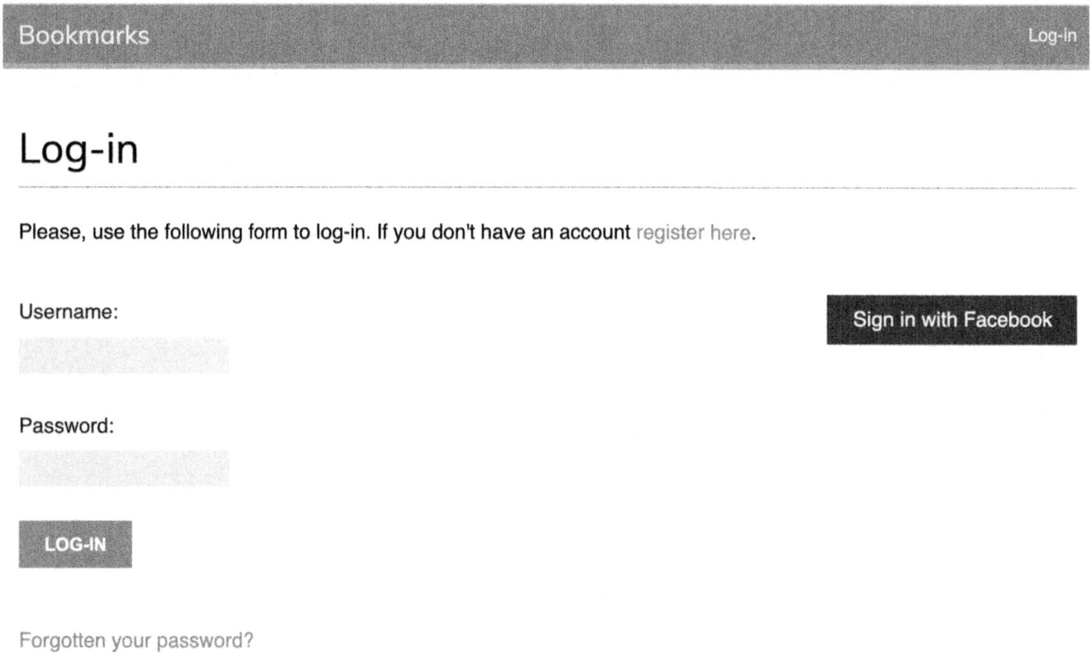

Bookmarks   Log-in

Log-in

Please, use the following form to log-in. If you don't have an account register here.

Username:

Sign in with Facebook

Password:

LOG-IN

Forgotten your password?

Figure 5.18: The login page including the button for Facebook authentication

Click on the **Sign in with Facebook** button. You will be redirected to Facebook, and you will see a modal dialog asking for your permission to let the *Bookmarks* application access your public Facebook profile:

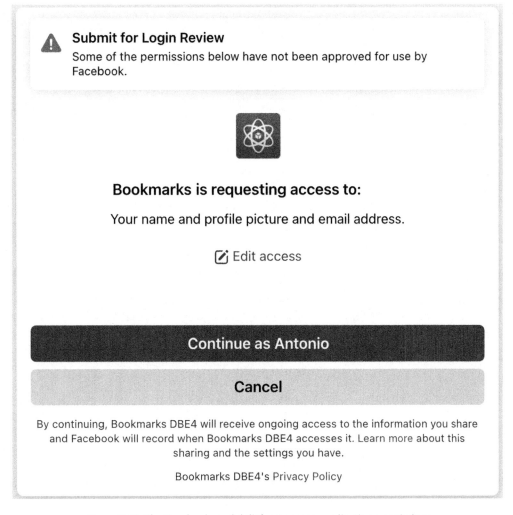

Figure 5.19: The Facebook modal dialog to grant application permissions

You will see a warning indicating that you need to submit the application for login review. Click on the **Continue as …** button.

You will be logged in and redirected to the dashboard page of your site. Remember that you have set this URL in the `LOGIN_REDIRECT_URL` setting. As you can see, adding social authentication to your site is pretty straightforward.

Authentication using Twitter

For social authentication using Twitter, add the following line highlighted in bold to the `AUTHENTICATION_BACKENDS` setting in the `settings.py` file of your project:

```
AUTHENTICATION_BACKENDS = [
    'django.contrib.auth.backends.ModelBackend',
    'account.authentication.EmailAuthBackend',
    'social_core.backends.facebook.FacebookOAuth2',
    'social_core.backends.twitter.TwitterOAuth',
]
```

You need a Twitter developer account. Open `https://developer.twitter.com/` in your browser and click on **Sign up**.

After creating a Twitter developer account, access the Developer Portal Dashboard at `https://developer.twitter.com/en/portal/dashboard`. The dashboard should look as follows:

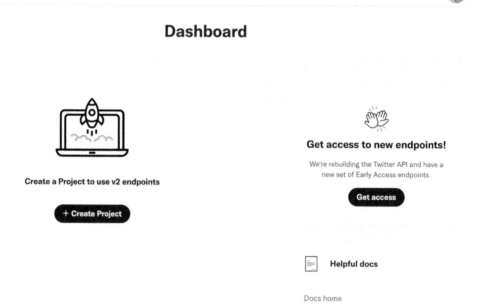

Figure 5.20: Twitter developer portal dashboard

Click on the **Create Project** button. You will see the following screen:

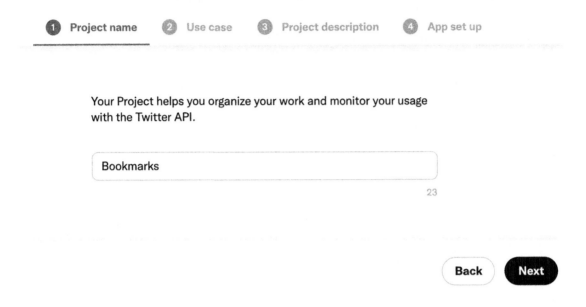

Figure 5.21: Twitter create project screen – Project name

Enter Bookmarks for the **Project name** and click on **Next**. You will see the following screen:

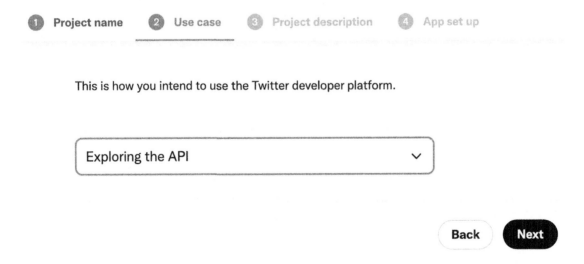

Figure 5.22: Twitter create project screen – Use case

Under **Use case**, select **Exploring the API** and click on **Next**. You can choose any other use case; it won't affect the configuration. Then you will see the following screen:

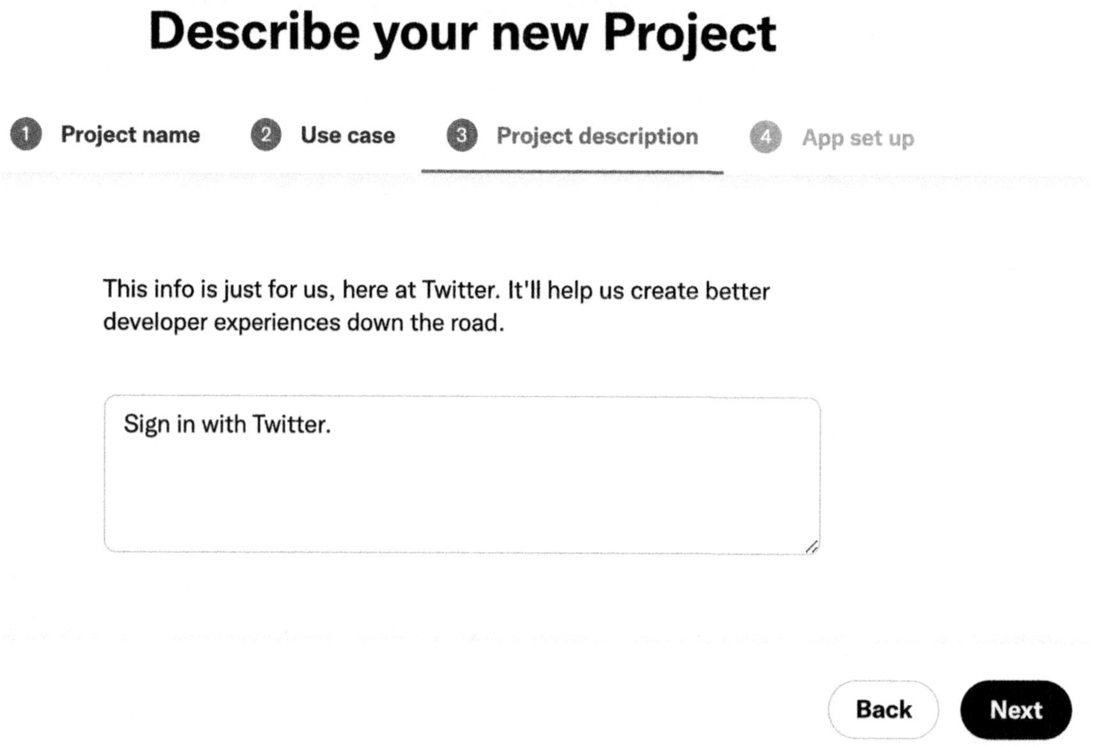

Describe your new Project

1 **Project name**   **2** **Use case**   **3** **Project description**   **4** App set up

This info is just for us, here at Twitter. It'll help us create better developer experiences down the road.

> Sign in with Twitter.

Back   Next

Figure 5.23: Twitter create project screen – Project description

Enter a short description for your project and click on **Next**. The project is now created, and you will see the following screen:

Add an existing App or create a new App

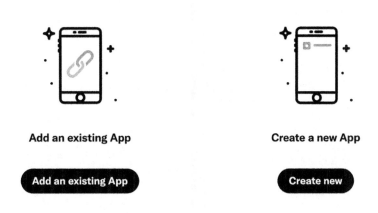

Figure 5.24: Twitter application configuration

We will create a new application. Click on **Create new**. You will see the following screen to configure the new application:

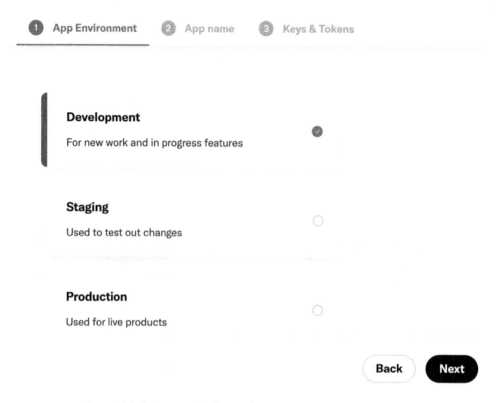

Figure 5.25: Twitter application configuration - environment selection

Under **App Environment**, select **Development** and click on **Next**. We are creating a development environment for the application. You will see the following screen:

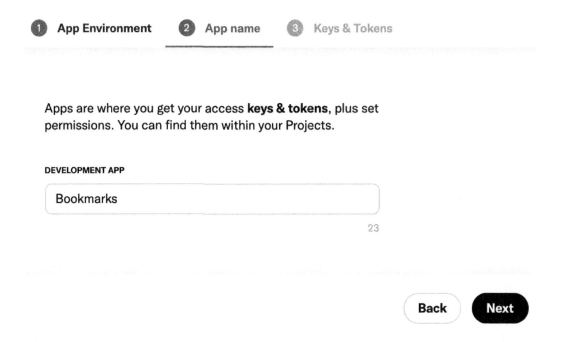

Figure 5.26: Twitter application configuration – App name

Under **App name**, enter Bookmarks followed by a suffix. Twitter won't allow you to use the name of an existing developer app within Twitter, so you need to enter a name that might be available. Click **Next**. Twitter will show you an error if the name you try to use for your app is already taken.

After choosing a name that is available, you will see the following screen:

Here are your keys & tokens

1 App Environment   2 App name   3 **Keys & Tokens**

For security, this will be the last time we'll fully display these. If something happens, you can always regenerate them. Learn more

API Key ⓘ

HUqeJUA9aplQIUJwwc3IUiBzd	Copy ⊞

API Key Secret ⓘ

XXXXXXXXXXXXXXXXXXXXXXXXXXXXXXXXXXXXXXXXX	Copy ⊞

Bearer Token ⓘ

XXXXXXXXXXXXXXXXXXXXXXXXXXXXXXXXXXXXXXXXXXXXXXXXXX XXXXXXXXXXXXXXXXXXXXXXXXXXXXXXXXXXXXXXXXXXXXXXXX	Copy ⊞

Go to dashboard   **App settings**

Figure 5.27: Twitter application configuration – generated API keys

Copy the **API Key** and **API Key Secret** into the following settings in the settings.py file of your project:

```
SOCIAL_AUTH_TWITTER_KEY = 'XXX' # Twitter API Key
SOCIAL_AUTH_TWITTER_SECRET = 'XXX' # Twitter API Secret
```

Then click on **App settings.** You will see a screen that includes the following section:

User authentication settings

Authentication not set up

OAuth 2.0 and OAuth 1.0a are authentication methods that allow users to sign in to your App with Twitter. They also allow your App to make specific requests on behalf of authenticated users. You can turn on one, or both methods.

Figure 5.28: Twitter application user authentication setup

Under **User authentication settings**, click on **Set up.** You will see the following screen:

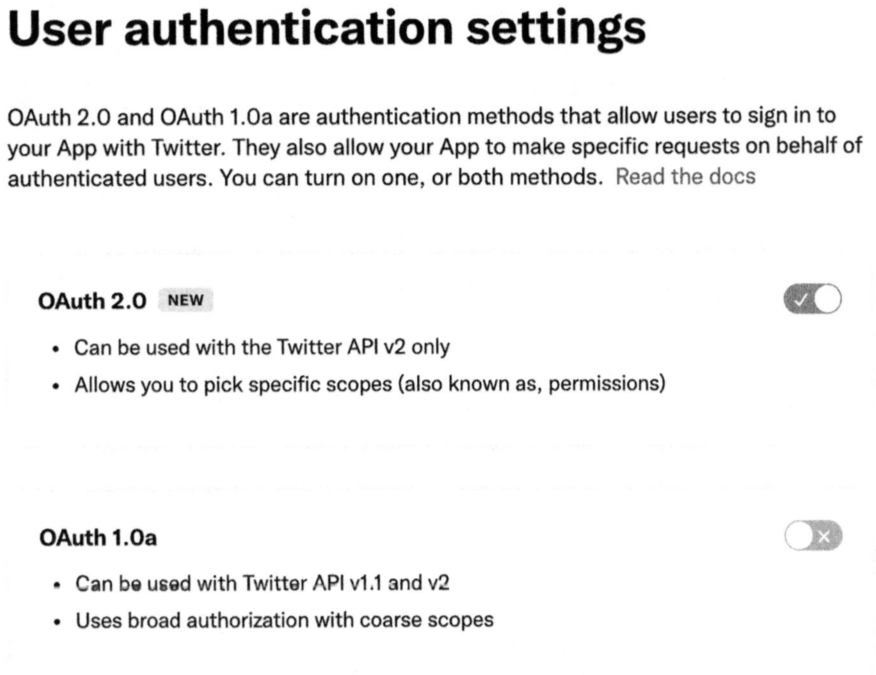

User authentication settings

OAuth 2.0 and OAuth 1.0a are authentication methods that allow users to sign in to your App with Twitter. They also allow your App to make specific requests on behalf of authenticated users. You can turn on one, or both methods. Read the docs

OAuth 2.0 NEW

- Can be used with the Twitter API v2 only
- Allows you to pick specific scopes (also known as, permissions)

OAuth 1.0a

- Can be used with Twitter API v1.1 and v2
- Uses broad authorization with coarse scopes

Figure 5.29: Twitter application OAuth 2.0 activation

Activate the **OAuth 2.0** option. This is the OAuth version that we will use. Then, under **OAuth 2.0 Settings**, select **Web App** for **Type of App** as follows:

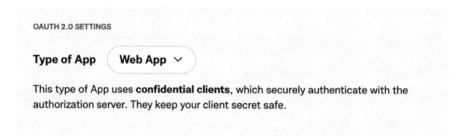

Figure 5.30: Twitter application OAuth 2.0 settings

Under **General Authentication Settings**, enter the following details of your application:

- **Callback URI / Redirect URL:** `https://mysite.com:8000/social-auth/complete/twitter/`
- **Website URL:** `https://mysite.com:8000/`

The settings should look as follows:

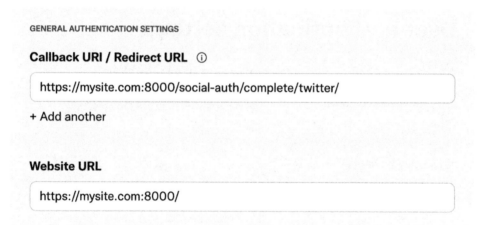

Figure 5.31: Twitter authentication URL configuration

Click on **Save.** Now, you will see the following screen including the **Client ID** and **Client Secret:**

Figure 5.32: Twitter application Client ID and Client Secret

You won't need them for client authentication because you will be using the **API Key** and **API Key Secret** instead. However, you can copy them and store the **Client Secret** in a safe place. Click on **Done.**

You will see another reminder to save the **Client Secret**:

Figure 5.33: Twitter Client Secret reminder

Click on **Yes, I saved it**. Now you will see that OAuth 2.0 authentication has been turned on like in the following screen:

Figure 5.34: Twitter application authentication settings

Now edit the `registration/login.html` template and add the following code highlighted in bold to the `<ul>` element:

```
<ul>
  <li class="facebook">
    <a href="{% url "social:begin" "facebook" %}">
      Sign in with Facebook
    </a>
  </li>
  <li class="twitter">
    <a href="{% url "social:begin" "twitter" %}">
      Sign in with Twitter
    </a>
  </li>
</ul>
```

Use the management command `runserver_plus` provided by Django Extensions to run the development server, as follows:

```
python manage.py runserver_plus --cert-file cert.crt
```

Open `https://mysite.com:8000/account/login/` in your browser. Now, the login page will look as follows:

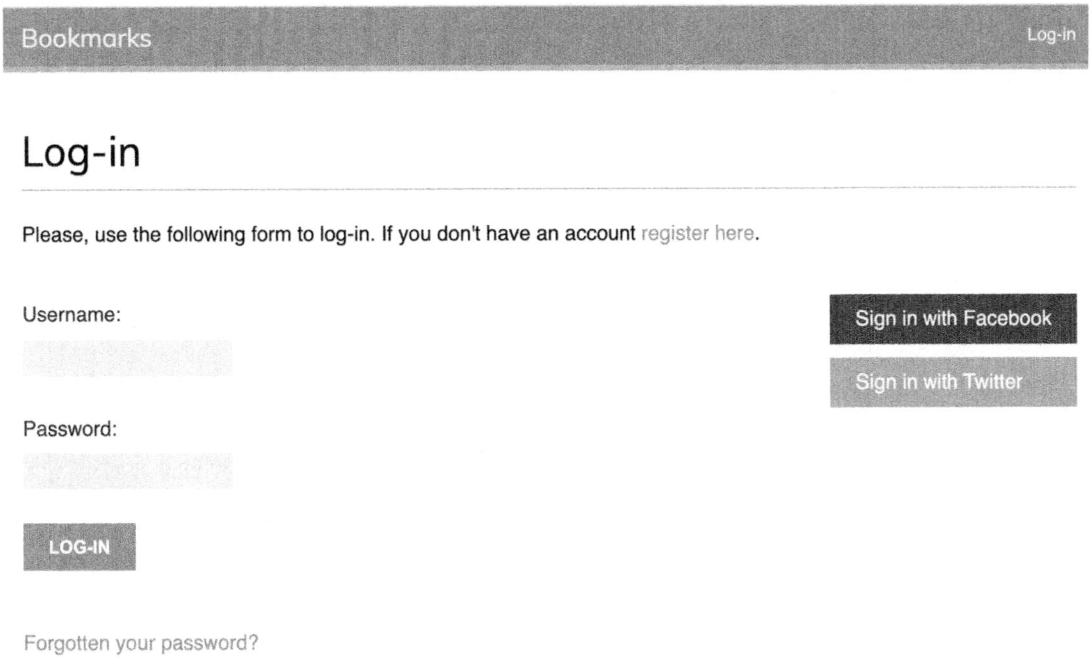

Figure 5.35: The login page including the button for Twitter authentication

Click on the **Sign in with Twitter** link. You will be redirected to Twitter, where you will be asked to authorize the application as follows:

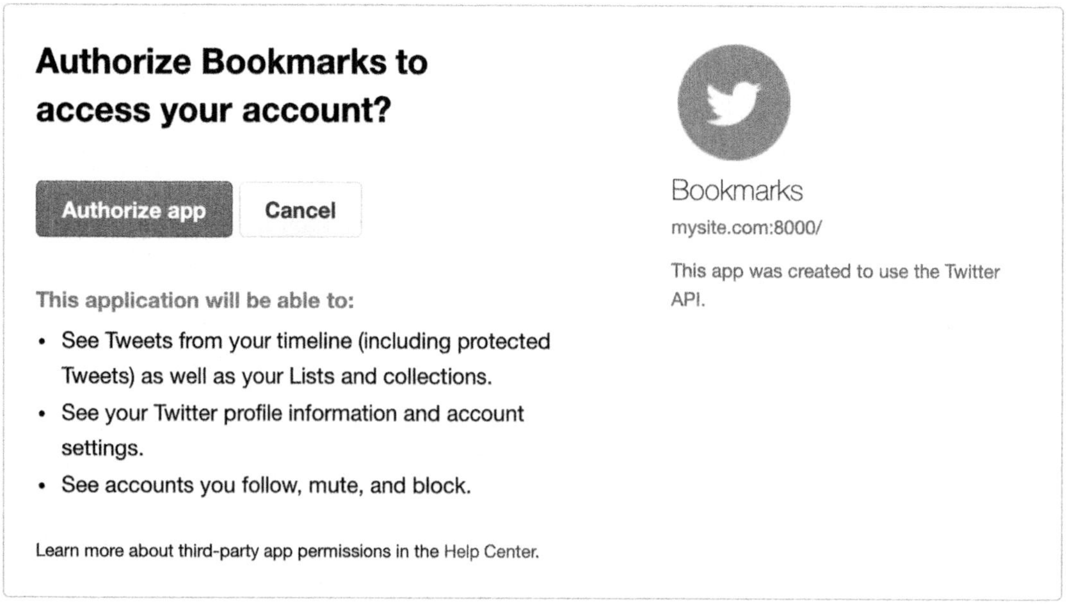

Authorize Bookmarks to access your account?

[Authorize app]   [Cancel]

Bookmarks
mysite.com:8000/

This app was created to use the Twitter API.

This application will be able to:

- See Tweets from your timeline (including protected Tweets) as well as your Lists and collections.
- See your Twitter profile information and account settings.
- See accounts you follow, mute, and block.

Learn more about third-party app permissions in the Help Center.

Figure 5.36: Twitter user authorization screen

Click on **Authorize app**. You will briefly see the following page while you are redirected to the dashboard page:

                                                                               zenxone

Redirecting you back to the application. This may take a few moments.   ⟩

We recommend reviewing the app's terms and privacy policy to understand how it will use data from your Twitter account. You can revoke access to any app at any time from the **Apps and sessions** section of your Twitter account settings.

By authorizing an app you continue to operate under Twitter's **Terms of Service**. In particular, some usage information will be shared back with Twitter. For more, see our **Privacy Policy**.

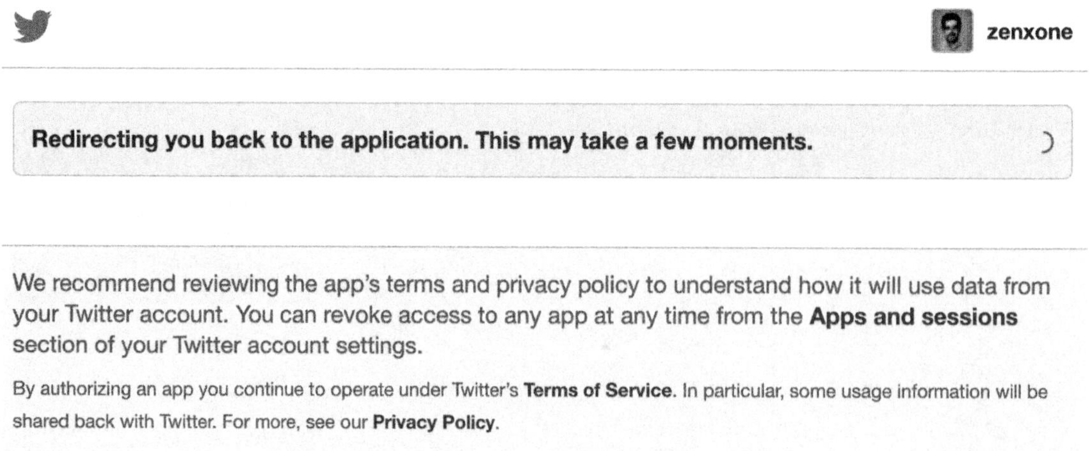

Figure 5.37: Twitter user authentication redirect page

You will then be redirected to the dashboard page of your application.

Authentication using Google

Google offers social authentication using OAuth2. You can read about Google's OAuth2 implementation at https://developers.google.com/identity/protocols/OAuth2.

To implement authentication using Google, add the following line highlighted in bold to the AUTHENTICATION_BACKENDS setting in the settings.py file of your project:

```python
AUTHENTICATION_BACKENDS = [
    'django.contrib.auth.backends.ModelBackend',
    'account.authentication.EmailAuthBackend',
    'social_core.backends.facebook.FacebookOAuth2',
    'social_core.backends.twitter.TwitterOAuth',
    'social_core.backends.google.GoogleOAuth2',
]
```

First, you will need to create an API key in your Google Developer Console. Open https://console.cloud.google.com/projectcreate in your browser. You will see the following screen:

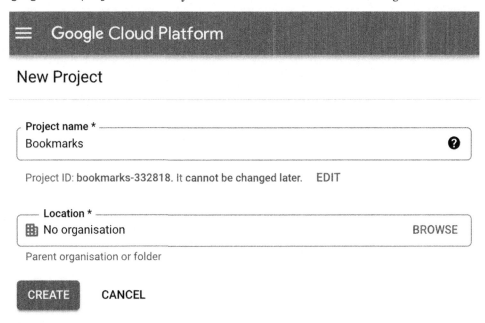

Figure 5.38: The Google project creation form

Under **Project name** enter Bookmarks and click the **CREATE** button.

When the new project is ready, make sure the project is selected in the top navigation bar as follows:

Figure 5.39: The Google Developer Console top navigation bar

After the project is created, under **APIs and services**, click on **Credentials** as follows:

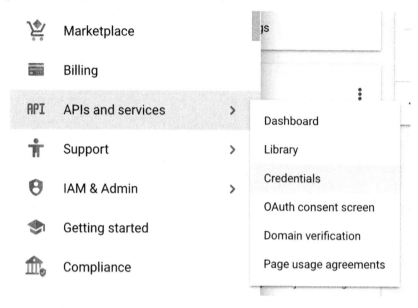

Figure 5.40: Google APIs and services menu

You will see the following screen:

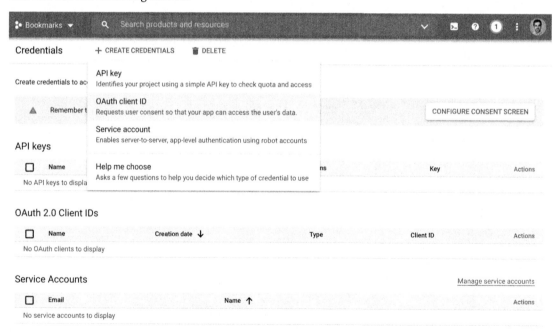

Figure 5.41: Google API creation of API credentials

Then click on **CREATE CREDENTIALS** and click on **OAuth client ID**.

Google will ask you to configure the consent screen first, like this:

⚠ To create an OAuth client ID, you must first configure your consent screen   [CONFIGURE CONSENT SCREEN]

Figure 5.42: The alert to configure the OAuth consent screen

We will configure the page that will be shown to users to give their consent to access your site with their Google account. Click on the **CONFIGURE CONSENT SCREEN** button. You will be redirected to the following screen:

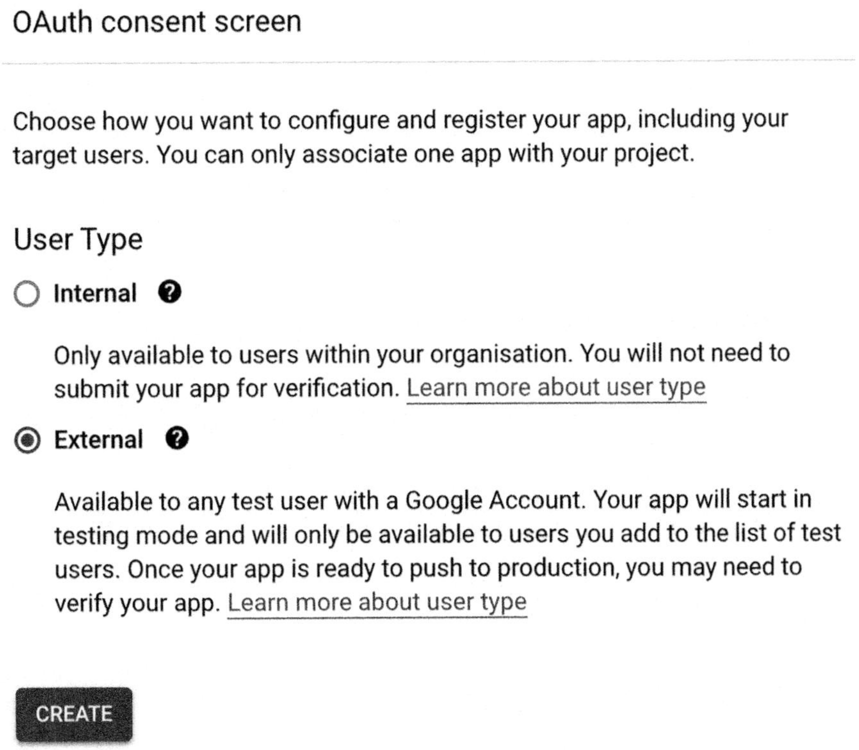

OAuth consent screen

Choose how you want to configure and register your app, including your target users. You can only associate one app with your project.

User Type

○ **Internal** ❷

Only available to users within your organisation. You will not need to submit your app for verification. Learn more about user type

◉ **External** ❷

Available to any test user with a Google Account. Your app will start in testing mode and will only be available to users you add to the list of test users. Once your app is ready to push to production, you may need to verify your app. Learn more about user type

Figure 5.43: User type selection in the Google OAuth consent screen setup

Choose **External** for **User Type** and click the **CREATE** button. You will see the following screen:

App information

This shows in the consent screen, and helps end users know who you are and contact you

```
┌─ App name * ──────────────────────────────────────────────┐
│  Bookmarks                                                  │
└─────────────────────────────────────────────────────────────┘
```
The name of the app asking for consent

```
┌─ User support email * ───────────────────────────────────┐
│  myacccount@gmail.com                                    ▼ │
└─────────────────────────────────────────────────────────────┘
```
For users to contact you with questions about their consent

Figure 5.44: Google OAuth consent screen setup

Under **App name**, enter Bookmarks and select your email for **User support email**.

Under **Authorised domains**, enter mysite.com as follows:

Authorised domains ❓

When a domain is used on the consent screen or in an OAuth client's configuration, it must be pre-registered here. If your app needs to go through verification, please go to the Google Search Console to check if your domains are authorised. Learn more about the authorised domain limit.

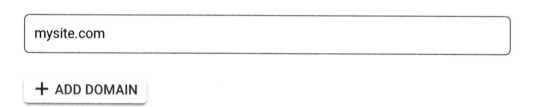

Figure 5.45: Google OAuth authorized domains

Enter your email under **Developer contact information** and click on **SAVE AND CONTINUE**.

In step **2. Scopes**, don't change anything and click on **SAVE AND CONTINUE**.

In step 3. **Test users,** add your Google user to **Test users** and click on **SAVE AND CONTINUE** as follows:

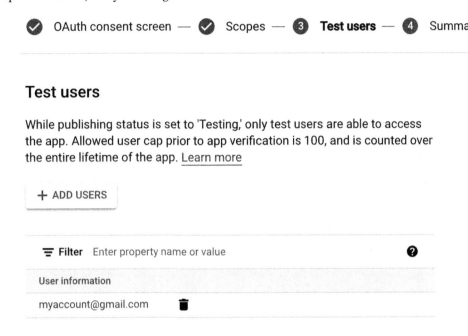

Figure 5.46: Google OAuth test users

You will see a summary of your consent screen configuration. Click on **Back to dashboard.**

In the menu on the left sidebar, click on **Credentials** and click again on **Create credentials** and then on **OAuth client ID.**

As the next step, enter the following information:

- **Application type:** Select **Web application**
- **Name:** Enter Bookmarks
- **Authorised JavaScript origins:** Add https://mysite.com:8000/
- **Authorised redirect URIs:** Add https://mysite.com:8000/social-auth/complete/google-oauth2/

The form should look like this:

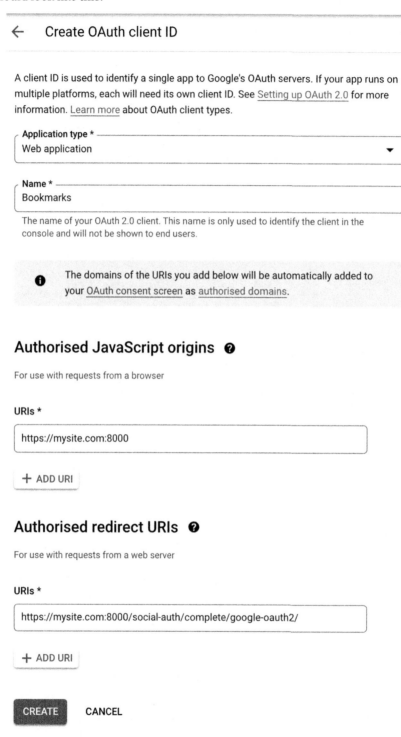

Figure 5.47: The Google OAuth client ID creation form

Click the **CREATE** button. You will get **Your Client ID** and **Your Client Secret** keys:

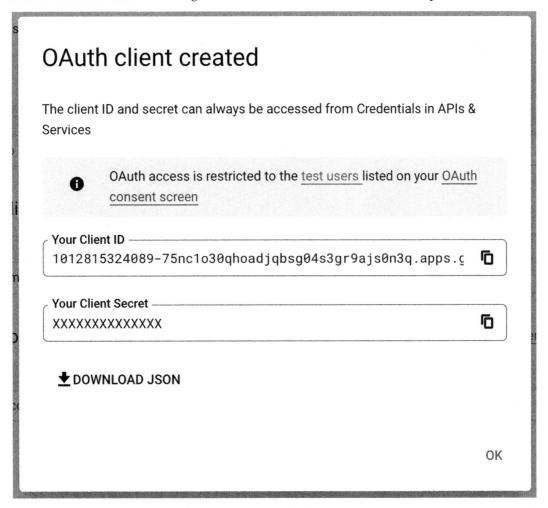

Figure 5.48: Google OAuth Client ID and Client Secret

Add both keys to your settings.py file, like this:

```
SOCIAL_AUTH_GOOGLE_OAUTH2_KEY = 'XXX' # Google Client ID
SOCIAL_AUTH_GOOGLE_OAUTH2_SECRET = 'XXX' # Google Client Secret
```

Edit the registration/login.html template and add the following code highlighted in bold to the `<ul>` element:

```
<ul>
  <li class="facebook">
    <a href="{% url "social:begin" "facebook" %}">
      Sign in with Facebook
    </a>
```

```
    </li>
    <li class="twitter">
      <a href="{% url "social:begin" "twitter" %}">
        Sign in with Twitter
      </a>
    </li>
    <li class="google">
      <a href="{% url "social:begin" "google-oauth2" %}">
        Sign in with Google
      </a>
    </li>
  </ul>
```

Use the management command `runserver_plus` provided by Django Extensions to run the development server, as follows:

```
python manage.py runserver_plus --cert-file cert.crt
```

Open `https://mysite.com:8000/account/login/` in your browser. The login page should now look as follows:

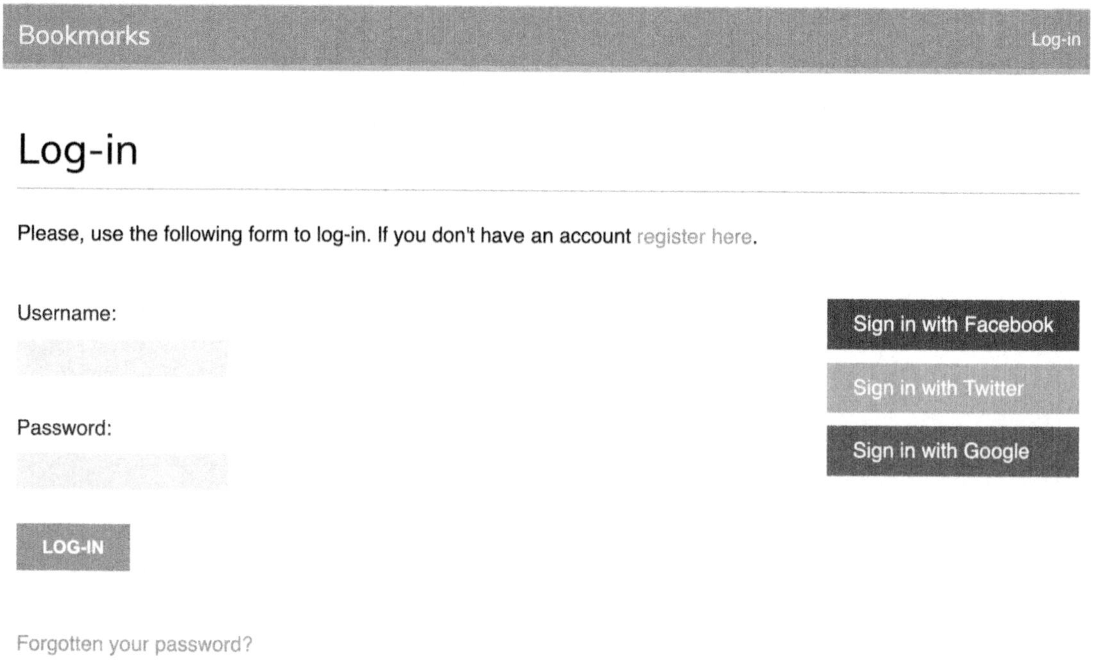

Figure 5.49: The login page including buttons for Facebook, Twitter, and Google authentication

Click on the **Sign in with Google** button. You will see the following screen:

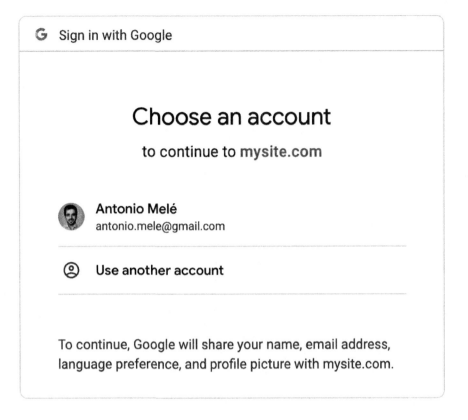

Figure 5.50: The Google application authorization screen

Click on your Google account to authorize the application. You will be logged in and redirected to the dashboard page of your website.

You have now added social authentication to your project with some of the most popular social platforms. You can easily implement social authentication with other online services using Python Social Auth.

Creating a profile for users that register with social authentication

When a user authenticates using social authentication, a new User object is created if there isn't an existing user associated with that social profile. Python Social Auth uses a pipeline consisting of a set of functions that are executed in a specific order executed during the authentication flow. These functions take care of retrieving any user details, creating a social profile in the database, and associating it to an existing user or creating a new one.

Currently, a no `Profile` object is created when new users are created via social authentication. We will add a new step to the pipeline, to automatically create a `Profile` object in the database when a new user is created.

Add the following `SOCIAL_AUTH_PIPELINE` setting to the `settings.py` file of your project:

```
SOCIAL_AUTH_PIPELINE = [
    'social_core.pipeline.social_auth.social_details',
    'social_core.pipeline.social_auth.social_uid',
    'social_core.pipeline.social_auth.auth_allowed',
    'social_core.pipeline.social_auth.social_user',
    'social_core.pipeline.user.get_username',
    'social_core.pipeline.user.create_user',
    'social_core.pipeline.social_auth.associate_user',
    'social_core.pipeline.social_auth.load_extra_data',
    'social_core.pipeline.user.user_details',
]
```

This is the default authentication pipeline used by Python Social Auth. It consists of several functions that perform different tasks when authenticating a user. You can find more details about the default authentication pipeline at https://python-social-auth.readthedocs.io/en/latest/pipeline.html.

Let's build a function that creates a `Profile` object in the database whenever a new user is created. We will then add this function to the social authentication pipeline.

Edit the `account/authentication.py` file and add the following code to it:

```
from account.models import Profile

def create_profile(backend, user, *args, **kwargs):
    """
    Create user profile for social authentication
    """
    Profile.objects.get_or_create(user=user)
```

The `create_profile` function takes two required arguments:

- backend: The social auth backend used for the user authentication. Remember you added the social authentication backends to the `AUTHENTICATION_BACKENDS` setting in your project.
- user: The `User` instance of the new or existing user authenticated.

You can check the different arguments that are passed to the pipeline functions at https://python-social-auth.readthedocs.io/en/latest/pipeline.html#extending-the-pipeline.

In the `create_profile` function, we check that a user object is present and we use the `get_or_create()` method to look up a `Profile` object for the given user, creating one if necessary.

Now, we need to add the new function to the authentication pipeline. Add the following line highlighted in bold to the SOCIAL_AUTH_PIPELINE setting in your settings.py file:

```
SOCIAL_AUTH_PIPELINE = [
    'social_core.pipeline.social_auth.social_details',
    'social_core.pipeline.social_auth.social_uid',
    'social_core.pipeline.social_auth.auth_allowed',
    'social_core.pipeline.social_auth.social_user',
    'social_core.pipeline.user.get_username',
    'social_core.pipeline.user.create_user',
    'account.authentication.create_profile',
    'social_core.pipeline.social_auth.associate_user',
    'social_core.pipeline.social_auth.load_extra_data',
    'social_core.pipeline.user.user_details',
]
```

We have added the create_profile function after social_core.pipeline.create_user. At this point, a User instance is available. The user can be an existing user or a new one created in this step of the pipeline. The create_profile function uses the User instance to look up the related Profile object and create a new one if necessary.

Access the user list in the administration site at https://mysite.com:8000/admin/auth/user/. Remove any users created through social authentication.

Then open https://mysite.com:8000/account/login/ and perform social authentication for the user you deleted. A new user will be created and now a Profile object will be created as well. Access https://mysite.com:8000/admin/account/profile/ to verify that a profile has been created for the new user.

We have successfully added the functionality to create the user profile automatically for social authentication.

Python Social Auth also offers a pipeline mechanism for the disconnection flow. You can find more details at https://python-social-auth.readthedocs.io/en/latest/pipeline.html#disconnection-pipeline.

Additional resources

The following resources provide additional information related to the topics covered in this chapter:

- Source code for this chapter – https://github.com/PacktPublishing/Django-4-by-example/tree/main/Chapter05
- Python Social Auth – https://github.com/python-social-auth
- Python Social Auth's authentication backends – https://python-social-auth.readthedocs.io/en/latest/backends/index.html#supported-backends

- Django allowed hosts setting – `https://docs.djangoproject.com/en/4.1/ref/settings/#allowed-hosts`
- Django Extensions documentation – `https://django-extensions.readthedocs.io/en/latest/`
- Facebook developer portal – `https://developers.facebook.com/apps/`
- Twitter apps – `https://developer.twitter.com/en/apps/create`
- Google's OAuth2 implementation – `https://developers.google.com/identity/protocols/OAuth2`
- Google APIs credentials – `https://console.developers.google.com/apis/credentials`
- Python Social Auth pipeline – `https://python-social-auth.readthedocs.io/en/latest/pipeline.html`
- Extending the Python Social Auth pipeline – `https://python-social-auth.readthedocs.io/en/latest/pipeline.html#extending-the-pipeline`
- Python Social Auth pipeline for disconnection – `https://python-social-auth.readthedocs.io/en/latest/pipeline.html#disconnection-pipeline`

Summary

In this chapter, you added social authentication to your site so that users can use their existing Facebook, Twitter, or Google accounts to log in. You used Python Social Auth and implemented social authentication using OAuth 2.0, the industry-standard protocol for authorization. You also learned how to serve your development server through HTTPS using Django Extensions. Finally, you customized the authentication pipeline to create user profiles for new users automatically.

In the next chapter, you will create an image bookmarking system. You will create models with many-to-many relationships and customize the behavior of forms. You will learn how to generate image thumbnails and how to build AJAX functionalities using JavaScript and Django.

6

Sharing Content on Your Website

In the previous chapter, you used Django Social Auth to add social authentication to your site using Facebook, Google, and Twitter. You learned how to run your development server with HTTPS on your local machine using Django Extensions. You customized the social authentication pipeline to create a user profile for new users automatically.

In this chapter, you will learn how to create a JavaScript bookmarklet to share content from other sites on your website, and you will implement AJAX features in your project using JavaScript and Django.

This chapter will cover the following points:

- Creating many-to-many relationships
- Customizing behavior for forms
- Using JavaScript with Django
- Building a JavaScript bookmarklet
- Generating image thumbnails using `easy-thumbnails`
- Implementing asynchronous HTTP requests with JavaScript and Django
- Building infinite scroll pagination

The source code for this chapter can be found at `https://github.com/PacktPublishing/Django-4-by-example/tree/main/Chapter06`.

All Python packages used in this chapter are included in the `requirements.txt` file in the source code for the chapter. You can follow the instructions to install each Python package in the following sections, or you can install all requirements at once with the command `pip install -r requirements.txt`.

Creating an image bookmarking website

We will now learn how to allow users to bookmark images that they find on other websites and share them on our site. To build this functionality, we will need the following elements:

1. A data model to store images and related information
2. A form and a view to handle image uploads

3.   JavaScript bookmarklet code that can be executed on any website. This code will find images across the page and allow users to select the image they want to bookmark

First, create a new application inside your bookmarks project directory by running the following command in the shell prompt:

```
django-admin startapp images
```

Add the new application to the INSTALLED_APPS setting in the settings.py file of the project, as follows:

```
INSTALLED_APPS = [
    # ...
    'images.apps.ImagesConfig',
]
```

We have activated the images application in the project.

Building the image model

Edit the models.py file of the images application and add the following code to it:

```
from django.db import models
from django.conf import settings


class Image(models.Model):
    user = models.ForeignKey(settings.AUTH_USER_MODEL,
                             related_name='images_created',
                             on_delete=models.CASCADE)
    title = models.CharField(max_length=200)
    slug = models.SlugField(max_length=200,
                            blank=True)
    url = models.URLField(max_length=2000)
    image = models.ImageField(upload_to='images/%Y/%m/%d/')
    description = models.TextField(blank=True)
    created = models.DateField(auto_now_add=True)

    class Meta:
        indexes = [
            models.Index(fields=['-created']),
        ]
        ordering = ['-created']

    def __str__(self):
        return self.title
```

This is the model that we will use to store images in the platform. Let's take a look at the fields of this model:

- `user`: This indicates the `User` object that bookmarked this image. This is a foreign key field because it specifies a one-to-many relationship: a user can post multiple images, but each image is posted by a single user. We have used `CASCADE` for the `on_delete` parameter so that related images are deleted when a user is deleted.
- `title`: A title for the image.
- `slug`: A short label that contains only letters, numbers, underscores, or hyphens to be used for building beautiful SEO-friendly URLs.
- `url`: The original URL for this image. We use `max_length` to define a maximum length of 2000 characters.
- `image`: The image file.
- `description`: An optional description for the image.
- `created`: The date and time that indicate when the object was created in the database. We have added `auto_now_add` to automatically set the current datetime when the object is created.

In the `Meta` class of the model, we have defined a database index in descending order for the `created` field. We have also added the `ordering` attribute to tell Django that it should sort results by the `created` field by default. We indicate descending order by using a hyphen before the field name, such as `-created`, so that new images will be displayed first.

> Database indexes improve query performance. Consider creating indexes for fields that you frequently query using `filter()`, `exclude()`, or `order_by()`. `ForeignKey` fields or fields with `unique=True` imply the creation of an index. You can learn more about database indexes at https://docs.djangoproject.com/en/4.1/ref/models/options/#django.db.models.Options.indexes.

We will override the `save()` method of the `Image` model to automatically generate the `slug` field based on the value of the `title` field. Import the `slugify()` function and add a `save()` method to the `Image` model, as follows. New lines are highlighted in bold:

```
from django.utils.text import slugify

class Image(models.Model):
    # ...
    def save(self, *args, **kwargs):
        if not self.slug:
            self.slug = slugify(self.title)
        super().save(*args, **kwargs)
```

When an `Image` object is saved, if the `slug` field doesn't have a value, the `slugify()` function is used to automatically generate a slug from the `title` field of the image. The object is then saved. By generating slugs automatically from the title, users won't have to provide a slug when they share images on our website.

Creating many-to-many relationships

Next, we will add another field to the `Image` model to store the users who like an image. We will need a many-to-many relationship in this case because a user might like multiple images and each image can be liked by multiple users.

Add the following field to the `Image` model:

```
users_like = models.ManyToManyField(settings.AUTH_USER_MODEL,
                     related_name='images_liked',
                     blank=True)
```

When we define a `ManyToManyField` field, Django creates an intermediary join table using the primary keys of both models. *Figure 6.1* shows the database table that will be created for this relationship:

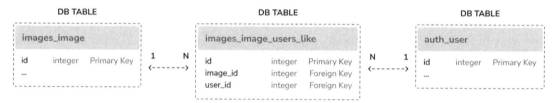

Figure 6.1: Intermediary database table for the many-to-many relationship

The `images_image_users_like` table is created by Django as an intermediary table that has references to the `images_image` table (`Image` model) and `auth_user` table (`User` model). The `ManyToManyField` field can be defined in either of the two related models.

As with `ForeignKey` fields, the `related_name` attribute of `ManyToManyField` allows you to name the relationship from the related object back to this one. `ManyToManyField` fields provide a many-to-many manager that allows you to retrieve related objects, such as `image.users_like.all()`, or get them from a user object, such as `user.images_liked.all()`.

You can learn more about many-to-many relationships at https://docs.djangoproject.com/en/4.1/topics/db/examples/many_to_many/.

Open the shell prompt and run the following command to create an initial migration:

```
python manage.py makemigrations images
```

The output should be similar to the following one:

```
Migrations for 'images':
   images/migrations/0001_initial.py
     - Create model Image
```

```
        - Create index images_imag_created_d57897_idx on field(s) -created of model
   image
```

Now run the following command to apply your migration:

```
python manage.py migrate images
```

You will get an output that includes the following line:

```
Applying images.0001_initial... OK
```

The Image model is now synced to the database.

Registering the image model in the administration site

Edit the admin.py file of the images application and register the Image model into the administration site, as follows:

```python
from django.contrib import admin
from .models import Image


@admin.register(Image)
class ImageAdmin(admin.ModelAdmin):
    list_display = ['title', 'slug', 'image', 'created']
    list_filter = ['created']
```

Start the development server with the following command:

```
python manage.py runserver_plus --cert-file cert.crt
```

Open https://127.0.0.1:8000/admin/ in your browser, and you will see the Image model in the administration site, like this:

Figure 6.2: The Images block on the Django administration site index page

You have completed the model to store images. Now you will learn how to implement a form to retrieve images by their URL and store them using the Image model.

Posting content from other websites

We will allow users to bookmark images from external websites and share them on our site. Users will provide the URL of the image, a title, and an optional description. We will create a form and a view to download the image and create a new Image object in the database.

Let's start by building a form to submit new images.

Create a new `forms.py` file inside the `images` application directory and add the following code to it:

```
from django import forms
from .models import Image


class ImageCreateForm(forms.ModelForm):
    class Meta:
        model = Image
        fields = ['title', 'url', 'description']
        widgets = {
            'url': forms.HiddenInput,
        }
```

We have defined a `ModelForm` form from the `Image` model, including only the `title`, `url`, and `description` fields. Users will not enter the image URL directly in the form. Instead, we will provide them with a JavaScript tool to choose an image from an external site, and the form will receive the image's URL as a parameter. We have overridden the default widget of the `url` field to use a `HiddenInput` widget. This widget is rendered as an HTML `input` element with a `type="hidden"` attribute. We use this widget because we don't want this field to be visible to users.

Cleaning form fields

In order to verify that the provided image URL is valid, we will check that the filename ends with a `.jpg`, `.jpeg`, or `.png` extension to allow sharing JPEG and PNG files only. In the previous chapter, we used the `clean_<fieldname>()` convention to implement field validation. This method is executed for each field, if present, when we call `is_valid()` on a form instance. In the `clean` method, you can alter the field's value or raise any validation errors for the field.

In the `forms.py` file of the `images` application, add the following method to the `ImageCreateForm` class:

```
def clean_url(self):
    url = self.cleaned_data['url']
    valid_extensions = ['jpg', 'jpeg', 'png']
    extension = url.rsplit('.', 1)[1].lower()
    if extension not in valid_extensions:
        raise forms.ValidationError('The given URL does not ' \
                                    'match valid image extensions.')
    return url
```

In the preceding code, we have defined a `clean_url()` method to clean the `url` field. The code works as follows:

1. The value of the `url` field is retrieved by accessing the `cleaned_data` dictionary of the form instance.
2. The URL is split to check whether the file has a valid extension. If the extension is invalid, a `ValidationError` is raised, and the form instance is not validated.

In addition to validating the given URL, we also need to download the image file and save it. We could, for example, use the view that handles the form to download the image file. Instead, let's take a more general approach by overriding the save() method of the model form to perform this task when the form is saved.

Installing the Requests library

When a user bookmarks an image, we will need to download the image file by its URL. We will use the Requests Python library for this purpose. Requests is the most popular HTTP library for Python. It abstracts the complexity of dealing with HTTP requests and provides a very simple interface to consume HTTP services. You can find the documentation for the Requests library at https://requests.readthedocs.io/en/master/.

Open the shell and install the Requests library with the following command:

```
pip install requests==2.28.1
```

We will now override the save() method of ImageCreateForm and use the Requests library to retrieve the image by its URL.

Overriding the save() method of a ModelForm

As you know, ModelForm provides a save() method to save the current model instance to the database and return the object. This method receives a Boolean commit parameter, which allows you to specify whether the object has to be persisted to the database. If commit is False, the save() method will return a model instance but will not save it to the database. We will override the form's save() method in order to retrieve the image file by the given URL and save it to the file system.

Add the following imports at the top of the forms.py file:

```python
from django.core.files.base import ContentFile
from django.utils.text import slugify
import requests
```

Then, add the following save() method to the ImageCreateForm form:

```python
def save(self, force_insert=False,
         force_update=False,
         commit=True):
    image = super().save(commit=False)
    image_url = self.cleaned_data['url']
    name = slugify(image.title)
    extension = image_url.rsplit('.', 1)[1].lower()
    image_name = f'{name}.{extension}'
    # download image from the given URL
    response = requests.get(image_url)
    image.image.save(image_name,
```

```
                    ContentFile(response.content),
                    save=False)
    if commit:
        image.save()
    return image
```

We have overridden the save() method, keeping the parameters required by ModelForm. The preceding code can be explained as follows:

1. A new image instance is created by calling the save() method of the form with commit=False.

2. The URL of the image is retrieved from the cleaned_data dictionary of the form.

3. An image name is generated by combining the image title slug with the original file extension of the image.

4. The Requests Python library is used to download the image by sending an HTTP GET request using the image URL. The response is stored in the response object.

5. The save() method of the image field is called, passing it a ContentFile object that is instantiated with the downloaded file content. In this way, the file is saved to the media directory of the project. The save=False parameter is passed to avoid saving the object to the database yet.

6. To maintain the same behavior as the original save() method of the model form, the form is only saved to the database if the commit parameter is True.

We will need a view to create an instance of the form and handle its submission.

Edit the views.py file of the images application and add the following code to it. New code is highlighted in bold:

```
from django.shortcuts import render, redirect
from django.contrib.auth.decorators import login_required
from django.contrib import messages
from .forms import ImageCreateForm


@login_required
def image_create(request):
    if request.method == 'POST':
        # form is sent
        form = ImageCreateForm(data=request.POST)
        if form.is_valid():
            # form data is valid
            cd = form.cleaned_data
            new_image = form.save(commit=False)
            # assign current user to the item
            new_image.user = request.user
            new_image.save()
```

```
            messages.success(request,
                             'Image added successfully')
            # redirect to new created item detail view
            return redirect(new_image.get_absolute_url())
    else:
        # build form with data provided by the bookmarklet via GET
        form = ImageCreateForm(data=request.GET)
    return render(request,
                  'images/image/create.html',
                  {'section': 'images',
                   'form': form})
```

In the preceding code, we have created a view to store images on the site. We have added the login_ required decorator to the image_create view to prevent access to unauthenticated users. This is how this view works:

1. Initial data has to be provided through a GET HTTP request in order to create an instance of the form. This data will consist of the url and title attributes of an image from an external website. Both parameters will be set in the GET request by the JavaScript bookmarklet that we will create later. For now, we can assume that this data will be available in the request.

2. When the form is submitted with a POST HTTP request, it is validated with form.is_valid(). If the form data is valid, a new Image instance is created by saving the form with form. save(commit=False). The new instance is not saved to the database because of commit=False.

3. A relationship to the current user performing the request is added to the new Image instance with new_image.user = request.user. This is how we will know who uploaded each image.

4. The Image object is saved to the database.

5. Finally, a success message is created using the Django messaging framework and the user is redirected to the canonical URL of the new image. We haven't yet implemented the get_ absolute_url() method of the Image model; we will do that later.

Create a new urls.py file inside the images application and add the following code to it:

```
from django.urls import path
from . import views


app_name = 'images'

urlpatterns = [
    path('create/', views.image_create, name='create'),
]
```

Edit the main `urls.py` file of the `bookmarks` project to include the patterns for the `images` application, as follows. The new code is highlighted in bold:

```
urlpatterns = [
    path('admin/', admin.site.urls),
    path('account/', include('account.urls')),
    path('social-auth/',
        include('social_django.urls', namespace='social')),
    path('images/', include('images.urls', namespace='images')),
]
```

Finally, we need to create a template to render the form. Create the following directory structure inside the `images` application directory:

```
templates/
  images/
    image/
      create.html
```

Edit the new `create.html` template and add the following code to it:

```
{% extends "base.html" %}

{% block title %}Bookmark an image{% endblock %}

{% block content %}
  <h1>Bookmark an image</h1>
  <img src="{{ request.GET.url }}" class="image-preview">
  <form method="post">
    {{ form.as_p }}
    {% csrf_token %}
    <input type="submit" value="Bookmark it!">
  </form>
{% endblock %}
```

Run the development server with the following command in the shell prompt:

```
python manage.py runserver_plus --cert-file cert.crt
```

Open `https://127.0.0.1:8000/images/create/?title=...&url=...` in your browser, including the title and url GET parameters, providing an existing JPEG image URL in the latter. For example, you can use the following URL: `https://127.0.0.1:8000/images/create/?title=%20Django%20and%20Duke&url=https://upload.wikimedia.org/wikipedia/commons/8/85/Django_Reinhardt_and_Duke_Ellington_%28Gottlieb%29.jpg`.

You will see the form with an image preview, like the following:

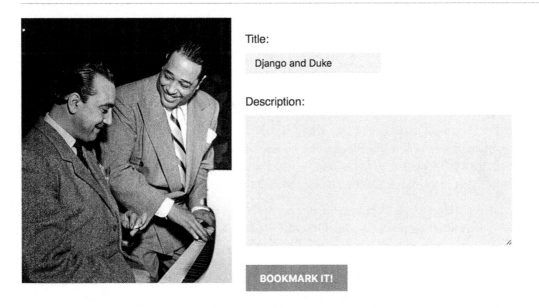

Figure 6.3: The create a new image bookmark page

Add a description and click on the **BOOKMARK IT!** button. A new Image object will be saved in your database. However, you will get an error that indicates that the Image model has no get_absolute_url() method, as follows:

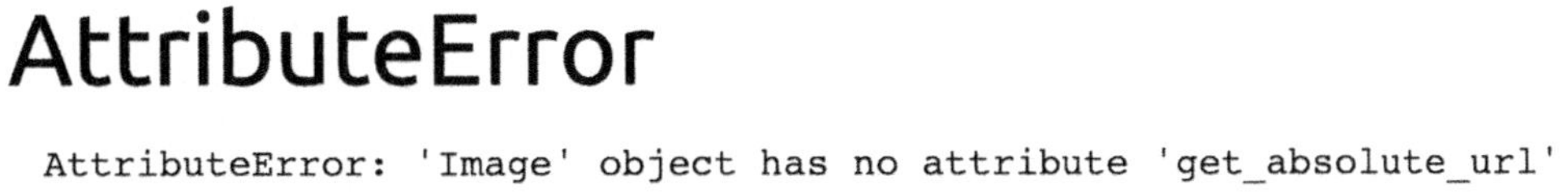

AttributeError

```
AttributeError: 'Image' object has no attribute 'get_absolute_url'
```

Figure 6.4: An error showing that the Image object has no attribute get_absolute_url

Don't worry about this error for now; we are going to implement the get_absolute_url method in the Image model later.

Open `https://127.0.0.1:8000/admin/images/image/` in your browser and verify that the new image object has been saved, like this:

Figure 6.5: The administration site image list page showing the Image object created

Building a bookmarklet with JavaScript

A bookmarklet is a bookmark stored in a web browser that contains JavaScript code to extend the browser's functionality. When you click on the bookmark in the bookmarks or favorites bar of your browser, the JavaScript code is executed on the website being displayed in the browser. This is very useful for building tools that interact with other websites.

Some online services, such as Pinterest, implement their own bookmarklet to let users share content from other sites onto their platform. The Pinterest bookmarklet, named *browser button*, is available at `https://about.pinterest.com/en/browser-button`. The Pinterest bookmarklet is provided as a Google Chrome extension, a Microsoft Edge add-on, or a plain JavaScript bookmarklet for Safari and other browsers that you can drag and drop to the bookmarks bar of your browser. The bookmarklet allows users to save images or websites to their Pinterest account.

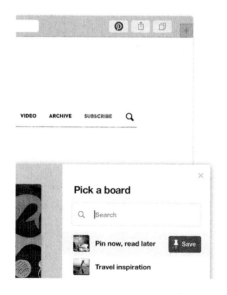

Figure 6.6: The Pin it bookmarklet from Pinterest

Let's create a bookmarklet in a similar way for your website. For that, we will be using JavaScript.

This is how your users will add the bookmarklet to their browser and use it:

1. The user drags a link from your site to their browser's bookmarks bar. The link contains JavaScript code in its `href` attribute. This code will be stored in the bookmark.

2. The user navigates to any website and clicks on the bookmark in the bookmarks or favorites bar. The JavaScript code of the bookmark is executed.

Since the JavaScript code will be stored as a bookmark, we will not be able to update it after the user has added it to their bookmarks bar. This is an important drawback that you can solve by implementing a launcher script. Users will save the launcher script as a bookmark, and the launcher script will load the actual JavaScript bookmarklet from a URL. By doing this, you will be able to update the code of the bookmarklet at any time. This is the approach that we will take to build the bookmarklet. Let's start!

Create a new template under `images/templates/` and name it `bookmarklet_launcher.js`. This will be the launcher script. Add the following JavaScript code to the new file:

```
(function(){
  if(!window.bookmarklet) {
    bookmarklet_js = document.body.appendChild(document.
createElement('script'));
    bookmarklet_js.src = '//127.0.0.1:8000/static/js/bookmarklet.js?r='+Math.
floor(Math.random()*9999999999999999);
    window.bookmarklet = true;
  }
  else {
    bookmarkletLaunch();
  }
})();
```

The preceding script checks whether the bookmarklet has already been loaded by checking the value of the bookmarklet window variable with `if(!window.bookmarklet)`:

*   If `window.bookmarklet` is not defined or doesn't have a truthy value (considered `true` in a Boolean context), a JavaScript file is loaded by appending a `<script>` element to the body of the HTML document loaded in the browser. The `src` attribute is used to load the URL of the `bookmarklet.js` script with a random 16-digit integer parameter generated with `Math.random()*9999999999999999`. Using a random number, we prevent the browser from loading the file from the browser's cache. If the bookmarklet JavaScript has been previously loaded, the different parameter value will force the browser to load the script from the source URL again. This way, we make sure the bookmarklet always runs the most up-to-date JavaScript code.

*   If `window.bookmarklet` is defined and has a truthy value, the function `bookmarkletLaunch()` is executed. We will define `bookmarkletLaunch()` as a global function in the `bookmarklet.js` script.

By checking the `bookmarklet` window variable, we prevent the bookmarklet JavaScript code from being loaded more than once if users click on the bookmarklet repeatedly.

You created the bookmarklet launcher code. The actual bookmarklet code will reside in the `bookmarklet.js` static file. Using launcher code allows you to update the bookmarklet code at any time without requiring users to change the bookmark they previously added to their browser.

Let's add the bookmarklet launcher to the dashboard pages so that users can add it to the bookmarks bar of their browser.

Edit the `account/dashboard.html` template of the `account` application and make it look like the following. New lines are highlighted in bold:

```
{% extends "base.html" %}

{% block title %}Dashboard{% endblock %}

{% block content %}
  <h1>Dashboard</h1>
  {% with total_images_created=request.user.images_created.count %}
    <p>Welcome to your dashboard. You have bookmarked {{ total_images_created }} image{{ total_images_created|pluralize }}.</p>
  {% endwith %}
  <p>Drag the following button to your bookmarks toolbar to bookmark images from other websites → <a href="javascript:{% include "bookmarklet_launcher.js" %}" class="button">Bookmark it</a></p>
  <p>You can also <a href="{% url "edit" %}">edit your profile</a> or <a href="{% url "password_change" %}">change your password</a>.</p>
{% endblock %}
```

Make sure that no template tag is split into multiple lines; Django doesn't support multiple-line tags.

The dashboard now displays the total number of images bookmarked by the user. We have added a `{% with %}` template tag to create a variable with the total number of images bookmarked by the current user. We have included a link with an `href` attribute that contains the bookmarklet launcher script. This JavaScript code is loaded from the `bookmarklet_launcher.js` template.

Open `https://127.0.0.1:8000/account/` in your browser. You should see the following page:

Dashboard

Welcome to your dashboard. You have bookmarked 1 image.

Drag the following button to your bookmarks toolbar to bookmark images from other websites →   **BOOKMARK IT**

You can also edit your profile or change your password.

Figure 6.7: The dashboard page, including the total images bookmarked and the button for the bookmarklet

Now create the following directories and files inside the `images` application directory:

```
static/
    js/
        bookmarklet.js
```

You will find a `static/css/` directory under the `images` application directory in the code that comes along with this chapter. Copy the `css/` directory into the `static/` directory of your code. You can find the contents of the directory at `https://github.com/PacktPublishing/Django-4-by-Example/tree/main/Chapter06/bookmarks/images/static`.

The `css/bookmarklet.css` file provides the styles for the JavaScript bookmarklet. The `static/` directory should contain the following file structure now:

```
css/
    bookmarklet.css
js/
    bookmarklet.js
```

Edit the `bookmarklet.js` static file and add the following JavaScript code to it:

```
const siteUrl = '//127.0.0.1:8000/';
const styleUrl = siteUrl + 'static/css/bookmarklet.css';
const minWidth = 250;
const minHeight = 250;
```

You have declared four different constants that will be used by the bookmarklet. These constants are:

- `siteUrl` and `staticUrl`: The base URL for the website and the base URL for static files.
- `minWidth` and `minHeight`: The minimum width and height in pixels for the images that the bookmarklet will collect from the site. The bookmarklet will identify images that have at least 250px width and 250px height.

Edit the `bookmarklet.js` static file and add the following code highlighted in bold:

```
const siteUrl = '//127.0.0.1:8000/';
const styleUrl = siteUrl + 'static/css/bookmarklet.css';
const minWidth = 250;
const minHeight = 250;

// Load CSS
var head = document.getElementsByTagName('head')[0];
var link = document.createElement('link');
link.rel = 'stylesheet';
link.type = 'text/css';
link.href = styleUrl + '?r=' + Math.floor(Math.random()*9999999999999999);
head.appendChild(link);
```

This section loads the CSS stylesheet for the bookmarklet. We use JavaScript to manipulate the **Document Object Model** (**DOM**). The DOM represents an HTML document in memory and it is created by the browser when a web page is loaded. The DOM is constructed as a tree of objects that comprise the structure and content of the HTML document.

The previous code generates an object equivalent to the following JavaScript code and appends it to the <head> element of the HTML page:

```
<link rel="stylesheet" type="text/css" href= "//127.0.0.1:8000/static/css/
bookmarklet.css?r=1234567890123456">
```

Let's review how this is done:

1. The <head> element of the site is retrieved with `document.getElementsByTagName()`. This function retrieves all HTML elements of the page with the given tag. By using [0] we access the first instance found. We access the first element because all HTML documents should have a single <head> element.
2. A <link> element is created with `document.createElement('link')`.
3. The `rel` and `type` attributes of the <link> element are set. This is equivalent to the HTML `<link rel="stylesheet" type="text/css">`.
4. The `href` attribute of the <link> element is set with the URL of the `bookmarklet.css` stylesheet. A 16-digit random number is used as a URL parameter to prevent the browser from loading the file from the cache.

5. The new <link> element is added to the <head> element of the HTML page using head. appendChild(link).

Now we will create the HTML element to display a container on the website where the bookmarklet is executed. The HTML container will be used to display all images found on the site and let users choose the image they want to share. It will use the CSS styles defined in the bookmarklet.css stylesheet.

Edit the bookmarklet.js static file and add the following code highlighted in bold:

```
const siteUrl = '//127.0.0.1:8000/';
const styleUrl = siteUrl + 'static/css/bookmarklet.css';
const minWidth = 250;
const minHeight = 250;

// Load CSS
var head = document.getElementsByTagName('head')[0];
var link = document.createElement('link');
link.rel = 'stylesheet';
link.type = 'text/css';
link.href = styleUrl + '?r=' + Math.floor(Math.random()*9999999999999999);
head.appendChild(link);

// Load HTML
var body = document.getElementsByTagName('body')[0];
boxHtml = '
  <div id="bookmarklet">
    <a href="#" id="close">&times;</a>
    <h1>Select an image to bookmark:</h1>
    <div class="images"></div>
  </div>';
body.innerHTML += boxHtml;
```

With this code the <body> element of the DOM is retrieved and new HTML is added to it by modifying its property innerHTML. A new <div> element is added to the body of the page. The <div> container consists of the following elements:

- A link to close the container defined with <a href="#" id="close">×</a>.
- A title defined with <h1>Select an image to bookmark:</h1>.
- An <div> element to list the images found on the site defined with <div class="images"></div>. This container is initially empty and will be filled with the images found on the site.

The HTML container, including the previously loaded CSS styles, will look like *Figure 6.8*:

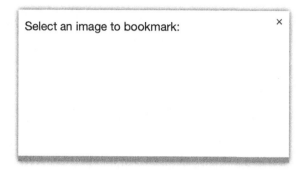

Figure 6.8: The image selection container

Now let's implement a function to launch the bookmarklet. Edit the bookmarklet.js static file and add the following code at the bottom:

```
function bookmarkletLaunch() {
    bookmarklet = document.getElementById('bookmarklet');
    var imagesFound = bookmarklet.querySelector('.images');

    // clear images found
    imagesFound.innerHTML = '';
    // display bookmarklet
    bookmarklet.style.display = 'block';

    // close event
    bookmarklet.querySelector('#close')
            .addEventListener('click', function(){
                bookmarklet.style.display = 'none'
            });
}

// launch the bookmkarklet
bookmarkletLaunch();
```

This is the bookmarkletLaunch() function. Before the definition of this function, the CSS for the bookmarklet is loaded and the HTML container is added to the DOM of the page. The bookmarkletLaunch() function works as follows:

1.   The bookmarklet main container is retrieved by getting the DOM element with the ID bookmarklet with document.getElementById().

2. The bookmarklet element is used to retrieve the child element with the class images. The querySelector() method allows you to retrieve DOM elements using CSS selectors. Selectors allow you to find DOM elements to which a set of CSS rules applies. You can find a list of CSS selectors at https://developer.mozilla.org/en-US/docs/Web/CSS/CSS_Selectors and you can read more information about how to locate DOM elements using selectors at https://developer.mozilla.org/en-US/docs/Web/API/Document_object_model/Locating_DOM_elements_using_selectors.

3. The images container is cleared by setting its innerHTML attribute to an empty string and the bookmarklet is displayed by setting the display CSS property to block.

4. The #close selector is used to find the DOM element with the ID close. A click event is attached to the element with the addEventListener() method. When users click the element, the bookmarklet main container is hidden by setting its display property to none.

The bookmarkletLaunch() function is executed after its definition.

After loading the CSS styles and the HTML container of the bookmarklet, you have to find image elements in the DOM of the current website. Images that have the minimum required dimension have to be added to the HTML container of the bookmarklet. Edit the bookmarklet.js static file and add the following code highlighted in bold to the bottom of the bookmarklet() function:

```
function bookmarkletLaunch() {
  bookmarklet = document.getElementById('bookmarklet');
  var imagesFound = bookmarklet.querySelector('.images');

  // clear images found
  imagesFound.innerHTML = '';
  // display bookmarklet
  bookmarklet.style.display = 'block';

  // close event
  bookmarklet.querySelector('#close')
            .addEventListener('click', function(){
              bookmarklet.style.display = 'none'
            });

  // find images in the DOM with the minimum dimensions
  images = document.querySelectorAll('img[src$=".jpg"], img[src$=".jpeg"],
img[src$=".png"]');
  images.forEach(image => {
    if(image.naturalWidth >= minWidth
      && image.naturalHeight >= minHeight)
    {
      var imageFound = document.createElement('img');
      imageFound.src = image.src;
      imagesFound.append(imageFound);
```

```
    }
  })
}
```

```
// Launch the bookmkarklet
bookmarkletLaunch();
```

The preceding code uses the img[src$=".jpg"], img[src$=".jpeg"], and img[src$=".png"] selectors to find all <img> DOM elements whose src attribute finishes with .jpg, .jpeg, or, .png respectively. Using these selectors with document.querySelectorAll() allows you to find all images with the JPEG and PNG format displayed on the website. Iteration over the results is performed with the forEach() method. Small images are filtered out because we don't consider them to be relevant. Only images with a size larger than the one specified with the minWidth and minHeight variables are used for the results. A new <img> element is created for each image found, where the src source URL attribute is copied from the original image and added to the imagesFound container.

For security reasons, your browser will prevent you from running the bookmarklet over HTTP on a site served through HTTPS. That's the reason we keep using RunServerPlus to run the development server using an auto-generated TLS/SSL certificate. Remember that you learned how to run the development server through HTTPS in *Chapter 5, Implementing Social Authentication*.

In a production environment, a valid TLS/SSL certificate will be required. When you own a domain name, you can apply for a trusted **Certification Authority** (CA) to issue a TLS/SSL certificate for it, so that browsers can verify its identity. If you want to obtain a trusted certificate for a real domain, you can use the *Let's Encrypt* service. *Let's Encrypt* is a nonprofit CA that simplifies obtaining and renewing trusted TLS/SSL certificates for free. You can find more information at https://letsencrypt.org.

Run the development server with the following command from the shell prompt:

```
python manage.py runserver_plus --cert-file cert.crt
```

Open https://127.0.0.1:8000/account/ in your browser. Log in with an existing user, then click and drag the **BOOKMARK IT** button to the bookmarks bar of your browser, as follows:

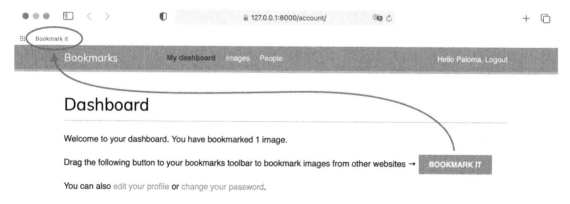

Figure 6.9: Adding the BOOKMARK IT button to the bookmarks bar

Open a website of your own choice in your browser and click on the **Bookmark it** bookmarklet in the bookmarks bar. You will see that a new white overlay appears on the website, displaying all JPEG and PNG images found with dimensions higher than 250×250 pixels. *Figure 6.10* shows the bookmarklet running on `https://amazon.com/`:

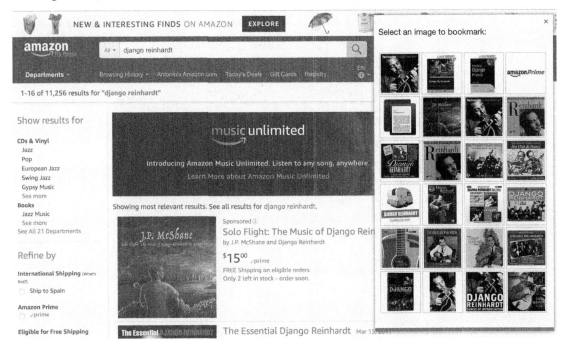

Figure 6.10: The bookmarklet loaded on amazon.com

If the HTML container doesn't appear, check the RunServer shell console log. If you see a MIME type error, it is most likely that your MIME map files are incorrect or need to be updated. You can apply the correct mapping for JavaScript and CSS files by adding the following lines to the `settings.py` file:

```
if DEBUG:
    import mimetypes
    mimetypes.add_type('application/javascript', '.js', True)
    mimetypes.add_type('text/css', '.css', True)
```

The HTML container includes the images that can be bookmarked. We will now implement the functionality for users to click on the desired image to bookmark it.

Edit the `js/bookmarklet.js` static file and add the following code at the bottom of the `bookmarklet()` function:

```
function bookmarkletLaunch() {
  bookmarklet = document.getElementById('bookmarklet');
  var imagesFound = bookmarklet.querySelector('.images');
```

```
   // clear images found
   imagesFound.innerHTML = '';
   // display bookmarklet
   bookmarklet.style.display = 'block';

   // close event
   bookmarklet.querySelector('#close')
           .addEventListener('click', function(){
               bookmarklet.style.display = 'none'
           });

   // find images in the DOM with the minimum dimensions
   images = document.querySelectorAll('img[src$=".jpg"], img[src$=".jpeg"],
img[src$=".png"]');
   images.forEach(image => {
     if(image.naturalWidth >= minWidth
        && image.naturalHeight >= minHeight)
     {
       var imageFound = document.createElement('img');
       imageFound.src = image.src;
       imagesFound.append(imageFound);
     }
   })

   // select image event
   imagesFound.querySelectorAll('img').forEach(image => {
     image.addEventListener('click', function(event){
       imageSelected = event.target;
       bookmarklet.style.display = 'none';
       window.open(siteUrl + 'images/create/?url='
                   + encodeURIComponent(imageSelected.src)
                   + '&title='
                   + encodeURIComponent(document.title),
                   '_blank');
     })
   })
}

// launch the bookmkarklet
bookmarkletLaunch();
```

The preceding code works as follows:

1. A `click()` event is attached to each image element within the `imagesFound` container.
2. When the user clicks on any of the images, the image element clicked is stored in the variable `imageSelected`.
3. The bookmarklet is then hidden by setting its `display` property to `none`.
4. A new browser window is opened with the URL to bookmark a new image on the site. The content of the `<title>` element of the website is passed to the URL in the `title` GET parameter and the selected image URL is passed in the `url` parameter.

Open a new URL with your browser, for example, `https://commons.wikimedia.org/`, as follows:

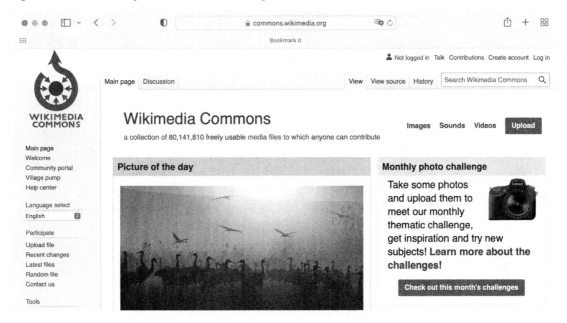

Figure 6.11: The Wikimedia Commons website

 Figures 6.11 to *6.14* image: *A flock of cranes (Grus grus) in Hula Valley, Northern Israel* by Tomere (Licence: Creative Commons Attribution-Share Alike 4.0 International: `https://creativecommons.org/licenses/by-sa/4.0/deed.en`)

Click on the **Bookmark it** bookmarklet to display the image selection overlay. You will see the image selection overlay like this:

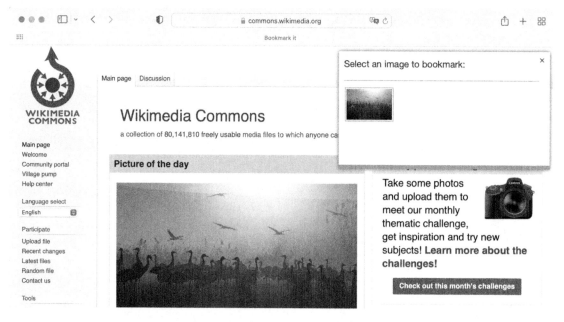

Figure 6.12: The bookmarklet loaded on an external website

If you click on an image, you will be redirected to the image creation page, passing the title of the website and the URL of the selected image as GET parameters. The page will look as follows:

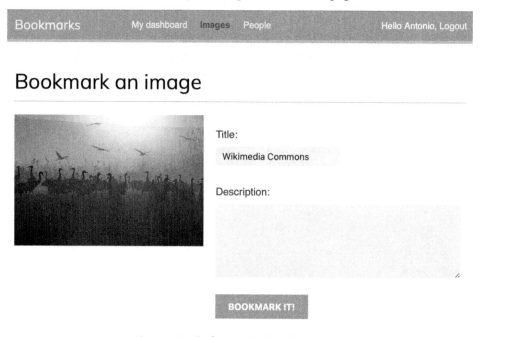

Figure 6.13: The form to bookmark an image

Congratulations! This is your first JavaScript bookmarklet, and it is fully integrated into your Django project. Next, we will create the detail view for images and implement the canonical URL for images.

Creating a detail view for images

Let's now create a simple detail view to display images that have been bookmarked on the site. Open the views.py file of the images application and add the following code to it:

```python
from django.shortcuts import get_object_or_404
from .models import Image


def image_detail(request, id, slug):
    image = get_object_or_404(Image, id=id, slug=slug)
    return render(request,
                  'images/image/detail.html',
                  {'section': 'images',
                   'image': image})
```

This is a simple view to display an image. Edit the urls.py file of the images application and add the following URL pattern highlighted in bold:

```python
urlpatterns = [
    path('create/', views.image_create, name='create'),
    path('detail/<int:id>/<slug:slug>/',
        views.image_detail, name='detail'),
]
```

Edit the models.py file of the images application and add the get_absolute_url() method to the Image model, as follows:

```python
from django.urls import reverse

class Image(models.Model):
    # ...
    def get_absolute_url(self):
        return reverse('images:detail', args=[self.id,
                                              self.slug])
```

Remember that the common pattern for providing canonical URLs for objects is to define a get_absolute_url() method in the model.

Finally, create a template inside the `/templates/images/image/` template directory for the `images` application and name it `detail.html`. Add the following code to it:

```
{% extends "base.html" %}

{% block title %}{{ image.title }}{% endblock %}

{% block content %}
  <h1>{{ image.title }}</h1>
  <img src="{{ image.image.url }}" class="image-detail">
  {% with total_likes=image.users_like.count %}
    <div class="image-info">
      <div>
        <span class="count">
          {{ total_likes }} like{{ total_likes|pluralize }}
        </span>
      </div>
      {{ image.description|linebreaks }}
    </div>
    <div class="image-likes">
      {% for user in image.users_like.all %}
        <div>
          {% if user.profile.photo %}
            <img src="{{ user.profile.photo.url }}">
          {% endif %}
          <p>{{ user.first_name }}</p>
        </div>
      {% empty %}
        Nobody likes this image yet.
      {% endfor %}
    </div>
  {% endwith %}
{% endblock %}
```

This is the template to display the detail view of a bookmarked image. We have used the `{% with %}` tag to create the `total_likes` variable with the result of a QuerySet that counts all user likes. By doing so, we avoid evaluating the same QuerySet twice (first to display the total number of likes, then to use the `pluralize` template filter). We have also included the image description and we have added a `{% for %}` loop to iterate over `image.users_like.all` to display all the users who like this image.

Whenever you need to repeat a query in your template, use the `{% with %}` template tag to avoid additional database queries.

Now, open an external URL in your browser and use the bookmarklet to bookmark a new image. You will be redirected to the image detail page after you post the image. The page will include a success message, as follows:

Bookmarks	My dashboard **Images** People	Hello Antonio, Logout

Image added successfully

Wikimedia Commons

A flock of cranes (Grus grus) in Hula Valley, Northern Israel.

Nobody likes this image yet.

Figure 6.14: The image detail page for the image bookmark

Great! You completed the bookmarklet functionality. Next, you will learn how to create thumbnails for images.

Creating image thumbnails using easy-thumbnails

We are displaying the original image on the detail page, but dimensions for different images may vary considerably. The file size for some images may be very large, and loading them might take too long. The best way to display optimized images in a uniform manner is to generate thumbnails. A thumbnail is a small image representation of a larger image. Thumbnails will load faster in the browser and are a great way to homogenize images of very different sizes. We will use a Django application called easy-thumbnails to generate thumbnails for the images bookmarked by users.

Open the terminal and install `easy-thumbnails` using the following command:

```
pip install easy-thumbnails==2.8.1
```

Edit the `settings.py` file of the bookmarks project and add `easy_thumbnails` to the `INSTALLED_APPS` setting, as follows:

```
INSTALLED_APPS = [
    # ...
    'easy_thumbnails',
]
```

Then, run the following command to sync the application with your database:

```
python manage.py migrate
```

You will see an output that includes the following lines:

```
Applying easy_thumbnails.0001_initial... OK
Applying easy_thumbnails.0002_thumbnaildimensions... OK
```

The `easy-thumbnails` application offers you different ways to define image thumbnails. The application provides a `{% thumbnail %}` template tag to generate thumbnails in templates and a custom `ImageField` if you want to define thumbnails in your models. Let's use the template tag approach.

Edit the `images/image/detail.html` template and consider the following line:

```
<img src="{{ image.image.url }}" class="image-detail">
```

The following lines should replace the preceding one:

```
{% load thumbnail %}
<a href="{{ image.image.url }}">
  <img src="{% thumbnail image.image 300x0 %}" class="image-detail">
</a>
```

We have defined a thumbnail with a fixed width of `300` pixels and a flexible height to maintain the aspect ratio by using the value `0`. The first time a user loads this page, a thumbnail image will be created. The thumbnail is stored in the same directory as the original file. The location is defined by the `MEDIA_ROOT` setting and the `upload_to` attribute of the `image` field of the `Image` model. The generated thumbnail will then be served in the following requests.

Run the development server with the following command from the shell prompt:

```
python manage.py runserver_plus --cert-file cert.crt
```

Access the image detail page for an existing image. The thumbnail will be generated and displayed on the site. Right-click on the image and open it in a new browser tab as follows:

Django and Duke

Figure 6.15: Open the image in a new browser tab

Check the URL of the generated image in your browser. It should look as follows:

🔒 127.0.0.1:8000/media/images/2022/01/10/django-and-duke.jpg.300x0_q85.jpg ↻

Figure 6.16: The URL of the generated image

The original filename is followed by additional details of the settings used to create the thumbnail. For a JPEG image, you will see a filename like `filename.jpg.300x0_q85.jpg`, where `300x0` are the size parameters used to generate the thumbnail, and `85` is the value for the default JPEG quality used by the library to generate the thumbnail.

You can use a different quality value using the `quality` parameter. To set the highest JPEG quality, you can use the value `100`, like this: `{% thumbnail image.image 300x0 quality=100 %}`. A higher quality will imply a larger file size.

The `easy-thumbnails` application offers several options to customize your thumbnails, including cropping algorithms and different effects that can be applied. If you run into any issues generating thumbnails, you can add `THUMBNAIL_DEBUG = True` to the `settings.py` file to obtain the debug information. You can read the full documentation of `easy-thumbnails` at `https://easy-thumbnails.readthedocs.io/`.

Adding asynchronous actions with JavaScript

We are going to add a *like* button to the image detail page to let users click on it to like an image. When users click the *like* button, we will send an HTTP request to the web server using JavaScript. This will perform the like action without reloading the whole page. For this functionality, we will implement a view that allows users to like/unlike images.

The JavaScript **Fetch API** is the built-in way to make asynchronous HTTP requests to web servers from web browsers. By using the Fetch API, you can send and retrieve data from the web server without the need for a whole page refresh. The Fetch API was launched as a modern successor to the browser built-in `XMLHttpRequest` (XHR) object, used to make HTTP requests without reloading the page. The set of web development techniques to send and retrieve data from a web server asynchronously without reloading the page is also known as **AJAX**, which stands for **Asynchronous JavaScript and XML**. AJAX is a misleading name because AJAX requests can exchange data not only in XML format but also in formats such as JSON, HTML, and plain text. You might find references to the Fetch API and AJAX indistinctively on the Internet.

You can find information about the Fetch API at `https://developer.mozilla.org/en-US/docs/Web/API/Fetch_API/Using_Fetch`.

We will start by implementing the view to perform the *like* and *unlike* actions, and then we will add the JavaScript code to the related template to perform asynchronous HTTP requests.

Edit the `views.py` file of the `images` application and add the following code to it:

```
from django.http import JsonResponse
from django.views.decorators.http import require_POST

@login_required
@require_POST
def image_like(request):
    image_id = request.POST.get('id')
    action = request.POST.get('action')
    if image_id and action:
        try:
            image = Image.objects.get(id=image_id)
```

```
            if action == 'like':
                image.users_like.add(request.user)
            else:
                image.users_like.remove(request.user)
            return JsonResponse({'status': 'ok'})
        except Image.DoesNotExist:
            pass
    return JsonResponse({'status': 'error'})
```

We have used two decorators for the new view. The login_required decorator prevents users who are not logged in from accessing this view. The require_POST decorator returns an HttpResponseNotAllowed object (status code 405) if the HTTP request is not done via POST. This way, you only allow POST requests for this view.

Django also provides a require_GET decorator to only allow GET requests and a require_http_methods decorator to which you can pass a list of allowed methods as an argument.

This view expects the following POST parameters:

- image_id: The ID of the image object on which the user is performing the action
- action: The action that the user wants to perform, which should be a string with the value like or unlike

We have used the manager provided by Django for the users_like many-to-many field of the Image model in order to add or remove objects from the relationship using the add() or remove() methods. If the add() method is called passing an object that is already present in the related object set, it will not be duplicated. If the remove() method is called with an object that is not in the related object set, nothing will happen. Another useful method of many-to-many managers is clear(), which removes all objects from the related object set.

To generate the view response, we have used the JsonResponse class provided by Django, which returns an HTTP response with an application/json content type, converting the given object into a JSON output.

Edit the urls.py file of the images application and add the following URL pattern highlighted in bold:

```
urlpatterns = [
    path('create/', views.image_create, name='create'),
    path('detail/<int:id>/<slug:slug>/',
        views.image_detail, name='detail'),
    path('like/', views.image_like, name='like'),
]
```

Loading JavaScript on the DOM

We need to add JavaScript code to the image detail template. To use JavaScript in our templates, we will add a base wrapper in the base.html template of the project first.

Edit the base.html template of the account application and include the following code highlighted in bold before the closing </body> HTML tag:

```html
<!DOCTYPE html>
<html>
<head>
  ...
</head>
<body>
  ...
  <script>
    document.addEventListener('DOMContentLoaded', (event) => {
      // DOM loaded
      {% block domready %}
      {% endblock %}
    })
  </script>
</body>
</html>
```

We have added a <script> tag to include JavaScript code. The document.addEventListener() method is used to define a function that will be called when the given event is triggered. We pass the event name DOMContentLoaded, which fires when the initial HTML document has been completely loaded and the **Document Object Model (DOM)** hierarchy has been fully constructed. By using this event, we make sure the DOM is fully constructed before we interact with any HTML elements and we manipulate the DOM. The code within the function will only be executed once the DOM is ready.

Inside the document-ready handler, we have included a Django template block called domready. Any template that extends the base.html template can use this block to include specific JavaScript code to execute when the DOM is ready.

Don't get confused by the JavaScript code and Django template tags. The Django template language is rendered on the server side to generate the HTML document, and JavaScript is executed in the browser on the client side. In some cases, it is useful to generate JavaScript code dynamically using Django, to be able to use the results of QuerySets or server-side calculations to define variables in JavaScript.

The examples in this chapter include JavaScript code in Django templates. The preferred method to add JavaScript code to your templates is by loading .js files, which are served as static files, especially if you are using large scripts.

Cross-site request forgery for HTTP requests in JavaScript

You learned about **cross-site request forgery (CSRF)** in *Chapter 2, Enhancing Your Blog with Advanced Features*. With CSRF protection active, Django looks for a CSRF token in all POST requests. When you submit forms, you can use the {% csrf_token %} template tag to send the token along with the form. HTTP requests made in JavaScript have to pass the CSRF token as well in every POST request.

Django allows you to set a custom `X-CSRFToken` header in your HTTP requests with the value of the CSRF token.

To include the token in HTTP requests that originate from JavaScript, we will need to retrieve the CSRF token from the `csrftoken` cookie, which is set by Django if the CSRF protection is active. To handle cookies, we will use the JavaScript Cookie library. JavaScript Cookie is a lightweight JavaScript API for handling cookies. You can learn more about it at `https://github.com/js-cookie/js-cookie`.

Edit the `base.html` template of the `account` application and add the following code highlighted in bold at the bottom of the `<body>` element like this:

```html
<!DOCTYPE html>
<html>
<head>
  ...
</head>
<body>
  ...
  <script src="//cdn.jsdelivr.net/npm/js-cookie@3.0.1/dist/js.cookie.min.js"></script>
  <script>
    const csrftoken = Cookies.get('csrftoken');
    document.addEventListener('DOMContentLoaded', (event) => {
      // DOM loaded
      {% block domready %}
      {% endblock %}
    })
  </script>
</body>
</html>
```

We have implemented the following functionality:

1. The JS Cookie plugin is loaded from a public **Content Delivery Network (CDN)**.
2. The value of the `csrftoken` cookie is retrieved with `Cookies.get()` and stored in the JavaScript constant `csrftoken`.

We have to include the CSRF token in all JavaScript fetch requests that use unsafe HTTP methods, such as `POST` or `PUT`. We will later include the `csrftoken` constant in a custom HTTP header named `X-CSRFToken` when sending HTTP `POST` requests.

You can find more information about Django's CSRF protection and AJAX at `https://docs.djangoproject.com/en/4.1/ref/csrf/#ajax`.

Next, we will implement the HTML and JavaScript code for users to like/unlike images.

Performing HTTP requests with JavaScript

Edit the images/image/detail.html template and add the following code highlighted in bold:

```
{% extends "base.html" %}

{% block title %}{{ image.title }}{% endblock %}

{% block content %}
  <h1>{{ image.title }}</h1>
  {% load thumbnail %}
  <a href="{{ image.image.url }}">
    <img src="{% thumbnail image.image 300x0 %}" class="image-detail">
  </a>
  {% with total_likes=image.users_like.count users_like=image.users_like.all %}
    <div class="image-info">
      <div>
        <span class="count">
        <span class="total">{{ total_likes }}</span>
        like{{ total_likes|pluralize }}
        </span>
        <a href="#" data-id="{{ image.id }}" data-action="{% if request.user in
users_like %}un{% endif %}like"
    class="like button">
          {% if request.user not in users_like %}
          Like
          {% else %}
          Unlike
          {% endif %}
        </a>
      </div>
      {{ image.description|linebreaks }}
    </div>
    <div class="image-likes">
      {% for user in users_like %}
        <div>
          {% if user.profile.photo %}
            <img src="{{ user.profile.photo.url }}">
          {% endif %}
          <p>{{ user.first_name }}</p>
        </div>
      {% empty %}
```

```
        Nobody likes this image yet.
      {% endfor %}
    </div>
  {% endwith %}
{% endblock %}
```

In the preceding code, we have added another variable to the {% with %} template tag to store the results of the image.users_like.all query and avoid executing the query against the database multiple times. This variable is used to check if the current user is in this list with {% if request.user in users_like %} and then with {% if request.user not in users_like %}. The same variable is then used to iterate over the users that like this image with {% for user in users_like %}.

We have added to this page the total number of users who like the image and have included a link for the user to like/unlike the image. The related object set, users_like, is used to check whether request.user is contained in the related object set, to display the text *Like* or *Unlike* based on the current relationship between the user and this image. We have added the following attributes to the <a> HTML link element:

- data-id: The ID of the image displayed.
- data-action: The action to perform when the user clicks on the link. This can be either like or unlike.

 Any attribute on any HTML element with a name that starts with data- is a data attribute. Data attributes are used to store custom data for your application.

We will send the value of the data-id and data-action attributes in the HTTP request to the image_like view. When a user clicks on the like/unlike link, we will need to perform the following actions in the browser:

1. Send an HTTP POST request to the image_like view, passing the image id and the action parameters to it.
2. If the HTTP request is successful, update the data-action attribute of the <a> HTML element with the opposite action (like / unlike), and modify its display text accordingly.
3. Update the total number of likes displayed on the page.

Add the following domready block at the bottom of the images/image/detail.html template:

```
{% block domready %}
  const url = '{% url "images:like" %}';
  var options = {
    method: 'POST',
    headers: {'X-CSRFToken': csrftoken},
    mode: 'same-origin'
```

```
    }

    document.querySelector('a.like')
            .addEventListener('click', function(e){
        e.preventDefault();
        var likeButton = this;
    });
{% endblock %}
```

The preceding code works as follows:

1. The `{% url %}` template tag is used to build the `images:like` URL. The generated URL is stored in the `url` JavaScript constant.
2. An `options` object is created with the options that will be passed to the HTTP request with the Fetch API. These are:

    •   `method`: The HTTP method to use. In this case, it's `POST`.
    •   `headers`: Additional HTTP headers to include in the request. We include the `X-CSRFToken` header with the value of the `csrftoken` constant that we defined in the `base.html` template.
    •   `mode`: The mode of the HTTP request. We use `same-origin` to indicate the request is made to the same origin. You can find more information about modes at `https://developer.mozilla.org/en-US/docs/Web/API/Request/mode`.

3. The `a.like` selector is used to find all `<a>` elements of the HTML document with the `like` class using `document.querySelector()`.
4. An event listener is defined for the `click` event on the elements targeted with the selector. This function is executed every time the user clicks on the `like/unlike` link.
5. Inside the handler function, `e.preventDefault()` is used to avoid the default behavior of the `<a>` element. This will prevent the default behavior of the link element, stopping the event propagation, and preventing the link from following the URL.
6. A variable `likeButton` is used to store the reference to `this`, the element on which the event was triggered.

Now we need to send the HTTP request using the Fetch API. Edit the `domready` block of the `images/image/detail.html` template and add the following code highlighted in bold:

```
{% block domready %}
  const url = '{% url "images:like" %}';
  var options = {
    method: 'POST',
    headers: {'X-CSRFToken': csrftoken},
    mode: 'same-origin'
  }
```

```
document.querySelector('a.like')
        .addEventListener('click', function(e){
    e.preventDefault();
    var likeButton = this;

    // add request body
    var formData = new FormData();
    formData.append('id', likeButton.dataset.id);
    formData.append('action', likeButton.dataset.action);
    options['body'] = formData;

    // send HTTP request
    fetch(url, options)
    .then(response => response.json())
    .then(data => {
      if (data['status'] === 'ok')
      {
      }
    })
  });
{% endblock %}
```

The new code works as follows:

1. A FormData object is created to construct a set of key/value pairs representing form fields and their values. The object is stored in the formData variable.

2. The id and action parameters expected by the image_like Django view are added to the formData object. The values for these parameters are retrieved from the likeButton element clicked. The data-id and data-action attributes are accessed with dataset.id and dataset.action.

3. A new body key is added to the options object that will be used for the HTTP request. The value for this key is the formData object.

4. The Fetch API is used by calling the fetch() function. The url variable defined previously is passed as the URL for the request, and the options object is passed as the options for the request.

5. The fetch() function returns a promise that resolves with a Response object, which is a representation of the HTTP response. The .then() method is used to define a handler for the promise. To extract the JSON body content we use response.json(). You can learn more about the Response object at https://developer.mozilla.org/en-US/docs/Web/API/Response.

6. The .then() method is used again to define a handler for the data extracted to JSON. In this handler, the status attribute of the data received is used to check whether its value is ok.

You added the functionality to send the HTTP request and handle the response. After a successful request, you need to change the button and its related action to the opposite: from *like* to *unlike*, or from *unlike* to *like*. By doing so, users are able to undo their action.

Edit the `domready` block of the `images/image/detail.html` template and add the following code highlighted in bold:

```
{% block domready %}
  var url = '{% url "images:like" %}';
  var options = {
    method: 'POST',
    headers: {'X-CSRFToken': csrftoken},
    mode: 'same-origin'
  }

  document.querySelector('a.like')
          .addEventListener('click', function(e){
    e.preventDefault();
    var likeButton = this;

    // add request body
    var formData = new FormData();
    formData.append('id', likeButton.dataset.id);
    formData.append('action', likeButton.dataset.action);
    options['body'] = formData;

    // send HTTP request
    fetch(url, options)
    .then(response => response.json())
    .then(data => {
      if (data['status'] === 'ok')
      {
        var previousAction = likeButton.dataset.action;

        // toggle button text and data-action
        var action = previousAction === 'like' ? 'unlike' : 'like';
        likeButton.dataset.action = action;
        likeButton.innerHTML = action;

        // update like count
        var likeCount = document.querySelector('span.count .total');
        var totalLikes = parseInt(likeCount.innerHTML);
```

```
        likeCount.innerHTML = previousAction === 'like' ? totalLikes + 1 :
totalLikes - 1;
      }
    })
  });
{% endblock %}
```

The preceding code works as follows:

1. The previous action of the button is retrieved from the `data-action` attribute of the link and it is stored in the `previousAction` variable.

2. The `data-action` attribute of the link and the link text are toggled. This allows users to undo their action.

3. The total like count is retrieved from the DOM by using the selector `span.count.total` and the value is parsed to an integer with `parseInt()`. The total like count is increased or decreased according to the action performed (*like* or *unlike*).

Open the image detail page in your browser for an image that you have uploaded. You should be able to see the following initial likes count and the **LIKE** button, as follows:

Figure 6.17: The likes count and LIKE button in the image detail template

Click on the **LIKE** button. You will note that the total likes count increases by one and the button text changes to **UNLIKE**, as follows:

Figure 6.18: The likes count and button after clicking the LIKE button

If you click on the **UNLIKE** button, the action is performed, and then the button's text changes back to **LIKE** and the total count changes accordingly.

When programming JavaScript, especially when performing AJAX requests, it is recommended to use a tool for debugging JavaScript and HTTP requests. Most modern browsers include developer tools to debug JavaScript. Usually, you can right-click anywhere on the website to open the contextual menu and click on **Inspect** or **Inspect Element** to access the web developer tools of your browser.

In the next section, you will learn how to use asynchronous HTTP requests with JavaScript and Django to implement infinite scroll pagination.

Adding infinite scroll pagination to the image list

Next, we need to list all bookmarked images on the website. We will use JavaScript requests to build an infinite scroll functionality. Infinite scroll is achieved by loading the next results automatically when the user scrolls to the bottom of the page.

Let's implement an image list view that will handle both standard browser requests and requests originating from JavaScript. When the user initially loads the image list page, we will display the first page of images. When they scroll to the bottom of the page, we will retrieve the following page of items with JavaScript and append it to the bottom of the main page.

The same view will handle both standard and AJAX infinite scroll pagination. Edit the `views.py` file of the `images` application and add the following code highlighted in bold:

```python
from django.http import HttpResponse
from django.core.paginator import Paginator, EmptyPage, \
                                  PageNotAnInteger

# ...

@login_required
def image_list(request):
    images = Image.objects.all()
    paginator = Paginator(images, 8)
    page = request.GET.get('page')
    images_only = request.GET.get('images_only')
    try:
        images = paginator.page(page)
    except PageNotAnInteger:
        # If page is not an integer deliver the first page
        images = paginator.page(1)
    except EmptyPage:
        if images_only:
            # If AJAX request and page out of range
            # return an empty page
            return HttpResponse('')
        # If page out of range return last page of results
        images = paginator.page(paginator.num_pages)
    if images_only:
        return render(request,
                      'images/image/list_images.html',
                      {'section': 'images',
                       'images': images})
```

```
    return render(request,
                  'images/image/list.html',
                  {'section': 'images',
                   'images': images})
```

In this view, a QuerySet is created to retrieve all images from the database. Then, a `Paginator` object is created to paginate over the results, retrieving eight images per page. The `page` HTTP GET parameter is retrieved to get the requested page number. The `images_only` HTTP GET parameter is retrieved to know if the whole page has to be rendered or only the new images. We will render the whole page when it is requested by the browser. However, we will only render the HTML with new images for Fetch API requests, since we will be appending them to the existing HTML page.

An `EmptyPage` exception will be triggered if the requested page is out of range. If this is the case and only images have to be rendered, an empty `HttpResponse` will be returned. This will allow you to stop the AJAX pagination on the client side when reaching the last page. The results are rendered using two different templates:

- For JavaScript HTTP requests, that will include the `images_only` parameter, the `list_images.html` template will be rendered. This template will only contain the images of the requested page.
- For browser requests, the `list.html` template will be rendered. This template will extend the `base.html` template to display the whole page and will include the `list_images.html` template to include the list of images.

Edit the `urls.py` file of the `images` application and add the following URL pattern highlighted in bold:

```
urlpatterns = [
    path('create/', views.image_create, name='create'),
    path('detail/<int:id>/<slug:slug>/',
         views.image_detail, name='detail'),
    path('like/', views.image_like, name='like'),
    path('', views.image_list, name='list'),
]
```

Finally, you need to create the templates mentioned here. Inside the `images/image/` template directory, create a new template and name it `list_images.html`. Add the following code to it:

```
{% load thumbnail %}
{% for image in images %}
  <div class="image">
    <a href="{{ image.get_absolute_url }}">
      {% thumbnail image.image 300x300 crop="smart" as im %}
      <a href="{{ image.get_absolute_url }}">
        <img src="{{ im.url }}">
      </a>
    </a>
```

```
      <div class="info">
        <a href="{{ image.get_absolute_url }}" class="title">
          {{ image.title }}
        </a>
      </div>
    </div>
  {% endfor %}
```

The preceding template displays the list of images. You will use it to return results for AJAX requests. In this code, you iterate over images and generate a square thumbnail for each image. You normalize the size of the thumbnails to 300x300 pixels. You also use the smart cropping option. This option indicates that the image has to be incrementally cropped down to the requested size by removing slices from the edges with the least entropy.

Create another template in the same directory and name it images/image/list.html. Add the following code to it:

```
{% extends "base.html" %}

{% block title %}Images bookmarked{% endblock %}

{% block content %}
  <h1>Images bookmarked</h1>
  <div id="image-list">
    {% include "images/image/list_images.html" %}
  </div>
{% endblock %}
```

The list template extends the base.html template. To avoid repeating code, you include the images/image/list_images.html template for displaying images. The images/image/list.html template will hold the JavaScript code for loading additional pages when scrolling to the bottom of the page.

Edit the images/image/list.html template and add the following code highlighted in bold:

```
{% extends "base.html" %}

{% block title %}Images bookmarked{% endblock %}

{% block content %}
  <h1>Images bookmarked</h1>
  <div id="image-list">
    {% include "images/image/list_images.html" %}
  </div>
{% endblock %}
```

```
{% block domready %}
  var page = 1;
  var emptyPage = false;
  var blockRequest = false;

  window.addEventListener('scroll', function(e) {
    var margin = document.body.clientHeight - window.innerHeight - 200;
    if(window.pageYOffset > margin && !emptyPage && !blockRequest) {
      blockRequest = true;
      page += 1;

      fetch('?images_only=1&page=' + page)
      .then(response => response.text())
      .then(html => {
        if (html === '') {
          emptyPage = true;
        }
        else {
          var imageList = document.getElementById('image-list');
          imageList.insertAdjacentHTML('beforeEnd', html);
          blockRequest = false;
        }
      })
    }
  });

  // Launch scroll event
  const scrollEvent = new Event('scroll');
  window.dispatchEvent(scrollEvent);
{% endblock %}
```

The preceding code provides the infinite scroll functionality. You include the JavaScript code in the domready block that you defined in the base.html template. The code is as follows:

1. You define the following variables:

   - page: Stores the current page number.
   - empty_page: Allows you to know whether the user is on the last page and retrieves an empty page. As soon as you get an empty page, you will stop sending additional HTTP requests because you will assume that there are no more results.
   - block_request: Prevents you from sending additional requests while an HTTP request is in progress.

2. You use `window.addEventListener()` to capture the `scroll` event and to define a handler function for it.

3. You calculate the `margin` variable to get the difference between the total document height and the window inner height, because that's the height of the remaining content for the user to scroll. You subtract a value of `200` from the result so that you load the next page when the user is closer than 200 pixels to the bottom of the page.

4. Before sending an HTTP request, you check that:

    *   The offset `window.pageYOffset` is higher than the calculated margin.
    *   The user didn't get to the last page of results (`emptyPage` has to be `false`).
    *   There is no other ongoing HTTP request (`blockRequest` has to be `false`).

5. If the previous conditions are met, you set `blockRequest` to `true` to prevent the `scroll` event from triggering additional HTTP requests, and you increase the page counter by `1` to retrieve the next page.

6. You use `fetch()` to send an HTTP `GET` request, setting the URL parameters `image_only=1` to retrieve only the HTML for images instead of the whole HTML page, and `page` for the requested page number.

7. The body content is extracted from the HTTP response with `response.text()` and the HTML returned is treated accordingly:

    *   **If the response has no content:** You got to the end of the results, and there are no more pages to load. You set `emptyPage` to `true` to prevent additional HTTP requests.
    *   **If the response contains data:** You append the data to the HTML element with the `image-list` ID. The page content expands vertically, appending results when the user approaches the bottom of the page. You remove the lock for additional HTTP requests by setting `blockRequest` to `false`.

8. Below the event listener, you simulate an initial `scroll` event when the page is loaded. You create the event by creating a new `Event` object, and then you launch it with `window.dispatchEvent()`. By doing this, you ensure that the event is triggered if the initial content fits the window and has no scroll.

Open `https://127.0.0.1:8000/images/` in your browser. You will see the list of images that you have bookmarked so far. It should look similar to this:

Figure 6.19: The image list page with infinite scroll pagination

Figure 6.19 image attributions:

- *Chick Corea* by ataelw (license: Creative Commons Attribution 2.0 Generic: https://creativecommons.org/licenses/by/2.0/)
- *Al Jarreau – Düsseldorf 1981* by Eddi Laumanns aka RX-Guru (license: Creative Commons Attribution 3.0 Unported: https://creativecommons.org/licenses/by/3.0/)
- *Al Jarreau* by Kingkongphoto & www.celebrity-photos.com (license: Creative Commons Attribution-ShareAlike 2.0 Generic: https://creativecommons.org/licenses/by-sa/2.0/)

Scroll to the bottom of the page to load additional pages. Ensure that you have bookmarked more than eight images using the bookmarklet, because that's the number of images you are displaying per page.

You can use your browser developer tools to track the AJAX requests. Usually, you can right-click anywhere on the website to open the contextual menu and click on **Inspect** or **Inspect Element** to access the web developer tools of your browser. Look for the panel for network requests. Reload the page and scroll to the bottom of the page to load new pages. You will see the request for the first page and the AJAX requests for additional pages, like in *Figure 6.20*:

Name	Status	Type	▲	Initiator	Size	Time
▤ images/	200	document		Other	6.7 kB	205 ms
☐ ?images_only=1&page=2	200	fetch		(index):170	4.8 kB	674 ms
☐ ?images_only=1&page=3	200	fetch		(index):170	993 B	6 ms
☐ ?images_only=1&page=4	200	fetch		(index):170	295 B	4 ms

Figure 6.20: HTTP requests registered in the developer tools of the browser

In the shell where you are running Django, you will see the requests as well like this:

```
[08/Aug/2022 08:14:20] "GET /images/ HTTP/1.1" 200
[08/Aug/2022 08:14:25] "GET /images/?images_only=1&page=2 HTTP/1.1" 200
[08/Aug/2022 08:14:26] "GET /images/?images_only=1&page=3 HTTP/1.1" 200
[08/Aug/2022 08:14:26] "GET /images/?images_only=1&page=4 HTTP/1.1" 200
```

Finally, edit the base.html template of the account application and add the URL for the images item highlighted in bold:

```
<ul class="menu">
  ...
  <li {% if section == "images" %}class="selected"{% endif %}>
    <a href="{% url "images:list" %}">Images</a>
  </li>
  ...
</ul>
```

Now you can access the image list from the main menu.

Additional resources

The following resources provide additional information related to the topics covered in this chapter:

- Source code for this chapter – https://github.com/PacktPublishing/Django-4-by-example/tree/main/Chapter06

- Database indexes – https://docs.djangoproject.com/en/4.1/ref/models/options/#django.db.models.Options.indexes

- Many-to-many relationships – https://docs.djangoproject.com/en/4.1/topics/db/examples/many_to_many/

- Requests HTTP library for Python – https://docs.djangoproject.com/en/4.1/topics/db/examples/many_to_many/

- Pinterest browser button – https://about.pinterest.com/en/browser-button

- Static content for the account application – https://github.com/PacktPublishing/Django-4-by-Example/tree/main/Chapter06/bookmarks/images/static

- CSS selectors – https://developer.mozilla.org/en-US/docs/Web/CSS/CSS_Selectors

- Locate DOM elements using CSS selectors – https://developer.mozilla.org/en-US/docs/Web/API/Document_object_model/Locating_DOM_elements_using_selectors

- *Let's Encrypt* free automated certificate authority – https://letsencrypt.org

- Django easy-thumbnails app – https://easy-thumbnails.readthedocs.io/

- JavaScript Fetch API usage – https://developer.mozilla.org/en-US/docs/Web/API/Fetch_API/Using_Fetch

- JavaScript Cookie library – https://github.com/js-cookie/js-cookie

- Django's CSRF protection and AJAX – https://docs.djangoproject.com/en/4.1/ref/csrf/#ajax

- JavaScript Fetch API Request mode – https://developer.mozilla.org/en-US/docs/Web/API/Request/mode

- JavaScript Fetch API Response – https://developer.mozilla.org/en-US/docs/Web/API/Response

Summary

In this chapter, you created models with many-to-many relationships and learned how to customize the behavior of forms. You built a JavaScript bookmarklet to share images from other websites on your site. This chapter has also covered the creation of image thumbnails using the `easy-thumbnails` application. Finally, you implemented AJAX views using the JavaScript Fetch API and added infinite scroll pagination to the image list view.

In the next chapter, you will learn how to build a follow system and an activity stream. You will work with generic relations, signals, and denormalization. You will also learn how to use Redis with Django to count image views and generate an image ranking.

7

Tracking User Actions

In the previous chapter, you built a JavaScript bookmarklet to share content from other websites on your platform. You also implemented asynchronous actions with JavaScript in your project and created an infinite scroll.

In this chapter, you will learn how to build a follow system and create a user activity stream. You will also discover how Django signals work and integrate Redis's fast I/O storage into your project to store item views.

This chapter will cover the following points:

- Building a follow system
- Creating many-to-many relationships with an intermediary model
- Creating an activity stream application
- Adding generic relations to models
- Optimizing QuerySets for related objects
- Using signals for denormalizing counts
- Using Django Debug Toolbar to obtain relevant debug information
- Counting image views with Redis
- Creating a ranking of the most viewed images with Redis

The source code for this chapter can be found at https://github.com/PacktPublishing/Django-4-by-example/tree/main/Chapter07.

All Python packages used in this chapter are included in the requirements.txt file in the source code for the chapter. You can follow the instructions to install each Python package in the following sections, or you can install all requirements at once with the command pip install -r requirements.txt.

Building a follow system

Let's build a follow system in your project. This means that your users will be able to follow each other and track what other users share on the platform. The relationship between users is a many-to-many relationship: a user can follow multiple users and they, in turn, can be followed by multiple users.

Creating many-to-many relationships with an intermediary model

In previous chapters, you created many-to-many relationships by adding the ManyToManyField to one of the related models and letting Django create the database table for the relationship. This is suitable for most cases, but sometimes you may need to create an intermediary model for the relationship. Creating an intermediary model is necessary when you want to store additional information about the relationship, for example, the date when the relationship was created, or a field that describes the nature of the relationship.

Let's create an intermediary model to build relationships between users. There are two reasons for using an intermediary model:

- You are using the User model provided by Django and you want to avoid altering it
- You want to store the time when the relationship was created

Edit the models.py file of the account application and add the following code to it:

```
class Contact(models.Model):
    user_from = models.ForeignKey('auth.User',
                                  related_name='rel_from_set',
                                  on_delete=models.CASCADE)
    user_to = models.ForeignKey('auth.User',
                                related_name='rel_to_set',
                                on_delete=models.CASCADE)
    created = models.DateTimeField(auto_now_add=True)

    class Meta:
        indexes = [
            models.Index(fields=['-created']),
        ]
        ordering = ['-created']

    def __str__(self):
        return f'{self.user_from} follows {self.user_to}'
```

The preceding code shows the Contact model that you will use for user relationships. It contains the following fields:

- user_from: A ForeignKey for the user who creates the relationship
- user_to: A ForeignKey for the user being followed
- created: A DateTimeField field with auto_now_add=True to store the time when the relationship was created

A database index is automatically created on the ForeignKey fields. In the Meta class of the model, we have defined a database index in descending order for the created field. We have also added the ordering attribute to tell Django that it should sort results by the created field by default. We indicate descending order by using a hyphen before the field name, like -created.

Using the ORM, you could create a relationship for a user, user1, following another user, user2, like this:

```
user1 = User.objects.get(id=1)
user2 = User.objects.get(id=2)
Contact.objects.create(user_from=user1, user_to=user2)
```

The related managers, rel_from_set and rel_to_set, will return a QuerySet for the Contact model. In order to access the end side of the relationship from the User model, it would be desirable for User to contain a ManyToManyField, as follows:

```
following = models.ManyToManyField('self',
                                    through=Contact,
                                    related_name='followers',
                                    symmetrical=False)
```

In the preceding example, you tell Django to use your custom intermediary model for the relationship by adding through=Contact to the ManyToManyField. This is a many-to-many relationship from the User model to itself; you refer to 'self' in the ManyToManyField field to create a relationship to the same model.

 When you need additional fields in a many-to-many relationship, create a custom model with a ForeignKey for each side of the relationship. Add a ManyToManyField in one of the related models and indicate to Django that your intermediary model should be used by including it in the through parameter.

If the User model was part of your application, you could add the previous field to the model. However, you can't alter the User class directly because it belongs to the django.contrib.auth application. Let's take a slightly different approach by adding this field dynamically to the User model.

Edit the models.py file of the account application and add the following lines highlighted in bold:

```
from django.contrib.auth import get_user_model


# ...


# Add following field to User dynamically
user_model = get_user_model()
user_model.add_to_class('following',
                        models.ManyToManyField('self',
                        through=Contact,
                        related_name='followers',
                        symmetrical=False))
```

In the preceding code, you retrieve the user model by using the generic function get_user_model(), which is provided by Django. You use the add_to_class() method of Django models to monkey patch the User model.

Be aware that using add_to_class() is not the recommended way of adding fields to models. However, you take advantage of using it in this case to avoid creating a custom user model, keeping all the advantages of Django's built-in User model.

You also simplify the way that you retrieve related objects using the Django ORM with user.followers. all() and user.following.all(). You use the intermediary Contact model and avoid complex queries that would involve additional database joins, as would have been the case had you defined the relationship in your custom Profile model. The table for this many-to-many relationship will be created using the Contact model. Thus, the ManyToManyField, added dynamically, will not imply any database changes for the Django User model.

Keep in mind that, in most cases, it is preferable to add fields to the Profile model you created before, instead of monkey patching the User model. Ideally, you shouldn't alter the existing Django User model. Django allows you to use custom user models. If you want to use a custom user model, take a look at the documentation at https://docs.djangoproject.com/en/4.1/topics/auth/ customizing/#specifying-a-custom-user-model.

Note that the relationship includes symmetrical=False. When you define a ManyToManyField in the model creating a relationship with itself, Django forces the relationship to be symmetrical. In this case, you are setting symmetrical=False to define a non-symmetrical relationship (if I follow you, it doesn't mean that you automatically follow me).

 When you use an intermediary model for many-to-many relationships, some of the related manager's methods are disabled, such as add(), create(), or remove(). You need to create or delete instances of the intermediary model instead.

Run the following command to generate the initial migrations for the account application:

```
python manage.py makemigrations account
```

You will obtain an output like the following one:

```
Migrations for 'account':
  account/migrations/0002_auto_20220124_1106.py
    - Create model Contact
    - Create index account_con_created_8bdae6_idx on field(s) -created of model
contact
```

Now, run the following command to sync the application with the database:

```
python manage.py migrate account
```

You should see an output that includes the following line:

```
Applying account.0002_auto_20220124_1106... OK
```

The `Contact` model is now synced to the database, and you are able to create relationships between users. However, your site doesn't offer a way to browse users or see a particular user's profile yet. Let's build list and detail views for the `User` model.

Creating list and detail views for user profiles

Open the `views.py` file of the `account` application and add the following code highlighted in bold:

```python
from django.shortcuts import get_object_or_404
from django.contrib.auth.models import User


# ...


@login_required
def user_list(request):
    users = User.objects.filter(is_active=True)
    return render(request,
                  'account/user/list.html',
                  {'section': 'people',
                   'users': users})


@login_required
def user_detail(request, username):
    user = get_object_or_404(User,
                             username=username,
                             is_active=True)
    return render(request,
                  'account/user/detail.html',
                  {'section': 'people',
                   'user': user})
```

These are simple list and detail views for `User` objects. The `user_list` view gets all active users. The Django `User` model contains an `is_active` flag to designate whether the user account is considered active. You filter the query by `is_active=True` to return only active users. This view returns all results, but you can improve it by adding pagination in the same way as you did for the `image_list` view.

The `user_detail` view uses the `get_object_or_404()` shortcut to retrieve the active user with the given username. The view returns an HTTP 404 response if no active user with the given username is found.

Edit the `urls.py` file of the `account` application, and add a URL pattern for each view, as follows. New code is highlighted in bold:

```python
urlpatterns = [
    # ...
    path('', include('django.contrib.auth.urls')),
```

```
    path('', views.dashboard, name='dashboard'),
    path('register/', views.register, name='register'),
    path('edit/', views.edit, name='edit'),
    path('users/', views.user_list, name='user_list'),
    path('users/<username>/', views.user_detail, name='user_detail'),
]
```

You will use the user_detail URL pattern to generate the canonical URL for users. You have already defined a get_absolute_url() method in a model to return the canonical URL for each object. Another way to specify the URL for a model is by adding the ABSOLUTE_URL_OVERRIDES setting to your project.

Edit the settings.py file of your project and add the following code highlighted in bold:

```
from django.urls import reverse_lazy


# ...


ABSOLUTE_URL_OVERRIDES = {
    'auth.user': lambda u: reverse_lazy('user_detail',
                                        args=[u.username])
}
```

Django adds a get_absolute_url() method dynamically to any models that appear in the ABSOLUTE_URL_OVERRIDES setting. This method returns the corresponding URL for the given model specified in the setting. You return the user_detail URL for the given user. Now, you can use get_absolute_url() on a User instance to retrieve its corresponding URL.

Open the Python shell with the following command:

```
python manage.py shell
```

Then run the following code to test it:

```
>>> from django.contrib.auth.models import User
>>> user = User.objects.latest('id')
>>> str(user.get_absolute_url())
'/account/users/ellington/'
```

The returned URL follows the expected format /account/users/<username>/.

You will need to create templates for the views that you just built. Add the following directory and files to the templates/account/ directory of the account application:

```
/user/
    detail.html
    list.html
```

Edit the `account/user/list.html` template and add the following code to it:

```
{% extends "base.html" %}
{% load thumbnail %}

{% block title %}People{% endblock %}

{% block content %}
  <h1>People</h1>
  <div id="people-list">
    {% for user in users %}
      <div class="user">
        <a href="{{ user.get_absolute_url }}">
          <img src="{% thumbnail user.profile.photo 180x180 %}">
        </a>
        <div class="info">
          <a href="{{ user.get_absolute_url }}" class="title">
            {{ user.get_full_name }}
          </a>
        </div>
      </div>
    {% endfor %}
  </div>
{% endblock %}
```

The preceding template allows you to list all the active users on the site. You iterate over the given users and use the `{% thumbnail %}` template tag from `easy-thumbnails` to generate profile image thumbnails.

Note that the users need to have a profile image. To use a default image for users that don't have a profile image, you can add an `if/else` statement to check whether the user has a profile photo, like `{% if user.profile.photo %} {# photo thumbnail #} {% else %} {# default image #} {% endif %}`.

Open the `base.html` template of your project and include the `user_list` URL in the `href` attribute of the following menu item. New code is highlighted in bold:

```
<ul class="menu">
  ...
  <li {% if section == "people" %}class="selected"{% endif %}>
    <a href="{% url "user_list" %}">People</a>
  </li>
</ul>
```

Start the development server with the following command:

```
python manage.py runserver
```

Open `http://127.0.0.1:8000/account/users/` in your browser. You should see a list of users like the following one:

People

Tesla   Einstein   Turing

Figure 7.1: The user list page with profile image thumbnails

Remember that if you have any difficulty generating thumbnails, you can add `THUMBNAIL_DEBUG = True` to your `settings.py` file in order to obtain debug information in the shell.

Edit the `account/user/detail.html` template of the account application and add the following code to it:

```
{% extends "base.html" %}
{% load thumbnail %}

{% block title %}{{ user.get_full_name }}{% endblock %}

{% block content %}
  <h1>{{ user.get_full_name }}</h1>
  <div class="profile-info">
    <img src="{% thumbnail user.profile.photo 180x180 %}" class="user-detail">
  </div>
  {% with total_followers=user.followers.count %}
    <span class="count">
      <span class="total">{{ total_followers }}</span>
      follower{{ total_followers|pluralize }}
    </span>
    <a href="#" data-id="{{ user.id }}" data-action="{% if request.user in
user.followers.all %}un{% endif %}follow" class="follow button">
```

```
        {% if request.user not in user.followers.all %}
          Follow
        {% else %}
          Unfollow
        {% endif %}
      </a>
      <div id="image-list" class="image-container">
        {% include "images/image/list_images.html" with images=user.images_
  created.all %}
      </div>
    {% endwith %}
  {% endblock %}
```

Make sure that no template tag is split onto multiple lines; Django doesn't support multiple-line tags.

In the detail template, the user profile is displayed and the {% thumbnail %} template tag is used to show the profile image. The total number of followers is presented and a link to follow or unfollow the user. This link will be used to follow/unfollow a particular user. The data-id and data-action attributes of the <a> HTML element contain the user ID and the initial action to perform when the link element is clicked – follow or unfollow. The initial action (*follow* or *unfollow*) depends on whether the user requesting the page is already a follower of the user. The images bookmarked by the user are displayed by including the images/image/list_images.html template.

Open your browser again and click on a user who has bookmarked some images. The user page will look as follows:

Figure 7.2: The user detail page

Image of *Chick Corea* by ataelw (license: Creative Commons Attribution 2.0 Generic: `https://creativecommons.org/licenses/by/2.0/`)

Adding user follow/unfollow actions with JavaScript

Let's add functionality to follow/unfollow users. We will create a new view to follow/unfollow users and implement an asynchronous HTTP request with JavaScript for the follow/unfollow action.

Edit the `views.py` file of the `account` application and add the following code highlighted in bold:

```python
from django.http import JsonResponse
from django.views.decorators.http import require_POST
from .models import Contact


# ...


@require_POST
@login_required
def user_follow(request):
    user_id = request.POST.get('id')
    action = request.POST.get('action')
    if user_id and action:
        try:
            user = User.objects.get(id=user_id)
            if action == 'follow':
                Contact.objects.get_or_create(
                    user_from=request.user,
                    user_to=user)
            else:
                Contact.objects.filter(user_from=request.user,
                                       user_to=user).delete()
            return JsonResponse({'status':'ok'})
        except User.DoesNotExist:
            return JsonResponse({'status':'error'})
    return JsonResponse({'status':'error'})
```

The `user_follow` view is quite similar to the `image_like` view that you created in *Chapter 6, Sharing Content on Your Website*. Since you are using a custom intermediary model for the user's many-to-many relationship, the default `add()` and `remove()` methods of the automatic manager of `ManyToManyField` are not available. Instead, the intermediary `Contact` model is used to create or delete user relationships.

Edit the `urls.py` file of the `account` application and add the following URL pattern highlighted in bold:

```
urlpatterns = [
    path('', include('django.contrib.auth.urls')),
    path('', views.dashboard, name='dashboard'),
    path('register/', views.register, name='register'),
    path('edit/', views.edit, name='edit'),
    path('users/', views.user_list, name='user_list'),
    path('users/follow/', views.user_follow, name='user_follow'),
    path('users/<username>/', views.user_detail, name='user_detail'),

]
```

Ensure that you place the preceding pattern before the `user_detail` URL pattern. Otherwise, any requests to `/users/follow/` will match the regular expression of the `user_detail` pattern and that view will be executed instead. Remember that in every HTTP request, Django checks the requested URL against each pattern in order of appearance and stops at the first match.

Edit the `user/detail.html` template of the `account` application and append the following code to it:

```
{% block domready %}
  var const = '{% url "user_follow" %}';
  var options = {
    method: 'POST',
    headers: {'X-CSRFToken': csrftoken},
    mode: 'same-origin'
  }

  document.querySelector('a.follow')
          .addEventListener('click', function(e){
    e.preventDefault();
    var followButton = this;

    // add request body
    var formData = new FormData();
    formData.append('id', followButton.dataset.id);
    formData.append('action', followButton.dataset.action);
    options['body'] = formData;

    // send HTTP request
    fetch(url, options)
    .then(response => response.json())
    .then(data => {
      if (data['status'] === 'ok')
```

```
    {
        var previousAction = followButton.dataset.action;

        // toggle button text and data-action
        var action = previousAction === 'follow' ? 'unfollow' : 'follow';
        followButton.dataset.action = action;
        followButton.innerHTML = action;

        // update follower count
        var followerCount = document.querySelector('span.count .total');
        var totalFollowers = parseInt(followerCount.innerHTML);
        followerCount.innerHTML = previousAction === 'follow' ? totalFollowers
+ 1 : totalFollowers - 1;
    }
  })
});
{% endblock %}
```

The preceding template block contains the JavaScript code to perform the asynchronous HTTP request to follow or unfollow a particular user and also to toggle the follow/unfollow link. The Fetch API is used to perform the AJAX request and set both the data-action attribute and the text of the HTML <a> element based on its previous value. When the action is completed, the total number of followers displayed on the page is updated as well.

Open the user detail page of an existing user and click on the **FOLLOW** link to test the functionality you just built. You will see that the followers count is increased:

Figure 7.3: The followers count and follow/unfollow button

The follow system is now complete, and users can follow each other. Next, we will build an activity stream creating relevant content for each user that is based on the people they follow.

Building a generic activity stream application

Many social websites display an activity stream to their users so that they can track what other users do on the platform. An activity stream is a list of recent activities performed by a user or a group of users. For example, Facebook's News Feed is an activity stream. Sample actions can be *user X bookmarked image Y* or *user X is now following user Y*.

You are going to build an activity stream application so that every user can see the recent interactions of the users they follow. To do so, you will need a model to save the actions performed by users on the website and a simple way to add actions to the feed.

Create a new application named actions inside your project with the following command:

```
python manage.py startapp actions
```

Add the new application to INSTALLED_APPS in the settings.py file of your project to activate the application in your project. The new line is highlighted in bold:

```
INSTALLED_APPS = [
    # ...
    'actions.apps.ActionsConfig',
]
```

Edit the models.py file of the actions application and add the following code to it:

```python
from django.db import models


class Action(models.Model):
    user = models.ForeignKey('auth.User',
                             related_name='actions',
                             on_delete=models.CASCADE)
    verb = models.CharField(max_length=255)
    created = models.DateTimeField(auto_now_add=True)

    class Meta:
        indexes = [
            models.Index(fields=['-created']),
        ]
        ordering = ['-created']
```

The preceding code shows the Action model that will be used to store user activities. The fields of this model are as follows:

- user: The user who performed the action; this is a ForeignKey to the Django User model.
- verb: The verb describing the action that the user has performed.
- created: The date and time when this action was created. We use auto_now_add=True to automatically set this to the current datetime when the object is saved for the first time in the database.

In the Meta class of the model, we have defined a database index in descending order for the created field. We have also added the ordering attribute to tell Django that it should sort results by the created field in descending order by default.

With this basic model, you can only store actions such as *user X did something*. You need an extra ForeignKey field to save actions that involve a target object, such as *user X bookmarked image Y* or *user X is now following user Y*. As you already know, a normal ForeignKey can point to only one model. Instead, you will need a way for the action's target object to be an instance of an existing model. This is what the Django contenttypes framework will help you to do.

Using the contenttypes framework

Django includes a `contenttypes` framework located at `django.contrib.contenttypes`. This application can track all models installed in your project and provides a generic interface to interact with your models.

The `django.contrib.contenttypes` application is included in the `INSTALLED_APPS` setting by default when you create a new project using the `startproject` command. It is used by other `contrib` packages, such as the authentication framework and the administration application.

The `contenttypes` application contains a `ContentType` model. Instances of this model represent the actual models of your application, and new instances of `ContentType` are automatically created when new models are installed in your project. The `ContentType` model has the following fields:

- `app_label`: This indicates the name of the application that the model belongs to. This is automatically taken from the `app_label` attribute of the model `Meta` options. For example, your `Image` model belongs to the `images` application.
- `model`: The name of the model class.
- `name`: This indicates the human-readable name of the model. This is automatically taken from the `verbose_name` attribute of the model `Meta` options.

Let's take a look at how you can interact with `ContentType` objects. Open the shell using the following command:

```
python manage.py shell
```

You can obtain the `ContentType` object corresponding to a specific model by performing a query with the `app_label` and `model` attributes, as follows:

```
>>> from django.contrib.contenttypes.models import ContentType
>>> image_type = ContentType.objects.get(app_label='images', model='image')
>>> image_type
<ContentType: images | image>
```

You can also retrieve the model class from a `ContentType` object by calling its `model_class()` method:

```
>>> image_type.model_class()
<class 'images.models.Image'>
```

It's also common to obtain the `ContentType` object for a particular model class, as follows:

```
>>> from images.models import Image
>>> ContentType.objects.get_for_model(Image)
<ContentType: images | image>
```

These are just some examples of using `contenttypes`. Django offers more ways to work with them. You can find the official documentation for the `contenttypes` framework at `https://docs.djangoproject.com/en/4.1/ref/contrib/contenttypes/`.

Adding generic relations to your models

In generic relations, ContentType objects play the role of pointing to the model used for the relationship. You will need three fields to set up a generic relation in a model:

- A ForeignKey field to ContentType: This will tell you the model for the relationship
- A field to store the primary key of the related object: This will usually be a PositiveIntegerField to match Django's automatic primary key fields
- A field to define and manage the generic relation using the two previous fields: The contenttypes framework offers a GenericForeignKey field for this purpose

Edit the models.py file of the actions application and add the following code highlighted in bold:

```python
from django.db import models
from django.contrib.contenttypes.models import ContentType
from django.contrib.contenttypes.fields import GenericForeignKey


class Action(models.Model):
    user = models.ForeignKey('auth.User',
                                related_name='actions',
                                on_delete=models.CASCADE)
    verb = models.CharField(max_length=255)
    created = models.DateTimeField(auto_now_add=True)
    target_ct = models.ForeignKey(ContentType,
                                    blank=True,
                                    null=True,
                                    related_name='target_obj',
                                    on_delete=models.CASCADE)
    target_id = models.PositiveIntegerField(null=True,
                                                blank=True)
    target = GenericForeignKey('target_ct', 'target_id')

    class Meta:
        indexes = [
            models.Index(fields=['-created']),
            models.Index(fields=['target_ct', 'target_id']),
        ]
        ordering = ['-created']
```

We have added the following fields to the `Action` model:

- `target_ct`: A `ForeignKey` field that points to the `ContentType` model
- `target_id`: A `PositiveIntegerField` for storing the primary key of the related object
- `target`: A `GenericForeignKey` field to the related object based on the combination of the two previous fields

We have also added a multiple-field index including the `target_ct` and `target_id` fields.

Django does not create `GenericForeignKey` fields in the database. The only fields that are mapped to database fields are `target_ct` and `target_id`. Both fields have `blank=True` and `null=True` attributes, so that a `target` object is not required when saving `Action` objects.

 You can make your applications more flexible by using generic relations instead of foreign keys.

Run the following command to create initial migrations for this application:

```
python manage.py makemigrations actions
```

You should see the following output:

```
Migrations for 'actions':
  actions/migrations/0001_initial.py
    - Create model Action
    - Create index actions_act_created_64f10d_idx on field(s) -created of model
action
    - Create index actions_act_target__f20513_idx on field(s) target_ct,
target_id of model action
```

Then, run the next command to sync the application with the database:

```
python manage.py migrate
```

The output of the command should indicate that the new migrations have been applied, as follows:

```
Applying actions.0001_initial... OK
```

Let's add the `Action` model to the administration site. Edit the `admin.py` file of the `actions` application and add the following code to it:

```python
from django.contrib import admin
from .models import Action


@admin.register(Action)
class ActionAdmin(admin.ModelAdmin):
```

```
list_display = ['user', 'verb', 'target', 'created']
list_filter = ['created']
search_fields = ['verb']
```

You just registered the Action model on the administration site.

Start the development server with the following command:

```
python manage.py runserver
```

Open http://127.0.0.1:8000/admin/actions/action/add/ in your browser. You should see the page for creating a new Action object, as follows:

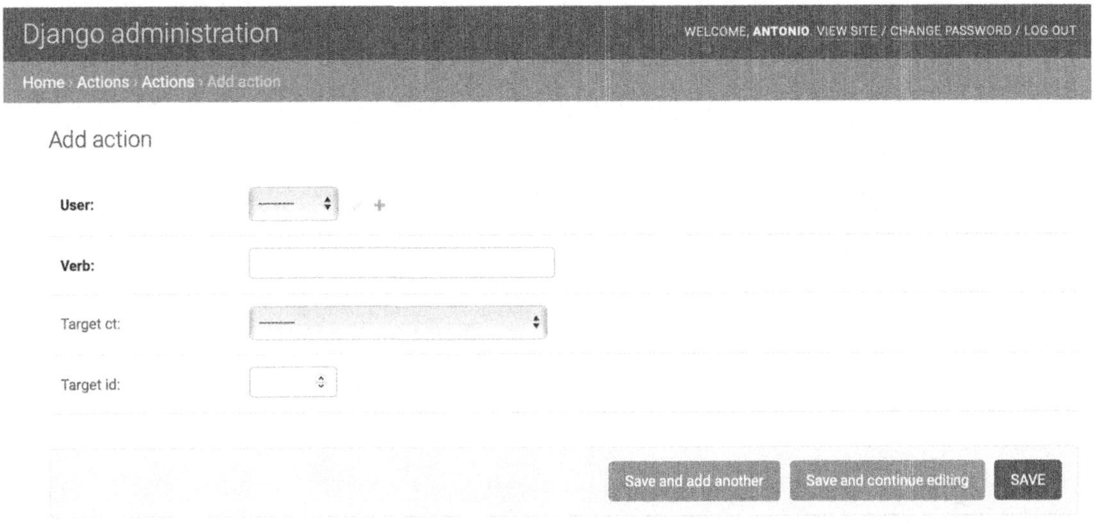

Figure 7.4: The Add action page on the Django administration site

As you will notice in the preceding screenshot, only the target_ct and target_id fields that are mapped to actual database fields are shown. The GenericForeignKey field does not appear in the form. The target_ct field allows you to select any of the registered models of your Django project. You can restrict the content types to choose from a limited set of models using the limit_choices_to attribute in the target_ct field; the limit_choices_to attribute allows you to restrict the content of ForeignKey fields to a specific set of values.

Create a new file inside the actions application directory and name it utils.py. You need to define a shortcut function that will allow you to create new Action objects in a simple way. Edit the new utils. py file and add the following code to it:

```
from django.contrib.contenttypes.models import ContentType
from .models import Action

def create_action(user, verb, target=None):
    action = Action(user=user, verb=verb, target=target)
    action.save()
```

The create_action() function allows you to create actions that optionally include a target object. You can use this function anywhere in your code as a shortcut to add new actions to the activity stream.

Avoiding duplicate actions in the activity stream

Sometimes, your users might click several times on the **Like** or **Unlike** button or perform the same action multiple times in a short period of time. This will easily lead to storing and displaying duplicate actions. To avoid this, let's improve the create_action() function to skip obvious duplicated actions.

Edit the utils.py file of the actions application, as follows:

```python
import datetime
from django.utils import timezone
from django.contrib.contenttypes.models import ContentType
from .models import Action


def create_action(user, verb, target=None):
    # check for any similar action made in the last minute
    now = timezone.now()
    last_minute = now - datetime.timedelta(seconds=60)
    similar_actions = Action.objects.filter(user_id=user.id,
                                            verb= verb,
                                            created__gte=last_minute)
    if target:
        target_ct = ContentType.objects.get_for_model(target)
        similar_actions = similar_actions.filter(
                                            target_ct=target_ct,
                                            target_id=target.id)
    if not similar_actions:
        # no existing actions found
        action = Action(user=user, verb=verb, target=target)
        action.save()
        return True
    return False
```

You have changed the create_action() function to avoid saving duplicate actions and return a Boolean to tell you whether the action was saved. This is how you avoid duplicates:

1. First, you get the current time using the timezone.now() method provided by Django. This method does the same as datetime.datetime.now() but returns a timezone-aware object. Django provides a setting called USE_TZ to enable or disable timezone support. The default settings.py file created using the startproject command includes USE_TZ=True.

2. You use the last_minute variable to store the datetime from one minute ago and retrieve any identical actions performed by the user since then.

3. You create an `Action` object if no identical action already exists in the last minute. You return `True` if an `Action` object was created, or `False` otherwise.

Adding user actions to the activity stream

It's time to add some actions to your views to build the activity stream for your users. You will store an action for each of the following interactions:

- A user bookmarks an image
- A user likes an image
- A user creates an account
- A user starts following another user

Edit the `views.py` file of the `images` application and add the following import:

```
from actions.utils import create_action
```

In the `image_create` view, add `create_action()` after saving the image, like this. The new line is highlighted in bold:

```
@login_required
def image_create(request):
    if request.method == 'POST':
        # form is sent
        form = ImageCreateForm(data=request.POST)
        if form.is_valid():
            # form data is valid
            cd = form.cleaned_data
            new_image = form.save(commit=False)
            # assign current user to the item
            new_image.user = request.user
            new_image.save()
            create_action(request.user, 'bookmarked image', new_image)
            messages.success(request, 'Image added successfully')
            # redirect to new created image detail view
            return redirect(new_image.get_absolute_url())
    else:
        # build form with data provided by the bookmarklet via GET
        form = ImageCreateForm(data=request.GET)
    return render(request,
                  'images/image/create.html',
                  {'section': 'images',
                   'form': form})
```

In the `image_like` view, add `create_action()` after adding the user to the `users_like` relationship, as follows. The new line is highlighted in bold:

```python
@login_required
@require_POST
def image_like(request):
    image_id = request.POST.get('id')
    action = request.POST.get('action')
    if image_id and action:
        try:
            image = Image.objects.get(id=image_id)
            if action == 'like':
                image.users_like.add(request.user)
                create_action(request.user, 'likes', image)
            else:
                image.users_like.remove(request.user)
            return JsonResponse({'status':'ok'})
        except Image.DoesNotExist:
            pass
    return JsonResponse({'status':'error'})
```

Now, edit the `views.py` file of the account application and add the following import:

```python
from actions.utils import create_action
```

In the `register` view, add `create_action()` after creating the `Profile` object, as follows. The new line is highlighted in bold:

```python
def register(request):
    if request.method == 'POST':
        user_form = UserRegistrationForm(request.POST)
        if user_form.is_valid():
            # Create a new user object but avoid saving it yet
            new_user = user_form.save(commit=False)
            # Set the chosen password
            new_user.set_password(
                user_form.cleaned_data['password'])
            # Save the User object
            new_user.save()
            # Create the user profile
            Profile.objects.create(user=new_user)
            create_action(new_user, 'has created an account')
            return render(request,
```

```
                              'account/register_done.html',
                              {'new_user': new_user})
    else:
        user_form = UserRegistrationForm()
    return render(request,
                  'account/register.html',
                  {'user_form': user_form})
```

In the user_follow view, add create_action() as follows. The new line is highlighted in bold:

```
@require_POST
@login_required
def user_follow(request):
    user_id = request.POST.get('id')
    action = request.POST.get('action')
    if user_id and action:
        try:
            user = User.objects.get(id=user_id)
            if action == 'follow':
                Contact.objects.get_or_create(
                    user_from=request.user,
                    user_to=user)
                create_action(request.user, 'is following', user)
            else:
                Contact.objects.filter(user_from=request.user,
                                       user_to=user).delete()
            return JsonResponse({'status':'ok'})
        except User.DoesNotExist:
            return JsonResponse({'status':'error'})
    return JsonResponse({'status':'error'})
```

As you can see in the preceding code, thanks to the Action model and the helper function, it's very easy to save new actions to the activity stream.

Displaying the activity stream

Finally, you need a way to display the activity stream for each user. You will include the activity stream on the user's dashboard. Edit the views.py file of the account application. Import the Action model and modify the dashboard view, as follows. New code is highlighted in bold:

```
from actions.models import Action

# ...
```

```
@login_required
def dashboard(request):
    # Display all actions by default
    actions = Action.objects.exclude(user=request.user)
    following_ids = request.user.following.values_list('id',
                                                        flat=True)
    if following_ids:
        # If user is following others, retrieve only their actions
        actions = actions.filter(user_id__in=following_ids)
    actions = actions[:10]
    return render(request,
                  'account/dashboard.html',
                  {'section': 'dashboard',
                   'actions': actions})
```

In the preceding view, you retrieve all actions from the database, excluding the ones performed by the current user. By default, you retrieve the latest actions performed by all users on the platform. If the user is following other users, you restrict the query to retrieve only the actions performed by the users they follow. Finally, you limit the result to the first 10 actions returned. You don't use order_by() in the QuerySet because you rely on the default ordering that you provided in the Meta options of the Action model. Recent actions will come first since you set ordering = ['-created'] in the Action model.

Optimizing QuerySets that involve related objects

Every time you retrieve an Action object, you will usually access its related User object and the user's related Profile object. The Django ORM offers a simple way to retrieve related objects at the same time, thereby avoiding additional queries to the database.

Using select_related()

Django offers a QuerySet method called select_related() that allows you to retrieve related objects for one-to-many relationships. This translates to a single, more complex QuerySet, but you avoid additional queries when accessing the related objects. The select_related method is for ForeignKey and OneToOne fields. It works by performing a SQL JOIN and including the fields of the related object in the SELECT statement.

To take advantage of select_related(), edit the following line of the preceding code in the views.py file of the account application to add select_related, including the fields that you will use, like this. Edit the views.py file of the account application. New code is highlighted in bold:

```
@login_required
def dashboard(request):
    # Display all actions by default
    actions = Action.objects.exclude(user=request.user)
    following_ids = request.user.following.values_list('id',
                                                        flat=True)
```

```
    if following_ids:
        # If user is following others, retrieve only their actions
        actions = actions.filter(user_id__in=following_ids)
    actions = actions.select_related('user', 'user__profile')[:10]
    return render(request,
                  'account/dashboard.html',
                  {'section': 'dashboard',
                   'actions': actions})
```

You use user__profile to join the Profile table in a single SQL query. If you call select_related() without passing any arguments to it, it will retrieve objects from all ForeignKey relationships. Always limit select_related() to the relationships that will be accessed afterward.

 Using select_related() carefully can vastly improve execution time.

Using prefetch_related()

select_related() will help you boost the performance for retrieving related objects in one-to-many relationships. However, select_related() doesn't work for many-to-many or many-to-one relationships (ManyToMany or reverse ForeignKey fields). Django offers a different QuerySet method called prefetch_related that works for many-to-many and many-to-one relationships in addition to the relationships supported by select_related(). The prefetch_related() method performs a separate lookup for each relationship and joins the results using Python. This method also supports the prefetching of GenericRelation and GenericForeignKey.

Edit the views.py file of the account application and complete your query by adding prefetch_related() to it for the target GenericForeignKey field, as follows. The new code is highlighted in bold:

```
@login_required
def dashboard(request):
    # Display all actions by default
    actions = Action.objects.exclude(user=request.user)
    following_ids = request.user.following.values_list('id',
                                                       flat=True)
    if following_ids:
        # If user is following others, retrieve only their actions
        actions = actions.filter(user_id__in=following_ids)
    actions = actions.select_related('user', 'user__profile')\
                     .prefetch_related('target')[:10]
    return render(request,
                  'account/dashboard.html',
```

```
                        {'section': 'dashboard',
                         'actions': actions})

    actions = actions.select_related('user', 'user__profile'
```

This query is now optimized for retrieving the user actions, including related objects.

Creating templates for actions

Let's now create the template to display a particular Action object. Create a new directory inside the actions application directory and name it templates. Add the following file structure to it:

```
actions/
    action/
        detail.html
```

Edit the actions/action/detail.html template file and add the following lines to it:

```
{% load thumbnail %}

{% with user=action.user profile=action.user.profile %}
<div class="action">
  <div class="images">
    {% if profile.photo %}
      {% thumbnail user.profile.photo "80x80" crop="100%" as im %}
      <a href="{{ user.get_absolute_url }}">
        <img src="{{ im.url }}" alt="{{ user.get_full_name }}"
        class="item-img">
      </a>
    {% endif %}
    {% if action.target %}
      {% with target=action.target %}
        {% if target.image %}
          {% thumbnail target.image "80x80" crop="100%" as im %}
          <a href="{{ target.get_absolute_url }}">
            <img src="{{ im.url }}" class="item-img">
          </a>
        {% endif %}
      {% endwith %}
    {% endif %}
  </div>
  <div class="info">
    <p>
      <span class="date">{{ action.created|timesince }} ago</span>
```

```
        <br />
        <a href="{{ user.get_absolute_url }}">
          {{ user.first_name }}
        </a>
        {{ action.verb }}
        {% if action.target %}
          {% with target=action.target %}
            <a href="{{ target.get_absolute_url }}">{{ target }}</a>
          {% endwith %}
        {% endif %}
      </p>
    </div>
  </div>
{% endwith %}
```

This is the template used to display an Action object. First, you use the {% with %} template tag to retrieve the user performing the action and the related Profile object. Then, you display the image of the target object if the Action object has a related target object. Finally, you display the link to the user who performed the action, the verb, and the target object, if any.

Edit the account/dashboard.html template of the account application and append the following code highlighted in bold to the bottom of the content block:

```
{% extends "base.html" %}

{% block title %}Dashboard{% endblock %}

{% block content %}

  ...

  <h2>What's happening</h2>
  <div id="action-list">
    {% for action in actions %}
      {% include "actions/action/detail.html" %}
    {% endfor %}
  </div>
{% endblock %}
```

Open http://127.0.0.1:8000/account/ in your browser. Log in as an existing user and perform several actions so that they get stored in the database. Then, log in using another user, follow the previous user, and take a look at the generated action stream on the dashboard page.

It should look like the following:

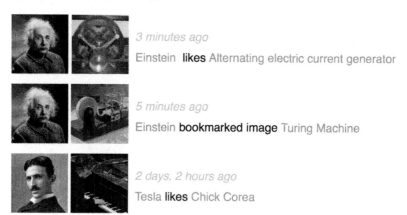

What's happening

3 minutes ago
Einstein **likes** Alternating electric current generator

5 minutes ago
Einstein **bookmarked image** Turing Machine

2 days, 2 hours ago
Tesla **likes** Chick Corea

Figure 7.5: The activity stream for the current user

Figure 7.5 image attributions:

- *Tesla's induction motor by Ctac (license: Creative Commons Attribution Share-Alike 3.0 Unported:* https://creativecommons.org/licenses/by-sa/3.0/)
- *Turing Machine Model Davey 2012 by Rocky Acosta (license: Creative Commons Attribution 3.0 Unported:* https://creativecommons.org/licenses/by/3.0/)
- *Chick Corea* by ataelw (license: Creative Commons Attribution 2.0 Generic: https://creativecommons.org/licenses/by/2.0/)

You just created a complete activity stream for your users, and you can easily add new user actions to it. You can also add infinite scroll functionality to the activity stream by implementing the same AJAX paginator that you used for the image_list view. Next, you will learn how to use Django signals to denormalize action counts.

Using signals for denormalizing counts

There are some cases when you may want to denormalize your data. Denormalization is making data redundant in such a way that it optimizes read performance. For example, you might be copying related data to an object to avoid expensive read queries to the database when retrieving the related data. You have to be careful about denormalization and only start using it when you really need it. The biggest issue you will find with denormalization is that it's difficult to keep your denormalized data updated.

Let's take a look at an example of how to improve your queries by denormalizing counts. You will denormalize data from your Image model and use Django signals to keep the data updated.

Working with signals

Django comes with a signal dispatcher that allows receiver functions to get notified when certain actions occur. Signals are very useful when you need your code to do something every time something else happens. Signals allow you to decouple logic: you can capture a certain action, regardless of the application or code that triggered that action, and implement logic that gets executed whenever that action occurs. For example, you can build a signal receiver function that gets executed every time a User object is saved. You can also create your own signals so that others can get notified when an event happens.

Django provides several signals for models located at `django.db.models.signals`. Some of these signals are as follows:

- `pre_save` and `post_save` are sent before or after calling the `save()` method of a model
- `pre_delete` and `post_delete` are sent before or after calling the `delete()` method of a model or QuerySet
- `m2m_changed` is sent when a `ManyToManyField` on a model is changed

These are just a subset of the signals provided by Django. You can find a list of all built-in signals at `https://docs.djangoproject.com/en/4.1/ref/signals/`.

Let's say you want to retrieve images by popularity. You can use the Django aggregation functions to retrieve images ordered by the number of users who like them. Remember that you used Django aggregation functions in *Chapter 3, Extending Your Blog Application*. The following code example will retrieve images according to their number of likes:

```
from django.db.models import Count
from images.models import Image
images_by_popularity = Image.objects.annotate(
    total_likes=Count('users_like')).order_by('-total_likes')
```

However, ordering images by counting their total `likes` is more expensive in terms of performance than ordering them by a field that stores total counts. You can add a field to the `Image` model to denormalize the total number of likes to boost performance in queries that involve this field. The issue is how to keep this field updated.

Edit the `models.py` file of the `images` application and add the following `total_likes` field to the `Image` model. The new code is highlighted in bold:

```
class Image(models.Model):
    # ...
    total_likes = models.PositiveIntegerField(default=0)

    class Meta:
        indexes = [
            models.Index(fields=['-created']),
```

```
            models.Index(fields=['-total_likes']),
    ]
    ordering = ['-created']
```

The `total_likes` field will allow you to store the total count of users who like each image. Denormalizing counts is useful when you want to filter or order QuerySets by them. We have added a database index for the `total_likes` field in descending order because we plan to retrieve images ordered by their total likes in descending order.

 There are several ways to improve performance that you have to take into account before denormalizing fields. Consider database indexes, query optimization, and caching before starting to denormalize your data.

Run the following command to create the migrations for adding the new field to the database table:

```
python manage.py makemigrations images
```

You should see the following output:

```
Migrations for 'images':
    images/migrations/0002_auto_20220124_1757.py
        - Add field total_likes to image
        - Create index images_imag_total_l_0bcd7e_idx on field(s) -total_likes of
model image
```

Then, run the following command to apply the migration:

```
python manage.py migrate images
```

The output should include the following line:

```
Applying images.0002_auto_20220124_1757... OK
```

You need to attach a `receiver` function to the m2m_changed signal.

Create a new file inside the images application directory and name it `signals.py`. Add the following code to it:

```
from django.db.models.signals import m2m_changed
from django.dispatch import receiver
from .models import Image


@receiver(m2m_changed, sender=Image.users_like.through)
def users_like_changed(sender, instance, **kwargs):
    instance.total_likes = instance.users_like.count()
    instance.save()
```

First, you register the users_like_changed function as a receiver function using the receiver() decorator. You attach it to the m2m_changed signal. Then, you connect the function to Image.users_like.
through so that the function is only called if the m2m_changed signal has been launched by this sender.
There is an alternate method for registering a receiver function; it consists of using the connect()
method of the Signal object.

 Django signals are synchronous and blocking. Don't confuse signals with asynchronous
tasks. However, you can combine both to launch asynchronous tasks when your code
gets notified by a signal. You will learn how to create asynchronous tasks with Celery in
Chapter 8, Building an Online Shop.

You have to connect your receiver function to a signal so that it gets called every time the signal is
sent. The recommended method for registering your signals is by importing them into the ready()
method of your application configuration class. Django provides an application registry that allows
you to configure and introspect your applications.

Application configuration classes

Django allows you to specify configuration classes for your applications. When you create an application using the startapp command, Django adds an apps.py file to the application directory, including
a basic application configuration that inherits from the AppConfig class.

The application configuration class allows you to store metadata and the configuration for the application, and it provides introspection for the application. You can find more information about application
configurations at https://docs.djangoproject.com/en/4.1/ref/applications/.

In order to register your signal receiver functions, when you use the receiver() decorator, you just
need to import the signals module of your application inside the ready() method of the application
configuration class. This method is called as soon as the application registry is fully populated. Any
other initializations for your application should also be included in this method.

Edit the apps.py file of the images application and add the following code highlighted in bold:

```
from django.apps import AppConfig


class ImagesConfig(AppConfig):
    default_auto_field = 'django.db.models.BigAutoField'
    name = 'images'

    def ready(self):
        # import signal handlers
        import images.signals
```

You import the signals for this application in the ready() method so that they are imported when the
images application is loaded.

Run the development server with the following command:

```
python manage.py runserver
```

Open your browser to view an image detail page and click on the **Like** button.

Go to the administration site, navigate to the edit image URL, such as `http://127.0.0.1:8000/admin/images/image/1/change/`, and take a look at the `total_likes` attribute. You should see that the `total_likes` attribute is updated with the total number of users who like the image, as follows:

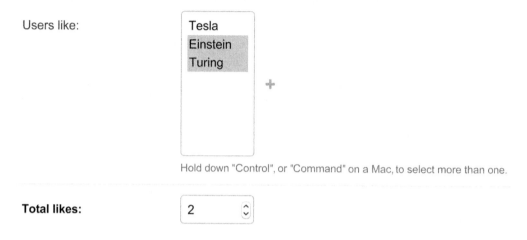

Figure 7.6: The image edit page on the administration site, including denormalization for total likes

Now, you can use the `total_likes` attribute to order images by popularity or display the value anywhere, avoiding using complex queries to calculate it.

Consider the following query to get images ordered by their likes count in descending order:

```
from django.db.models import Count
images_by_popularity = Image.objects.annotate(
    likes=Count('users_like')).order_by('-likes')
```

The preceding query can now be written as follows:

```
images_by_popularity = Image.objects.order_by('-total_likes')
```

This results in a less expensive SQL query thanks to denormalizing the total likes for images. You have also learned how you can use Django signals.

 Use signals with caution since they make it difficult to know the control flow. In many cases, you can avoid using signals if you know which receivers need to be notified.

You will need to set initial counts for the rest of the `Image` objects to match the current status of the database.

Open the shell with the following command:

```
python manage.py shell
```

Execute the following code in the shell:

```
>>> from images.models import Image
>>> for image in Image.objects.all():
...     image.total_likes = image.users_like.count()
...     image.save()
```

You have manually updated the likes count for the existing images in the database. From now on, the users_like_changed signal receiver function will handle updating the total_likes field whenever the many-to-many related objects change.

Next, you will learn how to use Django Debug Toolbar to obtain relevant debug information for requests, including execution time, SQL queries executed, templates rendered, signals registered, and much more.

Using Django Debug Toolbar

At this point, you will already be familiar with Django's debug page. Throughout the previous chapters, you have seen the distinctive yellow and grey Django debug page several times. For example, in *Chapter 2, Enhancing Your Blog with Advanced Features*, in the *Handling pagination errors* section, the debug page showed information related to unhandled exceptions when implementing object pagination.

The Django debug page provides useful debug information. However, there is a Django application that includes more detailed debug information and can be really helpful when developing.

Django Debug Toolbar is an external Django application that allows you to see relevant debug information about the current request/response cycle. The information is divided into multiple panels that show different information, including request/response data, Python package versions used, execution time, settings, headers, SQL queries, templates used, cache, signals, and logging.

You can find the documentation for Django Debug Toolbar at https://django-debug-toolbar.readthedocs.io/.

Installing Django Debug Toolbar

Install django-debug-toolbar via pip using the following command:

```
pip install django-debug-toolbar==3.6.0
```

Edit the settings.py file of your project and add debug_toolbar to the INSTALLED_APPS setting, as follows. The new line is highlighted in bold:

```
INSTALLED_APPS = [
    # ...
    'debug_toolbar',
]
```

In the same file, add the following line highlighted in bold to the `MIDDLEWARE` setting:

```
MIDDLEWARE = [
    'debug_toolbar.middleware.DebugToolbarMiddleware',
    'django.middleware.security.SecurityMiddleware',
    'django.contrib.sessions.middleware.SessionMiddleware',
    'django.middleware.common.CommonMiddleware',
    'django.middleware.csrf.CsrfViewMiddleware',
    'django.contrib.auth.middleware.AuthenticationMiddleware',
    'django.contrib.messages.middleware.MessageMiddleware',
    'django.middleware.clickjacking.XFrameOptionsMiddleware',
]
```

Django Debug Toolbar is mostly implemented as middleware. The order of `MIDDLEWARE` is important. `DebugToolbarMiddleware` has to be placed before any other middleware, except for middleware that encodes the response's content, such as `GZipMiddleware`, which, if present, should come first.

Add the following lines at the end of the `settings.py` file:

```
INTERNAL_IPS = [
    '127.0.0.1',
]
```

Django Debug Toolbar will only display if your IP address matches an entry in the `INTERNAL_IPS` setting. To prevent showing debug information in production, Django Debug Toolbar checks that the `DEBUG` setting is `True`.

Edit the main `urls.py` file of your project and add the following URL pattern highlighted in bold to the `urlpatterns`:

```
urlpatterns = [
    path('admin/', admin.site.urls),
    path('account/', include('account.urls')),
    path('social-auth/',
        include('social_django.urls', namespace='social')),
    path('images/', include('images.urls', namespace='images')),
    path('__debug__/', include('debug_toolbar.urls')),
]
```

Django Debug Toolbar is now installed in your project. Let's try it out!

Run the development server with the following command:

```
python manage.py runserver
```

Open `http://127.0.0.1:8000/images/` with your browser. You should now see a collapsible sidebar on the right. It should look as follows:

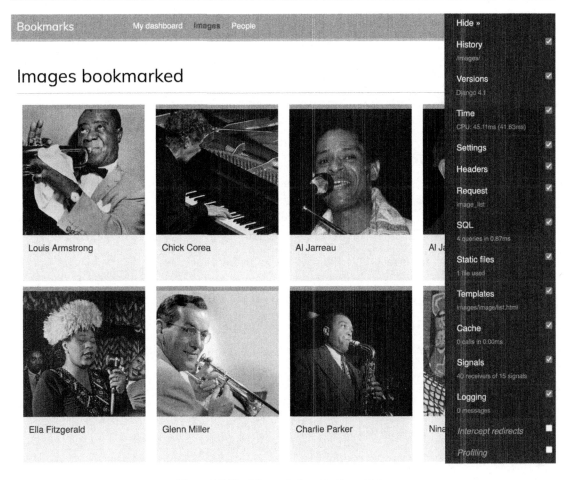

Figure 7.7: The Django Debug Toolbar sidebar

Figure 7.7 image attributions:

- *Chick Corea* by ataelw (license: Creative Commons Attribution 2.0 Generic: `https://creativecommons.org/licenses/by/2.0/`)
- *Al Jarreau – Düsseldorf 1981* by Eddi Laumanns aka RX-Guru (license: Creative Commons Attribution 3.0 Unported: `https://creativecommons.org/licenses/by/3.0/`)
- *Al Jarreau* by Kingkongphoto & www.celebrity-photos.com (license: Creative Commons Attribution-ShareAlike 2.0 Generic: `https://creativecommons.org/licenses/by-sa/2.0/`)

If the debug toolbar doesn't appear, check the RunServer shell console log. If you see a MIME type error, it is most likely that your MIME map files are incorrect or need to be updated.

You can apply the correct mapping for JavaScript and CSS files by adding the following lines to the settings.py file:

```
if DEBUG:
    import mimetypes
    mimetypes.add_type('application/javascript', '.js', True)
    mimetypes.add_type('text/css', '.css', True)
```

Django Debug Toolbar panels

Django Debug Toolbar features multiple panels that organize the debug information for the request/response cycle. The sidebar contains links to each panel, and you can use the checkbox of any panel to activate or deactivate it. The change will be applied to the next request. This is useful when we are not interested in a specific panel, but the calculation adds too much overhead to the request.

Click on **Time** in the sidebar menu. You will see the following panel:

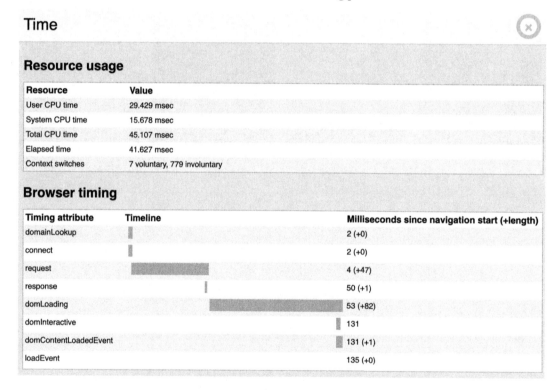

Figure 7.8: Time panel – Django Debug Toolbar

The **Time** panel includes a timer for the different phases of the request/response cycle. It also shows CPU, elapsed time, and the number of context switches. If you are using WIndows, you won't be able to see the **Time** panel. In Windows, only the total time is available and displayed in the toolbar.

Click on **SQL** in the sidebar menu. You will see the following panel:

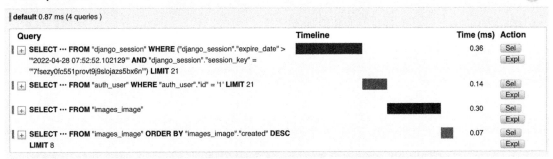

Figure 7.9: SQL panel – Django Debug Toolbar

Here you can see the different SQL queries that have been executed. This information can help you identify unnecessary queries, duplicated queries that can be reused, or long-running queries that can be optimized. Based on your findings, you can improve QuerySets in your views, create new indexes on model fields if necessary, or cache information when needed. In this chapter, you learned how to optimize queries that involve relationships using `select_related()` and `prefetch_related()`. You will learn how to cache data in *Chapter 14, Rendering and Caching Content*.

Click on **Templates** in the sidebar menu. You will see the following panel:

Templates (3 rendered)

Template paths
None

Templates

`images/image/list.html`
/Users/amele/Documents/Django-4-by-example/Chapter07/bookmarks/images/templates/images/image/list.html
▶ Toggle context

`base.html`
/Users/amele/Documents/Django-4-by-example/Chapter07/bookmarks/account/templates/base.html
▶ Toggle context

`images/image/list_images.html`
/Users/amele/Documents/Django-4-by-example/Chapter07/bookmarks/images/templates/images/image/list_images.html
▶ Toggle context

Context processors

django.template.context_processors.csrf
▶ Toggle context

django.template.context_processors.debug
▶ Toggle context

django.template.context_processors.request
▶ Toggle context

django.contrib.auth.context_processors.auth
▶ Toggle context

django.contrib.messages.context_processors.messages
▶ Toggle context

Figure 7.10: Templates panel – Django Debug Toolbar

This panel shows the different templates used when rendering the content, the template paths, and the context used. You can also see the different context processors used. You will learn about context processors in *Chapter 8*, *Building an Online Shop*.

Click on **Signals** in the sidebar menu. You will see the following panel:

Figure 7.11: Signals panel – Django Debug Toolbar

In this panel, you can see all the signals that are registered in your project and the receiver functions attached to each signal. For example, you can find the `users_like_changed` receiver function you created before, attached to the `m2m_changed` signal. The other signals and receivers are part of the different Django applications.

We have reviewed some of the panels that ship with Django Debug Toolbar. Besides the built-in panels, you can find additional third-party panels that you can download and use at https://django-debug-toolbar.readthedocs.io/en/latest/panels.html#third-party-panels.

Django Debug Toolbar commands

Besides the request/response debug panels, Django Debug Toolbar provides a management command to debug SQL for ORM calls. The management command `debugsqlshell` replicates the Django `shell` command but it outputs SQL statements for queries performed with the Django ORM.

Open the shell with the following command:

```
python manage.py debugsqlshell
```

Execute the following code:

```
>>> from images.models import Image
>>> Image.objects.get(id=1)
```

You will see the following output:

```
SELECT "images_image"."id",
       "images_image"."user_id",
       "images_image"."title",
       "images_image"."slug",
       "images_image"."url",
       "images_image"."image",
       "images_image"."description",
       "images_image"."created",
       "images_image"."total_likes"
FROM "images_image"
WHERE "images_image"."id" = 1
LIMIT 21 [0.44ms]
<Image: Django and Duke>
```

You can use this command to test ORM queries before adding them to your views. You can check the resulting SQL statement and the execution time for each ORM call.

In the next section, you will learn how to count image views using Redis, an in-memory database that provides low latency and high-throughput data access.

Counting image views with Redis

Redis is an advanced key/value database that allows you to save different types of data. It also has extremely fast I/O operations. Redis stores everything in memory, but the data can be persisted by dumping the dataset to disk every once in a while, or by adding each command to a log. Redis is very versatile compared to other key/value stores: it provides a set of powerful commands and supports diverse data structures, such as strings, hashes, lists, sets, ordered sets, and even bitmaps or Hyper-LogLogs.

Although SQL is best suited to schema-defined persistent data storage, Redis offers numerous advantages when dealing with rapidly changing data, volatile storage, or when a quick cache is needed. Let's take a look at how Redis can be used to build new functionality into your project.

You can find more information about Redis on its homepage at `https://redis.io/`.

Redis provides a Docker image that makes it very easy to deploy a Redis server with a standard configuration.

Installing Docker

Docker is a popular open-source containerization platform. It enables developers to package applications into containers, simplifying the process of building, running, managing, and distributing applications.

First, download and install Docker for your OS. You will find instructions for downloading and installing Docker on Linux, macOS, and Windows at `https://docs.docker.com/get-docker/`.

Installing Redis

After installing Docker on your Linux, macOS, or Windows machine, you can easily pull the Redis Docker image. Run the following command from the shell:

```
docker pull redis
```

This will download the Redis Docker image to your local machine. You can find information about the official Redis Docker image at `https://hub.docker.com/_/redis`. You can find other alternative methods to install Redis at `https://redis.io/download/`.

Execute the following command in the shell to start the Redis Docker container:

```
docker run -it --rm --name redis -p 6379:6379 redis
```

With this command, we run Redis in a Docker container. The `-it` option tells Docker to take you straight inside the container for interactive input. The `--rm` option tells Docker to automatically clean up the container and remove the file system when the container exits. The `--name` option is used to assign a name to the container. The `-p` option is used to publish the 6379 port, on which Redis runs, to the same host interface port. 6379 is the default port for Redis.

You should see an output that ends with the following lines:

```
# Server initialized
* Ready to accept connections
```

Keep the Redis server running on port 6379 and open another shell. Start the Redis client with the following command:

```
docker exec -it redis sh
```

You will see a line with the hash symbol:

```
#
```

Start the Redis client with the following command:

```
# redis-cli
```

You will see the Redis client shell prompt, like this:

```
127.0.0.1:6379>
```

The Redis client allows you to execute Redis commands directly from the shell. Let's try some commands. Enter the `SET` command in the Redis shell to store a value in a key:

```
127.0.0.1:6379> SET name "Peter"
OK
```

The preceding command creates a `name` key with the string value `"Peter"` in the Redis database. The `OK` output indicates that the key has been saved successfully.

Next, retrieve the value using the `GET` command, as follows:

```
127.0.0.1:6379> GET name
"Peter"
```

You can also check whether a key exists using the `EXISTS` command. This command returns 1 if the given key exists, and 0 otherwise:

```
127.0.0.1:6379> EXISTS name
(integer) 1
```

You can set the time for a key to expire using the `EXPIRE` command, which allows you to set the time-to-live in seconds. Another option is using the `EXPIREAT` command, which expects a Unix timestamp. Key expiration is useful for using Redis as a cache or to store volatile data:

```
127.0.0.1:6379> GET name
"Peter"
127.0.0.1:6379> EXPIRE name 2
(integer) 1
```

Wait for more than two seconds and try to get the same key again:

```
127.0.0.1:6379> GET name
(nil)
```

The `(nil)` response is a null response and means that no key has been found. You can also delete any key using the `DEL` command, as follows:

```
127.0.0.1:6379> SET total 1
OK
127.0.0.1:6379> DEL total
(integer) 1
127.0.0.1:6379> GET total
(nil)
```

These are just basic commands for key operations. You can find all Redis commands at `https://redis.io/commands/` and all Redis data types at `https://redis.io/docs/manual/data-types/`.

Using Redis with Python

You will need Python bindings for Redis. Install `redis-py` via `pip` using the following command:

```
pip install redis==4.3.4
```

You can find the `redis-py` documentation at `https://redis-py.readthedocs.io/`.

The `redis-py` package interacts with Redis, providing a Python interface that follows the Redis command syntax. Open the Python shell with the following command:

```
python manage.py shell
```

Execute the following code:

```
>>> import redis
>>> r = redis.Redis(host='localhost', port=6379, db=0)
```

The preceding code creates a connection with the Redis database. In Redis, databases are identified by an integer index instead of a database name. By default, a client is connected to database 0. The number of available Redis databases is set to 16, but you can change this in the `redis.conf` configuration file.

Next, set a key using the Python shell:

```
>>> r.set('foo', 'bar')
True
```

The command returns `True`, indicating that the key has been successfully created. Now you can retrieve the key using the `get()` command:

```
>>> r.get('foo')
b'bar'
```

As you will note from the preceding code, the methods of `Redis` follow the Redis command syntax.

Let's integrate Redis into your project. Edit the `settings.py` file of the `bookmarks` project and add the following settings to it:

```
REDIS_HOST = 'localhost'
REDIS_PORT = 6379
REDIS_DB = 0
```

These are the settings for the Redis server and the database that you will use for your project.

Storing image views in Redis

Let's find a way to store the total number of times an image has been viewed. If you implement this using the Django ORM, it will involve a SQL UPDATE query every time an image is displayed.

If you use Redis instead, you just need to increment a counter stored in memory, resulting in much better performance and less overhead.

Edit the `views.py` file of the `images` application and add the following code to it after the existing import statements:

```python
import redis
from django.conf import settings


# connect to redis
r = redis.Redis(host=settings.REDIS_HOST,
                port=settings.REDIS_PORT,
                db=settings.REDIS_DB)
```

With the preceding code, you establish the Redis connection in order to use it in your views. Edit the `views.py` file of the `images` application and modify the `image_detail` view, like this. The new code is highlighted in bold:

```python
def image_detail(request, id, slug):
    image = get_object_or_404(Image, id=id, slug=slug)
    # increment total image views by 1
    total_views = r.incr(f'image:{image.id}:views')
    return render(request,
                  'images/image/detail.html',
                  {'section': 'images',
                   'image': image,
                   'total_views': total_views})
```

In this view, you use the `incr` command, which increments the value of a given key by 1. If the key doesn't exist, the `incr` command creates it. The `incr()` method returns the final value of the key after performing the operation. You store the value in the `total_views` variable and pass it into the template context. You build the Redis key using a notation such as `object-type:id:field` (for example, `image:33:id`).

 The convention for naming Redis keys is to use a colon sign as a separator for creating namespaced keys. By doing so, the key names are especially verbose and related keys share part of the same schema in their names.

Edit the `images/image/detail.html` template of the `images` application and add the following code highlighted in bold:

```html
...
<div class="image-info">
  <div>
```

```
      <span class="count">
        <span class="total">{{ total_likes }}</span>
        like{{ total_likes|pluralize }}
      </span>
      <span class="count">
        {{ total_views }} view{{ total_views|pluralize }}
      </span>
      <a href="#" data-id="{{ image.id }}" data-action="{% if request.user in
users_like %}un{% endif %}like"
        class="like button">
          {% if request.user not in users_like %}
            Like
          {% else %}
            Unlike
          {% endif %}
      </a>
    </div>
    {{ image.description|linebreaks }}
  </div>
  ...
```

Run the development server with the following command:

```
python manage.py runserver
```

Open an image detail page in your browser and reload it several times. You will see that each time the view is processed, the total views displayed is incremented by 1. Take a look at the following example:

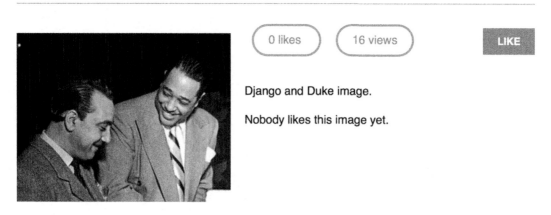

Figure 7.12: The image detail page, including the count of likes and views

Great! You have successfully integrated Redis into your project to count image views. In the next section, you will learn how to build a ranking of the most viewed images with Redis.

Storing a ranking in Redis

We will now create something more complex with Redis. We will use Redis to store a ranking of the most viewed images on the platform. We will use Redis sorted sets for this. A sorted set is a non-repeating collection of strings in which every member is associated with a score. Items are sorted by their score.

Edit the `views.py` file of the `images` application and add the following code highlighted in bold to the `image_detail` view:

```python
def image_detail(request, id, slug):
    image = get_object_or_404(Image, id=id, slug=slug)
    # increment total image views by 1
    total_views = r.incr(f'image:{image.id}:views')
    # increment image ranking by 1
    r.zincrby('image_ranking', 1, image.id)
    return render(request,
                  'images/image/detail.html',
                  {'section': 'images',
                   'image': image,
                   'total_views': total_views})
```

You use the `zincrby()` command to store image views in a sorted set with the `image:ranking` key. You will store the image `id` and a related score of `1`, which will be added to the total score of this element in the sorted set. This will allow you to keep track of all image views globally and have a sorted set ordered by the total number of views.

Now, create a new view to display the ranking of the most viewed images. Add the following code to the `views.py` file of the `images` application:

```python
@login_required
def image_ranking(request):
    # get image ranking dictionary
    image_ranking = r.zrange('image_ranking', 0, -1,
                             desc=True)[:10]
    image_ranking_ids = [int(id) for id in image_ranking]
    # get most viewed images
    most_viewed = list(Image.objects.filter(
                         id__in=image_ranking_ids))
    most_viewed.sort(key=lambda x: image_ranking_ids.index(x.id))
    return render(request,
                  'images/image/ranking.html',
                  {'section': 'images',
                   'most_viewed': most_viewed})
```

The `image_ranking` view works like this:

1. You use the `zrange()` command to obtain the elements in the sorted set. This command expects a custom range according to the lowest and highest scores. Using `0` as the lowest and `-1` as the highest score, you are telling Redis to return all elements in the sorted set. You also specify `desc=True` to retrieve the elements ordered by descending score. Finally, you slice the results using `[:10]` to get the first 10 elements with the highest score.

2. You build a list of returned image IDs and store it in the `image_ranking_ids` variable as a list of integers. You retrieve the `Image` objects for those IDs and force the query to be executed using the `list()` function. It is important to force the QuerySet execution because you will use the `sort()` list method on it (at this point, you need a list of objects instead of a QuerySet).

3. You sort the `Image` objects by their index of appearance in the image ranking. Now you can use the `most_viewed` list in your template to display the 10 most viewed images.

Create a new `ranking.html` template inside the `images/image/` template directory of the images application and add the following code to it:

```
{% extends "base.html" %}

{% block title %}Images ranking{% endblock %}

{% block content %}
  <h1>Images ranking</h1>
  <ol>
    {% for image in most_viewed %}
      <li>
        <a href="{{ image.get_absolute_url }}">
          {{ image.title }}
        </a>
      </li>
    {% endfor %}
  </ol>
{% endblock %}
```

The template is pretty straightforward. You iterate over the `Image` objects contained in the `most_viewed` list and display their names, including a link to the image detail page.

Finally, you need to create a URL pattern for the new view. Edit the `urls.py` file of the images application and add the following URL pattern highlighted in bold:

```
urlpatterns = [
    path('create/', views.image_create, name='create'),
    path('detail/<int:id>/<slug:slug>/',
        views.image_detail, name='detail'),
    path('like/', views.image_like, name='like'),
```

```
        path('', views.image_list, name='list'),
        path('ranking/', views.image_ranking, name='ranking'),
]
```

Run the development server, access your site in your web browser, and load the image detail page multiple times for different images. Then, access http://127.0.0.1:8000/images/ranking/ from your browser. You should be able to see an image ranking, as follows:

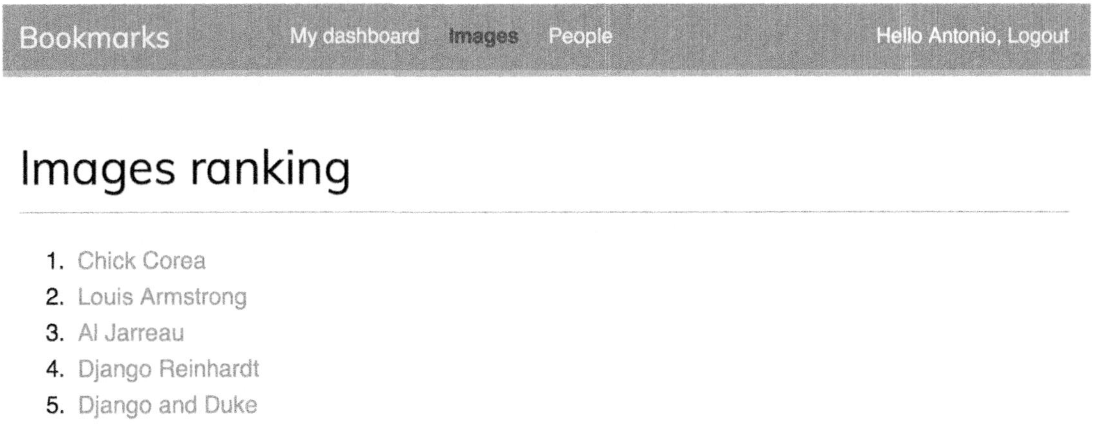

Bookmarks   My dashboard   **Images**   People   Hello Antonio, Logout

Images ranking

1. Chick Corea
2. Louis Armstrong
3. Al Jarreau
4. Django Reinhardt
5. Django and Duke

Figure 7.13: The ranking page built with data retrieved from Redis

Great! You just created a ranking with Redis.

Next steps with Redis

Redis is not a replacement for your SQL database, but it does offer fast in-memory storage that is more suitable for certain tasks. Add it to your stack and use it when you really feel it's needed. The following are some scenarios in which Redis could be useful:

- **Counting:** As you have seen, it is very easy to manage counters with Redis. You can use incr() and incrby() for counting stuff.
- **Storing the latest items:** You can add items to the start/end of a list using lpush() and rpush(). Remove and return the first/last element using lpop()/rpop(). You can trim the list's length using ltrim() to maintain its length.
- **Queues:** In addition to push and pop commands, Redis offers the blocking of queue commands.
- **Caching:** Using expire() and expireat() allows you to use Redis as a cache. You can also find third-party Redis cache backends for Django.
- **Pub/sub:** Redis provides commands for subscribing/unsubscribing and sending messages to channels.
- **Rankings and leaderboards:** Redis' sorted sets with scores make it very easy to create leaderboards.
- **Real-time tracking:** Redis's fast I/O makes it perfect for real-time scenarios.

Additional resources

The following resources provide additional information related to the topics covered in this chapter:

- Source code for this chapter – `https://github.com/PacktPublishing/Django-4-by-example/tree/main/Chapter07`
- Custom user models – `https://docs.djangoproject.com/en/4.1/topics/auth/customizing/#specifying-a-custom-user-model`
- The `contenttypes` framework – `https://docs.djangoproject.com/en/4.1/ref/contrib/contenttypes/`
- Built-in Django signals – `https://docs.djangoproject.com/en/4.1/ref/signals/`
- Application configuration classes – `https://docs.djangoproject.com/en/4.1/ref/applications/`
- Django Debug Toolbar documentation – `https://django-debug-toolbar.readthedocs.io/`
- Django Debug Toolbar third-party panels – `https://django-debug-toolbar.readthedocs.io/en/latest/panels.html#third-party-panels`
- Redis in-memory data store – `https://redis.io/`
- Docker download and install instructions – `https://docs.docker.com/get-docker/`
- Official Redis Docker image — `https://hub.docker.com/_/redis`.
- Redis download options – `https://redis.io/download/`
- Redis commands – `https://redis.io/commands/`
- Redis data types – `https://redis.io/docs/manual/data-types/`
- `redis-py` documentation – `https://redis-py.readthedocs.io/`

Summary

In this chapter, you built a follow system using many-to-many relationships with an intermediary model. You also created an activity stream using generic relations and you optimized QuerySets to retrieve related objects. This chapter then introduced you to Django signals, and you created a signal receiver function to denormalize related object counts. We covered application configuration classes, which you used to load your signal handlers. You added Django Debug Toolbar to your project. You also learned how to install and configure Redis in your Django project. Finally, you used Redis in your project to store item views, and you built an image ranking with Redis.

In the next chapter, you will learn how to build an online shop. You will create a product catalog and build a shopping cart using sessions. You will learn how to create custom context processors. You will also manage customer orders and send asynchronous notifications using Celery and RabbitMQ.

8

Building an Online Shop

In the previous chapter, you created a follow system and built a user activity stream. You also learned how Django signals work and integrated Redis into your project to count image views.

In this chapter, you will start a new Django project that consists of a fully featured online shop. This chapter and the following two chapters will show you how to build the essential functionalities of an e-commerce platform. Your online shop will enable clients to browse products, add them to the cart, apply discount codes, go through the checkout process, pay with a credit card, and obtain an invoice. You will also implement a recommendation engine to recommend products to your customers, and you will use internationalization to offer your site in multiple languages.

In this chapter, you will learn how to:

- Create a product catalog
- Build a shopping cart using Django sessions
- Create custom context processors
- Manage customer orders
- Configure Celery in your project with RabbitMQ as a message broker
- Send asynchronous notifications to customers using Celery
- Monitor Celery using Flower

The source code for this chapter can be found at `https://github.com/PacktPublishing/Django-4-by-example/tree/main/Chapter08`.

All Python modules used in this chapter are included in the `requirements.txt` file in the source code that comes along with this chapter. You can follow the instructions to install each Python module below or you can install all requirements at once with the command `pip install -r requirements.txt`.

Creating an online shop project

Let's start with a new Django project to build an online shop. Your users will be able to browse through a product catalog and add products to a shopping cart. Finally, they will be able to check out the cart and place an order. This chapter will cover the following functionalities of an online shop:

- Creating the product catalog models, adding them to the administration site, and building the basic views to display the catalog
- Building a shopping cart system using Django sessions to allow users to keep selected products while they browse the site
- Creating the form and functionality to place orders on the site
- Sending an asynchronous email confirmation to users when they place an order

Open a shell and use the following command to create a new virtual environment for this project within the env/ directory:

```
python -m venv env/myshop
```

If you are using Linux or macOS, run the following command to activate your virtual environment:

```
source env/myshop/bin/activate
```

If you are using Windows, use the following command instead:

```
.\env\myshop\Scripts\activate
```

The shell prompt will display your active virtual environment, as follows:

```
(myshop)laptop:~ zenx$
```

Install Django in your virtual environment with the following command:

```
pip install Django~=4.1.0
```

Start a new project called myshop with an application called shop by opening a shell and running the following command:

```
django-admin startproject myshop
```

The initial project structure has been created. Use the following commands to get into your project directory and create a new application named shop:

```
cd myshop/
django-admin startapp shop
```

Edit settings.py and add the following line highlighted in bold to the INSTALLED_APPS list:

```
INSTALLED_APPS = [
    'django.contrib.admin',
    'django.contrib.auth',
    'django.contrib.contenttypes',
```

```
    'django.contrib.sessions',
    'django.contrib.messages',
    'django.contrib.staticfiles',
    'shop.apps.ShopConfig',
]
```

Your application is now active for this project. Let's define the models for the product catalog.

Creating product catalog models

The catalog of your shop will consist of products that are organized into different categories. Each product will have a name, an optional description, an optional image, a price, and its availability.

Edit the models.py file of the shop application that you just created and add the following code:

```python
from django.db import models


class Category(models.Model):
    name = models.CharField(max_length=200)
    slug = models.SlugField(max_length=200,
                            unique=True)

    class Meta:
        ordering = ['name']
        indexes = [
            models.Index(fields=['name']),
        ]
        verbose_name = 'category'
        verbose_name_plural = 'categories'

    def __str__(self):
        return self.name

class Product(models.Model):
    category = models.ForeignKey(Category,
                                 related_name='products',
                                 on_delete=models.CASCADE)
    name = models.CharField(max_length=200)
    slug = models.SlugField(max_length=200)
    image = models.ImageField(upload_to='products/%Y/%m/%d',
                              blank=True)
    description = models.TextField(blank=True)
    price = models.DecimalField(max_digits=10,
                                decimal_places=2)
    available = models.BooleanField(default=True)
    created = models.DateTimeField(auto_now_add=True)
```

```
        updated = models.DateTimeField(auto_now=True)

    class Meta:
        ordering = ['name']
        indexes = [
            models.Index(fields=['id', 'slug']),
            models.Index(fields=['name']),
            models.Index(fields=['-created']),
        ]

    def __str__(self):
        return self.name
```

These are the `Category` and `Product` models. The `Category` model consists of a name field and a unique `slug` field (unique implies the creation of an index). In the `Meta` class of the `Category` model, we have defined an index for the `name` field.

The `Product` model fields are as follows:

- `category`: A `ForeignKey` to the `Category` model. This is a one-to-many relationship: a product belongs to one category and a category contains multiple products.
- `name`: The name of the product.
- `slug`: The slug for this product to build beautiful URLs.
- `image`: An optional product image.
- `description`: An optional description of the product.
- `price`: This field uses Python's `decimal.Decimal` type to store a fixed-precision decimal number. The maximum number of digits (including the decimal places) is set using the `max_digits` attribute and decimal places with the `decimal_places` attribute.
- `available`: A Boolean value that indicates whether the product is available or not. It will be used to enable/disable the product in the catalog.
- `created`: This field stores when the object was created.
- `updated`: This field stores when the object was last updated.

For the `price` field, we use `DecimalField` instead of `FloatField` to avoid rounding issues.

 Always use `DecimalField` to store monetary amounts. `FloatField` uses Python's `float` type internally, whereas `DecimalField` uses Python's `Decimal` type. By using the `Decimal` type, you will avoid `float` rounding issues.

In the `Meta` class of the `Product` model, we have defined a multiple-field index for the `id` and `slug` fields. Both fields are indexed together to improve performance for queries that utilize the two fields.

We plan to query products by both `id` and `slug`. We have added an index for the `name` field and an index for the `created` field. We have used a hyphen before the field name to define the index with a descending order.

Figure 8.1 shows the two data models you have created:

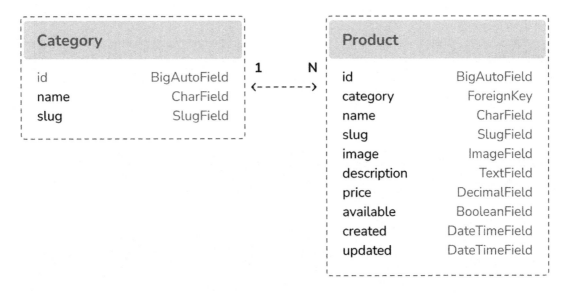

Figure 8.1: Models for the product catalog

In *Figure 8.1*, you can see the different fields of the data models and the one-to-many relationship between the `Category` and the `Product` models.

These models will result in the following database tables displayed in *Figure 8.2*:

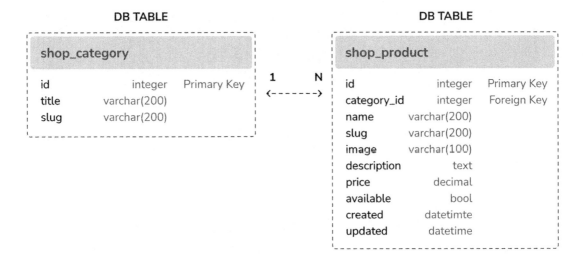

Figure 8.2: Database tables for the product catalog models

The one-to-many relationship between both tables is defined with the `category_id` field in the `shop_product` table, which is used to store the ID of the related `Category` for each `Product` object.

Let's create the initial database migrations for the `shop` application. Since you are going to deal with images in your models you will need to install the Pillow library. Remember that in *Chapter 4, Building a Social Website*, you learned how to install the Pillow library to manage images. Open the shell and install `Pillow` with the following command:

```
pip install Pillow==9.2.0
```

Now run the next command to create initial migrations for your project:

```
python manage.py makemigrations
```

You will see the following output:

```
Migrations for 'shop':
  shop/migrations/0001_initial.py
    - Create model Category
    - Create model Product
    - Create index shop_catego_name_289c7e_idx on field(s) name of model
category
    - Create index shop_produc_id_f21274_idx on field(s) id, slug of model
product
    - Create index shop_produc_name_a2070e_idx on field(s) name of model
product
    - Create index shop_produc_created_ef211c_idx on field(s) -created of model
product
```

Run the next command to sync the database:

```
python manage.py migrate
```

You will see output that includes the following line:

```
Applying shop.0001_initial... OK
```

The database is now synced with your models.

Registering catalog models on the administration site

Let's add your models to the administration site so that you can easily manage categories and products. Edit the admin.py file of the shop application and add the following code to it:

```python
from django.contrib import admin
from .models import Category, Product


@admin.register(Category)
class CategoryAdmin(admin.ModelAdmin):
    list_display = ['name', 'slug']
    prepopulated_fields = {'slug': ('name',)}


@admin.register(Product)
class ProductAdmin(admin.ModelAdmin):
    list_display = ['name', 'slug', 'price',
                    'available', 'created', 'updated']
    list_filter = ['available', 'created', 'updated']
    list_editable = ['price', 'available']
    prepopulated_fields = {'slug': ('name',)}
```

Remember that you use the prepopulated_fields attribute to specify fields where the value is automatically set using the value of other fields. As you have seen before, this is convenient for generating slugs.

You use the list_editable attribute in the ProductAdmin class to set the fields that can be edited from the list display page of the administration site. This will allow you to edit multiple rows at once. Any field in list_editable must also be listed in the list_display attribute, since only the fields displayed can be edited.

Now create a superuser for your site using the following command:

```
python manage.py createsuperuser
```

Enter the desired username, email, and password. Run the development server with the following command:

```
python manage.py runserver
```

Open `http://127.0.0.1:8000/admin/shop/product/add/` in your browser and log in with the user that you just created. Add a new category and product using the administration interface. The add product form should look as follows:

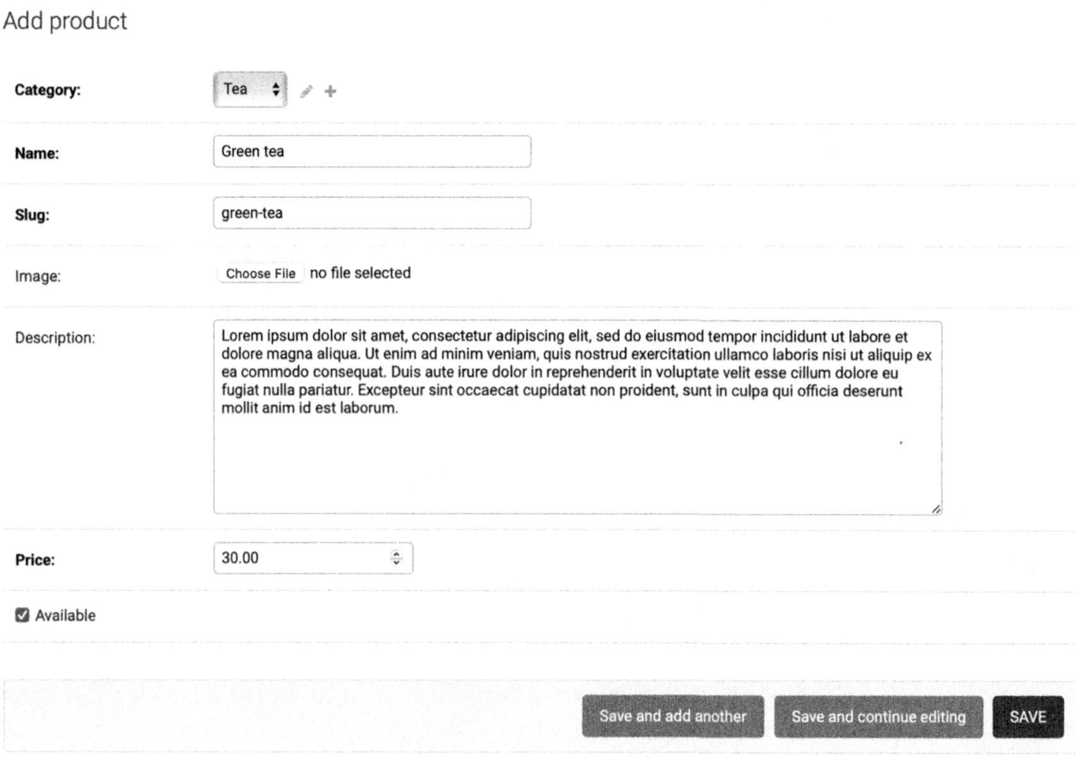

Add product

Category:	Tea ⇅ ✎ +
Name:	Green tea
Slug:	green-tea
Image:	Choose File no file selected
Description:	Lorem ipsum dolor sit amet, consectetur adipiscing elit, sed do eiusmod tempor incididunt ut labore et dolore magna aliqua. Ut enim ad minim veniam, quis nostrud exercitation ullamco laboris nisi ut aliquip ex ea commodo consequat. Duis aute irure dolor in reprehenderit in voluptate velit esse cillum dolore eu fugiat nulla pariatur. Excepteur sint occaecat cupidatat non proident, sunt in culpa qui officia deserunt mollit anim id est laborum.
Price:	30.00 ⇕
☑ Available	

Save and add another   Save and continue editing   SAVE

Figure 8.3: The product creation form

Click on the **Save** button. The product change list page of the administration page will then look like this:

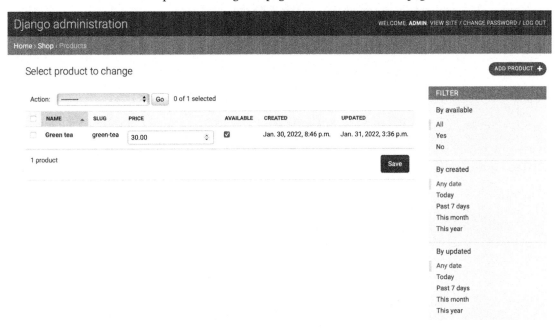

Figure 8.4: The product change list page

Building catalog views

In order to display the product catalog, you need to create a view to list all the products or filter products by a given category. Edit the views.py file of the shop application and add the following code highlighted in bold:

```python
from django.shortcuts import render, get_object_or_404
from .models import Category, Product


def product_list(request, category_slug=None):
    category = None
    categories = Category.objects.all()
    products = Product.objects.filter(available=True)
    if category_slug:
```

```
            category = get_object_or_404(Category,
                                          slug=category_slug)
        products = products.filter(category=category)
    return render(request,
                  'shop/product/list.html',
                  {'category': category,
                   'categories': categories,
                   'products': products})
```

In the preceding code, you filter the QuerySet with `available=True` to retrieve only available products. You use an optional `category_slug` parameter to optionally filter products by a given category.

You also need a view to retrieve and display a single product. Add the following view to the `views.py` file:

```
def product_detail(request, id, slug):
    product = get_object_or_404(Product,
                                id=id,
                                slug=slug,
                                available=True)
    return render(request,
                  'shop/product/detail.html',
                  {'product': product})
```

The `product_detail` view expects the `id` and `slug` parameters in order to retrieve the `Product` instance. You can get this instance just through the ID, since it's a unique attribute. However, you include the slug in the URL to build SEO-friendly URLs for products.

After building the product list and detail views, you have to define URL patterns for them. Create a new file inside the `shop` application directory and name it `urls.py`. Add the following code to it:

```
from django.urls import path
from . import views

app_name = 'shop'

urlpatterns = [
    path('', views.product_list, name='product_list'),
    path('<slug:category_slug>/', views.product_list,
        name='product_list_by_category'),
    path('<int:id>/<slug:slug>/', views.product_detail,
        name='product_detail'),
]
```

These are the URL patterns for your product catalog. You have defined two different URL patterns for the product_list view: a pattern named product_list, which calls the product_list view without any parameters, and a pattern named product_list_by_category, which provides a category_slug parameter to the view for filtering products according to a given category. You added a pattern for the product_detail view, which passes the id and slug parameters to the view in order to retrieve a specific product.

Edit the urls.py file of the myshop project to make it look like this:

```python
from django.contrib import admin
from django.urls import path, include

urlpatterns = [
    path('admin/', admin.site.urls),
    path('', include('shop.urls', namespace='shop')),
]
```

In the main URL patterns of the project, you include URLs for the shop application under a custom namespace named shop.

Next, edit the models.py file of the shop application, import the reverse() function, and add a get_absolute_url() method to the Category and Product models as follows. The new code is highlighted in bold:

```python
from django.db import models
from django.urls import reverse

class Category(models.Model):
    # ...
    def get_absolute_url(self):
        return reverse('shop:product_list_by_category',
                       args=[self.slug])

class Product(models.Model):
    # ...
    def get_absolute_url(self):
        return reverse('shop:product_detail',
                       args=[self.id, self.slug])
```

As you already know, get_absolute_url() is the convention to retrieve the URL for a given object. Here, you use the URL patterns that you just defined in the urls.py file.

Creating catalog templates

Now you need to create templates for the product list and detail views. Create the following directory and file structure inside the shop application directory:

```
templates/
    shop/
        base.html
        product/
            list.html
            detail.html
```

You need to define a base template and then extend it in the product list and detail templates. Edit the shop/base.html template and add the following code to it:

```
{% load static %}
<!DOCTYPE html>
<html>
  <head>
    <meta charset="utf-8" />
    <title>{% block title %}My shop{% endblock %}</title>
    <link href="{% static "css/base.css" %}" rel="stylesheet">
  </head>
  <body>
    <div id="header">
      <a href="/" class="logo">My shop</a>
    </div>
    <div id="subheader">
      <div class="cart">
        Your cart is empty.
      </div>
    </div>
    <div id="content">
      {% block content %}
      {% endblock %}
    </div>
  </body>
</html>
```

This is the base template that you will use for your shop. In order to include the CSS styles and images that are used by the templates, you need to copy the static files that accompany this chapter, which are located in the static/ directory of the shop application. Copy them to the same location in your project. You can find the contents of the directory at https://github.com/PacktPublishing/Django-4-by-Example/tree/main/Chapter08/myshop/shop/static.

Edit the shop/product/list.html template and add the following code to it:

```
{% extends "shop/base.html" %}
{% load static %}

{% block title %}
  {% if category %}{{ category.name }}{% else %}Products{% endif %}
{% endblock %}

{% block content %}
  <div id="sidebar">
    <h3>Categories</h3>
    <ul>
      <li {% if not category %}class="selected"{% endif %}>
        <a href="{% url "shop:product_list" %}">All</a>
      </li>
      {% for c in categories %}
        <li {% if category.slug == c.slug %}class="selected"
        {% endif %}>
          <a href="{{ c.get_absolute_url }}">{{ c.name }}</a>
        </li>
      {% endfor %}
    </ul>
  </div>
  <div id="main" class="product-list">
    <h1>{% if category %}{{ category.name }}{% else %}Products
    {% endif %}</h1>
    {% for product in products %}
      <div class="item">
        <a href="{{ product.get_absolute_url }}">
          <img src="{% if product.image %}{{ product.image.url }}{% else %}{%
static "img/no_image.png" %}{% endif %}">
        </a>
        <a href="{{ product.get_absolute_url }}">{{ product.name }}</a>
        <br>
        ${{ product.price }}
      </div>
    {% endfor %}
  </div>
{% endblock %}
```

Make sure that no template tag is split into multiple lines.

This is the product list template. It extends the shop/base.html template and uses the categories context variable to display all the categories in a sidebar, and products to display the products of the current page. The same template is used for both listing all available products and listing products filtered by a category. Since the image field of the Product model can be blank, you need to provide a default image for the products that don't have an image. The image is located in your static files directory with the relative path img/no_image.png.

Since you are using ImageField to store product images, you need the development server to serve uploaded image files.

Edit the settings.py file of myshop and add the following settings:

```
MEDIA_URL = 'media/'
MEDIA_ROOT = BASE_DIR / 'media'
```

MEDIA_URL is the base URL that serves media files uploaded by users. MEDIA_ROOT is the local path where these files reside, which you build by dynamically prepending the BASE_DIR variable.

For Django to serve the uploaded media files using the development server, edit the main urls.py file of myshop and add the following code highlighted in bold:

```
from django.contrib import admin
from django.urls import path, include
from django.conf import settings
from django.conf.urls.static import static

urlpatterns = [
    path('admin/', admin.site.urls),
    path('', include('shop.urls', namespace='shop')),
]

if settings.DEBUG:
    urlpatterns += static(settings.MEDIA_URL,
                          document_root=settings.MEDIA_ROOT)
```

Remember that you only serve static files this way during development. In a production environment, you should never serve static files with Django; the Django development server doesn't serve static files in an efficient manner. *Chapter 17, Going Live*, will teach you how to serve static files in a production environment.

Run the development server with the following command:

```
python manage.py runserver
```

Add a couple of products to your shop using the administration site and open http://127.0.0.1:8000/ in your browser. You will see the product list page, which will look similar to this:

My shop

Your cart is empty.

Products

Categories

All

Tea

Green tea
$30.00

Red tea
$45.50

Tea powder
$21.20

Figure 8.5: The product list page

Images in this chapter:

- *Green tea*: Photo by Jia Ye on Unsplash
- *Red tea*: Photo by Manki Kim on Unsplash
- *Tea powder*: Photo by Phuong Nguyen on Unsplash

If you create a product using the administration site and don't upload any image for it, the default no_image.png image will be displayed instead:

Green tea
$30.00

Red tea
$45.50

Tea powder
$21.20

Figure 8.6: The product list displaying a default image for products that have no image

Edit the `shop/product/detail.html` template and add the following code to it:

```
{% extends "shop/base.html" %}
{% load static %}

{% block title %}
  {{ product.name }}
{% endblock %}
{% block content %}
  <div class="product-detail">
    <img src="{% if product.image %}{{ product.image.url }}{% else %}
    {% static "img/no_image.png" %}{% endif %}">
    <h1>{{ product.name }}</h1>
    <h2>
      <a href="{{ product.category.get_absolute_url }}">
        {{ product.category }}
      </a>
    </h2>
    <p class="price">${{ product.price }}</p>
    {{ product.description|linebreaks }}
  </div>
{% endblock %}
```

In the preceding code, you call the `get_absolute_url()` method on the related category object to display the available products that belong to the same category.

Now open `http://127.0.0.1:8000/` in your browser and click on any product to see the product detail page. It will look as follows:

My shop

Your cart is empty.

Red tea

Tea

$45.50

Lorem ipsum dolor sit amet, consectetur adipiscing elit, sed do eiusmod tempor incididunt ut labore et dolore magna aliqua. Ut enim ad minim veniam, quis nostrud exercitation ullamco laboris nisi ut aliquip ex ea commodo consequat. Duis aute irure dolor in reprehenderit in voluptate velit esse cillum dolore eu fugiat nulla pariatur. Excepteur sint occaecat cupidatat non proident, sunt in culpa qui officia deserunt mollit anim id est laborum.

Figure 8.7: The product detail page

You have now created a basic product catalog. Next, you will implement a shopping cart that allows users to add any product to it while browsing the online shop.

Building a shopping cart

After building the product catalog, the next step is to create a shopping cart so that users can pick the products that they want to purchase. A shopping cart allows users to select products and set the amount they want to order, and then store this information temporarily while they browse the site, until they eventually place an order. The cart has to be persisted in the session so that the cart items are maintained during a user's visit.

You will use Django's session framework to persist the cart. The cart will be kept in the session until it finishes or the user checks out of the cart. You will also need to build additional Django models for the cart and its items.

Using Django sessions

Django provides a session framework that supports anonymous and user sessions. The session framework allows you to store arbitrary data for each visitor. Session data is stored on the server side, and cookies contain the session ID unless you use the cookie-based session engine. The session middleware manages the sending and receiving of cookies. The default session engine stores session data in the database, but you can choose other session engines.

To use sessions, you have to make sure that the MIDDLEWARE setting of your project contains 'django.contrib.sessions.middleware.SessionMiddleware'. This middleware manages sessions. It's added by default to the MIDDLEWARE setting when you create a new project using the startproject command.

The session middleware makes the current session available in the request object. You can access the current session using request.session, treating it like a Python dictionary to store and retrieve session data. The session dictionary accepts any Python object by default that can be serialized to JSON. You can set a variable in the session like this:

```
request.session['foo'] = 'bar'
```

Retrieve a session key as follows:

```
request.session.get('foo')
```

Delete a key you previously stored in the session as follows:

```
del request.session['foo']
```

 When users log in to the site, their anonymous session is lost, and a new session is created for authenticated users. If you store items in an anonymous session that you need to keep after the user logs in, you will have to copy the old session data into the new session. You can do this by retrieving the session data before you log in the user using the login() function of the Django authentication system and storing it in the session after that.

Session settings

There are several settings you can use to configure sessions for your project. The most important is SESSION_ENGINE. This setting allows you to set the place where sessions are stored. By default, Django stores sessions in the database using the Session model of the django.contrib.sessions application.

Django offers the following options for storing session data:

- **Database sessions:** Session data is stored in the database. This is the default session engine.
- **File-based sessions:** Session data is stored in the filesystem.
- **Cached sessions:** Session data is stored in a cache backend. You can specify cache backends using the CACHES setting. Storing session data in a cache system provides the best performance.
- **Cached database sessions:** Session data is stored in a write-through cache and database. Reads only use the database if the data is not already in the cache.
- **Cookie-based sessions:** Session data is stored in the cookies that are sent to the browser.

 For better performance use a cache-based session engine. Django supports Memcached out of the box and you can find third-party cache backends for Redis and other cache systems.

You can customize sessions with specific settings. Here are some of the important session-related settings:

- SESSION_COOKIE_AGE: The duration of session cookies in seconds. The default value is 1209600 (two weeks).
- SESSION_COOKIE_DOMAIN: The domain used for session cookies. Set this to mydomain.com to enable cross-domain cookies or use None for a standard domain cookie.
- SESSION_COOKIE_HTTPONLY: Whether to use HttpOnly flag on the session cookie. If this is set to True, client-side JavaScript will not be able to access the session cookie. The default value is True for increased security against user session hijacking.
- SESSION_COOKIE_SECURE: A Boolean indicating that the cookie should only be sent if the connection is an HTTPS connection. The default value is False.
- SESSION_EXPIRE_AT_BROWSER_CLOSE: A Boolean indicating that the session has to expire when the browser is closed. The default value is False.
- SESSION_SAVE_EVERY_REQUEST: A Boolean that, if True, will save the session to the database on every request. The session expiration is also updated each time it's saved. The default value is False.

You can see all the session settings and their default values at https://docs.djangoproject.com/en/4.1/ref/settings/#sessions.

Session expiration

You can choose to use browser-length sessions or persistent sessions using the SESSION_EXPIRE_AT_ BROWSER_CLOSE setting. This is set to False by default, forcing the session duration to the value stored in the SESSION_COOKIE_AGE setting. If you set SESSION_EXPIRE_AT_BROWSER_CLOSE to True, the session will expire when the user closes the browser, and the SESSION_COOKIE_AGE setting will not have any effect.

You can use the set_expiry() method of request.session to overwrite the duration of the current session.

Storing shopping carts in sessions

You need to create a simple structure that can be serialized to JSON for storing cart items in a session. The cart has to include the following data for each item contained in it:

- The ID of a Product instance
- The quantity selected for the product
- The unit price for the product

Since product prices may vary, let's take the approach of storing the product's price along with the product itself when it's added to the cart. By doing so, you use the current price of the product when users add it to their cart, no matter whether the product's price is changed afterward. This means that the price that the item has when the client adds it to the cart is maintained for that client in the session until checkout is completed or the session finishes.

Next, you have to build functionality to create shopping carts and associate them with sessions. This has to work as follows:

- When a cart is needed, you check whether a custom session key is set. If no cart is set in the session, you create a new cart and save it in the cart session key.
- For successive requests, you perform the same check and get the cart items from the cart session key. You retrieve the cart items from the session and their related Product objects from the database.

Edit the settings.py file of your project and add the following setting to it:

```
CART_SESSION_ID = 'cart'
```

This is the key that you are going to use to store the cart in the user session. Since Django sessions are managed per visitor, you can use the same cart session key for all sessions.

Let's create an application for managing shopping carts. Open the terminal and create a new application, running the following command from the project directory:

```
python manage.py startapp cart
```

Then, edit the `settings.py` file of your project and add the new application to the `INSTALLED_APPS` setting with the following line highlighted in bold:

```
INSTALLED_APPS = [
    # ...
    'shop.apps.ShopConfig',
    'cart.apps.CartConfig',
]
```

Create a new file inside the `cart` application directory and name it `cart.py`. Add the following code to it:

```
from decimal import Decimal
from django.conf import settings
from shop.models import Product


class Cart:
    def __init__(self, request):
        """
        Initialize the cart.
        """
        self.session = request.session
        cart = self.session.get(settings.CART_SESSION_ID)
        if not cart:
            # save an empty cart in the session
            cart = self.session[settings.CART_SESSION_ID] = {}
        self.cart = cart
```

This is the `Cart` class that will allow you to manage the shopping cart. You require the cart to be initialized with a request object. You store the current session using `self.session = request.session` to make it accessible to the other methods of the `Cart` class.

First, you try to get the cart from the current session using `self.session.get(settings.CART_SESSION_ID)`. If no cart is present in the session, you create an empty cart by setting an empty dictionary in the session.

You will build your cart dictionary with product IDs as keys, and for each product key, a dictionary will be a value that includes quantity and price. By doing this, you can guarantee that a product will not be added more than once to the cart. This way, you can also simplify retrieving cart items.

Let's create a method to add products to the cart or update their quantity. Add the following `add()` and `save()` methods to the `Cart` class:

```
class Cart:
    # ...
    def add(self, product, quantity=1, override_quantity=False):
```

```
        """
        Add a product to the cart or update its quantity.
        """
        product_id = str(product.id)
        if product_id not in self.cart:
            self.cart[product_id] = {'quantity': 0,
                                     'price': str(product.price)}
        if override_quantity:
            self.cart[product_id]['quantity'] = quantity
        else:
            self.cart[product_id]['quantity'] += quantity
        self.save()

    def save(self):
        # mark the session as "modified" to make sure it gets saved
        self.session.modified = True
```

The add() method takes the following parameters as input:

- product: The product instance to add or update in the cart.
- quantity: An optional integer with the product quantity. This defaults to 1.
- override_quantity: This is a Boolean that indicates whether the quantity needs to be overridden with the given quantity (True), or whether the new quantity has to be added to the existing quantity (False).

You use the product ID as a key in the cart's content dictionary. You convert the product ID into a string because Django uses JSON to serialize session data, and JSON only allows string key names. The product ID is the key, and the value that you persist is a dictionary with quantity and price figures for the product. The product's price is converted from decimal into a string to serialize it. Finally, you call the save() method to save the cart in the session.

The save() method marks the session as modified using session.modified = True. This tells Django that the session has changed and needs to be saved.

You also need a method for removing products from the cart. Add the following method to the Cart class:

```
class Cart:
    # ...
    def remove(self, product):
        """
        Remove a product from the cart.
        """
        product_id = str(product.id)
```

```
            if product_id in self.cart:
                del self.cart[product_id]
                self.save()
```

The remove() method removes a given product from the cart dictionary and calls the save() method to update the cart in the session.

You will have to iterate through the items contained in the cart and access the related Product instances. To do so, you can define an __iter__() method in your class. Add the following method to the Cart class:

```
class Cart:
    # ...
    def __iter__(self):
        """
        Iterate over the items in the cart and get the products
        from the database.
        """
        product_ids = self.cart.keys()
        # get the product objects and add them to the cart
        products = Product.objects.filter(id__in=product_ids)
        cart = self.cart.copy()
        for product in products:
            cart[str(product.id)]['product'] = product
        for item in cart.values():
            item['price'] = Decimal(item['price'])
            item['total_price'] = item['price'] * item['quantity']
            yield item
```

In the __iter__() method, you retrieve the Product instances that are present in the cart to include them in the cart items. You copy the current cart in the cart variable and add the Product instances to it. Finally, you iterate over the cart items, converting each item's price back into decimal, and adding a total_price attribute to each item. This __iter__() method will allow you to easily iterate over the items in the cart in views and templates.

You also need a way to return the number of total items in the cart. When the len() function is executed on an object, Python calls its __len__() method to retrieve its length. Next, you are going to define a custom __len__() method to return the total number of items stored in the cart.

Add the following __len__() method to the Cart class:

```
class Cart:
    # ...
    def __len__(self):
        """
```

```
        Count all items in the cart.
        """
        return sum(item['quantity'] for item in self.cart.values())
```

You return the sum of the quantities of all the cart items.

Add the following method to calculate the total cost of the items in the cart:

```
class Cart:
    # ...
    def get_total_price(self):
        return sum(Decimal(item['price']) * item['quantity'] for item in self.
cart.values())
```

Finally, add a method to clear the cart session:

```
class Cart:
    # ...
    def clear(self):
        # remove cart from session
        del self.session[settings.CART_SESSION_ID]
        self.save()
```

Your Cart class is now ready to manage shopping carts.

Creating shopping cart views

Now that you have a Cart class to manage the cart, you need to create the views to add, update, or remove items from it. You need to create the following views:

- A view to add or update items in the cart that can handle current and new quantities
- A view to remove items from the cart
- A view to display cart items and totals

Adding items to the cart

To add items to the cart, you need a form that allows the user to select a quantity. Create a forms.py file inside the cart application directory and add the following code to it:

```
from django import forms

PRODUCT_QUANTITY_CHOICES = [(i, str(i)) for i in range(1, 21)]

class CartAddProductForm(forms.Form):
    quantity = forms.TypedChoiceField(
                            choices=PRODUCT_QUANTITY_CHOICES,
                            coerce=int)
```

```
        override = forms.BooleanField(required=False,
                                       initial=False,
                                       widget=forms.HiddenInput)
```

You will use this form to add products to the cart. Your `CartAddProductForm` class contains the following two fields:

*   `quantity`: This allows the user to select a quantity between 1 and 20. You use a `TypedChoiceField` field with `coerce=int` to convert the input into an integer.
*   `override`: This allows you to indicate whether the quantity has to be added to any existing quantity in the cart for this product (`False`), or whether the existing quantity has to be overridden with the given quantity (`True`). You use a `HiddenInput` widget for this field, since you don't want to display it to the user.

Let's create a view for adding items to the cart. Edit the `views.py` file of the `cart` application and add the following code highlighted in bold:

```
from django.shortcuts import render, redirect, get_object_or_404
from django.views.decorators.http import require_POST
from shop.models import Product
from .cart import Cart
from .forms import CartAddProductForm


@require_POST
def cart_add(request, product_id):
    cart = Cart(request)
    product = get_object_or_404(Product, id=product_id)
    form = CartAddProductForm(request.POST)
    if form.is_valid():
        cd = form.cleaned_data
        cart.add(product=product,
                 quantity=cd['quantity'],
                 override_quantity=cd['override'])
    return redirect('cart:cart_detail')
```

This is the view for adding products to the cart or updating quantities for existing products. You use the `require_POST` decorator to allow only `POST` requests. The view receives the product ID as a parameter. You retrieve the `Product` instance with the given ID and validate `CartAddProductForm`. If the form is valid, you either add or update the product in the cart. The view redirects to the `cart_detail` URL, which will display the contents of the cart. You are going to create the `cart_detail` view shortly.

You also need a view to remove items from the cart. Add the following code to the `views.py` file of the cart application:

```
@require_POST
def cart_remove(request, product_id):
```

```
        cart = Cart(request)
        product = get_object_or_404(Product, id=product_id)
        cart.remove(product)
        return redirect('cart:cart_detail')
```

The cart_remove view receives the product ID as a parameter. You use the require_POST decorator to allow only POST requests. You retrieve the Product instance with the given ID and remove the product from the cart. Then, you redirect the user to the cart_detail URL.

Finally, you need a view to display the cart and its items. Add the following view to the views.py file of the cart application:

```
    def cart_detail(request):
        cart = Cart(request)
        return render(request, 'cart/detail.html', {'cart': cart})
```

The cart_detail view gets the current cart to display it.

You have created views to add items to the cart, update quantities, remove items from the cart, and display the cart's contents. Let's add URL patterns for these views. Create a new file inside the cart application directory and name it urls.py. Add the following URLs to it:

```
    from django.urls import path
    from . import views


    app_name = 'cart'


    urlpatterns = [
        path('', views.cart_detail, name='cart_detail'),
        path('add/<int:product_id>/', views.cart_add, name='cart_add'),
        path('remove/<int:product_id>/', views.cart_remove,
                                        name='cart_remove'),

    ]
```

Edit the main urls.py file of the myshop project and add the following URL pattern highlighted in bold to include the cart URLs:

```
    urlpatterns = [
        path('admin/', admin.site.urls),
        path('cart/', include('cart.urls', namespace='cart')),
        path('', include('shop.urls', namespace='shop')),

    ]
```

Make sure that you include this URL pattern before the `shop.urls` pattern, since it's more restrictive than the latter.

Building a template to display the cart

The `cart_add` and `cart_remove` views don't render any templates, but you need to create a template for the `cart_detail` view to display cart items and totals.

Create the following file structure inside the `cart` application directory:

```
templates/
    cart/
        detail.html
```

Edit the `cart/detail.html` template and add the following code to it:

```
{% extends "shop/base.html" %}
{% load static %}

{% block title %}
  Your shopping cart
{% endblock %}

{% block content %}
  <h1>Your shopping cart</h1>
  <table class="cart">
    <thead>
      <tr>
        <th>Image</th>
        <th>Product</th>
        <th>Quantity</th>
        <th>Remove</th>
        <th>Unit price</th>
        <th>Price</th>
      </tr>
    </thead>
    <tbody>
      {% for item in cart %}
        {% with product=item.product %}
          <tr>
            <td>
              <a href="{{ product.get_absolute_url }}">
                <img src="{% if product.image %}{{ product.image.url }}
                {% else %}{% static "img/no_image.png" %}{% endif %}">
              </a>
            </td>
```

```
                    <td>{{ product.name }}</td>
                    <td>{{ item.quantity }}</td>
                    <td>
                      <form action="{% url "cart:cart_remove" product.id %}"
  method="post">
                          <input type="submit" value="Remove">
                          {% csrf_token %}
                      </form>
                    </td>
                    <td class="num">${{ item.price }}</td>
                    <td class="num">${{ item.total_price }}</td>
                  </tr>
                {% endwith %}
              {% endfor %}
              <tr class="total">
                <td>Total</td>
                <td colspan="4"></td>
                <td class="num">${{ cart.get_total_price }}</td>
              </tr>
            </tbody>
          </table>
          <p class="text-right">
            <a href="{% url "shop:product_list" %}" class="button
            light">Continue shopping</a>
            <a href="#" class="button">Checkout</a>
          </p>
        {% endblock %}
```

Make sure that no template tag is split into multiple lines.

This is the template that is used to display the cart's contents. It contains a table with the items stored in the current cart. You allow users to change the quantity of the selected products using a form that is posted to the cart_add view. You also allow users to remove items from the cart by providing a **Remove** button for each of them. Finally, you use an HTML form with an action attribute that points to the cart_remove URL including the product ID.

Adding products to the cart

Now you need to add an **Add to cart** button to the product detail page. Edit the views.py file of the shop application and add CartAddProductForm to the product_detail view, as follows:

```
from cart.forms import CartAddProductForm


# ...


def product_detail(request, id, slug):
```

```
    product = get_object_or_404(Product, id=id,
                                         slug=slug,
                                         available=True)
    cart_product_form = CartAddProductForm()
    return render(request,
                'shop/product/detail.html',
                {'product': product,
                 'cart_product_form': cart_product_form})
```

Edit the `shop/product/detail.html` template of the `shop` application and add the following form to the product price as follows. New lines are highlighted in bold:

```
...
<p class="price">${{ product.price }}</p>
<form action="{% url "cart:cart_add" product.id %}" method="post">
  {{ cart_product_form }}
  {% csrf_token %}
  <input type="submit" value="Add to cart">
</form>
{{ product.description|linebreaks }}
...
```

Run the development server with the following command:

```
python manage.py runserver
```

Now open `http://127.0.0.1:8000/` in your browser and navigate to a product's detail page. It will contain a form to choose a quantity before adding the product to the cart. The page will look like this:

Figure 8.8: The product detail page, including the Add to cart form

Choose a quantity and click on the **Add to cart** button. The form is submitted to the cart_add view via POST. The view adds the product to the cart in the session, including its current price and the selected quantity. Then, it redirects the user to the cart detail page, which will look like *Figure 8.9*:

Your shopping cart

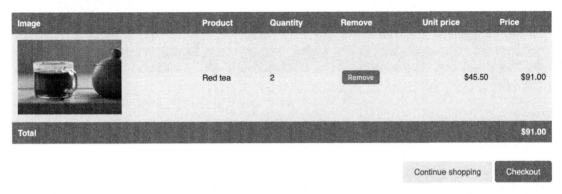

Figure 8.9: The cart detail page

Updating product quantities in the cart

When users see the cart, they might want to change product quantities before placing an order. You are going to allow users to change quantities from the cart detail page.

Edit the views.py file of the cart application and add the following lines highlighted in bold to the cart_detail view:

```
def cart_detail(request):
    cart = Cart(request)
    for item in cart:
        item['update_quantity_form'] = CartAddProductForm(initial={
                            'quantity': item['quantity'],
                            'override': True})
    return render(request, 'cart/detail.html', {'cart': cart})
```

You create an instance of CartAddProductForm for each item in the cart to allow changing product quantities. You initialize the form with the current item quantity and set the override field to True so that when you submit the form to the cart_add view, the current quantity is replaced with the new one.

Now edit the cart/detail.html template of the cart application and find the following line:

```
<td>{{ item.quantity }}</td>
```

Replace the previous line with the following code:

```
<td>
    <form action="{% url "cart:cart_add" product.id %}" method="post">
```

```
        {{ item.update_quantity_form.quantity }}
        {{ item.update_quantity_form.override }}
        <input type="submit" value="Update">
        {% csrf_token %}
      </form>
  </td>
```

Run the development server with the following command:

```
python manage.py runserver
```

Open `http://127.0.0.1:8000/cart/` in your browser.

You will see a form to edit the quantity for each cart item, as follows:

Your shopping cart

Figure 8.10: The cart detail page, including the form to update product quantities

Change the quantity of an item and click on the **Update** button to test the new functionality. You can also remove an item from the cart by clicking the **Remove** button.

Creating a context processor for the current cart

You might have noticed that the message **Your cart is empty** is displayed in the header of the site, even when the cart contains items. You should display the total number of items in the cart and the total cost instead. Since this has to be displayed on all pages, you need to build a context processor to include the current cart in the request context, regardless of the view that processes the request.

Context processors

A context processor is a Python function that takes the `request` object as an argument and returns a dictionary that gets added to the request context. Context processors come in handy when you need to make something available globally to all templates.

By default, when you create a new project using the startproject command, your project contains the following template context processors in the context_processors option inside the TEMPLATES setting:

- django.template.context_processors.debug: This sets the Boolean debug and sql_queries variables in the context, representing the list of SQL queries executed in the request.
- django.template.context_processors.request: This sets the request variable in the context.
- django.contrib.auth.context_processors.auth: This sets the user variable in the request.
- django.contrib.messages.context_processors.messages: This sets a messages variable in the context containing all the messages that have been generated using the messages framework.

Django also enables django.template.context_processors.csrf to avoid **cross-site request forgery (CSRF)** attacks. This context processor is not present in the settings, but it is always enabled and can't be turned off for security reasons.

You can see the list of all built-in context processors at https://docs.djangoproject.com/en/4.1/ref/templates/api/#built-in-template-context-processors.

Setting the cart into the request context

Let's create a context processor to set the current cart into the request context. With it, you will be able to access the cart in any template.

Create a new file inside the cart application directory and name it context_processors.py. Context processors can reside anywhere in your code but creating them here will keep your code well organized. Add the following code to the file:

```python
from .cart import Cart


def cart(request):
    return {'cart': Cart(request)}
```

In your context processor, you instantiate the cart using the request object and make it available for the templates as a variable named cart.

Edit the settings.py file of your project and add cart.context_processors.cart to the context_processors option inside the TEMPLATES setting, as follows. The new line is highlighted in bold:

```python
TEMPLATES = [
    {
        'BACKEND': 'django.template.backends.django.DjangoTemplates',
        'DIRS': [],
        'APP_DIRS': True,
        'OPTIONS': {
            'context_processors': [
                'django.template.context_processors.debug',
                'django.template.context_processors.request',
```

```
            'django.contrib.auth.context_processors.auth',
            'django.contrib.messages.context_processors.messages',
            'cart.context_processors.cart',
        ],
    },
  },
]
```

The cart context processor will be executed every time a template is rendered using Django's RequestContext. The cart variable will be set in the context of your templates. You can read more about RequestContext at https://docs.djangoproject.com/en/4.1/ref/templates/api/#django.template.RequestContext.

 Context processors are executed in all the requests that use RequestContext. You might want to create a custom template tag instead of a context processor if your functionality is not needed in all templates, especially if it involves database queries.

Next, edit the shop/base.html template of the shop application and find the following lines:

```
<div class="cart">
  Your cart is empty.
</div>
```

Replace the previous lines with the following code:

```
<div class="cart">
  {% with total_items=cart|length %}
    {% if total_items > 0 %}
      Your cart:
      <a href="{% url "cart:cart_detail" %}">
          {{ total_items }} item{{ total_items|pluralize }},
          ${{ cart.get_total_price }}
      </a>
    {% else %}
      Your cart is empty.
    {% endif %}
  {% endwith %}
</div>
```

Restart the development server with the following command:

```
python manage.py runserver
```

Open http://127.0.0.1:8000/ in your browser and add some products to the cart.

In the header of the website, you can now see the total number of items in the cart and the total cost, as follows:

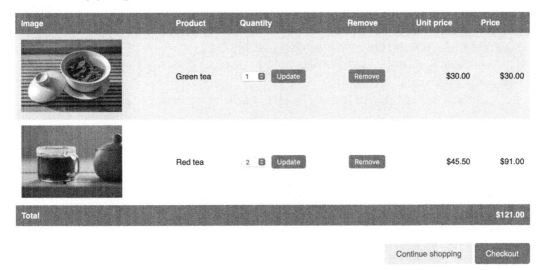

Figure 8.11: The site header displaying the current items in the cart

You have completed the cart functionality. Next, you are going to create the functionality to register customer orders.

Registering customer orders

When a shopping cart is checked out, you need to save an order in the database. Orders will contain information about customers and the products they are buying.

Create a new application for managing customer orders using the following command:

```
python manage.py startapp orders
```

Edit the settings.py file of your project and add the new application to the INSTALLED_APPS setting, as follows:

```
INSTALLED_APPS = [
    # ...
    'shop.apps.ShopConfig',
    'cart.apps.CartConfig',
    'orders.apps.OrdersConfig',
]
```

You have activated the orders application.

Creating order models

You will need a model to store the order details and a second model to store items bought, including their price and quantity. Edit the models.py file of the orders application and add the following code to it:

```python
from django.db import models
from shop.models import Product


class Order(models.Model):
    first_name = models.CharField(max_length=50)
    last_name = models.CharField(max_length=50)
    email = models.EmailField()
    address = models.CharField(max_length=250)
    postal_code = models.CharField(max_length=20)
    city = models.CharField(max_length=100)
    created = models.DateTimeField(auto_now_add=True)
    updated = models.DateTimeField(auto_now=True)
    paid = models.BooleanField(default=False)

    class Meta:
        ordering = ['-created']
        indexes = [
            models.Index(fields=['-created']),
        ]

    def __str__(self):
        return f'Order {self.id}'

    def get_total_cost(self):
        return sum(item.get_cost() for item in self.items.all())

class OrderItem(models.Model):
    order = models.ForeignKey(Order,
                              related_name='items',
                              on_delete=models.CASCADE)
    product = models.ForeignKey(Product,
                                related_name='order_items',
                                on_delete=models.CASCADE)
    price = models.DecimalField(max_digits=10,
                                decimal_places=2)
    quantity = models.PositiveIntegerField(default=1)

    def __str__(self):
```

```
                return str(self.id)

        def get_cost(self):
            return self.price * self.quantity
```

The `Order` model contains several fields to store customer information and a paid Boolean field, which defaults to `False`. Later on, you are going to use this field to differentiate between paid and unpaid orders. We have also defined a `get_total_cost()` method to obtain the total cost of the items bought in this order.

The `OrderItem` model allows you to store the product, quantity, and price paid for each item. We have defined a `get_cost()` method that returns the cost of the item by multiplying the item price with the quantity.

Run the next command to create initial migrations for the `orders` application:

```
python manage.py makemigrations
```

You will see output similar to the following:

```
Migrations for 'orders':
  orders/migrations/0001_initial.py
    - Create model Order
    - Create model OrderItem
    - Create index orders_orde_created_743fca_idx on field(s) -created of model
order
```

Run the following command to apply the new migration:

```
python manage.py migrate
```

You will see the following output:

```
Applying orders.0001_initial... OK
```

Your order models are now synced to the database.

Including order models in the administration site

Let's add the order models to the administration site. Edit the `admin.py` file of the `orders` application and add the following code highlighted in bold:

```
from django.contrib import admin
from .models import Order, OrderItem


class OrderItemInline(admin.TabularInline):
    model = OrderItem
    raw_id_fields = ['product']


@admin.register(Order)
```

```
class OrderAdmin(admin.ModelAdmin):
    list_display = ['id', 'first_name', 'last_name', 'email',
                    'address', 'postal_code', 'city', 'paid',
                    'created', 'updated']
    list_filter = ['paid', 'created', 'updated']
    inlines = [OrderItemInline]
```

You use a `ModelInline` class for the `OrderItem` model to include it as an *inline* in the `OrderAdmin` class. An inline allows you to include a model on the same edit page as its related model.

Run the development server with the following command:

```
python manage.py runserver
```

Open `http://127.0.0.1:8000/admin/orders/order/add/` in your browser. You will see the following page:

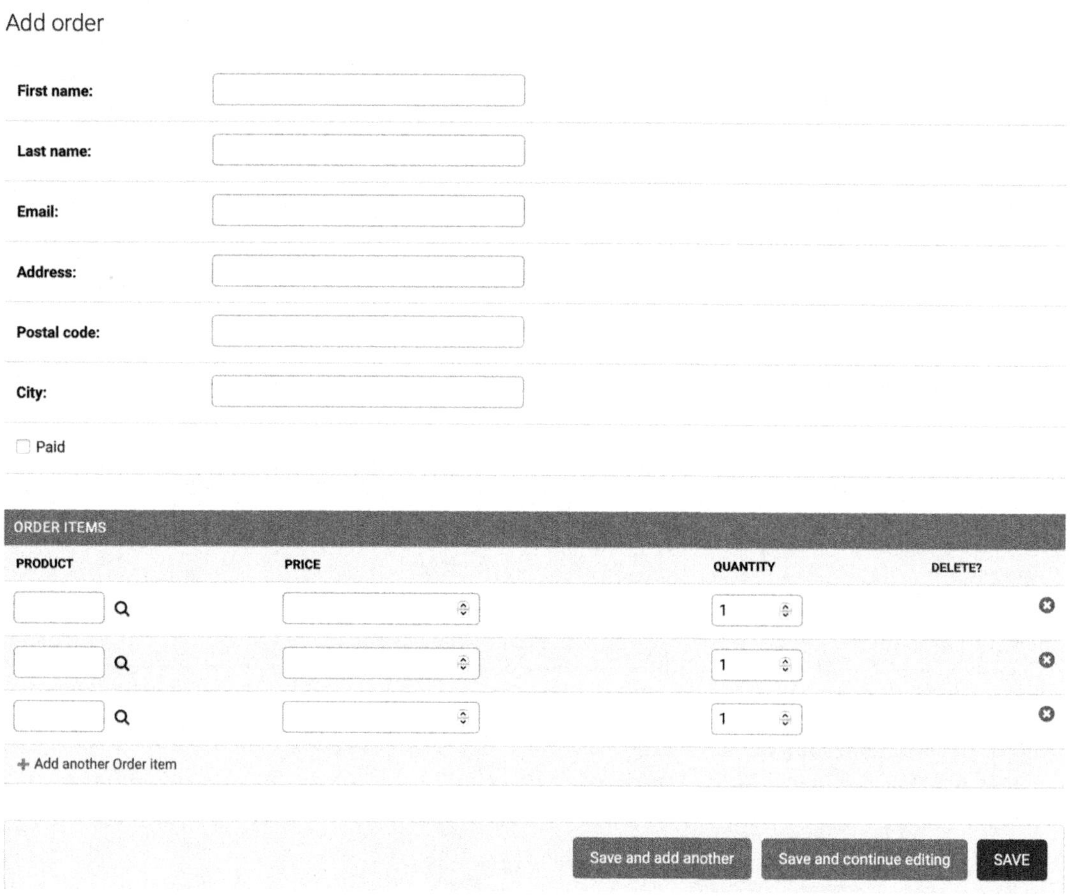

Figure 8.12: The Add order form, including OrderItemInline

Creating customer orders

You will use the order models that you created to persist the items contained in the shopping cart when the user finally places an order. A new order will be created following these steps:

1. Present a user with an order form to fill in their data
2. Create a new Order instance with the data entered, and create an associated OrderItem instance for each item in the cart
3. Clear all the cart's contents and redirect the user to a success page

First, you need a form to enter the order details. Create a new file inside the orders application directory and name it forms.py. Add the following code to it:

```
from django import forms
from .models import Order


class OrderCreateForm(forms.ModelForm):
    class Meta:
        model = Order
        fields = ['first_name', 'last_name', 'email', 'address',
                  'postal_code', 'city']
```

This is the form that you are going to use to create new Order objects. Now you need a view to handle the form and create a new order. Edit the views.py file of the orders application and add the following code highlighted in bold:

```
from django.shortcuts import render
from .models import OrderItem
from .forms import OrderCreateForm
from cart.cart import Cart


def order_create(request):
    cart = Cart(request)
    if request.method == 'POST':
        form = OrderCreateForm(request.POST)
        if form.is_valid():
            order = form.save()
            for item in cart:
                OrderItem.objects.create(order=order,
                                         product=item['product'],
                                         price=item['price'],
                                         quantity=item['quantity'])
            # clear the cart
            cart.clear()
```

```
            return render(request,
                          'orders/order/created.html',
                          {'order': order})
        else:
            form = OrderCreateForm()
        return render(request,
                      'orders/order/create.html',
                      {'cart': cart, 'form': form})
```

In the order_create view, you obtain the current cart from the session with cart = Cart(request). Depending on the request method, you perform the following tasks:

- **GET request**: Instantiates the OrderCreateForm form and renders the orders/order/create. html template.

- **POST request**: Validates the data sent in the request. If the data is valid, you create a new order in the database using order = form.save(). You iterate over the cart items and create an OrderItem for each of them. Finally, you clear the cart's contents and render the template orders/order/created.html.

Create a new file inside the orders application directory and name it urls.py. Add the following code to it:

```
from django.urls import path
from . import views

app_name = 'orders'

urlpatterns = [
    path('create/', views.order_create, name='order_create'),
]
```

This is the URL pattern for the order_create view.

Edit the urls.py file of myshop and include the following pattern. Remember to place it before the shop.urls pattern as follows. The new line is highlighted in bold:

```
urlpatterns = [
    path('admin/', admin.site.urls),
    path('cart/', include('cart.urls', namespace='cart')),
    path('orders/', include('orders.urls', namespace='orders')),
    path('', include('shop.urls', namespace='shop')),
]
```

Edit the cart/detail.html template of the cart application and find this line:

```
<a href="#" class="button">Checkout</a>
```

Add the `order_create` URL to the `href` HTML attribute as follows:

```
<a href="{% url "orders:order_create" %}" class="button">
  Checkout
</a>
```

Users can now navigate from the cart detail page to the order form.

You still need to define templates for creating orders. Create the following file structure inside the `orders` application directory:

```
templates/
    orders/
        order/
            create.html
            created.html
```

Edit the `orders/order/create.html` template and add the following code:

```
{% extends "shop/base.html" %}

{% block title %}
  Checkout
{% endblock %}

{% block content %}
  <h1>Checkout</h1>
  <div class="order-info">
    <h3>Your order</h3>
    <ul>
      {% for item in cart %}
        <li>
          {{ item.quantity }}x {{ item.product.name }}
          <span>${{ item.total_price }}</span>
        </li>
      {% endfor %}
    </ul>
    <p>Total: ${{ cart.get_total_price }}</p>
  </div>
  <form method="post" class="order-form">
    {{ form.as_p }}
    <p><input type="submit" value="Place order"></p>
    {% csrf_token %}
  </form>
{% endblock %}
```

This template displays the cart items, including totals and the form to place an order.

Edit the `orders/order/created.html` template and add the following code:

```
{% extends "shop/base.html" %}

{% block title %}
  Thank you
{% endblock %}

{% block content %}
  <h1>Thank you</h1>
  <p>Your order has been successfully completed. Your order number is
  <strong>{{ order.id }}</strong>.</p>
{% endblock %}
```

This is the template that you render when the order is successfully created.

Start the web development server to load new files. Open `http://127.0.0.1:8000/` in your browser, add a couple of products to the cart, and continue to the checkout page. You will see the following form:

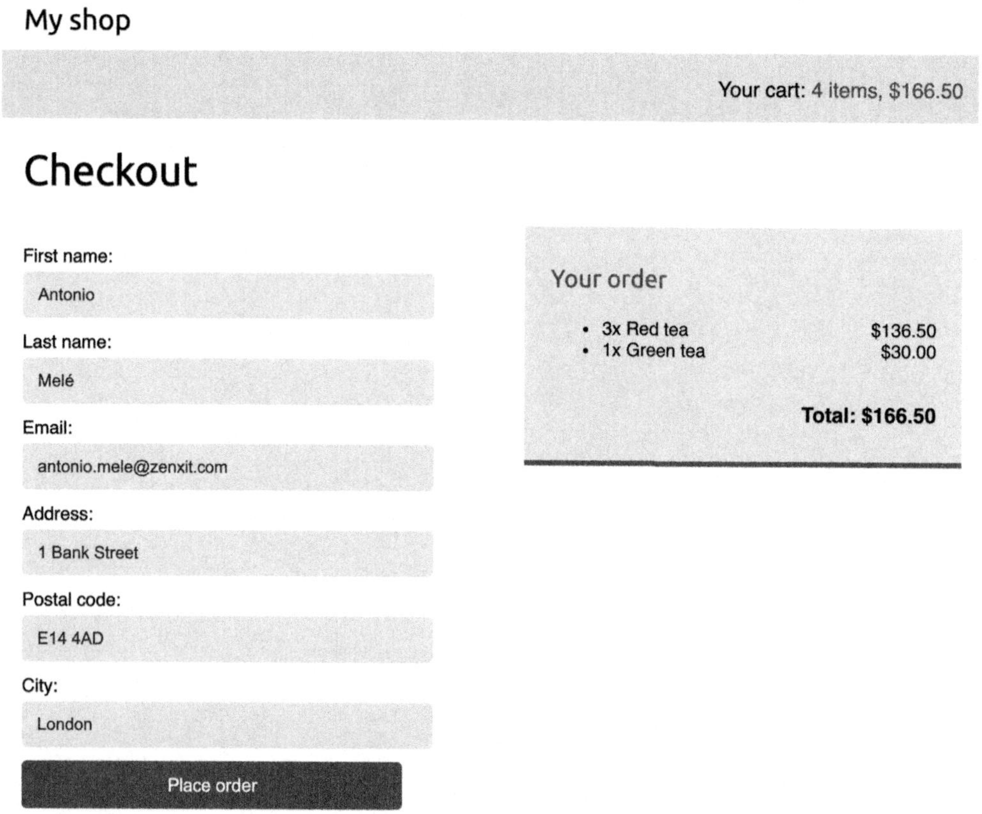

Figure 8.13: The order creation page, including the chart checkout form and order details

Fill in the form with valid data and click on the **Place order** button. The order will be created, and you will see a success page like this:

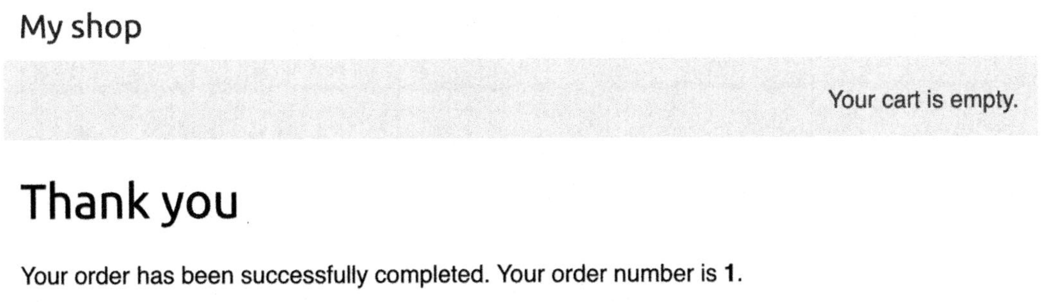

My shop

Your cart is empty.

Thank you

Your order has been successfully completed. Your order number is **1**.

Figure 8.14: The order created template displaying the order number

The order has been registered and the cart has been cleared.

You might have noticed that the message **Your cart is empty** is displayed in the header when an order is completed. This is because the cart has been cleared. We can easily avoid this message for views that have an order object in the template context.

Edit the shop/base.html template of the shop application and replace the following line highlighted in bold:

```
...
<div class="cart">
  {% with total_items=cart|length %}
    {% if total_items > 0 %}
      Your cart:
      <a href="{% url "cart:cart_detail" %}">
        {{ total_items }} item{{ total_items|pluralize }},
        ${{ cart.get_total_price }}
      </a>
    {% elif not order %}
      Your cart is empty.
    {% endif %}
  {% endwith %}
</div>
...
```

The message **Your cart is empty** will not be displayed anymore when an order is created.

Now open the administration site at `http://127.0.0.1:8000/admin/orders/order/`. You will see that the order has been successfully created, like this:

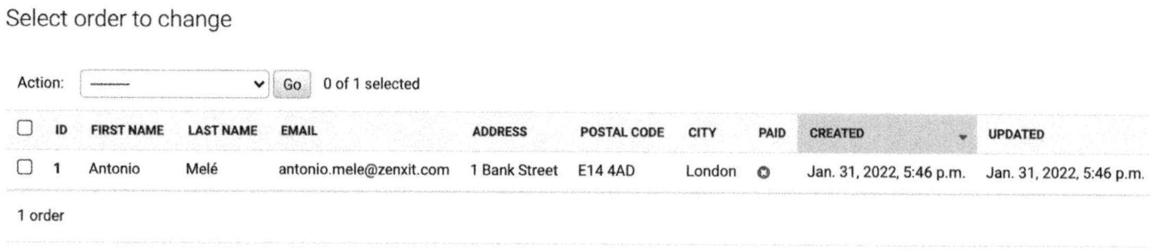

Select order to change

	ID	FIRST NAME	LAST NAME	EMAIL	ADDRESS	POSTAL CODE	CITY	PAID	CREATED	UPDATED
☐	1	Antonio	Melé	antonio.mele@zenxit.com	1 Bank Street	E14 4AD	London	◯	Jan. 31, 2022, 5:46 p.m.	Jan. 31, 2022, 5:46 p.m.

Action: [——— ▾] [Go] 0 of 1 selected

1 order

Figure 8.15: The order change list section of the administration site including the order created

You have implemented the order system. Now you will learn how to create asynchronous tasks to send confirmation emails to users when they place an order.

Asynchronous tasks

When receiving an HTTP request, you need to return a response to the user as quickly as possible. Remember that in *Chapter 7, Tracking User Actions*, you used the Django Debug Toolbar to check the time for the different phases of the request/response cycle and the execution time for the SQL queries performed. Every task executed during the course of the request/response cycle adds up to the total response time. Long-running tasks can seriously slow down the server response. How do we return a fast response to the user while still completing time-consuming tasks? We can do it with asynchronous execution.

Working with asynchronous tasks

We can offload work from the request/response cycle by executing certain tasks in the background. For example, a video-sharing platform allows users to upload videos but requires a long time to transcode uploaded videos. When the user uploads a video, the site might return a response informing that the transcoding will start soon and start transcoding the video asynchronously. Another example is sending emails to users. If your site sends email notifications from a view, the **Simple Mail Transfer Protocol (SMTP)** connection might fail or slow down the response. By sending the email asynchronously, you avoid blocking the code execution.

Asynchronous execution is especially relevant for data-intensive, resource-intensive, and time-consuming processes or processes subject to failure, which might require a retry policy.

Workers, message queues, and message brokers

While your web server processes requests and returns responses, you need a second task-based server, named **worker**, to process the asynchronous tasks. One or multiple workers can be running and executing tasks in the background. These workers can access the database, process files, send e-mails, etc. Workers can even queue future tasks. All while keeping the main web server free to process HTTP requests.

To tell the workers what tasks to execute we need to send **messages**. We communicate with brokers by adding messages to a **message queue**, which is basically a **first in, first out** (**FIFO**) data structure. When a broker becomes available, it takes the first message from the queue and starts executing the corresponding task. When finished, the broker takes the next message from the queue and executes the corresponding task. Brokers become idle when the message queue is empty. When using multiple brokers, each broker takes the first available message in order when they become available. The queue ensures each broker only gets one task at a time, and that no task is processed by more than one worker.

Figure 8.16 shows how a message queue works:

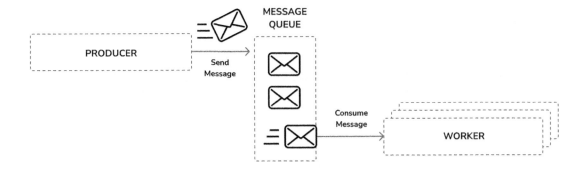

Figure 8.16: Asynchronous execution using a message queue and workers

A producer sends a message to the queue, and the worker(s) consume the messages on a first-come, first-served basis; the first message added to the message queue is the first message to be processed by the worker(s).

In order to manage the message queue, we need a **message broker**. The message broker is used to translate messages to a formal messaging protocol and manage message queues for multiple receivers. It provides reliable storage and guaranteed message delivery. The message broker allows us to create message queues, route messages, distribute messages among workers, etc.

Using Django with Celery and RabbitMQ

Celery is a distributed task queue that can process vast amounts of messages. We will use Celery to define asynchronous tasks as Python functions within our Django applications. We will run Celery workers that will listen to the message broker to get new messages to process asynchronous tasks.

Using Celery, not only can you create asynchronous tasks easily and let them be executed by workers as soon as possible, but you can also schedule them to run at a specific time. You can find the Celery documentation at `https://docs.celeryq.dev/en/stable/index.html`.

Celery communicates via messages and requires a message broker to mediate between clients and workers. There are several options for a message broker for Celery, including key/value stores such as Redis, or an actual message broker such as RabbitMQ.

RabbitMQ is the most widely deployed message broker. It supports multiple messaging protocols, such as the **Advanced Message Queuing Protocol (AMQP)**, and it is the recommended message worker for Celery. RabbitMQ is lightweight, easy to deploy, and can be configured for scalability and high availability.

Figure 8.17 shows how we will use Django, Celery, and RabbitMQ to execute asynchronous tasks:

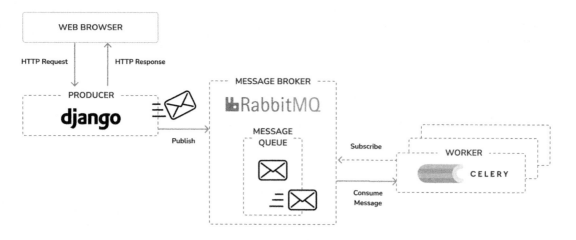

Figure 8.17: Architecture for asynchronous tasks with Django, RabbitMQ, and Celery

Installing Celery

Let's install Celery and integrate it into the project. Install Celery via `pip` using the following command:

```
pip install celery==5.2.7
```

You can find an introduction to Celery at https://docs.celeryq.dev/en/stable/getting-started/introduction.html.

Installing RabbitMQ

The RabbitMQ community provides a Docker image that makes it very easy to deploy a RabbitMQ server with a standard configuration. Remember that you learned how to install Docker in *Chapter 7, Tracking User Actions*.

After installing Docker on your machine, you can easily pull the RabbitMQ Docker image by running the following command from the shell:

```
docker pull rabbitmq
```

This will download the RabbitMQ Docker image to your local machine. You can find information about the official RabbitMQ Docker image at `https://hub.docker.com/_/rabbitmq`.

If you want to install RabbitMQ natively on your machine instead of using Docker, you will find detailed installation guides for different operating systems at `https://www.rabbitmq.com/download.html`.

Execute the following command in the shell to start the RabbitMQ server with Docker:

```
docker run -it --rm --name rabbitmq -p 5672:5672 -p 15672:15672
rabbitmq:management
```

With this command, we are telling RabbitMQ to run on port 5672, and we are running its web-based management user interface on port 15672.

You will see output that includes the following lines:

```
Starting broker...
...
completed with 4 plugins.
Server startup complete; 4 plugins started.
```

RabbitMQ is running on port 5672 and ready to receive messages.

Accessing RabbitMQ's management interface

Open `http://127.0.0.1:15672/` in your browser. You will see the login screen for the management UI of RabbitMQ. It will look like this:

Figure 8.18: The RabbitMQ management UI login screen

Enter guest as both the username and the password and click on **Login**. You will see the following screen:

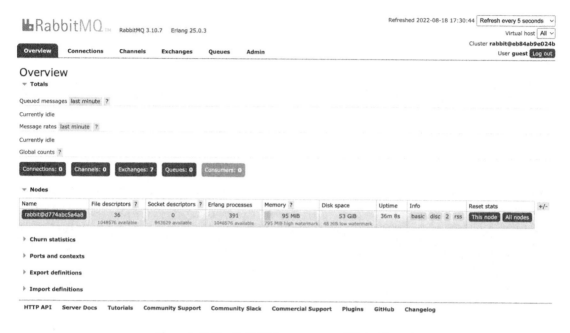

Figure 8.19: The RabbitMQ management UI dashboard

This is the default admin user for RabbitMQ. In this screen you can monitor the current activity for RabbitMQ. You can see that there is one node running with no connections or queues registered.

If you use RabbitMQ in a production environment, you will need to create a new admin user and remove the default guest user. You can do that in the **Admin** section of the management UI.

Now we will add Celery to the project. Then, we will run Celery and test the connection to RabbitMQ.

Adding Celery to your project

You have to provide a configuration for the Celery instance. Create a new file next to the settings.py file of myshop and name it celery.py. This file will contain the Celery configuration for your project. Add the following code to it:

```
import os
from celery import Celery

# set the default Django settings module for the 'celery' program.
os.environ.setdefault('DJANGO_SETTINGS_MODULE', 'myshop.settings')
```

```
app = Celery('myshop')
app.config_from_object('django.conf:settings', namespace='CELERY')
app.autodiscover_tasks()
```

In this code, you do the following:

- You set the DJANGO_SETTINGS_MODULE variable for the Celery command-line program.
- You create an instance of the application with app = Celery('myshop').
- You load any custom configuration from your project settings using the config_from_object() method. The namespace attribute specifies the prefix that Celery-related settings will have in your settings.py file. By setting the CELERY namespace, all Celery settings need to include the CELERY_ prefix in their name (for example, CELERY_BROKER_URL).
- Finally, you tell Celery to auto-discover asynchronous tasks for your applications. Celery will look for a tasks.py file in each application directory of applications added to INSTALLED_APPS in order to load asynchronous tasks defined in it.

You need to import the celery module in the __init__.py file of your project to ensure it is loaded when Django starts.

Edit the myshop/__init__.py file and add the following code to it:

```
# import celery
from .celery import app as celery_app


__all__ = ['celery_app']
```

You have added Celery to the Django project, and you can now start using it.

Running a Celery worker

A Celery worker is a process that handles bookkeeping features like sending/receiving queue messages, registering tasks, killing hung tasks, tracking status, etc. A worker instance can consume from any number of message queues.

Open another shell and start a Celery worker from your project directory, using the following command:

```
celery -A myshop worker -l info
```

The Celery worker is now running and ready to process tasks. Let's check if there is a connection between Celery and RabbitMQ.

Open `http://127.0.0.1:15672/` in your browser to access the RabbitMQ management UI. You will now see a graph under **Queued messages** and another graph under **Message rates**, like in *Figure 8.20*:

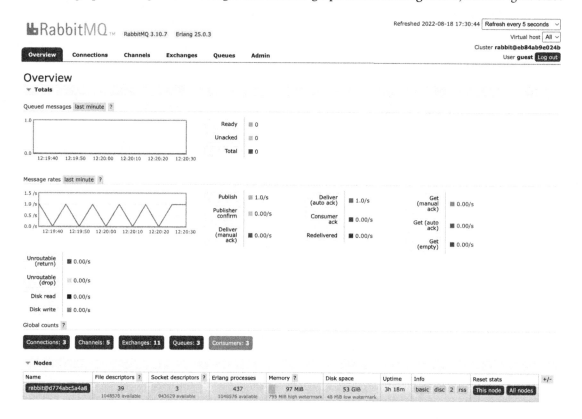

Figure 8.20: The RabbitMQ management dashboard displaying connections and queues

Obviously, there are no queued messages as we didn't send any messages to the message queue yet. The graph under **Message rates** should update every five seconds; you can see the refresh rate on the top right of the screen. This time, both **Connections** and **Queues** should display a number higher than zero.

Now we can start programming asynchronous tasks.

 The `CELERY_ALWAYS_EAGER` setting allows you to execute tasks locally in a synchronous manner, instead of sending them to the queue. This is useful for running unit tests or executing the application in your local environment without running Celery.

Adding asynchronous tasks to your application

Let's send a confirmation email to the user whenever an order is placed in the online shop. We will implement sending the email in a Python function and register it as a task with Celery. Then, we will add it to the `order_create` view to execute the task asynchronously.

When the `order_create` view is executed, Celery will send the message to a message queue managed by RabbitMQ and then a Celery broker will execute the asynchronous task that we defined with a Python function.

The convention for easy task discovery by Celery is to define asynchronous tasks for your application in a `tasks` module within the application directory.

Create a new file inside the `orders` application and name it `tasks.py`. This is the place where Celery will look for asynchronous tasks. Add the following code to it:

```python
from celery import shared_task
from django.core.mail import send_mail
from .models import Order


@shared_task
def order_created(order_id):
    """
    Task to send an e-mail notification when an order is
    successfully created.
    """
    order = Order.objects.get(id=order_id)
    subject = f'Order nr. {order.id}'
    message = f'Dear {order.first_name},\n\n' \
              f'You have successfully placed an order.' \
              f'Your order ID is {order.id}.'
    mail_sent = send_mail(subject,
                          message,
                          'admin@myshop.com',
                          [order.email])
    return mail_sent
```

We have defined the `order_created` task by using the `@shared_task` decorator. As you can see, a Celery task is just a Python function decorated with `@shared_task`. The `order_created` task function receives an `order_id` parameter. It's always recommended to only pass IDs to task functions and retrieve objects from the database when the task is executed. By doing so we avoid accessing outdated information, since the data in the database might have changed while the task was queued. We have used the `send_mail()` function provided by Django to send an email notification to the user who placed the order.

You learned how to configure Django to use your SMTP server in *Chapter 2, Enhancing Your Blog with Advanced Features*. If you don't want to set up email settings, you can tell Django to write emails to the console by adding the following setting to the `settings.py` file:

```python
EMAIL_BACKEND = 'django.core.mail.backends.console.EmailBackend'
```

Use asynchronous tasks not only for time-consuming processes, but also for other processes that do not take so much time to be executed but that are subject to connection failures or require a retry policy.

Now you have to add the task to your `order_create` view. Edit the `views.py` file of the `orders` application, import the task, and call the `order_created` asynchronous task after clearing the cart, as follows:

```python
from .tasks import order_created
#...


def order_create(request):
    # ...
    if request.method == 'POST':
        # ...
        if form.is_valid():
            # ...
            cart.clear()
            # Launch asynchronous task
            order_created.delay(order.id)
        # ...
```

You call the `delay()` method of the task to execute it asynchronously. The task will be added to the message queue and executed by the Celery worker as soon as possible.

Make sure RabbitMQ is running. Then, stop the Celery worker process and start it again with the following command:

```
celery -A myshop worker -l info
```

The Celery worker has now registered the task. In another shell, start the development server from the project directory with the following command:

```
python manage.py runserver
```

Open `http://127.0.0.1:8000/` in your browser, add some products to your shopping cart, and complete an order. In the shell where you started the Celery worker you will see output similar to the following:

```
[2022-02-03 20:25:19,569: INFO/MainProcess] Task orders.tasks.order_
created[a94dc22e-372b-4339-bff7-52bc83161c5c] received
...
[2022-02-03 20:25:19,605: INFO/ForkPoolWorker-8] Task orders.tasks.
order_created[a94dc22e-372b-4339-bff7-52bc83161c5c] succeeded in
0.015824042027816176s: 1
```

The order_created task has been executed and an email notification for the order has been sent. If you are using the email backend console.EmailBackend, no email is sent but you should see the rendered text of the email in the output of the console.

Monitoring Celery with Flower

Besides the RabbitMQ management UI, you can use other tools to monitor the asynchronous tasks that are executed with Celery. Flower is a useful web-based tool for monitoring Celery.

Install Flower using the following command:

```
pip install flower==1.1.0
```

Once installed, you can launch Flower by running the following command in a new shell from your project directory:

```
celery -A myshop flower
```

Open http://localhost:5555/dashboard in your browser. You will be able to see the active Celery workers and asynchronous task statistics. The screen should look as follows:

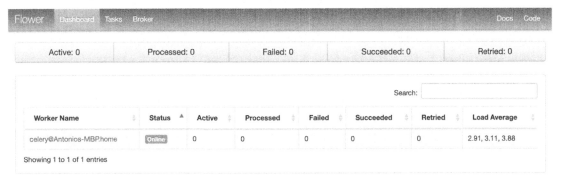

Figure 8.21: The Flower dashboard

You will see an active worker, whose name starts with **celery@** and whose status is **Online**.

Click on the worker's name and then click on the **Queues** tab. You will see the following screen:

Figure 8.22: Flower – Worker Celery task queues

Here you can see the active queue named **celery**. This is the active queue consumer connected to the message broker.

Click the **Tasks** tab. You will see the following screen:

Figure 8.23: Flower – Worker Celery tasks

Here you can see the tasks that have been processed and the number of times that they have been executed. You should see the order_created task and the total times that it has been executed. This number might vary depending on how many orders you have placed.

Open http://localhost:8000/ in your browser. Add some items to the cart, and then complete the checkout process.

Open http://localhost:5555/dashboard in your browser. Flower has registered the task as processed. You should now see 1 under **Processed** and 1 under **Succeeded** as well:

Figure 8.24: Flower – Celery workers

Under **Tasks** you can see additional details about each task registered with Celery:

Figure 8.25: Flower – Celery tasks

You can find the documentation for Flower at https://flower.readthedocs.io/.

Additional resources

The following resources provide additional information related to the topics covered in this chapter:

- Source code for this chapter – `https://github.com/PacktPublishing/Django-4-by-example/tree/main/Chapter08`
- Static files for the project – `https://github.com/PacktPublishing/Django-4-by-Example/tree/main/Chapter08/myshop/shop/static`
- Django session settings – `https://docs.djangoproject.com/en/4.1/ref/settings/#sessions`
- Django built-in context processors – `https://docs.djangoproject.com/en/4.1/ref/templates/api/#built-in-template-context-processors`
- Information about `RequestContext` – `https://docs.djangoproject.com/en/4.1/ref/templates/api/#django.template.RequestContext`
- Celery documentation – `https://docs.celeryq.dev/en/stable/index.html`
- Introduction to Celery – `https://docs.celeryq.dev/en/stable/getting-started/introduction.html`
- Official RabbitMQ Docker image — `https://hub.docker.com/_/rabbitmq`
- RabbitMQ installation instructions – `https://www.rabbitmq.com/download.html`
- Flower documentation – `https://flower.readthedocs.io/`

Summary

In this chapter, you created a basic e-commerce application. You made a product catalog and built a shopping cart using sessions. You implemented a custom context processor to make the cart available to all templates and created a form for placing orders. You also learned how to implement asynchronous tasks using Celery and RabbitMQ.

In the next chapter, you will discover how to integrate a payment gateway into your shop, add custom actions to the administration site, export data in CSV format, and generate PDF files dynamically.

Join us on Discord

Read this book alongside other users and the author.

Ask questions, provide solutions to other readers, chat with the author via *Ask Me Anything* sessions, and much more. Scan the QR code or visit the link to join the book community.

`https://packt.link/django`

Managing Payments and Orders

In the previous chapter, you created a basic online shop with a product catalog and a shopping cart. You learned how to use Django sessions and built a custom context processor. You also learned how to launch asynchronous tasks using Celery and RabbitMQ.

In this chapter, you will learn how to integrate a payment gateway into your site to let users pay by credit card. You will also extend the administration site with different features.

In this chapter, you will:

- Integrate the Stripe payment gateway into your project
- Process credit card payments with Stripe
- Handle payment notifications
- Export orders to CSV files
- Create custom views for the administration site
- Generate PDF invoices dynamically

The source code for this chapter can be found at https://github.com/PacktPublishing/Django-4-by-example/tree/main/Chapter09.

All Python packages used in this chapter are included in the requirements.txt file in the source code for the chapter. You can follow the instructions to install each Python package in the following sections, or you can install all the requirements at once with the command pip install -r requirements.txt.

Integrating a payment gateway

A payment gateway is a technology used by merchants to process payments from customers online. Using a payment gateway, you can manage customers' orders and delegate payment processing to a reliable, secure third party. By using a trusted payment gateway, you won't have to worry about the technical, security, and regulatory complexity of processing credit cards in your own system.

There are several payment gateway providers to choose from. We are going to integrate Stripe, which is a very popular payment gateway used by online services such as Shopify, Uber, Twitch, and GitHub, among others.

Stripe provides an **Application Programming Interface (API)** that allows you to process online payments with multiple payment methods, such as credit card, Google Pay, and Apple Pay. You can learn more about Stripe at `https://www.stripe.com/`.

Stripe provides different products related to payment processing. It can manage one-off payments, recurring payments for subscription services, multiparty payments for platforms and marketplaces, and more.

Stripe offers different integration methods, from Stripe-hosted payment forms to fully customizable checkout flows. We will integrate the *Stripe Checkout* product, which consists of a payment page optimized for conversion. Users will be able to easily pay with a credit card or other payment methods for the items they order. We will receive payment notifications from Stripe. You can see the *Stripe Checkout* documentation at `https://stripe.com/docs/payments/checkout`.

By leveraging *Stripe Checkout* to process payments, you rely on a solution that is secure and compliant with **Payment Card Industry (PCI)** requirements. You will be able to collect payments from Google Pay, Apple Pay, Afterpay, Alipay, SEPA direct debits, Bacs direct debit, BECS direct debit, iDEAL, Sofort, GrabPay, FPX, and other payment methods.

Creating a Stripe account

You need a Stripe account to integrate the payment gateway into your site. Let's create an account to test the Stripe API. Open `https://dashboard.stripe.com/register` in your browser. You will see a form like the following one:

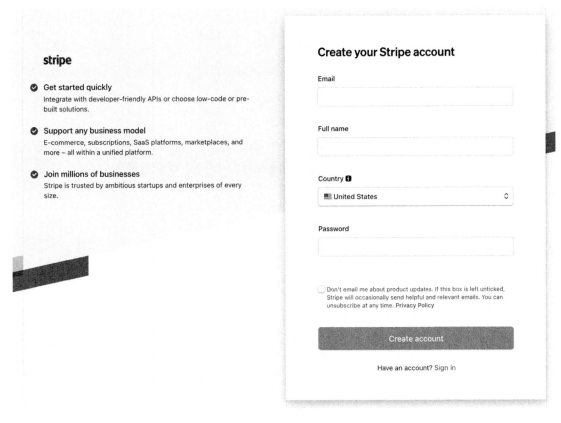

Figure 9.1: The Stripe signup form

Fill in the form with your own data and click on **Create account**. You will receive an email from Stripe with a link to verify your email address. The email will look like this:

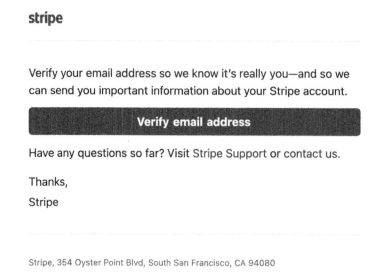

Figure 9.2: The verification email to verify your email address

Open the email in your inbox and click on **Verify email address.**

You will be redirected to the Stripe dashboard screen, which will look like this:

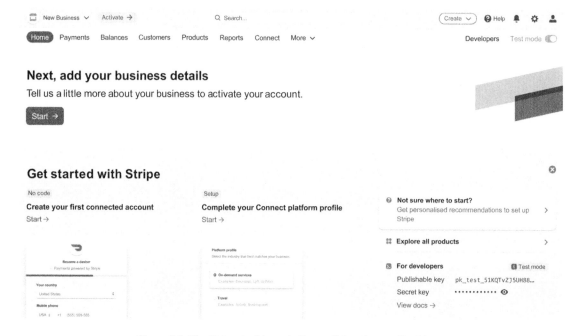

Figure 9.3: The Stripe dashboard after verifying the email address

In the top right of the screen, you can see that **Test mode** is activated. Stripe provides you with a test environment and a production environment. If you own a business or are a freelancer, you can add your business details to activate the account and get access to process real payments. However, this is not necessary to implement and test payments through Stripe, as we will be working on the test environment.

You need to add an account name to process payments. Open `https://dashboard.stripe.com/settings/account` in your browser. You will see the following screen:

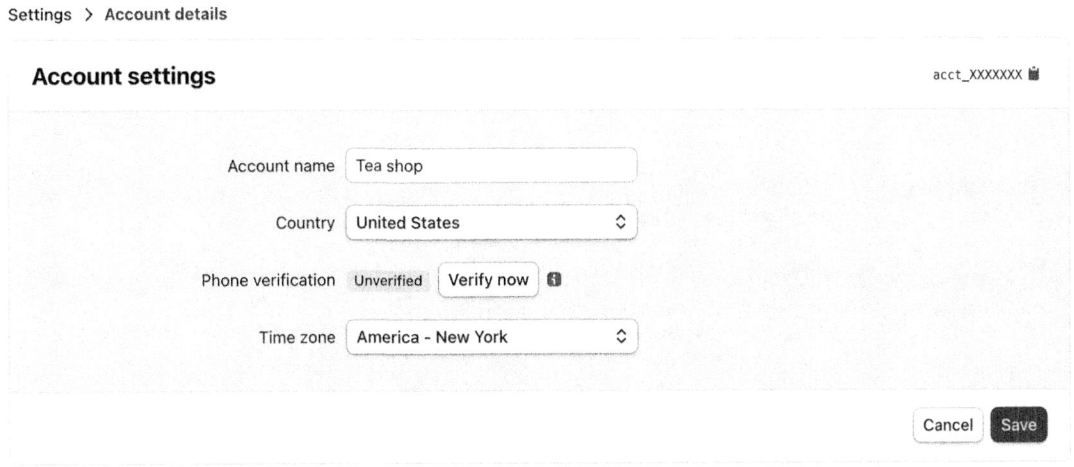

Settings > Account details
Account settings
acct_XXXXXXX
Account name
Tea shop
Country
United States
Phone verification
Unverified
Verify now
Time zone
America - New York
Cancel
Save

Figure 9.4: The Stripe account settings

Under **Account name**, enter the name of your choice and then click on **Save**. Go back to the Stripe dashboard. You will see your account name displayed in the header:

Tea shop
Activate →
Search...
Home
Payments
Balances
Customers
Products
Reports
Connect
More
TEST DATA

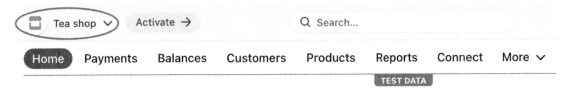

Figure 9.5: The Stripe dashboard header including the account name

We will continue by installing the Stripe Python SDK and adding Stripe to our Django project.

Installing the Stripe Python library

Stripe provides a Python library that simplifies dealing with its API. We are going to integrate the payment gateway into the project using the `stripe` library.

You can find the source code for the Stripe Python library at `https://github.com/stripe/stripe-python`.

Install the `stripe` library from the shell using the following command:

```
pip install stripe==4.0.2
```

Adding Stripe to your project

Open `https://dashboard.stripe.com/test/apikeys` in your browser. You can also access this page from the Stripe dashboard by clicking on **Developers** and then clicking on **API keys**. You will see the following screen:

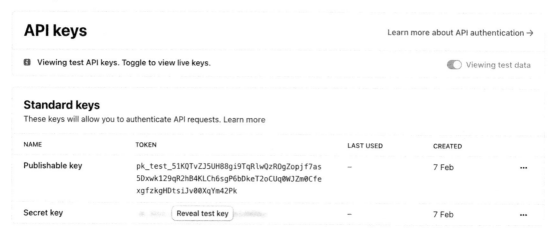

Figure 9.6: The Stripe test API keys screen

Stripe provides a key pair for two different environments, test and production. There is a **Publishable key** and a **Secret key** for each environment. Test mode publishable keys have the prefix `pk_test_` and live mode publishable keys have the prefix `pk_live_`. Test mode secret keys have the prefix `sk_test_` and live mode secret keys have the prefix `sk_live_`.

You will need this information to authenticate requests to the Stripe API. You should always keep your private key secret and store it securely. The publishable key can be used in client-side code such as JavaScript scripts. You can read more about Stripe API keys at `https://stripe.com/docs/keys`.

Add the following settings to the `settings.py` file of your project:

```
# Stripe settings
STRIPE_PUBLISHABLE_KEY = '' # Publishable key
STRIPE_SECRET_KEY = ''      # Secret key
STRIPE_API_VERSION = '2022-08-01'
```

Replace the `STRIPE_PUBLISHABLE_KEY` and `STRIPE_SECRET_KEY` values with the test **Publishable key** and the **Secret key** provided by Stripe. You will use Stripe API version `2022-08-01`. You can see the release notes for this API version at `https://stripe.com/docs/upgrades#2022-08-01`.

You are using the test environment keys for the project. Once you go live and validate your Stripe account, you will obtain the production environment keys. In *Chapter 17, Going Live*, you will learn how to configure settings for multiple environments.

Let's integrate the payment gateway into the checkout process. You can find the Python documentation for Stripe at `https://stripe.com/docs/api?lang=python`.

Building the payment process

The checkout process will work as follows:

1. Add items to the shopping cart
2. Check out the shopping cart
3. Enter credit card details and pay

We are going to create a new application to manage payments. Create a new application in your project using the following command:

```
python manage.py startapp payment
```

Edit the `settings.py` file of the project and add the new application to the `INSTALLED_APPS` setting, as follows. The new line is highlighted in bold:

```
INSTALLED_APPS = [
    # ...
    'shop.apps.ShopConfig',
    'cart.apps.CartConfig',
    'orders.apps.OrdersConfig',
    'payment.apps.PaymentConfig',
]
```

The payment application is now active in the project.

Currently, users are able to place orders but they cannot pay for them. After clients place an order, we need to redirect them to the payment process.

Edit the `views.py` file of the `orders` application and include the following imports:

```
from django.urls import reverse
from django.shortcuts import render, redirect
```

In the same file, find the following lines of the `order_create` view:

```
# launch asynchronous task
order_created.delay(order.id)
return render(request,
              'orders/order/created.html',
              locals())
```

Replace them with the following code:

```python
# launch asynchronous task
order_created.delay(order.id)
# set the order in the session
request.session['order_id'] = order.id
# redirect for payment
return redirect(reverse('payment:process'))
```

The edited view should look as follows:

```python
from django.urls import reverse
from django.shortcuts import render, redirect
# ...

def order_create(request):
    cart = Cart(request)
    if request.method == 'POST':
        form = OrderCreateForm(request.POST)
        if form.is_valid():
            order = form.save()
            for item in cart:
                OrderItem.objects.create(order=order,
                                         product=item['product'],
                                         price=item['price'],
                                         quantity=item['quantity'])
            # clear the cart
            cart.clear()
            # launch asynchronous task
            order_created.delay(order.id)
            # set the order in the session
            request.session['order_id'] = order.id
            # redirect for payment
            return redirect(reverse('payment:process'))
    else:
        form = OrderCreateForm()
    return render(request,
                  'orders/order/create.html',
                  {'cart': cart, 'form': form})
```

Instead of rendering the template orders/order/created.html when placing a new order, the order ID is stored in the user session and the user is redirected to the payment:process URL. We are going to implement this URL later. Remember that Celery has to be running for the order_created task to be queued and executed.

Let's integrate the payment gateway.

Integrating Stripe Checkout

The Stripe Checkout integration consists of a checkout page hosted by Stripe that allows the user to enter the payment details, usually a credit card, and collects the payment. If the payment is successful, Stripe redirects the client to a success page. If the payment is canceled by the client, it redirects the client to a cancel page.

We will implement three views:

- payment_process: Creates a Stripe **Checkout Session** and redirects the client to the Stripe-hosted payment form. A checkout session is a programmatic representation of what the client sees when they are redirected to the payment form, including the products, quantities, currency, and amount to charge
- payment_completed: Displays a message for successful payments. The user is redirected to this view if the payment is successful
- payment_canceled: Displays a message for canceled payments. The user is redirected to this view if the payment is canceled

Figure 9.7 shows the checkout payment flow:

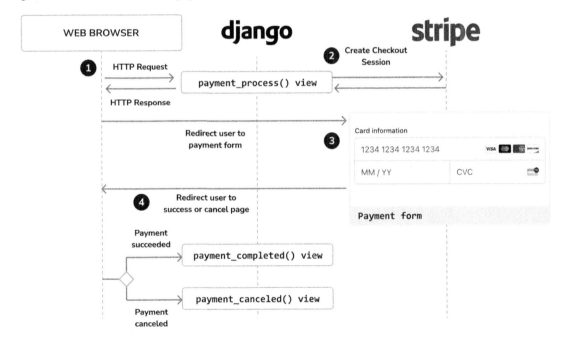

Figure 9.7: The checkout payment flow

The complete checkout process will work as follows:

1. After an order is created, the user is redirected to the payment_process view. The user is presented with an order summary and a button to proceed with the payment.
2. When the user proceeds to pay, a Stripe checkout session is created. The checkout session includes the list of items that the user will purchase, a URL to redirect the user to after a successful payment, and a URL to redirect the user to if the payment is canceled.
3. The view redirects the user to the Stripe-hosted checkout page. This page includes the payment form. The client enters their credit card details and submits the form.
4. Stripe processes the payment and redirects the client to the payment_completed view. If the client doesn't complete the payment, Stripe redirects the client to the payment_canceled view instead.

Let's start building the payment views. Edit the views.py file of the payment application and add the following code to it:

```python
from decimal import Decimal
import stripe
from django.conf import settings
from django.shortcuts import render, redirect, reverse,\
                             get_object_or_404
from orders.models import Order

# create the Stripe instance
stripe.api_key = settings.STRIPE_SECRET_KEY
stripe.api_version = settings.STRIPE_API_VERSION

def payment_process(request):
    order_id = request.session.get('order_id', None)
    order = get_object_or_404(Order, id=order_id)

    if request.method == 'POST':
        success_url = request.build_absolute_uri(
                        reverse('payment:completed'))
        cancel_url = request.build_absolute_uri(
                        reverse('payment:canceled'))
        # Stripe checkout session data
        session_data = {
            'mode': 'payment',
            'client_reference_id': order.id,
            'success_url': success_url,
            'cancel_url': cancel_url,
            'line_items': []
        }
```

```
            # create Stripe checkout session
            session = stripe.checkout.Session.create(**session_data)
            # redirect to Stripe payment form
            return redirect(session.url, code=303)

    else:
        return render(request, 'payment/process.html', locals())
```

In the previous code, the `stripe` module is imported and the Stripe API key is set using the value of the `STRIPE_SECRET_KEY` setting. The API version to use is also set using the value of the `STRIPE_API_VERSION` setting.

The `payment_process` view performs the following tasks:

1. The current `Order` object is retrieved from the database using the `order_id` session key, which was stored previously in the session by the `order_create` view.

2. The `Order` object for the given ID is retrieved. By using the shortcut function `get_object_or_404()`, an `Http404` (page not found) exception is raised if no order is found with the given ID.

3. If the view is loaded with a `GET` request, the template `payment/process.html` is rendered and returned. This template will include the order summary and a button to proceed with the payment, which will generate a `POST` request to the view.

4. If the view is loaded with a `POST` request, a Stripe checkout session is created with `stripe.checkout.Session.create()` using the following parameters:

    *   `mode`: The mode of the checkout session. We use payment for a one-time payment. You can see the different values accepted for this parameter at https://stripe.com/docs/api/checkout/sessions/object#checkout_session_object-mode.

    *   `client_reference_id`: The unique reference for this payment. We will use this to reconcile the Stripe checkout session with our order. By passing the order ID, we link Stripe payments to orders in our system, and we will be able to receive payment notifications from Stripe to mark the orders as paid.

    *   `success_url`: The URL for Stripe to redirect the user to if the payment is successful. We use `request.build_absolute_uri()` to generate an absolute URI from the URL path. You can see the documentation for this method at https://docs.djangoproject.com/en/4.1/ref/request-response/#django.http.HttpRequest.build_absolute_uri.

    *   `cancel_url`: The URL for Stripe to redirect the user to if the payment is canceled.

    *   `line_items`: This is an empty list. We will next populate it with the order items to be purchased.

5. After creating the checkout session, an HTTP redirect with status code `303` is returned to redirect the user to Stripe. The status code `303` is recommended to redirect web applications to a new URI after an HTTP `POST` has been performed.

You can see all the parameters to create a Stripe session object at https://stripe.com/docs/api/checkout/sessions/create.

Let's populate the line_items list with the order items to create the checkout session. Each item will contain the name of the item, the amount to charge, the currency to use, and the quantity purchased.

Add the following code highlighted in bold to the payment_process view:

```python
def payment_process(request):
    order_id = request.session.get('order_id', None)
    order = get_object_or_404(Order, id=order_id)

    if request.method == 'POST':
        success_url = request.build_absolute_uri(
                        reverse('payment:completed'))
        cancel_url = request.build_absolute_uri(
                        reverse('payment:canceled'))
        # Stripe checkout session data
        session_data = {
            'mode': 'payment',
            'success_url': success_url,
            'cancel_url': cancel_url,
            'line_items': []
        }
        # add order items to the Stripe checkout session
        for item in order.items.all():
            session_data['line_items'].append({
                'price_data': {
                    'unit_amount': int(item.price * Decimal('100')),
                    'currency': 'usd',
                    'product_data': {
                        'name': item.product.name,
                    },
                },
                'quantity': item.quantity,
            })
        # create Stripe checkout session
        session = stripe.checkout.Session.create(**session_data)
        # redirect to Stripe payment form
        return redirect(session.url, code=303)

    else:
        return render(request, 'payment/process.html', locals())
```

We use the following information for each item:

- `price_data`: Price-related information.

  - `unit_amount`: The amount in cents to be collected by the payment. This is a positive integer representing how much to charge in the smallest currency unit with no decimal places. For example, to charge $10.00, this would be 1000 (that is, 1,000 cents). The item price, item.price, is multiplied by Decimal('100') to obtain the value in cents and then it is converted into an integer.

  - `currency`: The currency to use in three-letter ISO format. We use usd for US dollars. You can see a list of supported currencies at `https://stripe.com/docs/currencies`.

  - `product_data`: Product-related information.

    - `name`: The name of the product.

- `quantity`: The number of units to purchase.

The `payment_process` view is now ready. Let's create simple views for the payment success and cancel pages.

Add the following code to the `views.py` file of the payment application:

```python
def payment_completed(request):
    return render(request, 'payment/completed.html')


def payment_canceled(request):
    return render(request, 'payment/canceled.html')
```

Create a new file inside the payment application directory and name it urls.py. Add the following code to it:

```python
from django.urls import path
from . import views

app_name = 'payment'

urlpatterns = [
    path('process/', views.payment_process, name='process'),
    path('completed/', views.payment_completed, name='completed'),
    path('canceled/', views.payment_canceled, name='canceled'),
]
```

These are the URLs for the payment workflow. We have included the following URL patterns:

- process: The view that displays the order summary to the user, creates the Stripe checkout session, and redirects the user to the Stripe-hosted payment form

- completed: The view for Stripe to redirect the user to if the payment is successful
- canceled: The view for Stripe to redirect the user to if the payment is canceled

Edit the main urls.py file of the myshop project and include the URL patterns for the payment application, as follows:

```python
urlpatterns = [
    path('admin/', admin.site.urls),
    path('cart/', include('cart.urls', namespace='cart')),
    path('orders/', include('orders.urls', namespace='orders')),
    path('payment/', include('payment.urls', namespace='payment')),
    path('', include('shop.urls', namespace='shop')),
]
```

We have placed the new path before the shop.urls pattern to avoid an unintended pattern match with a pattern defined in shop.urls. Remember that Django runs through each URL pattern in order and stops at the first one that matches the requested URL.

Let's build a template for each view. Create the following file structure inside the payment application directory:

```
templates/
    payment/
        process.html
        completed.html
        canceled.html
```

Edit the payment/process.html template and add the following code to it:

```html
{% extends "shop/base.html" %}
{% load static %}

{% block title %}Pay your order{% endblock %}

{% block content %}
  <h1>Order summary</h1>
  <table class="cart">
    <thead>
      <tr>
        <th>Image</th>
        <th>Product</th>
        <th>Price</th>
        <th>Quantity</th>
        <th>Total</th>
      </tr>
    </thead>
```

```
    <tbody>
      {% for item in order.items.all %}
        <tr class="row{% cycle "1" "2" %}">
          <td>
            <img src="{% if item.product.image %}{{ item.product.image.url }}
            {% else %}{% static "img/no_image.png" %}{% endif %}">
          </td>
          <td>{{ item.product.name }}</td>
          <td class="num">${{ item.price }}</td>
          <td class="num">{{ item.quantity }}</td>
          <td class="num">${{ item.get_cost }}</td>
        </tr>
      {% endfor %}
      <tr class="total">
        <td colspan="4">Total</td>
        <td class="num">${{ order.get_total_cost }}</td>
      </tr>
    </tbody>
  </table>
  <form action="{% url "payment:process" %}" method="post">
    <input type="submit" value="Pay now">
    {% csrf_token %}
  </form>
{% endblock %}
```

This is the template to display the order summary to the user and allow the client to proceed with the payment. It includes a form and a **Pay now** button to submit it via POST. When the form is submitted, the payment_process view creates the Stripe checkout session and redirects the user to the Stripe-hosted payment form.

Edit the payment/completed.html template and add the following code to it:

```
{% extends "shop/base.html" %}

{% block title %}Payment successful{% endblock %}

{% block content %}
  <h1>Your payment was successful</h1>
  <p>Your payment has been processed successfully.</p>
{% endblock %}
```

This is the template for the page that the user is redirected to after a successful payment.

Edit the `payment/canceled.html` template and add the following code to it:

```
{% extends "shop/base.html" %}

{% block title %}Payment canceled{% endblock %}

{% block content %}
  <h1>Your payment has not been processed</h1>
  <p>There was a problem processing your payment.</p>
{% endblock %}
```

This is the template for the page that the user is redirected to when the payment is canceled.

We have implemented the necessary views to process payments, including their URL patterns and templates. It's time to try out the checkout process.

Testing the checkout process

Execute the following command in the shell to start the RabbitMQ server with Docker:

```
docker run -it --rm --name rabbitmq -p 5672:5672 -p 15672:15672
rabbitmq:management
```

This will run RabbitMQ on port 5672 and the web-based management interface on port 15672.

Open another shell and start the Celery worker from your project directory with the following command:

```
celery -A myshop worker -l info
```

Open one more shell and start the development server from your project directory with this command:

```
python manage.py runserver
```

Open `http://127.0.0.1:8000/` in your browser, add some products to the shopping cart, and fill in the checkout form. Click the **Place order** button. The order will be persisted to the database, the order ID will be saved in the current session, and you will be redirected to the payment process page.

The payment process page will look as follows:

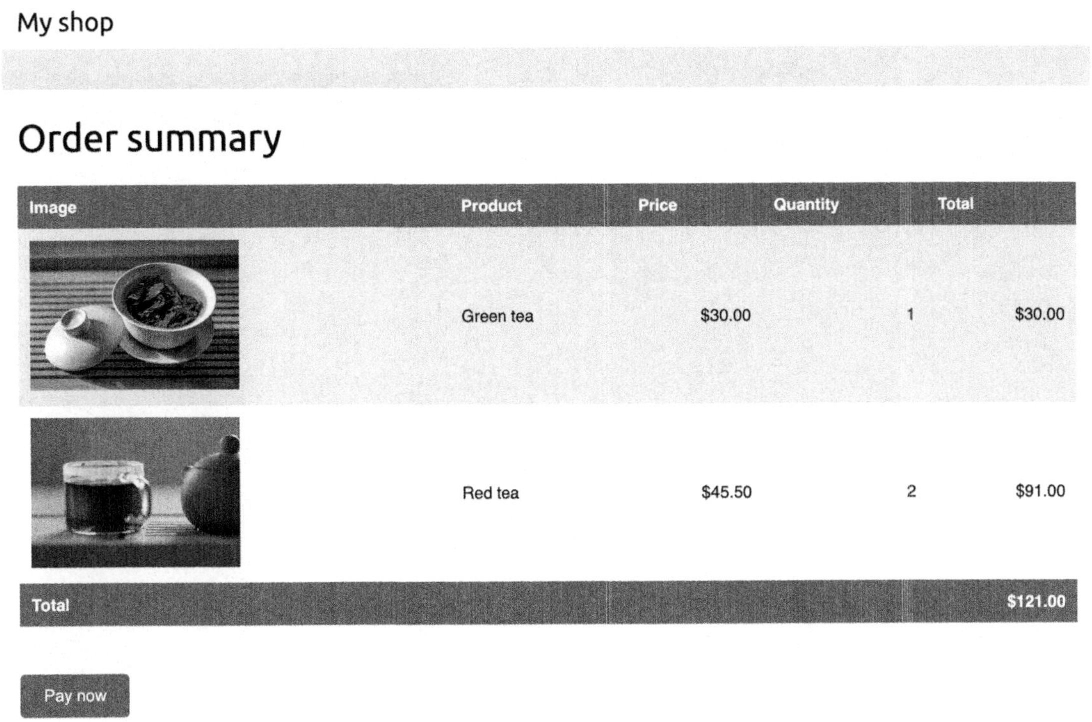

My shop

Order summary

Image	Product	Price	Quantity	Total
	Green tea	$30.00	1	$30.00
	Red tea	$45.50	2	$91.00
Total				**$121.00**

`Pay now`

Figure 9.8: The payment process page including an order summary

Images in this chapter:

- *Green tea*: Photo by Jia Ye on Unsplash
- *Red tea*: Photo by Manki Kim on Unsplash

On this page, you can see an order summary and a **Pay now** button. Click on **Pay now**. The payment_ process view will create a Stripe checkout session and you will be redirected to the Stripe-hosted payment form. You will see the following page:

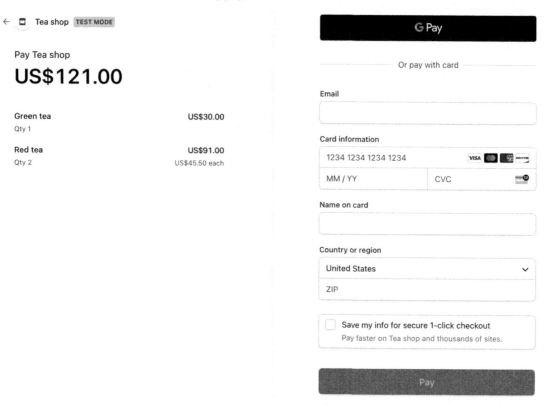

Figure 9.9: The Stripe checkout payment from

Using test credit cards

Stripe provides different test credit cards from different card issuers and countries, which allows you to simulate payments to test all possible scenarios (successful payment, declined payment, etc.). The following table shows some of the cards you can test for different scenarios:

Result	Test Credit Card	CVC	Expiry date
Successful payment	4242 4242 4242 4242	Any 3 digits	Any future date
Failed payment	4000 0000 0000 0002	Any 3 digits	Any future date
Requires 3D secure authentication	4000 0025 0000 3155	Any 3 digits	Any future date

You can find the complete list of credit cards for testing at `https://stripe.com/docs/testing`.

We are going to use the test card 4242 4242 4242 4242, which is a Visa card that returns a successful purchase. We will use the CVC 123 and any future expiration date, such as 12/29. Enter the credit card details in the payment form as follows:

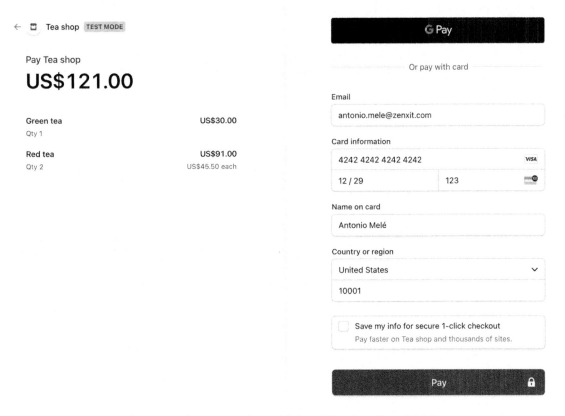

Figure 9.10: The payment form with the valid test credit card details

Click the **Pay** button. The button text will change to **Processing...**, as in *Figure 9.11*:

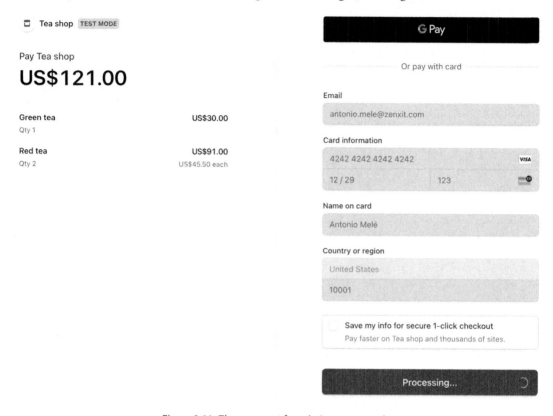

Figure 9.11: The payment form being processed

After a couple of seconds, you will see the button turns green like in *Figure 9.12*:

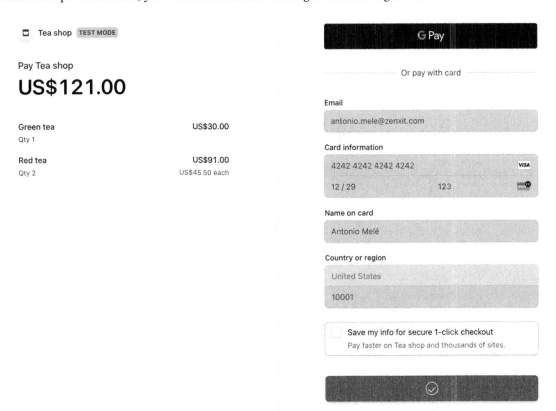

Figure 9.12: The payment form after the payment is successful

Then Stripe redirects your browser to the payment completed URL you provided when creating the checkout session. You will see the following page:

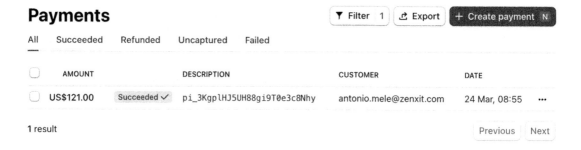

Figure 9.13: The successful payment page

Checking the payment information in the Stripe dashboard

Access the Stripe dashboard at `https://dashboard.stripe.com/test/payments`. Under **Payments**, you will be able to see the payment like in *Figure 9.14*:

Payments

Filter 1   Export   + Create payment N

All   Succeeded   Refunded   Uncaptured   Failed

AMOUNT		DESCRIPTION	CUSTOMER	DATE	
US$121.00	Succeeded ✓	pi_3KgplHJ5UH88gi9T0e3c8Nhy	antonio.mele@zenxit.com	24 Mar, 08:55	...

1 result   Previous   Next

Figure 9.14: The payment object with status Succeeded in the Stripe dashboard

The payment status is **Succeeded**. The payment description includes the **payment intent** ID that starts with `pi_`. When a checkout session is confirmed, Stripe creates a payment intent associated with the session. A payment intent is used to collect a payment from the user. Stripe records all attempted payments as payment intents. Each payment intent has a unique ID, and it encapsulates the details of the transaction, such as the supported payment methods, the amount to collect, and the desired currency. Click on the transaction to access the payment details.

You will see the following screen:

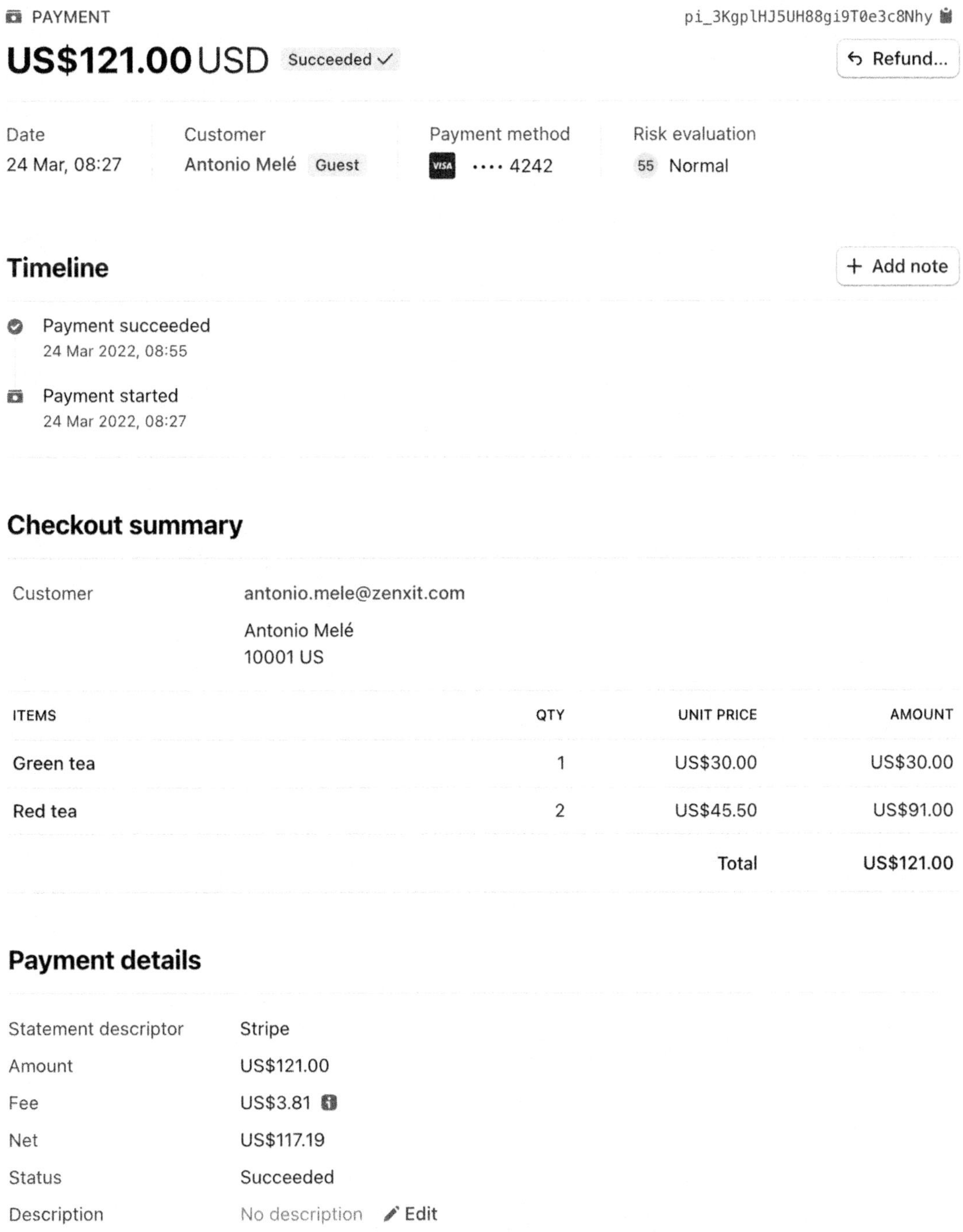

PAYMENT pi_3KgplHJ5UH88gi9T0e3c8Nhy

US$121.00 USD   Succeeded ✓   ↩ Refund...

Date	Customer	Payment method	Risk evaluation
24 Mar, 08:27	Antonio Melé Guest	VISA •••• 4242	55 Normal

Timeline   + Add note

✓ **Payment succeeded**
24 Mar 2022, 08:55

▣ **Payment started**
24 Mar 2022, 08:27

Checkout summary

Customer   antonio.mele@zenxit.com

                  Antonio Melé
                  10001 US

ITEMS	QTY	UNIT PRICE	AMOUNT
Green tea	1	US$30.00	US$30.00
Red tea	2	US$45.50	US$91.00
		Total	US$121.00

Payment details

Statement descriptor	Stripe
Amount	US$121.00
Fee	US$3.81 ⓘ
Net	US$117.19
Status	Succeeded
Description	No description ✎ Edit

Figure 9.15: Payment details for a Stripe transaction

Here you can see the payment information and the payment timeline, including payment changes. Under **Checkout summary**, you can find the line items purchased, including name, quantity, unit price, and amount. Under **Payment details**, you can see a breakdown of the amount paid and the Stripe fee for processing the payment.

Under this section, you will find a **Payment method** section including details about the payment method and the credit card checks performed by Stripe, like in *Figure 9.16*:

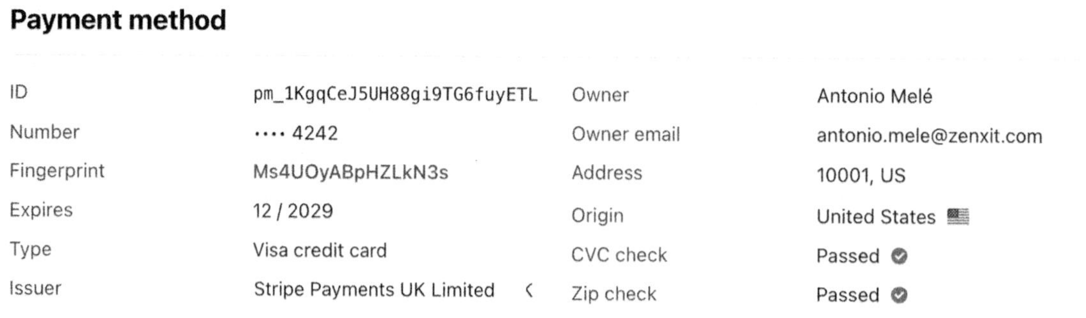

Payment method

ID	pm_1KgqCeJ5UH88gi9TG6fuyETL	Owner	Antonio Melé
Number	•••• 4242	Owner email	antonio.mele@zenxit.com
Fingerprint	Ms4UOyABpHZLkN3s	Address	10001, US
Expires	12 / 2029	Origin	United States 🇺🇸
Type	Visa credit card	CVC check	Passed ✅
Issuer	Stripe Payments UK Limited ‹	Zip check	Passed ✅

Figure 9.16: Payment method used in the Stripe transaction

Under this section, you will find another section named **Events and logs**, like in *Figure 9.17*:

Events and logs

LATEST ACTIVITY

PaymentIntent status: succeeded

ALL ACTIVITY

A Checkout Session was completed
24/03/2022, 08:55:51

The payment pi_3KgplHJ5UH88gi9T0e3c8Nhy for US$121.00 has succeeded
24/03/2022, 08:55:50

ch_3LXk4dJ5UH88gi9T1BeplYFX was charged US$121.00
24/03/2022, 08:55:50

A new payment pi_3KgplHJ5UH88gi9T0e3c8Nhy for US$121.00 was created
24/03/2022, 08:55:49

200 OK A request to confirm a Checkout Session completed
24/03/2022, 08:55:31

200 OK A request to create a Checkout Session completed
24/03/2022, 08:55:30

⮂ From Stripe

checkout.session.completed

View event detail

Event data

```
1   {
2       "id": "cs_test_a1cCmTfq07pHKkqJJ7uW9F4RJMdfHCvYNasrQnOPXrk4xti",
3       "object": "checkout.session",
4       "livemode": false,
5       "payment_intent": pi_3KgplHJ5UH88gi9T0e3c8Nhy,
6       "status": "complete",
7       "after_expiration": null,
8       "allow_promotion_codes": null,
9       "amount_subtotal": 12100,
10      "amount_total": 12100,
```

⊘ See all 72 lines

Figure 9.17: Events and logs for a Stripe transaction

This section contains all the activity related to the transaction, including requests to the Stripe API. You can click on any request to see the HTTP request to the Stripe API and the response in JSON format.

Let's review the activity events in chronological order, from bottom to top:

1. First, a new checkout session is created by sending a POST request to the Stripe API endpoint /v1/checkout/sessions. The Stripe SDK method stripe.checkout.Session.create() that is used in the payment_process view builds and sends the request to the Stripe API and handles the response to return a session object.

2. The user is redirected to the checkout page where they submit the payment form. A request to confirm the checkout session is sent by the Stripe checkout page.

3. A new payment intent is created.

4. A charge related to the payment intent is created.

5. The payment intent is now completed with a successful payment.

6. The checkout session is completed.

Congratulations! You have successfully integrated Stripe Checkout into your project. Next, you will learn how to receive payment notifications from Stripe and how to reference Stripe payments in your shop orders.

Using webhooks to receive payment notifications

Stripe can push real-time events to our application by using webhooks. A **webhook**, also called a callback, can be thought of as an event-driven API instead of a request-driven API. Instead of polling the Stripe API frequently to know when a new payment is completed, Stripe can send an HTTP request to a URL of our application to notify of successful payments in real time. These notification of these events will be asynchronous, when the event occurs, regardless of our synchronous calls to the Stripe API.

We will build a webhook endpoint to receive Stripe events. The webhook will consist of a view that will receive a JSON payload with the event information to process it. We will use the event information to mark orders as paid when the checkout session is successfully completed.

Creating a webhook endpoint

You can add webhook endpoint URLs to your Stripe account to receive events. Since we are using webhooks and we don't have a hosted website accessible through a public URL, we will use the Stripe **Command-Line Interface (CLI)** to listen to events and forward them to our local environment.

Open `https://dashboard.stripe.com/test/webhooks` in your browser. You will see the following screen:

Webhooks

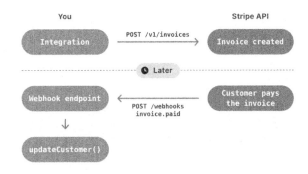

Listen to Stripe events

Create webhook endpoints, so that Stripe can notify your integration when asynchronous events occur.

Add an endpoint | Test in a local environment

Learn about webhooks

Figure 9.18: The Stripe webhooks default screen

Here you can see a schema of how Stripe notifies your integration asynchronously. You will get Stripe notifications in real time whenever an event happens. Stripe sends different types of events like checkout session created, payment intent created, payment intent updated, or checkout session completed. You can find a list of all the types of events that Stripe sends at `https://stripe.com/docs/api/events/types`.

Click on **Test in a local environment**. You will see the following screen:

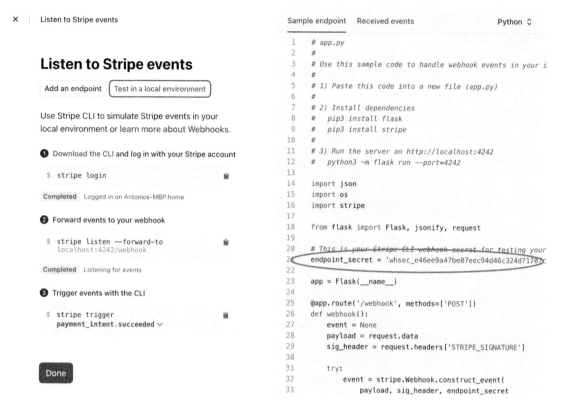

Figure 9.19: The Stripe webhook setup screen

This screen shows the steps to listen to Stripe events from your local environment. It also includes a sample Python webhook endpoint. Copy just the endpoint_secret value.

Edit the settings.py file of the myshop project and add the following setting to it:

```
STRIPE_WEBHOOK_SECRET = ''
```

Replace the STRIPE_WEBHOOK_SECRET value with the endpoint_secret value provided by Stripe.

To build a webhook endpoint, we will create a view that receives a JSON payload with the event details. We will check the event details to identify when a checkout session is completed and mark the related order as paid.

Stripe signs the webhook events it sends to your endpoints by including a Stripe-Signature header with a signature in each event. By checking the Stripe signature, you can verify that events were sent by Stripe and not by a third party. If you don't check the signature, an attacker could send fake events to your webhooks intentionally. The Stripe SDK provides a method to verify signatures. We will use it to create a webhook that verifies the signature.

Add a new file to the payment/ application directory and name it webhooks.py. Add the following code to the new webhooks.py file:

```python
import stripe
from django.conf import settings
from django.http import HttpResponse
from django.views.decorators.csrf import csrf_exempt
from orders.models import Order


@csrf_exempt
def stripe_webhook(request):
    payload = request.body
    sig_header = request.META['HTTP_STRIPE_SIGNATURE']
    event = None

    try:
        event = stripe.Webhook.construct_event(
                    payload,
                    sig_header,
                    settings.STRIPE_WEBHOOK_SECRET)
    except ValueError as e:
        # Invalid payload
        return HttpResponse(status=400)
    except stripe.error.SignatureVerificationError as e:
        # Invalid signature
        return HttpResponse(status=400)

    return HttpResponse(status=200)
```

The @csrf_exempt decorator is used to prevent Django from performing the CSRF validation that is done by default for all POST requests. We use the method stripe.Webhook.construct_event() of the stripe library to verify the event's signature header. If the event's payload or the signature is invalid, we return an HTTP 400 Bad Request response. Otherwise, we return an HTTP 200 OK response. This is the basic functionality required to verify the signature and construct the event from the JSON payload. Now we can implement the actions of the webhook endpoint.

Add the following code highlighted in bold to the stripe_webhook view:

```python
@csrf_exempt
def stripe_webhook(request):
    payload = request.body
    sig_header = request.META['HTTP_STRIPE_SIGNATURE']
```

```
        event = None

        try:
            event = stripe.Webhook.construct_event(
                        payload,
                        sig_header,
                        settings.STRIPE_WEBHOOK_SECRET)
        except ValueError as e:
            # Invalid payload
            return HttpResponse(status=400)
        except stripe.error.SignatureVerificationError as e:
            # Invalid signature
            return HttpResponse(status=400)

        if event.type == 'checkout.session.completed':
            session = event.data.object
            if session.mode == 'payment' and session.payment_status == 'paid':
                try:
                    order = Order.objects.get(id=session.client_reference_id)
                except Order.DoesNotExist:
                    return HttpResponse(status=404)
                # mark order as paid
                order.paid = True
                order.save()

        return HttpResponse(status=200)
```

In the new code, we check if the event received is checkout.session.completed. This event indicates that the checkout session has been successfully completed. If we receive this event, we retrieve the session object and check whether the session mode is payment because this is the expected mode for one-off payments. Then we get the client_reference_id attribute that we used when we created the checkout session and use the Django ORM to retrieve the Order object with the given id. If the order does not exist, we raise an HTTP 404 exception. Otherwise, we mark the order as paid with order.paid = True and we save the order to the database.

Edit the `urls.py` file of the payment application and add the following code highlighted in bold:

```
from django.urls import path
from . import views
from . import webhooks

app_name = 'payment'

urlpatterns = [
    path('process/', views.payment_process, name='process'),
    path('completed/', views.payment_completed, name='completed'),
    path('canceled/', views.payment_canceled, name='canceled'),
    path('webhook/', webhooks.stripe_webhook, name='stripe-webhook'),
]
```

We have imported the webhooks module and added the URL pattern for the Stripe webhook.

Testing webhook notifications

To test webhooks, you need to install the Stripe CLI. The Stripe CLI is a developer tool that allows you to test and manage your integration with Stripe directly from your shell. You will find installation instructions at `https://stripe.com/docs/stripe-cli#install`.

If you are using macOS or Linux, you can install the Stripe CLI with Homebrew using the following command:

```
brew install stripe/stripe-cli/stripe
```

If you are using Windows, or you are using macOS or Linux without Homebrew, download the latest Stripe CLI release for macOS, Linux, or Windows from `https://github.com/stripe/stripe-cli/releases/latest` and unzip the file. If you are using Windows, run the unzipped `.exe` file.

After installing the Stripe CLI, run the following command from a shell:

```
stripe login
```

You will see the following output:

```
Your pairing code is: xxxx-yyyy-zzzz-oooo
This pairing code verifies your authentication with Stripe.
Press Enter to open the browser or visit https://dashboard.stripe.com/
stripecli/confirm_auth?t=....
```

Press *Enter* or open the URL in your browser. You will see the following screen:

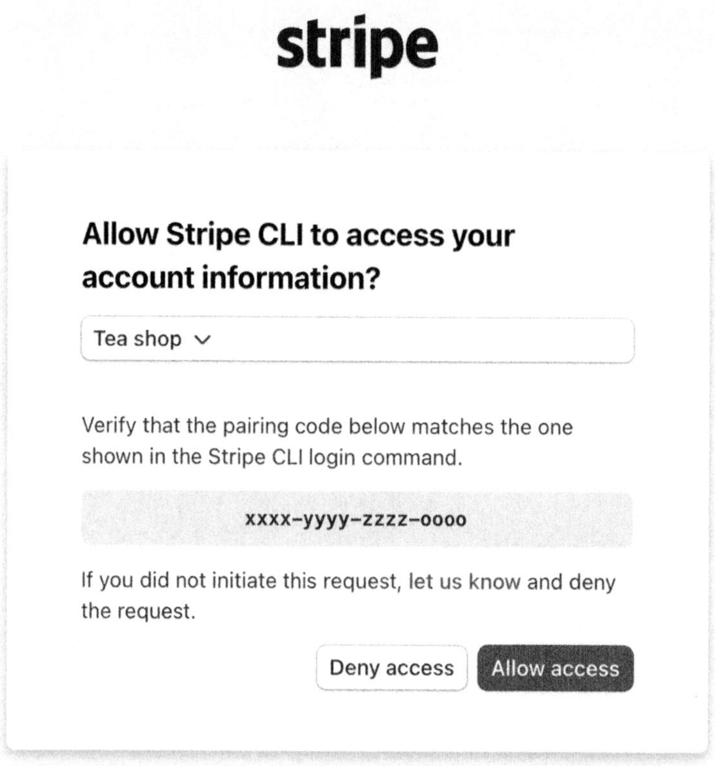

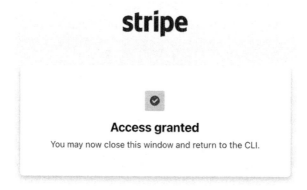

Figure 9.20: The Stripe CLI pairing screen

Verify that the pairing code in the Stripe CLI matches the one shown on the website and click on **Allow access.** You will see the following message:

stripe

Access granted
You may now close this window and return to the CLI.

Figure 9.21: The Stripe CLI pairing confirmation

Now run the following command from your shell:

```
stripe listen --forward-to localhost:8000/payment/webhook/
```

We use this command to tell Stripe to listen to events and forward them to our local host. We use port 8000, where the Django development server is running, and the path /payment/webhook/, which matches the URL pattern of our webhook.

You will see the following output:

```
Getting ready... > Ready! You are using Stripe API Version [2022-08-01]. Your
webhook signing secret is xxxxxxxxxxxxxxxxxxx (^C to quit)
```

Here, you can see the webhook secret. Check that the webhook signing secret matches the STRIPE_WEBHOOK_SECRET setting in the settings.py file of your project.

Open https://dashboard.stripe.com/test/webhooks in your browser. You will see the following screen:

Webhooks

Hosted endpoints   + Add endpoint

Listen to live Stripe events by creating a hosted webhook endpoint when your app is deployed online.

Local listeners   + Add local listener

DEVICE		VERSION	STATUS
🖥 Antonios-MacBook-Pro.local	localhost:8000/payment/webhook/	1.11.0	Listening

Figure 9.22: The Stripe Webhooks page

Under **Local listeners**, you will see the local listener that we created.

 In a production environment, the Stripe CLI is not needed. Instead, you would need to add a hosted webhook endpoint using the URL of your hosted application.

Open http://127.0.0.1:8000/ in your browser, add some products to the shopping cart, and complete the checkout process.

Check the shell where you are running the Stripe CLI:

```
2022-08-17 13:06:13   --> payment_intent.created [evt_...]
2022-08-17 13:06:13  <-- [200] POST http://localhost:8000/payment/webhook/
[evt_...]

2022-08-17 13:06:13   --> payment_intent.succeeded [evt_...]
2022-08-17 13:06:13  <-- [200] POST http://localhost:8000/payment/webhook/
[evt_...]

2022-08-17 13:06:13   --> charge.succeeded [evt_...]
2022-08-17 13:06:13  <-- [200] POST http://localhost:8000/payment/webhook/
[evt_...]

2022-08-17 13:06:14   --> checkout.session.completed [evt_...]
2022-08-17 13:06:14  <-- [200] POST http://localhost:8000/payment/webhook/
[evt_...]
```

You can see the different events that have been sent by Stripe to the local webhook endpoint. These are, in chronological order:

- payment_intent.created: The payment intent has been created.
- payment_intent.succeeded: The payment intent succeeded.
- charge.succeeded: The charge associated with the payment intent succeeded.
- checkout.session.completed: The checkout session has been completed. This is the event that we use to mark the order as paid.

The stripe_webhook webhook returns an HTTP 200 OK response to all of the requests sent by Stripe. However, we only process the event checkout.session.completed to mark the order related to the payment as paid.

Next, open http://127.0.0.1:8000/admin/orders/order/ in your browser. The order should now be marked as paid:

PAID

Figure 9.23: An order marked as paid in the order list of the administration site

Now orders get automatically marked as paid with Stripe payment notifications. Next, you are going to learn how to reference Stripe payments in your shop orders.

Referencing Stripe payments in orders

Each Stripe payment has a unique identifier. We can use the payment ID to associate each order with its corresponding Stripe payment. We will add a new field to the Order model of the orders application, so that we can reference the related payment by its ID. This will allow us to link each order with the related Stripe transaction.

Edit the models.py file of the orders application and add the following field to the Order model. The new field is highlighted in bold:

```python
class Order(models.Model):
    # ...
    stripe_id = models.CharField(max_length=250, blank=True)
```

Let's sync this field with the database. Use the following command to generate the database migrations for the project:

```
python manage.py makemigrations
```

You will see the following output:

```
Migrations for 'orders':
  orders/migrations/0002_order_stripe_id.py
    - Add field stripe_id to order
```

Apply the migration to the database with the following command:

```
python manage.py migrate
```

You will see output that ends with the following line:

```
Applying orders.0002_order_stripe_id... OK
```

The model changes are now synced with the database. Now you will be able to store the Stripe payment ID for each order.

Edit the stripe_webhook function in the views.py file of the payment application and add the following lines highlighted in bold:

```python
# ...
@csrf_exempt
def stripe_webhook(request):
    # ...

    if event.type == 'checkout.session.completed':
        session = event.data.object
        if session.mode == 'payment' and session.payment_status == 'paid':
            try:
```

```
                  order = Order.objects.get(id=session.client_reference_id)
              except Order.DoesNotExist:
                  return HttpResponse(status=404)
              # mark order as paid
              order.paid = True
              # store Stripe payment ID
              order.stripe_id = session.payment_intent
              order.save()
              # Launch asynchronous task
              payment_completed.delay(order.id)

      return HttpResponse(status=200)
```

With this change, when receiving a webhook notification for a completed checkout session, the payment intent ID is stored in the `stripe_id` field of the order object.

Open `http://127.0.0.1:8000/` in your browser, add some products to the shopping cart, and complete the checkout process. Then, access `http://127.0.0.1:8000/admin/orders/order/` in your browser and click on the latest order ID to edit it. The `stripe_id` field should contain the payment intent ID as in *Figure 9.24*:

Stripe id: pi_3KgzdDJ5UH88gi9T15cZLTrO

Figure 9.24: The Stripe ID field with the payment intent ID

Great! We are successfully referencing Stripe payments in orders. Now, we can add Stripe payment IDs to the order list on the administration site. We can also include a link to each payment ID to see the payment details in the Stripe dashboard.

Edit the `models.py` file of the orders application and add the following code highlighted in bold:

```
from django.db import models
from django.conf import settings
from shop.models import Product


class Order(models.Model):
    # ...

    class Meta:
        # ...

    def __str__(self):
```

```
                return f'Order {self.id}'

        def get_total_cost(self):
            return sum(item.get_cost() for item in self.items.all())

        def get_stripe_url(self):
            if not self.stripe_id:
                # no payment associated
                return ''
            if '_test_' in settings.STRIPE_SECRET_KEY:
                # Stripe path for test payments
                path = '/test/'
            else:
                # Stripe path for real payments
                path = '/'
            return f'https://dashboard.stripe.com{path}payments/{self.stripe_id}'
```

We have added the new get_stripe_url() method to the Order model. This method is used to return the Stripe dashboard's URL for the payment associated with the order. If no payment ID is stored in the stripe_id field of the Order object, an empty string is returned. Otherwise, the URL for the payment in the Stripe dashboard is returned. We check if the string _test_ is present in the STRIPE_SECRET_KEY setting to discriminate the production environment from the test environment. Payments in the production environment follow the pattern https://dashboard.stripe.com/payments/{id}, whereas test payments follow the pattern https://dashboard.stripe.com/payments/test/{id}.

Let's add a link to each Order object on the list display page of the administration site.

Edit the admin.py file of the orders application and add the following code highlighted in bold:

```
from django.utils.safestring import mark_safe

def order_payment(obj):
    url = obj.get_stripe_url()
    if obj.stripe_id:
        html = f'<a href="{url}" target="_blank">{obj.stripe_id}</a>'
        return mark_safe(html)
    return ''
order_payment.short_description = 'Stripe payment'

@admin.register(Order)
class OrderAdmin(admin.ModelAdmin):
    list_display = ['id', 'first_name', 'last_name', 'email',
```

```
                        'address', 'postal_code', 'city', 'paid',
                    order_payment, 'created', 'updated']
    # ...
```

The order_stripe_payment() function takes an Order object as an argument and returns an HTML link with the payment URL in Stripe. Django escapes HTML output by default. We use the mark_safe function to avoid auto-escaping.

 Avoid using mark_safe on input that has come from the user to avoid **Cross-Site Scripting (XSS)**. XSS enables attackers to inject client-side scripts into web content viewed by other users.

Open http://127.0.0.1:8000/admin/orders/order/ in your browser. You will see a new column named **STRIPE PAYMENT**. You will see the related Stripe payment ID for the latest order. If you click on the payment ID, you will be taken to the payment URL in Stripe, where you can find the additional payment details.

PAID	STRIPE PAYMENT
✔	pi_3KgzZVJ5UH88gi9T1l8ofnc6

Figure 9.25: The Stripe payment ID for an order object in the administration site

Now you automatically store Stripe payment IDs in orders when receiving payment notifications. You have successfully integrated Stripe into your project.

Going live

Once you have tested your integration, you can apply for a production Stripe account. When you are ready to move into production, remember to replace your test Stripe credentials with the live ones in the settings.py file. You will also need to add a webhook endpoint for your hosted website at https://dashboard.stripe.com/webhooks instead of using the Stripe CLI. *Chapter 17, Going Live*, will teach you how to configure project settings for multiple environments.

Exporting orders to CSV files

Sometimes, you might want to export the information contained in a model to a file so that you can import it into another system. One of the most widely used formats to export/import data is **Comma-Separated Values (CSV)**. A CSV file is a plain text file consisting of a number of records. There is usually one record per line and some delimiter character, usually a literal comma, separating the record fields. We are going to customize the administration site to be able to export orders to CSV files.

Adding custom actions to the administration site

Django offers a wide range of options to customize the administration site. You are going to modify the object list view to include a custom administration action. You can implement custom administration actions to allow staff users to apply actions to multiple elements at once in the change list view.

An administration action works as follows: a user selects objects from the administration object list page with checkboxes, then they select an action to perform on all of the selected items, and execute the actions. *Figure 9.26* shows where actions are located in the administration site:

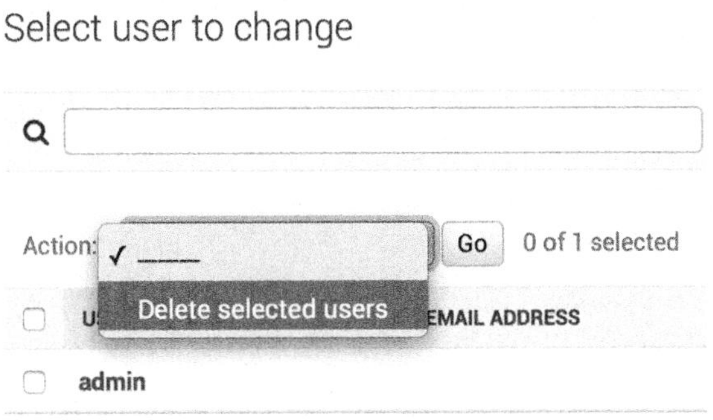

Figure 9.26: The drop-down menu for Django administration actions

You can create a custom action by writing a regular function that receives the following parameters:

- The current `ModelAdmin` being displayed
- The current request object as an `HttpRequest` instance
- A QuerySet for the objects selected by the user

This function will be executed when the action is triggered from the administration site.

You are going to create a custom administration action to download a list of orders as a CSV file.

Edit the `admin.py` file of the `orders` application and add the following code before the `OrderAdmin` class:

```python
import csv
import datetime
from django.http import HttpResponse

def export_to_csv(modeladmin, request, queryset):
    opts = modeladmin.model._meta
    content_disposition = f'attachment; filename={opts.verbose_name}.csv'
    response = HttpResponse(content_type='text/csv')
    response['Content-Disposition'] = content_disposition
    writer = csv.writer(response)
    fields = [field for field in opts.get_fields() if not \
              field.many_to_many and not field.one_to_many]
```

```
    # Write a first row with header information
    writer.writerow([field.verbose_name for field in fields])
    # Write data rows
    for obj in queryset:
        data_row = []
        for field in fields:
            value = getattr(obj, field.name)
            if isinstance(value, datetime.datetime):
                value = value.strftime('%d/%m/%Y')
            data_row.append(value)
        writer.writerow(data_row)
    return response
export_to_csv.short_description = 'Export to CSV'
```

In this code, you perform the following tasks:

1. You create an instance of HttpResponse, specifying the text/csv content type, to tell the browser that the response has to be treated as a CSV file. You also add a Content-Disposition header to indicate that the HTTP response contains an attached file.
2. You create a CSV writer object that will write to the response object.
3. You get the model fields dynamically using the get_fields() method of the model's _meta options. You exclude many-to-many and one-to-many relationships.
4. You write a header row including the field names.
5. You iterate over the given QuerySet and write a row for each object returned by the QuerySet. You take care of formatting datetime objects because the output value for CSV has to be a string.
6. You customize the display name for the action in the actions drop-down element of the administration site by setting a short_description attribute on the function.

You have created a generic administration action that can be added to any ModelAdmin class.

Finally, add the new export_to_csv administration action to the OrderAdmin class, as follows. New code is highlighted in bold:

```
@admin.register(Order)
class OrderAdmin(admin.ModelAdmin):
    list_display = ['id', 'first_name', 'last_name', 'email',
                    'address', 'postal_code', 'city', 'paid',
                    order_payment, 'created', 'updated']
    list_filter = ['paid', 'created', 'updated']
    inlines = [OrderItemInline]
    actions = [export_to_csv]
```

Start the development server with the command:

```
python manage.py runserver
```

Open `http://127.0.0.1:8000/admin/orders/order/` in your browser. The resulting administration action should look like this:

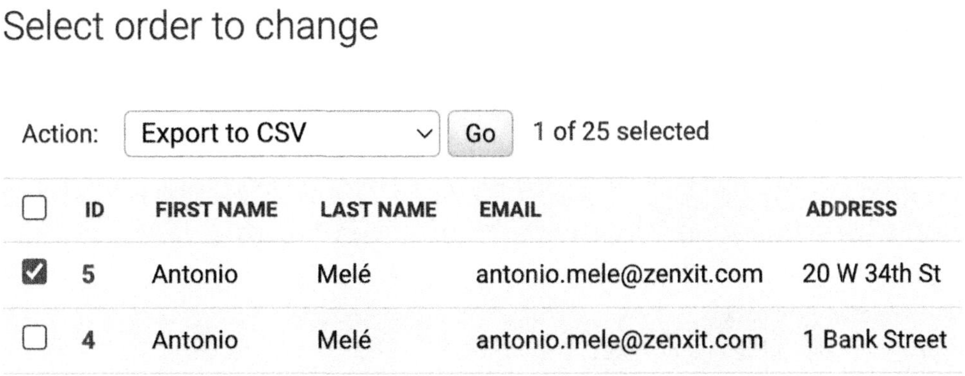

Select order to change

	ID	FIRST NAME	LAST NAME	EMAIL	ADDRESS
☑	5	Antonio	Melé	antonio.mele@zenxit.com	20 W 34th St
☐	4	Antonio	Melé	antonio.mele@zenxit.com	1 Bank Street

Action: Export to CSV ⌄ Go 1 of 25 selected

Figure 9.27: Using the custom Export to CSV administration action

Select some orders and choose the **Export to CSV** action from the select box, then click the **Go** button. Your browser will download the generated CSV file named `order.csv`. Open the downloaded file using a text editor. You should see content with the following format, including a header row and a row for each `Order` object you selected:

```
ID,first name,last name,email,address,postal
code,city,created,updated,paid,stripe id
5,Antonio,Melé,antonio.mele@zenxit.com,20 W 34th St,10001,New
York,24/03/2022,24/03/2022,True,pi_3KgzZVJ5UH88gi9T1l8ofnc6
...
```

As you can see, creating administration actions is pretty straightforward. You can learn more about generating CSV files with Django at `https://docs.djangoproject.com/en/4.1/howto/outputting-csv/`.

Next, you are going to customize the administration site further by creating a custom administration view.

Extending the administration site with custom views

Sometimes, you may want to customize the administration site beyond what is possible through configuring `ModelAdmin`, creating administration actions, and overriding administration templates. You might want to implement additional functionalities that are not available in existing administration views or templates. If this is the case, you need to create a custom administration view. With a custom view, you can build any functionality you want; you just have to make sure that only staff users can access your view and that you maintain the administration look and feel by making your template extend an administration template.

Let's create a custom view to display information about an order. Edit the `views.py` file of the orders application and add the following code highlighted in bold:

```python
from django.urls import reverse
from django.shortcuts import render, redirect, get_object_or_404
from django.contrib.admin.views.decorators import staff_member_required
from .models import OrderItem, Order
from .forms import OrderCreateForm
, from .tasks import order_created
from cart.cart import Cart


def order_create(request):
    # ...


@staff_member_required
def admin_order_detail(request, order_id):
    order = get_object_or_404(Order, id=order_id)
    return render(request,
                  'admin/orders/order/detail.html',
                  {'order': order})
```

The `staff_member_required` decorator checks that both the `is_active` and `is_staff` fields of the user requesting the page are set to `True`. In this view, you get the `Order` object with the given ID and render a template to display the order.

Next, edit the `urls.py` file of the orders application and add the following URL pattern highlighted in bold:

```python
urlpatterns = [
    path('create/', views.order_create, name='order_create'),
    path('admin/order/<int:order_id>/', views.admin_order_detail,
                              name='admin_order_detail'),
]
```

Create the following file structure inside the `templates/` directory of the orders application:

```
admin/
    orders/
        order/
            detail.html
```

Edit the `detail.html` template and add the following content to it:

```
{% extends "admin/base_site.html" %}

{% block title %}
```

```
      Order {{ order.id }} {{ block.super }}
  {% endblock %}

  {% block breadcrumbs %}
    <div class="breadcrumbs">
      <a href="{% url "admin:index" %}">Home</a> &rsaquo;
      <a href="{% url "admin:orders_order_changelist" %}">Orders</a>
      &rsaquo;
      <a href="{% url "admin:orders_order_change" order.id %}">Order {{ order.id
  }}</a>
      &rsaquo; Detail
    </div>
  {% endblock %}

  {% block content %}
  <div class="module">
    <h1>Order {{ order.id }}</h1>
    <ul class="object-tools">
      <li>
        <a href="#" onclick="window.print();">
          Print order
        </a>
      </li>
    </ul>
    <table>
      <tr>
        <th>Created</th>
        <td>{{ order.created }}</td>
      </tr>
      <tr>
        <th>Customer</th>
        <td>{{ order.first_name }} {{ order.last_name }}</td>
      </tr>
      <tr>
        <th>E-mail</th>
        <td><a href="mailto:{{ order.email }}">{{ order.email }}</a></td>
      </tr>
      <tr>
        <th>Address</th>
      <td>
        {{ order.address }},
        {{ order.postal_code }} {{ order.city }}
      </td>
```

```
      </tr>
      <tr>
        <th>Total amount</th>
        <td>${{ order.get_total_cost }}</td>
      </tr>
      <tr>
        <th>Status</th>
        <td>{% if order.paid %}Paid{% else %}Pending payment{% endif %}</td>
      </tr>
      <tr>
        <th>Stripe payment</th>
        <td>
          {% if order.stripe_id %}
            <a href="{{ order.get_stripe_url }}" target="_blank">
              {{ order.stripe_id }}
            </a>
          {% endif %}
        </td>
      </tr>
    </table>
</div>
<div class="module">
  <h2>Items bought</h2>
  <table style="width:100%">
    <thead>
      <tr>
        <th>Product</th>
        <th>Price</th>
        <th>Quantity</th>
        <th>Total</th>
      </tr>
    </thead>
    <tbody>
      {% for item in order.items.all %}
        <tr class="row{% cycle "1" "2" %}">
          <td>{{ item.product.name }}</td>
          <td class="num">${{ item.price }}</td>
          <td class="num">{{ item.quantity }}</td>
          <td class="num">${{ item.get_cost }}</td>
        </tr>
      {% endfor %}
      <tr class="total">
        <td colspan="3">Total</td>
```

```
          <td class="num">${{ order.get_total_cost }}</td>
        </tr>
      </tbody>
    </table>
  </div>
{% endblock %}
```

Make sure that no template tag is split into multiple lines.

This is the template to display the details of an order on the administration site. This template extends the `admin/base_site.html` template of Django's administration site, which contains the main HTML structure and CSS styles. You use the blocks defined in the parent template to include your own content. You display information about the order and the items bought.

When you want to extend an administration template, you need to know its structure and identify existing blocks. You can find all administration templates at `https://github.com/django/django/tree/4.0/django/contrib/admin/templates/admin`.

You can also override an administration template if you need to. To do so, copy a template into your `templates/` directory, keeping the same relative path and filename. Django's administration site will use your custom template instead of the default one.

Finally, let's add a link to each `Order` object on the list display page of the administration site. Edit the `admin.py` file of the `orders` application and add the following code to it, above the `OrderAdmin` class:

```python
from django.urls import reverse

def order_detail(obj):
    url = reverse('orders:admin_order_detail', args=[obj.id])
    return mark_safe(f'<a href="{url}">View</a>')
```

This is a function that takes an `Order` object as an argument and returns an HTML link for the `admin_order_detail` URL. Django escapes HTML output by default. You have to use the `mark_safe` function to avoid auto-escaping.

Then, edit the `OrderAdmin` class to display the link as follows. New code is highlighted in bold:

```python
class OrderAdmin(admin.ModelAdmin):
    list_display = ['id', 'first_name', 'last_name', 'email',
                    'address', 'postal_code', 'city', 'paid',
                    order_payment, 'created', 'updated',
                    order_detail]
    # ...
```

Start the development server with the command:

```
python manage.py runserver
```

Open `http://127.0.0.1:8000/admin/orders/order/` in your browser. Each row includes a **View** link, as follows:

PAID	STRIPE PAYMENT	CREATED ▼	UPDATED	ORDER DETAIL
✓	pi_3KgzZVJ5UH88gi9T1l8ofnc6	March 24, 2022, 10:55 p.m.	March 24, 2022, 7:44 p.m.	View

Figure 9.28: The View link included in each order row

Click on the **View** link for any order to load the custom order detail page. You should see a page like the following one:

Figure 9.29: The custom order detail page on the administration site

Now that you have created the product detail page, you will learn how to generate order invoices in PDF format dynamically.

Generating PDF invoices dynamically

Now that you have a complete checkout and payment system, you can generate a PDF invoice for each order. There are several Python libraries to generate PDF files. One popular library to generate PDFs with Python code is ReportLab. You can find information about how to output PDF files with ReportLab at `https://docs.djangoproject.com/en/4.1/howto/outputting-pdf/`.

In most cases, you will have to add custom styles and formatting to your PDF files. You will find it more convenient to render an HTML template and convert it into a PDF file, keeping Python away from the presentation layer. You are going to follow this approach and use a module to generate PDF files with Django. You will use WeasyPrint, which is a Python library that can generate PDF files from HTML templates.

Installing WeasyPrint

First, install WeasyPrint's dependencies for your operating system from `https://doc.courtbouillon.`
`org/weasyprint/stable/first_steps.html`. Then, install WeasyPrint via `pip` using the following
command:

```
pip install WeasyPrint==56.1
```

Creating a PDF template

You need an HTML document as input for WeasyPrint. You are going to create an HTML template,
render it using Django, and pass it to WeasyPrint to generate the PDF file.

Create a new template file inside the `templates/orders/order/` directory of the orders application
and name it `pdf.html`. Add the following code to it:

```html
<html>
<body>
  <h1>My Shop</h1>
  <p>
    Invoice no. {{ order.id }}<br>
    <span class="secondary">
      {{ order.created|date:"M d, Y" }}
    </span>
  </p>
  <h3>Bill to</h3>
  <p>
    {{ order.first_name }} {{ order.last_name }}<br>
    {{ order.email }}<br>
    {{ order.address }}<br>
    {{ order.postal_code }}, {{ order.city }}
  </p>
  <h3>Items bought</h3>
  <table>
    <thead>
      <tr>
        <th>Product</th>
        <th>Price</th>
        <th>Quantity</th>
        <th>Cost</th>
      </tr>
    </thead>
    <tbody>
      {% for item in order.items.all %}
```

```
            <tr class="row{% cycle "1" "2" %}">
              <td>{{ item.product.name }}</td>
              <td class="num">${{ item.price }}</td>
              <td class="num">{{ item.quantity }}</td>
              <td class="num">${{ item.get_cost }}</td>
            </tr>
          {% endfor %}
          <tr class="total">
            <td colspan="3">Total</td>
            <td class="num">${{ order.get_total_cost }}</td>
          </tr>
        </tbody>
      </table>

      <span class="{% if order.paid %}paid{% else %}pending{% endif %}">
        {% if order.paid %}Paid{% else %}Pending payment{% endif %}
      </span>
    </body>
  </html>
```

This is the template for the PDF invoice. In this template, you display all order details and an HTML `<table>` element including the products. You also include a message to display whether the order has been paid.

Rendering PDF files

You are going to create a view to generate PDF invoices for existing orders using the administration site. Edit the `views.py` file inside the `orders` application directory and add the following code to it:

```python
from django.conf import settings
from django.http import HttpResponse
from django.template.loader import render_to_string
import weasyprint


@staff_member_required
def admin_order_pdf(request, order_id):
    order = get_object_or_404(Order, id=order_id)
    html = render_to_string('orders/order/pdf.html',
                            {'order': order})
    response = HttpResponse(content_type='application/pdf')
    response['Content-Disposition'] = f'filename=order_{order.id}.pdf'
    weasyprint.HTML(string=html).write_pdf(response,
        stylesheets=[weasyprint.CSS(
```

```
            settings.STATIC_ROOT / 'css/pdf.css')])
    return response
```

This is the view to generate a PDF invoice for an order. You use the `staff_member_required` decorator to make sure only staff users can access this view.

You get the `Order` object with the given ID and you use the `render_to_string()` function provided by Django to render `orders/order/pdf.html`. The rendered HTML is saved in the `html` variable.

Then, you generate a new `HttpResponse` object specifying the `application/pdf` content type and including the `Content-Disposition` header to specify the filename. You use WeasyPrint to generate a PDF file from the rendered HTML code and write the file to the `HttpResponse` object.

You use the static file `css/pdf.css` to add CSS styles to the generated PDF file. Then, you load it from the local path by using the `STATIC_ROOT` setting. Finally, you return the generated response.

If you are missing the CSS styles, remember to copy the static files located in the `static/` directory of the `shop` application to the same location of your project.

You can find the contents of the directory at `https://github.com/PacktPublishing/Django-4-by-Example/tree/main/Chapter09/myshop/shop/static`.

Since you need to use the `STATIC_ROOT` setting, you have to add it to your project. This is the project's path where static files reside. Edit the `settings.py` file of the `myshop` project and add the following setting:

```
STATIC_ROOT = BASE_DIR / 'static'
```

Then, run the following command:

```
python manage.py collectstatic
```

You should see output that ends like this:

```
131 static files copied to 'code/myshop/static'.
```

The `collectstatic` command copies all static files from your applications into the directory defined in the `STATIC_ROOT` setting. This allows each application to provide its own static files using a `static/` directory containing them. You can also provide additional static file sources in the `STATICFILES_DIRS` setting. All of the directories specified in the `STATICFILES_DIRS` list will also be copied to the `STATIC_ROOT` directory when `collectstatic` is executed. Whenever you execute `collectstatic` again, you will be asked if you want to override the existing static files.

Edit the `urls.py` file inside the `orders` application directory and add the following URL pattern highlighted in bold:

```
urlpatterns = [
    # ...
    path('admin/order/<int:order_id>/pdf/',
        views.admin_order_pdf,
```

```
        name='admin_order_pdf'),
]
```

Now you can edit the administration list display page for the `Order` model to add a link to the PDF file for each result. Edit the `admin.py` file inside the `orders` application and add the following code above the `OrderAdmin` class:

```
def order_pdf(obj):
    url = reverse('orders:admin_order_pdf', args=[obj.id])
    return mark_safe(f'<a href="{url}">PDF</a>')
order_pdf.short_description = 'Invoice'
```

If you specify a `short_description` attribute for your callable, Django will use it for the name of the column.

Add `order_pdf` to the `list_display` attribute of the `OrderAdmin` class, as follows:

```
class OrderAdmin(admin.ModelAdmin):
    list_display = ['id', 'first_name', 'last_name', 'email',
                    'address', 'postal_code', 'city', 'paid',
                    order_payment, 'created', 'updated',
                    order_detail, order_pdf]
```

Make sure the development server is running. Open `http://127.0.0.1:8000/admin/orders/order/` in your browser. Each row should now include a **PDF** link, like this:

CREATED	UPDATED	ORDER DETAIL	INVOICE
March 24, 2022, 10:55 p.m.	March 24, 2022, 7:44 p.m.	View	PDF

Figure 9.30: The PDF link included in each order row

Click on the **PDF** link for any order. You should see a generated PDF file like the following one for orders that have not been paid yet:

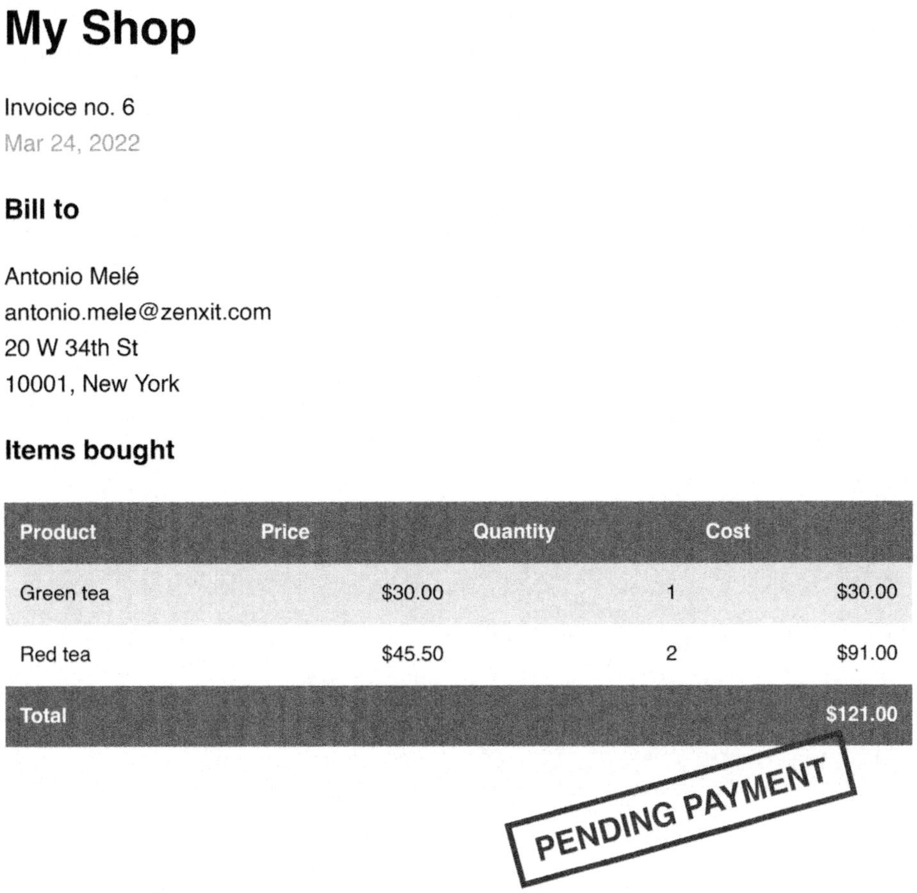

My Shop

Invoice no. 6
Mar 24, 2022

Bill to

Antonio Melé
antonio.mele@zenxit.com
20 W 34th St
10001, New York

Items bought

Product	Price	Quantity	Cost
Green tea	$30.00	1	$30.00
Red tea	$45.50	2	$91.00
Total			$121.00

PENDING PAYMENT

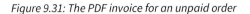

Figure 9.31: The PDF invoice for an unpaid order

For paid orders, you will see the following PDF file:

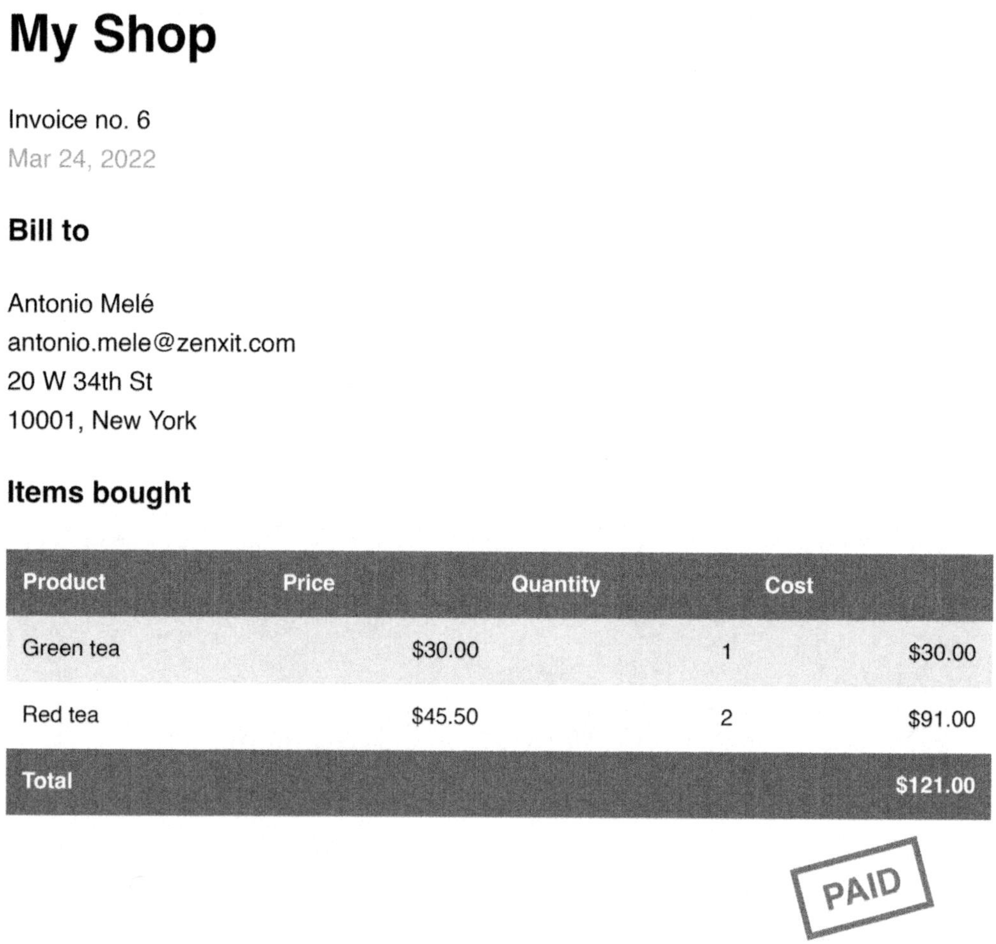

My Shop

Invoice no. 6
Mar 24, 2022

Bill to

Antonio Melé
antonio.mele@zenxit.com
20 W 34th St
10001, New York

Items bought

Product	Price	Quantity	Cost
Green tea	$30.00	1	$30.00
Red tea	$45.50	2	$91.00
Total			$121.00

Figure 9.32: The PDF invoice for a paid order

Sending PDF files by email

When a payment is successful, you will send an automatic email to your customer including the generated PDF invoice. You will create an asynchronous task to perform this action.

Create a new file inside the payment application directory and name it `tasks.py`. Add the following code to it:

```
from io import BytesIO
from celery import shared_task
import weasyprint
from django.template.loader import render_to_string
from django.core.mail import EmailMessage
```

```python
from django.conf import settings
from orders.models import Order


@shared_task
def payment_completed(order_id):
    """
    Task to send an e-mail notification when an order is
    successfully paid.
    """
    order = Order.objects.get(id=order_id)
    # create invoice e-mail
    subject = f'My Shop - Invoice no. {order.id}'
    message = 'Please, find attached the invoice for your recent purchase.'
    email = EmailMessage(subject,
                         message,
                         'admin@myshop.com',
                         [order.email])
    # generate PDF
    html = render_to_string('orders/order/pdf.html', {'order': order})
    out = BytesIO()
    stylesheets=[weasyprint.CSS(settings.STATIC_ROOT / 'css/pdf.css')]
    weasyprint.HTML(string=html).write_pdf(out,
                                           stylesheets=stylesheets)
    # attach PDF file
    email.attach(f'order_{order.id}.pdf',
                 out.getvalue(),
                 'application/pdf')
    # send e-mail
    email.send()
```

You define the payment_completed task by using the @shared_task decorator. In this task, you use the EmailMessage class provided by Django to create an email object. Then, you render the template into the html variable. You generate the PDF file from the rendered template and output it to a BytesIO instance, which is an in-memory bytes buffer. Then, you attach the generated PDF file to the EmailMessage object using the attach() method, including the contents of the out buffer. Finally, you send the email.

Remember to set up your **Simple Mail Transfer Protocol (SMTP)** settings in the settings.py file of the project to send emails. You can refer to *Chapter 2, Enhancing Your Blog with Advanced Features*, to see a working example of an SMTP configuration. If you don't want to set up email settings, you can tell Django to write emails to the console by adding the following setting to the settings.py file:

```python
EMAIL_BACKEND = 'django.core.mail.backends.console.EmailBackend'
```

Let's add the `payment_completed` task to the webhook endpoint that handles payment completion events.

Edit the `webhooks.py` file of the payment application and modify it to make it look like this:

```python
import stripe
from django.conf import settings
from django.http import HttpResponse
from django.views.decorators.csrf import csrf_exempt
from orders.models import Order
from .tasks import payment_completed


@csrf_exempt
def stripe_webhook(request):
    payload = request.body
    sig_header = request.META['HTTP_STRIPE_SIGNATURE']
    event = None

    try:
        event = stripe.Webhook.construct_event(
                    payload,
                    sig_header,
                    settings.STRIPE_WEBHOOK_SECRET)
    except ValueError as e:
        # Invalid payload
        return HttpResponse(status=400)
    except stripe.error.SignatureVerificationError as e:
        # Invalid signature
        return HttpResponse(status=400)

    if event.type == 'checkout.session.completed':
        session = event.data.object
        if session.mode == 'payment' and session.payment_status == 'paid':
            try:
                order = Order.objects.get(id=session.client_reference_id)
            except Order.DoesNotExist:
                return HttpResponse(status=404)
            # mark order as paid
            order.paid = True
            # store Stripe payment ID
            order.stripe_id = session.payment_intent
            order.save()
```

```
    # Launch asynchronous task
    payment_completed.delay(order.id)

    return HttpResponse(status=200)
```

The payment_completed task is queued by calling its delay() method. The task will be added to the queue and will be executed asynchronously by a Celery worker as soon as possible.

Now you can complete a new checkout process in order to receive the PDF invoice in your email. If you are using the console.EmailBackend for your email backend, in the shell where you are running Celery you will be able to see the following output:

```
MIME-Version: 1.0
Subject: My Shop - Invoice no. 7
From: admin@myshop.com
To: antonio.mele@zenxit.com
Date: Sun, 27 Mar 2022 20:15:24 -0000
Message-ID: <164841212458.94972.10344068999595916799@antonios-mbp.home>


--===============8908668108717577350==
Content-Type: text/plain; charset="utf-8"
MIME-Version: 1.0
Content-Transfer-Encoding: 7bit

Please, find attached the invoice for your recent purchase.
--===============8908668108717577350==
Content-Type: application/pdf
MIME-Version: 1.0
Content-Transfer-Encoding: base64
Content-Disposition: attachment; filename="order_7.pdf"

JVBERi0xLjcKJfCflqQKMSAwIG9iago8PAovVHlwZSA...
```

This output shows that the email contains an attachment. You have learned how to attach files to emails and send them programmatically.

Congratulations! You have completed the Stripe integration and have added valuable functionality to your shop.

Additional resources

The following resources provide additional information related to the topics covered in this chapter:

- Source code for this chapter – https://github.com/PacktPublishing/Django-4-by-example/tree/main/Chapter09

- Stripe website – `https://www.stripe.com/`
- Stripe Checkout documentation – `https://stripe.com/docs/payments/checkout`
- Creating a Stripe account – `https://dashboard.stripe.com/register`
- Stripe account settings – `https://dashboard.stripe.com/settings/account`
- Stripe Python library – `https://github.com/stripe/stripe-python`
- Stripe test API keys – `https://dashboard.stripe.com/test/apikeys`
- Stripe API keys documentation – `https://stripe.com/docs/keys`
- Stripe API version 2022-08-01 release notes – `https://stripe.com/docs/upgrades#2022-08-01`
- Stripe checkout session modes – `https://stripe.com/docs/api/checkout/sessions/object#checkout_session_object-mode`
- Building absolute URIs with Django – `https://docs.djangoproject.com/en/4.1/ref/request-response/#django.http.HttpRequest.build_absolute_uri`
- Creating Stripe sessions – `https://stripe.com/docs/api/checkout/sessions/create`
- Stripe-supported currencies – `https://stripe.com/docs/currencies`
- Stripe Payments dashboard – `https://dashboard.stripe.com/test/payments`
- Credit cards for testing payments with Stripe – `https://stripe.com/docs/testing`
- Stripe webhooks – `https://dashboard.stripe.com/test/webhooks`
- Types of events sent by Stripe – `https://stripe.com/docs/api/events/types`
- Installing the Stripe CLI – `https://stripe.com/docs/stripe-cli#install`
- Latest Stripe CLI release – `https://github.com/stripe/stripe-cli/releases/latest`
- Generating CSV files with Django – `https://docs.djangoproject.com/en/4.1/howto/outputting-csv/`
- Django administration templates – `https://github.com/django/django/tree/4.0/django/contrib/admin/templates/admin`
- Outputting PDF files with ReportLab – `https://docs.djangoproject.com/en/4.1/howto/outputting-pdf/`
- Installing WeasyPrint – `https://weasyprint.readthedocs.io/en/latest/install.html`
- Static files for this chapter – `https://github.com/PacktPublishing/Django-4-by-Example/tree/main/Chapter09/myshop/shop/static`

Summary

In this chapter, you integrated the Stripe payment gateway into your project and created a webhook endpoint to receive payment notifications. You built a custom administration action to export orders to CSV. You also customized the Django administration site using custom views and templates. Finally, you learned how to generate PDF files with WeasyPrint and how to attach them to emails.

The next chapter will teach you how to create a coupon system using Django sessions and you will build a product recommendation engine with Redis.

10

Extending Your Shop

In the previous chapter, you learned how to integrate a payment gateway into your shop. You also learned how to generate CSV and PDF files.

In this chapter, you will add a coupon system to your shop and create a product recommendation engine.

This chapter will cover the following points:

- Creating a coupon system
- Applying coupons to the shopping cart
- Applying coupons to orders
- Creating coupons for Stripe Checkout
- Storing products that are usually bought together
- Building a product recommendation engine with Redis

The source code for this chapter can be found at `https://github.com/PacktPublishing/Django-4-by-example/tree/main/Chapter10`.

All the Python packages used in this chapter are included in the `requirements.txt` file in the source code for the chapter. You can follow the instructions to install each Python package in the following sections, or you can install all the requirements at once with the command `pip install -r requirements.txt`.

Creating a coupon system

Many online shops give out coupons to customers that can be redeemed for discounts on their purchases. An online coupon usually consists of a code that is given to users and is valid for a specific time frame.

You are going to create a coupon system for your shop. Your coupons will be valid for customers during a certain time frame. The coupons will not have any limitations in terms of the number of times they can be redeemed, and they will be applied to the total value of the shopping cart.

For this functionality, you will need to create a model to store the coupon code, a valid time frame, and the discount to apply.

Create a new application inside the myshop project using the following command:

```
python manage.py startapp coupons
```

Edit the settings.py file of myshop and add the application to the INSTALLED_APPS setting, as follows:

```
INSTALLED_APPS = [
    # ...
    'coupons.apps.CouponsConfig',
]
```

The new application is now active in your Django project.

Building the coupon model

Let's start by creating the Coupon model. Edit the models.py file of the coupons application and add the following code to it:

```
from django.db import models
from django.core.validators import MinValueValidator, \
                                    MaxValueValidator


class Coupon(models.Model):
    code = models.CharField(max_length=50,
                            unique=True)
    valid_from = models.DateTimeField()
    valid_to = models.DateTimeField()
    discount = models.IntegerField(
                validators=[MinValueValidator(0),
                            MaxValueValidator(100)],
                help_text='Percentage value (0 to 100)')
    active = models.BooleanField()

    def __str__(self):
        return self.code
```

This is the model that you are going to use to store coupons. The Coupon model contains the following fields:

- code: The code that users have to enter in order to apply the coupon to their purchase.
- valid_from: The datetime value that indicates when the coupon becomes valid.

- • valid_to: The datetime value that indicates when the coupon becomes invalid.
- • discount: The discount rate to apply (this is a percentage, so it takes values from 0 to 100). You use validators for this field to limit the minimum and maximum accepted values.
- • active: A Boolean that indicates whether the coupon is active.

Run the following command to generate the initial migration for the coupons application:

```
python manage.py makemigrations
```

The output should include the following lines:

```
Migrations for 'coupons':
  coupons/migrations/0001_initial.py
    - Create model Coupon
```

Then, execute the next command to apply migrations:

```
python manage.py migrate
```

You should see an output that includes the following line:

```
Applying coupons.0001_initial... OK
```

The migrations have now been applied to the database. Let's add the Coupon model to the administration site. Edit the admin.py file of the coupons application and add the following code to it:

```python
from django.contrib import admin
from .models import Coupon


@admin.register(Coupon)
class CouponAdmin(admin.ModelAdmin):
    list_display = ['code', 'valid_from', 'valid_to',
                    'discount', 'active']
    list_filter = ['active', 'valid_from', 'valid_to']
    search_fields = ['code']
```

The Coupon model is now registered on the administration site. Ensure that your local server is running with the following command:

```
python manage.py runserver
```

Open http://127.0.0.1:8000/admin/coupons/coupon/add/ in your browser.

You should see the following form:

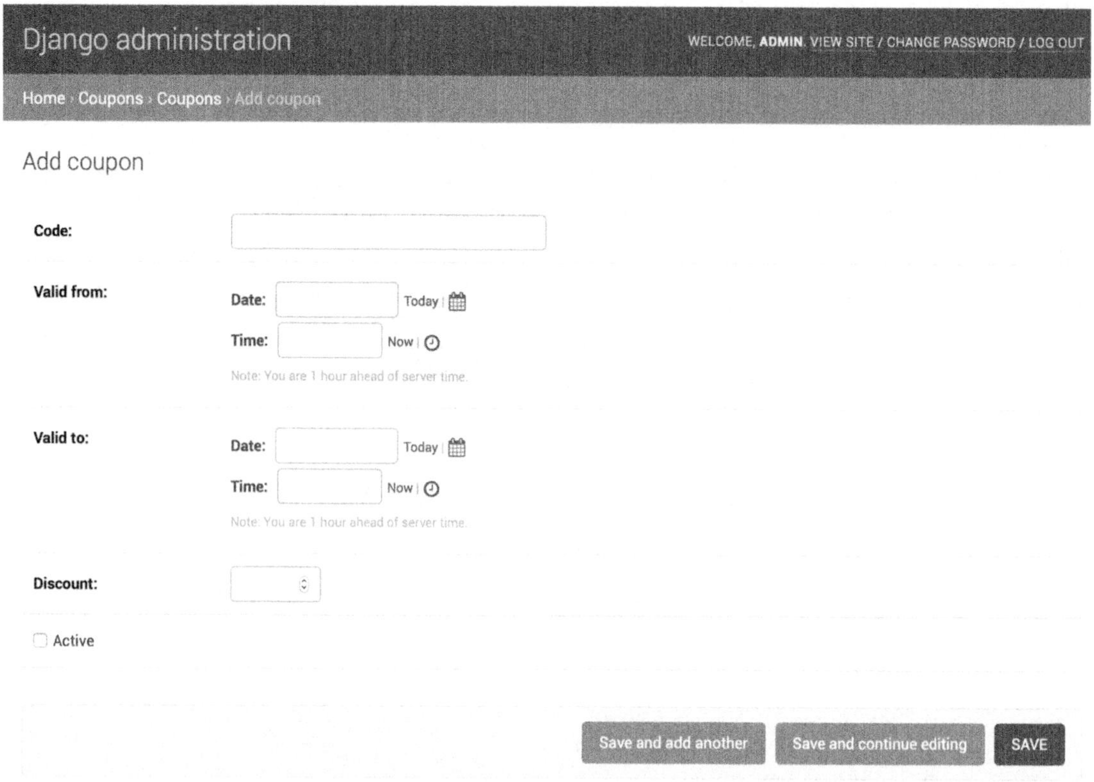
Django administration
WELCOME, ADMIN. VIEW SITE / CHANGE PASSWORD / LOG OUT
Home › Coupons › Coupons › Add coupon
Add coupon
Code:
Valid from:
Date:
Today
Time:
Now
Note: You are 1 hour ahead of server time.
Valid to:
Date:
Today
Time:
Now
Note: You are 1 hour ahead of server time.
Discount:
Active
Save and add another
Save and continue editing
SAVE

Figure 10.1: The Add coupon form on the Django administration site

Fill in the form to create a new coupon that is valid for the current date, make sure that you check the **Active** checkbox, and click the **SAVE** button. *Figure 10.2* shows an example of creating a coupon:

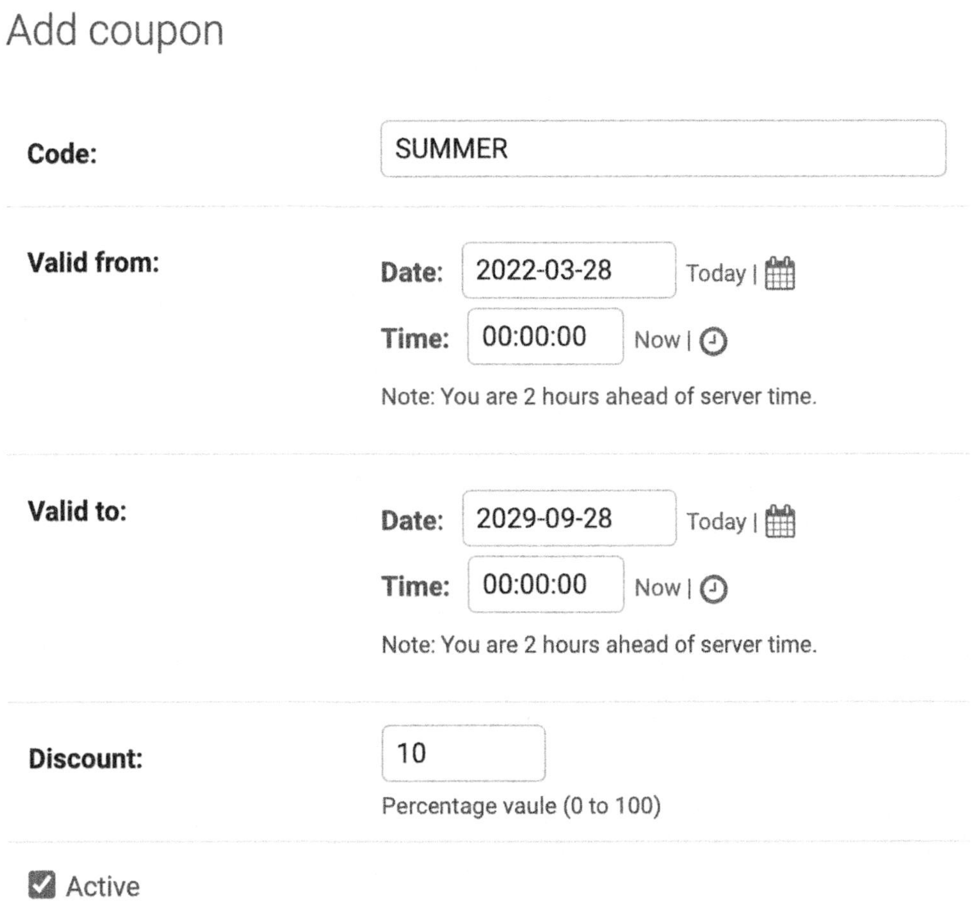

Add coupon

Code: SUMMER

Valid from:

Date: 2022-03-28 Today | 📅

Time: 00:00:00 Now | 🕐

Note: You are 2 hours ahead of server time.

Valid to:

Date: 2029-09-28 Today | 📅

Time: 00:00:00 Now | 🕐

Note: You are 2 hours ahead of server time.

Discount: 10

Percentage vaule (0 to 100)

☑ Active

Figure 10.2: The Add coupon form with sample data

After creating the coupon, the coupon change list page on the administration site will look similar to *Figure 10.3*:

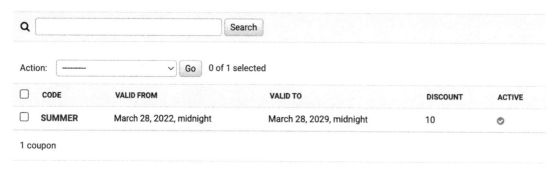

Figure 10.3: The coupon change list page on the Django administration site

Next, we will implement the functionality to apply coupons to the shopping cart.

Applying a coupon to the shopping cart

You can store new coupons and make queries to retrieve existing coupons. Now you need a way for customers to apply coupons to their purchases. The functionality to apply a coupon would be as follows:

1. The user adds products to the shopping cart.
2. The user can enter a coupon code in a form displayed on the shopping cart details page.
3. When the user enters a coupon code and submits the form, you look for an existing coupon with the given code that is currently valid. You have to check that the coupon code matches the one entered by the user, that the active attribute is True, and that the current datetime is between the valid_from and valid_to values.
4. If a coupon is found, you save it in the user's session and display the cart, including the discount applied to it and the updated total amount.
5. When the user places an order, you save the coupon to the given order.

Create a new file inside the coupons application directory and name it forms.py. Add the following code to it:

```python
from django import forms

class CouponApplyForm(forms.Form):
    code = forms.CharField()
```

This is the form that you are going to use for the user to enter a coupon code. Edit the views.py file inside the coupons application and add the following code to it:

```python
from django.shortcuts import render, redirect
from django.utils import timezone
from django.views.decorators.http import require_POST
from .models import Coupon
from .forms import CouponApplyForm


@require_POST
def coupon_apply(request):
    now = timezone.now()
    form = CouponApplyForm(request.POST)
    if form.is_valid():
        code = form.cleaned_data['code']
        try:
            coupon = Coupon.objects.get(code__iexact=code,
                                        valid_from__lte=now,
                                        valid_to__gte=now,
                                        active=True)
            request.session['coupon_id'] = coupon.id
        except Coupon.DoesNotExist:
            request.session['coupon_id'] = None
    return redirect('cart:cart_detail')
```

The coupon_apply view validates the coupon and stores it in the user's session. You apply the require_POST decorator to this view to restrict it to POST requests. In the view, you perform the following tasks:

1. You instantiate the CouponApplyForm form using the posted data and check that the form is valid.
2. If the form is valid, you get the code entered by the user from the form's cleaned_data dictionary. You try to retrieve the Coupon object with the given code. You use the iexact field lookup to perform a case-insensitive exact match. The coupon has to be currently active (active=True) and valid for the current datetime. You use Django's timezone.now() function to get the current timezone-aware datetime, and you compare it with the valid_from and valid_to fields by performing the lte (less than or equal to) and gte (greater than or equal to) field lookups, respectively.
3. You store the coupon ID in the user's session.
4. You redirect the user to the cart_detail URL to display the cart with the coupon applied.

You need a URL pattern for the `coupon_apply` view. Create a new file inside the `coupons` application directory and name it `urls.py`. Add the following code to it:

```python
from django.urls import path
from . import views

app_name = 'coupons'

urlpatterns = [
    path('apply/', views.coupon_apply, name='apply'),
]
```

Then, edit the main `urls.py` of the `myshop` project and include the `coupons` URL patterns with the following line highlighted in bold:

```python
urlpatterns = [
    path('admin/', admin.site.urls),
    path('cart/', include('cart.urls', namespace='cart')),
    path('orders/', include('orders.urls', namespace='orders')),
    path('payment/', include('payment.urls', namespace='payment')),
    path('coupons/', include('coupons.urls', namespace='coupons')),
    path('', include('shop.urls', namespace='shop')),
]
```

Remember to place this pattern before the `shop.urls` pattern.

Now, edit the `cart.py` file of the `cart` application. Include the following import:

```python
from coupons.models import Coupon
```

Add the following code highlighted in bold to the end of the __init__() method of the `Cart` class to initialize the coupon from the current session:

```python
class Cart:
    def __init__(self, request):
        """
        Initialize the cart.
        """
        self.session = request.session
        cart = self.session.get(settings.CART_SESSION_ID)
        if not cart:
            # save an empty cart in the session
            cart = self.session[settings.CART_SESSION_ID] = {}
        self.cart = cart
        # store current applied coupon
        self.coupon_id = self.session.get('coupon_id')
```

In this code, you try to get the `coupon_id` session key from the current session and store its value in the `Cart` object. Add the following methods highlighted in bold to the `Cart` object:

```python
class Cart:
    # ...

    @property
    def coupon(self):
        if self.coupon_id:
            try:
                return Coupon.objects.get(id=self.coupon_id)
            except Coupon.DoesNotExist:
                pass
        return None

    def get_discount(self):
        if self.coupon:
            return (self.coupon.discount / Decimal(100)) \
                * self.get_total_price()
        return Decimal(0)

    def get_total_price_after_discount(self):
        return self.get_total_price() - self.get_discount()
```

These methods are as follows:

- `coupon()`: You define this method as a property. If the cart contains a `coupon_id` attribute, the Coupon object with the given ID is returned.
- `get_discount()`: If the cart contains a coupon, you retrieve its discount rate and return the amount to be deducted from the total amount of the cart.
- `get_total_price_after_discount()`: You return the total amount of the cart after deducting the amount returned by the `get_discount()` method.

The `Cart` class is now prepared to handle a coupon applied to the current session and apply the corresponding discount.

Let's include the coupon system in the cart's detail view. Edit the `views.py` file of the `cart` application and add the following import to the top of the file:

```python
from coupons.forms import CouponApplyForm
```

Further down, edit the `cart_detail` view and add the new form to it, as follows:

```python
def cart_detail(request):
    cart = Cart(request)
    for item in cart:
```

```
                item['update_quantity_form'] = CartAddProductForm(initial={
                                    'quantity': item['quantity'],
                                    'override': True})
        coupon_apply_form = CouponApplyForm()
        return render(request,
                        'cart/detail.html',
                        {'cart': cart,
                        'coupon_apply_form': coupon_apply_form})
```

Edit the `cart/detail.html` template of the cart application and locate the following lines:

```
<tr class="total">
  <td>Total</td>
  <td colspan="4"></td>
  <td class="num">${{ cart.get_total_price }}</td>
</tr>
```

Replace them with the following code:

```
{% if cart.coupon %}
  <tr class="subtotal">
    <td>Subtotal</td>
    <td colspan="4"></td>
    <td class="num">${{ cart.get_total_price|floatformat:2 }}</td>
  </tr>
  <tr>
    <td>
        "{{ cart.coupon.code }}" coupon
        ({{ cart.coupon.discount }}% off)
    </td>
    <td colspan="4"></td>
    <td class="num neg">
      - ${{ cart.get_discount|floatformat:2 }}
    </td>
  </tr>
{% endif %}
<tr class="total">
  <td>Total</td>
  <td colspan="4"></td>
  <td class="num">
    ${{ cart.get_total_price_after_discount|floatformat:2 }}
  </td>
</tr>
```

This is the code for displaying an optional coupon and its discount rate. If the cart contains a coupon, you display the first row, including the total amount of the cart as the subtotal. Then, you use a second row to display the current coupon applied to the cart. Finally, you display the total price, including any discount, by calling the `get_total_price_after_discount()` method of the `cart` object.

In the same file, include the following code after the `</table>` HTML tag:

```
<p>Apply a coupon:</p>
<form action="{% url "coupons:apply" %}" method="post">
  {{ coupon_apply_form }}
  <input type="submit" value="Apply">
  {% csrf_token %}
</form>
```

This will display the form to enter a coupon code and apply it to the current cart.

Open `http://127.0.0.1:8000/` in your browser and add a product to the cart. You will see that the shopping cart page now includes a form to apply a coupon:

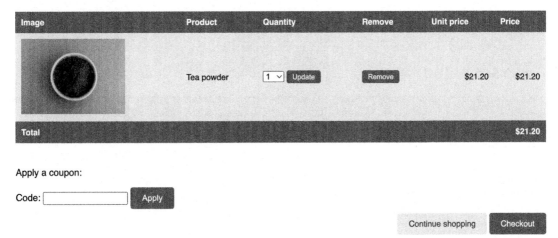

Figure 10.4: The cart detail page, including a form to apply a coupon

 Image of *Tea powder*: Photo by Phuong Nguyen on Unsplash

In the **Code** field, enter the coupon code you created using the administration site:

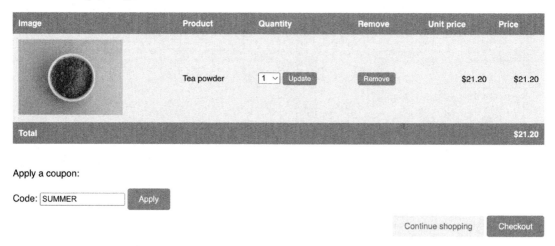

Figure 10.5: The cart detail page, including a coupon code on the form

Click the **Apply** button. The coupon will be applied, and the cart will display the coupon discount as follows:

Figure 10.6: The cart detail page, including the coupon applied

Let's add the coupon to the next step of the purchase process. Edit the `orders/order/create.html` template of the `orders` application and locate the following lines:

```
<ul>
  {% for item in cart %}
    <li>
      {{ item.quantity }}x {{ item.product.name }}
      <span>${{ item.total_price }}</span>
    </li>
  {% endfor %}
</ul>
```

Replace them with the following code:

```
<ul>
  {% for item in cart %}
    <li>
      {{ item.quantity }}x {{ item.product.name }}
      <span>${{ item.total_price|floatformat:2 }}</span>
    </li>
  {% endfor %}
  {% if cart.coupon %}
    <li>
      "{{ cart.coupon.code }}" ({{ cart.coupon.discount }}% off)
      <span class="neg">- ${{ cart.get_discount|floatformat:2 }}</span>
    </li>
  {% endif %}
</ul>
```

The order summary should now include the coupon applied, if there is one. Now find the following line:

```
<p>Total: ${{ cart.get_total_price }}</p>
```

Replace it with the following:

```
<p>Total: ${{ cart.get_total_price_after_discount|floatformat:2 }}</p>
```

By doing this, the total price will also be calculated by applying the discount of the coupon.

Open `http://127.0.0.1:8000/orders/create/` in your browser. You should see that the order summary includes the applied coupon, as follows:

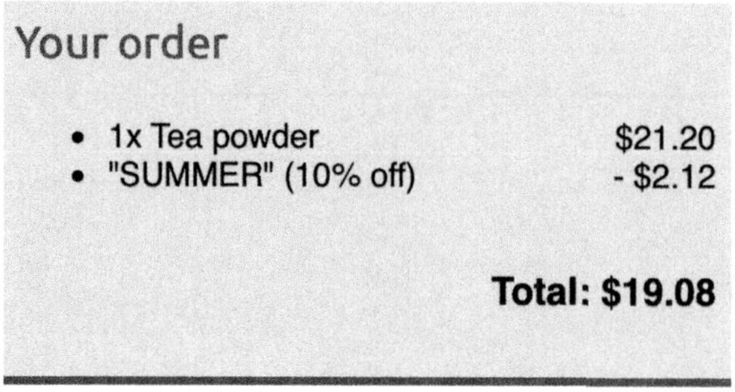

Your order

- 1x Tea powder $21.20
- "SUMMER" (10% off)   - $2.12

Total: $19.08

Figure 10.7: The order summary, including the coupon applied to the cart

Users can now apply coupons to their shopping cart. However, you still need to store coupon information in the order that it is created when users check out the cart.

Applying coupons to orders

You are going to store the coupon that was applied to each order. First, you need to modify the `Order` model to store the related `Coupon` object, if there is one.

Edit the `models.py` file of the `orders` application and add the following imports to it:

```python
from decimal import Decimal
from django.core.validators import MinValueValidator, \
                                    MaxValueValidator
from coupons.models import Coupon
```

Then, add the following fields to the `Order` model:

```python
class Order(models.Model):
    # ...
    coupon = models.ForeignKey(Coupon,
                               related_name='orders',
                               null=True,
                               blank=True,
                               on_delete=models.SET_NULL)
    discount = models.IntegerField(default=0,
                                   validators=[MinValueValidator(0),
                                   MaxValueValidator(100)])
```

These fields allow you to store an optional coupon for the order and the discount percentage applied with the coupon. The discount is stored in the related `Coupon` object, but you can include it in the `Order` model to preserve it if the coupon has been modified or deleted. You set `on_delete` to `models.SET_NULL` so that if the coupon gets deleted, the coupon field is set to `Null`, but the discount is preserved.

You need to create a migration to include the new fields of the Order model. Run the following command from the command line:

```
python manage.py makemigrations
```

You should see an output like the following:

```
Migrations for 'orders':
  orders/migrations/0003_order_coupon_order_discount.py
    - Add field coupon to order
    - Add field discount to order
```

Apply the new migration with the following command:

```
python manage.py migrate orders
```

You should see the following confirmation indicating that the new migration has been applied:

```
Applying orders.0003_order_coupon_order_discount... OK
```

The Order model field changes are now synced with the database.

Edit the models.py file, and add two new methods, get_total_cost_before_discount() and get_discount(), to the Order model like this. The new code is highlighted in bold:

```python
class Order(models.Model):
    # ...
    def get_total_cost_before_discount(self):
        return sum(item.get_cost() for item in self.items.all())

    def get_discount(self):
        total_cost = self.get_total_cost_before_discount()
        if self.discount:
            return total_cost * (self.discount / Decimal(100))
        return Decimal(0)
```

Then, edit the get_total_cost() method of the Order model as follows. The new code is highlighted in bold:

```python
    def get_total_cost(self):
        total_cost = self.get_total_cost_before_discount()
        return total_cost - self.get_discount()
```

The get_total_cost() method of the Order model will now take into account the discount applied, if there is one.

Edit the `views.py` file of the `orders` application and modify the `order_create` view to save the related coupon and its discount when creating a new order. Add the following code highlighted in bold to the `order_create` view:

```python
def order_create(request):
    cart = Cart(request)
    if request.method == 'POST':
        form = OrderCreateForm(request.POST)
        if form.is_valid():
            order = form.save(commit=False)
            if cart.coupon:
                order.coupon = cart.coupon
                order.discount = cart.coupon.discount
            order.save()
            for item in cart:
                OrderItem.objects.create(order=order,
                                         product=item['product'],
                                         price=item['price'],
                                         quantity=item['quantity'])
            # clear the cart
            cart.clear()
            # launch asynchronous task
            order_created.delay(order.id)
            # set the order in the session
            request.session['order_id'] = order.id
            # redirect for payment
            return redirect(reverse('payment:process'))
    else:
        form = OrderCreateForm()
    return render(request,
                  'orders/order/create.html',
                  {'cart': cart, 'form': form})
```

In the new code, you create an `Order` object using the `save()` method of the `OrderCreateForm` form. You avoid saving it to the database yet by using `commit=False`. If the cart contains a coupon, you store the related coupon and the discount that was applied. Then, you save the `order` object to the database.

Edit the `payment/process.html` template of the payment application and locate the following lines:

```html
<tr class="total">
  <td>Total</td>
  <td colspan="4"></td>
  <td class="num">${{ order.get_total_cost }}</td>
</tr>
```

Replace them with the following code. New lines are highlighted in bold:

```
{% if order.coupon %}
  <tr class="subtotal">
    <td>Subtotal</td>
    <td colspan="3"></td>
    <td class="num">
      ${{ order.get_total_cost_before_discount|floatformat:2 }}
    </td>
  </tr>
  <tr>
    <td>
      "{{ order.coupon.code }}" coupon
      ({{ order.discount }}% off)
    </td>
    <td colspan="3"></td>
    <td class="num neg">
      - ${{ order.get_discount|floatformat:2 }}
    </td>
  </tr>
{% endif %}
<tr class="total">
  <td>Total</td>
  <td colspan="3"></td>
  <td class="num">
    ${{ order.get_total_cost|floatformat:2 }}
  </td>
</tr>
```

We have updated the order summary before payment.

Make sure that the development server is running with the following command:

```
python manage.py runserver
```

Make sure Docker is running, and execute the following command in another shell to start the RabbitMQ server with Docker:

```
docker run -it --rm --name rabbitmq -p 5672:5672 -p 15672:15672
rabbitmq:management
```

Open another shell and start the Celery worker from your project directory with the following command:

```
celery -A myshop worker -l info
```

Open an additional shell and execute the following command to forward Stripe events to your local webhook URL:

```
stripe listen --forward-to localhost:8000/payment/webhook/
```

Open `http://127.0.0.1:8000/` in your browser and create an order using the coupon you created. After validating the items in the shopping cart, on the **Order summary** page, you will see the coupon applied to the order:

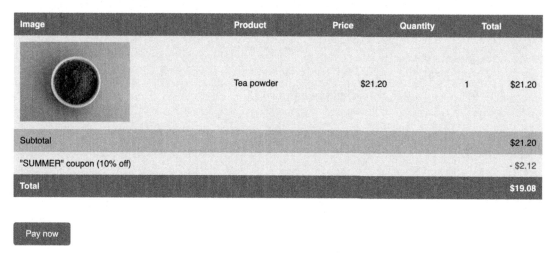

Figure 10.8: The Order summary page, including the coupon applied to the order

If you click on **Pay now**, you will see that Stripe is not aware of the discount applied, as displayed in *Figure 10.9*:

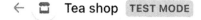

Figure 10.9: The item details of the Stripe Checkout page, including no discount coupon

Stripe shows the full amount to be paid without any deduction. This is because we are not passing on the discount to Stripe. Remember that in the `payment_process` view, we pass the order items as `line_items` to Stripe, including the cost and quantity of each order item.

Creating coupons for Stripe Checkout

Stripe allows you to define discount coupons and link them to one-time payments. You can find more information about creating discounts for Stripe Checkout at `https://stripe.com/docs/payments/checkout/discounts`.

Let's edit the payment_process view to create a coupon for Stripe Checkout. Edit the `views.py` file of the payment application and add the following code highlighted in bold to the payment_process view:

```python
def payment_process(request):
    order_id = request.session.get('order_id', None)
    order = get_object_or_404(Order, id=order_id)

    if request.method == 'POST':
        success_url = request.build_absolute_uri(
                        reverse('payment:completed'))
        cancel_url = request.build_absolute_uri(
                        reverse('payment:canceled'))

        # Stripe checkout session data
        session_data = {
            'mode': 'payment',
            'client_reference_id': order.id,
            'success_url': success_url,
            'cancel_url': cancel_url,
            'line_items': []
        }
        # add order items to the Stripe checkout session
        for item in order.items.all():
            session_data['line_items'].append({
                'price_data': {
                    'unit_amount': int(item.price * Decimal('100')),
                    'currency': 'usd',
                    'product_data': {
                        'name': item.product.name,
                    },
                },
                'quantity': item.quantity,
            })

        # Stripe coupon
        if order.coupon:
```

```
            stripe_coupon = stripe.Coupon.create(
                                name=order.coupon.code,
                                percent_off=order.discount,
                                duration='once')
            session_data['discounts'] = [{
                'coupon': stripe_coupon.id
            }]

        # create Stripe checkout session
        session = stripe.checkout.Session.create(**session_data)

        # redirect to Stripe payment form
        return redirect(session.url, code=303)

    else:
        return render(request, 'payment/process.html', locals())
```

In the new code, you check if the order has a related coupon. In that case, you use the Stripe SDK to create a Stripe coupon using `stripe.Coupon.create()`. You use the following attributes for the coupon:

- name: The code of the coupon related to the order object is used.
- percent_off: The discount of the order object is issued.
- duration: The value once is used. This indicates to Stripe that this is a coupon for a one-time payment.

After creating the coupon, its `id` is added to the `session_data` dictionary used to create the Stripe Checkout session. This links the coupon to the checkout session.

Open `http://127.0.0.1:8000/` in your browser and complete a purchase using the coupon you created. When redirected to the Stripe Checkout page, you will see the coupon applied:

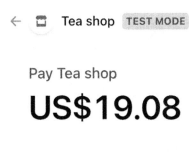

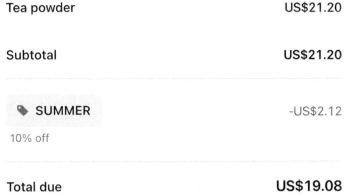

Figure 10.10: The item details of the Stripe Checkout page, including a discount coupon named SUMMER

The Stripe Checkout page now includes the order coupon, and the total amount to pay now includes the amount deducted using the coupon.

Complete the purchase and then open `http://127.0.0.1:8000/admin/orders/order/` in your browser. Click on the order object for which the coupon was used. The edit form will display the discount applied, as shown in *Figure 10.11*:

Stripe id:	pi_3KuKlYJ5UH88gi9T0aShmjvC
Coupon:	SUMMER ∨ ✎ + ✕
Discount:	10

ORDER ITEMS

PRODUCT	PRICE	QUANTITY	DELETE?
4			
1 Q Tea powder	21,20	1	☐

Figure 10.11: The order edit form, including the coupon and discount applied

You are successfully storing coupons for orders and processing payments with discounts. Next, you will add coupons to the order detail view of the administration site and to PDF invoices for orders.

Adding coupons to orders on the administration site and to PDF invoices

Let's add the coupon to the order detail page on the administration site. Edit the `admin/orders/order/detail.html` template of the `orders` application and add the following code highlighted in bold:

```
...
<table style="width:100%">
  ...
  <tbody>
    {% for item in order.items.all %}
      <tr class="row{% cycle "1" "2" %}">
        <td>{{ item.product.name }}</td>
        <td class="num">${{ item.price }}</td>
        <td class="num">{{ item.quantity }}</td>
        <td class="num">${{ item.get_cost }}</td>
      </tr>
    {% endfor %}

    {% if order.coupon %}
      <tr class="subtotal">
        <td colspan="3">Subtotal</td>
        <td class="num">
          ${{ order.get_total_cost_before_discount|floatformat:2 }}
```

```
            </td>
        </tr>
        <tr>
            <td colspan="3">
                "{{ order.coupon.code }}" coupon
                ({{ order.discount }}% off)
            </td>
            <td class="num neg">
                - ${{ order.get_discount|floatformat:2 }}
            </td>
        </tr>
    {% endif %}

    <tr class="total">
      <td colspan="3">Total</td>
      <td class="num">
        ${{ order.get_total_cost|floatformat:2 }}
      </td>
    </tr>
  </tbody>
</table>
...
```

Access http://127.0.0.1:8000/admin/orders/order/ with your browser, and click on the **View** link of the latest order. The **Items bought** table will now include the coupon used, as shown in *Figure 10.12*:

Items bought			
PRODUCT	**PRICE**	**QUANTITY**	**TOTAL**
Tea powder	$21.20	2	$42.40
Subtotal			$42.40
"SUMMER" coupon (10% off)			- $4.24
Total			$38.16

Figure 10.12: The product detail page on the administration site, including the coupon used

Now, let's modify the order invoice template to include the coupon used for the order. Edit the orders/order/detail.pdf template of the orders application and add the following code highlighted in bold:

```
...
<table>
  <thead>
    <tr>
```

```
      <th>Product</th>
      <th>Price</th>
      <th>Quantity</th>
      <th>Cost</th>
    </tr>
  </thead>
  <tbody>
    {% for item in order.items.all %}
      <tr class="row{% cycle "1" "2" %}">
        <td>{{ item.product.name }}</td>
        <td class="num">${{ item.price }}</td>
        <td class="num">{{ item.quantity }}</td>
        <td class="num">${{ item.get_cost }}</td>
      </tr>
    {% endfor %}

    {% if order.coupon %}
      <tr class="subtotal">
        <td colspan="3">Subtotal</td>
        <td class="num">
          ${{ order.get_total_cost_before_discount|floatformat:2 }}
        </td>
      </tr>
      <tr>
        <td colspan="3">
          "{{ order.coupon.code }}" coupon
          ({{ order.discount }}% off)
        </td>
        <td class="num neg">
          - ${{ order.get_discount|floatformat:2 }}
        </td>
      </tr>
    {% endif %}

    <tr class="total">
      <td colspan="3">Total</td>
      <td class="num">${{ order.get_total_cost|floatformat:2 }}</td>
    </tr>
  </tbody>
</table>

...
```

Access `http://127.0.0.1:8000/admin/orders/order/` with your browser, and click on the **PDF** link of the latest order. The **Items bought** table will now include the coupon used, as shown in *Figure 10.13*:

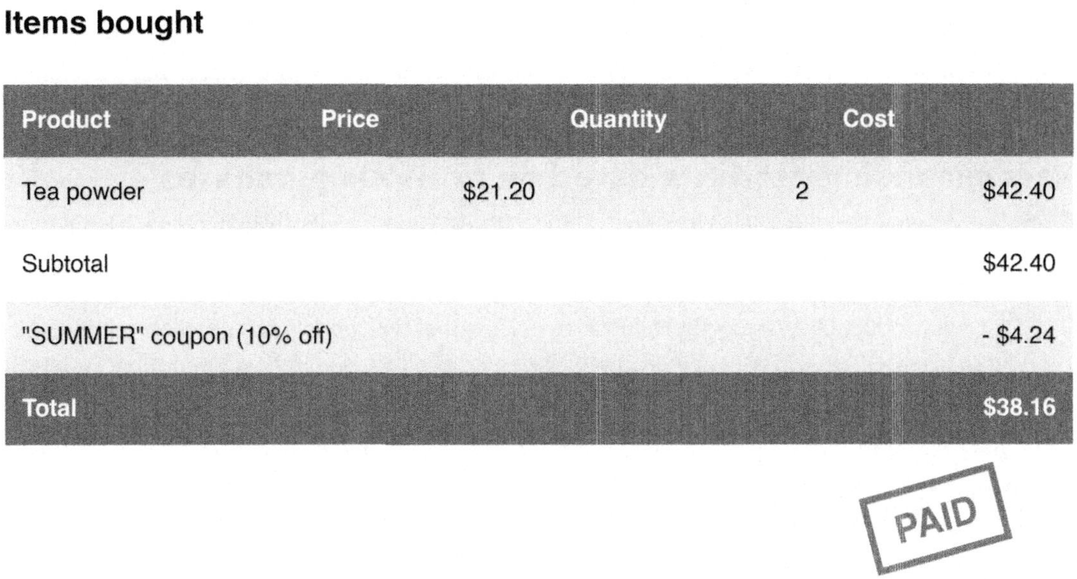

Items bought

Product	Price	Quantity	Cost
Tea powder	$21.20	2	$42.40
Subtotal			$42.40
"SUMMER" coupon (10% off)			- $4.24
Total			**$38.16**

Figure 10.13: The PDF order invoice, including the coupon used

You successfully added a coupon system to your shop. Next, you are going to build a product recommendation engine.

Building a recommendation engine

A recommendation engine is a system that predicts the preference or rating that a user would give to an item. The system selects relevant items for a user based on their behavior and the knowledge it has about them. Nowadays, recommendation systems are used in many online services. They help users by selecting the stuff they might be interested in from the vast amount of available data that is irrelevant to them. Offering good recommendations enhances user engagement. E-commerce sites also benefit from offering relevant product recommendations by increasing their average revenue per user.

You are going to create a simple, yet powerful, recommendation engine that suggests products that are usually bought together. You will suggest products based on historical sales, thus identifying products that are usually bought together. You are going to suggest complementary products in two different scenarios:

- **Product detail page:** You will display a list of products that are usually bought with the given product. This will be displayed as *users who bought this also bought X, Y, and Z*. You need a data structure that allows you to store the number of times each product has been bought together with the product being displayed.

- **Cart detail page:** Based on the products that users add to the cart, you are going to suggest products that are usually bought together with these ones. In this case, the score you calculate to obtain related products has to be aggregated.

You are going to use Redis to store products that are usually purchased together. Remember that you already used Redis in *Chapter 7, Tracking User Actions*. If you haven't installed Redis yet, you can find installation instructions in that chapter.

Recommending products based on previous purchases

We will recommend products to users based on the items that are frequently bought together. For that, we are going to store a key in Redis for each product bought on the site. The product key will contain a Redis sorted set with scores. Every time a new purchase is completed, we will increment the score by 1 for each product bought together. The sorted set will allow you to give scores to products that are bought together. We will use the number of times the product is bought with another product as the score for that item.

Remember to install redis-py in your environment using the following command:

```
pip install redis==4.3.4
```

Edit the settings.py file of your project and add the following settings to it:

```
# Redis settings
REDIS_HOST = 'localhost'
REDIS_PORT = 6379
REDIS_DB = 1
```

These are the settings required to establish a connection with the Redis server. Create a new file inside the shop application directory and name it recommender.py. Add the following code to it:

```
import redis
from django.conf import settings
from .models import Product

# connect to redis
r = redis.Redis(host=settings.REDIS_HOST,
                port=settings.REDIS_PORT,
                db=settings.REDIS_DB)

class Recommender:
    def get_product_key(self, id):
        return f'product:{id}:purchased_with'

    def products_bought(self, products):
        product_ids = [p.id for p in products]
```

```
            for product_id in product_ids:
                for with_id in product_ids:
                    # get the other products bought with each product
                    if product_id != with_id:
                        # increment score for product purchased together
                        r.zincrby(self.get_product_key(product_id),
                                  1,
                                  with_id)
```

This is the `Recommender` class, which will allow you to store product purchases and retrieve product suggestions for a given product or products.

The `get_product_key()` method receives an ID of a `Product` object and builds the Redis key for the sorted set where related products are stored, which looks like `product:[id]:purchased_with`.

The `products_bought()` method receives a list of `Product` objects that have been bought together (that is, belong to the same order).

In this method, you perform the following tasks:

1. You get the product IDs for the given `Product` objects.
2. You iterate over the product IDs. For each ID, you iterate again over the product IDs and skip the same product so that you get the products that are bought together with each product.
3. You get the Redis product key for each product bought using the `get_product_id()` method. For a product with an ID of 33, this method returns the key `product:33:purchased_with`. This is the key for the sorted set that contains the product IDs of products that were bought together with this one.
4. You increment the score of each product ID contained in the sorted set by 1. The score represents the number of times another product has been bought together with the given product.

You now have a method to store and score the products that were bought together. Next, you need a method to retrieve the products that were bought together for a list of given products. Add the following `suggest_products_for()` method to the `Recommender` class:

```
def suggest_products_for(self, products, max_results=6):
    product_ids = [p.id for p in products]
    if len(products) == 1:
        # only 1 product
        suggestions = r.zrange(
                        self.get_product_key(product_ids[0]),
                        0, -1, desc=True)[:max_results]
    else:
        # generate a temporary key
        flat_ids = ''.join([str(id) for id in product_ids])
        tmp_key = f'tmp_{flat_ids}'
```

```
        # multiple products, combine scores of all products
        # store the resulting sorted set in a temporary key
        keys = [self.get_product_key(id) for id in product_ids]
        r.zunionstore(tmp_key, keys)
        # remove ids for the products the recommendation is for
        r.zrem(tmp_key, *product_ids)
        # get the product ids by their score, descendant sort
        suggestions = r.zrange(tmp_key, 0, -1,
                                    desc=True)[:max_results]
        # remove the temporary key
        r.delete(tmp_key)
    suggested_products_ids = [int(id) for id in suggestions]
    # get suggested products and sort by order of appearance
    suggested_products = list(Product.objects.filter(
        id__in=suggested_products_ids))
    suggested_products.sort(key=lambda x: suggested_products_ids.index(x.id))
    return suggested_products
```

The suggest_products_for() method receives the following parameters:

- products: This is a list of Product objects to get recommendations for. It can contain one or more products.

- max_results: This is an integer that represents the maximum number of recommendations to return.

In this method, you perform the following actions:

1. You get the product IDs for the given Product objects.

2. If only one product is given, you retrieve the ID of the products that were bought together with the given product, ordered by the total number of times that they were bought together. To do so, you use Redis' ZRANGE command. You limit the number of results to the number specified in the max_results attribute (6 by default).

3. If more than one product is given, you generate a temporary Redis key built with the IDs of the products.

4. Combine and sum all scores for the items contained in the sorted set of each of the given products. This is done using the Redis ZUNIONSTORE command. The ZUNIONSTORE command performs a union of the sorted sets with the given keys and stores the aggregated sum of scores of the elements in a new Redis key. You can read more about this command at https://redis.io/commands/zunionstore/. You save the aggregated scores in the temporary key.

5. Since you are aggregating scores, you might obtain the same products you are getting recommendations for. You remove them from the generated sorted set using the ZREM command.

6. You retrieve the IDs of the products from the temporary key, ordered by their scores using the ZRANGE command. You limit the number of results to the number specified in the max_results attribute. Then, you remove the temporary key.

7. Finally, you get the Product objects with the given IDs, and you order the products in the same order as them.

For practical purposes, let's also add a method to clear the recommendations. Add the following method to the Recommender class:

```python
def clear_purchases(self):
    for id in Product.objects.values_list('id', flat=True):
        r.delete(self.get_product_key(id))
```

Let's try the recommendation engine. Make sure you include several Product objects in the database and initialize the Redis Docker container using the following command:

```
docker run -it --rm --name redis -p 6379:6379 redis
```

Open another shell and run the following command to open the Python shell:

```
python manage.py shell
```

Make sure that you have at least four different products in your database. Retrieve four different products by their names:

```python
>>> from shop.models import Product
>>> black_tea = Product.objects.get(name='Black tea')
>>> red_tea = Product.objects.get(name='Red tea')
>>> green_tea = Product.objects.get(name='Green tea')
>>> tea_powder = Product.objects.get(name='Tea powder')
```

Then, add some test purchases to the recommendation engine:

```python
>>> from shop.recommender import Recommender
>>> r = Recommender()
>>> r.products_bought([black_tea, red_tea])
>>> r.products_bought([black_tea, green_tea])
>>> r.products_bought([red_tea, black_tea, tea_powder])
>>> r.products_bought([green_tea, tea_powder])
>>> r.products_bought([black_tea, tea_powder])
>>> r.products_bought([red_tea, green_tea])
```

You have stored the following scores:

```
black_tea:  red_tea (2), tea_powder (2), green_tea (1)
red_tea:    black_tea (2), tea_powder (1), green_tea (1)
green_tea:  black_tea (1), tea_powder (1), red_tea(1)
tea_powder: black_tea (2), red_tea (1), green_tea (1)
```

This is a representation of products that have been bought together with each of the products, including how many times they have been bought together.

Let's retrieve product recommendations for a single product:

```
>>> r.suggest_products_for([black_tea])
[<Product: Tea powder>, <Product: Red tea>, <Product: Green tea>]
>>> r.suggest_products_for([red_tea])
[<Product: Black tea>, <Product: Tea powder>, <Product: Green tea>]
>>> r.suggest_products_for([green_tea])
[<Product: Black tea>, <Product: Tea powder>, <Product: Red tea>]
>>> r.suggest_products_for([tea_powder])
[<Product: Black tea>, <Product: Red tea>, <Product: Green tea>]
```

You can see that the order for recommended products is based on their score. Let's get recommendations for multiple products with aggregated scores:

```
>>> r.suggest_products_for([black_tea, red_tea])
[<Product: Tea powder>, <Product: Green tea>]
>>> r.suggest_products_for([green_tea, red_tea])
[<Product: Black tea>, <Product: Tea powder>]
>>> r.suggest_products_for([tea_powder, black_tea])
[<Product: Red tea>, <Product: Green tea>]
```

You can see that the order of the suggested products matches the aggregated scores. For example, products suggested for black_tea and red_tea are tea_powder (2+1) and green_tea (1+1).

You have verified that your recommendation algorithm works as expected. Let's now display recommendations for products on your site.

Edit the views.py file of the shop application. Add the functionality to retrieve a maximum of four recommended products into the product_detail view, as follows:

```
from .recommender import Recommender

def product_detail(request, id, slug):
    product = get_object_or_404(Product,
                                id=id,
                                slug=slug,
                                available=True)
    cart_product_form = CartAddProductForm()
    r = Recommender()
    recommended_products = r.suggest_products_for([product], 4)
    return render(request,
                  'shop/product/detail.html',
                  {'product': product,
                   'cart_product_form': cart_product_form,
                   'recommended_products': recommended_products})
```

Edit the shop/product/detail.html template of the shop application and add the following code after
{{ product.description|linebreaks }}:

```
{% if recommended_products %}
  <div class="recommendations">
    <h3>People who bought this also bought</h3>
    {% for p in recommended_products %}
      <div class="item">
        <a href="{{ p.get_absolute_url }}">
          <img src="{% if p.image %}{{ p.image.url }}{% else %}
          {% static  "img/no_image.png" %}{% endif %}">
        </a>
        <p><a href="{{ p.get_absolute_url }}">{{ p.name }}</a></p>
      </div>
    {% endfor %}
  </div>
{% endif %}
```

Run the development server, and open http://127.0.0.1:8000/ in your browser. Click on any product to view its details. You should see that recommended products are displayed below the product,
as shown in *Figure 10.14*:

Tea powder

Tea

$21.20

Quantity: 1

Add to cart

People who bought this also bought

Black tea

Red tea

Green tea

Figure 10.14: The product detail page, including recommended products

Images in this chapter:

- *Green tea*: Photo by Jia Ye on Unsplash
- *Red tea*: Photo by Manki Kim on Unsplash
- *Tea powder*: Photo by Phuong Nguyen on Unsplash

You are also going to include product recommendations in the cart. The recommendations will be based on the products that the user has added to the cart.

Edit `views.py` inside the `cart` application, import the `Recommender` class, and edit the `cart_detail` view to make it look like the following:

```python
from shop.recommender import Recommender


def cart_detail(request):
    cart = Cart(request)
    for item in cart:
        item['update_quantity_form'] = CartAddProductForm(initial={
                          'quantity': item['quantity'],
                          'override': True})
    coupon_apply_form = CouponApplyForm()

    r = Recommender()
    cart_products = [item['product'] for item in cart]
    if(cart_products):
        recommended_products = r.suggest_products_for(
                                    cart_products,
                                    max_results=4)
    else:
        recommended_products = []
    return render(request,
                  'cart/detail.html',
                  {'cart': cart,
                   'coupon_apply_form': coupon_apply_form,
                   'recommended_products': recommended_products})
```

Edit the `cart/detail.html` template of the cart application and add the following code just after the `</table>` HTML tag:

```html
{% if recommended_products %}
  <div class="recommendations cart">
    <h3>People who bought this also bought</h3>
    {% for p in recommended_products %}
```

```
      <div class="item">
        <a href="{{ p.get_absolute_url }}">
          <img src="{% if p.image %}{{ p.image.url }}{% else %}
          {% static "img/no_image.png" %}{% endif %}">
        </a>
        <p><a href="{{ p.get_absolute_url }}">{{ p.name }}</a></p>
      </div>
    {% endfor %}
  </div>
{% endif %}
```

Open http://127.0.0.1:8000/en/ in your browser and add a couple of products to your cart. When you navigate to http://127.0.0.1:8000/en/cart/, you should see the aggregated product recommendations for the items in the cart, as follows:

Your shopping cart

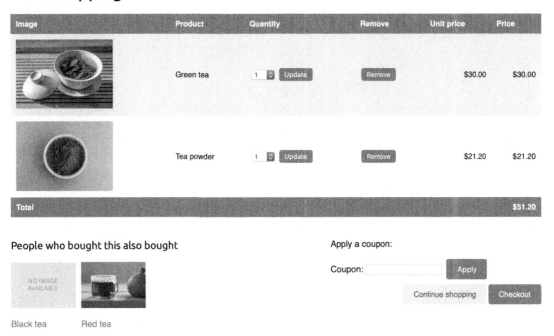

Figure 10.15: The shopping cart details page, including recommended products

Congratulations! You have built a complete recommendation engine using Django and Redis.

Additional resources

The following resources provide additional information related to the topics covered in this chapter:

- Source code for this chapter – `https://github.com/PacktPublishing/Django-4-by-example/tree/main/Chapter10`
- Discounts for Stripe Checkout – `https://stripe.com/docs/payments/checkout/discounts`
- The Redis `ZUNIONSTORE` command – `https://redis.io/commands/zunionstore/`

Summary

In this chapter, you created a coupon system using Django sessions and integrated it with Stripe. You also built a recommendation engine using Redis to recommend products that are usually purchased together.

The next chapter will give you an insight into the internationalization and localization of Django projects. You will learn how to translate code and manage translations with Rosetta. You will implement URLs for translations and build a language selector. You will also implement model translations using `django-parler` and you will validate localized form fields using `django-localflavor`.

11

Adding Internationalization to Your Shop

In the previous chapter, you added a coupon system to your shop and built a product recommendation engine.

In this chapter, you will learn how internationalization and localization work.

This chapter will cover the following points:

- Preparing your project for internationalization
- Managing translation files
- Translating Python code
- Translating templates
- Using Rosetta to manage translations
- Translating URL patterns and using a language prefix in URLs
- Allowing users to switch language
- Translating models using `django-parler`
- Using translations with the ORM
- Adapting views to use translations
- Using localized form fields of `django-localflavor`

The source code for this chapter can be found at https://github.com/PacktPublishing/Django-4-by-example/tree/main/Chapter11.

All the Python modules used in this chapter are included in the `requirements.txt` file in the source code that comes with this chapter. You can follow the instructions to install each Python module below or you can install all the requirements at once with the command `pip install -r requirements.txt`.

478   *Adding Internationalization to Your Shop*

Internationalization with Django

Django offers full internationalization and localization support. It allows you to translate your application into multiple languages and it handles locale-specific formatting for dates, times, numbers, and time zones. Let's clarify the difference between internationalization and localization:

Internationalization (frequently abbreviated to **i18n**) is the process of adapting software for the potential use of different languages and locales so that it isn't hardwired to a specific language or locale.

Localization (abbreviated to **l10n**) is the process of actually translating the software and adapting it to a particular locale. Django itself is translated into more than 50 languages using its internationalization framework.

The internationalization framework allows you to easily mark strings for translation, both in Python code and in your templates. It relies on the GNU gettext toolset to generate and manage message files. A **message file** is a plain text file that represents a language. It contains a part, or all, of the translation strings found in your application and their respective translations for a single language. Message files have the `.po` extension. Once the translation is done, message files are compiled to offer rapid access to translated strings. The compiled translation files have the `.mo` extension.

Internationalization and localization settings

Django provides several settings for internationalization. The following settings are the most relevant ones:

- `USE_I18N`: A Boolean that specifies whether Django's translation system is enabled. This is `True` by default.

- `USE_L10N`: A Boolean indicating whether localized formatting is enabled. When active, localized formats are used to represent dates and numbers. This is `False` by default.

- `USE_TZ`: A Boolean that specifies whether datetimes are time-zone-aware. When you create a project with the `startproject` command, this is set to `True`.

- `LANGUAGE_CODE`: The default language code for the project. This is in the standard language ID format, for example, `'en-us'` for American English, or `'en-gb'` for British English. This setting requires `USE_I18N` to be set to `True` in order to take effect. You can find a list of valid language IDs at `http://www.i18nguy.com/unicode/language-identifiers.html`.

- `LANGUAGES`: A tuple that contains available languages for the project. They come in two tuples of a **language code** and a **language name**. You can see the list of available languages at `django.conf.global_settings`. When you choose which languages your site will be available in, you set `LANGUAGES` to a subset of that list.

- `LOCALE_PATHS`: A list of directories where Django looks for message files containing translations for the project.

- `TIME_ZONE`: A string that represents the time zone for the project. This is set to `'UTC'` when you create a new project using the `startproject` command. You can set it to any other time zone, such as `'Europe/Madrid'`.

These are some of the internationalization and localization settings available. You can find the full list at https://docs.djangoproject.com/en/4.1/ref/settings/#globalization-i18n-l10n.

Internationalization management commands

Django includes the following management commands to manage translations:

- makemessages: This runs over the source tree to find all the strings marked for translation and creates or updates the .po message files in the locale directory. A single .po file is created for each language.
- compilemessages: This compiles the existing .po message files to .mo files, which are used to retrieve translations.

Installing the gettext toolkit

You will need the gettext toolkit to be able to create, update, and compile message files. Most Linux distributions include the gettext toolkit. If you are using macOS, the simplest way to install it is via Homebrew, at https://brew.sh/, with the following command:

```
brew install gettext
```

You might also need to force link it with the following command:

```
brew link --force gettext
```

If you are using Windows, follow the steps at https://docs.djangoproject.com/en/4.1/topics/i18n/translation/#gettext-on-windows. You can download a precompiled gettext binary installer for Windows from https://mlocati.github.io/articles/gettext-iconv-windows.html.

How to add translations to a Django project

Let's take a look at the process of internationalizing your project. You will need to do the following:

1. Mark the strings for translation in your Python code and your templates.
2. Run the makemessages command to create or update message files that include all the translation strings from your code.
3. Translate the strings contained in the message files and compile them using the compilemessages management command.

How Django determines the current language

Django comes with a middleware that determines the current language based on the request data. This is the LocaleMiddleware middleware that resides in django.middleware.locale.LocaleMiddleware, which performs the following tasks:

1. If you are using i18n_patterns, that is, you are using translated URL patterns, it looks for a language prefix in the requested URL to determine the current language.
2. If no language prefix is found, it looks for an existing LANGUAGE_SESSION_KEY in the current user's session.

3. If the language is not set in the session, it looks for an existing cookie with the current language. A custom name for this cookie can be provided in the `LANGUAGE_COOKIE_NAME` setting. By default, the name for this cookie is `django_language`.

4. If no cookie is found, it looks for the `Accept-Language` HTTP header of the request.

5. If the `Accept-Language` header does not specify a language, Django uses the language defined in the `LANGUAGE_CODE` setting.

By default, Django will use the language defined in the `LANGUAGE_CODE` setting unless you are using `LocaleMiddleware`. The process described here only applies when using this middleware.

Preparing your project for internationalization

Let's prepare your project to use different languages. You are going to create an English and a Spanish version for your shop. Edit the `settings.py` file of your project and add the following `LANGUAGES` setting to it. Place it next to the `LANGUAGE_CODE` setting:

```
LANGUAGES = [
    ('en', 'English'),
    ('es', 'Spanish'),
]
```

The `LANGUAGES` setting contains two tuples that consist of a language code and a name. Language codes can be locale-specific, such as en-us or en-gb, or generic, such as en. With this setting, you specify that your application will only be available in English and Spanish. If you don't define a custom `LANGUAGES` setting, the site will be available in all the languages that Django is translated into.

Make your `LANGUAGE_CODE` setting look like the following:

```
LANGUAGE_CODE = 'en'
```

Add `'django.middleware.locale.LocaleMiddleware'` to the `MIDDLEWARE` setting. Make sure that this middleware comes after `SessionMiddleware` because `LocaleMiddleware` needs to use session data. It also has to be placed before `CommonMiddleware` because the latter needs an active language to resolve the requested URL. The `MIDDLEWARE` setting should now look like the following:

```
MIDDLEWARE = [
    'django.middleware.security.SecurityMiddleware',
    'django.contrib.sessions.middleware.SessionMiddleware',
    'django.middleware.locale.LocaleMiddleware',
    'django.middleware.common.CommonMiddleware',
    'django.middleware.csrf.CsrfViewMiddleware',
    'django.contrib.auth.middleware.AuthenticationMiddleware',
    'django.contrib.messages.middleware.MessageMiddleware',
    'django.middleware.clickjacking.XFrameOptionsMiddleware',
]
```

The order of middleware classes is very important because each middleware can depend on data set by another middleware that was executed previously. Middleware is applied for requests in order of appearance in MIDDLEWARE, and in reverse order for responses.

Create the following directory structure inside the main project directory, next to the manage.py file:

```
locale/
    en/
    es/
```

The locale directory is the place where message files for your application will reside. Edit the settings.py file again and add the following setting to it:

```
LOCALE_PATHS = [
    BASE_DIR / 'locale',
]
```

The LOCALE_PATHS setting specifies the directories where Django has to look for translation files. Locale paths that appear first have the highest precedence.

When you use the makemessages command from your project directory, message files will be generated in the locale/ path you created. However, for applications that contain a locale/ directory, message files will be generated in that directory.

Translating Python code

To translate literals in your Python code, you can mark strings for translation using the gettext() function included in django.utils.translation. This function translates the message and returns a string. The convention is to import this function as a shorter alias named _ (the underscore character).

You can find all the documentation about translations at https://docs.djangoproject.com/en/4.1/topics/i18n/translation/.

Standard translations

The following code shows how to mark a string for translation:

```
from django.utils.translation import gettext as _
output = _('Text to be translated.')
```

Lazy translations

Django includes **lazy** versions for all of its translation functions, which have the suffix _lazy(). When using the lazy functions, strings are translated when the value is accessed, rather than when the function is called (this is why they are translated **lazily**). The lazy translation functions come in handy when the strings marked for translation are in paths that are executed when modules are loaded.

Using gettext_lazy() instead of gettext() means that strings are translated when the value is accessed. Django offers a lazy version for all translation functions.

Translations including variables

The strings marked for translation can include placeholders to include variables in the translations. The following code is an example of a translation string with a placeholder:

```
from django.utils.translation import gettext as _
month = _('April')
day = '14'
output = _('Today is %(month)s %(day)s') % {'month': month,
                                            'day': day}
```

By using placeholders, you can reorder the text variables. For example, an English translation of the previous example might be *today is April 14*, while the Spanish one might be *hoy es 14 de Abril*. Always use string interpolation instead of positional interpolation when you have more than one parameter for the translation string. By doing so, you will be able to reorder the placeholder text.

Plural forms in translations

For plural forms, you can use ngettext() and ngettext_lazy(). These functions translate singular and plural forms depending on an argument that indicates the number of objects. The following example shows how to use them:

```
output = ngettext('there is %(count)d product',
                  'there are %(count)d products',
                  count) % {'count': count}
```

Now that you know the basics of translating literals in your Python code, it's time to apply translations to your project.

Translating your own code

Edit the settings.py file of your project, import the gettext_lazy() function, and change the LANGUAGES setting, as follows, to translate the language names:

```
from django.utils.translation import gettext_lazy as _
# ...

LANGUAGES = [
    ('en', _('English')),
    ('es', _('Spanish')),
]
```

Here, you use the `gettext_lazy()` function instead of `gettext()` to avoid a circular import, thus translating the languages' names when they are accessed.

Open the shell and run the following command from your project directory:

```
django-admin makemessages --all
```

You should see the following output:

```
processing locale es
processing locale en
```

Take a look at the `locale/` directory. You should see a file structure like the following:

```
en/
     LC_MESSAGES/
          django.po
es/
     LC_MESSAGES/
          django.po
```

A `.po` message file has been created for each language. Open `es/LC_MESSAGES/django.po` with a text editor. At the end of the file, you should be able to see the following:

```
#: myshop/settings.py:118
msgid "English"
msgstr ""
#: myshop/settings.py:119
msgid "Spanish"
msgstr ""
```

Each translation string is preceded by a comment showing details about the file and the line where it was found. Each translation includes two strings:

- `msgid`: The translation string as it appears in the source code.
- `msgstr`: The language translation, which is empty by default. This is where you have to enter the actual translation for the given string.

Fill in the `msgstr` translations for the given `msgid` string, as follows:

```
#: myshop/settings.py:118
msgid "English"
msgstr "Inglés"
#: myshop/settings.py:119
msgid "Spanish"
msgstr "Español"
```

Save the modified message file, open the shell, and run the following command:

```
django-admin compilemessages
```

If everything goes well, you should see an output like the following:

```
processing file django.po in myshop/locale/en/LC_MESSAGES
processing file django.po in myshop/locale/es/LC_MESSAGES
```

The output gives you information about the message files that are being compiled. Take a look at the locale directory of the myshop project again. You should see the following files:

```
en/
    LC_MESSAGES/
        django.mo
        django.po
es/
    LC_MESSAGES/
        django.mo
        django.po
```

You can see that a .mo compiled message file has been generated for each language.

You have translated the language names. Now, let's translate the model field names that are displayed on the site. Edit the models.py file of the orders application, and add names marked for translation to the Order model fields as follows:

```
from django.utils.translation import gettext_lazy as _

class Order(models.Model):
    first_name = models.CharField(_('first name'),
                                  max_length=50)
    last_name = models.CharField(_('last name'),
                                 max_length=50)
    email = models.EmailField(_('e-mail'))
    address = models.CharField(_('address'),
                               max_length=250)
    postal_code = models.CharField(_('postal code'),
                                   max_length=20)
    city = models.CharField(_('city'),
                            max_length=100)
    # ...
```

You have added names for the fields that are displayed when a user is placing a new order. These are first_name, last_name, email, address, postal_code, and city. Remember that you can also use the verbose_name attribute to name the fields.

Create the following directory structure inside the `orders` application directory:

```
locale/
    en/
    es/
```

By creating a `locale` directory, the translation strings of this application will be stored in a message file under this directory instead of the main messages file. In this way, you can generate separate translation files for each application.

Open the shell from the project directory and run the following command:

```
django-admin makemessages --all
```

You should see the following output:

```
processing locale es
processing locale en
```

Open the `locale/es/LC_MESSAGES/django.po` file of the order application using a text editor. You will see the translation strings for the `Order` model. Fill in the following `msgstr` translations for the given `msgid` strings:

```
#: orders/models.py:12
msgid "first name"
msgstr "nombre"
#: orders/models.py:14
msgid "last name"
msgstr "apellidos"
#: orders/models.py:16
msgid "e-mail"
msgstr "e-mail"
#: orders/models.py:17
msgid "address"
msgstr "dirección"
#: orders/models.py:19
msgid "postal code"
msgstr "código postal"
#: orders/models.py:21
msgid "city"
msgstr "ciudad"
```

After you have finished adding the translations, save the file.

Besides a text editor, you can use Poedit to edit translations. Poedit is a piece of software for editing translations that uses gettext. It is available for Linux, Windows, and macOS. You can download Poedit from https://poedit.net/.

Let's also translate the forms of your project. The `OrderCreateForm` of the orders application does not have to be translated. That's because it is a `ModelForm` and it uses the `verbose_name` attribute of the `Order` model fields for the form field labels. You are going to translate the forms of the cart and coupons applications.

Edit the `forms.py` file inside the cart application directory and add a `label` attribute to the `quantity` field of the `CartAddProductForm`. Then, mark this field for translation, as follows:

```
from django import forms
from django.utils.translation import gettext_lazy as _


PRODUCT_QUANTITY_CHOICES = [(i, str(i)) for i in range(1, 21)]


class CartAddProductForm(forms.Form):
    quantity = forms.TypedChoiceField(
                    choices=PRODUCT_QUANTITY_CHOICES,
                    coerce=int,
                    label=_('Quantity'))
    override = forms.BooleanField(required=False,
                                  initial=False,
                                  widget=forms.HiddenInput)
```

Edit the `forms.py` file of the coupons application and translate the `CouponApplyForm` form, as follows:

```
from django import forms
from django.utils.translation import gettext_lazy as _


class CouponApplyForm(forms.Form):
    code = forms.CharField(label=_('Coupon'))
```

You have added a label to the code field and marked it for translation.

Translating templates

Django offers the {% trans %} and {% blocktrans %} template tags to translate the strings in templates. In order to use the translation template tags, you have to add {% load i18n %} to the top of your template to load them.

The {% trans %} template tag

The {% trans %} template tag allows you to mark a literal for translation. Internally, Django executes `gettext()` on the given text. This is how to mark a string for translation in a template:

```
{% trans "Text to be translated" %}
```

You can use as to store the translated content in a variable that you can use throughout your template. The following example stores the translated text in a variable called greeting:

```
{% trans "Hello!" as greeting %}
<h1>{{ greeting }}</h1>
```

The {% trans %} tag is useful for simple translation strings, but it can't handle content for translation that includes variables.

The {% blocktrans %} template tag

The {% blocktrans %} template tag allows you to mark content that includes literals and variable content using placeholders. The following example shows you how to use the {% blocktrans %} tag, including a name variable in the content for translation:

```
{% blocktrans %}Hello {{ name }}!{% endblocktrans %}
```

You can use with to include template expressions, such as accessing object attributes or applying template filters to variables. You always have to use placeholders for these. You can't access expressions or object attributes inside the blocktrans block. The following example shows you how to use with to include an object attribute to which the capfirst filter has been applied:

```
{% blocktrans with name=user.name|capfirst %}
  Hello {{ name }}!
{% endblocktrans %}
```

 Use the {% blocktrans %} tag instead of {% trans %} when you need to include variable content in your translation string.

Translating the shop templates

Edit the shop/base.html template of the shop application. Make sure that you load the i18n tag at the top of the template and mark the strings for translation, as follows. New code is highlighted in bold:

```
{% load i18n %}
{% load static %}
<!DOCTYPE html>
<html>
<head>
  <meta charset="utf-8" />
  <title>
    {% block title %}{% trans "My shop" %}{% endblock %}
  </title>
  <link href="{% static "css/base.css" %}" rel="stylesheet">
```

```
    </head>
    <body>
      <div id="header">
        <a href="/" class="logo">{% trans "My shop" %}</a>
      </div>
      <div id="subheader">
        <div class="cart">
          {% with total_items=cart|length %}
            {% if total_items > 0 %}
              {% trans "Your cart" %}:
              <a href="{% url "cart:cart_detail" %}">
                {% blocktrans with total=cart.get_total_price count items=total_
items %}
                  {{ items }} item, ${{ total }}
                {% plural %}
                  {{ items }} items, ${{ total }}
                {% endblocktrans %}
              </a>
            {% elif not order %}
              {% trans "Your cart is empty." %}
            {% endif %}
          {% endwith %}
        </div>
      </div>
      <div id="content">
        {% block content %}
        {% endblock %}
      </div>
    </body>
    </html>
```

Make sure that no template tag is split across multiple lines.

Notice the {% blocktrans %} tag to display the cart's summary. The cart's summary was previously as follows:

```
{{ total_items }} item{{ total_items|pluralize }},
${{ cart.get_total_price }}
```

You changed it, and now you use {% blocktrans with ... %} to set up the placeholder total with the value of cart.get_total_price (the object method called here). You also use count, which allows you to set a variable for counting objects for Django to select the right plural form. You set the items variable to count objects with the value of total_items.

This allows you to set a translation for the singular and plural forms, which you separate with the {% plural %} tag within the {% blocktrans %} block. The resulting code is:

```
{% blocktrans with total=cart.get_total_price count items=total_items %}
  {{ items }} item, ${{ total }}
{% plural %}
  {{ items }} items, ${{ total }}
{% endblocktrans %}
```

Next, edit the shop/product/detail.html template of the shop application and load the i18n tags at the top of it, but after the {% extends %} tag, which always has to be the first tag in the template:

```
{% extends "shop/base.html" %}
{% load i18n %}
{% load static %}
...
```

Then, find the following line:

```
<input type="submit" value="Add to cart">
```

Replace it with the following:

```
<input type="submit" value="{% trans "Add to cart" %}">
```

Then, find the following line:

```
<h3>People who bought this also bought</h3>
```

Replace it with the following:

```
<h3>{% trans "People who bought this also bought" %}</h3>
```

Now, translate the orders application template. Edit the orders/order/create.html template of the orders application and mark the text for translation, as follows:

```
{% extends "shop/base.html" %}
{% load i18n %}
{% block title %}
  {% trans "Checkout" %}
{% endblock %}
{% block content %}
  <h1>{% trans "Checkout" %}</h1>
  <div class="order-info">
    <h3>{% trans "Your order" %}</h3>
    <ul>
      {% for item in cart %}
        <li>
          {{ item.quantity }}x {{ item.product.name }}
```

```
                <span>${{ item.total_price }}</span>
            </li>
        {% endfor %}
        {% if cart.coupon %}
            <li>
                {% blocktrans with code=cart.coupon.code discount=cart.coupon.
discount %}
                    "{{ code }}" ({{ discount }}% off)
                {% endblocktrans %}
                <span class="neg">- ${{ cart.get_discount|floatformat:2 }}</span>
            </li>
        {% endif %}
    </ul>
    <p>{% trans "Total" %}: ${{
    cart.get_total_price_after_discount|floatformat:2 }}</p>
    </div>
    <form method="post" class="order-form">
        {{ form.as_p }}
        <p><input type="submit" value="{% trans "Place order" %}"></p>
        {% csrf_token %}
    </form>
{% endblock %}
```

Make sure that no template tag is split across multiple lines. Take a look at the following files in the code that accompanies this chapter to see how the strings have been marked for translation:

- The shop application: Template shop/product/list.html
- The orders application: Template orders/order/pdf.html
- The cart application: Template cart/detail.html
- The payments application: Templates payment/process.html, payment/completed.html, and payment/canceled.html

Remember that you can find the source code for this chapter at https://github.com/PacktPublishing/Django-4-by-Example/tree/master/Chapter11.

Let's update the message files to include the new translation strings. Open the shell and run the following command:

```
django-admin makemessages --all
```

The .po files are inside the locale directory of the myshop project, and you'll see that the orders application now contains all the strings that you marked for translation.

Edit the .po translation files of the project and the orders application and include Spanish translations in msgstr. You can also use the translated .po files in the source code that accompanies this chapter.

Run the following command to compile the translation files:

```
django-admin compilemessages
```

You will see the following output:

```
processing file django.po in myshop/locale/en/LC_MESSAGES
processing file django.po in myshop/locale/es/LC_MESSAGES
processing file django.po in myshop/orders/locale/en/LC_MESSAGES
processing file django.po in myshop/orders/locale/es/LC_MESSAGES
```

A .mo file containing compiled translations has been generated for each .po translation file.

Using the Rosetta translation interface

Rosetta is a third-party application that allows you to edit translations using the same interface as the Django administration site. Rosetta makes it easy to edit .po files, and it updates compiled translation files. Let's add it to your project.

Install Rosetta via pip using this command:

```
pip install django-rosetta==0.9.8
```

Then, add 'rosetta' to the INSTALLED_APPS setting in your project's settings.py file, as follows:

```
INSTALLED_APPS = [
    # ...
    'rosetta',
]
```

You need to add Rosetta's URLs to your main URL configuration. Edit the main urls.py file of your project and add the following URL pattern highlighted in bold:

```
urlpatterns = [
    path('admin/', admin.site.urls),
    path('cart/', include('cart.urls', namespace='cart')),
    path('orders/', include('orders.urls', namespace='orders')),
    path('payment/', include('payment.urls', namespace='payment')),
    path('coupons/', include('coupons.urls', namespace='coupons')),
    path('rosetta/', include('rosetta.urls')),
    path('', include('shop.urls', namespace='shop')),
]
```

Make sure you place it before the shop.urls pattern to avoid an undesired pattern match.

Open http://127.0.0.1:8000/admin/ and log in with a superuser. Then, navigate to http://127.0.0.1:8000/rosetta/ in your browser. In the **Filter** menu, click **THIRD PARTY** to display all the available message files, including those that belong to the orders application.

You should see a list of existing languages, as follows:

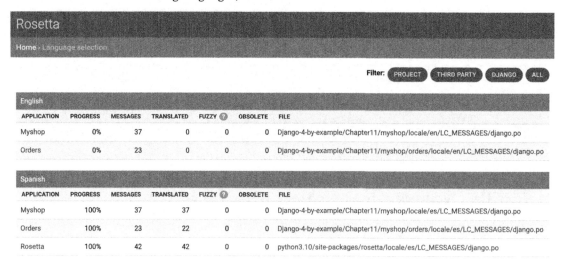

Figure 11.1: The Rosetta administration interface

Click the **Myshop** link under the **Spanish** section to edit the Spanish translations. You should see a list of translation strings, as follows:

ORIGINAL	SPANISH	FUZZY	OCCURRENCES(S)
Quantity	Cantidad	☐	cart/forms.py:12 cart/templates/cart/detail.html:16 payment/templates/payment/process.html:15
Your shopping cart	Su carro	☐	cart/templates/cart/detail.html:6 cart/templates/cart/detail.html:10
Image	Imagen	☐	cart/templates/cart/detail.html:14 payment/templates/payment/process.html:12
Product	Producto	☐	cart/templates/cart/detail.html:15 payment/templates/payment/process.html:13
Remove	Eliminar	☐	cart/templates/cart/detail.html:17 cart/templates/cart/detail.html:43
Unit price	Precio unitario	☐	cart/templates/cart/detail.html:18
Price	Precio	☐	cart/templates/cart/detail.html:19 payment/templates/payment/process.html:14
Update	Actualizar	☐	cart/templates/cart/detail.html:37

Figure 11.2: Editing Spanish translations using Rosetta

You can enter the translations under the **SPANISH** column. The **OCCURRENCE(S)** column displays the files and lines of code where each translation string was found.

Translations that include placeholders will appear as follows:

0:

%(items)s producto, $%(total)s

%(items)s item, $%(total)s

1:

%(items)s productos, $%(total)s

%(items)s items, $%(total)s

Figure 11.3: Translations including placeholders

Rosetta uses a different background color to display placeholders. When you translate content, make sure that you keep placeholders untranslated. For example, take the following string:

```
%(items)s items, $%(total)s
```

It can be translated into Spanish as follows:

```
%(items)s productos, $%(total)s
```

You can take a look at the source code that comes with this chapter to use the same Spanish translations for your project.

When you finish editing translations, click the **Save and translate next block** button to save the translations to the `.po` file. Rosetta compiles the message file when you save translations, so there is no need for you to run the `compilemessages` command. However, Rosetta requires write access to the `locale` directories to write the message files. Make sure that the directories have valid permissions.

If you want other users to be able to edit translations, open `http://127.0.0.1:8000/admin/auth/group/add/` in your browser and create a new group named `translators`. Then, access `http://127.0.0.1:8000/admin/auth/user/` to edit the users to whom you want to grant permissions so that they can edit translations. When editing a user, under the **Permissions** section, add the `translators` group to the **Chosen Groups** for each user. Rosetta is only available to superusers or users who belong to the `translators` group.

You can read Rosetta's documentation at `https://django-rosetta.readthedocs.io/`.

 When you add new translations to your production environment, if you serve Django with a real web server, you will have to reload your server after running the `compilemessages` command, or after saving the translations with Rosetta, for any changes to take effect.

When editing translations, a translation can be marked as *fuzzy*. Let's review what fuzzy translations are.

Fuzzy translations

When editing translations in Rosetta, you can see a **FUZZY** column. This is not a Rosetta feature; it is provided by gettext. If the **FUZZY** flag is active for a translation, it will not be included in the compiled message files. This flag marks translation strings that need to be reviewed by a translator. When .po files are updated with new translation strings, it is possible that some translation strings will automatically be flagged as fuzzy. This happens when gettext finds some msgid that has been slightly modified. gettext pairs it with what it thinks was the old translation and flags it as fuzzy for review. The translator should then review the fuzzy translations, remove the **FUZZY** flag, and compile the translation file again.

URL patterns for internationalization

Django offers internationalization capabilities for URLs. It includes two main features for internationalized URLs:

- **Language prefix in URL patterns:** Adding a language prefix to URLs to serve each language version under a different base URL.
- **Translated URL patterns:** Translating URL patterns so that every URL is different for each language.

One reason for translating URLs is to optimize your site for search engines. By adding a language prefix to your patterns, you will be able to index a URL for each language instead of a single URL for all of them. Furthermore, by translating URLs into each language, you will provide search engines with URLs that will rank better for each language.

Adding a language prefix to URL patterns

Django allows you to add a language prefix to your URL patterns. For example, the English version of your site can be served under a path starting with /en/, and the Spanish version under /es/. To use languages in URL patterns, you have to use the LocaleMiddleware provided by Django. The framework will use it to identify the current language from the requested URL. Previously, you added it to the MIDDLEWARE setting of your project, so you don't need to do it now.

Let's add a language prefix to your URL patterns. Edit the main urls.py file of the myshop project and add i18n_patterns(), as follows:

```python
from django.conf.urls.i18n import i18n_patterns

urlpatterns = i18n_patterns(
    path('admin/', admin.site.urls),
    path('cart/', include('cart.urls', namespace='cart')),
    path('orders/', include('orders.urls', namespace='orders')),
    path('payment/', include('payment.urls', namespace='payment')),
    path('coupons/', include('coupons.urls', namespace='coupons')),
    path('rosetta/', include('rosetta.urls')),
    path('', include('shop.urls', namespace='shop')),
)
```

You can combine non-translatable standard URL patterns and patterns under i18n_patterns so that some patterns include a language prefix and others don't. However, it's better to use translated URLs only to avoid the possibility that a carelessly translated URL matches a non-translated URL pattern.

Run the development server and open http://127.0.0.1:8000/ in your browser. Django will perform the steps described in the *How Django determines the current language* section to determine the current language, and it will redirect you to the requested URL, including the language prefix. Take a look at the URL in your browser; it should now look like http://127.0.0.1:8000/en/. The current language is the one set by the Accept-Language header of your browser if it is Spanish or English; otherwise, it is the default LANGUAGE_CODE (English) defined in your settings.

Translating URL patterns

Django supports translated strings in URL patterns. You can use a different translation for each language for a single URL pattern. You can mark URL patterns for translation in the same way as you would with literals, using the gettext_lazy() function.

Edit the main urls.py file of the myshop project and add translation strings to the regular expressions of the URL patterns for the cart, orders, payment, and coupons applications, as follows:

```
from django.utils.translation import gettext_lazy as _

urlpatterns = i18n_patterns(
    path('admin/', admin.site.urls),
    path(_('cart/'), include('cart.urls', namespace='cart')),
    path(_('orders/'), include('orders.urls', namespace='orders')),
    path(_('payment/'), include('payment.urls', namespace='payment')),
    path(_('coupons/'), include('coupons.urls', namespace='coupons')),
    path('rosetta/', include('rosetta.urls')),
    path('', include('shop.urls', namespace='shop')),
)
```

Edit the urls.py file of the orders application and mark the order_create URL pattern for translation, as follows:

```
from django.utils.translation import gettext_lazy as _

urlpatterns = [
    path(_('create/'), views.order_create, name='order_create'),
    # ...
]
```

Edit the `urls.py` file of the payment application and change the code to the following:

```python
from django.utils.translation import gettext_lazy as _

urlpatterns = [
    path(_('process/'), views.payment_process, name='process'),
    path(_('done/'), views.payment_done, name='done'),
    path(_('canceled/'), views.payment_canceled, name='canceled'),
    path('webhook/', webhooks.stripe_webhook, name='stripe-webhook'),
]
```

Note that these URL patterns will include a language prefix because they are included under `i18n_patterns()` in the main `urls.py` file of the project. This will make each URL pattern have a different URI for each available language, one starting with /en/, another one with /es/, and so on. However, we need a single URL for Stripe to notify events, and we need to avoid language prefixes in the webhook URL.

Remove the webhook URL pattern from the `urls.py` file of the payment application. The file should now look like the following:

```python
from django.utils.translation import gettext_lazy as _

urlpatterns = [
    path(_('process/'), views.payment_process, name='process'),
    path(_('done/'), views.payment_done, name='done'),
    path(_('canceled/'), views.payment_canceled, name='canceled'),
]
```

Then, add the following webhook URL pattern to the main `urls.py` file of the `myshop` project. The new code is highlighted in bold:

```python
from django.utils.translation import gettext_lazy as _
from payment import webhooks

urlpatterns = i18n_patterns(
    path('admin/', admin.site.urls),
    path(_('cart/'), include('cart.urls', namespace='cart')),
    path(_('orders/'), include('orders.urls', namespace='orders')),
    path(_('payment/'), include('payment.urls', namespace='payment')),
    path(_('coupons/'), include('coupons.urls', namespace='coupons')),
    path('rosetta/', include('rosetta.urls')),
    path('', include('shop.urls', namespace='shop')),
)

urlpatterns += [
```

```
        path('payment/webhook/', webhooks.stripe_webhook,
                            name='stripe-webhook'),
]


if settings.DEBUG:
    urlpatterns += static(settings.MEDIA_URL,
                          document_root=settings.MEDIA_ROOT)
```

We have added the `webhook` URL pattern to `urlpatterns` outside of `i18n_patterns()` to ensure we maintain a single URL for Stripe event notifications.

You don't need to translate the URL patterns of the `shop` application, as they are built with variables and do not include any other literals.

Open the shell and run the next command to update the message files with the new translations:

```
django-admin makemessages --all
```

Make sure the development server is running with the following command:

```
python manage.py runserver
```

Open `http://127.0.0.1:8000/en/rosetta/` in your browser and click the **Myshop** link under the **Spanish** section. Click on **UNTRANSLATED ONLY** to only see the strings that have not been translated yet. Now you will see the URL patterns for translation, as shown in *Figure 11.4*:

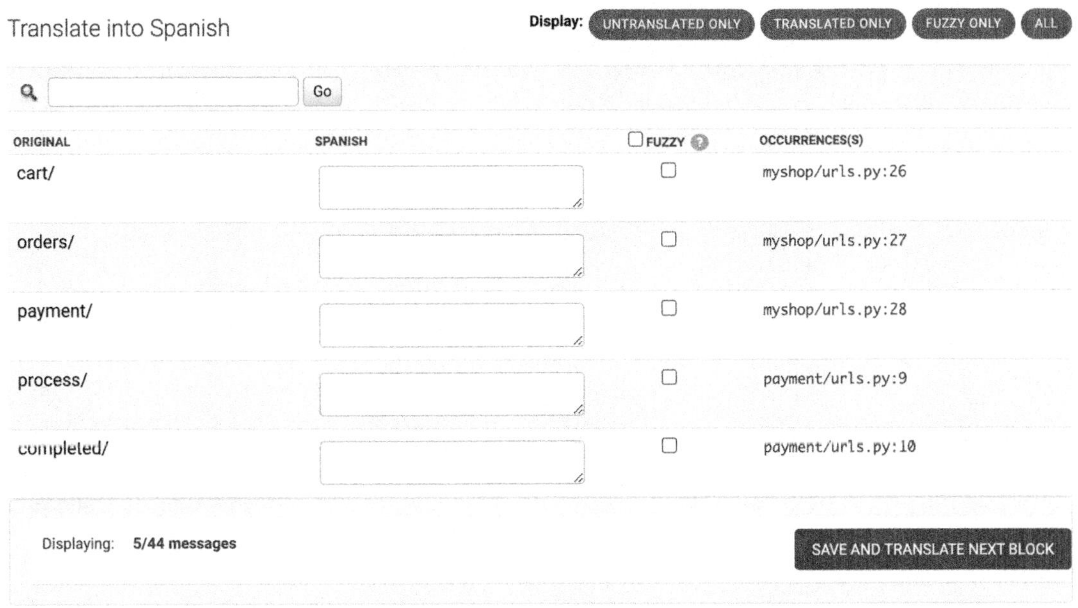

Figure 11.4: URL patterns for translation in the Rosetta interface

Add a different translation string for each URL. Don't forget to include a slash character / at the end of each URL, as shown in *Figure 11.5*:

Figure 11.5: Spanish translations for URL patterns in the Rosetta interface

When you have finished, click **SAVE AND TRANSLATE NEXT BLOCK**.

Then, click on **FUZZY ONLY**. You will see translations that have been flagged as fuzzy because they were paired with the old translation of a similar original string. In the case displayed in *Figure 11.6*, the translations are incorrect and need to be corrected:

Figure 11.6: Fuzzy translations in the Rosetta interface

Enter the correct text for the fuzzy translations. Rosetta will automatically uncheck the **FUZZY** select box when you enter new text for a translation. When you have finished, click **SAVE AND TRANSLATE NEXT BLOCK**:

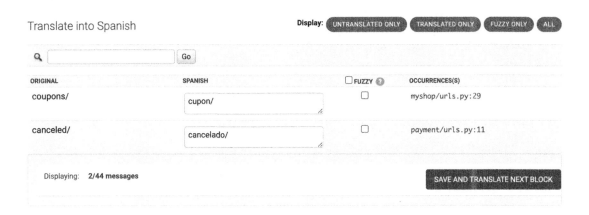

Figure 11.7: Correcting fuzzy translations in the Rosetta interface

You can now go back to http://127.0.0.1:8000/en/rosetta/files/third-party/ and edit the Spanish translation for the orders application as well.

Allowing users to switch language

Since you are serving content that is available in multiple languages, you should let your users switch the site's language. You are going to add a language selector to your site. The language selector will consist of a list of available languages displayed using links.

Edit the shop/base.html template of the shop application and locate the following lines:

```
<div id="header">
  <a href="/" class="logo">{% trans "My shop" %}</a>
</div>
```

Replace them with the following code:

```
<div id="header">
  <a href="/" class="logo">{% trans "My shop" %}</a>
  {% get_current_language as LANGUAGE_CODE %}
  {% get_available_languages as LANGUAGES %}
  {% get_language_info_list for LANGUAGES as languages %}
  <div class="languages">
    <p>{% trans "Language" %}:</p>
    <ul class="languages">
      {% for language in languages %}
        <li>
          <a href="/{{ language.code }}/"
          {% if language.code == LANGUAGE_CODE %} class="selected"{% endif %}>
            {{ language.name_local }}
          </a>
        </li>
```

```
        {% endfor %}
     </ul>
   </div>
</div>
```

Make sure that no template tag is split into multiple lines.

This is how you build your language selector:

1. You load the internationalization tags using `{% load i18n %}`.
2. You use the `{% get_current_language %}` tag to retrieve the current language.
3. You get the languages defined in the LANGUAGES setting using the `{% get_available_languages %}` template tag.
4. You use the tag `{% get_language_info_list %}` to provide easy access to the language attributes.
5. You build an HTML list to display all available languages, and you add a `selected` class attribute to the current active language.

In the code for the language selector, you used the template tags provided by i18n, based on the languages available in the settings of your project. Now open `http://127.0.0.1:8000/` in your browser and take a look. You should see the language selector in the top right-hand corner of the site, as follows:

Figure 11.8: The product list page, including a language selector in the site header

 Images in this chapter:

- *Green tea*: Photo by Jia Ye on Unsplash
- *Red tea*: Photo by Manki Kim on Unsplash
- *Tea powder*: Photo by Phuong Nguyen on Unsplash

Users can now easily switch to their preferred language by clicking on it.

Translating models with django-parler

Django does not provide a solution for translating models out of the box. You have to implement your own solution to manage content stored in different languages, or use a third-party module for model translation. There are several third-party applications that allow you to translate model fields. Each of them takes a different approach to storing and accessing translations. One of these applications is django-parler. This module offers a very effective way to translate models, and it integrates smoothly with Django's administration site.

django-parler generates a separate database table for each model that contains translations. This table includes all the translated fields and a foreign key for the original object that the translation belongs to. It also contains a language field, since each row stores the content for a single language.

Installing django-parler

Install django-parler via pip using the following command:

```
pip install django-parler==2.3
```

Edit the settings.py file of your project and add 'parler' to the INSTALLED_APPS setting, as follows:

```
INSTALLED_APPS = [
    # ...
    'parler',
]
```

Also, add the following code to your settings:

```
# django-parler settings
PARLER_LANGUAGES = {
    None: (
        {'code': 'en'},
        {'code': 'es'},
    ),
    'default': {
        'fallback': 'en',
        'hide_untranslated': False,
    }
}
```

This setting defines the available languages, en and es, for django-parler. You specify the default language en and indicate that django-parler should not hide untranslated content.

Translating model fields

Let's add translations to your product catalog. django-parler provides a TranslatableModel model class and a TranslatedFields wrapper to translate model fields.

Edit the `models.py` file inside the `shop` application directory and add the following import:

```python
from parler.models import TranslatableModel, TranslatedFields
```

Then, modify the `Category` model to make the `name` and `slug` fields translatable, as follows:

```python
class Category(TranslatableModel):
    translations = TranslatedFields(
        name = models.CharField(max_length=200),
        slug = models.SlugField(max_length=200,
                                unique=True),
    )
```

The `Category` model now inherits from `TranslatableModel` instead of `models.Model`, and both the `name` and `slug` fields are included in the `TranslatedFields` wrapper.

Edit the `Product` model to add translations for the `name`, `slug`, and `description` fields, as follows:

```python
class Product(TranslatableModel):
    translations = TranslatedFields(
        name = models.CharField(max_length=200),
        slug = models.SlugField(max_length=200),
        description = models.TextField(blank=True)
    )
    category = models.ForeignKey(Category,
                                 related_name='products',
                                 on_delete=models.CASCADE)
    image = models.ImageField(upload_to='products/%Y/%m/%d',
                              blank=True)
    price = models.DecimalField(max_digits=10,
                                decimal_places=2)
    available = models.BooleanField(default=True)
    created = models.DateTimeField(auto_now_add=True)
    updated = models.DateTimeField(auto_now=True)
```

`django-parler` manages translations by generating another model for each translatable model. In the following schema, you can see the fields of the `Product` model and what the generated `ProductTranslation` model will look like:

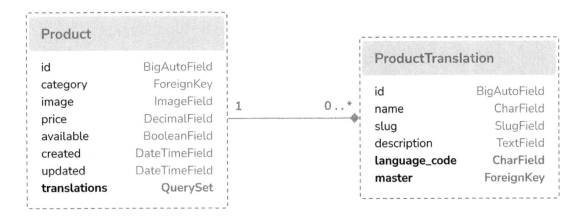

Figure 11.9: The Product model and related ProductTranslation model generated by django-parler

The ProductTranslation model generated by django-parler includes the name, slug, and description translatable fields, a language_code field, and a ForeignKey for the master Product object. There is a one-to-many relationship from Product to ProductTranslation. A ProductTranslation object will exist for each available language of each Product object.

Since Django uses a separate table for translations, there are some Django features that you can't use. It is not possible to use a default ordering by a translated field. You can filter by translated fields in queries, but you can't include a translatable field in the ordering Meta options. Also, you can't use indexes for the fields that are translated, as these fields will not exist in the original model, because they will reside in the translation model.

Edit the models.py file of the shop application and comment out the ordering and indexes attributes of the Category Meta class:

```
class Category(TranslatableModel):
    # ...
    class Meta:
        # ordering = ['name']
        # indexes = [
        #     models.Index(fields=['name']),
        # ]
        verbose_name = 'category'
        verbose_name_plural = 'categories'
```

You also have to comment out the `ordering` and attribute of the `Product` `Meta` class and the indexes that refer to the translated fields. Comment out the following lines of the `Product` `Meta` class:

```
class Product(TranslatableModel):
    # ...
    class Meta:
        # ordering = ['name']
        indexes = [
            # models.Index(fields=['id', 'slug']),
            # models.Index(fields=['name']),
            models.Index(fields=['-created']),
        ]
```

You can read more about the `django-parler` module's compatibility with Django at `https://django-parler.readthedocs.io/en/latest/compatibility.html`.

Integrating translations into the administration site

`django-parler` integrates smoothly with the Django administration site. It includes a `TranslatableAdmin` class that overrides the `ModelAdmin` class provided by Django to manage model translations.

Edit the `admin.py` file of the `shop` application and add the following import to it:

```
from parler.admin import TranslatableAdmin
```

Modify the `CategoryAdmin` and `ProductAdmin` classes to inherit from `TranslatableAdmin` instead of `ModelAdmin`. `django-parler` doesn't support the `prepopulated_fields` attribute, but it does support the `get_prepopulated_fields()` method that provides the same functionality. Let's change this accordingly. Edit the `admin.py` file to make it look like the following:

```
from django.contrib import admin
from parler.admin import TranslatableAdmin
from .models import Category, Product

@admin.register(Category)
class CategoryAdmin(TranslatableAdmin):
    list_display = ['name', 'slug']

    def get_prepopulated_fields(self, request, obj=None):
        return {'slug': ('name',)}

@admin.register(Product)
class ProductAdmin(TranslatableAdmin):
    list_display = ['name', 'slug', 'price',
                    'available', 'created', 'updated']
```

```
        list_filter = ['available', 'created', 'updated']
        list_editable = ['price', 'available']

    def get_prepopulated_fields(self, request, obj=None):
        return {'slug': ('name',)}
```

You have adapted the administration site to work with the new translated models. You can now sync the database with the model changes that you made.

Creating migrations for model translations

Open the shell and run the following command to create a new migration for the model translations:

```
python manage.py makemigrations shop --name "translations"
```

You will see the following output:

```
Migrations for 'shop':
  shop/migrations/0002_translations.py
    - Create model CategoryTranslation
    - Create model ProductTranslation
    - Change Meta options on category
    - Change Meta options on product
    - Remove index shop_catego_name_289c7e_idx from category
    - Remove index shop_produc_id_f21274_idx from product
    - Remove index shop_produc_name_a2070e_idx from product
    - Remove field name from category
    - Remove field slug from category
    - Remove field description from product
    - Remove field name from product
    - Remove field slug from product
    - Add field master to producttranslation
    - Add field master to categorytranslation
    - Alter unique_together for producttranslation (1 constraint(s))
    - Alter unique_together for categorytranslation (1 constraint(s))
```

This migration automatically includes the `CategoryTranslation` and `ProductTranslation` models created dynamically by `django-parler`. It's important to note that this migration deletes the previous existing fields from your models. This means that you will lose that data and will need to set your categories and products again on the administration site after running it.

Edit the file `migrations/0002_translations.py` of the `shop` application and replace the two occurrences of the following line:

```
bases=(parler.models.TranslatedFieldsModelMixin, models.Model),
```

with the following one:

```
bases=(parler.models.TranslatableModel, models.Model),
```

This is a fix for a minor issue found in the django-parler version you are using. This change is necessary to prevent the migration from failing when applying it. This issue is related to creating translations for existing fields in the model and will probably be fixed in newer django-parler versions.

Run the following command to apply the migration:

```
python manage.py migrate shop
```

You will see an output that ends with the following line:

```
Applying shop.0002_translations... OK
```

Your models are now synchronized with the database.

Run the development server using the following command:

```
python manage.py runserver
```

Open `http://127.0.0.1:8000/en/admin/shop/category/` in your browser. You will see that existing categories lost their name and slug due to deleting those fields and using the translatable models generated by django-parler instead. You will just see a dash under each column like in *Figure 11.10*:

Select category to change

Action: [--------- ⌄] [Go] 0 of 1 selected

☐	NAME	SLUG
☐	-	-

1 category

Figure 11.10: The category list on the Django administration site after creating the translation models

Click on the dash under the category name to edit it. You will see that the **Change category** page includes two different tabs, one for English and one for Spanish translations:

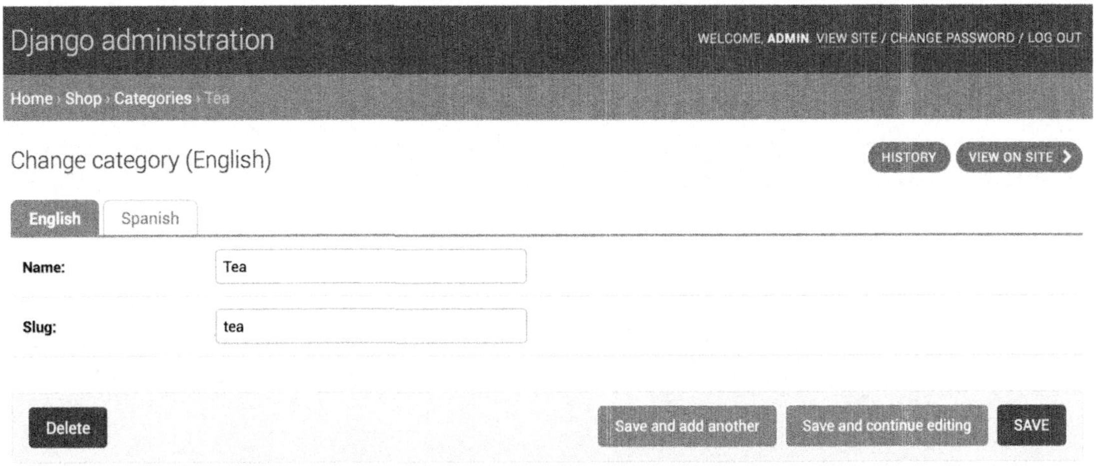

Figure 11.11: The category edit form, including the language tabs added by django-parler

Make sure that you fill in a name and slug for all existing categories. When you edit a category, enter the English details and click on **Save and continue editing**. Then, click on **Spanish**, add the Spanish translation for the fields, and click on **SAVE**:

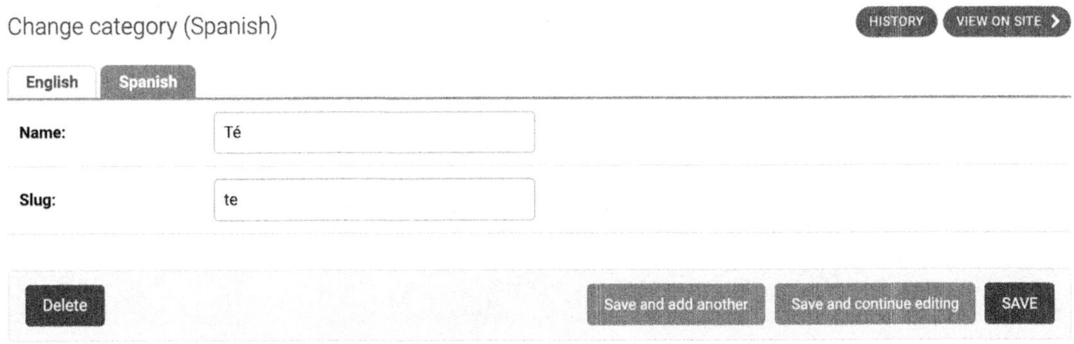

Figure 11.12: The Spanish translation of the category edit form

Make sure to save the changes before switching between the language tabs.

After completing the data for existing categories, open `http://127.0.0.1:8000/en/admin/shop/product/` and edit each of the products, providing an English and Spanish name, a slug, and a description.

Using translations with the ORM

You have to adapt your shop views to use translation QuerySets. Run the following command to open the Python shell:

```
python manage.py shell
```

Let's take a look at how you can retrieve and query translation fields. To get the object with translatable fields translated into a specific language, you can use Django's `activate()` function, as follows:

```
>>> from shop.models import Product
>>> from django.utils.translation import activate
>>> activate('es')
>>> product=Product.objects.first()
>>> product.name
'Té verde'
```

Another way to do this is by using the `language()` manager provided by `django-parler`, as follows:

```
>>> product=Product.objects.language('en').first()
>>> product.name
'Green tea'
```

When you access translated fields, they are resolved using the current language. You can set a different current language for an object to access that specific translation, as follows:

```
>>> product.set_current_language('es')
>>> product.name
'Té verde'
>>> product.get_current_language()
'es'
```

When performing a QuerySet using `filter()`, you can filter using the related translation objects with the `translations__` syntax, as follows:

```
>>> Product.objects.filter(translations__name='Green tea')
<TranslatableQuerySet [<Product: Té verde>]>
```

Adapting views for translations

Let's adapt the product catalog views. Edit the `views.py` file of the `shop` application and add the following code highlighted in bold to the `product_list` view:

```
def product_list(request, category_slug=None):
    category = None
    categories = Category.objects.all()
```

```
    products = Product.objects.filter(available=True)
    if category_slug:
        language = request.LANGUAGE_CODE
        category = get_object_or_404(Category,
                                     translations__language_code=language,
                                     translations__slug=category_slug)
        products = products.filter(category=category)
    return render(request,
                  'shop/product/list.html',
                  {'category': category,
                   'categories': categories,
                   'products': products})
```

Then, edit the product_detail view and add the following code highlighted in bold:

```
def product_detail(request, id, slug):
    language = request.LANGUAGE_CODE
    product = get_object_or_404(Product,
                                id=id,
                                translations__language_code=language,
                                translations__slug=slug,
                                available=True)
    cart_product_form = CartAddProductForm()
    r = Recommender()
    recommended_products = r.suggest_products_for([product], 4)
    return render(request,
                  'shop/product/detail.html',
                  {'product': product,
                   'cart_product_form': cart_product_form,
                   'recommended_products': recommended_products})
```

The product_list and product_detail views are now adapted to retrieve objects using translated fields.

Run the development server with the following command:

```
python manage.py runserver
```

Open `http://127.0.0.1:8000/es/` in your browser. You should see the product list page, including all products translated into Spanish:

Figure 11.13: The Spanish version of the product list page

Now, each product's URL is built using the `slug` field translated into the current language. For example, the URL for a product in Spanish is `http://127.0.0.1:8000/es/2/te-rojo/`, whereas, in English, the URL is `http://127.0.0.1:8000/en/2/red-tea/`. If you navigate to a product details page, you will see the translated URL and the contents of the selected language, as shown in the following example:

Té rojo

Té

$45,50

Cantidad: 1 ⌄   Añadir al carro

Figure 11.14: The Spanish version of the product details page

If you want to know more about django-parler, you can find the full documentation at https://django-parler.readthedocs.io/en/latest/.

You have learned how to translate Python code, templates, URL patterns, and model fields. To complete the internationalization and localization process, you need to use localized formatting for dates, times, and numbers as well.

Format localization

Depending on the user's locale, you might want to display dates, times, and numbers in different formats. Localized formatting can be activated by changing the USE_L10N setting to True in the settings.py file of your project.

When USE_L10N is enabled, Django will try to use a locale-specific format whenever it outputs a value in a template. You can see that decimal numbers in the English version of your site are displayed with a dot separator for decimal places, while in the Spanish version, they are displayed using a comma. This is due to the locale formats specified for the es locale by Django. You can take a look at the Spanish formatting configuration at https://github.com/django/django/blob/stable/4.0.x/django/conf/locale/es/formats.py.

Normally, you will set the USE_L10N setting to True and let Django apply the format localization for each locale. However, there might be situations in which you don't want to use localized values. This is especially relevant when outputting JavaScript or JSON, which has to provide a machine-readable format.

Django offers a {% localize %} template tag that allows you to turn on/off localization for template fragments. This gives you control over localized formatting. You will have to load the l10n tags to be able to use this template tag. The following is an example of how to turn localization on and off in a template:

```
{% load l10n %}

{% localize on %}
  {{ value }}
{% endlocalize %}

{% localize off %}
  {{ value }}
{% endlocalize %}
```

Django also offers the localize and unlocalize template filters to force or avoid the localization of a value. These filters can be applied as follows:

```
{{ value|localize }}
{{ value|unlocalize }}
```

You can also create custom format files to specify locale formatting. You can find further information about format localization at https://docs.djangoproject.com/en/4.1/topics/i18n/formatting/.

Next, you will learn how to create localized form fields.

Using django-localflavor to validate form fields

django-localflavor is a third-party module that contains a collection of utilities, such as form fields or model fields, that are specific for each country. It's very useful for validating local regions, local phone numbers, identity card numbers, social security numbers, and so on. The package is organized into a series of modules named after ISO 3166 country codes.

Install django-localflavor using the following command:

```
pip install django-localflavor==3.1
```

Edit the settings.py file of your project and add localflavor to the INSTALLED_APPS setting, as follows:

```
INSTALLED_APPS = [
    # ...
    'localflavor',
]
```

You are going to add the United States zip code field so that a valid United States zip code is required to create a new order.

Edit the forms.py file of the orders application and make it look like the following:

```python
from django import forms
from localflavor.us.forms import USZipCodeField
from .models import Order

class OrderCreateForm(forms.ModelForm):
    postal_code = USZipCodeField()
    class Meta:
        model = Order
        fields = ['first_name', 'last_name', 'email', 'address',
                  'postal_code', 'city']
```

You import the USZipCodeField field from the us package of localflavor and use it for the postal_code field of the OrderCreateForm form.

Run the development server with the following command:

```
python manage.py runserver
```

Open http://127.0.0.1:8000/en/orders/create/ in your browser. Fill in all the fields, enter a three-letter zip code, and then submit the form. You will get the following validation error, which is raised by USZipCodeField:

```
Enter a zip code in the format XXXXX or XXXXX-XXXX.
```

Figure 11.15 shows the form validation error:

- Enter a zip code in the format XXXXX or XXXXX-XXXX.

Postal code:

ABC

Figure 11.15: The validation error for an invalid US zip code

This is just a brief example of how to use a custom field from localflavor in your own project for validation purposes. The local components provided by localflavor are very useful for adapting your application to specific countries. You can read the django-localflavor documentation and see all the available local components for each country at https://django-localflavor.readthedocs.io/en/latest/.

Additional resources

The following resources provide additional information related to the topics covered in this chapter:

- Source code for this chapter – `https://github.com/PacktPublishing/Django-4-by-example/tree/main/Chapter11`
- List of valid language IDs – `http://www.i18nguy.com/unicode/language-identifiers.html`
- List of internationalization and localization settings – `https://docs.djangoproject.com/en/4.1/ref/settings/#globalization-i18n-l10n`
- Homebrew package manager – `https://brew.sh/`
- Installing gettext on Windows – `https://docs.djangoproject.com/en/4.1/topics/i18n/translation/#gettext-on-windows`
- Precompiled gettext binary installer for Windows – `https://mlocati.github.io/articles/gettext-iconv-windows.html`
- Documentation about translations – `https://docs.djangoproject.com/en/4.1/topics/i18n/translation/`
- Poedit translation file editor – `https://poedit.net/`
- Documentation for Django Rosetta – `https://django-rosetta.readthedocs.io/`
- The `django-parler` module's compatibility with Django – `https://django-parler.readthedocs.io/en/latest/compatibility.html`
- Documentation for `django-parler` – `https://django-parler.readthedocs.io/en/latest/`
- Django formatting configuration for the Spanish locale – `https://github.com/django/django/blob/stable/4.0.x/django/conf/locale/es/formats.py`
- Django format localization – `https://docs.djangoproject.com/en/4.1/topics/i18n/formatting/`
- Documentation for `django-localflavor` – `https://django-localflavor.readthedocs.io/en/latest/`

Summary

In this chapter, you learned the basics of the internationalization and localization of Django projects. You marked code and template strings for translation, and you discovered how to generate and compile translation files. You also installed Rosetta in your project to manage translations through a web interface. You translated URL patterns, and you created a language selector to allow users to switch the language of the site. Then, you used `django-parler` to translate models, and you used `django-localflavor` to validate localized form fields.

In the next chapter, you will start a new Django project that will consist of an e-learning platform. You will create the application models, and you will learn how to create and apply fixtures to provide initial data for the models. You will build a custom model field and use it in your models. You will also build authentication views for your new application.

12

Building an E-Learning Platform

In the previous chapter, you learned the basics of the internationalization and localization of Django projects. You added internationalization to your online shop project. You learned how to translate Python strings, templates, and models. You also learned how to manage translations, and you created a language selector and added localized fields to your forms.

In this chapter, you will start a new Django project that will consist of an e-learning platform with your own **content management system (CMS)**. Online learning platforms are a great example of applications where you need to provide tools to generate content with flexibility in mind.

In this chapter, you will learn how to:

- Create models for the CMS
- Create fixtures for your models and apply them
- Use model inheritance to create data models for polymorphic content
- Create custom model fields
- Order course contents and modules
- Build authentication views for the CMS

The source code for this chapter can be found at `https://github.com/PacktPublishing/Django-4-by-example/tree/main/Chapter12`.

All the Python modules used in this chapter are included in the `requirements.txt` file in the source code that comes with this chapter. You can follow the instructions to install each Python module below, or you can install all the requirements at once with the command `pip install r requirements.txt`.

Setting up the e-learning project

Your final practical project will be an e-learning platform. First, create a virtual environment for your new project within the env/ directory with the following command:

```
python -m venv env/educa
```

If you are using Linux or macOS, run the following command to activate your virtual environment:

```
source env/educa/bin/activate
```

If you are using Windows, use the following command instead:

```
.\env\educa\Scripts\activate
```

Install Django in your virtual environment with the following command:

```
pip install Django~=4.1.0
```

You are going to manage image uploads in your project, so you also need to install `Pillow` with the following command:

```
pip install Pillow==9.2.0
```

Create a new project using the following command:

```
django-admin startproject educa
```

Enter the new educa directory and create a new application using the following commands:

```
cd educa
django-admin startapp courses
```

Edit the settings.py file of the educa project and add `courses` to the `INSTALLED_APPS` setting, as follows. The new line is highlighted in bold:

```
INSTALLED_APPS = [
    'courses.apps.CoursesConfig',
    'django.contrib.admin',
    'django.contrib.auth',
    'django.contrib.contenttypes',
    'django.contrib.sessions',
    'django.contrib.messages',
    'django.contrib.staticfiles',
]
```

The courses application is now active for the project. Next, we are going to prepare our project to serve media files, and we will define the models for the courses and course contents.

Serving media files

Before creating the models for courses and course contents, we will prepare the project to serve media files. Course instructors will be able to upload media files to course contents using the CMS that we will build. Therefore, we will configure the project to serve media files.

Edit the settings.py file of the project and add the following lines:

```
MEDIA_URL = 'media/'
MEDIA_ROOT = BASE_DIR / 'media'
```

This will enable Django to manage file uploads and serve media files. MEDIA_URL is the base URL used to serve the media files uploaded by users. MEDIA_ROOT is the local path where they reside. Paths and URLs for files are built dynamically by prepending the project path or the media URL to them for portability.

Now, edit the main urls.py file of the educa project and modify the code, as follows. New lines are highlighted in bold:

```
from django.contrib import admin
from django.urls import path
from django.conf import settings
from django.conf.urls.static import static

urlpatterns = [
    path('admin/', admin.site.urls),
]

if settings.DEBUG:
    urlpatterns += static(settings.MEDIA_URL,
                          document_root=settings.MEDIA_ROOT)
```

We have added the static() helper function to serve media files with the Django development server during development (that is, when the DEBUG setting is set to True).

 Remember that the static() helper function is suitable for development but not for production use. Django is very inefficient at serving static files. Never serve your static files with Django in a production environment. You will learn how to serve static files in a production environment in *Chapter 17, Going Live*.

The project is now ready to serve media files. Let's create the models for the courses and course contents.

Building the course models

Your e-learning platform will offer courses on various subjects. Each course will be divided into a configurable number of modules, and each module will contain a configurable number of contents. The contents will be of various types: text, files, images, or videos. The following example shows what the data structure of your course catalog will look like:

```
Subject 1
  Course 1
    Module 1
```

```
        Content 1 (image)
        Content 2 (text)
    Module 2
        Content 3 (text)
        Content 4 (file)
        Content 5 (video)
    ...
```

Let's build the course models. Edit the models.py file of the courses application and add the following code to it:

```python
from django.db import models
from django.contrib.auth.models import User


class Subject(models.Model):
    title = models.CharField(max_length=200)
    slug = models.SlugField(max_length=200, unique=True)

    class Meta:
        ordering = ['title']

    def __str__(self):
        return self.title



class Course(models.Model):
    owner = models.ForeignKey(User,
                              related_name='courses_created',
                              on_delete=models.CASCADE)
    subject = models.ForeignKey(Subject,
                                related_name='courses',
                                on_delete=models.CASCADE)
    title = models.CharField(max_length=200)
    slug = models.SlugField(max_length=200, unique=True)
    overview = models.TextField()
    created = models.DateTimeField(auto_now_add=True)

    class Meta:
        ordering = ['-created']

    def __str__(self):
        return self.title
```

```python
class Module(models.Model):
    course = models.ForeignKey(Course,
                               related_name='modules',
                               on_delete=models.CASCADE)
    title = models.CharField(max_length=200)
    description = models.TextField(blank=True)

    def __str__(self):
        return self.title
```

These are the initial `Subject`, `Course`, and `Module` models. The `Course` model fields are as follows:

- `owner`: The instructor who created this course.
- `subject`: The subject that this course belongs to. It is a `ForeignKey` field that points to the `Subject` model.
- `title`: The title of the course.
- `slug`: The slug of the course. This will be used in URLs later.
- `overview`: A `TextField` column to store an overview of the course.
- `created`: The date and time when the course was created. It will be automatically set by Django when creating new objects because of `auto_now_add=True`.

Each course is divided into several modules. Therefore, the `Module` model contains a `ForeignKey` field that points to the `Course` model.

Open the shell and run the following command to create the initial migration for this application:

```
python manage.py makemigrations
```

You will see the following output:

```
Migrations for 'courses':
  courses/migrations/0001_initial.py:
    - Create model Course
    - Create model Module
    - Create model Subject
    - Add field subject to course
```

Then, run the following command to apply all migrations to the database:

```
python manage.py migrate
```

You should see output that includes all applied migrations, including those of Django. The output will contain the following line:

```
Applying courses.0001_initial... OK
```

The models of your courses application have been synced with the database.

Registering the models in the administration site

Let's add the course models to the administration site. Edit the admin.py file inside the courses application directory and add the following code to it:

```python
from django.contrib import admin
from .models import Subject, Course, Module


@admin.register(Subject)
class SubjectAdmin(admin.ModelAdmin):
    list_display = ['title', 'slug']
    prepopulated_fields = {'slug': ('title',)}


class ModuleInline(admin.StackedInline):
    model = Module


@admin.register(Course)
class CourseAdmin(admin.ModelAdmin):
    list_display = ['title', 'subject', 'created']
    list_filter = ['created', 'subject']
    search_fields = ['title', 'overview']
    prepopulated_fields = {'slug': ('title',)}
    inlines = [ModuleInline]
```

The models for the course application are now registered on the administration site. Remember that you use the @admin.register() decorator to register models on the administration site.

Using fixtures to provide initial data for models

Sometimes, you might want to prepopulate your database with hardcoded data. This is useful for automatically including initial data in the project setup, instead of having to add it manually. Django comes with a simple way to load and dump data from the database into files that are called **fixtures**. Django supports fixtures in JSON, XML, or YAML formats. You are going to create a fixture to include several initial Subject objects for your project.

First, create a superuser using the following command:

```
python manage.py createsuperuser
```

Then, run the development server using the following command:

```
python manage.py runserver
```

Open `http://127.0.0.1:8000/admin/courses/subject/` in your browser. Create several subjects using the administration site. The change list page should look as follows:

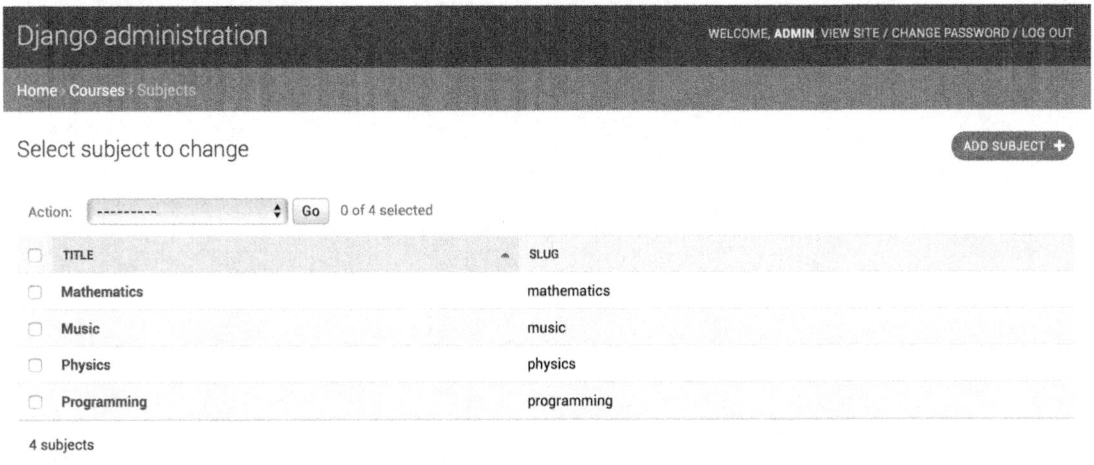

Django administration   WELCOME, **ADMIN**. VIEW SITE / CHANGE PASSWORD / LOG OUT

Home › Courses › Subjects

Select subject to change   ADD SUBJECT +

Action: [---------] [Go]   0 of 4 selected

☐ TITLE ▲	SLUG
☐ Mathematics	mathematics
☐ Music	music
☐ Physics	physics
☐ Programming	programming

4 subjects

Figure 12.1: The subject change list view on the administration site

Run the following command from the shell:

```
python manage.py dumpdata courses --indent=2
```

You will see an output similar to the following:

```
[
{
  "model": "courses.subject",
  "pk": 1,
  "fields": {
    "title": "Mathematics",
    "slug": "mathematics"
  }
},
{
  "model": "courses.subject",
  "pk": 2,
  "fields": {
    "title": "Music",
    "slug": "music"
  }
}
```

```json
  },
  {
    "model": "courses.subject",
    "pk": 3,
    "fields": {
      "title": "Physics",
      "slug": "physics"
    }
  },
  {
    "model": "courses.subject",
    "pk": 4,
    "fields": {
      "title": "Programming",
      "slug": "programming"
    }
  }
]
```

The `dumpdata` command dumps data from the database into the standard output, serialized in JSON format by default. The resulting data structure includes information about the model and its fields for Django to be able to load it into the database.

You can limit the output to the models of an application by providing the application names to the command, or specifying single models for outputting data using the `app.Model` format. You can also specify the format using the `--format` flag. By default, `dumpdata` outputs the serialized data to the standard output. However, you can indicate an output file using the `--output` flag. The `--indent` flag allows you to specify indentations. For more information on `dumpdata` parameters, run `python manage.py dumpdata --help`.

Save this dump to a fixtures file in a new `fixtures/` directory in the `courses` application using the following commands:

```
mkdir courses/fixtures
python manage.py dumpdata courses --indent=2 --output=courses/fixtures/
subjects.json
```

Run the development server and use the administration site to remove the subjects you created, as shown in *Figure 12.2*:

Select subject to change
ADD SUBJECT
Action

Delete selected subjects
Go
4 of 4 selected
TITLE
SLUG
Mathematics
mathematics
Music
music
Physics
physics
Programming
programming
4 subjects

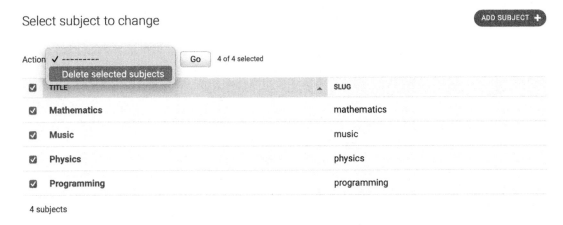

Figure 12.2: Deleting all existing subjects

After deleting all subjects, load the fixture into the database using the following command:

```
python manage.py loaddata subjects.json
```

All `Subject` objects included in the fixture are loaded into the database again:

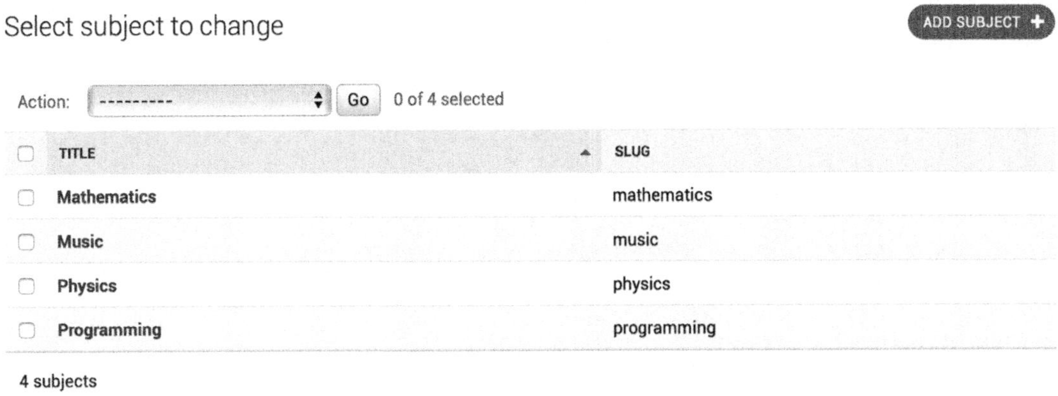

Select subject to change
ADD SUBJECT
Action:

Go
0 of 4 selected
TITLE
SLUG
Mathematics
mathematics
Music
music
Physics
physics
Programming
programming
4 subjects

Figure 12.3: Subjects from the fixture are now loaded into the database

By default, Django looks for files in the `fixtures/` directory of each application, but you can specify the complete path to the fixture file for the `loaddata` command. You can also use the `FIXTURE_DIRS` setting to tell Django additional directories to look in for fixtures.

 Fixtures are not only useful for setting up initial data, but also for providing sample data for your application or data required for your tests.

You can read about how to use fixtures for testing at `https://docs.djangoproject.com/en/4.1/topics/testing/tools/#fixture-loading`.

If you want to load fixtures in model migrations, look at Django's documentation about data migrations. You can find the documentation for migrating data at `https://docs.djangoproject.com/en/4.1/topics/migrations/#data-migrations`.

You have created the models to manage course subjects, courses, and course modules. Next, you will create models to manage different types of module contents.

Creating models for polymorphic content

You plan to add different types of content to the course modules, such as text, images, files, and videos. **Polymorphism** is the provision of a single interface to entities of different types. You need a versatile data model that allows you to store diverse content that is accessible through a single interface. In *Chapter 7, Tracking User Actions*, you learned about the convenience of using generic relations to create foreign keys that can point to the objects of any model. You are going to create a `Content` model that represents the modules' contents and define a generic relation to associate any object with the content object.

Edit the `models.py` file of the `courses` application and add the following imports:

```
from django.contrib.contenttypes.models import ContentType
from django.contrib.contenttypes.fields import GenericForeignKey
```

Then, add the following code to the end of the file:

```
class Content(models.Model):
    module = models.ForeignKey(Module,
                               related_name='contents',
                               on_delete=models.CASCADE)
    content_type = models.ForeignKey(ContentType,
                                     on_delete=models.CASCADE)
    object_id = models.PositiveIntegerField()
    item = GenericForeignKey('content_type', 'object_id')
```

This is the Content model. A module contains multiple contents, so you define a ForeignKey field that points to the Module model. You can also set up a generic relation to associate objects from different models that represent different types of content. Remember that you need three different fields to set up a generic relation. In your Content model, these are:

- content_type: A ForeignKey field to the ContentType model.
- object_id: A PositiveIntegerField to store the primary key of the related object.
- item: A GenericForeignKey field to the related object combining the two previous fields.

Only the content_type and object_id fields have a corresponding column in the database table of this model. The item field allows you to retrieve or set the related object directly, and its functionality is built on top of the other two fields.

You are going to use a different model for each type of content. Your Content models will have some common fields, but they will differ in the actual data they can store. This is how you will create a single interface for different types of content.

Using model inheritance

Django supports model inheritance. It works in a similar way to standard class inheritance in Python. Django offers the following three options to use model inheritance:

- **Abstract models:** Useful when you want to put some common information into several models.
- **Multi-table model inheritance:** Applicable when each model in the hierarchy is considered a complete model by itself.
- **Proxy models:** Useful when you need to change the behavior of a model, for example, by including additional methods, changing the default manager, or using different meta options.

Let's take a closer look at each of them.

Abstract models

An abstract model is a base class in which you define the fields you want to include in all child models. Django doesn't create any database tables for abstract models. A database table is created for each child model, including the fields inherited from the abstract class and the ones defined in the child model.

To mark a model as abstract, you need to include abstract=True in its Meta class. Django will recognize that it is an abstract model and will not create a database table for it. To create child models, you just need to subclass the abstract model.

The following example shows an abstract Content model and a child Text model:

```
from django.db import models

class BaseContent(models.Model):
    title = models.CharField(max_length=100)
    created = models.DateTimeField(auto_now_add=True)
    class Meta:
```

```
        abstract = True

class Text(BaseContent):
    body = models.TextField()
```

In this case, Django would create a table for the Text model only, including the title, created, and body fields.

Multi-table model inheritance

In multi-table inheritance, each model corresponds to a database table. Django creates a OneToOneField field for the relationship between the child model and its parent model. To use multi-table inheritance, you have to subclass an existing model. Django will create a database table for both the original model and the sub-model. The following example shows multi-table inheritance:

```
from django.db import models

class BaseContent(models.Model):
    title = models.CharField(max_length=100)
    created = models.DateTimeField(auto_now_add=True)

class Text(BaseContent):
    body = models.TextField()
```

Django will include an automatically generated OneToOneField field in the Text model and create a database table for each model.

Proxy models

A proxy model changes the behavior of a model. Both models operate on the database table of the original model. To create a proxy model, add proxy=True to the Meta class of the model. The following example illustrates how to create a proxy model:

```
from django.db import models
from django.utils import timezone

class BaseContent(models.Model):
    title = models.CharField(max_length=100)
    created = models.DateTimeField(auto_now_add=True)

class OrderedContent(BaseContent):
    class Meta:
        proxy = True
        ordering = ['created']
```

```
def created_delta(self):
    return timezone.now() - self.created
```

Here, you define an `OrderedContent` model that is a proxy model for the `Content` model. This model provides a default ordering for QuerySets and an additional `created_delta()` method. Both models, `Content` and `OrderedContent`, operate on the same database table, and objects are accessible via the ORM through either model.

Creating the Content models

The `Content` model of your `courses` application contains a generic relation to associate different types of content with it. You will create a different model for each type of content. All `Content` models will have some fields in common and additional fields to store custom data. You are going to create an abstract model that provides the common fields for all `Content` models.

Edit the `models.py` file of the `courses` application and add the following code to it:

```python
class ItemBase(models.Model):
    owner = models.ForeignKey(User,
                              related_name='%(class)s_related',
                              on_delete=models.CASCADE)
    title = models.CharField(max_length=250)
    created = models.DateTimeField(auto_now_add=True)
    updated = models.DateTimeField(auto_now=True)

    class Meta:
        abstract = True

    def __str__(self):
        return self.title

class Text(ItemBase):
    content = models.TextField()

class File(ItemBase):
    file = models.FileField(upload_to='files')

class Image(ItemBase):
    file = models.FileField(upload_to='images')

class Video(ItemBase):
    url = models.URLField()
```

In this code, you define an abstract model named `ItemBase`. Therefore, you set `abstract=True` in its `Meta` class.

In this model, you define the `owner`, `title`, `created`, and `updated` fields. These common fields will be used for all types of content.

The `owner` field allows you to store which user created the content. Since this field is defined in an abstract class, you need a different `related_name` for each sub-model. Django allows you to specify a placeholder for the model class name in the `related_name` attribute as `%(class)s`. By doing so, the `related_name` for each child model will be generated automatically. Since you are using `'%(class)s_related'` as the `related_name`, the reverse relationship for child models will be `text_related`, `file_related`, `image_related`, and `video_related`, respectively.

You have defined four different `Content` models that inherit from the `ItemBase` abstract model. They are as follows:

- Text: To store text content
- File: To store files, such as PDFs
- Image: To store image files
- Video: To store videos; you use an `URLField` field to provide a video URL in order to embed it

Each child model contains the fields defined in the `ItemBase` class in addition to its own fields. A database table will be created for the `Text`, `File`, `Image`, and `Video` models, respectively. There will be no database table associated with the `ItemBase` model since it is an abstract model.

Edit the `Content` model you created previously and modify its `content_type` field, as follows:

```python
content_type = models.ForeignKey(ContentType,
                    on_delete=models.CASCADE,
                    limit_choices_to={'model__in':(
                                        'text',
                                        'video',
                                        'image',
                                        'file')})
```

You add a `limit_choices_to` argument to limit the `ContentType` objects that can be used for the generic relation. You use the `model__in` field lookup to filter the query to the `ContentType` objects with a `model` attribute that is `'text'`, `'video'`, `'image'`, or `'file'`.

Let's create a migration to include the new models you have added. Run the following command from the command line:

```
python manage.py makemigrations
```

You will see the following output:

```
Migrations for 'courses':
  courses/migrations/0002_video_text_image_file_content.py
```

```
    - Create model Video
    - Create model Text
    - Create model Image
    - Create model File
    - Create model Content
```

Then, run the following command to apply the new migration:

```
python manage.py migrate
```

The output you see should end with the following line:

```
Applying courses.0002_video_text_image_file_content... OK
```

You have created models that are suitable for adding diverse content to the course modules. However, there is still something missing in your models: the course modules and contents should follow a particular order. You need a field that allows you to order them easily.

Creating custom model fields

Django comes with a complete collection of model fields that you can use to build your models. However, you can also create your own model fields to store custom data or alter the behavior of existing fields.

You need a field that allows you to define an order for the objects. An easy way to specify an order for objects using existing Django fields is by adding a PositiveIntegerField to your models. Using integers, you can easily specify the order of the objects. You can create a custom order field that inherits from PositiveIntegerField and provides additional behavior.

There are two relevant functionalities that you will build into your order field:

- **Automatically assign an order value when no specific order is provided:** When saving a new object with no specific order, your field should automatically assign the number that comes after the last existing ordered object. If there are two objects with orders 1 and 2 respectively, when saving a third object, you should automatically assign order 3 to it if no specific order has been provided.
- **Order objects with respect to other fields:** Course modules will be ordered with respect to the course they belong to and module contents with respect to the module they belong to.

Create a new fields.py file inside the courses application directory and add the following code to it:

```python
from django.db import models
from django.core.exceptions import ObjectDoesNotExist


class OrderField(models.PositiveIntegerField):
    def __init__(self, for_fields=None, *args, **kwargs):
        self.for_fields = for_fields
        super().__init__(*args, **kwargs)
```

```
def pre_save(self, model_instance, add):
    if getattr(model_instance, self.attname) is None:
        # no current value
        try:
            qs = self.model.objects.all()
            if self.for_fields:
                # filter by objects with the same field values
                # for the fields in "for_fields"
                query = {field: getattr(model_instance, field)\
                for field in self.for_fields}
                qs = qs.filter(**query)
            # get the order of the last item
            last_item = qs.latest(self.attname)
            value = last_item.order + 1
        except ObjectDoesNotExist:
            value = 0
        setattr(model_instance, self.attname, value)
        return value
    else:
        return super().pre_save(model_instance, add)
```

This is the custom `OrderField`. It inherits from the `PositiveIntegerField` field provided by Django. Your `OrderField` field takes an optional `for_fields` parameter, which allows you to indicate the fields used to order the data.

Your field overrides the `pre_save()` method of the `PositiveIntegerField` field, which is executed before saving the field to the database. In this method, you perform the following actions:

1. You check whether a value already exists for this field in the model instance. You use `self.attname`, which is the attribute name given to the field in the model. If the attribute's value is different from `None`, you calculate the order you should give it as follows:

    1. You build a QuerySet to retrieve all objects for the field's model. You retrieve the model class the field belongs to by accessing `self.model`.

    2. If there are any field names in the `for_fields` attribute of the field, you filter the QuerySet by the current value of the model fields in `for_fields`. By doing so, you calculate the order with respect to the given fields.

    3. You retrieve the object with the highest order with `last_item = qs.latest(self.attname)` from the database. If no object is found, you assume this object is the first one and assign order `0` to it.

    4. If an object is found, you add 1 to the highest order found.

    5. You assign the calculated order to the field's value in the model instance using `setattr()` and return it.

2. If the model instance has a value for the current field, you use it instead of calculating it.

 When you create custom model fields, make them generic. Avoid hardcoding data that depends on a specific model or field. Your field should work in any model.

You can find more information about writing custom model fields at https://docs.djangoproject.com/en/4.1/howto/custom-model-fields/.

Adding ordering to module and content objects

Let's add the new field to your models. Edit the models.py file of the courses application, and import the OrderField class and a field to the Module model, as follows:

```
from .fields import OrderField

class Module(models.Model):
    # ...
    order = OrderField(blank=True, for_fields=['course'])
```

You name the new field order and specify that the ordering is calculated with respect to the course by setting for_fields=['course']. This means that the order for a new module will be assigned by adding 1 to the last module of the same Course object.

Now, you can edit the __str__() method of the Module model to include its order, as follows:

```
class Module(models.Model):
    # ...
    def __str__(self):
        return f'{self.order}. {self.title}'
```

Module contents also need to follow a particular order. Add an OrderField field to the Content model, as follows:

```
class Content(models.Model):
    # ...
    order = OrderField(blank=True, for_fields=['module'])
```

This time, you specify that the order is calculated with respect to the module field.

Finally, let's add a default ordering for both models. Add the following Meta class to the Module and Content models:

```
class Module(models.Model):
    # ...
    class Meta:
        ordering = ['order']
```

```
class Content(models.Model):
    # ...
    class Meta:
        ordering = ['order']
```

The Module and Content models should now look as follows:

```
class Module(models.Model):
    course = models.ForeignKey(Course,
                               related_name='modules',
                               on_delete=models.CASCADE)
    title = models.CharField(max_length=200)
    description = models.TextField(blank=True)
    order = OrderField(blank=True, for_fields=['course'])

    class Meta:
        ordering = ['order']

    def __str__(self):
        return f'{self.order}. {self.title}'


class Content(models.Model):
    module = models.ForeignKey(Module,
                               related_name='contents',
                               on_delete=models.CASCADE)
    content_type = models.ForeignKey(ContentType,
                         on_delete=models.CASCADE,
                         limit_choices_to={'model__in':(
                                                'text',
                                                'video',
                                                'image',
                                                'file')})
    object_id = models.PositiveIntegerField()
    item = GenericForeignKey('content_type', 'object_id')
    order = OrderField(blank=True, for_fields=['module'])

    class Meta:
            ordering = ['order']
```

Let's create a new model migration that reflects the new order fields. Open the shell and run the following command:

```
python manage.py makemigrations courses
```

You will see the following output:

```
It is impossible to add a non-nullable field 'order' to content without
specifying a default. This is because the database needs something to populate
existing rows.
Please select a fix:
 1) Provide a one-off default now (will be set on all existing rows with a null
value for this column)
 2) Quit and manually define a default value in models.py.
Select an option:
```

Django is telling you that you have to provide a default value for the new order field for existing rows in the database. If the field includes null=True, it accepts null values and Django creates the migration automatically instead of asking for a default value. You can specify a default value, or cancel the migration and add a default attribute to the order field in the models.py file before creating the migration.

Enter 1 and press *Enter* to provide a default value for existing records. You will see the following output:

```
Please enter the default value as valid Python.
The datetime and django.utils.timezone modules are available, so it is possible
to provide e.g. timezone.now as a value.
Type 'exit' to exit this prompt
>>>
```

Enter 0 so that this is the default value for existing records and press *Enter*. Django will ask you for a default value for the Module model too. Choose the first option and enter 0 as the default value again. Finally, you will see an output similar to the following one:

```
Migrations for 'courses':
courses/migrations/0003_alter_content_options_alter_module_options_and_more.py
    - Change Meta options on content
    - Change Meta options on module
    - Add field order to content
    - Add field order to module
```

Then, apply the new migrations with the following command:

```
python manage.py migrate
```

The output of the command will inform you that the migration was successfully applied, as follows:

```
Applying courses.0003_alter_content_options_alter_module_options_and_more... OK
```

Let's test your new field. Open the shell with the following command:

```
python manage.py shell
```

Create a new course, as follows:

```
>>> from django.contrib.auth.models import User
>>> from courses.models import Subject, Course, Module
>>> user = User.objects.last()
>>> subject = Subject.objects.last()
>>> c1 = Course.objects.create(subject=subject, owner=user, title='Course 1',
slug='course1')
```

You have created a course in the database. Now, you will add modules to the course and see how their order is automatically calculated. You create an initial module and check its order:

```
>>> m1 = Module.objects.create(course=c1, title='Module 1')
>>> m1.order
0
```

OrderField sets its value to 0, since this is the first Module object created for the given course. You can create a second module for the same course:

```
>>> m2 = Module.objects.create(course=c1, title='Module 2')
>>> m2.order
1
```

OrderField calculates the next order value, adding 1 to the highest order for existing objects. Let's create a third module, forcing a specific order:

```
>>> m3 = Module.objects.create(course=c1, title='Module 3', order=5)
>>> m3.order
5
```

If you provide a custom order when creating or saving an object, OrderField will use that value instead of calculating the order.

Let's add a fourth module:

```
>>> m4 = Module.objects.create(course=c1, title='Module 4')
>>> m4.order
6
```

The order for this module has been automatically set. Your OrderField field does not guarantee that all order values are consecutive. However, it respects existing order values and always assigns the next order based on the highest existing order.

Let's create a second course and add a module to it:

```
>>> c2 = Course.objects.create(subject=subject, title='Course 2',
slug='course2', owner=user)
>>> m5 = Module.objects.create(course=c2, title='Module 1')
>>> m5.order
0
```

To calculate the new module's order, the field only takes into consideration existing modules that belong to the same course. Since this is the first module of the second course, the resulting order is 0. This is because you specified for_fields=['course'] in the order field of the Module model.

Congratulations! You have successfully created your first custom model field. Next, you are going to create an authentication system for the CMS.

Adding authentication views

Now that you have created a polymorphic data model, you are going to build a CMS to manage the courses and their contents. The first step is to add an authentication system for the CMS.

Adding an authentication system

You are going to use Django's authentication framework for users to authenticate to the e-learning platform. Both instructors and students will be instances of Django's User model, so they will be able to log in to the site using the authentication views of django.contrib.auth.

Edit the main urls.py file of the educa project and include the login and logout views of Django's authentication framework:

```
from django.contrib import admin
from django.urls import path
from django.conf import settings
from django.conf.urls.static import static
from django.contrib.auth import views as auth_views

urlpatterns = [
    path('accounts/login/', auth_views.LoginView.as_view(),
        name='login'),
    path('accounts/logout/', auth_views.LogoutView.as_view(),
        name='logout'),
    path('admin/', admin.site.urls),
]

if settings.DEBUG:
    urlpatterns += static(settings.MEDIA_URL,
                        document_root=settings.MEDIA_ROOT)
```

Creating the authentication templates

Create the following file structure inside the `courses` application directory:

```
templates/
    base.html
    registration/
        login.html
        logged_out.html
```

Before building the authentication templates, you need to prepare the base template for your project. Edit the `base.html` template file and add the following content to it:

```
{% load static %}
<!DOCTYPE html>
<html>
  <head>
    <meta charset="utf-8" />
    <title>{% block title %}Educa{% endblock %}</title>
    <link href="{% static "css/base.css" %}" rel="stylesheet">
  </head>
  <body>
    <div id="header">
      <a href="/" class="logo">Educa</a>
      <ul class="menu">
        {% if request.user.is_authenticated %}
          <li><a href="{% url "logout" %}">Sign out</a></li>
        {% else %}
          <li><a href="{% url "login" %}">Sign in</a></li>
        {% endif %}
      </ul>
    </div>
    <div id="content">
      {% block content %}
      {% endblock %}
    </div>
    <script>
      document.addEventListener('DOMContentLoaded', (event) => {
        // DOM Loaded
        {% block domready %}
        {% endblock %}
      })
    </script>
```

```
    </body>
  </html>
```

This is the base template that will be extended by the rest of the templates. In this template, you define the following blocks:

- `title`: The block for other templates to add a custom title for each page.
- `content`: The main block for content. All templates that extend the base template should add content to this block.
- `domready`: Located inside the JavaScript event listener for the `DOMContentLoaded` event. It allows you to execute code when the **Document Object Model** (**DOM**) has finished loading.

The CSS styles used in this template are located in the `static/` directory of the `courses` application in the code that comes with this chapter. Copy the `static/` directory into the same directory of your project to use them. You can find the contents of the directory at https://github.com/PacktPublishing/Django-4-by-Example/tree/main/Chapter12/educa/courses/static.

Edit the `registration/login.html` template and add the following code to it:

```
{% extends "base.html" %}

{% block title %}Log-in{% endblock %}

{% block content %}
  <h1>Log-in</h1>
  <div class="module">
    {% if form.errors %}
      <p>Your username and password didn't match. Please try again.</p>
    {% else %}
      <p>Please, use the following form to log-in:</p>
    {% endif %}
    <div class="login-form">
      <form action="{% url 'login' %}" method="post">
        {{ form.as_p }}
        {% csrf_token %}
        <input type="hidden" name="next" value="{{ next }}" />
        <p><input type="submit" value="Log in"></p>
      </form>
    </div>
  </div>
{% endblock %}
```

This is a standard login template for Django's `login` view.

Edit the `registration/logged_out.html` template and add the following code to it:

```
{% extends "base.html" %}

{% block title %}Logged out{% endblock %}

{% block content %}
  <h1>Logged out</h1>
  <div class="module">
    <p>
      You have been successfully logged out.
      You can <a href="{% url "login" %}">log-in again</a>.
    </p>
  </div>
{% endblock %}
```

This is the template that will be displayed to the user after logging out. Run the development server with the following command:

```
python manage.py runserver
```

Open `http://127.0.0.1:8000/accounts/login/` in your browser. You should see the login page:

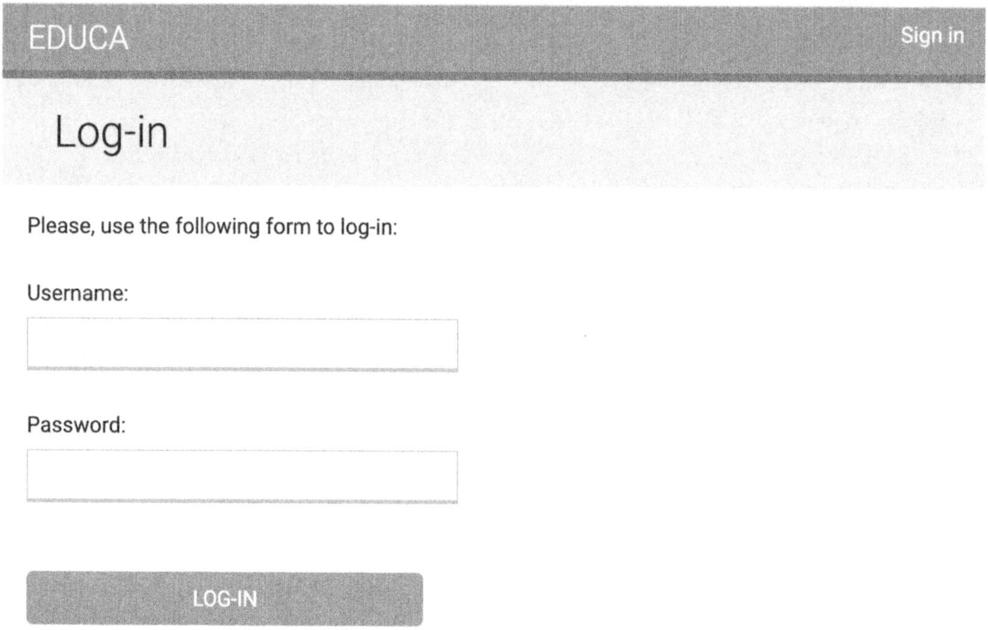

Figure 12.4: The account login page

Open `http://127.0.0.1:8000/accounts/logout/` in your browser. You should see the **Logged out** page now, as shown in *Figure 12.5*:

Figure 12.5: The account logged out page

You have successfully created an authentication system for the CMS.

Additional resources

The following resources provide additional information related to the topics covered in this chapter:

- Source code for this chapter — `https://github.com/PacktPublishing/Django-4-by-example/tree/main/Chapter12`
- Using Django fixtures for testing — `https://docs.djangoproject.com/en/4.1/topics/testing/tools/#fixture-loading`
- Data migrations — `https://docs.djangoproject.com/en/4.1/topics/migrations/#data-migrations`
- Creating custom model fields – `https://docs.djangoproject.com/en/4.1/howto/custom-model-fields/`
- Static directory for the e-learning project –`https://github.com/PacktPublishing/Django-4-by-Example/tree/main/Chapter12/educa/courses/static`

Summary

In this chapter, you learned how to use fixtures to provide initial data for models. By using model inheritance, you created a flexible system to manage different types of content for the course modules. You also implemented a custom model field on order objects and created an authentication system for the e-learning platform.

In the next chapter, you will implement the CMS functionality to manage course contents using class-based views. You will use the Django groups and permissions system to restrict access to views, and you will implement formsets to edit the content of courses. You will also create a drag-and-drop functionality to reorder course modules and their content using JavaScript and Django.

Join us on Discord

Read this book alongside other users and the author.

Ask questions, provide solutions to other readers, chat with the author via *Ask Me Anything* sessions, and much more. Scan the QR code or visit the link to join the book community.

`https://packt.link/django`

13

Creating a Content Management System

In the previous chapter, you created the application models for the e-learning platform and learned how to create and apply data fixtures for models. You created a custom model field to order objects and implemented user authentication.

In this chapter, you will learn how to build the functionality for instructors to create courses and manage the contents of those courses in a versatile and efficient manner.

In this chapter, you will learn how to:

- Create a content management system using class-based views and mixins
- Build formsets and model formsets to edit course modules and module contents
- Manage groups and permissions
- Implement a drag-and-drop functionality to reorder modules and content

The source code for this chapter can be found at https://github.com/PacktPublishing/Django-4-by-example/tree/main/Chapter13.

All Python modules used in this chapter are included in the requirements.txt file in the source code that comes along with this chapter. You can follow the instructions to install each Python module below or you can install all the requirements at once with the command pip install -r requirements.txt.

Creating a CMS

Now that you have created a versatile data model, you are going to build the CMS. The CMS will allow instructors to create courses and manage their content. You need to provide the following functionality:

- List the courses created by the instructor
- Create, edit, and delete courses
- Add modules to a course and reorder them

- Add different types of content to each module
- Reorder course modules and content

Let's start with the basic CRUD views.

Creating class-based views

You are going to build views to create, edit, and delete courses. You will use class-based views for this. Edit the views.py file of the courses application and add the following code:

```
from django.views.generic.list import ListView
from .models import Course


class ManageCourseListView(ListView):
    model = Course
    template_name = 'courses/manage/course/list.html'


    def get_queryset(self):
        qs = super().get_queryset()
        return qs.filter(owner=self.request.user)
```

This is the ManageCourseListView view. It inherits from Django's generic ListView. You override the get_queryset() method of the view to retrieve only courses created by the current user. To prevent users from editing, updating, or deleting courses they didn't create, you will also need to override the get_queryset() method in the create, update, and delete views. When you need to provide a specific behavior for several class-based views, it is recommended that you use *mixins*.

Using mixins for class-based views

Mixins are a special kind of multiple inheritance for a class. You can use them to provide common discrete functionality that, when added to other mixins, allows you to define the behavior of a class. There are two main situations to use mixins:

- You want to provide multiple optional features for a class
- You want to use a particular feature in several classes

Django comes with several mixins that provide additional functionality to your class-based views. You can learn more about mixins at https://docs.djangoproject.com/en/4.1/topics/class-based-views/mixins/.

You are going to implement common behavior for multiple views in mixin classes and use it for the course views. Edit the views.py file of the courses application and modify it as follows:

```
from django.views.generic.list import ListView
from django.views.generic.edit import CreateView, \
    UpdateView, DeleteView
from django.urls import reverse_lazy
```

```
from .models import Course

class OwnerMixin:
    def get_queryset(self):
        qs = super().get_queryset()
        return qs.filter(owner=self.request.user)

class OwnerEditMixin:
    def form_valid(self, form):
        form.instance.owner = self.request.user
        return super().form_valid(form)

class OwnerCourseMixin(OwnerMixin):
    model = Course
    fields = ['subject', 'title', 'slug', 'overview']
    success_url = reverse_lazy('manage_course_list')

class OwnerCourseEditMixin(OwnerCourseMixin, OwnerEditMixin):
    template_name = 'courses/manage/course/form.html'

class ManageCourseListView(OwnerCourseMixin, ListView):
    template_name = 'courses/manage/course/list.html'

class CourseCreateView(OwnerCourseEditMixin, CreateView):
    pass

class CourseUpdateView(OwnerCourseEditMixin, UpdateView):
    pass

class CourseDeleteView(OwnerCourseMixin, DeleteView):
    template_name = 'courses/manage/course/delete.html'
```

In this code, you create the OwnerMixin and OwnerEditMixin mixins. You will use these mixins together with the ListView, CreateView, UpdateView, and DeleteView views provided by Django. OwnerMixin implements the get_queryset() method, which is used by the views to get the base QuerySet. Your mixin will override this method to filter objects by the owner attribute to retrieve objects that belong to the current user (request.user).

OwnerEditMixin implements the form_valid() method, which is used by views that use Django's ModelFormMixin mixin, that is, views with forms or model forms such as CreateView and UpdateView. form_valid() is executed when the submitted form is valid.

The default behavior for this method is saving the instance (for model forms) and redirecting the user to `success_url`. You override this method to automatically set the current user in the `owner` attribute of the object being saved. By doing so, you set the owner for an object automatically when it is saved.

Your `OwnerMixin` class can be used for views that interact with any model that contains an `owner` attribute.

You also define an `OwnerCourseMixin` class that inherits `OwnerMixin` and provides the following attributes for child views:

- `model`: The model used for QuerySets; it is used by all views.
- `fields`: The fields of the model to build the model form of the `CreateView` and `UpdateView` views.
- `success_url`: Used by `CreateView`, `UpdateView`, and `DeleteView` to redirect the user after the form is successfully submitted or the object is deleted. You use a URL with the name `manage_course_list`, which you are going to create later.

You define an `OwnerCourseEditMixin` mixin with the following attribute:

- `template_name`: The template you will use for the `CreateView` and `UpdateView` views.

Finally, you create the following views that subclass `OwnerCourseMixin`:

- `ManageCourseListView`: Lists the courses created by the user. It inherits from `OwnerCourseMixin` and `ListView`. It defines a specific `template_name` attribute for a template to list courses.
- `CourseCreateView`: Uses a model form to create a new `Course` object. It uses the fields defined in `OwnerCourseMixin` to build a model form and also subclasses `CreateView`. It uses the template defined in `OwnerCourseEditMixin`.
- `CourseUpdateView`: Allows the editing of an existing `Course` object. It uses the fields defined in `OwnerCourseMixin` to build a model form and also subclasses `UpdateView`. It uses the template defined in `OwnerCourseEditMixin`.
- `CourseDeleteView`: Inherits from `OwnerCourseMixin` and the generic `DeleteView`. It defines a specific `template_name` attribute for a template to confirm the course deletion.

You have created the basic views to manage courses. Next, you are going to use the Django authentication groups and permissions to limit access to these views.

Working with groups and permissions

Currently, any user can access the views to manage courses. You want to restrict these views so that only instructors have permission to create and manage courses.

Django's authentication framework includes a permission system that allows you to assign permissions to users and groups. You are going to create a group for instructor users and assign permissions to create, update, and delete courses.

Run the development server using the following command:

```
python manage.py runserver
```

Open `http://127.0.0.1:8000/admin/auth/group/add/` in your browser to create a new Group object. Add the name `Instructors` and choose all permissions of the `courses` application, except those of the `Subject` model, as follows:

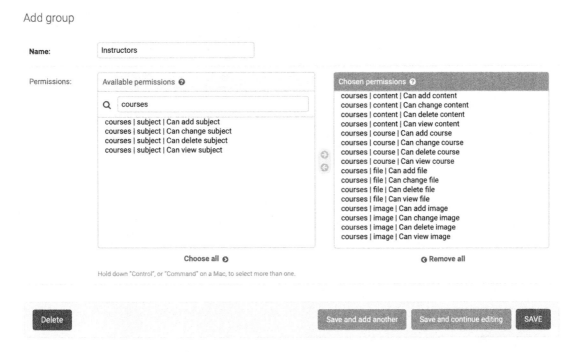

Figure 13.1: The Instructors group permissions

As you can see, there are four different permissions for each model: *can view*, *can add*, *can change*, and *can delete*. After choosing permissions for this group, click the **SAVE** button.

Django creates permissions for models automatically, but you can also create custom permissions. You will learn how to create custom permissions in *Chapter 15, Building an API*. You can read more about adding custom permissions at `https://docs.djangoproject.com/en/4.1/topics/auth/customizing/#custom-permissions`.

Open `http://127.0.0.1:8000/admin/auth/user/add/` and create a new user. Edit the user and add it to the **Instructors** group, as follows:

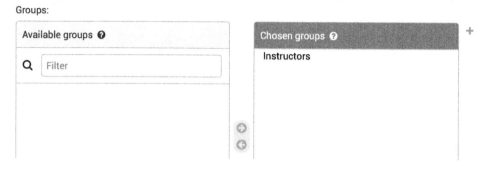

Figure 13.2: User group selection

Users inherit the permissions of the groups they belong to, but you can also add individual permissions to a single user using the administration site. Users that have `is_superuser` set to `True` have all permissions automatically.

Restricting access to class-based views

You are going to restrict access to the views so that only users with the appropriate permissions can add, change, or delete `Course` objects. You are going to use the following two mixins provided by `django.contrib.auth` to limit access to views:

- `LoginRequiredMixin`: Replicates the `login_required` decorator's functionality.
- `PermissionRequiredMixin`: Grants access to the view to users with a specific permission. Remember that superusers automatically have all permissions.

Edit the `views.py` file of the `courses` application and add the following import:

```
from django.contrib.auth.mixins import LoginRequiredMixin, \
                                       PermissionRequiredMixin
```

Make `OwnerCourseMixin` inherit `LoginRequiredMixin` and `PermissionRequiredMixin`, like this:

```
class OwnerCourseMixin(OwnerMixin,
                       LoginRequiredMixin,
                       PermissionRequiredMixin):
    model = Course
    fields = ['subject', 'title', 'slug', 'overview']
    success_url = reverse_lazy('manage_course_list')
```

Then, add a `permission_required` attribute to the course views, as follows:

```
class ManageCourseListView(OwnerCourseMixin, ListView):
    template_name = 'courses/manage/course/list.html'
    permission_required = 'courses.view_course'
```

```
class CourseCreateView(OwnerCourseEditMixin, CreateView):
    permission_required = 'courses.add_course'

class CourseUpdateView(OwnerCourseEditMixin, UpdateView):
    permission_required = 'courses.change_course'

class CourseDeleteView(OwnerCourseMixin, DeleteView):
    template_name = 'courses/manage/course/delete.html'
    permission_required = 'courses.delete_course'
```

PermissionRequiredMixin checks that the user accessing the view has the permission specified in the permission_required attribute. Your views are now only accessible to users with the proper permissions.

Let's create URLs for these views. Create a new file inside the courses application directory and name it urls.py. Add the following code to it:

```
from django.urls import path
from . import views

urlpatterns = [
    path('mine/',
         views.ManageCourseListView.as_view(),
         name='manage_course_list'),
    path('create/',
         views.CourseCreateView.as_view(),
         name='course_create'),
    path('<pk>/edit/',
         views.CourseUpdateView.as_view(),
         name='course_edit'),
    path('<pk>/delete/',
         views.CourseDeleteView.as_view(),
         name='course_delete'),
]
```

These are the URL patterns for the list, create, edit, and delete course views. The pk parameter refers to the primary key field. Remember that pk is a short for primary key. Every Django model has a field that serves as its primary key. By default, the primary key is the automatically generated id field. The Django generic views for single objects retrieve an object by its pk field. Edit the main urls.py file of the educa project and include the URL patterns of the courses application, as follows.

New code is highlighted in bold:

```
from django.contrib import admin
from django.urls import path, include
from django.conf import settings
from django.conf.urls.static import static
from django.contrib.auth import views as auth_views

urlpatterns = [
    path('accounts/login/',
            auth_views.LoginView.as_view(),
            name='login'),
    path('accounts/logout/',
            auth_views.LogoutView.as_view(),
            name='logout'),
    path('admin/', admin.site.urls),
    path('course/', include('courses.urls')),
]

if settings.DEBUG:
    urlpatterns += static(settings.MEDIA_URL,
                            document_root=settings.MEDIA_ROOT)
```

You need to create the templates for these views. Create the following directories and files inside the templates/ directory of the courses application:

```
courses/
    manage/
        course/
            list.html
            form.html
            delete.html
```

Edit the courses/manage/course/list.html template and add the following code to it:

```
{% extends "base.html" %}

{% block title %}My courses{% endblock %}

{% block content %}
  <h1>My courses</h1>
  <div class="module">
    {% for course in object_list %}
```

```
      <div class="course-info">
        <h3>{{ course.title }}</h3>
        <p>
          <a href="{% url "course_edit" course.id %}">Edit</a>
          <a href="{% url "course_delete" course.id %}">Delete</a>
        </p>
      </div>
    {% empty %}
      <p>You haven't created any courses yet.</p>
    {% endfor %}
    <p>
      <a href="{% url "course_create" %}" class="button">Create new course</a>
    </p>
  </div>
{% endblock %}
```

This is the template for the `ManageCourseListView` view. In this template, you list the courses created by the current user. You include links to edit or delete each course, and a link to create new courses.

Run the development server using the command:

```
python manage.py runserver
```

Open `http://127.0.0.1:8000/accounts/login/?next=/course/mine/` in your browser and log in with a user belonging to the `Instructors` group. After logging in, you will be redirected to the `http://127.0.0.1:8000/course/mine/` URL and you should see the following page:

Figure 13.3: The instructor courses page with no courses

This page will display all courses created by the current user.

Let's create the template that displays the form for the create and update course views. Edit the `courses/manage/course/form.html` template and write the following code:

```
{% extends "base.html" %}

{% block title %}
  {% if object %}
    Edit course "{{ object.title }}"
  {% else %}
    Create a new course
  {% endif %}
{% endblock %}

{% block content %}
  <h1>
    {% if object %}
      Edit course "{{ object.title }}"
    {% else %}
      Create a new course
    {% endif %}
  </h1>
  <div class="module">
    <h2>Course info</h2>
    <form method="post">
      {{ form.as_p }}
      {% csrf_token %}
      <p><input type="submit" value="Save course"></p>
    </form>
  </div>
{% endblock %}
```

The `form.html` template is used for both the `CourseCreateView` and `CourseUpdateView` views. In this template, you check whether an `object` variable is in the context. If `object` exists in the context, you know that you are updating an existing course, and you use it in the page title. Otherwise, you are creating a new `Course` object.

Open `http://127.0.0.1:8000/course/mine/` in your browser and click the **CREATE NEW COURSE** button. You will see the following page:

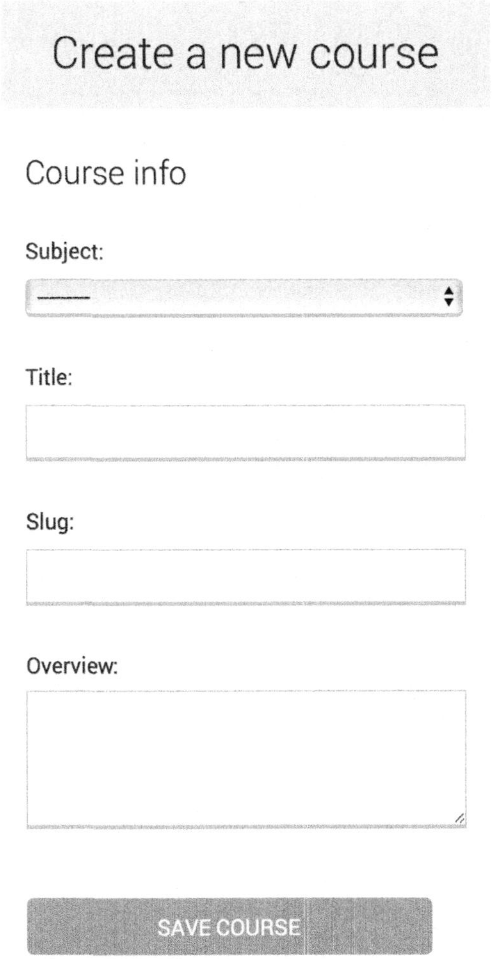

Figure 13.4: The form to create a new course

Fill in the form and click the **SAVE COURSE** button. The course will be saved, and you will be redirected to the course list page. It should look as follows:

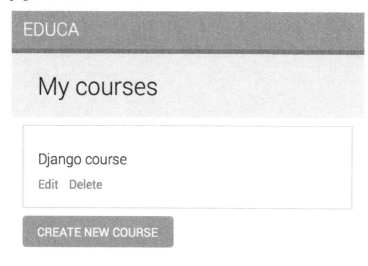

Figure 13.5: The instructor courses page with one course

Then, click the **Edit** link for the course you have just created. You will see the form again, but this time you are editing an existing Course object instead of creating one.

Finally, edit the courses/manage/course/delete.html template and add the following code:

```
{% extends "base.html" %}

{% block title %}Delete course{% endblock %}

{% block content %}
  <h1>Delete course "{{ object.title }}"</h1>
  <div class="module">
    <form action="" method="post">
      {% csrf_token %}
      <p>Are you sure you want to delete "{{ object }}"?</p>
      <input type="submit" value="Confirm">
    </form>
  </div>
{% endblock %}
```

This is the template for the CourseDeleteView view. This view inherits from DeleteView, provided by Django, which expects user confirmation to delete an object.

Open the course list in the browser and click the **Delete** link of your course. You should see the following confirmation page:

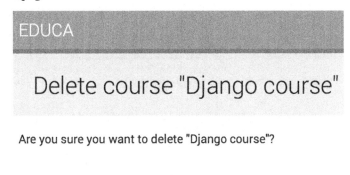

Figure 13.6: The delete course confirmation page

Click the **CONFIRM** button. The course will be deleted, and you will be redirected to the course list page again.

Instructors can now create, edit, and delete courses. Next, you need to provide them with a CMS to add course modules and their contents. You will start by managing course modules.

Managing course modules and their contents

You are going to build a system to manage course modules and their contents. You will need to build forms that can be used for managing multiple modules per course and different types of content for each module. Both modules and their contents will have to follow a specific order and you should be able to reorder them using the CMS.

Using formsets for course modules

Django comes with an abstraction layer to work with multiple forms on the same page. These groups of forms are known as *formsets*. Formsets manage multiple instances of a certain Form or ModelForm. All forms are submitted at once and the formset takes care of the initial number of forms to display, limiting the maximum number of forms that can be submitted and validating all the forms.

Formsets include an is_valid() method to validate all forms at once. You can also provide initial data for the forms and specify how many additional empty forms to display. You can learn more about formsets at https://docs.djangoproject.com/en/4.1/topics/forms/formsets/ and about model formsets at https://docs.djangoproject.com/en/4.1/topics/forms/modelforms/#model-formsets.

Since a course is divided into a variable number of modules, it makes sense to use formsets to manage them. Create a forms.py file in the courses application directory and add the following code to it:

```
from django import forms
from django.forms.models import inlineformset_factory
from .models import Course, Module
```

```
ModuleFormSet = inlineformset_factory(Course,
                                      Module,
                                      fields=['title',
                                              'description'],
                                      extra=2,
                                      can_delete=True)
```

This is the `ModuleFormSet` formset. You build it using the `inlineformset_factory()` function provided by Django. Inline formsets are a small abstraction on top of formsets that simplify working with related objects. This function allows you to build a model formset dynamically for the `Module` objects related to a `Course` object.

You use the following parameters to build the formset:

- `fields`: The fields that will be included in each form of the formset.
- `extra`: Allows you to set the number of empty extra forms to display in the formset.
- `can_delete`: If you set this to `True`, Django will include a Boolean field for each form that will be rendered as a checkbox input. It allows you to mark the objects that you want to delete.

Edit the `views.py` file of the `courses` application and add the following code to it:

```python
from django.shortcuts import redirect, get_object_or_404
from django.views.generic.base import TemplateResponseMixin, View
from .forms import ModuleFormSet


class CourseModuleUpdateView(TemplateResponseMixin, View):
    template_name = 'courses/manage/module/formset.html'
    course = None

    def get_formset(self, data=None):
        return ModuleFormSet(instance=self.course,
                             data=data)

    def dispatch(self, request, pk):
        self.course = get_object_or_404(Course,
                                        id=pk,
                                        owner=request.user)
        return super().dispatch(request, pk)

    def get(self, request, *args, **kwargs):
        formset = self.get_formset()
        return self.render_to_response({
                        'course': self.course,
```

```
                                          'formset': formset})

    def post(self, request, *args, **kwargs):
        formset = self.get_formset(data=request.POST)
        if formset.is_valid():
            formset.save()
            return redirect('manage_course_list')
        return self.render_to_response({
                                    'course': self.course,
                                    'formset': formset})
```

The `CourseModuleUpdateView` view handles the formset to add, update, and delete modules for a specific course. This view inherits from the following mixins and views:

- `TemplateResponseMixin`: This mixin takes charge of rendering templates and returning an HTTP response. It requires a `template_name` attribute that indicates the template to be rendered and provides the `render_to_response()` method to pass it a context and render the template.
- `View`: The basic class-based view provided by Django.

In this view, you implement the following methods:

- `get_formset()`: You define this method to avoid repeating the code to build the formset. You create a `ModuleFormSet` object for the given `Course` object with optional data.
- `dispatch()`: This method is provided by the `View` class. It takes an HTTP request and its parameters and attempts to delegate to a lowercase method that matches the HTTP method used. A GET request is delegated to the `get()` method and a POST request to `post()`, respectively. In this method, you use the `get_object_or_404()` shortcut function to get the `Course` object for the given `id` parameter that belongs to the current user. You include this code in the `dispatch()` method because you need to retrieve the course for both GET and POST requests. You save it into the `course` attribute of the view to make it accessible to other methods.
- `get()`: Executed for GET requests. You build an empty `ModuleFormSet` formset and render it to the template together with the current `Course` object using the `render_to_response()` method provided by `TemplateResponseMixin`.
- `post()`: Executed for POST requests.
- In this method, you perform the following actions:

    1. You build a `ModuleFormSet` instance using the submitted data.
    2. You execute the `is_valid()` method of the formset to validate all of its forms.
    3. If the formset is valid, you save it by calling the `save()` method. At this point, any changes made, such as adding, updating, or marking modules for deletion, are applied to the database. Then, you redirect users to the `manage_course_list` URL. If the formset is not valid, you render the template to display any errors instead.

Edit the `urls.py` file of the courses application and add the following URL pattern to it:

```
path('<pk>/module/',
     views.CourseModuleUpdateView.as_view(),
     name='course_module_update'),
```

Create a new directory inside the courses/manage/ template directory and name it `module`. Create a courses/manage/module/formset.html template and add the following code to it:

```
{% extends "base.html" %}

{% block title %}
  Edit "{{ course.title }}"
{% endblock %}

{% block content %}
  <h1>Edit "{{ course.title }}"</h1>
  <div class="module">
    <h2>Course modules</h2>
    <form method="post">
      {{ formset }}
      {{ formset.management_form }}
      {% csrf_token %}
      <input type="submit" value="Save modules">
    </form>
  </div>
{% endblock %}
```

In this template, you create a `<form>` HTML element in which you include `formset`. You also include the management form for the formset with the variable `{{ formset.management_form }}`. The management form includes hidden fields to control the initial, total, minimum, and maximum number of forms. You can see that it's very easy to create a formset.

Edit the courses/manage/course/list.html template and add the following link for the `course_module_update` URL below the course **Edit** and **Delete** links:

```
<a href="{% url "course_edit" course.id %}">Edit</a>
<a href="{% url "course_delete" course.id %}">Delete</a>
<a href="{% url "course_module_update" course.id %}">Edit modules</a>
```

You have included the link to edit the course modules.

Open `http://127.0.0.1:8000/course/mine/` in your browser. Create a course and click the **Edit modules** link for it. You should see a formset, as follows:

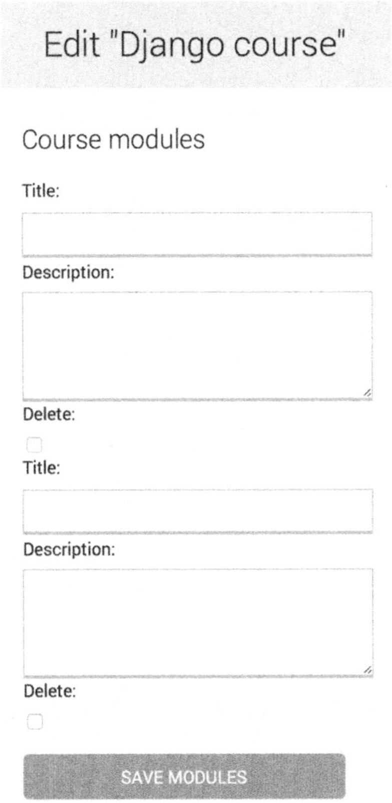

Edit "Django course"

Course modules

Title:

Description:

Delete:

Title:

Description:

Delete:

SAVE MODULES

Figure 13.7: The course edit page, including the formset for course modules

The formset includes a form for each `Module` object contained in the course. After these, two empty extra forms are displayed because you set `extra=2` for `ModuleFormSet`. When you save the formset, Django will include another two extra fields to add new modules.

Adding content to course modules

Now, you need a way to add content to course modules. You have four different types of content: text, video, image, and file. You could consider creating four different views to create content, with one for each model. However, you are going to take a more generic approach and create a view that handles creating or updating the objects of any content model.

Edit the `views.py` file of the `courses` application and add the following code to it:

```
from django.forms.models import modelform_factory
from django.apps import apps
from .models import Module, Content
```

```python
class ContentCreateUpdateView(TemplateResponseMixin, View):
    module = None
    model = None
    obj = None
    template_name = 'courses/manage/content/form.html'

    def get_model(self, model_name):
        if model_name in ['text', 'video', 'image', 'file']:
            return apps.get_model(app_label='courses',
                                  model_name=model_name)
        return None

    def get_form(self, model, *args, **kwargs):
        Form = modelform_factory(model, exclude=['owner',
                                                 'order',
                                                 'created',
                                                 'updated'])
        return Form(*args, **kwargs)

    def dispatch(self, request, module_id, model_name, id=None):
        self.module = get_object_or_404(Module,
                                        id=module_id,
                                        course__owner=request.user)
        self.model = self.get_model(model_name)
        if id:
            self.obj = get_object_or_404(self.model,
                                         id=id,
                                         owner=request.user)
        return super().dispatch(request, module_id, model_name, id)
```

This is the first part of `ContentCreateUpdateView`. It will allow you to create and update different models' contents. This view defines the following methods:

- `get_model()`: Here, you check that the given model name is one of the four content models: Text, Video, Image, or File. Then, you use Django's apps module to obtain the actual class for the given model name. If the given model name is not one of the valid ones, you return None.

- `get_form()`: You build a dynamic form using the `modelform_factory()` function of the form's framework. Since you are going to build a form for the Text, Video, Image, and File models, you use the `exclude` parameter to specify the common fields to exclude from the form and let all other attributes be included automatically. By doing so, you don't have to know which fields to include depending on the model.

- dispatch(): It receives the following URL parameters and stores the corresponding module, model, and content object as class attributes:

    - module_id: The ID for the module that the content is/will be associated with.
    - model_name: The model name of the content to create/update.
    - id: The ID of the object that is being updated. It's None to create new objects.

Add the following get() and post() methods to ContentCreateUpdateView:

```
def get(self, request, module_id, model_name, id=None):
    form = self.get_form(self.model, instance=self.obj)
    return self.render_to_response({'form': form,
                                    'object': self.obj})


def post(self, request, module_id, model_name, id=None):
    form = self.get_form(self.model,
                         instance=self.obj,
                         data=request.POST,
                         files=request.FILES)
    if form.is_valid():
        obj = form.save(commit=False)
        obj.owner = request.user
        obj.save()
        if not id:
            # new content
            Content.objects.create(module=self.module,
                                   item=obj)
        return redirect('module_content_list', self.module.id)
    return self.render_to_response({'form': form,
                                    'object': self.obj})
```

These methods are as follows:

- get(): Executed when a GET request is received. You build the model form for the Text, Video, Image, or File instance that is being updated. Otherwise, you pass no instance to create a new object, since self.obj is None if no ID is provided.
- post(): Executed when a POST request is received. You build the model form, passing any submitted data and files to it. Then, you validate it. If the form is valid, you create a new object and assign request.user as its owner before saving it to the database. You check for the id parameter. If no ID is provided, you know the user is creating a new object instead of updating an existing one. If this is a new object, you create a Content object for the given module and associate the new content with it.

Edit the `urls.py` file of the courses application and add the following URL patterns to it:

```python
path('module/<int:module_id>/content/<model_name>/create/',
    views.ContentCreateUpdateView.as_view(),
    name='module_content_create'),
path('module/<int:module_id>/content/<model_name>/<id>/',
    views.ContentCreateUpdateView.as_view(),
    name='module_content_update'),
```

The new URL patterns are as follows:

- `module_content_create`: To create new text, video, image, or file objects and add them to a module. It includes the `module_id` and `model_name` parameters. The first one allows linking the new content object to the given module. The latter specifies the content model to build the form for.

- `module_content_update`: To update an existing text, video, image, or file object. It includes the `module_id` and `model_name` parameters and an `id` parameter to identify the content that is being updated.

Create a new directory inside the `courses/manage/` template directory and name it content. Create the template `courses/manage/content/form.html` and add the following code to it:

```html
{% extends "base.html" %}

{% block title %}
  {% if object %}
    Edit content "{{ object.title }}"
  {% else %}
    Add new content
  {% endif %}
{% endblock %}

{% block content %}
  <h1>
    {% if object %}
      Edit content "{{ object.title }}"
    {% else %}
      Add new content
    {% endif %}
  </h1>
  <div class="module">
    <h2>Course info</h2>
    <form action="" method="post" enctype="multipart/form-data">
      {{ form.as_p }}
      {% csrf_token %}
      <p><input type="submit" value="Save content"></p>
```

```
      </form>
    </div>
  {% endblock %}
```

This is the template for the `ContentCreateUpdateView` view. In this template, you check whether an `object` variable is in the context. If `object` exists in the context, you are updating an existing object. Otherwise, you are creating a new object.

You include `enctype="multipart/form-data"` in the `<form>` HTML element because the form contains a file upload for the `File` and `Image` content models.

Run the development server, open `http://127.0.0.1:8000/course/mine/`, click **Edit modules** for an existing course, and create a module.

Then open the Python shell with the following command:

```
python manage.py shell
```

Obtain the ID of the most recently created module, as follows:

```
>>> from courses.models import Module
>>> Module.objects.latest('id').id
6
```

Run the development server and open `http://127.0.0.1:8000/course/module/6/content/image/ create/` in your browser, replacing the module ID with the one you obtained before. You will see the form to create an `Image` object, as follows:

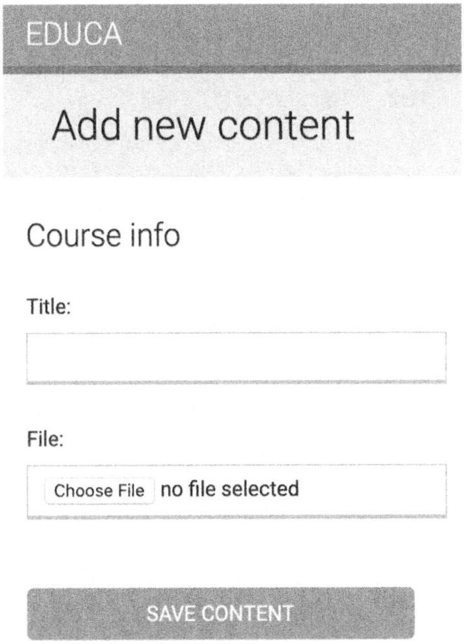

Figure 13.8: The course add new image content form

Don't submit the form yet. If you try to do so, it will fail because you haven't defined the module_content_list URL yet. You are going to create it in a bit.

You also need a view for deleting content. Edit the views.py file of the courses application and add the following code:

```
class ContentDeleteView(View):
    def post(self, request, id):
        content = get_object_or_404(Content,
                        id=id,
                        module__course__owner=request.user)
        module = content.module
        content.item.delete()
        content.delete()
        return redirect('module_content_list', module.id)
```

The ContentDeleteView class retrieves the Content object with the given ID. It deletes the related Text, Video, Image, or File object. Finally, it deletes the Content object and redirects the user to the module_content_list URL to list the other contents of the module.

Edit the urls.py file of the courses application and add the following URL pattern to it:

```
path('content/<int:id>/delete/',
    views.ContentDeleteView.as_view(),
    name='module_content_delete'),
```

Now instructors can create, update, and delete content easily.

Managing modules and their contents

You have built views to create, edit, and delete course modules and their contents. Next, you need a view to display all modules for a course and list the contents of a specific module.

Edit the views.py file of the courses application and add the following code to it:

```
class ModuleContentListView(TemplateResponseMixin, View):
    template_name = 'courses/manage/module/content_list.html'

    def get(self, request, module_id):
        module = get_object_or_404(Module,
                                    id=module_id,
                                    course__owner=request.user)
        return self.render_to_response({'module': module})
```

This is the ModuleContentListView view. This view gets the Module object with the given ID that belongs to the current user and renders a template with the given module.

Edit the `urls.py` file of the courses application and add the following URL pattern to it:

```
path('module/<int:module_id>/',
     views.ModuleContentListView.as_view(),
     name='module_content_list'),
```

Create a new template inside the `templates/courses/manage/module/` directory and name it `content_list.html`. Add the following code to it:

```
{% extends "base.html" %}

{% block title %}
  Module {{ module.order|add:1 }}: {{ module.title }}
{% endblock %}

{% block content %}
{% with course=module.course %}
  <h1>Course "{{ course.title }}"</h1>
  <div class="contents">
    <h3>Modules</h3>
    <ul id="modules">
      {% for m in course.modules.all %}
        <li data-id="{{ m.id }}" {% if m == module %}
        class="selected"{% endif %}>
          <a href="{% url "module_content_list" m.id %}">
            <span>
              Module <span class="order">{{ m.order|add:1 }}</span>
            </span>
            <br>
            {{ m.title }}
          </a>
        </li>
      {% empty %}
        <li>No modules yet.</li>
      {% endfor %}
    </ul>
    <p><a href="{% url "course_module_update" course.id %}">
    Edit modules</a></p>
  </div>
  <div class="module">
    <h2>Module {{ module.order|add:1 }}: {{ module.title }}</h2>
    <h3>Module contents:</h3>
```

```
<div id="module-contents">
  {% for content in module.contents.all %}
    <div data-id="{{ content.id }}">
      {% with item=content.item %}
        <p>{{ item }}</p>
        <a href="#">Edit</a>
        <form action="{% url "module_content_delete" content.id %}"
         method="post">
          <input type="submit" value="Delete">
          {% csrf_token %}
        </form>
      {% endwith %}
    </div>
  {% empty %}
    <p>This module has no contents yet.</p>
  {% endfor %}
</div>
<h3>Add new content:</h3>
<ul class="content-types">
  <li>
    <a href="{% url "module_content_create" module.id "text" %}">
      Text
    </a>
  </li>
  <li>
    <a href="{% url "module_content_create" module.id "image" %}">
      Image
    </a>
  </li>
  <li>
    <a href="{% url "module_content_create" module.id "video" %}">
      Video
    </a>
  </li>
  <li>
    <a href="{% url "module_content_create" module.id "file" %}">
      File
    </a>
  </li>
</ul>
```

```
    </div>
    {% endwith %}
    {% endblock %}
```

Make sure that no template tag is split into multiple lines.

This is the template that displays all modules for a course and the contents of the selected module. You iterate over the course modules to display them in a sidebar. You iterate over a module's contents and access `content.item` to get the related `Text`, `Video`, `Image`, or `File` object. You also include links to create new text, video, image, or file content.

You want to know which type of object each of the `item` objects is: `Text`, `Video`, `Image`, or `File`. You need the model name to build the URL to edit the object. Besides this, you could display each item in the template differently based on the type of content it is. You can get the model name for an object from the model's `Meta` class by accessing the object's `_meta` attribute. Nevertheless, Django doesn't allow accessing variables or attributes starting with an underscore in templates to prevent retrieving private attributes or calling private methods. You can solve this by writing a custom template filter.

Create the following file structure inside the `courses` application directory:

```
templatetags/
    __init__.py
    course.py
```

Edit the `course.py` module and add the following code to it:

```python
from django import template

register = template.Library()

@register.filter
def model_name(obj):
    try:
        return obj._meta.model_name
    except AttributeError:
        return None
```

This is the `model_name` template filter. You can apply it in templates as `object|model_name` to get the model name for an object.

Edit the `templates/courses/manage/module/content_list.html` template and add the following line below the `{% extends %}` template tag:

```
{% load course %}
```

This will load the course template tags. Then, find the following lines:

```
<p>{{ item }}</p>
<a href="#">Edit</a>
```

Replace them with the following ones:

```
<p>{{ item }} ({{ item|model_name }})</p>
<a href="{% url "module_content_update" module.id item|model_name item.id %}">
  Edit
</a>
```

In the preceding code, you display the item model name in the template and also use the model name to build the link to edit the object.

Edit the `courses/manage/course/list.html` template and add a link to the `module_content_list` URL, like this:

```
<a href="{% url "course_module_update" course.id %}">Edit modules</a>
{% if course.modules.count > 0 %}
  <a href="{% url "module_content_list" course.modules.first.id %}">
    Manage contents
  </a>
{% endif %}
```

The new link allows users to access the contents of the first module of the course, if there are any.

Stop the development server and run it again using the command:

```
python manage.py runserver
```

By stopping and running the development server, you make sure that the `course` template tags file gets loaded.

Open `http://127.0.0.1:8000/course/mine/` and click the **Manage contents** link for a course that contains at least one module. You will see a page like the following one:

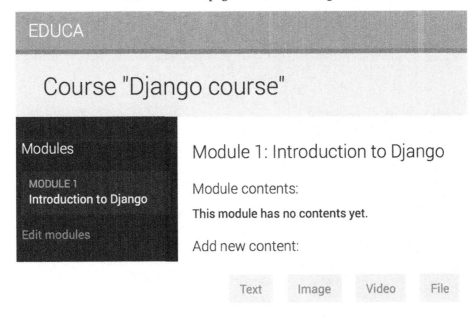

Figure 13.9: The page to manage course module contents

When you click on a module in the left sidebar, its contents are displayed in the main area. The template also includes links to add new text, video, image, or file content for the module being displayed.

Add a couple of different types of content to the module and look at the result. Module contents will appear below **Module contents:**

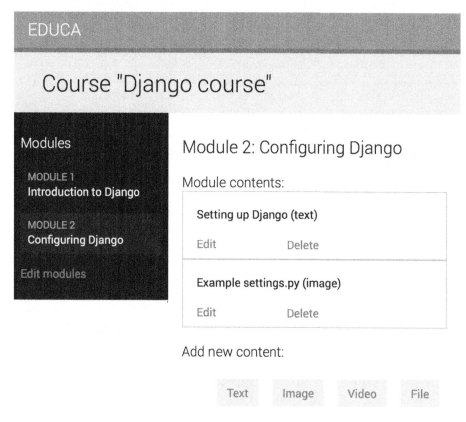

Figure 13.10: Managing different module contents

Next, we will allow course instructors to reorder modules and module contents with a simple drag-and-drop functionality.

Reordering modules and their contents

We will implement a JavaScript drag-and-drop functionality to let course instructors reorder the modules of a course by dragging them.

To implement this feature, we will use the HTML5 Sortable library, which simplifies the process of creating sortable lists using the native HTML5 Drag and Drop API.

When users finish dragging a module, you will use the JavaScript Fetch API to send an asynchronous HTTP request to the server that stores the new module order.

You can read more information about the HTML5 Drag and Drop API at `https://www.w3schools.com/html/html5_draganddrop.asp`. You can find examples built with the HTML5 Sortable library at `https://lukasoppermann.github.io/html5sortable/`. Documentation for the HTML5 Sortable library is available at `https://github.com/lukasoppermann/html5sortable`.

Using mixins from django-braces

`django-braces` is a third-party module that contains a collection of generic mixins for Django. These mixins provide additional features for class-based views. You can see a list of all mixins provided by `django-braces` at `https://django-braces.readthedocs.io/`.

You will use the following mixins of `django-braces`:

- `CsrfExemptMixin`: Used to avoid checking the **cross-site request forgery** (**CSRF**) token in the POST requests. You need this to perform AJAX POST requests without the need to pass a `csrf_token`.
- `JsonRequestResponseMixin`: Parses the request data as JSON and also serializes the response as JSON and returns an HTTP response with the `application/json` content type.

Install `django-braces` via `pip` using the following command:

```
pip install django-braces==1.15.0
```

You need a view that receives the new order of module IDs encoded in JSON and updates the order accordingly. Edit the `views.py` file of the `courses` application and add the following code to it:

```python
from braces.views import CsrfExemptMixin, JsonRequestResponseMixin


class ModuleOrderView(CsrfExemptMixin,
                      JsonRequestResponseMixin,
                      View):
    def post(self, request):
        for id, order in self.request_json.items():
            Module.objects.filter(id=id,
                course__owner=request.user).update(order=order)
        return self.render_json_response({'saved': 'OK'})
```

This is the `ModuleOrderView` view, which allows you to update the order of course modules.

You can build a similar view to order a module's contents. Add the following code to the `views.py` file:

```python
class ContentOrderView(CsrfExemptMixin,
                       JsonRequestResponseMixin,
                       View):
    def post(self, request):
        for id, order in self.request_json.items():
            Content.objects.filter(id=id,
```

```
                              module__course__owner=request.user) \
                          .update(order=order)
              return self.render_json_response({'saved': 'OK'})
```

Now, edit the `urls.py` file of the `courses` application and add the following URL patterns to it:

```python
path('module/order/',
     views.ModuleOrderView.as_view(),
     name='module_order'),
path('content/order/',
     views.ContentOrderView.as_view(),
     name='content_order'),
```

Finally, you need to implement the drag-and-drop functionality in the template. We will use the HTML5 Sortable library, which simplifies the creation of sortable elements using the standard HTML Drag and Drop API.

Edit the `base.html` template located in the `templates/` directory of the `courses` application and add the following block highlighted in bold:

```html
{% load static %}
<!DOCTYPE html>
<html>
  <head>
    # ...
  </head>
  <body>
    <div id="header">
      # ...
    </div>
    <div id="content">
      {% block content %}
      {% endblock %}
    </div>
    {% block include_js %}
    {% endblock %}
    <script>
      document.addEventListener('DOMContentLoaded', (event) => {
        // DOM Loaded
        {% block domready %}
        {% endblock %}
      })
    </script>
  </body>
</html>
```

This new block named `include_js` will allow you to insert JavaScript files in any template that extends the `base.html` template.

Next, edit the `courses/manage/module/content_list.html` template and add the following code highlighted in bold to the bottom of the template:

```
# ...
{% block content %}
  # ...
{% endblock %}

{% block include_js %}
  <script src="https://cdnjs.cloudflare.com/ajax/libs/html5sortable/0.13.3/
html5sortable.min.js"></script>
{% endblock %}
```

In this code, you load the HTML5 Sortable library from a public CDN. Remember you loaded a JavaScript library from a content delivery network before in *Chapter 6, Sharing Content on Your Website*.

Now add the following domready block highlighted in bold to the `courses/manage/module/content_list.html` template:

```
# ...
{% block content %}
  # ...
{% endblock %}

{% block include_js %}
  <script src="https://cdnjs.cloudflare.com/ajax/libs/html5sortable/0.13.3/
html5sortable.min.js"></script>
{% endblock %}

{% block domready %}
  var options = {
      method: 'POST',
      mode: 'same-origin'
  }
  const moduleOrderUrl = '{% url "module_order" %}';
{% endblock %}
```

In these new lines, you add JavaScript code to the {% block domready %} block that was defined in the event listener for the DOMContentLoaded event in the base.html template. This guarantees that your JavaScript code will be executed once the page has been loaded. With this code, you define the options for the HTTP request to reorder modules that you will implement next. You will send a POST request using the Fetch API to update the module order. The module_order URL path is built and stored in the JavaScript constant moduleOrderUrl.

Add the following code highlighted in bold to the domready block:

```
{% block domready %}
  var options = {
      method: 'POST',
      mode: 'same-origin'
  }
  const moduleOrderUrl = '{% url "module_order" %}';

  sortable('#modules', {
    forcePlaceholderSize: true,
    placeholderClass: 'placeholder'
  });
{% endblock %}
```

In the new code, you define a sortable element for the HTML element with id="modules", which is the module list in the sidebar. Remember that you use a CSS selector # to select the element with the given id. When you start dragging an item, the HTML5 Sortable library creates a placeholder item so that you can easily see where the element will be placed.

You set the forcePlacehoderSize option to true, to force the placeholder element to have a height, and you use the placeholderClass to define the CSS class for the placeholder element. You use the class named placeholder that is defined in the css/base.css static file loaded in the base.html template.

Open `http://127.0.0.1:8000/course/mine/` in your browser and click on **Manage contents** for any course. Now you can drag and drop the course modules in the left sidebar, as in *Figure 13.11*:

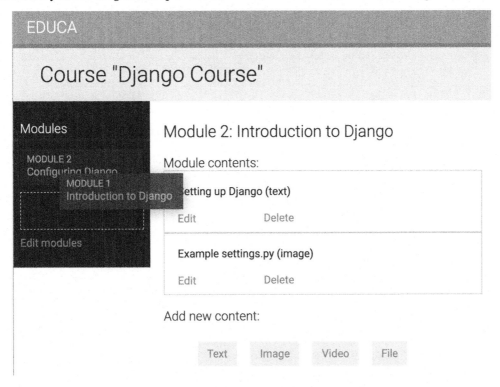

Figure 13.11: Reordering modules with the drag-and-drop functionality

While you drag the element, you will see the placeholder item created by the Sortable library, which has a dashed-line border. The placeholder element allows you to identify the position where the dragged element will be dropped.

When you drag a module to a different position, you need to send an HTTP request to the server to store the new order. This can be done by attaching an event handler to the sortable element and sending a request to the server using the JavaScript Fetch API.

Edit the domready block of the `courses/manage/module/content_list.html` template and add the following code highlighted in bold:

```
{% block domready %}
  var options = {
      method: 'POST',
      mode: 'same-origin'
  }
  const moduleOrderUrl = '{% url "module_order" %}';

  sortable('#modules', {
    forcePlaceholderSize: true,
    placeholderClass: 'placeholder'
  })[0].addEventListener('sortupdate', function(e) {

      modulesOrder = {};
      var modules = document.querySelectorAll('#modules li');
      modules.forEach(function (module, index) {
          // update module index
          modulesOrder[module.dataset.id] = index;
          // update index in HTML element
          module.querySelector('.order').innerHTML = index + 1;
          // add new order to the HTTP request options
          options['body'] = JSON.stringify(modulesOrder);

          // send HTTP request
          fetch(moduleOrderUrl, options)
      });
  });

{% endblock %}
```

In the new code, an event listener is created for the `sortupdate` event of the sortable element. The `sortupdate` event is triggered when an element is dropped in a different position. The following tasks are performed in the event function:

1. An empty `modulesOrder` dictionary is created. The keys for this dictionary will be the module IDs, and the values will contain the index of each module.
2. The list elements of the `#modules` HTML element are selected with `document.querySelectorAll()`, using the `#modules li` CSS selector.
3. `forEach()` is used to iterate over each list element.

4. The new index for each module is stored in the modulesOrder dictionary. The ID of each module is retrieved from the HTML data-id attribute by accessing module.dataset.id. You use the ID as the key of the modulesOrder dictionary and the new index of the module as the value.

5. The order displayed for each module is updated by selecting the element with the order CSS class. Since the index is zero-based and we want to display a one-based index, we add 1 to index.

6. A key named body is added to the options dictionary with the new order contained in modulesOrder. The JSON.stringify() method converts the JavaScript object into a JSON string. This is the body for the HTTP request to update the module order.

7. The Fetch API is used by creating a fetch() HTTP request to update the module order. The view ModuleOrderView that corresponds to the module_order URL takes care of updating the order of the modules.

You can now drag and drop modules. When you finish dragging a module, an HTTP request is sent to the module_order URL to update the order of the modules. If you refresh the page, the latest module order will be kept because it was updated in the database. *Figure 13.12* shows a different order for the modules in the sidebar after sorting them using drag and drop:

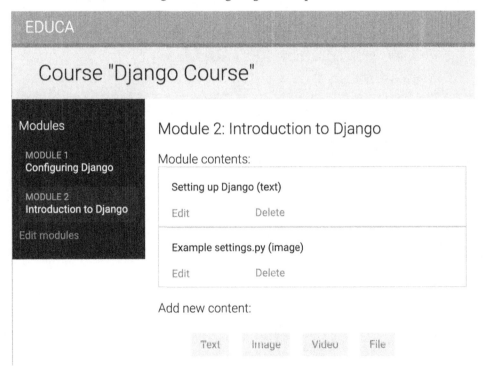

Figure 13.12: New order for modules after reordering them with drag and drop

If you run into any issues, remember to use your browser's developer tools to debug JavaScript and HTTP requests. Usually, you can right-click anywhere on the website to open the contextual menu and click on **Inspect** or **Inspect Element** to access the web developer tools of your browser.

Let's add the same drag-and-drop functionality to allow course instructors to sort module contents as well.

Edit the `domready` block of the `courses/manage/module/content_list.html` template and add the following code highlighted in bold:

```
{% block domready %}


  // ...


  const contentOrderUrl = '{% url "content_order" %}';

  sortable('#module-contents', {
    forcePlaceholderSize: true,
    placeholderClass: 'placeholder'
  })[0].addEventListener('sortupdate', function(e) {

    contentOrder = {};
    var contents = document.querySelectorAll('#module-contents div');
    contents.forEach(function (content, index) {
      // update content index
      contentOrder[content.dataset.id] = index;
      // add new order to the HTTP request options
      options['body'] = JSON.stringify(contentOrder);

      // send HTTP request
      fetch(contentOrderUrl, options)
    });
  });


{% endblock %}
```

In this case, you use the `content_order` URL instead of `module_order` and build the `sortable` functionality on the HTML element with the ID `module-contents`. The functionality is mainly the same as for ordering course modules. In this case, you don't need to update the numbering of the contents because they don't include any visible index.

Now you can drag and drop both modules and module contents, as in *Figure 13.13*:

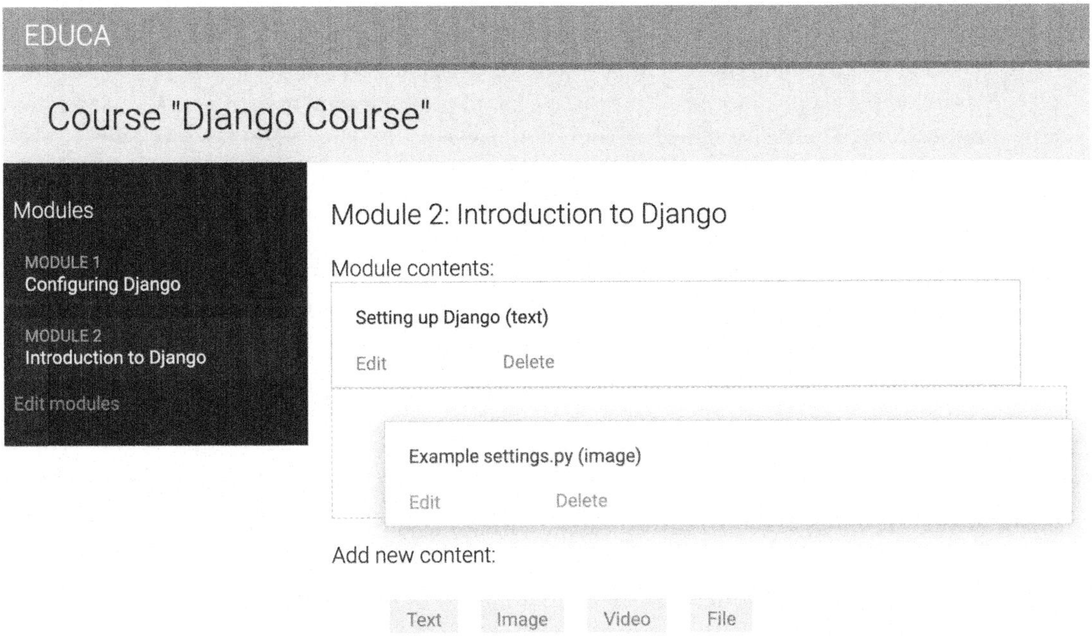

Figure 13.13: Reordering module contents with the drag-and-drop functionality

Great! You built a very versatile content management system for the course instructors.

Additional resources

The following resources provide additional information related to the topics covered in this chapter:

- Source code for this chapter – https://github.com/PacktPublishing/Django-4-by-example/tree/main/Chapter13

- Django mixins documentation – https://docs.djangoproject.com/en/4.1/topics/class-based-views/mixins/

- Creating custom permissions – https://docs.djangoproject.com/en/4.1/topics/auth/customizing/#custom-permissions

- Django formsets – https://docs.djangoproject.com/en/4.1/topics/forms/formsets/

- Django model formsets –https://docs.djangoproject.com/en/4.1/topics/forms/modelforms/#model-formsets

- HTML5 drag-and-drop API – https://www.w3schools.com/html/html5_draganddrop.asp

- HTML5 Sortable library documentation – https://github.com/lukasoppermann/html5sortable

- HTML5 Sortable library examples – https://lukasoppermann.github.io/html5sortable/

- django-braces documentation – https://django-braces.readthedocs.io/

Summary

In this chapter, you learned how to use class-based views and mixins to create a content management system. You also worked with groups and permissions to restrict access to your views. You learned how to use formsets and model formsets to manage course modules and their content. You also built a drag-and-drop functionality with JavaScript to reorder course modules and their contents.

In the next chapter, you will create a student registration system and manage student enrollment onto courses. You will also learn how to render different kinds of content and cache content using Django's cache framework.

14

Rendering and Caching Content

In the previous chapter, you used model inheritance and generic relations to create flexible course content models. You implemented a custom model field, and you built a course management system using class-based views. Finally, you created a JavaScript drag-and-drop functionality using asynchronous HTTP requests to order course modules and their contents.

In this chapter, you will build the functionality to access course contents, create a student registration system, and manage student enrollment onto courses. You will also learn how to cache data using the Django cache framework.

In this chapter, you will:

- Create public views for displaying course information
- Build a student registration system
- Manage student enrollment onto courses
- Render diverse content for course modules
- Install and configure Memcached
- Cache content using the Django cache framework
- Use the Memcached and Redis cache backends
- Monitor your Redis server in the Django administration site

Let's start by creating a course catalog for students to browse existing courses and enroll on them.

The source code for this chapter can be found at https://github.com/PacktPublishing/Django-4-by-example/tree/main/Chapter14.

All Python modules used in this chapter are included in the requirements.txt file in the source code that comes along with this chapter. You can follow the instructions to install each Python module below or you can install all requirements at once with the command pip install -r requirements.txt.

Displaying courses

For your course catalog, you have to build the following functionalities:

- List all available courses, optionally filtered by subject
- Display a single course overview

Edit the `views.py` file of the `courses` application and add the following code:

```
from django.db.models import Count
from .models import Subject


class CourseListView(TemplateResponseMixin, View):
    model = Course
    template_name = 'courses/course/list.html'
    def get(self, request, subject=None):
        subjects = Subject.objects.annotate(
                        total_courses=Count('courses'))
        courses = Course.objects.annotate(
                        total_modules=Count('modules'))
        if subject:
            subject = get_object_or_404(Subject, slug=subject)
            courses = courses.filter(subject=subject)
        return self.render_to_response({'subjects': subjects,
                                        'subject': subject,
                                        'courses': courses})
```

This is the `CourseListView` view. It inherits from `TemplateResponseMixin` and `View`. In this view, you perform the following tasks:

1. You retrieve all subjects, using the ORM's `annotate()` method with the `Count()` aggregation function to include the total number of courses for each subject.
2. You retrieve all available courses, including the total number of modules contained in each course.
3. If a subject slug URL parameter is given, you retrieve the corresponding `subject` object and limit the query to the courses that belong to the given subject.
4. You use the `render_to_response()` method provided by `TemplateResponseMixin` to render the objects to a template and return an HTTP response.

Let's create a detail view for displaying a single course overview. Add the following code to the `views.py` file:

```
from django.views.generic.detail import DetailView


class CourseDetailView(DetailView):
```

```
    model = Course
    template_name = 'courses/course/detail.html'
```

This view inherits from the generic `DetailView` provided by Django. You specify the `model` and `template_name` attributes. Django's `DetailView` expects a primary key (pk) or slug URL parameter to retrieve a single object for the given model. The view renders the template specified in `template_name`, including the `Course` object in the template context variable `object`.

Edit the main `urls.py` file of the `educa` project and add the following URL pattern to it:

```
from courses.views import CourseListView

urlpatterns = [
    # ...
    path('', CourseListView.as_view(), name='course_list'),
]
```

You add the `course_list` URL pattern to the main `urls.py` file of the project because you want to display the list of courses in the URL `http://127.0.0.1:8000/`, and all other URLs for the courses application have the `/course/` prefix.

Edit the `urls.py` file of the `courses` application and add the following URL patterns:

```
path('subject/<slug:subject>/',
    views.CourseListView.as_view(),
    name='course_list_subject'),
path('<slug:slug>/',
    views.CourseDetailView.as_view(),
    name='course_detail'),
```

You define the following URL patterns:

- `course_list_subject`: For displaying all courses for a subject
- `course_detail`: For displaying a single course overview

Let's build templates for the `CourseListView` and `CourseDetailView` views.

Create the following file structure inside the `templates/courses/` directory of the `courses` application:

```
course/
    list.html
    detail.html
```

Edit the `courses/course/list.html` template of the `courses` application and write the following code:

```
{% extends "base.html" %}

{% block title %}
```

```
    {% if subject %}
      {{ subject.title }} courses
    {% else %}
      All courses
    {% endif %}
{% endblock %}

{% block content %}
  <h1>
    {% if subject %}
      {{ subject.title }} courses
    {% else %}
      All courses
    {% endif %}
  </h1>
  <div class="contents">
    <h3>Subjects</h3>
    <ul id="modules">
      <li {% if not subject %}class="selected"{% endif %}>
        <a href="{% url "course_list" %}">All</a>
      </li>
      {% for s in subjects %}
        <li {% if subject == s %}class="selected"{% endif %}>
          <a href="{% url "course_list_subject" s.slug %}">
            {{ s.title }}
            <br>
            <span>
              {{ s.total_courses }} course{{ s.total_courses|pluralize }}
            </span>
          </a>
        </li>
      {% endfor %}
    </ul>
  </div>
  <div class="module">
    {% for course in courses %}
      {% with subject=course.subject %}
        <h3>
          <a href="{% url "course_detail" course.slug %}">
            {{ course.title }}
          </a>
        </h3>
```

```
        <p>
          <a href="{% url "course_list_subject" subject.slug %}">{{ subject
}}</a>.
            {{ course.total_modules }} modules.
            Instructor: {{ course.owner.get_full_name }}
        </p>
      {% endwith %}
    {% endfor %}
  </div>
{% endblock %}
```

Make sure that no template tag is split into multiple lines.

This is the template for listing the available courses. You create an HTML list to display all `Subject` objects and build a link to the `course_list_subject` URL for each of them. You also include the total number of courses for each subject and use the `pluralize` template filter to add a plural suffix to the word **course** when the number is different than 1, to show *0 courses, 1 course, 2 courses*, etc. You add a `selected` HTML class to highlight the current subject if a subject is selected. You iterate over every `Course` object, displaying the total number of modules and the instructor's name.

Run the development server and open `http://127.0.0.1:8000/` in your browser. You should see a page similar to the following one:

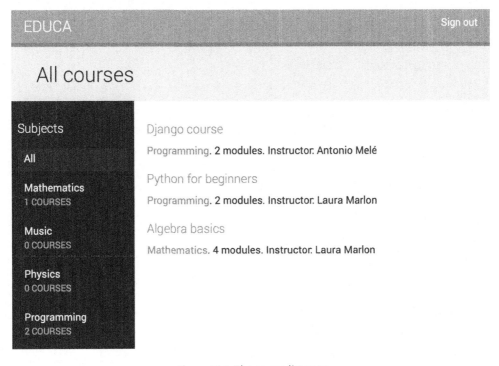

Figure 14.1: The course list page

The left sidebar contains all subjects, including the total number of courses for each of them. You can click any subject to filter the courses displayed.

Edit the `courses/course/detail.html` template and add the following code to it:

```
{% extends "base.html" %}

{% block title %}
  {{ object.title }}
{% endblock %}

{% block content %}
  {% with subject=object.subject %}
    <h1>
      {{ object.title }}
    </h1>
    <div class="module">
      <h2>Overview</h2>
      <p>
        <a href="{% url "course_list_subject" subject.slug %}">
        {{ subject.title }}</a>.
        {{ object.modules.count }} modules.
        Instructor: {{ object.owner.get_full_name }}
      </p>
      {{ object.overview|linebreaks }}
    </div>
  {% endwith %}
{% endblock %}
```

In this template, you display the overview and details for a single course. Open `http://127.0.0.1:8000/` in your browser and click on one of the courses. You should see a page with the following structure:

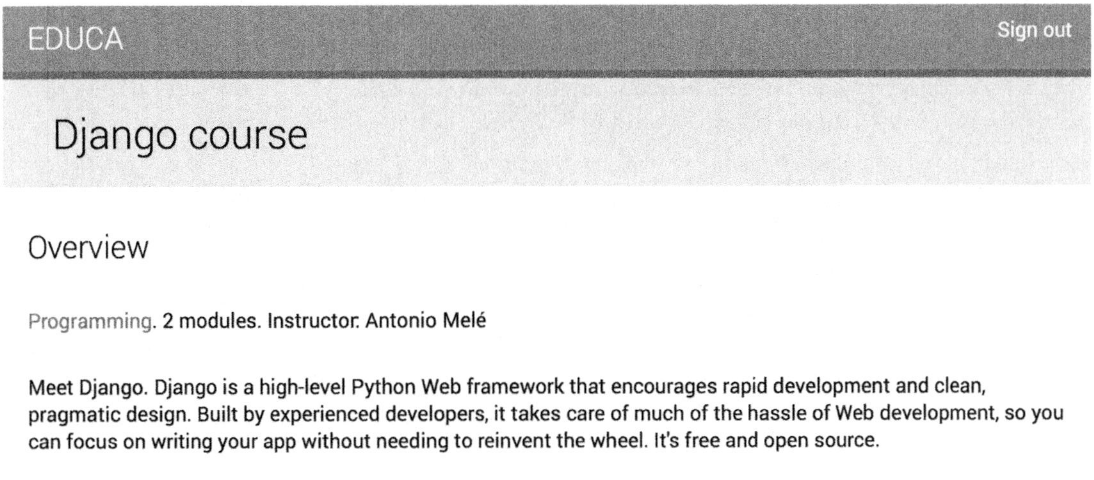

EDUCA   Sign out

Django course

Overview

Programming. **2 modules. Instructor:** Antonio Melé

Meet Django. Django is a high-level Python Web framework that encourages rapid development and clean, pragmatic design. Built by experienced developers, it takes care of much of the hassle of Web development, so you can focus on writing your app without needing to reinvent the wheel. It's free and open source.

Figure 14.2: The course overview page

You have created a public area for displaying courses. Next, you need to allow users to register as students and enroll on courses.

Adding student registration

Create a new application using the following command:

```
python manage.py startapp students
```

Edit the settings.py file of the educa project and add the new application to the INSTALLED_APPS setting, as follows:

```
INSTALLED_APPS = [
    # ...
    'students.apps.StudentsConfig',
]
```

Creating a student registration view

Edit the views.py file of the students application and write the following code:

```
from django.urls import reverse_lazy
from django.views.generic.edit import CreateView
from django.contrib.auth.forms import UserCreationForm
from django.contrib.auth import authenticate, login
```

```
class StudentRegistrationView(CreateView):
    template_name = 'students/student/registration.html'
    form_class = UserCreationForm
    success_url = reverse_lazy('student_course_list')

    def form_valid(self, form):
        result = super().form_valid(form)
        cd = form.cleaned_data
        user = authenticate(username=cd['username'],
                            password=cd['password1'])
        login(self.request, user)
        return result
```

This is the view that allows students to register on your site. You use the generic `CreateView`, which provides the functionality for creating model objects. This view requires the following attributes:

- `template_name`: The path of the template to render this view.
- `form_class`: The form for creating objects, which has to be `ModelForm`. You use Django's `UserCreationForm` as the registration form to create `User` objects.
- `success_url`: The URL to redirect the user to when the form is successfully submitted. You reverse the URL named `student_course_list`, which you are going to create in the *Accessing the course contents* section for listing the courses that students are enrolled on.

The `form_valid()` method is executed when valid form data has been posted. It has to return an HTTP response. You override this method to log the user in after they have successfully signed up.

Create a new file inside the `students` application directory and name it `urls.py`. Add the following code to it:

```
from django.urls import path
from . import views

urlpatterns = [
    path('register/',
         views.StudentRegistrationView.as_view(),
         name='student_registration'),
]
```

Then, edit the main `urls.py` of the educa project and include the URLs for the `students` application by adding the following pattern to your URL configuration:

```
urlpatterns = [
    # ...
    path('students/', include('students.urls')),
]
```

Create the following file structure inside the `students` application directory:

```
templates/
    students/
        student/
            registration.html
```

Edit the `students/student/registration.html` template and add the following code to it:

```
{% extends "base.html" %}

{% block title %}
  Sign up
{% endblock %}

{% block content %}
  <h1>
    Sign up
  </h1>
  <div class="module">
    <p>Enter your details to create an account:</p>
    <form method="post">
      {{ form.as_p }}
      {% csrf_token %}
      <p><input type="submit" value="Create my account"></p>
    </form>
  </div>
{% endblock %}
```

Run the development server and open `http://127.0.0.1:8000/students/register/` in your browser. You should see a registration form like this:

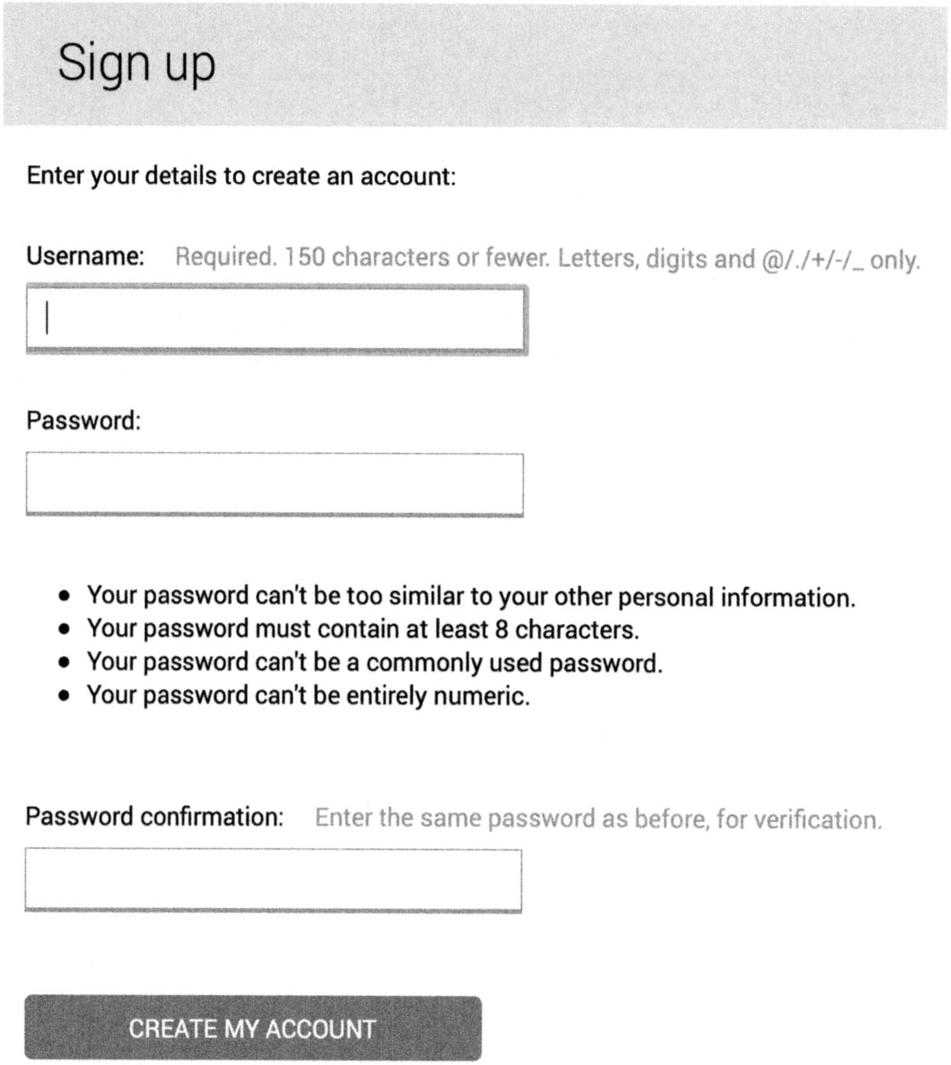

Sign up

Enter your details to create an account:

Username: Required. 150 characters or fewer. Letters, digits and @/./+/-/_ only.

Password:

- Your password can't be too similar to your other personal information.
- Your password must contain at least 8 characters.
- Your password can't be a commonly used password.
- Your password can't be entirely numeric.

Password confirmation: Enter the same password as before, for verification.

CREATE MY ACCOUNT

Figure 14.3: The student registration form

Note that the `student_course_list` URL specified in the `success_url` attribute of the `StudentRegistrationView` view doesn't exist yet. If you submit the form, Django won't find the URL to redirect you to after a successful registration. As mentioned, you will create this URL in the *Accessing the course contents* section.

Enrolling on courses

After users create an account, they should be able to enroll on courses. To store enrollments, you need to create a many-to-many relationship between the Course and User models.

Edit the models.py file of the courses application and add the following field to the Course model:

```
students = models.ManyToManyField(User,
                                    related_name='courses_joined',
                                    blank=True)
```

From the shell, execute the following command to create a migration for this change:

```
python manage.py makemigrations
```

You will see output similar to this:

```
Migrations for 'courses':
    courses/migrations/0004_course_students.py
      - Add field students to course
```

Then, execute the next command to apply pending migrations:

```
python manage.py migrate
```

You should see output that ends with the following line:

```
Applying courses.0004_course_students... OK
```

You can now associate students with the courses on which they are enrolled. Let's create the functionality for students to enroll on courses.

Create a new file inside the students application directory and name it forms.py. Add the following code to it:

```
from django import forms
from courses.models import Course

class CourseEnrollForm(forms.Form):
    course = forms.ModelChoiceField(
                queryset=Course.objects.all(),
                widget=forms.HiddenInput)
```

You are going to use this form for students to enroll on courses. The course field is for the course on which the user will be enrolled; therefore, it's a ModelChoiceField. You use a HiddenInput widget because you are not going to show this field to the user. You are going to use this form in the CourseDetailView view to display a button to enroll.

Edit the `views.py` file of the `students` application and add the following code:

```python
from django.views.generic.edit import FormView
from django.contrib.auth.mixins import LoginRequiredMixin
from .forms import CourseEnrollForm


class StudentEnrollCourseView(LoginRequiredMixin,
                             FormView):
    course = None
    form_class = CourseEnrollForm

    def form_valid(self, form):
        self.course = form.cleaned_data['course']
        self.course.students.add(self.request.user)
        return super().form_valid(form)

    def get_success_url(self):
        return reverse_lazy('student_course_detail',
                           args=[self.course.id])
```

This is the `StudentEnrollCourseView` view. It handles students enrolling on courses. The view inherits from the `LoginRequiredMixin` mixin so that only logged-in users can access the view. It also inherits from Django's `FormView` view, since you handle a form submission. You use the `CourseEnrollForm` form for the `form_class` attribute and also define a `course` attribute for storing the given `Course` object. When the form is valid, you add the current user to the students enrolled on the course.

The `get_success_url()` method returns the URL that the user will be redirected to if the form was successfully submitted. This method is equivalent to the `success_url` attribute. Then, you reverse the URL named `student_course_detail`.

Edit the `urls.py` file of the `students` application and add the following URL pattern to it:

```python
path('enroll-course/',
    views.StudentEnrollCourseView.as_view(),
    name='student_enroll_course'),
```

Let's add the enroll button form to the course overview page. Edit the `views.py` file of the `courses` application and modify `CourseDetailView` to make it look as follows:

```python
from students.forms import CourseEnrollForm


class CourseDetailView(DetailView):
    model = Course
```

```
        template_name = 'courses/course/detail.html'

    def get_context_data(self, **kwargs):
        context = super().get_context_data(**kwargs)
        context['enroll_form'] = CourseEnrollForm(
                            initial={'course':self.object})
        return context
```

You use the get_context_data() method to include the enrollment form in the context for rendering the templates. You initialize the hidden course field of the form with the current Course object so that it can be submitted directly.

Edit the courses/course/detail.html template and locate the following line:

```
{{ object.overview|linebreaks }}
```

Replace it with the following code:

```
{{ object.overview|linebreaks }}
{% if request.user.is_authenticated %}
  <form action="{% url "student_enroll_course" %}" method="post">
    {{ enroll_form }}
    {% csrf_token %}
    <input type="submit" value="Enroll now">
  </form>
{% else %}
  <a href="{% url "student_registration" %}" class="button">
    Register to enroll
  </a>
{% endif %}
```

This is the button for enrolling on courses. If the user is authenticated, you display the enrollment button, including the hidden form that points to the student_enroll_course URL. If the user is not authenticated, you display a link to register on the platform.

Make sure that the development server is running, open `http://127.0.0.1:8000/` in your browser, and click a course. If you are logged in, you should see an **ENROLL NOW** button placed below the course overview, as follows:

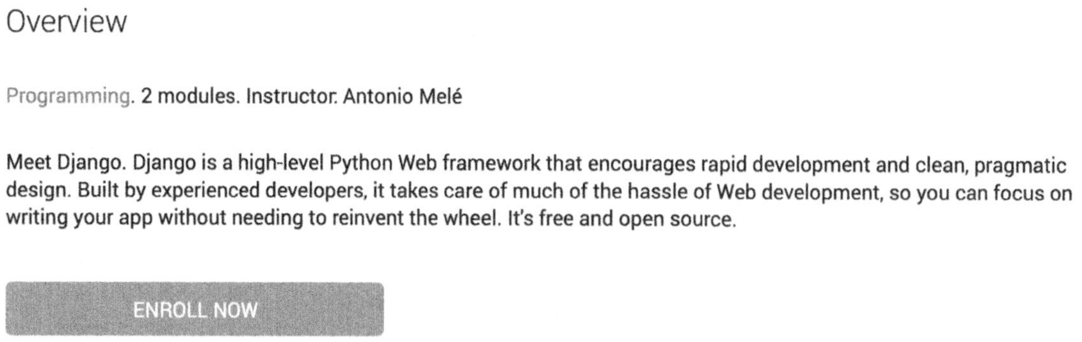

Overview

Programming. **2 modules. Instructor.** Antonio Melé

Meet Django. Django is a high-level Python Web framework that encourages rapid development and clean, pragmatic design. Built by experienced developers, it takes care of much of the hassle of Web development, so you can focus on writing your app without needing to reinvent the wheel. It's free and open source.

ENROLL NOW

Figure 14.4: The course overview page, including an ENROLL NOW button

If you are not logged in, you will see a **REGISTER TO ENROLL** button instead.

Accessing the course contents

You need a view for displaying the courses that students are enrolled on, and a view for accessing the actual course contents. Edit the `views.py` file of the `students` application and add the following code to it:

```python
from django.views.generic.list import ListView
from courses.models import Course

class StudentCourseListView(LoginRequiredMixin, ListView):
    model = Course
    template_name = 'students/course/list.html'

    def get_queryset(self):
        qs = super().get_queryset()
        return qs.filter(students__in=[self.request.user])
```

This is the view to see courses that students are enrolled on. It inherits from `LoginRequiredMixin` to make sure that only logged-in users can access the view. It also inherits from the generic `ListView` for displaying a list of `Course` objects. You override the `get_queryset()` method to retrieve only the courses that a student is enrolled on; you filter the QuerySet by the student's `ManyToManyField` field to do so.

Then, add the following code to the `views.py` file of the `students` application:

```python
from django.views.generic.detail import DetailView

class StudentCourseDetailView(DetailView):
```

```
    model = Course
    template_name = 'students/course/detail.html'

    def get_queryset(self):
        qs = super().get_queryset()
        return qs.filter(students__in=[self.request.user])

    def get_context_data(self, **kwargs):
        context = super().get_context_data(**kwargs)
        # get course object
        course = self.get_object()
        if 'module_id' in self.kwargs:
            # get current module
            context['module'] = course.modules.get(
                id=self.kwargs['module_id'])
        else:
            # get first module
            context['module'] = course.modules.all()[0]
        return context
```

This is the `StudentCourseDetailView` view. You override the `get_queryset()` method to limit the base QuerySet to courses on which the student is enrolled. You also override the `get_context_data()` method to set a course module in the context if the `module_id` URL parameter is given. Otherwise, you set the first module of the course. This way, students will be able to navigate through modules inside a course.

Edit the `urls.py` file of the `students` application and add the following URL patterns to it:

```
path('courses/',
     views.StudentCourseListView.as_view(),
     name='student_course_list'),
path('course/<pk>/',
     views.StudentCourseDetailView.as_view(),
     name='student_course_detail'),
path('course/<pk>/<module_id>/',
     views.StudentCourseDetailView.as_view(),
     name='student_course_detail_module'),
```

Create the following file structure inside the `templates/students/` directory of the `students` application:

```
course/
    detail.html
    list.html
```

Edit the `students/course/list.html` template and add the following code to it:

```
{% extends "base.html" %}

{% block title %}My courses{% endblock %}

{% block content %}
  <h1>My courses</h1>
  <div class="module">
    {% for course in object_list %}
      <div class="course-info">
        <h3>{{ course.title }}</h3>
        <p><a href="{% url "student_course_detail" course.id %}">
        Access contents</a></p>
      </div>
    {% empty %}
      <p>
        You are not enrolled in any courses yet.
        <a href="{% url "course_list" %}">Browse courses</a>
        to enroll on a course.
      </p>
    {% endfor %}
  </div>
{% endblock %}
```

This template displays the courses that the student is enrolled on. Remember that when a new student successfully registers with the platform, they will be redirected to the `student_course_list` URL. Let's also redirect students to this URL when they log in to the platform.

Edit the `settings.py` file of the educa project and add the following code to it:

```
from django.urls import reverse_lazy
LOGIN_REDIRECT_URL = reverse_lazy('student_course_list')
```

This is the setting used by the `auth` module to redirect the student after a successful login if no next parameter is present in the request. After a successful login, a student will be redirected to the `student_course_list` URL to view the courses that they are enrolled on.

Edit the `students/course/detail.html` template and add the following code to it:

```
{% extends "base.html" %}

{% block title %}
  {{ object.title }}
{% endblock %}
```

```
{% block content %}
  <h1>
    {{ module.title }}
  </h1>
  <div class="contents">
    <h3>Modules</h3>
    <ul id="modules">
      {% for m in object.modules.all %}
        <li data-id="{{ m.id }}" {% if m == module %}class="selected"{% endif
%}>
          <a href="{% url "student_course_detail_module" object.id m.id %}">
            <span>
              Module <span class="order">{{ m.order|add:1 }}</span>
            </span>
            <br>
            {{ m.title }}
          </a>
        </li>
      {% empty %}
        <li>No modules yet.</li>
      {% endfor %}
    </ul>
  </div>
  <div class="module">
    {% for content in module.contents.all %}
      {% with item=content.item %}
        <h2>{{ item.title }}</h2>
        {{ item.render }}
      {% endwith %}
    {% endfor %}
  </div>
{% endblock %}
```

Make sure no template tag is split across multiple lines. This is the template for enrolled students to access the contents of a course. First, you build an HTML list including all course modules and highlighting the current module. Then, you iterate over the current module contents and access each content item to display it using {{ item.render }}. You will add the render() method to the content models next. This method will take care of rendering the content properly.

You can now access http://127.0.0.1:8000/students/register/, register a new student account, and enroll on any course.

Rendering different types of content

To display the course contents, you need to render the different content types that you created: *text*, *image*, *video*, and *file*.

Edit the `models.py` file of the `courses` application and add the following `render()` method to the `ItemBase` model:

```python
from django.template.loader import render_to_string


class ItemBase(models.Model):
    # ...
    def render(self):
        return render_to_string(
            f'courses/content/{self._meta.model_name}.html',
            {'item': self})
```

This method uses the `render_to_string()` function for rendering a template and returning the rendered content as a string. Each kind of content is rendered using a template named after the content model. You use `self._meta.model_name` to generate the appropriate template name for each content model dynamically. The `render()` method provides a common interface for rendering diverse content.

Create the following file structure inside the `templates/courses/` directory of the `courses` application:

```
content/
    text.html
    file.html
    image.html
    video.html
```

Edit the `courses/content/text.html` template and write this code:

```
{{ item.content|linebreaks }}
```

This is the template to render text content. The `linebreaks` template filter replaces line breaks in plain text with HTML line breaks.

Edit the `courses/content/file.html` template and add the following:

```html
<p>
   <a href="{{ item.file.url }}" class="button">Download file</a>
</p>
```

This is the template to render files. You generate a link to download the file.

Edit the `courses/content/image.html` template and write:

```
<p>
  <img src="{{ item.file.url }}" alt="{{ item.title }}">
</p>
```

This is the template to render images.

You also have to create a template for rendering `Video` objects. You will use `django-embed-video` for embedding video content. `django-embed-video` is a third-party Django application that allows you to embed videos in your templates, from sources such as YouTube or Vimeo, by simply providing their public URL.

Install the package with the following command:

```
pip install django-embed-video==1.4.4
```

Edit the `settings.py` file of your project and add the application to the `INSTALLED_APPS` setting, as follows:

```
INSTALLED_APPS = [
    # ...
    'embed_video',
]
```

You can find the `django-embed-video` application's documentation at `https://django-embed-video.readthedocs.io/en/latest/`.

Edit the `courses/content/video.html` template and write the following code:

```
{% load embed_video_tags %}
{% video item.url "small" %}
```

This is the template to render videos.

Now, run the development server and access `http://127.0.0.1:8000/course/mine/` in your browser. Access the site with a user that belongs to the `Instructors` group, and add multiple contents to a course. To include video content, you can just copy any YouTube URL, such as `https://www.youtube.com/watch?v=bgV39DlmZ2U`, and include it in the `url` field of the form.

After adding contents to the course, open `http://127.0.0.1:8000/`, click the course, and click on the **ENROLL NOW** button. You should be enrolled on the course and redirected to the `student_course_detail` URL. *Figure 14.5* shows a sample course contents page:

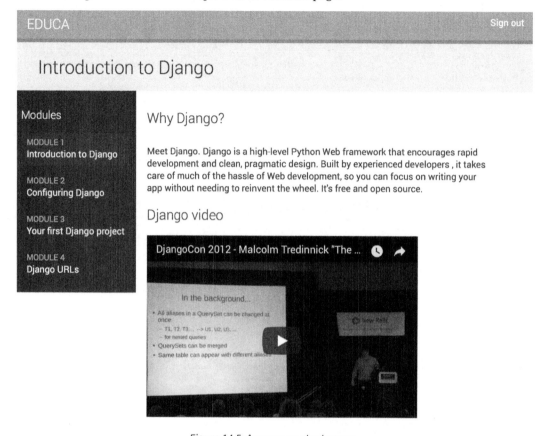

Figure 14.5: A course contents page

Great! You have created a common interface for rendering courses with different types of content.

Using the cache framework

Processing HTTP requests to your web application usually entails database access, data manipulation, and template rendering. It is much more expensive in terms of processing than just serving a static website. The overhead in some requests can be significant when your site starts getting more and more traffic. This is where caching becomes precious. By caching queries, calculation results, or rendered content in an HTTP request, you will avoid expensive operations in the following requests that need to return the same data. This translates into shorter response times and less processing on the server side.

Django includes a robust cache system that allows you to cache data with different levels of granularity. You can cache a single query, the output of a specific view, parts of rendered template content, or your entire site. Items are stored in the cache system for a default time, but you can specify the timeout when you cache data.

This is how you will usually use the cache framework when your application processes an HTTP request:

1. Try to find the requested data in the cache.
2. If found, return the cached data.
3. If not found, perform the following steps:

    1. Perform the database query or processing required to generate the data.
    2. Save the generated data in the cache.
    3. Return the data.

You can read detailed information about Django's cache system at `https://docs.djangoproject.com/en/4.1/topics/cache/`.

Available cache backends

Django comes with the following cache backends:

- `backends.memcached.PyMemcacheCache` or `backends.memcached.PyLibMCCache`: Memcached backends. Memcached is a fast and efficient memory-based cache server. The backend to use depends on the Memcached Python bindings you choose.
- `backends.redis.RedisCache`: A Redis cache backend. This backend has been added in Django 4.0.
- `backends.db.DatabaseCache`: Use the database as a cache system.
- `backends.filebased.FileBasedCache`: Use the file storage system. This serializes and stores each cache value as a separate file.
- `backends.locmem.LocMemCache`: A local memory cache backend. This is the default cache backend.
- `backends.dummy.DummyCache`: A dummy cache backend intended only for development. It implements the cache interface without actually caching anything. This cache is per-process and thread-safe.

 For optimal performance, use a memory-based cache backend such as the Memcached or Redis backends.

Installing Memcached

Memcached is a popular high-performance, memory-based cache server. We are going to use Memcached and the `PyMemcacheCache` Memcached backend.

Installing the Memcached Docker image

Run the following command from the shell to pull the Memcached Docker image:

```
docker pull memcached
```

This will download the Memcached Docker image to your local machine. If you don't want to use Docker, you can also download Memcached from `https://memcached.org/downloads`.

Run the Memcached Docker container with the following command:

```
docker run -it --rm --name memcached -p 11211:11211 memcached -m 64
```

Memcached runs on port 11211 by default. The -p option is used to publish the 11211 port to the same host interface port. The -m option is used to limit the memory for the container to 64 MB. Memcached runs in memory, and it is allotted a specified amount of RAM. When the allotted RAM is full, Memcached starts removing the oldest data to store new data. If you want to run the command in detached mode (in the background of your terminal) you can use the -d option.

You can find more information about Memcached at `https://memcached.org`.

Installing the Memcached Python binding

After installing Memcached, you have to install a Memcached Python binding. We will install pymemcache, which is a fast, pure-Python Memcached client. Run the following command in the shell:

```
pip install pymemcache==3.5.2
```

You can read more information about the pymemcache library at `https://github.com/pinterest/pymemcache`.

Django cache settings

Django provides the following cache settings:

- CACHES: A dictionary containing all available caches for the project.
- CACHE_MIDDLEWARE_ALIAS: The cache alias to use for storage.
- CACHE_MIDDLEWARE_KEY_PREFIX: The prefix to use for cache keys. Set a prefix to avoid key collisions if you share the same cache between several sites.
- CACHE_MIDDLEWARE_SECONDS: The default number of seconds to cache pages.

The caching system for the project can be configured using the CACHES setting. This setting allows you to specify the configuration for multiple caches. Each cache included in the CACHES dictionary can specify the following data:

- BACKEND: The cache backend to use.
- KEY_FUNCTION: A string containing a dotted path to a callable that takes a prefix, version, and key as arguments and returns a final cache key.
- KEY_PREFIX: A string prefix for all cache keys, to avoid collisions.

- LOCATION: The location of the cache. Depending on the cache backend, this might be a directory, a host and port, or a name for the in-memory backend.
- OPTIONS: Any additional parameters to be passed to the cache backend.
- TIMEOUT: The default timeout, in seconds, for storing the cache keys. It is 300 seconds by default, which is 5 minutes. If set to None, cache keys will not expire.
- VERSION: The default version number for the cache keys. Useful for cache versioning.

Adding Memcached to your project

Let's configure the cache for your project. Edit the settings.py file of the educa project and add the following code to it:

```
CACHES = {
    'default': {
        'BACKEND': 'django.core.cache.backends.memcached.PyMemcacheCache',
        'LOCATION': '127.0.0.1:11211',
    }
}
```

You are using the PyMemcacheCache backend. You specify its location using the address:port notation. If you have multiple Memcached instances, you can use a list for LOCATION.

You have set up Memcached for your project. Let's start caching data!

Cache levels

Django provides the following levels of caching, listed here by ascending order of granularity:

- **Low-level cache API:** Provides the highest granularity. Allows you to cache specific queries or calculations.
- **Template cache:** Allows you to cache template fragments.
- **Per-view cache:** Provides caching for individual views.
- **Per-site cache:** The highest-level cache. It caches your entire site.

 Think about your cache strategy before implementing caching. Focus first on expensive queries or calculations that are not calculated on a per-user basis.

Let's start by learning how to use the low-level cache API in your Python code.

Using the low-level cache API

The low-level cache API allows you to store objects in the cache with any granularity. It is located at django.core.cache. You can import it like this:

```
from django.core.cache import cache
```

This uses the default cache. It's equivalent to `caches['default']`. Accessing a specific cache is also possible via its alias:

```
from django.core.cache import caches
my_cache = caches['alias']
```

Let's take a look at how the cache API works. Open the Django shell with the following command:

```
python manage.py shell
```

Execute the following code:

```
>>> from django.core.cache import cache
>>> cache.set('musician', 'Django Reinhardt', 20)
```

You access the default cache backend and use `set(key, value, timeout)` to store a key named `'musician'` with a value that is the string `'Django Reinhardt'` for 20 seconds. If you don't specify a timeout, Django uses the default timeout specified for the cache backend in the `CACHES` setting. Now, execute the following code:

```
>>> cache.get('musician')
'Django Reinhardt'
```

You retrieve the key from the cache. Wait for 20 seconds and execute the same code:

```
>>> cache.get('musician')
```

No value is returned this time. The `'musician'` cache key has expired and the `get()` method returns `None` because the key is not in the cache anymore.

 Always avoid storing a `None` value in a cache key because you won't be able to distinguish between the actual value and a cache miss.

Let's cache a QuerySet with the following code:

```
>>> from courses.models import Subject
>>> subjects = Subject.objects.all()
>>> cache.set('my_subjects', subjects)
```

You perform a QuerySet on the `Subject` model and store the returned objects in the `'my_subjects'` key. Let's retrieve the cached data:

```
>>> cache.get('my_subjects')
<QuerySet [<Subject: Mathematics>, <Subject: Music>, <Subject: Physics>,
<Subject: Programming>]>
```

You are going to cache some queries in your views. Edit the `views.py` file of the `courses` application and add the following import:

```
from django.core.cache import cache
```

In the `get()` method of the `CourseListView`, find the following lines:

```
subjects = Subject.objects.annotate(
                total_courses=Count('courses'))
```

Replace the lines with the following ones:

```
subjects = cache.get('all_subjects')
if not subjects:
    subjects = Subject.objects.annotate(
                   total_courses=Count('courses'))
    cache.set('all_subjects', subjects)
```

In this code, you try to get the `all_students` key from the cache using `cache.get()`. This returns `None` if the given key is not found. If no key is found (not cached yet or cached but timed out), you perform the query to retrieve all `Subject` objects and their number of courses, and you cache the result using `cache.set()`.

Checking cache requests with Django Debug Toolbar

Let's add Django Debug Toolbar to the project to check the cache queries. You learned how to use Django Debug Toolbar in *Chapter 7, Tracking User Actions*.

First install Django Debug Toolbar with the following command:

```
pip install django-debug-toolbar==3.6.0
```

Edit the `settings.py` file of your project and add `debug_toolbar` to the `INSTALLED_APPS` setting as follows. The new line is highlighted in bold:

```
INSTALLED_APPS = [
    # ...
    'debug_toolbar',
]
```

In the same file, add the following line highlighted in bold to the `MIDDLEWARE` setting:

```
MIDDLEWARE = [
    'debug_toolbar.middleware.DebugToolbarMiddleware',
    'django.middleware.security.SecurityMiddleware',
    'django.contrib.sessions.middleware.SessionMiddleware',
    'django.middleware.common.CommonMiddleware',
    'django.middleware.csrf.CsrfViewMiddleware',
```

```
    'django.contrib.auth.middleware.AuthenticationMiddleware',
    'django.contrib.messages.middleware.MessageMiddleware',
    'django.middleware.clickjacking.XFrameOptionsMiddleware',
]
```

Remember that `DebugToolbarMiddleware` has to be placed before any other middleware, except for middleware that encodes the response's content, such as `GZipMiddleware`, which, if present, should come first.

Add the following lines at the end of the `settings.py` file:

```
INTERNAL_IPS = [
    '127.0.0.1',
]
```

Django Debug Toolbar will only display if your IP address matches an entry in the `INTERNAL_IPS` setting.

Edit the main `urls.py` file of the project and add the following URL pattern to `urlpatterns`:

```
path('__debug__/', include('debug_toolbar.urls')),]
```

Run the development server and open `http://127.0.0.1:8000/` in your browser.

You should now see Django Debug Toolbar on the right side of the page. Click on **Cache** in the sidebar menu. You will see the following panel:

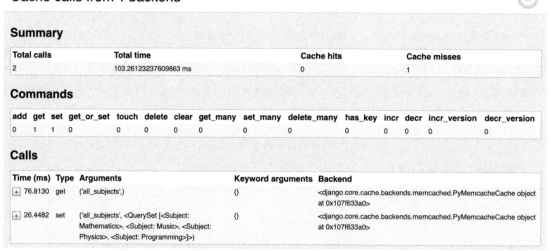

Figure 14.6: The Cache panel of Django Debug Toolbar including cache requests for CourseListView
on a cache miss

Under **Total calls** you should see 2. The first time the `CourseListView` view is executed there are two cache requests. Under **Commands** you will see that the get command has been executed once, and that the set command has been executed once as well. The get command corresponds to the call that retrieves the `all_subjects` cache key. This is the first call displayed under **Calls**. The first time the view is executed a cache miss occurs because no data is cached yet. That's why there is 1 under **Cache misses**. Then, the set command is used to store the results of the subjects QuerySet in the cache using the `all_subjects` cache key. This is the second call displayed under **Calls**.

In the **SQL** menu item of Django Debug Toolbar, you will see the total number of SQL queries executed in this request. This includes the query to retrieve all subjects that are then stored in the cache:

Figure 14.7: SQL queries executed for CourseListView on a cache miss

Reload the page in the browser and click on **Cache** in the sidebar menu:

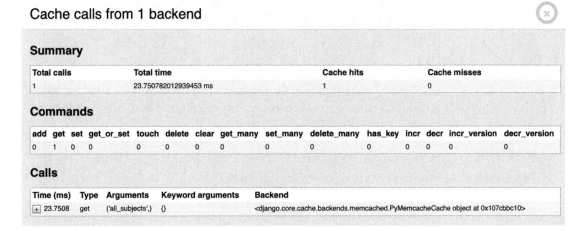

Figure 14.8: The Cache panel of Django Debug Toolbar, including cache requests for CourseListView view on a cache hit

Now, there is only a single cache request. Under **Total calls** you should see 1. And under **Commands** you can see that the cache request corresponds to a get command. In this case there is a cache hit (see **Cache hits**) instead of a cache miss because the data has been found in the cache. Under **Calls** you can see the get request to retrieve the `all_subjects` cache key.

Check the **SQL** menu item of the debug toolbar. You should see that there is one less SQL query in this request. You are saving one SQL query because the view finds the data in the cache and doesn't need to retrieve it from the database:

Figure 14.9: SQL queries executed for CourseListView on a cache hit

In this example, for a single request, it takes more time to retrieve the item from the cache than the time saved on the additional SQL query. However, when you have many users accessing your site, you will find significant time reductions by retrieving the data from the cache instead of hitting the database, and you will be able to serve the site to more concurrent users.

Successive requests to the same URL will retrieve the data from the cache. Since we didn't specify a timeout when caching data with `cache.set('all_subjects', subjects)` in the `CourseListView` view, the default timeout will be used (300 seconds by default, which is 5 minutes). When the timeout is reached, the next request to the URL will generate a cache miss, the QuerySet will be executed, and data will be cached for another 5 minutes. You can define a different default timeout in the `TIMEOUT` element of the `CACHES` setting.

Caching based on dynamic data

Often, you will want to cache something that is based on dynamic data. In these cases, you have to build dynamic keys that contain all the information required to uniquely identify the cached data.

Edit the `views.py` file of the `courses` application and modify the `CourseListView` view to make it look like this:

```
class CourseListView(TemplateResponseMixin, View):
    model = Course
    template_name = 'courses/course/list.html'

    def get(self, request, subject=None):
        subjects = cache.get('all_subjects')
        if not subjects:
            subjects = Subject.objects.annotate(
                        total_courses=Count('courses'))
            cache.set('all_subjects', subjects)
        all_courses = Course.objects.annotate(
                        total_modules=Count('modules'))
        if subject:
            subject = get_object_or_404(Subject, slug=subject)
```

```
                    key = f'subject_{subject.id}_courses'
                    courses = cache.get(key)
                    if not courses:
                            courses = all_courses.filter(subject=subject)
                            cache.set(key, courses)
            else:
                    courses = cache.get('all_courses')
                    if not courses:
                            courses = all_courses
                            cache.set('all_courses', courses)
        return self.render_to_response({'subjects': subjects,
                                        'subject': subject,
                                        'courses': courses})
```

In this case, you also cache both all courses and courses filtered by subject. You use the all_courses cache key for storing all courses if no subject is given. If there is a subject, you build the key dynamically with f'subject_{subject.id}_courses'.

It's important to note that you can't use a cached QuerySet to build other QuerySets, since what you cached are actually the results of the QuerySet. So you can't do the following:

```
courses = cache.get('all_courses')
courses.filter(subject=subject)
```

Instead, you have to create the base QuerySet Course.objects.annotate(total_modules=Count('modules')), which is not going to be executed until it is forced, and use it to further restrict the QuerySet with all_courses.filter(subject=subject) in case the data was not found in the cache.

Caching template fragments

Caching template fragments is a higher-level approach. You need to load the cache template tags in your template using {% load cache %}. Then, you will be able to use the {% cache %} template tag to cache specific template fragments. You will usually use the template tag as follows:

```
{% cache 300 fragment_name %}
    ...
{% endcache %}
```

The {% cache %} template tag has two required arguments: the timeout in seconds and a name for the fragment. If you need to cache content depending on dynamic data, you can do so by passing additional arguments to the {% cache %} template tag to uniquely identify the fragment.

Edit the /students/course/detail.html of the students application. Add the following code at the top of it, just after the {% extends %} tag:

```
{% load cache %}
```

Then, find the following lines:

```
{% for content in module.contents.all %}
  {% with item=content.item %}
    <h2>{{ item.title }}</h2>
    {{ item.render }}
  {% endwith %}
{% endfor %}
```

Replace them with the following ones:

```
{% cache 600 module_contents module %}
  {% for content in module.contents.all %}
    {% with item=content.item %}
      <h2>{{ item.title }}</h2>
      {{ item.render }}
    {% endwith %}
  {% endfor %}
{% endcache %}
```

You cache this template fragment using the name `module_contents` and pass the current `Module` object to it. Thus, you uniquely identify the fragment. This is important to avoid caching a module's contents and serving the wrong content when a different module is requested.

If the `USE_I18N` setting is set to `True`, the per-site middleware cache will respect the active language. If you use the `{% cache %}` template tag, you have to use one of the translation-specific variables available in templates to achieve the same result, such as `{% cache 600 name request.LANGUAGE_CODE %}`.

Caching views

You can cache the output of individual views using the `cache_page` decorator located at `django.views.decorators.cache`. The decorator requires a `timeout` argument (in seconds).

Let's use it in your views. Edit the `urls.py` file of the `students` application and add the following import:

```
from django.views.decorators.cache import cache_page
```

Then, apply the `cache_page` decorator to the `student_course_detail` and `student_course_detail_module` URL patterns, as follows:

```
path('course/<pk>/',
    cache_page(60 * 15)(views.StudentCourseDetailView.as_view()),
        name='student_course_detail'),
path('course/<pk>/<module_id>/',
    cache_page(60 * 15)(views.StudentCourseDetailView.as_view()),
        name='student_course_detail_module'),
```

Now, the complete content returned by the StudentCourseDetailView is cached for 15 minutes.

 The per-view cache uses the URL to build the cache key. Multiple URLs pointing to the same view will be cached separately.

Using the per-site cache

This is the highest-level cache. It allows you to cache your entire site. To allow the per-site cache, edit the settings.py file of your project and add the UpdateCacheMiddleware and FetchFromCacheMiddleware classes to the MIDDLEWARE setting, as follows:

```
MIDDLEWARE = [
    'debug_toolbar.middleware.DebugToolbarMiddleware',
    'django.middleware.security.SecurityMiddleware',
    'django.contrib.sessions.middleware.SessionMiddleware',
    'django.middleware.cache.UpdateCacheMiddleware',
    'django.middleware.common.CommonMiddleware',
    'django.middleware.cache.FetchFromCacheMiddleware',
    'django.middleware.csrf.CsrfViewMiddleware',
    'django.contrib.auth.middleware.AuthenticationMiddleware',
    'django.contrib.messages.middleware.MessageMiddleware',
    'django.middleware.clickjacking.XFrameOptionsMiddleware',
]
```

Remember that middleware is executed in the given order during the request phase, and in reverse order during the response phase. UpdateCacheMiddleware is placed before CommonMiddleware because it runs during response time, when middleware is executed in reverse order. FetchFromCacheMiddleware is placed after CommonMiddleware intentionally because it needs to access request data set by the latter.

Next, add the following settings to the settings.py file:

```
CACHE_MIDDLEWARE_ALIAS = 'default'
CACHE_MIDDLEWARE_SECONDS = 60 * 15  # 15 minutes
CACHE_MIDDLEWARE_KEY_PREFIX = 'educa'
```

In these settings, you use the default cache for your cache middleware and set the global cache timeout to 15 minutes. You also specify a prefix for all cache keys to avoid collisions in case you use the same Memcached backend for multiple projects. Your site will now cache and return cached content for all GET requests.

You can access the different pages and check the cache requests using Django Debug Toolbar. The per-site cache is not viable for many sites because it affects all views, even the ones that you might not want to cache, like management views where you want data to be returned from the database to reflect the latest changes.

In this project, the best approach is to cache the templates or views that are used to display course contents to students, while keeping the content management views for instructors without any cache.

Let's deactivate the per-site cache. Edit the `settings.py` file of your project and comment out the `UpdateCacheMiddleware` and `FetchFromCacheMiddleware` classes in the `MIDDLEWARE` setting, as follows:

```
MIDDLEWARE = [
    'debug_toolbar.middleware.DebugToolbarMiddleware',
    'django.middleware.security.SecurityMiddleware',
    'django.contrib.sessions.middleware.SessionMiddleware',
    # 'django.middleware.cache.UpdateCacheMiddleware',
    'django.middleware.common.CommonMiddleware',
    # 'django.middleware.cache.FetchFromCacheMiddleware',
    'django.middleware.csrf.CsrfViewMiddleware',
    'django.contrib.auth.middleware.AuthenticationMiddleware',
    'django.contrib.messages.middleware.MessageMiddleware',
    'django.middleware.clickjacking.XFrameOptionsMiddleware',
]
```

You have seen an overview of the different methods provided by Django to cache data. You should always define your cache strategy wisely, taking into account expensive QuerySets or calculations, data that won't change frequently, and data that will be accessed concurrently by many users.

Using the Redis cache backend

Django 4.0 introduced a Redis cache backend. Let's change the settings to use Redis instead of Memcached as the cache backend for the project. Remember that you already used Redis in *Chapter 7, Tracking User Actions*, and in *Chapter 10, Extending Your Shop*.

Install `redis-py` in your environment using the following command:

```
pip install redis==4.3.4
```

Then, edit the `settings.py` file of the educa project and modify the `CACHES` setting, as follows:

```
CACHES = {
    'default': {
        'BACKEND': 'django.core.cache.backends.redis.RedisCache',
        'LOCATION': 'redis://127.0.0.1:6379',
    }
}
```

The project will now use the RedisCache cache backend. The location is defined in the format redis://
[host]:[port]. You use 127.0.0.1 to point to the local host and 6379, which is the default port for Redis.

Initialize the Redis Docker container using the following command:

```
docker run -it --rm --name redis -p 6379:6379 redis
```

If you want to run the command in the background (in detached mode) you can use the -d option.

Run the development server and open http://127.0.0.1:8000/ in your browser. Check the cache
requests in the **Cache** panel of Django Debug Toolbar. You are now using Redis as your project's cache
backend instead of Memcached.

Monitoring Redis with Django Redisboard

You can monitor your Redis server using Django Redisboard. Django Redisboard adds Redis statistics
to the Django administration site. You can find more information about Django Redisboard at https://
github.com/ionelmc/django-redisboard.

Install django-redisboard in your environment using the following command:

```
pip install django-redisboard==8.3.0
```

Install the attrs Python library used by django-redisboard in your environment with the following
command:

```
pip install attrs
```

Edit the settings.py file of your project and add the application to the INSTALLED_APPS setting, as
follows:

```
INSTALLED_APPS = [
    # ...
    'redisboard',
]
```

Run the following command from your project's directory to run the Django Redisboard migrations:

```
python manage.py migrate redisboard
```

Run the development server and open `http://127.0.0.1:8000/admin/redisboard/redisserver/add/` in your browser to add a Redis server to monitor. Under the **Label**, enter `redis`, and under **URL**, enter `redis://localhost:6379/0`, as in *Figure 14.10*:

Add Redis Server

Label:	redis

URL:	redis://localhost:6379/0

IANA-compliant URL. Examples:

```
redis://[[username]:[password]]@localhost:6379/0
rediss://[[username]:[password]]@localhost:6379/0
unix://[[username]:[password]]@/path/to/socket.sock?db=0
```

Password:	

You can also specify the password here (the field is masked).

Figure 14.10: The form to add a Redis server for Django Redisboard in the administration site

We will monitor the Redis instance running on our local host, which runs on port 6379 and uses the Redis database numbered 0. Click on **SAVE**. The information will be saved to the database, and you will be able to see the Redis configuration and metrics on the Django administration site:

Select Redis Server to change

Action: [_____ ▾] [Go] 0 of 1 selected

	NAME	STATUS	MEMORY	CLIENTS	DETAILS		CPU UTILIZATION		SLOWLOG	TOOLS
☐	redis	UP	1.29M (peak: 1.34M)	7	redis version	7.0.4	cpu utilization	0.002%%	**Total: 3 items**	Inspect Details
					redis mode	standalone	used cpu sys	2318.116634	**13.7ms** INFO	
					os	Linux 5.10.104-linuxkit aarch64	used cpu sys children	0.123416	**13.6ms** INFO	
					multiplexing api	epoll	used cpu user	1732.266923	**11.2ms** ZUNIONSTORE tmp_34 2 product:3:purchased_with product:4:purchased_with	
					atomicvar api	c11-builtin	used cpu user children	0.060922		
					gcc version	10.2.1				
					used memory human	1.29M				
					used memory rss human	8.14M				
					used memory peak human	1.34M				
					total system memory human	7.76G				
					used memory lua human	31.00K				
					used memory vm total human	63.00K				
					used memory scripts human	184B				
					maxmemory human	0B				
					maxmemory policy	noeviction				
					expired keys	32				

Figure 14.11: The Redis monitoring of Django Redisboard on the administration site

Congratulations! You have successfully implemented caching for your project.

Additional resources

The following resources provide additional information related to the topics covered in this chapter:

- Source code for this chapter – `https://github.com/PacktPublishing/Django-4-by-example/tree/main/Chapter14`
- `django-embed-video` documentation – `https://django-embed-video.readthedocs.io/en/latest/`
- Django's cache framework documentation – `https://docs.djangoproject.com/en/4.1/topics/cache/`
- Memcached downloads – `https://memcached.org/downloads`
- Memcached official website – `https://memcached.org`
- Pymemcache's source code – `https://github.com/pinterest/pymemcache`
- Django Redisboard's source code – `https://github.com/ionelmc/django-redisboard`

Summary

In this chapter, you implemented the public views for the course catalog. You built a system for students to register and enroll on courses. You also created the functionality to render different types of content for the course modules. Finally, you learned how to use the Django cache framework and you used the Memcached and Redis cache backends for your project.

In the next chapter, you will build a RESTful API for your project using Django REST framework and consume it using the Python Requests library.

15

Building an API

In the previous chapter, you built a system for student registration and enrollment on courses. You created views to display course contents and learned how to use Django's cache framework.

In this chapter, you will create a RESTful API for your e-learning platform. An API allows you to build a common core that can be used on multiple platforms like websites, mobile applications, plugins, and so on. For example, you can create an API to be consumed by a mobile application for your e-learning platform. If you provide an API to third parties, they will be able to consume information and operate with your application programmatically. An API allows developers to automate actions on your platform and integrate your service with other applications or online services. You will build a fully featured API for your e-learning platform.

In this chapter, you will:

- Install Django REST framework
- Create serializers for your models
- Build a RESTful API
- Create nested serializers
- Build custom API views
- Handle API authentication
- Add permissions to API views
- Create a custom permission
- Implement ViewSets and routers
- Use the Requests library to consume the API

Let's start with the setup of your API.

The source code for this chapter can be found at https://github.com/PacktPublishing/Django-4-by-example/tree/main/Chapter15.

All Python modules used in this chapter are included in the requirements.txt file in the source code that comes along with this chapter. You can follow the instructions to install each Python module below or you can install all requirements at once with the command pip install -r requirements.txt.

Building a RESTful API

When building an API, there are several ways you can structure its endpoints and actions, but following REST principles is encouraged. The **REST** architecture comes from **Representational State Transfer**. RESTful APIs are resource-based; your models represent resources and HTTP methods such as GET, POST, PUT, or DELETE are used to retrieve, create, update, or delete objects. HTTP response codes are also used in this context. Different HTTP response codes are returned to indicate the result of the HTTP request, for example, 2XX response codes for success, 4XX for errors, and so on.

The most common formats to exchange data in RESTful APIs are JSON and XML. You will build a RESTful API with JSON serialization for your project. Your API will provide the following functionality:

- Retrieve subjects
- Retrieve available courses
- Retrieve course contents
- Enroll on a course

You can build an API from scratch with Django by creating custom views. However, there are several third-party modules that simplify creating an API for your project; the most popular among them is Django REST framework.

Installing Django REST framework

Django REST framework allows you to easily build RESTful APIs for your project. You can find all the information about REST framework at https://www.django-rest-framework.org/.

Open the shell and install the framework with the following command:

```
pip install djangorestframework==3.13.1
```

Edit the settings.py file of the educa project and add rest_framework to the INSTALLED_APPS setting to activate the application, as follows:

```
INSTALLED_APPS = [
    # ...
    'rest_framework',
]
```

Then, add the following code to the settings.py file:

```
REST_FRAMEWORK = {
    'DEFAULT_PERMISSION_CLASSES': [
        'rest_framework.permissions.DjangoModelPermissionsOrAnonReadOnly'
    ]
}
```

You can provide a specific configuration for your API using the REST_FRAMEWORK setting. REST framework offers a wide range of settings to configure default behaviors. The DEFAULT_PERMISSION_CLASSES setting specifies the default permissions to read, create, update, or delete objects. You set DjangoModelPermissionsOrAnonReadOnly as the only default permission class. This class relies on Django's permissions system to allow users to create, update, or delete objects while providing read-only access for anonymous users. You will learn more about permissions later, in the *Adding permissions to views* section.

For a complete list of available settings for REST framework, you can visit https://www.django-rest-framework.org/api-guide/settings/.

Defining serializers

After setting up REST framework, you need to specify how your data will be serialized. Output data has to be serialized in a specific format, and input data will be deserialized for processing. The framework provides the following classes to build serializers for single objects:

- Serializer: Provides serialization for normal Python class instances
- ModelSerializer: Provides serialization for model instances
- HyperlinkedModelSerializer: The same as ModelSerializer, but it represents object relationships with links rather than primary keys

Let's build your first serializer. Create the following file structure inside the courses application directory:

```
api/
    __init__.py
    serializers.py
```

You will build all the API functionality inside the api directory to keep everything well organized. Edit the serializers.py file and add the following code:

```python
from rest_framework import serializers
from courses.models import Subject


class SubjectSerializer(serializers.ModelSerializer):
    class Meta:
        model = Subject
        fields = ['id', 'title', 'slug']
```

This is the serializer for the Subject model. Serializers are defined in a similar fashion to Django's Form and ModelForm classes. The Meta class allows you to specify the model to serialize and the fields to be included for serialization. All model fields will be included if you don't set a fields attribute.

Let's try the serializer. Open the command line and start the Django shell with the following command:

```
python manage.py shell
```

Run the following code:

```
>>> from courses.models import Subject
>>> from courses.api.serializers import SubjectSerializer
>>> subject = Subject.objects.latest('id')
>>> serializer = SubjectSerializer(subject)
>>> serializer.data
{'id': 4, 'title': 'Programming', 'slug': 'programming'}
```

In this example, you get a `Subject` object, create an instance of `SubjectSerializer`, and access the serialized data. You can see that the model data is translated into Python native data types.

Understanding parsers and renderers

The serialized data has to be rendered in a specific format before you return it in an HTTP response. Likewise, when you get an HTTP request, you have to parse the incoming data and deserialize it before you can operate with it. REST framework includes renderers and parsers to handle that.

Let's see how to parse incoming data. Execute the following code in the Python shell:

```
>>> from io import BytesIO
>>> from rest_framework.parsers import JSONParser
>>> data = b'{"id":4,"title":"Programming","slug":"programming"}'
>>> JSONParser().parse(BytesIO(data))
{'id': 4, 'title': 'Programming', 'slug': 'programming'}
```

Given a JSON string input, you can use the `JSONParser` class provided by REST framework to convert it to a Python object.

REST framework also includes `Renderer` classes that allow you to format API responses. The framework determines which renderer to use through content negotiation by inspecting the request's `Accept` header to determine the expected content type for the response. Optionally, the renderer is determined by the format suffix of the URL. For example, the URL `http://127.0.0.1:8000/api/data.json` might be an endpoint that triggers the `JSONRenderer` in order to return a JSON response.

Go back to the shell and execute the following code to render the `serializer` object from the previous serializer example:

```
>>> from rest_framework.renderers import JSONRenderer
>>> JSONRenderer().render(serializer.data)
```

You will see the following output:

```
b'{"id":4,"title":"Programming","slug":"programming"}'
```

You use the `JSONRenderer` to render the serialized data into JSON. By default, REST framework uses two different renderers: `JSONRenderer` and `BrowsableAPIRenderer`. The latter provides a web interface to easily browse your API. You can change the default renderer classes with the `DEFAULT_RENDERER_CLASSES` option of the `REST_FRAMEWORK` setting.

You can find more information about renderers and parsers at https://www.django-rest-framework. org/api-guide/renderers/ and https://www.django-rest-framework.org/api-guide/parsers/, respectively.

Next, you are going to learn how to build API views and use serializers in views.

Building list and detail views

REST framework comes with a set of generic views and mixins that you can use to build your API views. They provide the functionality to retrieve, create, update, or delete model objects. You can see all the generic mixins and views provided by REST framework at https://www.django-rest-framework. org/api-guide/generic-views/.

Let's create list and detail views to retrieve Subject objects. Create a new file inside the courses/api/ directory and name it views.py. Add the following code to it:

```
from rest_framework import generics
from courses.models import Subject
from courses.api.serializers import SubjectSerializer


class SubjectListView(generics.ListAPIView):
    queryset = Subject.objects.all()
    serializer_class = SubjectSerializer


class SubjectDetailView(generics.RetrieveAPIView):
    queryset = Subject.objects.all()
    serializer_class = SubjectSerializer
```

In this code, you are using the generic ListAPIView and RetrieveAPIView views of REST framework. You include a pk URL parameter for the detail view to retrieve the object for the given primary key. Both views have the following attributes:

* queryset: The base QuerySet to use to retrieve objects
* serializer_class: The class to serialize objects

Let's add URL patterns for your views. Create a new file inside the courses/api/ directory, name it urls.py, and make it look as follows:

```
from django.urls import path
from . import views


app_name = 'courses'


urlpatterns = [
    path('subjects/',
        views.SubjectListView.as_view(),
```

```
                    name='subject_list'),
        path('subjects/<pk>/',
            views.SubjectDetailView.as_view(),
            name='subject_detail'),
]
```

Edit the main `urls.py` file of the educa project and include the API patterns, as follows:

```
urlpatterns = [
    # ...
    path('api/', include('courses.api.urls', namespace='api')),
]
```

Our initial API endpoints are now ready to be used.

Consuming the API

You use the api namespace for your API URLs. Ensure that your server is running with the following command:

```
python manage.py runserver
```

We are going to use `curl` to consume the API. `curl` is a command-line tool that allows you to transfer data to and from a server. If you are using Linux, macOS, or Windows 10/11, `curl` is very likely included in your system. However, you can download `curl` from https://curl.se/download.html.

Open the shell and retrieve the URL http://127.0.0.1:8000/api/subjects/ with `curl`, as follows:

```
curl http://127.0.0.1:8000/api/subjects/
```

You will get a response similar to the following one:

```
[
    {
        "id":1,
        "title":"Mathematics",
        "slug":"mathematics"
    },
    {
        "id":2,
        "title":"Music",
        "slug":"music"
    },
    {
        "id":3,
        "title":"Physics",
        "slug":"physics"
    },
```

```
    {
        "id":4,
        "title":"Programming",
        "slug":"programming"
    }
]
```

To obtain a more readable, well-indented JSON response, you can use `curl` with the `json_pp` utility, as follows:

```
curl http://127.0.0.1:8000/api/subjects/ | json_pp
```

The HTTP response contains a list of `Subject` objects in JSON format.

Instead of `curl`, you can also use any other tool to send custom HTTP requests, including a browser extension such as Postman, which you can get at `https://www.getpostman.com/`.

Open `http://127.0.0.1:8000/api/subjects/` in your browser. You will see REST framework's browsable API, as follows:

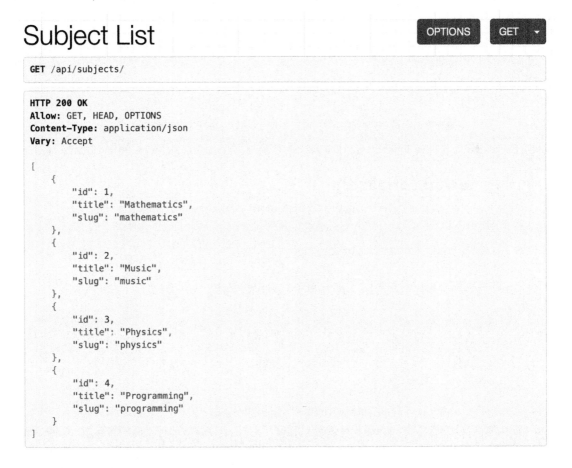

Figure 15.1: The subject list page in the REST framework browsable API

This HTML interface is provided by the `BrowsableAPIRenderer` renderer. It displays the result headers and content, and it allows you to perform requests. You can also access the API detail view for a `Subject` object by including its ID in the URL.

Open `http://127.0.0.1:8000/api/subjects/1/` in your browser. You will see a single `Subject` object rendered in JSON format.

Subject Detail   OPTIONS   GET ▾

```
GET /api/subjects/1/
```

```
HTTP 200 OK
Allow: GET, HEAD, OPTIONS
Content-Type: application/json
Vary: Accept

{
    "id": 1,
    "title": "Mathematics",
    "slug": "mathematics"
}
```

Figure 15.2: The subject detail page in the REST framework browsable API

This is the response for the `SubjectDetailView`. Next, we are going to dig deeper into model serializers.

Creating nested serializers

We are going to create a serializer for the `Course` model. Edit the `api/serializers.py` file of the courses application and add the following code highlighted in bold:

```python
from courses.models import Subject, Course

class CourseSerializer(serializers.ModelSerializer):
    class Meta:
        model = Course
        fields = ['id', 'subject', 'title', 'slug',
                  'overview', 'created', 'owner',
                  'modules']
```

Let's take a look at how a `Course` object is serialized. Open the shell and execute the following command:

```
python manage.py shell
```

Run the following code:

```
>>> from rest_framework.renderers import JSONRenderer
>>> from courses.models import Course
>>> from courses.api.serializers import CourseSerializer
>>> course = Course.objects.latest('id')
>>> serializer = CourseSerializer(course)
>>> JSONRenderer().render(serializer.data)
```

You will get a JSON object with the fields that you included in CourseSerializer. You can see that the related objects of the modules manager are serialized as a list of primary keys, as follows:

```
"modules": [6, 7, 9, 10]
```

You want to include more information about each module, so you need to serialize Module objects and nest them. Modify the previous code of the api/serializers.py file of the courses application to make it look as follows:

```
from rest_framework import serializers
from courses.models import Subject, Course, Module


class ModuleSerializer(serializers.ModelSerializer):
    class Meta:
        model = Module
        fields = ['order', 'title', 'description']


class CourseSerializer(serializers.ModelSerializer):
    modules = ModuleSerializer(many=True, read_only=True)

    class Meta:
        model = Course
        fields = ['id', 'subject', 'title', 'slug',
                  'overview', 'created', 'owner',
                  'modules']
```

In the new code, you define ModuleSerializer to provide serialization for the Module model. Then, you add a modules attribute to CourseSerializer to nest the ModuleSerializer serializer. You set many=True to indicate that you are serializing multiple objects. The read_only parameter indicates that this field is read-only and should not be included in any input to create or update objects.

Open the shell and create an instance of `CourseSerializer` again. Render the serializer's data attribute with `JSONRenderer`. This time, the listed modules are being serialized with the nested `ModuleSerializer` serializer, as follows:

```
"modules": [
    {
        "order": 0,
        "title": "Introduction to overview",
        "description": "A brief overview about the Web Framework."
    },
    {
        "order": 1,
        "title": "Configuring Django",
        "description": "How to install Django."
    },
    ...
]
```

You can read more about serializers at `https://www.django-rest-framework.org/api-guide/serializers/`.

Generic API views are very useful to build REST APIs based on your models and serializers. However, you might also need to implement your own views with custom logic. Let's learn how to create a custom API view.

Building custom API views

REST framework provides an `APIView` class that builds API functionality on top of Django's `View` class. The `APIView` class differs from `View` by using REST framework's custom `Request` and `Response` objects and handling `APIException` exceptions to return the appropriate HTTP responses. It also has a built-in authentication and authorization system to manage access to views.

You are going to create a view for users to enroll on courses. Edit the `api/views.py` file of the courses application and add the following code highlighted in bold:

```
from django.shortcuts import get_object_or_404
from rest_framework.views import APIView
from rest_framework.response import Response
from rest_framework import generics
from courses.models import Subject, Course
from courses.api.serializers import SubjectSerializer

# ...

class CourseEnrollView(APIView):
```

```
def post(self, request, pk, format=None):
    course = get_object_or_404(Course, pk=pk)
    course.students.add(request.user)
    return Response({'enrolled': True})
```

The `CourseEnrollView` view handles user enrollment on courses. The preceding code is as follows:

1. You create a custom view that subclasses `APIView`.
2. You define a `post()` method for `POST` actions. No other HTTP method will be allowed for this view.
3. You expect a `pk` URL parameter containing the ID of a course. You retrieve the course by the given `pk` parameter and raise a `404` exception if it's not found.
4. You add the current user to the `students` many-to-many relationship of the `Course` object and return a successful response.

Edit the `api/urls.py` file and add the following URL pattern for the `CourseEnrollView` view:

```
path('courses/<pk>/enroll/',
    views.CourseEnrollView.as_view(),
    name='course_enroll'),
```

Theoretically, you could now perform a `POST` request to enroll the current user on a course. However, you need to be able to identify the user and prevent unauthenticated users from accessing this view. Let's see how API authentication and permissions work.

Handling authentication

REST framework provides authentication classes to identify the user performing the request. If authentication is successful, the framework sets the authenticated `User` object in `request.user`. If no user is authenticated, an instance of Django's `AnonymousUser` is set instead.

REST framework provides the following authentication backends:

- `BasicAuthentication`: This is HTTP basic authentication. The user and password are sent by the client in the `Authorization` HTTP header encoded with Base64. You can learn more about it at https://en.wikipedia.org/wiki/Basic_access_authentication.
- `TokenAuthentication`: This is token-based authentication. A `Token` model is used to store user tokens. Users include the token in the `Authorization` HTTP header for authentication.
- `SessionAuthentication`: This uses Django's session backend for authentication. This backend is useful for performing authenticated AJAX requests to the API from your website's frontend.
- `RemoteUserAuthentication`: This allows you to delegate authentication to your web server, which sets a `REMOTE_USER` environment variable.

You can build a custom authentication backend by subclassing the `BaseAuthentication` class provided by REST framework and overriding the `authenticate()` method.

You can set authentication on a per-view basis, or set it globally with the DEFAULT_AUTHENTICATION_ CLASSES setting.

 Authentication only identifies the user performing the request. It won't allow or deny access to views. You have to use permissions to restrict access to views.

You can find all the information about authentication at https://www.django-rest-framework.org/ api-guide/authentication/.

Let's add BasicAuthentication to your view. Edit the api/views.py file of the courses application and add an authentication_classes attribute to CourseEnrollView, as follows:

```python
# ...
from rest_framework.authentication import BasicAuthentication

class CourseEnrollView(APIView):
    authentication_classes = [BasicAuthentication]
    # ...
```

Users will be identified by the credentials set in the Authorization header of the HTTP request.

Adding permissions to views

REST framework includes a permission system to restrict access to views. Some of the built-in permissions of REST framework are:

- AllowAny: Unrestricted access, regardless of whether a user is authenticated or not.
- IsAuthenticated: Allows access to authenticated users only.
- IsAuthenticatedOrReadOnly: Complete access to authenticated users. Anonymous users are only allowed to execute read methods such as GET, HEAD, or OPTIONS.
- DjangoModelPermissions: Permissions tied to django.contrib.auth. The view requires a queryset attribute. Only authenticated users with model permissions assigned are granted permission.
- DjangoObjectPermissions: Django permissions on a per-object basis.

If users are denied permission, they will usually get one of the following HTTP error codes:

- HTTP 401: Unauthorized
- HTTP 403: Permission denied

You can read more information about permissions at https://www.django-rest-framework.org/ api-guide/permissions/.

Edit the api/views.py file of the courses application and add a permission_classes attribute to CourseEnrollView, as follows:

```
# ...
from rest_framework.authentication import BasicAuthentication
from rest_framework.permissions import IsAuthenticated

class CourseEnrollView(APIView):
    authentication_classes = [BasicAuthentication]
    permission_classes = [IsAuthenticated]
    # ...
```

You include the IsAuthenticated permission. This will prevent anonymous users from accessing the view. Now, you can perform a POST request to your new API method.

Make sure the development server is running. Open the shell and run the following command:

```
curl -i -X POST http://127.0.0.1:8000/api/courses/1/enroll/
```

You will get the following response:

```
HTTP/1.1 401 Unauthorized
...
{"detail": "Authentication credentials were not provided."}
```

You got a 401 HTTP code as expected since you are not authenticated. Let's use basic authentication with one of your users. Run the following command, replacing student:password with the credentials of an existing user:

```
curl -i -X POST -u student:password http://127.0.0.1:8000/api/courses/1/enroll/
```

You will get the following response:

```
HTTP/1.1 200 OK
...
{"enrolled": true}
```

You can access the administration site and check that the user is now enrolled in the course.

Next, you are going to learn a different way to build common views by using ViewSets.

Creating ViewSets and routers

ViewSets allow you to define the interactions of your API and let REST framework build the URLs dynamically with a Router object. By using ViewSets, you can avoid repeating logic for multiple views. ViewSets include actions for the following standard operations:

- Create operation: create()
- Retrieve operation: list() and retrieve()

- Update operation: `update()` and `partial_update()`
- Delete operation: `destroy()`

Let's create a `ViewSet` for the `Course` model. Edit the `api/views.py` file and add the following code to it:

```python
# ...
from rest_framework import viewsets
from courses.api.serializers import SubjectSerializer,
        CourseSerializer


class CourseViewSet(viewsets.ReadOnlyModelViewSet):
    queryset = Course.objects.all()
    serializer_class = CourseSerializer
```

You subclass `ReadOnlyModelViewSet`, which provides the read-only actions `list()` and `retrieve()` to both list objects, or retrieves a single object.

Edit the `api/urls.py` file and create a router for your `ViewSet`, as follows:

```python
from django.urls import path, include
from rest_framework import routers
from . import views


router = routers.DefaultRouter()
router.register('courses', views.CourseViewSet)

urlpatterns = [
    # ...
    path('', include(router.urls)),
]
```

You create a `DefaultRouter` object and register your `ViewSet` with the courses prefix. The router takes charge of generating URLs automatically for your `ViewSet`.

Open http://127.0.0.1:8000/api/ in your browser. You will see that the router lists all ViewSets in its base URL, as shown in *Figure 15.3*:

Figure 15.3: The API root page of the REST framework browsable API

You can access http://127.0.0.1:8000/api/courses/ to retrieve the list of courses.

You can learn more about ViewSets at https://www.django-rest-framework.org/api-guide/viewsets/. You can also find more information about routers at https://www.django-rest-framework.org/api-guide/routers/.

Adding additional actions to ViewSets

You can add extra actions to ViewSets. Let's change your previous CourseEnrollView view into a custom ViewSet action. Edit the api/views.py file and modify the CourseViewSet class to look as follows:

```
# ...
from rest_framework.decorators import action

class CourseViewSet(viewsets.ReadOnlyModelViewSet):
    queryset = Course.objects.all()
    serializer_class = CourseSerializer
```

```
@action(detail=True,
        methods=['post'],
        authentication_classes=[BasicAuthentication],
        permission_classes=[IsAuthenticated])
def enroll(self, request, *args, **kwargs):
    course = self.get_object()
    course.students.add(request.user)
    return Response({'enrolled': True})
```

In the preceding code, you add a custom enroll() method that represents an additional action for this ViewSet. The preceding code is as follows:

1. You use the action decorator of the framework with the parameter detail=True to specify that this is an action to be performed on a single object.
2. The decorator allows you to add custom attributes for the action. You specify that only the post() method is allowed for this view and set the authentication and permission classes.
3. You use self.get_object() to retrieve the Course object.
4. You add the current user to the students many-to-many relationship and return a custom success response.

Edit the api/urls.py file and remove or comment out the following URL, since you don't need it anymore:

```
path('courses/<pk>/enroll/',
    views.CourseEnrollView.as_view(),
    name='course_enroll'),
```

Then, edit the api/views.py file and remove or comment out the CourseEnrollView class.

The URL to enroll on courses is now automatically generated by the router. The URL remains the same since it's built dynamically using the action name enroll.

After students are enrolled in a course, they need to access the course's content. Next, you are going to learn how to ensure only students that enrolled can access the course.

Creating custom permissions

You want students to be able to access the contents of the courses they are enrolled on. Only students enrolled on a course should be able to access its contents. The best way to do this is with a custom permission class. REST Framework provides a BasePermission class that allows you to define the following methods:

- has_permission(): View-level permission check
- has_object_permission(): Instance-level permission check

These methods should return True to grant access, or False otherwise.

Create a new file inside the `courses/api/` directory and name it `permissions.py`. Add the following code to it:

```
from rest_framework.permissions import BasePermission


class IsEnrolled(BasePermission):
    def has_object_permission(self, request, view, obj):
        return obj.students.filter(id=request.user.id).exists()
```

You subclass the `BasePermission` class and override the `has_object_permission()`. You check that the user performing the request is present in the `students` relationship of the `Course` object. You are going to use the `IsEnrolled` permission next.

Serializing course contents

You need to serialize course contents. The `Content` model includes a generic foreign key that allows you to associate objects of different content models. Yet, you added a common `render()` method for all content models in the previous chapter. You can use this method to provide rendered content to your API.

Edit the `api/serializers.py` file of the `courses` application and add the following code to it:

```
from courses.models import Subject, Course, Module, Content


class ItemRelatedField(serializers.RelatedField):
    def to_representation(self, value):
        return value.render()


class ContentSerializer(serializers.ModelSerializer):
    item = ItemRelatedField(read_only=True)
    class Meta:
        model = Content
        fields = ['order', 'item']
```

In this code, you define a custom field by subclassing the `RelatedField` serializer field provided by REST framework and overriding the `to_representation()` method. You define the `ContentSerializer` serializer for the `Content` model and use the custom field for the `item` generic foreign key.

You need an alternative serializer for the `Module` model that includes its contents, and an extended `Course` serializer as well. Edit the `api/serializers.py` file and add the following code to it:

```
class ModuleWithContentsSerializer(
        serializers.ModelSerializer):
    contents = ContentSerializer(many=True)
    class Meta:
```

```
            model = Module
            fields = ['order', 'title', 'description',
                        'contents']


class CourseWithContentsSerializer(
    serializers.ModelSerializer):
    modules = ModuleWithContentsSerializer(many=True)
    class Meta:
        model = Course
        fields = ['id', 'subject', 'title', 'slug',
                    'overview', 'created', 'owner',
                    'modules']
```

Let's create a view that mimics the behavior of the retrieve() action, but includes the course contents. Edit the api/views.py file and add the following method to the CourseViewSet class:

```
from courses.api.permissions import IsEnrolled
from courses.api.serializers import CourseWithContentsSerializer


class CourseViewSet(viewsets.ReadOnlyModelViewSet):
    # ...
    @action(detail=True,
            methods=['get'],
            serializer_class=CourseWithContentsSerializer,
            authentication_classes=[BasicAuthentication],
            permission_classes=[IsAuthenticated, IsEnrolled])
    def contents(self, request, *args, **kwargs):
        return self.retrieve(request, *args, **kwargs)
```

The description of this method is as follows:

1. You use the action decorator with the parameter detail=True to specify an action that is performed on a single object.

2. You specify that only the GET method is allowed for this action.

3. You use the new CourseWithContentsSerializer serializer class that includes rendered course contents.

4. You use both IsAuthenticated and your custom IsEnrolled permissions. By doing so, you make sure that only users enrolled in the course are able to access its contents.

5. You use the existing retrieve() action to return the Course object.

Open `http://127.0.0.1:8000/api/courses/1/contents/` in your browser. If you access the view with the right credentials, you will see that each module of the course includes the rendered HTML for course contents, as follows:

```
{
    "order": 0,
    "title": "Introduction to Django",
    "description": "Brief introduction to the Django Web Framework.",
    "contents": [
        {
            "order": 0,
            "item": "<p>Meet Django. Django is a high-level
            Python Web framework
            ...</p>"
        },
        {
            "order": 1,
            "item": "\n<iframe width=\"480\" height=\"360\"
            src=\"http://www.youtube.com/embed/bgV39DlmZ2U?
            wmode=opaque\"
            frameborder=\"0\" allowfullscreen></iframe>\n"
        }
    ]
}
```

You have built a simple API that allows other services to access the course application programmatically. REST framework also allows you to handle creating and editing objects with the `ModelViewSet` class. We have covered the main aspects of Django REST framework, but you will find further information about its features in its extensive documentation at `https://www.django-rest-framework.org/`.

Consuming the RESTful API

Now that you have implemented an API, you can consume it in a programmatic manner from other applications. You can interact with the API using the JavaScript Fetch API in the frontend of your application, in a similar fashion to the functionalities you built in *Chapter 6, Sharing Content on Your Website*. You can also consume the API from applications built with Python or any other programming language.

You are going to create a simple Python application that uses the RESTful API to retrieve all available courses and then enroll a student in all of them. You will learn how to authenticate against the API using HTTP basic authentication and perform `GET` and `POST` requests.

We will use the Python Requests library to consume the API. We used Requests in *Chapter 6, Sharing Content on Your Website* to retrieve images by their URL. Requests abstracts the complexity of dealing with HTTP requests and provides a very simple interface to consume HTTP services. You can find the documentation for the Requests library at `https://requests.readthedocs.io/en/master/`.

Open the shell and install the Requests library with the following command:

```
pip install requests==2.28.1
```

Create a new directory next to the educa project directory and name it `api_examples`. Create a new file inside the `api_examples/` directory and name it `enroll_all.py`. The file structure should now look like this:

```
api_examples/
    enroll_all.py
educa/
    ...
```

Edit the `enroll_all.py` file and add the following code to it:

```python
import requests

base_url = 'http://127.0.0.1:8000/api/'

# retrieve all courses
r = requests.get(f'{base_url}courses/')
courses = r.json()

available_courses = ', '.join([course['title'] for course in courses])
print(f'Available courses: {available_courses}')
```

In this code, you perform the following actions:

1. You import the Requests library and define the base URL for the API.
2. You use `requests.get()` to retrieve data from the API by sending a `GET` request to the URL `http://127.0.0.1:8000/api/courses/`. This API endpoint is publicly accessible, so it does not require any authentication.
3. You use the `json()` method of the response object to decode the JSON data returned by the API.
4. You print the title attribute of each course.

Start the development server from the educa project directory with the following command:

```
python manage.py runserver
```

In another shell, run the following command from the `api_examples/` directory:

```
python enroll_all.py
```

You will see output with a list of all course titles, like this:

```
Available courses: Introduction to Django, Python for beginners, Algebra basics
```

This is your first automated call to your API.

Edit the enroll_all.py file and change it to make it look like this:

```
import requests

username = ''
password = ''
base_url = 'http://127.0.0.1:8000/api/'

# retrieve all courses
r = requests.get(f'{base_url}courses/')
courses = r.json()
available_courses = ', '.join([course['title'] for course in courses])
print(f'Available courses: {available_courses}')

for course in courses:
    course_id = course['id']
    course_title = course['title']
    r = requests.post(f'{base_url}courses/{course_id}/enroll/',
                        auth=(username, password))
    if r.status_code == 200:
        # successful request
        print(f'Successfully enrolled in {course_title}')
```

Replace the values for the username and password variables with the credentials of an existing user.

With the new code, you perform the following actions:

1. You define the username and password of the student you want to enroll on courses.
2. You iterate over the available courses retrieved from the API.
3. You store the course ID attribute in the course_id variable and the title attribute in the course_title variable.
4. You use requests.post() to send a POST request to the URL http://127.0.0.1:8000/api/courses/[id]/enroll/ for each course. This URL corresponds to the CourseEnrollView API view, which allows you to enroll a user on a course. You build the URL for each course using the course_id variable. The CourseEnrollView view requires authentication. It uses the IsAuthenticated permission and the BasicAuthentication authentication class. The Requests library supports HTTP basic authentication out of the box. You use the auth parameter to pass a tuple with the username and password to authenticate the user using HTTP basic authentication.
5. If the status code of the response is 200 OK, you print a message to indicate that the user has been successfully enrolled on the course.

You can use different kinds of authentication with Requests. You can find more information on authentication with Requests at https://requests.readthedocs.io/en/master/user/authentication/.

Run the following command from the `api_examples/` directory:

```
python enroll_all.py
```

You will now see output like this:

```
Available courses: Introduction to Django, Python for beginners, Algebra basics
Successfully enrolled in Introduction to Django
Successfully enrolled in Python for beginners
Successfully enrolled in Algebra basics
```

Great! You have successfully enrolled the user on all available courses using the API. You will see a `Successfully enrolled` message for each course on the platform. As you can see, it's very easy to consume the API from any other application. You can effortlessly build other functionalities based on the API and let others integrate your API into their applications.

Additional resources

The following resources provide additional information related to the topics covered in this chapter:

- Source code for this chapter – `https://github.com/PacktPublishing/Django-4-by-example/tree/main/Chapter15`
- REST framework website – `https://www.django-rest-framework.org/`
- REST framework settings – `https://www.django-rest-framework.org/api-guide/settings/`
- REST framework renderers – `https://www.django-rest-framework.org/api-guide/renderers/`
- REST framework parsers – `https://www.django-rest-framework.org/api-guide/parsers/`
- REST framework generic mixins and views – `https://www.django-rest-framework.org/api-guide/generic-views/`
- Download `curl` – `https://curl.se/download.html`
- Postman API platform – `https://www.getpostman.com/`
- REST framework serializers – `https://www.django-rest-framework.org/api-guide/serializers/`
- HTTP basic authentication – `https://en.wikipedia.org/wiki/Basic_access_authentication`
- REST framework authentication – `https://www.django-rest-framework.org/api-guide/authentication/`
- REST framework permissions – `https://www.django-rest-framework.org/api-guide/permissions/`
- REST framework ViewSets – `https://www.django-rest-framework.org/api-guide/viewsets/`
- REST framework routers – `https://www.django-rest-framework.org/api-guide/routers/`
- Python Requests library documentation – `https://requests.readthedocs.io/en/master/`
- Authentication with the Requests library – `https://requests.readthedocs.io/en/master/user/authentication/`

Summary

In this chapter, you learned how to use Django REST framework to build a RESTful API for your project. You created serializers and views for models, and you built custom API views. You also added authentication to your API and restricted access to API views using permissions. Next, you discovered how to create custom permissions, and you implemented ViewSets and routers. Finally, you used the Requests library to consume the API from an external Python script.

The next chapter will teach you how to build a chat server using Django Channels. You will implement asynchronous communication using WebSockets and you will use Redis to set up a channel layer.

16

Building a Chat Server

In the previous chapter, you created a RESTful API for your project. In this chapter, you will build a chat server for students using Django Channels. Students will be able to access a different chat room for each course they are enrolled on. To create the chat server, you will learn how to serve your Django project through **Asynchronous Server Gateway Interface** (**ASGI**), and you will implement asynchronous communication.

In this chapter, you will:

- Add Channels to your project
- Build a WebSocket consumer and appropriate routing
- Implement a WebSocket client
- Enable a channel layer with Redis
- Make your consumer fully asynchronous

The source code for this chapter can be found at `https://github.com/PacktPublishing/Django-4-by-example/tree/main/Chapter16`.

All Python modules used in this chapter are included in the `requirements.txt` file in the source code that comes along with this chapter. You can follow the instructions to install each Python module below or you can install all requirements at once with the command `pip install -r requirements.txt`.

Creating a chat application

You are going to implement a chat server to provide students with a chat room for each course. Students enrolled on a course will be able to access the course chat room and exchange messages in real time. You will use Channels to build this functionality. Channels is a Django application that extends Django to handle protocols that require long-running connections, such as WebSockets, chatbots, or MQTT (a lightweight publish/subscribe message transport commonly used in **Internet of Things** (**IoT**) projects).

Using Channels, you can easily implement real-time or asynchronous functionalities into your project in addition to your standard HTTP synchronous views. You will start by adding a new application to your project. The new application will contain the logic for the chat server.

You can the documentation for Django Channels at `https://channels.readthedocs.io/`.

Let's start implementing the chat server. Run the following command from the project educa directory to create the new application file structure:

```
django-admin startapp chat
```

Edit the `settings.py` file of the educa project and activate the `chat` application in your project by editing the `INSTALLED_APPS` setting, as follows:

```python
INSTALLED_APPS = [
    # ...
    'chat',
]
```

The new `chat` application is now active in your project.

Implementing the chat room view

You will provide students with a different chat room for each course. You need to create a view for students to join the chat room of a given course. Only students who are enrolled on a course will be able to access the course chat room.

Edit the `views.py` file of the new `chat` application and add the following code to it:

```python
from django.shortcuts import render, get_object_or_404
from django.http import HttpResponseForbidden
from django.contrib.auth.decorators import login_required


@login_required
def course_chat_room(request, course_id):
    try:
        # retrieve course with given id joined by the current user
        course = request.user.courses_joined.get(id=course_id)
    except:
        # user is not a student of the course or course does not exist
        return HttpResponseForbidden()
    return render(request, 'chat/room.html', {'course': course})
```

This is the `course_chat_room` view. In this view, you use the `@login_required` decorator to prevent any non-authenticated user from accessing the view. The view receives a required `course_id` parameter that is used to retrieve the course with the given `id`.

You access the courses that the user is enrolled on through the relationship `courses_joined` and you retrieve the course with the given `id` from that subset of courses. If the course with the given `id` does not exist or the user is not enrolled on it, you return an `HttpResponseForbidden` response, which translates to an HTTP response with status 403.

If the course with the given `id` exists and the user is enrolled on it, you render the `chat/room.html` template, passing the `course` object to the template context.

You need to add a URL pattern for this view. Create a new file inside the chat application directory and name it `urls.py`. Add the following code to it:

```
from django.urls import path
from . import views


app_name = 'chat'


urlpatterns = [
    path('room/<int:course_id>/', views.course_chat_room,
        name='course_chat_room'),
]
```

This is the initial URL patterns file for the `chat` application. You define the `course_chat_room` URL pattern, including the `course_id` parameter with the `int` prefix, as you only expect an integer value here.

Include the new URL patterns of the chat application in the main URL patterns of the project. Edit the main `urls.py` file of the `educa` project and add the following line to it:

```
urlpatterns = [
    # ...
    path('chat/', include('chat.urls', namespace='chat')),
]
```

URL patterns for the `chat` application are added to the project under the `chat/` path.

You need to create a template for the `course_chat_room` view. This template will contain an area to visualize the messages that are exchanged in the chat, and a text input with a submit button to send text messages to the chat.

Create the following file structure within the `chat` application directory:

```
templates/
    chat/
        room.html
```

Edit the `chat/room.html` template and add the following code to it:

```
{% extends "base.html" %}

{% block title %}Chat room for "{{ course.title }}"{% endblock %}

{% block content %}
  <div id="chat">
```

```
  </div>
  <div id="chat-input">
    <input id="chat-message-input" type="text">
    <input id="chat-message-submit" type="submit" value="Send">
  </div>
{% endblock %}


{% block include_js %}
{% endblock %}


{% block domready %}
{% endblock %}
```

This is the template for the course chat room. In this template, you extend the base.html template of your project and fill its content block. In the template, you define a <div> HTML element with the chat ID that you will use to display the chat messages sent by the user and by other students. You also define a second <div> element with a text input and a submit button that will allow the user to send messages. You add the include_js and domready blocks defined in the base.html template, which you are going to implement later, to establish a connection with a WebSocket and send or receive messages.

Run the development server and open http://127.0.0.1:8000/chat/room/1/ in your browser, replacing 1 with the id of an existing course in the database. Access the chat room with a logged-in user who is enrolled on the course. You will see the following screen:

Figure 16.1: The course chat room page

This is the course chat room screen that students will use to discuss topics within a course.

Real-time Django with Channels

You are building a chat server to provide students with a chat room for each course. Students enrolled on a course will be able to access the course chat room and exchange messages. This functionality requires real-time communication between the server and the client. The client should be able to connect to the chat and send or receive data at any time. There are several ways you could implement this feature, using AJAX polling or long polling in combination with storing the messages in your database or Redis. However, there is no efficient way to implement a chat server using a standard synchronous web application. You are going to build a chat server using asynchronous communication through ASGI.

Asynchronous applications using ASGI

Django is usually deployed using **Web Server Gateway Interface (WSGI)**, which is the standard interface for Python applications to handle HTTP requests. However, to work with asynchronous applications, you need to use another interface called ASGI, which can handle WebSocket requests as well. ASGI is the emerging Python standard for asynchronous web servers and applications.

You can find an introduction to ASGI at `https://asgi.readthedocs.io/en/latest/introduction.html`.

Django comes with support for running asynchronous Python through ASGI. Writing asynchronous views is supported since Django 3.1 and Django 4.1 introduces asynchronous handlers for class-based views. Channels builds upon the native ASGI support available in Django and provides additional functionalities to handle protocols that require long-running connections, such as WebSockets, IoT protocols, and chat protocols.

WebSockets provide full-duplex communication by establishing a persistent, open, bidirectional **Transmission Control Protocol (TCP)** connection between servers and clients. You are going to use WebSockets to implement your chat server.

You can find more information about deploying Django with ASGI at `https://docs.djangoproject.com/en/4.1/howto/deployment/asgi/`.

You can find more information about Django's support for writing asynchronous views at `https://docs.djangoproject.com/en/4.1/topics/async/` and Django's support for asynchronous class-based views at `https://docs.djangoproject.com/en/4.1/topics/class-based-views/#async-class-based-views`.

The request/response cycle using Channels

It's important to understand the differences in a request cycle between a standard synchronous request cycle and a Channels implementation. The following schema shows the request cycle of a synchronous Django setup:

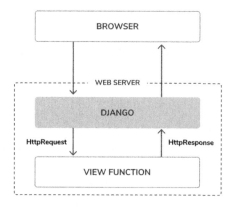

Figure 16.2: The Django request/response cycle

When an HTTP request is sent by the browser to the web server, Django handles the request and passes the HttpRequest object to the corresponding view. The view processes the request and returns an HttpResponse object that is sent back to the browser as an HTTP response. There is no mechanism to maintain an open connection or send data to the browser without an associated HTTP request.

The following schema shows the request cycle of a Django project using Channels with WebSockets:

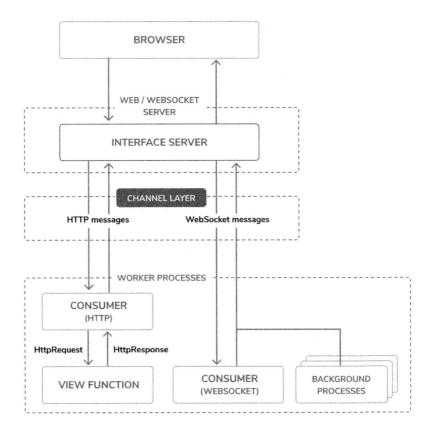

Figure 16.3: The Django Channels request/response cycle

Channels replaces Django's request/response cycle with messages that are sent across channels. HTTP requests are still routed to view functions using Django, but they get routed over channels. This allows for WebSockets message handling as well, where you have producers and consumers that exchange messages across a channel layer. Channels preserves Django's synchronous architecture, allowing you to choose between writing synchronous code and asynchronous code, or a combination of both.

Installing Channels

You are going to add Channels to your project and set up the required basic ASGI application routing for it to manage HTTP requests.

Install Channels in your virtual environment with the following command:

```
pip install channels==3.0.5
```

Edit the `settings.py` file of the `educa` project and add `channels` to the `INSTALLED_APPS` setting as follows:

```python
INSTALLED_APPS = [
    # ...
    'channels',
]
```

The `channels` application is now activated in your project.

Channels expects you to define a single root application that will be executed for all requests. You can define the root application by adding the `ASGI_APPLICATION` setting to your project. This is similar to the `ROOT_URLCONF` setting that points to the base URL patterns of your project. You can place the root application anywhere in your project, but it is recommended to put it in a project-level file. You can add your root routing configuration to the `asgi.py` file directly, where the ASGI application will be defined.

Edit the `asgi.py` file in the `educa` project directory and add the following code highlighted in bold:

```python
import os

from django.core.asgi import get_asgi_application
from channels.routing import ProtocolTypeRouter

os.environ.setdefault('DJANGO_SETTINGS_MODULE', 'educa.settings')

django_asgi_app = get_asgi_application()

application = ProtocolTypeRouter({
    'http': django_asgi_app,
})
```

In the previous code, you define the main ASGI application that will be executed when serving the Django project through ASGI. You use the `ProtocolTypeRouter` class provided by Channels as the main entry point of your routing system. `ProtocolTypeRouter` takes a dictionary that maps communication types like `http` or `websocket` to ASGI applications. You instantiate this class with the default application for the HTTP protocol. Later, you will add a protocol for the WebSocket.

Add the following line to the settings.py file of your project:

```
ASGI_APPLICATION = 'educa.routing.application'
```

The ASGI_APPLICATION setting is used by Channels to locate the root routing configuration.

When Channels is added to the INSTALLED_APPS setting, it takes control over the runserver command, replacing the standard Django development server. Besides handling URL routing to Django views for synchronous requests, the Channels development server also manages routes to WebSocket consumers.

Start the development server using the following command:

```
python manage.py runserver
```

You will see output similar to the following:

```
Watching for file changes with StatReloader
Performing system checks...

System check identified no issues (0 silenced).
May 30, 2022 - 08:02:57
Django version 4.0.4, using settings 'educa.settings'
Starting ASGI/Channels version 3.0.4 development server at
http://127.0.0.1:8000/
Quit the server with CONTROL-C.
```

Check that the output contains the line Starting ASGI/Channels version 3.0.4 development server. This line confirms that you are using the Channels development server, which is capable of managing synchronous and asynchronous requests, instead of the standard Django development server. HTTP requests continue to behave the same as before, but they get routed over Channels.

Now that Channels is installed in your project, you can build the chat server for courses. To implement the chat server for your project, you will need to take the following steps:

1. **Set up a consumer:** Consumers are individual pieces of code that can handle WebSockets in a very similar way to traditional HTTP views. You will build a consumer to read and write messages to a communication channel.

2. **Configure routing:** Channels provides routing classes that allow you to combine and stack your consumers. You will configure URL routing for your chat consumer.

3. **Implement a WebSocket client:** When the student accesses the chat room, you will connect to the WebSocket from the browser and send or receive messages using JavaScript.

4. **Enable a channel layer:** Channel layers allow you to talk between different instances of an application. They're a useful part of making a distributed real-time application. You will set up a channel layer using Redis.

Let's start by writing your own consumer to handle connecting to a WebSocket, receiving and sending messages, and disconnecting.

Writing a consumer

Consumers are the equivalent of Django views for asynchronous applications. As mentioned, they handle WebSockets in a very similar way to how traditional views handle HTTP requests. Consumers are ASGI applications that can handle messages, notifications, and other things. Unlike Django views, consumers are built for long-running communication. URLs are mapped to consumers through routing classes that allow you to combine and stack consumers.

Let's implement a basic consumer that can accept WebSocket connections and echoes every message it receives from the WebSocket back to it. This initial functionality will allow the student to send messages to the consumer and receive back the messages it sends.

Create a new file inside the chat application directory and name it consumers.py. Add the following code to it:

```python
import json
from channels.generic.websocket import WebsocketConsumer

class ChatConsumer(WebsocketConsumer):
    def connect(self):
        # accept connection
        self.accept()

    def disconnect(self, close_code):
        pass

    # receive message from WebSocket
    def receive(self, text_data):
        text_data_json = json.loads(text_data)
        message = text_data_json['message']
        # send message to WebSocket
        self.send(text_data=json.dumps({'message': message}))
```

This is the ChatConsumer consumer. This class inherits from the Channels WebsocketConsumer class to implement a basic WebSocket consumer. In this consumer, you implement the following methods:

- connnect(): Called when a new connection is received. You accept any connection with self.accept(). You can also reject a connection by calling self.close().
- disconnect(): Called when the socket closes. You use pass because you don't need to implement any action when a client closes the connection.
- receive(): Called whenever data is received. You expect text to be received as text_data (this could also be binary_data for binary data). You treat the text data received as JSON. Therefore, you use json.loads() to load the received JSON data into a Python dictionary. You access the message key, which you expect to be present in the JSON structure received. To echo the message, you send the message back to the WebSocket with self.send(), transforming it into JSON format again through json.dumps().

The initial version of your `ChatConsumer` consumer accepts any WebSocket connection and echoes to the WebSocket client every message it receives. Note that the consumer does not broadcast messages to other clients yet. You will build this functionality by implementing a channel layer later.

Routing

You need to define a URL to route connections to the `ChatConsumer` consumer you have implemented. Channels provides routing classes that allow you to combine and stack consumers to dispatch based on what the connection is. You can think of them as the URL routing system of Django for asynchronous applications.

Create a new file inside the `chat` application directory and name it `routing.py`. Add the following code to it:

```
from django.urls import re_path
from . import consumers

websocket_urlpatterns = [
    re_path(r'ws/chat/room/(?P<course_id>\d+)/$',
            consumers.ChatConsumer.as_asgi()),
]
```

In this code, you map a URL pattern with the `ChatConsumer` class that you defined in the `chat/consumers.py` file. You use Django's `re_path` to define the path with regular expressions. You use the `re_path` function instead of the common `path` function because of the limitations of Channels' URL routing. The URL includes an integer parameter called `course_id`. This parameter will be available in the scope of the consumer and will allow you to identify the course chat room that the user is connecting to. You call the `as_asgi()` method of the consumer class in order to get an ASGI application that will instantiate an instance of the consumer for each user connection. This behavior is similar to Django's `as_view()` method for class-based views.

 It is a good practice to prepend WebSocket URLs with `/ws/` to differentiate them from URLs used for standard synchronous HTTP requests. This also simplifies the production setup when an HTTP server routes requests based on the path.

Edit the global `asgi.py` file located next to the `settings.py` file so that it looks like this:

```
import os

from django.core.asgi import get_asgi_application
from channels.routing import ProtocolTypeRouter, URLRouter
from channels.auth import AuthMiddlewareStack
import chat.routing
```

```
os.environ.setdefault('DJANGO_SETTINGS_MODULE', 'educa.settings')

django_asgi_app = get_asgi_application()

application = ProtocolTypeRouter({
    'http': django_asgi_app,
    'websocket': AuthMiddlewareStack(
        URLRouter(chat.routing.websocket_urlpatterns)
    ),
})
```

In this code, you add a new route for the websocket protocol. You use URLRouter to map websocket connections to the URL patterns defined in the websocket_urlpatterns list of the chat application routing.py file. You also use AuthMiddlewareStack. The AuthMiddlewareStack class provided by Channels supports standard Django authentication, where the user details are stored in the session. Later, you will access the user instance in the scope of the consumer to identify the user who sends a message.

Implementing the WebSocket client

So far, you have created the course_chat_room view and its corresponding template for students to access the course chat room. You have implemented a WebSocket consumer for the chat server and tied it with URL routing. Now, you need to build a WebSocket client to establish a connection with the WebSocket in the course chat room template and be able to send/receive messages.

You are going to implement the WebSocket client with JavaScript to open and maintain a connection in the browser. You will interact with the **Document Object Model (DOM)** using JavaScript.

Edit the chat/room.html template of the chat application and modify the include_js and domready blocks, as follows:

```
{% block include_js %}
  {{ course.id|json_script:"course-id" }}
{% endblock %}

{% block domready %}
  const courseId = JSON.parse(
    document.getElementById('course-id').textContent
  );
  const url = 'ws://' + window.location.host +
              '/ws/chat/room/' + courseId + '/';
  const chatSocket = new WebSocket(url);
{% endblock %}
```

In the include_js block, you use the json_script template filter to securely use the value of course.id with JavaScript. The json_script template filter provided by Django outputs a Python object as JSON, wrapped in a <script> tag, so that you can safely use it with JavaScript. The code {{ course.id|json_script:"course-id" }} is rendered as <script id="course-id" type="application/json">6</script>. This value is then retrieved in the domready block by parsing the content of the element with id="course-id" using JSON.parse(). This is the safe way to use Python objects in JavaScript.

You can find more information about the json_script template filter at https://docs.djangoproject.com/en/4.1/ref/templates/builtins/#json-script.

In the domready block, you define an URL with the WebSocket protocol, which looks like ws:// (or wss:// for secure WebSockets, just like https://). You build the URL using the current location of the browser, which you obtain from window.location.host. The rest of the URL is built with the path for the chat room URL pattern that you defined in the routing.py file of the chat application.

You write the URL instead of building it with a resolver because Channels does not provide a way to reverse URLs. You use the current course ID to generate the URL for the current course and store the URL in a new constant named url.

You then open a WebSocket connection to the stored URL using new WebSocket(url). You assign the instantiated WebSocket client object to the new constant chatSocket.

You have created a WebSocket consumer, you have included routing for it, and you have implemented a basic WebSocket client. Let's try the initial version of your chat.

Start the development server using the following command:

```
python manage.py runserver
```

Open the URL http://127.0.0.1:8000/chat/room/1/ in your browser, replacing 1 with the id of an existing course in the database. Take a look at the console output. Besides the HTTP GET requests for the page and its static files, you should see two lines including WebSocket HANDSHAKING and WebSocket CONNECT, like the following output:

```
HTTP GET /chat/room/1/ 200 [0.02, 127.0.0.1:57141]
HTTP GET /static/css/base.css 200 [0.01, 127.0.0.1:57141]
WebSocket HANDSHAKING /ws/chat/room/1/ [127.0.0.1:57144]
WebSocket CONNECT /ws/chat/room/1/ [127.0.0.1:57144]
```

The Channels development server listens for incoming socket connections using a standard TCP socket. The handshake is the bridge from HTTP to WebSockets. In the handshake, details of the connection are negotiated and either party can close the connection before completion. Remember that you are using self.accept() to accept any connection in the connect() method of the ChatConsumer class, implemented in the consumers.py file of the chat application. The connection is accepted, and therefore, you see the WebSocket CONNECT message in the console.

If you use the browser developer tools to track network connections, you can also see information for the WebSocket connection that has been established.

It should look like *Figure 16.4*:

| Resources | Timelines | Storage | Canvas | Audit | Console | Search | + ⚙ |

| CSS | Image | Font | JS | XHR | Other | ☐ Group Media Requests | ↓ Import | ↑ Export | ⊘ | 🗑 |

| Preview | Headers | Cookies | Sizes | Timing | Security |

Data	Time
WebSocket Connection Established	10:45:00 PM

Figure 16.4: The browser developer tools showing that the WebSocket connection has been established

Now that you can connect to the WebSocket, it's time to interact with it. You will implement the methods to handle common events, such as receiving a message and closing the connection. Edit the chat/ room.html template of the chat application and modify the domready block, as follows:

```
{% block domready %}
  const courseId = JSON.parse(
    document.getElementById('course-id').textContent
  );
  const url = 'ws://' + window.location.host +
              '/ws/chat/room/' + courseId + '/';
  const chatSocket = new WebSocket(url);

  chatSocket.onmessage = function(event) {
    const data = JSON.parse(event.data);
    const chat = document.getElementById('chat');

    chat.innerHTML += '<div class="message">' +
                      data.message + '</div>';
    chat.scrollTop = chat.scrollHeight;
  };

  chatSocket.onclose = function(event) {
    console.error('Chat socket closed unexpectedly');
  };

{% endblock %}
```

In this code, you define the following events for the WebSocket client:

- onmessage: Fired when data is received through the WebSocket. You parse the message, which you expect in JSON format, and access its message attribute. You then append a new <div> element with the message received to the HTML element with the chat ID. This will add new messages to the chat log, while keeping all previous messages that have been added to the log. You scroll the chat log <div> to the bottom to ensure that the new message gets visibility. You achieve this by scrolling to the total scrollable height of the chat log, which can be obtained by accessing its scrollHeight attribute.

- onclose: Fired when the connection with the WebSocket is closed. You don't expect to close the connection, and therefore, you write the error Chat socket closed unexpectedly to the console log if this happens.

You have implemented the action to display the message when a new message is received. You need to implement the functionality to send messages to the socket as well.

Edit the chat/room.html template of the chat application and add the following JavaScript code to the bottom of the domready block:

```
const input = document.getElementById('chat-message-input');
const submitButton = document.getElementById('chat-message-submit');

submitButton.addEventListener('click', function(event) {
  const message = input.value;
  if(message) {
    // send message in JSON format
    chatSocket.send(JSON.stringify({'message': message}));
    // clear input
    input.innerHTML = '';
    input.focus();
  }
});
```

In this code, you define an event listener for the click event of the submit button, which you select by its ID chat-message-submit. When the button is clicked, you perform the following actions:

1. You read the message entered by the user from the value of the text input element with the ID chat-message-input.
2. You check whether the message has any content with if(message).
3. If the user has entered a message, you form JSON content such as {'message': 'string entered by the user'} by using JSON.stringify().
4. You send the JSON content through the WebSocket, calling the send() method of chatSocket client.
5. You clear the contents of the text input by setting its value to an empty string with input. innerHTML = ''.
6. You return the focus to the text input with input.focus() so that the user can write a new message straightaway.

The user is now able to send messages using the text input and by clicking the submit button.

To improve the user experience, you will give focus to the text input as soon as the page loads so that the user can type directly in it. You will also capture keyboard keypress events to identify the *Enter* key and fire the click event on the submit button. The user will be able to either click the button or press the *Enter* key to send a message.

Edit the `chat/room.html` template of the `chat` application and add the following JavaScript code to the bottom of the `domready` block:

```
input.addEventListener('keypress', function(event) {
    if (event.key === 'Enter') {
        // cancel the default action, if needed
        event.preventDefault();
        // trigger click event on button
        submitButton.click();
    }
});


input.focus();
```

In this code, you also define a function for the `keypress` event of the `input` element. For any key that the user presses, you check whether its key is `Enter`. You prevent the default behavior for this key with `event.preventDefault()`. If the *Enter* key is pressed, you fire the `click` event on the submit button to send the message to the WebSocket.

Outside of the event handler, in the main JavaScript code for the `domready` block, you give the focus to the text input with `input.focus()`. By doing so, when the DOM is loaded, the focus will be set on the `input` element for the user to type a message.

The `domready` block of the `chat/room.html` template should now look as follows:

```
{% block domready %}
  const courseId = JSON.parse(
    document.getElementById('course-id').textContent
  );
  const url = 'ws://' + window.location.host +
              '/ws/chat/room/' + courseId + '/';
  const chatSocket = new WebSocket(url);

  chatSocket.onmessage = function(event) {
    const data = JSON.parse(event.data);
    const chat = document.getElementById('chat');

    chat.innerHTML += '<div class="message">' +
                      data.message + '</div>';
    chat.scrollTop = chat.scrollHeight;
  };
```

```
    chatSocket.onclose = function(event) {
      console.error('Chat socket closed unexpectedly');
    };

    const input = document.getElementById('chat-message-input');
    const submitButton = document.getElementById('chat-message-submit');

    submitButton.addEventListener('click', function(event) {
      const message = input.value;
      if(message) {
        // send message in JSON format
        chatSocket.send(JSON.stringify({'message': message}));
        // clear input
        input.value = '';
        input.focus();
      }
    });

    input.addEventListener('keypress', function(event) {
      if (event.key === 'Enter') {
        // cancel the default action, if needed
        event.preventDefault();
        // trigger click event on button
        submitButton.click();
      }
    });

    input.focus();
  {% endblock %}
```

Open the URL http://127.0.0.1:8000/chat/room/1/ in your browser, replacing 1 with the id of an existing course in the database. With a logged-in user who is enrolled on the course, write some text in the input field and click the **SEND** button or press the *Enter* key.

You will see that your message appears in the chat log:

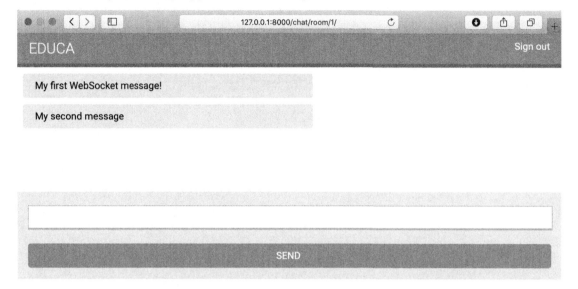

Figure 16.5: The chat room page, including messages sent through the WebSocket

Great! The message has been sent through the WebSocket and the ChatConsumer consumer has received the message and has sent it back through the WebSocket. The chatSocket client has received a message event and the onmessage function has been fired, adding the message to the chat log.

You have implemented the functionality with a WebSocket consumer and a WebSocket client to establish client/server communication and can send or receive events. However, the chat server is not able to broadcast messages to other clients. If you open a second browser tab and enter a message, the message will not appear on the first tab. In order to build communication between consumers, you have to enable a channel layer.

Enabling a channel layer

Channel layers allow you to communicate between different instances of an application. A channel layer is the transport mechanism that allows multiple consumer instances to communicate with each other and with other parts of Django.

In your chat server, you plan to have multiple instances of the ChatConsumer consumer for the same course chat room. Each student who joins the chat room will instantiate the WebSocket client in their browser, and that will open a connection with an instance of the WebSocket consumer. You need a common channel layer to distribute messages between consumers.

Channels and groups

Channel layers provide two abstractions to manage communications: channels and groups:

*   **Channel:** You can think of a channel as an inbox where messages can be sent to or as a task queue. Each channel has a name. Messages are sent to a channel by anyone who knows the channel name and then given to consumers listening on that channel.
*   **Group:** Multiple channels can be grouped into a group. Each group has a name. A channel can be added or removed from a group by anyone who knows the group name. Using the group name, you can also send a message to all channels in the group.

You will work with channel groups to implement the chat server. By creating a channel group for each course chat room, the ChatConsumer instances will be able to communicate with each other.

Setting up a channel layer with Redis

Redis is the preferred option for a channel layer, though Channels has support for other types of channel layers. Redis works as the communication store for the channel layer. Remember that you already used Redis in *Chapter 7, Tracking User Actions, Chapter 10, Extending Your Shop*, and *Chapter 14, Rendering and Caching Content*.

If you haven't installed Redis yet, you can find installation instructions in *Chapter 7, Tracking User Actions*.

To use Redis as a channel layer, you have to install the channels-redis package. Install channels-redis in your virtual environment with the following command:

```
pip install channels-redis==3.4.1
```

Edit the settings.py file of the educa project and add the following code to it:

```
CHANNEL_LAYERS = {
    'default': {
        'BACKEND': 'channels_redis.core.RedisChannelLayer',
        'CONFIG': {
            'hosts': [('127.0.0.1', 6379)],
        },
    },
}
```

The CHANNEL_LAYERS setting defines the configuration for the channel layers available to the project. You define a default channel layer using the RedisChannelLayer backend provided by channels-redis and specify the host 127.0.0.1 and the port 6379, on which Redis is running.

Let's try the channel layer. Initialize the Redis Docker container using the following command:

```
docker run -it --rm --name redis -p 6379:6379 redis
```

If you want to run the command in the background (in detached mode) you can use the -d option.

Open the Django shell using the following command from the project directory:

```
python manage.py shell
```

To verify that the channel layer can communicate with Redis, write the following code to send a message to a test channel named test_channel and receive it back:

```
>>> import channels.layers
>>> from asgiref.sync import async_to_sync
>>> channel_layer = channels.layers.get_channel_layer()
>>> async_to_sync(channel_layer.send)('test_channel', {'message': 'hello'})
>>> async_to_sync(channel_layer.receive)('test_channel')
```

You should get the following output:

```
{'message': 'hello'}
```

In the previous code, you send a message to a test channel through the channel layer, and then you retrieve it from the channel layer. The channel layer is communicating successfully with Redis.

Updating the consumer to broadcast messages

Let's edit the ChatConsumer consumer to use the channel layer. You will use a channel group for each course chat room. Therefore, you will use the course id to build the group name. ChatConsumer instances will know the group name and will be able to communicate with each other.

Edit the consumers.py file of the chat application, import the async_to_sync() function, and modify the connect() method of the ChatConsumer class, as follows:

```
import json
from channels.generic.websocket import WebsocketConsumer
from asgiref.sync import async_to_sync

class ChatConsumer(WebsocketConsumer):
    def connect(self):
        self.id = self.scope['url_route']['kwargs']['course_id']
        self.room_group_name = f'chat_{self.id}'
        # join room group
        async_to_sync(self.channel_layer.group_add)(
            self.room_group_name,
            self.channel_name
        )
        # accept connection
        self.accept()
    # ...
```

In this code, you import the async_to_sync() helper function to wrap calls to asynchronous channel layer methods. ChatConsumer is a synchronous WebsocketConsumer consumer, but it needs to call asynchronous methods of the channel layer.

In the new connect() method, you perform the following tasks:

1. You retrieve the course id from the scope to know the course that the chat room is associated with. You access self.scope['url_route']['kwargs ']['course_id'] to retrieve the course_id parameter from the URL. Every consumer has a scope with information about its connection, arguments passed by the URL, and the authenticated user, if any.

2. You build the group name with the id of the course that the group corresponds to. Remember that you will have a channel group for each course chat room. You store the group name in the room_group_name attribute of the consumer.

3. You join the group by adding the current channel to the group. You obtain the channel name from the channel_name attribute of the consumer. You use the group_add method of the channel layer to add the channel to the group. You use the async_to_sync() wrapper to use the channel layer asynchronous method.

4. You keep the self.accept() call to accept the WebSocket connection.

When the ChatConsumer consumer receives a new WebSocket connection, it adds the channel to the group associated with the course in its scope. The consumer is now able to receive any messages sent to the group.

In the same consumers.py file, modify the disconnect() method of the ChatConsumer class, as follows:

```python
class ChatConsumer(WebsocketConsumer):
    # ...
    def disconnect(self, close_code):
        # Leave room group
        async_to_sync(self.channel_layer.group_discard)(
            self.room_group_name,
            self.channel_name
        )
    # ...
```

When the connection is closed, you call the group_discard() method of the channel layer to leave the group. You use the async_to_sync() wrapper to use the channel layer asynchronous method.

In the same consumers.py file, modify the receive() method of the ChatConsumer class, as follows:

```python
class ChatConsumer(WebsocketConsumer):
    # ...
    # receive message from WebSocket
    def receive(self, text_data):
        text_data_json = json.loads(text_data)
```

```
        message = text_data_json['message']
        # send message to room group
        async_to_sync(self.channel_layer.group_send)(
            self.room_group_name,
            {
                'type': 'chat_message',
                'message': message,
            }
        )
```

When you receive a message from the WebSocket connection, instead of sending the message to the associated channel, you send the message to the group. You do this by calling the group_send() method of the channel layer. You use the async_to_sync() wrapper to use the channel layer asynchronous method. You pass the following information in the event sent to the group:

- type: The event type. This is a special key that corresponds to the name of the method that should be invoked on consumers that receive the event. You can implement a method in the consumer named the same as the message type so that it gets executed every time a message with that specific type is received.
- message: The actual message you are sending.

In the same consumers.py file, add a new chat_message() method in the ChatConsumer class, as follows:

```
class ChatConsumer(WebsocketConsumer):
    # ...
    # receive message from room group
    def chat_message(self, event):
        # send message to WebSocket
        self.send(text_data=json.dumps(event))
```

You name this method chat_message() to match the type key that is sent to the channel group when a message is received from the WebSocket. When a message with type chat_message is sent to the group, all consumers subscribed to the group will receive the message and will execute the chat_message() method. In the chat_message() method, you send the event message received to the WebSocket.

The complete consumers.py file should now look like this:

```
import json
from channels.generic.websocket import WebsocketConsumer
from asgiref.sync import async_to_sync

class ChatConsumer(WebsocketConsumer):
    def connect(self):
        self.id = self.scope['url_route']['kwargs']['course_id']
        self.room_group_name = f'chat_{self.id}'
```

```
        # join room group
        async_to_sync(self.channel_layer.group_add)(
            self.room_group_name,
            self.channel_name
        )
        # accept connection
        self.accept()

    def disconnect(self, close_code):
        # leave room group
        async_to_sync(self.channel_layer.group_discard)(
            self.room_group_name,
            self.channel_name
        )

    # receive message from WebSocket
    def receive(self, text_data):
        text_data_json = json.loads(text_data)
        message = text_data_json['message']
        # send message to room group
        async_to_sync(self.channel_layer.group_send)(
            self.room_group_name,
            {
                'type': 'chat_message',
                'message': message,
            }
        )

    # receive message from room group
    def chat_message(self, event):
        # send message to WebSocket
        self.send(text_data=json.dumps(event))
```

You have implemented a channel layer in `ChatConsumer`, allowing consumers to broadcast messages and communicate with each other.

Run the development server with the following command:

```
python manage.py runserver
```

Open the URL `http://127.0.0.1:8000/chat/room/1/` in your browser, replacing 1 with the `id` of an existing course in the database. Write a message and send it. Then, open a second browser window and access the same URL. Send a message from each browser window.

The result should look like this:

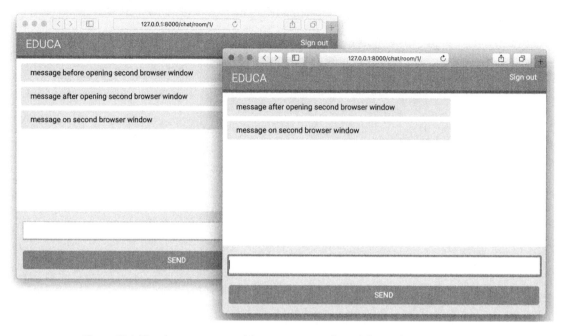

Figure 16.6: The chat room page with messages sent from different browser windows

You will see that the first message is only displayed in the first browser window. When you open a second browser window, messages sent in any of the browser windows are displayed in both of them. When you open a new browser window and access the chat room URL, a new WebSocket connection is established between the JavaScript WebSocket client in the browser and the WebSocket consumer in the server. Each channel gets added to the group associated with the course ID and passed through the URL to the consumer. Messages are sent to the group and received by all consumers.

Adding context to the messages

Now that messages can be exchanged between all users in a chat room, you probably want to display who sent which message and when it was sent. Let's add some context to the messages.

Edit the consumers.py file of the chat application and implement the following changes:

```python
import json
from channels.generic.websocket import WebsocketConsumer
from asgiref.sync import async_to_sync
from django.utils import timezone

class ChatConsumer(WebsocketConsumer):
    def connect(self):
        self.user = self.scope['user']
```

```python
        self.id = self.scope['url_route']['kwargs']['course_id']
        self.room_group_name = f'chat_{self.id}'
        # join room group
        async_to_sync(self.channel_layer.group_add)(
            self.room_group_name,
            self.channel_name
        )
        # accept connection
        self.accept()

    def disconnect(self, close_code):
        # leave room group
        async_to_sync(self.channel_layer.group_discard)(
            self.room_group_name,
            self.channel_name
        )

    # receive message from WebSocket
    def receive(self, text_data):
        text_data_json = json.loads(text_data)
        message = text_data_json['message']
        now = timezone.now()
        # send message to room group
        async_to_sync(self.channel_layer.group_send)(
            self.room_group_name,
            {
                'type': 'chat_message',
                'message': message,
                'user': self.user.username,
                'datetime': now.isoformat(),
            }
        )

    # receive message from room group
    def chat_message(self, event):
        # send message to WebSocket
        self.send(text_data=json.dumps(event))
```

You now import the `timezone` module provided by Django. In the `connect()` method of the consumer, you retrieve the current user from the scope with `self.scope['user']` and store them in a new user attribute of the consumer. When the consumer receives a message through the WebSocket, it gets the current time using `timezone.now()` and passes the current user and `datetime` in ISO 8601 format along with the message in the event sent to the channel group.

Edit the chat/room.html template of the chat application and add the following line highlighted in bold to the include_js block:

```
{% block include_js %}
  {{ course.id|json_script:"course-id" }}
  {{ request.user.username|json_script:"request-user" }}
{% endblock %}
```

Using the json_script template, you safely print the username of the request user to use it with JavaScript.

In the domready block of the chat/room.html template, add the following lines highlighted in bold:

```
{% block domready %}
  const courseId = JSON.parse(
    document.getElementById('course-id').textContent
  );
  const requestUser = JSON.parse(
    document.getElementById('request-user').textContent
  );
  # ...
{% endblock %}
```

In the new code, you safely parse the data of the element with the ID request-user and store it in the requestUser constant.

Then, in the domready block, find the following lines:

```
const data = JSON.parse(e.data);
const chat = document.getElementById('chat');

chat.innerHTML += '<div class="message">' +
                  data.message + '</div>';
chat.scrollTop = chat.scrollHeight;
```

Replace those lines with the following code:

```
const data = JSON.parse(e.data);
const chat = document.getElementById('chat');

const dateOptions = {hour: 'numeric', minute: 'numeric', hour12: true};
const datetime = new Date(data.datetime).toLocaleString('en', dateOptions);
const isMe = data.user === requestUser;
const source = isMe ? 'me' : 'other';
const name = isMe ? 'Me' : data.user;

chat.innerHTML += '<div class="message ' + source + '">' +
                  '<strong>' + name + '</strong> ' +
                  '<span class="date">' + datetime + '</span><br>' +
                  data.message + '</div>';
chat.scrollTop = chat.scrollHeight;
```

In this code, you implement the following changes:

1. You convert the datetime received in the message to a JavaScript Date object and format it with a specific locale.

2. You compare the username received in the message with two different constants as helpers to identify the user.

3. The constant source gets the value me if the user sending the message is the current user, or other otherwise.

4. The constant name gets the value Me if the user sending the message is the current user or the name of the user sending the message otherwise. You use it to display the name of the user sending the message.

5. You use the source value as a class of the main <div> message element to differentiate messages sent by the current user from messages sent by others. Different CSS styles are applied based on the class attribute. These CSS styles are declared in the css/base.css static file.

6. You use the username and the datetime in the message that you append to the chat log.

Open the URL http://127.0.0.1:8000/chat/room/1/ in your browser, replacing 1 with the id of an existing course in the database. With a logged-in user who is enrolled on the course, write a message and send it.

Then, open a second browser window in incognito mode to prevent the use of the same session. Log in with a different user, also enrolled on the same course, and send a message.

You will be able to exchange messages using the two different users and see the user and time, with a clear distinction between messages sent by the user and messages sent by others. The conversation between two users should look similar to the following one:

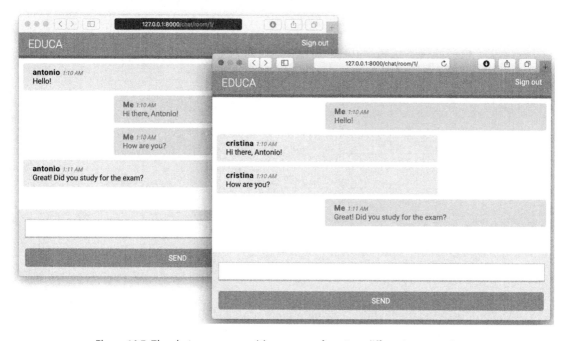

Figure 16.7: The chat room page with messages from two different user sessions

Great! You have built a functional real-time chat application using Channels. Next, you will learn how to improve the chat consumer by making it fully asynchronous.

Modifying the consumer to be fully asynchronous

The ChatConsumer you have implemented inherits from the base WebsocketConsumer class, which is synchronous. Synchronous consumers are convenient for accessing Django models and calling regular synchronous I/O functions. However, asynchronous consumers perform better, since they don't require additional threads when handling requests. Since you are using the asynchronous channel layer functions, you can easily rewrite the ChatConsumer class to be asynchronous.

Edit the consumers.py file of the chat application and implement the following changes:

```
import json
from channels.generic.websocket import AsyncWebsocketConsumer
from asgiref.sync import async_to_sync
from django.utils import timezone


class ChatConsumer(AsyncWebsocketConsumer):
```

```python
async def connect(self):
    self.user = self.scope['user']
    self.id = self.scope['url_route']['kwargs']['course_id']
    self.room_group_name = 'chat_%s' % self.id
    # join room group
    await self.channel_layer.group_add(
        self.room_group_name,
        self.channel_name
    )
    # accept connection
    await self.accept()

async def disconnect(self, close_code):
    # leave room group
    await self.channel_layer.group_discard(
        self.room_group_name,
        self.channel_name
    )

# receive message from WebSocket
async def receive(self, text_data):
    text_data_json = json.loads(text_data)
    message = text_data_json['message']
    now = timezone.now()
    # send message to room group
    await self.channel_layer.group_send(
        self.room_group_name,
        {
            'type': 'chat_message',
            'message': message,
            'user': self.user.username,
            'datetime': now.isoformat(),
        }
    )

# receive message from room group
async def chat_message(self, event):
    # send message to WebSocket
    await self.send(text_data=json.dumps(event))
```

You have implemented the following changes:

1. The `ChatConsumer` consumer now inherits from the `AsyncWebsocketConsumer` class to implement asynchronous calls

2. You have changed the definition of all methods from `def` to `async def`

3. You use `await` to call asynchronous functions that perform I/O operations

4. You no longer use the `async_to_sync()` helper function when calling methods on the channel layer

Open the URL `http://127.0.0.1:8000/chat/room/1/` with two different browser windows again and verify that the chat server still works. The chat server is now fully asynchronous!

Integrating the chat application with existing views

The chat server is now fully implemented, and students enrolled on a course can communicate with each other. Let's add a link for students to join the chat room for each course.

Edit the `students/course/detail.html` template of the `students` application and add the following `<h3>` HTML element code at the bottom of the `<div class="contents">` element:

```html
<div class="contents">
  ...
  <h3>
    <a href="{% url "chat:course_chat_room" object.id %}">
      Course chat room
    </a>
  </h3>
</div>
```

Open the browser and access any course that the student is enrolled on to view the course contents. The sidebar will now contain a **Course chat room** link that points to the course chat room view. If you click on it, you will enter the chat room:

EDUCA

Introduction to Django

Modules

MODULE 1
Introduction to Django

MODULE 2
Configuring Django

MODULE 3
Your first Django project

MODULE 4
Django URLs

Course chat room

Why Django?

Meet Django. Django is a high-level Python Web framework that encourages rapid development and clean, pragmatic design. Built by experienced developers , it takes care of much of the hassle of Web development, so you can focus on writing your app without needing to reinvent the wheel. It's free and open source.

Django video

Figure 16.8: The course detail page, including a link to the course chat room

Congratulations! You successfully built your first asynchronous application using Django Channels.

Additional resources

The following resources provide additional information related to the topics covered in this chapter:

*   Source code for this chapter – `https://github.com/PacktPublishing/Django-4-by-example/tree/main/Chapter16`
*   Introduction to ASGI – `https://asgi.readthedocs.io/en/latest/introduction.html`
*   Django support for asynchronous views – `https://docs.djangoproject.com/en/4.1/topics/async/`
*   Django support for asynchronous class-based views – `https://docs.djangoproject.com/en/4.1/topics/class-based-views/#async-class-based-views`
*   Django Channels documentation – `https://channels.readthedocs.io/`
*   Deploying Django with ASGI – `https://docs.djangoproject.com/en/4.1/howto/deployment/asgi/`
*   `json_script` template filter usage – `https://docs.djangoproject.com/en/4.1/ref/templates/builtins/#json-script`

Summary

In this chapter, you learned how to create a chat server using Channels. You implemented a WebSocket consumer and client. You also enabled communication between consumers using a channel layer with Redis and modified the consumer to be fully asynchronous.

The next chapter will teach you how to build a production environment for your Django project using NGINX, uWSGI, and Daphne with Docker Compose. You will also learn how to implement custom middleware and create custom management commands.

17

Going Live

In the previous chapter, you built a real-time chat server for students using Django Channels. Now that you have created a fully functional e-learning platform, you need to set up a production environment so that it can be accessed over the internet. Until now, you have been working in a development environment, using the Django development server to run your site. In this chapter, you will learn how to set up a production environment that is able to serve your Django project in a secure and efficient manner.

This chapter will cover the following topics:

- Configuring Django settings for multiple environments
- Using Docker Compose to run multiple services
- Setting up a web server with uWSGI and Django
- Serving PostgreSQL and Redis with Docker Compose
- Using the Django system check framework
- Serving NGINX with Docker
- Serving static assets through NGINX
- Securing connections through TLS/SSL
- Using the Daphne ASGI server for Django Channels
- Creating a custom Django middleware
- Implementing custom Django management commands

The source code for this chapter can be found at `https://github.com/PacktPublishing/Django-4-by-example/tree/main/Chapter17`.

All Python modules used in this chapter are included in the `requirements.txt` file in the source code that comes along with this chapter. You can follow the instructions to install each Python module below or you can install all requirements at once with the command `pip install -r requirements.txt`.

Creating a production environment

It's time to deploy your Django project in a production environment. You will start by configuring Django settings for multiple environments, and then you will set up a production environment.

Managing settings for multiple environments

In real-world projects, you will have to deal with multiple environments. You will usually have at least a local environment for development and a production environment for serving your application. You could have other environments as well, such as testing or staging environments.

Some project settings will be common to all environments, but others will be specific to each environment. Usually, you will use a base file that defines common settings, and a settings file per environment that overrides any necessary settings and defines additional ones.

We will manage the following environments:

- `local`: The local environment to run the project on your machine.
- `prod`: The environment for deploying your project on a production server.

Create a `settings/` directory next to the `settings.py` file of the educa project. Rename the `settings.py` file to `base.py` and move it into the new `settings/` directory.

Create the following additional files inside the `settings/` folder so that the new directory looks as follows:

```
settings/
    __init__.py
    base.py
    local.py
    prod.py
```

These files are as follows:

- `base.py`: The base settings file that contains common settings (previously `settings.py`)
- `local.py`: Custom settings for your local environment
- `prod.py`: Custom settings for the production environment

You have moved the settings files to a directory one level below, so you need to update the `BASE_DIR` setting in the `settings/base.py` file to point to the main project directory.

When handling multiple environments, create a base settings file and a settings file for each environment. Environment settings files should inherit the common settings and override environment-specific settings.

Edit the `settings/base.py` file and replace the following line:

```
BASE_DIR = Path(__file__).resolve().parent.parent
```

with the following one:

```
BASE_DIR = Path(__file__).resolve().parent.parent.parent
```

You point to one directory above by adding `.parent` to the `BASE_DIR` path. Let's configure the settings for the local environment.

Local environment settings

Instead of using a default configuration for the `DEBUG` and `DATABASES` settings, you will define them for each environment explicitly. These settings will be environment specific. Edit the `educa/settings/local.py` file and add the following lines:

```
from .base import *

DEBUG = True

DATABASES = {
    'default': {
        'ENGINE': 'django.db.backends.sqlite3',
        'NAME': BASE_DIR / 'db.sqlite3',
    }
}
```

This is the settings file for your local environment. In this file, you import all settings defined in the `base.py` file, and you define the `DEBUG` and `DATABASES` settings for this environment. The `DEBUG` and `DATABASES` settings remain the same as you have been using for development.

Now remove the `DATABASES` and `DEBUG` settings from the `base.py` settings file.

Django management commands won't automatically detect the settings file to use because the project settings file is not the default `settings.py` file. When running management commands, you need to indicate the settings module to use by adding a `--settings` option, as follows:

```
python manage.py runserver --settings=educa.settings.local
```

Next, we are going to validate the project and the local environment configuration.

Running the local environment

Let's run the local environment using the new settings structure. Make sure Redis is running or start the Redis Docker container in a shell with the following command:

```
docker run -it --rm --name redis -p 6379:6379 redis
```

Run the following management command in another shell, from the project directory:

```
python manage.py runserver --settings=educa.settings.local
```

Open http://127.0.0.1:8000/ in your browser and check that the site loads correctly. You are now serving your site using the settings for the local environment.

If don't want to pass the --settings option every time you run a management command, you can define the DJANGO_SETTINGS_MODULE environment variable. Django will use it to identify the settings module to use. If you are using Linux or macOS, you can define the environment variable by executing the following command in the shell:

```
export DJANGO_SETTINGS_MODULE=educa.settings.local
```

If you are using Windows, you can execute the following command in the shell:

```
set DJANGO_SETTINGS_MODULE=educa.settings.local
```

Any management command you execute after will use the settings defined in the DJANGO_SETTINGS_MODULE environment variable.

Stop the Django development server from the shell by pressing the keys *Ctrl + C* and stop the Redis Docker container from the shell by also pressing the keys *Ctrl + C*.

The local environment works well. Let's prepare the settings for the production environment.

Production environment settings

Let's start by adding initial settings for the production environment. Edit the educa/settings/prod.py file and make it look as follows:

```
from .base import *

DEBUG = False

ADMINS = [
    ('Antonio M', 'email@mydomain.com'),
]

ALLOWED_HOSTS = ['*']

DATABASES = {
    'default': {
    }
}
```

These are the settings for the production environment:

- DEBUG: Setting DEBUG to False is necessary for any production environment. Failing to do so will result in the traceback information and sensitive configuration data being exposed to everyone.

- **ADMINS:** When `DEBUG` is `False` and a view raises an exception, all information will be sent by email to the people listed in the `ADMINS` setting. Make sure that you replace the name/email tuple with your own information.
- **ALLOWED_HOSTS:** For security reasons, Django will only allow the hosts included in this list to serve the project. For now, you allow all hosts by using the asterisk symbol, *. You will limit the hosts that can be used for serving the project later.
- **DATABASES:** You keep `default` database settings empty because you will configure the production database later.

Over the next sections of this chapter, you will complete the settings file for your production environment.

You have successfully organized settings for handling multiple environments. Now you will build a complete production environment by setting up different services with Docker.

Using Docker Compose

Docker allows you to build, deploy, and run application containers. A Docker container combines application source code with operating system libraries and dependencies required to run the application. By using application containers, you can improve your application portability. You are already using a Redis Docker image to serve Redis in your local environment. This Docker image contains everything needed to run Redis and allows you to run it seamlessly on your machine. For the production environment, you will use Docker Compose to build and run different Docker containers.

Docker Compose is a tool for defining and running multi-container applications. You can create a configuration file to define the different services and use a single command to start all services from your configuration. You can find information about Docker Compose at `https://docs.docker.com/compose/`.

For the production environment, you will create a distributed application that runs across multiple Docker containers. Each Docker container will run a different service. You will initially define the following three services and you will add additional services in the next sections:

- Web service: A web server to serve the Django project
- Database service: A database service to run PostgreSQL
- Cache service: A service to run Redis

Let's start by installing Docker Compose.

Installing Docker Compose

You can run Docker Compose on macOS, 64-bit Linux, and Windows. The fastest way to install Docker Compose is by installing Docker Desktop. The installation includes Docker Engine, the command-line interface, and the Docker Compose plugin.

Install Docker Desktop by following the instructions at `https://docs.docker.com/compose/install/compose-desktop/`.

Open the Docker Desktop application and click on **Containers**. It will look as follows:

Figure 17.1: The Docker Desktop interface

After installing Docker Compose, you will need to create a Docker image for your Django project.

Creating a Dockerfile

You need to create a Docker image to run the Django project. A `Dockerfile` is a text file that contains the commands for Docker to assemble a Docker image. You will prepare a `Dockerfile` with the commands to build the Docker image for the Django project.

Next to the educa project directory, create a new file and name it `Dockerfile`. Add the following code to the new file:

```
# Pull official base Python Docker image
FROM python:3.10.6

# Set environment variables
ENV PYTHONDONTWRITEBYTECODE=1
ENV PYTHONUNBUFFERED=1

# Set work directory
WORKDIR /code

# Install dependencies
RUN pip install --upgrade pip
```

```
COPY requirements.txt /code/
RUN pip install -r requirements.txt

# Copy the Django project
COPY . /code/
```

This code performs the following tasks:

1. The Python 3.10.6 parent Docker image is used. You can find the official Python Docker image at https://hub.docker.com/_/python.

2. The following environment variables are set:

    a. PYTHONDONTWRITEBYTECODE: Prevents Python from writing out pyc files.

    b. PYTHONUNBUFFERED: Ensures that the Python stdout and stderr streams are sent straight to the terminal without first being buffered.

3. The WORKDIR command is used to define the working directory of the image.

4. The pip package of the image is upgraded.

5. The requirements.txt file is copied to the code directory of the parent Python image.

6. The Python packages in requirements.txt are installed in the image using pip.

7. The Django project source code is copied from the local directory to the code directory of the image.

With this Dockerfile, you have defined how the Docker image to serve Django will be assembled. You can find the Dockerfile reference at https://docs.docker.com/engine/reference/builder/.

Adding the Python requirements

A requirements.txt file is used in the Dockerfile you created to install all necessary Python packages for the project.

Next to the educa project directory, create a new file and name it requirements.txt. You may have already created this file before and copied the content for the requirements.txt file from https://github.com/PacktPublishing/Django-4-by-example/blob/main/Chapter17/requirements.txt. If you haven't done so, add the following lines to the newly created requirements.txt file:

```
asgiref==3.5.2
Django~=4.1
Pillow==9.2.0
sqlparse==0.4.2
django-braces==1.15.0
django-embed-video==1.4.4
pymemcache==3.5.2
django-debug-toolbar==3.6.0
redis==4.3.4
```

```
django-redisboard==8.3.0
djangorestframework==3.13.1
requests==2.28.1
channels==3.0.5
channels-redis==3.4.1
psycopg2==2.9.3
uwsgi==2.0.20
daphne==3.0.2
```

In addition to the Python packages that you have installed in the previous chapters, the requirements.txt includes the following packages:

- psycopg2: A PostgreSQL adapter. You will use PostgreSQL for the production environment.
- uwsgi: A WSGI web server. You will configure this web server later to serve Django in the production environment.
- daphne: An ASGI web server. You will use this web server later to serve Django Channels.

Let's start by setting up the Docker application in Docker Compose. We will create a Docker Compose file with the definition for the web server, database, and Redis services.

Creating a Docker Compose file

To define the services that will run in different Docker containers, we will use a Docker Compose file. The Compose file is a text file with YAML format, defining services, networks, and data volumes for a Docker application. YAML is a human-readable data-serialization language. You can see an example of a YAML file at https://yaml.org/.

Next to the educa project directory, create a new file and name it docker-compose.yml. Add the following code to it:

```
services:

  web:
    build: .
    command: python /code/educa/manage.py runserver 0.0.0.0:8000
    restart: always
    volumes:
      - .:/code
    ports:
      - "8000:8000"
    environment:
      - DJANGO_SETTINGS_MODULE=educa.settings.prod
```

In this file, you define a web service. The sections to define this service are as follows:

- build: Defines the build requirements for a service container image. This can be a single string defining a context path, or a detailed build definition. You provide a relative path with a single dot . to point to the same directory where the Compose file is located. Docker Compose will look for a Dockerfile at this location. You can read more about the build section at https:// docs.docker.com/compose/compose-file/build/.

- command: Overrides the default command of the container. You run the Django development server using the runserver management command. The project is served on host 0.0.0.0, which is the default Docker IP, on port 8000.

- restart: Defines the restart policy for the container. Using always, the container is restarted always if it stops. This is useful for a production environment, where you want to minimize downtime. You can read more about the restart policy at https://docs.docker.com/config/ containers/start-containers-automatically/.

- volumes: Data in Docker containers is not permanent. Each Docker container has a virtual filesystem that is populated with the files of the image and that is destroyed when the container is stopped. Volumes are the preferred method to persist data generated and used by Docker containers. In this section, you mount the local directory . to the /code directory of the image. You can read more about Docker volumes at https://docs.docker.com/storage/volumes/.

- ports: Exposes container ports. Host port 8000 is mapped to container port 8000, on which the Django development server is running.

- environment: Defines environment variables. You set the DJANGO_SETTINGS_MODULE environment variable to use the production Django settings file educa.settings.prod.

Note that in the Docker Compose file definition, you are using the Django development server to serve the application. The Django development server is not suitable for production use, so you will replace it later with a WSGI Python web server.

You can find information about the Docker Compose specification at https://docs.docker.com/ compose/compose-file/.

At this point, assuming your parent directory is named Chapter17, the file structure should look as follows:

```
Chapter17/
    Dockerfile
    docker-compose.yml
    educa/
        manage.py
        ...
    requirements.txt
```

Open a shell in the parent directory, where the `docker-compose.yml` file is located, and run the following command:

```
docker compose up
```

This will start the Docker app defined in the Docker Compose file. You will see an output that includes the following lines:

```
chapter17-web-1  | Performing system checks...
chapter17-web-1  |
chapter17-web-1  | System check identified no issues (0 silenced).
chapter17-web-1  | July 19, 2022 - 15:56:28
chapter17-web-1  | Django version 4.1, using settings 'educa.settings.prod'
chapter17-web-1  | Starting ASGI/Channels version 3.0.5 development server at
http://0.0.0.0:8000/
chapter17-web-1  | Quit the server with CONTROL-C.
```

The Docker container for your Django project is running!

Open `http://localhost:8000/admin/` with your browser. You should see the Django administration site login form. It should look like *Figure 17.2*:

Django administration

Username: [   ]
Password: [   ]
[Log in]

Figure 17.2: The Django administration site login form

CSS styles are not being loaded. You are using `DEBUG=False`, so URL patterns for serving static files are not being included in the main `urls.py` file of the project. Remember that the Django development server is not suitable for serving static files. You will configure a server for serving static files later in this chapter.

If you access any other URL of your site, you might get an HTTP `500` error because you haven't configured a database for the production environment yet.

Take a look at the Docker Desktop app. You will see the following containers:

			NAME	IMAGE ↑	⁞	STATUS	PORT(S)	STARTED	⁞				
☐													
☐	⌄	⬚	**chapter17** 1 container	-		Running (1/1)	-			‖	↻	■	🗑
☐		⬚	**web-1** a9d7ca5be970 ⧉	chapter17_web		Running	8000	37 seconds ag 🗗 🖻		‖	↻	■	

Figure 17.3: The chapter17 application and the web-1 container in Docker Desktop

The chapter17 Docker application is running and it has a single container named web-1, which is running on port 8000. The name for the Docker application is generated dynamically using the name of the directory where the Docker Compose file is located, in this case, chapter17.

Next, you are going to add a PostgreSQL service and a Redis service to your Docker application.

Configuring the PostgreSQL service

Throughout this book, you have mostly used the SQLite database. SQLite is simple and quick to set up, but for a production environment, you will need a more powerful database, such as PostgreSQL, MySQL, or Oracle. You learned how to install PostgreSQL in *Chapter 3, Extending Your Blog Application*. For the production environment, we will use a PostgreSQL Docker image instead. You can find information about the official PostgreSQL Docker image at https://hub.docker.com/_/postgres.

Edit the docker-compose.yml file and add the following lines highlighted in bold:

```
services:

  db:
    image: postgres:14.5
    restart: always
    volumes:
      - ./data/db:/var/lib/postgresql/data
    environment:
      - POSTGRES_DB=postgres
      - POSTGRES_USER=postgres
      - POSTGRES_PASSWORD=postgres

  web:
    build: .
    command: python /code/educa/manage.py runserver 0.0.0.0:8000
```

```
      restart: always
      volumes:
        - .:/code
      ports:
        - "8000:8000"
      environment:
        - DJANGO_SETTINGS_MODULE=educa.settings.prod
        - POSTGRES_DB=postgres
        - POSTGRES_USER=postgres
        - POSTGRES_PASSWORD=postgres
      depends_on:
        - db
```

With these changes, you define a service named db with the following subsections:

- image: The service uses the base postgres Docker image.

- restart: The restart policy is set to always.

- volumes: You mount the ./data/db directory to the image directory /var/lib/postgresql/data to persist the database so that data stored in the database is maintained after the Docker application is stopped. This will create the local data/db/ path.

- environment: You use the POSTGRES_DB (database name), POSTGRES_USER, and POSTGRES_PASSWORD variables with default values.

The definition for the web service now includes the PostgreSQL environment variables for Django. You create a service dependency using depends_on so that the web service is started after the db service. This will guarantee the order of the container initialization, but it won't guarantee that PostgreSQL is fully initiated before the Django web server is started. To solve this, you need to use a script that will wait on the availability of the database host and its TCP port. Docker recommends using the wait-for-it tool to control container initialization.

Download the wait-for-it.sh Bash script from https://github.com/vishnubob/wait-for-it/blob/master/wait-for-it.sh and save the file next to the docker-compose.yml file. Then edit the docker-compose.yml file and modify the web service definition as follows. New code is highlighted in bold:

```
web:
  build: .
  command: ["./wait-for-it.sh", "db:5432", "--",
            "python", "/code/educa/manage.py", "runserver",
            "0.0.0.0:8000"]
  restart: always
  volumes:
      - .:/code
    environment:
```

```
    - DJANGO_SETTINGS_MODULE=educa.settings.prod
    - POSTGRES_DB=postgres
    - POSTGRES_USER=postgres
    - POSTGRES_PASSWORD=postgres
  depends_on:
    - db
```

In this service definition, you use the `wait-for-it.sh` Bash script to wait for the db host to be ready and accepting connections on port 5432, the default port for PostgreSQL, before starting the Django development server. You can read more about the service startup order in Compose at `https://docs.docker.com/compose/startup-order/`.

Let's edit Django settings. Edit the `educa/settings/prod.py` file and add the following code highlighted in bold:

```python
import os
from .base import *

DEBUG = False

ADMINS = [
    ('Antonio M', 'email@mydomain.com'),
]

ALLOWED_HOSTS = ['*']

DATABASES = {
    'default': {
        'ENGINE': 'django.db.backends.postgresql',
        'NAME': os.environ.get('POSTGRES_DB'),
        'USER': os.environ.get('POSTGRES_USER'),
        'PASSWORD': os.environ.get('POSTGRES_PASSWORD'),
        'HOST': 'db',
        'PORT': 5432,
    }
}
```

In the production settings file, you use the following settings:

- `ENGINE`: You use the Django database backend for PostgreSQL.
- `NAME`, `USER`, and `PASSWORD`: You use `os.environ.get()` to retrieve the environment variables `POSTGRES_DB` (database name), `POSTGRES_USER`, and `POSTGRES_PASSWORD`. You have set these environment variables in the Docker Compose file.

- HOST: You use db, which is the container hostname for the database service defined in the Docker Compose file. A container hostname defaults to the container's ID in Docker. That's why you use the db hostname.
- PORT: You use the value 5432, which is the default port for PostgreSQL.

Stop the Docker application from the shell by pressing the keys *Ctrl + C* or using the stop button in the Docker Desktop app. Then start Compose again with the command:

```
docker compose up
```

The first execution after adding the db service to the Docker Compose file will take longer because PostgreSQL needs to initialize the database. The output will contain the following two lines:

```
chapter17-db-1    | database system is ready to accept connections
...
chapter17-web-1  | Starting ASGI/Channels version 3.0.5 development server at
http://0.0.0.0:8000/
```

Both the PostgreSQL database and the Django application are ready. The production database is empty, so you need to apply database migrations.

Applying database migrations and creating a superuser

Open a different shell in the parent directory, where the docker-compose.yml file is located, and run the following command:

```
docker compose exec web python /code/educa/manage.py migrate
```

The command docker compose exec allows you to execute commands in the container. You use this command to execute the migrate management command in the web Docker container.

Finally, create a superuser with the following command:

```
docker compose exec web python /code/educa/manage.py createsuperuser
```

Migrations have been applied to the database and you have created a superuser. You can access http://localhost:8000/admin/ with the superuser credentials. CSS styles still won't load because you haven't configured serving static files yet.

You have defined services to serve Django and PostgreSQL using Docker Compose. Next, you will add a service to serve Redis in the production environment.

Configuring the Redis service

Let's add a Redis service to the Docker Compose file. For this purpose, you will use the official Redis Docker image. You can find information about the official Redis Docker image at https://hub.docker.com/_/redis.

Edit the `docker-compose.yml` file and add the following lines highlighted in bold:

```
services:

  db:
    # ...

  cache:
    image: redis:7.0.4
    restart: always
    volumes:
      - ./data/cache:/data

  web:
    # ...
    depends_on:
      - db
      - cache
```

In the previous code, you define the `cache` service with the following subsections:

- `image`: The service uses the base `redis` Docker image.
- `restart`: The restart policy is set to `always`.
- `volumes`: You mount the `./data/cache` directory to the image directory `/data` where any Redis writes will be persisted. This will create the local `data/cache/` path.

In the web service definition, you add the `cache` service as a dependency, so that the `web` service is started after the `cache` service. The Redis server initializes fast, so you don't need to use the `wait-for-it` tool in this case.

Edit the `educa/settings/prod.py` file and add the following lines:

```
REDIS_URL = 'redis://cache:6379'
CACHES['default']['LOCATION'] = REDIS_URL
CHANNEL_LAYERS['default']['CONFIG']['hosts'] = [REDIS_URL]
```

In these settings, you use the `cache` hostname that is automatically generated by Docker Compose using the name of the cache service and port 6379 used by Redis. You modify the Django `CACHE` setting and the `CHANNEL_LAYERS` setting used by Channels to use the production Redis URL.

Stop the Docker application from the shell by pressing the keys *Ctrl + C* or using the stop button in the Docker Desktop app. Then start Compose again with the command:

```
docker compose up
```

Open the Docker Desktop application. You should see now the chapter17 Docker application running a container for each service defined in the Docker Compose file: db, cache, and web:

		NAME	IMAGE	STATUS	PORT(S)	STARTED	
☐	⌄ ⬢	chapter17 3 containers	-	Running (3/3)	-		‖ ⟳ ■ 🗑
☐	▦	db-1 9d0b376f0547 📋	postgres	Running	-	5 minutes agc	⊡ ‖ ⟳ ■
☐	▦	web-1 087abe150782 📋	chapter17_web	Running	8000	5 minutes agc ↗ ⊡ ‖ ⟳ ■
☐	▦	cache-1 0600a3fbf3cd 📋	redis	Running	-	5 minutes agc	⊡ ‖ ⟳ ■

Figure 17.4: The chapter17 application with the db-1, web-1, and cache-1 containers in Docker Desktop

You are still serving Django with the Django development server, which is not suitable for production use. Let's replace it with the WSGI Python web server.

Serving Django through WSGI and NGINX

Django's primary deployment platform is WSGI. **WSGI** stands for **Web Server Gateway Interface**, and it is the standard for serving Python applications on the web.

When you generate a new project using the startproject command, Django creates a wsgi.py file inside your project directory. This file contains a WSGI application callable, which is an access point to your application.

WSGI is used for both running your project with the Django development server and deploying your application with the server of your choice in a production environment. You can learn more about WSGI at https://wsgi.readthedocs.io/en/latest/.

Using uWSGI

Throughout this book, you have been using the Django development server to run projects in your local environment. However, you need a standard web server for deploying your application in a production environment.

uWSGI is an extremely fast Python application server. It communicates with your Python application using the WSGI specification. uWSGI translates web requests into a format that your Django project can process.

Let's configure uWSGI to serve the Django project. You already added uwsgi==2.0.20 to the requirements. txt file of the project, so uWSGI is already being installed in the Docker image of the web service.

Edit the docker-compose.yml file and modify the web service definition as follows. New code is high-lighted in bold:

```
web:
    build: .
    command: ["./wait-for-it.sh", "db:5432", "--",
              "uwsgi", "--ini", "/code/config/uwsgi/uwsgi.ini"]
    restart: always
    volumes:
      - .:/code
    environment:
      - DJANGO_SETTINGS_MODULE=educa.settings.prod
      - POSTGRES_DB=postgres
      - POSTGRES_USER=postgres
      - POSTGRES_PASSWORD=postgres
    depends_on:
      - db
      - cache
```

Make sure to remove the ports section. uWSGI will be reachable with a socket, so you don't need to expose a port in the container.

The new command for the image runs uwsgi passing the configuration file /code/config/uwsgi/uwsgi.ini to it. Let's create the configuration file for uWSGI.

Configuring uWSGI

uWSGI allows you to define a custom configuration in a .ini file. Next to the docker-compose.yml file, create the file path config/uwsgi/uwsgi.ini. Assuming your parent directory is named Chapter17, the file structure should look as follows:

```
Chapter17/
    config/
        uwsgi/
            uwsgi.ini
    Dockerfile
    docker-compose.yml
    educa/
        manage.py
        ...
    requirements.txt
```

Edit the `config/uwsgi/uwsgi.ini` file and add the following code to it:

```
[uwsgi]
socket=/code/educa/uwsgi_app.sock
chdir = /code/educa/
module=educa.wsgi:application
master=true
chmod-socket=666
uid=www-data
gid=www-data
vacuum=true
```

In the `uwsgi.ini` file, you define the following options:

- `socket`: The UNIX/TCP socket to bind the server.
- `chdir`: The path to your project directory, so that uWSGI changes to that directory before loading the Python application.
- `module`: The WSGI module to use. You set this to the `application` callable contained in the `wsgi` module of your project.
- `master`: Enable the master process.
- `chmod-socket`: The file permissions to apply to the socket file. In this case, you use 666 so that NGINX can read/write the socket.
- `uid`: The user ID of the process once it's started.
- `gid`: The group ID of the process once it's started.
- `vacuum`: Using `true` instructs uWSGI to clean up any temporary files or UNIX sockets it creates.

The `socket` option is intended for communication with some third-party router, such as NGINX. You are going to run uWSGI using a socket and you are going to configure NGINX as your web server, which will communicate with uWSGI through the socket.

You can find the list of available uWSGI options at `https://uwsgi-docs.readthedocs.io/en/latest/Options.html`.

You will not be able to access your uWSGI instance from your browser now, since it's running through a socket. Let's complete the production environment.

Using NGINX

When you are serving a website, you have to serve dynamic content, but you also need to serve static files, such as CSS style sheets, JavaScript files, and images. While uWSGI is capable of serving static files, it adds an unnecessary overhead to HTTP requests and therefore, it is encouraged to set up a web server, such as NGINX, in front of it.

NGINX is a web server focused on high concurrency, performance, and low memory usage. NGINX also acts as a reverse proxy, receiving HTTP and WebSocket requests and routing them to different backends.

Generally, you will use a web server, such as NGINX, in front of uWSGI for serving static files efficiently, and you will forward dynamic requests to uWSGI workers. By using NGINX, you can also apply different rules and benefit from its reverse proxy capabilities.

We will add the NGINX service to the Docker Compose file using the official NGINX Docker image. You can find information about the official NGINX Docker image at `https://hub.docker.com/_/nginx`.

Edit the `docker-compose.yml` file and add the following lines highlighted in bold:

```
services:

  db:
    # ...

  cache:
    # ...

  web:
    # ...

  nginx:
    image: nginx:1.23.1
    restart: always
    volumes:
      - ./config/nginx:/etc/nginx/templates
      - .:/code
    ports:
      - "80:80"
```

You have added the definition for the `nginx` service with the following subsections:

- `image`: The service uses the base `nginx` Docker image.
- `restart`: The restart policy is set to `always`.
- `volumes`: You mount the `./config/nginx` volume to the `/etc/nginx/templates` directory of the Docker image. This is where NGINX will look for a default configuration template. You also mount the local directory `.` to the `/code` directory of the image, so that NGINX can have access to static files.
- `ports`: You expose port `80`, which is mapped to container port `80`. This is the default port for HTTP.

Let's configure the NGINX web server.

Configuring NGINX

Create the following file path highlighted in bold under the `config/` directory:

```
config/
    uwsgi/
       uwsgi.ini
    nginx/
          default.conf.template
```

Edit the file `nginx/default.conf.template` and add the following code to it:

```
# upstream for uWSGI
upstream uwsgi_app {
    server unix:/code/educa/uwsgi_app.sock;
}

server {
    listen        80;
    server_name   www.educaproject.com educaproject.com;
    error_log     stderr warn;
    access_log    /dev/stdout main;

    location / {
        include      /etc/nginx/uwsgi_params;
        uwsgi_pass   uwsgi_app;
    }
}
```

This is the basic configuration for NGINX. In this configuration, you set up an upstream named `uwsgi_app`, which points to the socket created by uWSGI. You use the `server` block with the following configuration:

- You tell NGINX to listen on port `80`.
- You set the server name to both `www.educaproject.com` and `educaproject.com`. NGINX will serve incoming requests for both domains.
- You use `stderr` for the `error_log` directive to get error logs written to the standard error file. The second parameter determines the logging level. You use `warn` to get warnings and errors of higher severity.
- You point `access_log` to the standard output with `/dev/stdout`.
- You specify that any request under the `/` path has to be routed to the `uwsgi_app` socket to uWSGI.
- You include the default uWSGI configuration parameters that come with NGINX. These are located at `/etc/nginx/uwsgi_params`.

NGINX is now configured. You can find the NGINX documentation at `https://nginx.org/en/docs/`.

Stop the Docker application from the shell by pressing the keys *Ctrl + C* or using the stop button in the Docker Desktop app. Then start Compose again with the command:

```
docker compose up
```

Open the URL `http://localhost/` in your browser. It's not necessary to add a port to the URL because you are accessing the host through the standard HTTP port 80. You should see the course list page with no CSS styles, like *Figure 17.5*:

<u>Educa</u>

- <u>Sign in</u>

All courses

Subjects

- <u>All</u>

Figure 17.5: The course list page served with NGINX and uWSGI

The following diagram shows the request/response cycle of the production environment that you have set up:

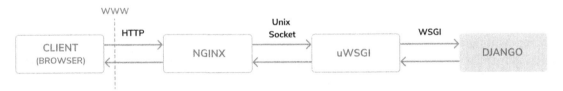

Figure 17.6: The production environment request/response cycle

The following happens when the client browser sends an HTTP request:

1. NGINX receives the HTTP request.
2. NGINX delegates the request to uWSGI through a socket.
3. uWSGI passes the request to Django for processing.
4. Django returns an HTTP response that is passed back to NGINX, which in turn passes it back to the client browser.

If you check the Docker Desktop application, you should see that there are 4 containers running:

- db service running PostgreSQL
- cache service running Redis
- web service running uWSGI + Django
- nginx service running NGINX

Let's continue with the production environment setup. Instead of accessing our project using `localhost`, we will configure the project to use the `educaproject.com` hostname.

Using a hostname

You will use the `educaproject.com` hostname for your site. Since you are using a sample domain name, you need to redirect it to your local host.

If you are using Linux or macOS, edit the `/etc/hosts` file and add the following line to it:

```
127.0.0.1 educaproject.com www.educaproject.com
```

If you are using Windows, edit the file `C:\Windows\System32\drivers\etc` and add the same line.

By doing so, you are routing the hostnames `educaproject.com` and `www.educaproject.com` to your local server. In a production server, you won't need to do this, since you will have a fixed IP address and you will point your hostname to your server in your domain's DNS configuration.

Open `http://educaproject.com/` in your browser. You should be able to see your site, still without any static assets loaded. Your production environment is almost ready.

Now you can restrict the hosts that can serve your Django project. Edit the production settings file `educa/settings/prod.py` of your project and change the `ALLOWED_HOSTS` setting, as follows:

```
ALLOWED_HOSTS = ['educaproject.com', 'www.educaproject.com']
```

Django will only serve your application if it's running under any of these hostnames. You can read more about the `ALLOWED_HOSTS` setting at `https://docs.djangoproject.com/en/4.1/ref/settings/#allowed-hosts`.

The production environment is almost ready. Let's continue by configuring NGINX to serve static files.

Serving static and media assets

uWSGI is capable of serving static files flawlessly, but it is not as fast and effective as NGINX. For the best performance, you will use NGINX to serve static files in your production environment. You will set up NGINX to serve both the static files of your application (CSS style sheets, JavaScript files, and images) and media files uploaded by instructors for the course contents.

Edit the `settings/base.py` file and add the following line just below the `STATIC_URL` setting:

```
STATIC_ROOT = BASE_DIR / 'static'
```

This is the root directory for all static files of the project. Next, you are going to collect the static files from the different Django applications into the common directory.

Collecting static files

Each application in your Django project may contain static files in a `static/` directory. Django provides a command to collect static files from all applications into a single location. This simplifies the setup for serving static files in production. The `collectstatic` command collects the static files from all applications of the project into the path defined with the `STATIC_ROOT` setting.

Stop the Docker application from the shell by pressing the keys *Ctrl + C* or using the stop button in the Docker Desktop app. Then start Compose again with the command:

```
docker compose up
```

Open another shell in the parent directory, where the `docker-compose.yml` file is located, and run the following command:

```
docker compose exec web python /code/educa/manage.py collectstatic
```

Note that you can alternatively run the following command in the shell, from the `educa/` project directory:

```
python manage.py collectstatic --settings=educa.settings.local
```

Both commands will have the same effect since the base local directory is mounted to the Docker image. Django will ask if you want to override any existing files in the root directory. Type yes and press *Enter*. You will see the following output:

```
171 static files copied to '/code/educa/static'.
```

Files located under the `static/` directory of each application present in the `INSTALLED_APPS` setting have been copied to the global `/educa/static/` project directory.

Serving static files with NGINX

Edit the `config/nginx/default.conf.template` file and add the following lines highlighted in bold to the `server` block:

```
server {
    # ...

    location / {
        include      /etc/nginx/uwsgi_params;
        uwsgi_pass   uwsgi_app;
    }

    location /static/ {
        alias /code/educa/static/;
```

```
    }
    location /media/ {
        alias /code/educa/media/;
    }
}
```

These directives tell NGINX to serve static files located under the /static/ and /media/ paths directly.
These paths are as follows:

- /static/: Corresponds to the path of the STATIC_URL setting. The target path corresponds to
  the value of the STATIC_ROOT setting. You use it to serve the static files of your application from
  the directory mounted to the NGINX Docker image.
- /media/: Corresponds to the path of the MEDIA_URL setting, and its target path corresponds to
  the value of the MEDIA_ROOT setting. You use it to serve the media files uploaded to the course
  contents from the directory mounted to the NGINX Docker image.

The schema of the production environment now looks like this:

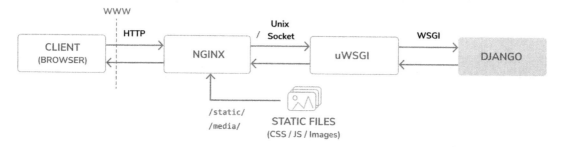

Figure 17.7: The production environment request/response cycle, including static files

Files under the /static/ and /media/ paths are now served by NGINX directly, instead of being forwarded to uWSGI. Requests to any other path are still passed by NGINX to uWSGI through the UNIX socket.

Stop the Docker application from the shell by pressing the keys *Ctrl + C* or using the stop button in the
Docker Desktop app. Then start Compose again with the command:

```
docker compose up
```

Open `http://educaproject.com/` in your browser. You should see the following screen:

Figure 17.8: The course list page served with NGINX and uWSGI

Static resources, such as CSS style sheets and images, are now loaded correctly. HTTP requests for static files are now being served by NGINX directly, instead of being forwarded to uWSGI.

You have successfully configured NGINX for serving static files. Next, you are going to check your Django project to deploy it in a production environment and you are going to serve your site under HTTPS.

Securing your site with SSL/TLS

The **Transport Layer Security (TLS)** protocol is the standard for serving websites through a secure connection. The TLS predecessor is **Secure Sockets Layer (SSL)**. Although SSL is now deprecated, in multiple libraries and online documentation, you will find references to both the terms TLS and SSL. It's strongly encouraged that you serve your websites over HTTPS.

In this section, you are going to check your Django project for a production deployment and prepare the project to be served over HTTPS. Then, you are going to configure an SSL/TLS certificate in NGINX to serve your site securely.

Checking your project for production

Django includes a system check framework for validating your project at any time. The check framework inspects the applications installed in your Django project and detects common problems. Checks are triggered implicitly when you run management commands like `runserver` and `migrate`. However, you can trigger checks explicitly with the `check` management command.

You can read more about Django's system check framework at `https://docs.djangoproject.com/en/4.1/topics/checks/`.

Let's confirm that the check framework does not raise any issues for your project. Open the shell in the educa project directory and run the following command to check your project:

```
python manage.py check --settings=educa.settings.prod
```

You will see the following output:

```
System check identified no issues (0 silenced).
```

The system check framework didn't identify any issues. If you use the `--deploy` option, the system check framework will perform additional checks that are relevant for a production deployment.

Run the following command from the educa project directory:

```
python manage.py check --deploy --settings=educa.settings.prod
```

You will see output like the following:

```
System check identified some issues:

WARNINGS:
(security.W004) You have not set a value for the SECURE_HSTS_SECONDS setting.
...
(security.W008) Your SECURE_SSL_REDIRECT setting is not set to True...
(security.W009) Your SECRET_KEY has less than 50 characters, less than 5 unique
characters, or it's prefixed with 'django-insecure-'...
(security.W012) SESSION_COOKIE_SECURE is not set to True. ...
(security.W016) You have 'django.middleware.csrf.CsrfViewMiddleware' in your
MIDDLEWARE, but you have not set CSRF_COOKIE_SECURE ...

System check identified 5 issues (0 silenced).
```

The check framework has identified five issues (0 errors, 5 warnings). All warnings are related to security-related settings.

Let's address issue `security.W009`. Edit the `educa/settings/base.py` file and modify the `SECRET_KEY` setting by removing the `django-insecure-` prefix and adding additional random characters to generate a string with at least 50 characters.

Run the `check` command again and verify that issue `security.W009` is not raised anymore. The rest of the warnings are related to SSL/TLS configuration. We will address them next.

Configuring your Django project for SSL/TLS

Django comes with specific settings for SSL/TLS support. You are going to edit the production settings to serve your site over HTTPS.

Edit the educa/settings/prod.py settings file and add the following settings to it:

```
# Security
CSRF_COOKIE_SECURE = True
SESSION_COOKIE_SECURE = True
SECURE_SSL_REDIRECT = True
```

These settings are as follows:

- CSRF_COOKIE_SECURE: Use a secure cookie for **cross-site request forgery** (CSRF) protection. With True, browsers will only transfer the cookie over HTTPS.
- SESSION_COOKIE_SECURE: Use a secure session cookie. With True, browsers will only transfer the cookie over HTTPS.
- SECURE_SSL_REDIRECT: Whether HTTP requests have to be redirected to HTTPS.

Django will now redirect HTTP requests to HTTPS; session and CSRF cookies will be sent only over HTTPS.

Run the following command from the main directory of your project:

```
python manage.py check --deploy --settings=educa.settings.prod
```

Only one warning remains, security.W004:

```
(security.W004) You have not set a value for the SECURE_HSTS_SECONDS setting.
...
```

This warning is related to the **HTTP Strict Transport Security** (HSTS) policy. The HSTS policy prevents users from bypassing warnings and connecting to a site with an expired, self-signed, or otherwise invalid SSL certificate. In the next section, we will use a self-signed certificate for our site, so we will ignore this warning. When you own a real domain, you can apply for a trusted **Certificate Authority** (**CA**) to issue an SSL/TLS certificate for it, so that browsers can verify its identity. In that case, you can give a value to SECURE_HSTS_SECONDS higher than 0, which is the default value. You can learn more about the HSTS policy at https://docs.djangoproject.com/en/4.1/ref/middleware/#http-strict-transport-security.

You have successfully fixed the rest of the issues raised by the check framework. You can read more about the Django deployment checklist at https://docs.djangoproject.com/en/4.1/howto/deployment/checklist/.

Creating an SSL/TLS certificate

Create a new directory inside the educa project directory and name it ssl. Then, generate an SSL/TLS certificate from the command line with the following command:

```
openssl req -x509 -newkey rsa:2048 -sha256 -days 3650 -nodes \
   -keyout ssl/educa.key -out ssl/educa.crt \
   -subj '/CN=*.educaproject.com' \
   -addext 'subjectAltName=DNS:*.educaproject.com'
```

This will generate a private key and a 2048-bit SSL/TLS certificate that is valid for 10 years. This certificate is issued for the hostname `*.educaproject.com`. This is a wildcard certificate; by using the wildcard character `*` in the domain name, the certificate can be used for any subdomain of `educaproject.com`, such as `www.educaproject.com` or `django.educaproject.com`. After generating the certificate, the `educa/ssl/` directory will contain two files: `educa.key` (the private key) and `educa.crt` (the certificate).

You will need at least OpenSSL 1.1.1 or LibreSSL 3.1.0 to use the `-addext` option. You can check the OpenSSL location in your machine with the command `which openssl` and you can check the version with the command `openssl version`.

Alternatively, you can use the SSL/TLS certificate provided in the source code for this chapter. You will find the certificate at `https://github.com/PacktPublishing/Django-4-by-example/blob/main/Chapter17/educa/ssl/`. Note that you should generate a private key and not use this certificate in production.

Configuring NGINX to use SSL/TLS

Edit the `docker-compose.yml` file and add the following line highlighted in bold:

```
services:
  # ...

  nginx:
    #...
    ports:
      - "80:80"
      - "443:443"
```

The NGINX container host will be accessible through port 80 (HTTP) and port 443 (HTTPS). The host port 443 is mapped to the container port 443.

Edit the `config/nginx/default.conf.template` file of the educa project and edit the server block to include SSL/TLS, as follows:

```
server {
    listen               80;
    listen               443 ssl;
    ssl_certificate      /code/educa/ssl/educa.crt;
    ssl_certificate_key  /code/educa/ssl/educa.key;
    server_name          www.educaproject.com educaproject.com;
    # ...
}
```

With the preceding code, NGINX now listens both to HTTP over port 80 and HTTPS over port 443. You indicate the path to the SSL/TLS certificate with `ssl_certificate` and the certificate key with `ssl_certificate_key`.

Stop the Docker application from the shell by pressing the keys *Ctrl* + *C* or using the stop button in the Docker Desktop app. Then start Compose again with the command:

```
docker compose up
```

Open `https://educaproject.com/` with your browser. You should see a warning message similar to the following one:

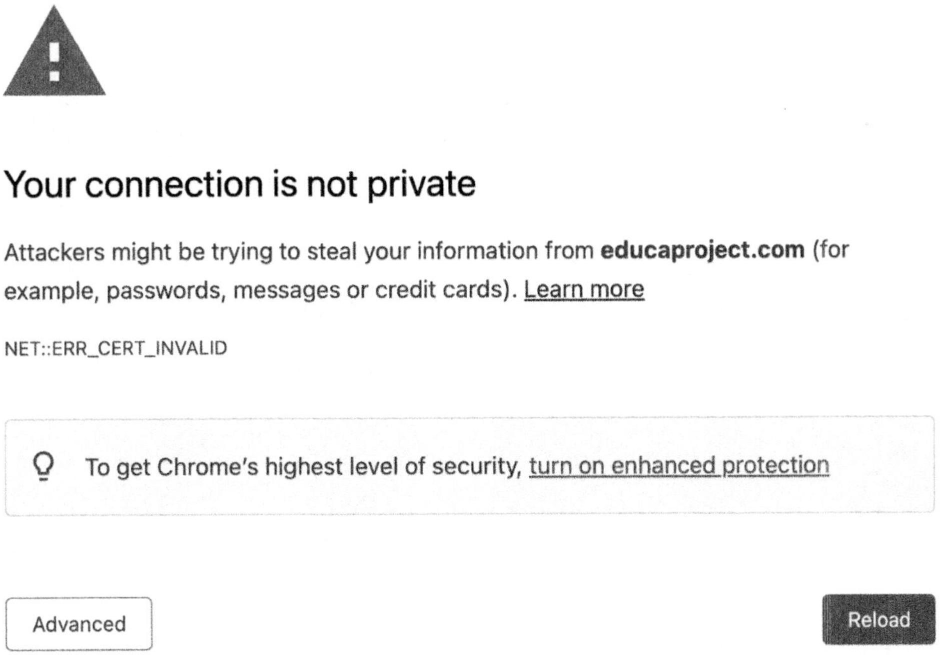

Your connection is not private

Attackers might be trying to steal your information from **educaproject.com** (for example, passwords, messages or credit cards). Learn more

NET::ERR_CERT_INVALID

> 💡   To get Chrome's highest level of security, turn on enhanced protection

Advanced   Reload

Figure 17.9: An invalid certificate warning

This screen might vary depending on your browser. It alerts you that your site is not using a trusted or valid certificate; the browser can't verify the identity of your site. This is because you signed your own certificate instead of obtaining one from a trusted CA. When you own a real domain, you can apply for a trusted CA to issue an SSL/TLS certificate for it, so that browsers can verify its identity. If you want to obtain a trusted certificate for a real domain, you can refer to the Let's Encrypt project created by the Linux Foundation. It is a nonprofit CA that simplifies obtaining and renewing trusted SSL/TLS certificates for free. You can find more information at `https://letsencrypt.org`.

Click on the link or button that provides additional information and choose to visit the website, ignoring warnings. The browser might ask you to add an exception for this certificate or verify that you trust it. If you are using Chrome, you might not see any option to proceed to the website. If this is the case, type thisisunsafe and press Enter directly in Chrome on the warning page. Chrome will then load the website. Note that you do this with your own issued certificate; don't trust any unknown certificate or bypass the browser SSL/TLS certificate checks for other domains.

When you access the site, the browser will display a lock icon next to the URL like *Figure 17.10*:

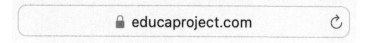

Figure 17.10: The browser address bar, including a secure connection padlock icon

Other browsers might display a warning indicating that the certificate is not trusted, like *Figure 17.11*:

Figure 17.11: The browser address bar, including a warning message

If you click the lock icon or the warning icon, the SSL/TLS certificate details will be displayed as follows:

Figure 17.12: TLS/SSL certificate details

In the certificate details, you will see it is a self-signed certificate and you will see its expiration date. Your browser might mark the certificate as unsafe, but you are using it for testing purposes only. You are now serving your site securely over HTTPS.

Redirecting HTTP traffic over to HTTPS

You are redirecting HTTP requests to HTTPS with Django using the SECURE_SSL_REDIRECT setting. Any request using http:// is redirected to the same URL using https://. However, this can be handled in a more efficient manner using NGINX.

Edit the config/nginx/default.conf.template file and add the following lines highlighted in bold:

```
# upstream for uWSGI
upstream uwsgi_app {
    server unix:/code/educa/uwsgi_app.sock;
}


server {
    listen       80;
    server_name www.educaproject.com educaproject.com;
    return 301 https://$host$request_uri;
}

server {
    listen                443 ssl;
    ssl_certificate       /code/educa/ssl/educa.crt;
    ssl_certificate_key   /code/educa/ssl/educa.key;
    server_name   www.educaproject.com educaproject.com;
    # ...
}
```

In this code, you remove the directive listen 80; from the original server block, so that the platform is only available over HTTPS (port 443). On top of the original server block, you add an additional server block that only listens on port 80 and redirects all HTTP requests to HTTPS. To achieve this, you return an HTTP response code 301 (permanent redirect) that redirects to the https:// version of the requested URL using the $host and $request_uri variables.

Open a shell in the parent directory, where the docker-compose.yml file is located, and run the following command to reload NGINX:

```
docker compose exec nginx nginx -s reload
```

This runs the nginx -s reload command in the nginx container. You are now redirecting all HTTP traffic to HTTPS using NGINX.

Your environment is now secured with TLS/SSL. To complete the production environment, you need to set up an asynchronous web server for Django Channels.

Using Daphne for Django Channels

In *Chapter 16, Building a Chat Server,* you used Django Channels to build a chat server using WebSockets. uWSGI is suitable for running Django or any other WSGI application, but it doesn't support asynchronous communication using **Asynchronous Server Gateway Interface (ASGI)** or WebSockets. In order to run Channels in production, you need an ASGI web server that is capable of managing WebSockets.

Daphne is an HTTP, HTTP2, and WebSocket server for ASGI developed to serve Channels. You can run Daphne alongside uWSGI to serve both ASGI and WSGI applications efficiently. You can find more information about Daphne at `https://github.com/django/daphne`.

You already added `daphne==3.0.2` to the `requirements.txt` file of the project. Let's create a new service in the Docker Compose file to run the Daphne web server.

Edit the `docker-compose.yml` file and add the following lines:

```
daphne:
    build: .
    working_dir: /code/educa/
    command: ["../wait-for-it.sh", "db:5432", "--",
              "daphne", "-u", "/code/educa/daphne.sock",
              "educa.asgi:application"]
    restart: always
    volumes:
      - .:/code
    environment:
      - DJANGO_SETTINGS_MODULE=educa.settings.prod
      - POSTGRES_DB=postgres
      - POSTGRES_USER=postgres
      - POSTGRES_PASSWORD=postgres
    depends_on:
      - db
      - cache
```

The daphne service definition is very similar to the web service. The image for the daphne service is also built with the Dockerfile you previously created for the web service. The main differences are:

- `working_dir` changes the working directory of the image to /code/educa/.
- `command` runs the `educa.asgi:application` application defined in the educa/asgi.py file with daphne using a UNIX socket. It also uses the wait-for-it Bash script to wait for the PostgreSQL database to be ready before initializing the web server.

Since you are running Django on production, Django checks the ALLOWED_HOSTS when receiving HTTP requests. We will implement the same validation for WebSocket connections.

Edit the educa/asgi.py file of your project and add the following lines highlighted in bold:

```
import os

from django.core.asgi import get_asgi_application
from channels.routing import ProtocolTypeRouter, URLRouter
from channels.security.websocket import AllowedHostsOriginValidator
from channels.auth import AuthMiddlewareStack
import chat.routing

os.environ.setdefault('DJANGO_SETTINGS_MODULE', 'educa.settings')

django_asgi_app = get_asgi_application()

application = ProtocolTypeRouter({
    'http': django_asgi_app,
    'websocket': AllowedHostsOriginValidator(
        AuthMiddlewareStack(
            URLRouter(chat.routing.websocket_urlpatterns)
        )
    ),
})
```

The Channels configuration is now ready for production.

Using secure connections for WebSockets

You have configured NGINX to use secure connections with SSL/TLS. You need to change ws (WebSocket) connections to use the wss (WebSocket Secure) protocol now, in the same way that HTTP connections are now being served over HTTPS.

Edit the chat/room.html template of the chat application and find the following line in the domready block:

```
const url = 'ws://' + window.location.host +
```

Replace that line with the following one:

```
const url = 'wss://' + window.location.host +
```

By using wss:// instead of ws://, you are explicitly connecting to a secure WebSocket.

Including Daphne in the NGINX configuration

In your production setup, you will run Daphne on a UNIX socket and use NGINX in front of it. NGINX will pass requests to Daphne based on the requested path. You will expose Daphne to NGINX through a UNIX socket interface, just like the uWSGI setup.

Edit the `config/nginx/default.conf.template` file and make it look as follows:

```
# upstream for uWSGI
upstream uwsgi_app {
    server unix:/code/educa/uwsgi_app.sock;
}

# upstream for Daphne
upstream daphne {
    server unix:/code/educa/daphne.sock;
}

server {
    listen        80;
    server_name www.educaproject.com educaproject.com;
    return 301 https://$host$request_uri;
}

server {
    listen              443 ssl;
    ssl_certificate     /code/educa/ssl/educa.crt;
    ssl_certificate_key /code/educa/ssl/educa.key;
    server_name www.educaproject.com educaproject.com;
    error_log    stderr warn;
    access_log   /dev/stdout main;

    location / {
        include      /etc/nginx/uwsgi_params;
        uwsgi_pass   uwsgi_app;
    }

    location /ws/ {
        proxy_http_version  1.1;
        proxy_set_header    Upgrade $http_upgrade;
        proxy_set_header    Connection "upgrade";
        proxy_redirect      off;
```

```
        proxy_pass              http://daphne;
    }


    location /static/ {
        alias /code/educa/static/;
    }
    location /media/ {
        alias /code/educa/media/;
    }


}
```

In this configuration, you set up a new upstream named daphne, which points to a UNIX socket created by Daphne. In the server block, you configure the /ws/ location to forward requests to Daphne. You use the proxy_pass directive to pass requests to Daphne and you include some additional proxy directives.

With this configuration, NGINX will pass any URL request that starts with the /ws/ prefix to Daphne and the rest to uWSGI, except for files under the /static/ or /media/ paths, which will be served directly by NGINX.

The production setup including Daphne now looks like this:

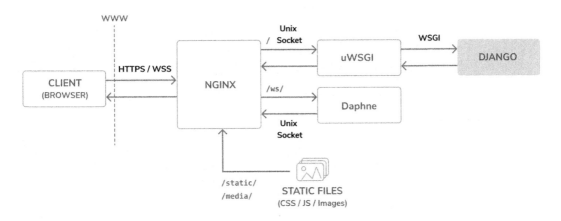

Figure 17.13: The production environment request/response cycle, including Daphne

NGINX runs in front of uWSGI and Daphne as a reverse proxy server. NGINX faces the web and passes requests to the application server (uWSGI or Daphne) based on their path prefix. Besides this, NGINX also serves static files and redirects non-secure requests to secure ones. This setup reduces downtime, consumes less server resources, and provides greater performance and security.

Stop the Docker application from the shell by pressing the keys *Ctrl* + *C* or using the stop button in the Docker Desktop app. Then start Compose again with the command:

```
docker compose up
```

Use your browser to create a sample course with an instructor user, log in with a user who is enrolled on the course, and open `https://educaproject.com/chat/room/1/` with your browser. You should be able to send and receive messages like the following example:

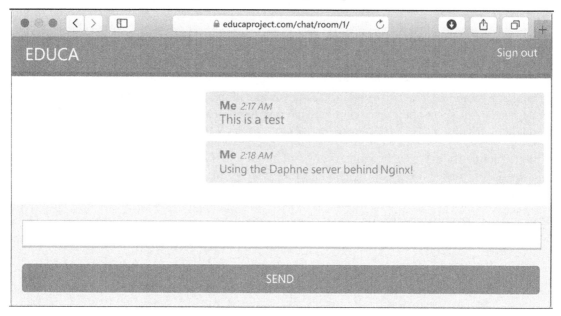

Figure 17.14: Course chat room messages served with NGINX and Daphne

Daphne is working correctly, and NGINX is passing WebSocket requests to it. All connections are secured with SSL/TLS.

Congratulations! You have built a custom production-ready stack using NGINX, uWSGI, and Daphne. You could do further optimization for additional performance and enhanced security through configuration settings in NGINX, uWSGI, and Daphne. However, this production setup is a great start!

You have used Docker Compose to define and run services in multiple containers. Note that you can use Docker Compose both for local development environments as well as production environments. You can find additional information on using Docker Compose in production at `https://docs.docker.com/compose/production/`.

For more advanced production environments, you will need to dynamically distribute containers across a varying number of machines. For that, instead of Docker Compose, you will need an orchestrator like Docker Swarm mode or Kubernetes. You can find information about Docker Swarm mode at `https://docs.docker.com/engine/swarm/`, and about Kubernetes at `https://kubernetes.io/docs/home/`.

Creating a custom middleware

You already know the MIDDLEWARE setting, which contains the middleware for your project. You can think of it as a low-level plugin system, allowing you to implement hooks that get executed in the request/response process. Each middleware is responsible for some specific action that will be executed for all HTTP requests or responses.

Avoid adding expensive processing to middleware, since they are executed in every single request.

When an HTTP request is received, middleware is executed in order of appearance in the MIDDLEWARE setting. When an HTTP response has been generated by Django, the response passes through all middleware back in reverse order.

A middleware can be written as a function, as follows:

```
def my_middleware(get_response):
    def middleware(request):
        # Code executed for each request before
        # the view (and later middleware) are called.
        response = get_response(request)
        # Code executed for each request/response after
        # the view is called.
        return response
    return middleware
```

A middleware factory is a callable that takes a get_response callable and returns a middleware. A middleware is a callable that takes a request and returns a response, just like a view. The get_response callable might be the next middleware in the chain or the actual view in the case of the last listed middleware.

If any middleware returns a response without calling its get_response callable, it short-circuits the process; no further middleware gets executed (also not the view), and the response returns through the same layers that the request passed in through.

The order of middleware in the MIDDLEWARE setting is very important because middleware can depend on data set in the request by other middleware that has been executed previously.

When adding a new middleware to the MIDDLEWARE setting, make sure to place it in the right position. Middleware is executed in order of appearance in the setting during the request phase, and in reverse order for responses.

You can find more information about middleware at https://docs.djangoproject.com/en/4.1/topics/http/middleware/.

Creating a subdomain middleware

You are going to create a custom middleware to allow courses to be accessible through a custom subdomain. Each course detail URL, which looks like `https://educaproject.com/course/django/`, will also be accessible through the subdomain that makes use of the course slug, such as `https://django.educaproject.com/`. Users will be able to use the subdomain as a shortcut to access the course details. Any requests to subdomains will be redirected to each corresponding course detail URL.

Middleware can reside anywhere within your project. However, it's recommended to create a `middleware.py` file in your application directory.

Create a new file inside the `courses` application directory and name it `middleware.py`. Add the following code to it:

```python
from django.urls import reverse
from django.shortcuts import get_object_or_404, redirect
from .models import Course


def subdomain_course_middleware(get_response):
    """
    Subdomains for courses
    """
    def middleware(request):
        host_parts = request.get_host().split('.')
        if len(host_parts) > 2 and host_parts[0] != 'www':
            # get course for the given subdomain
            course = get_object_or_404(Course, slug=host_parts[0])
            course_url = reverse('course_detail',
                                 args=[course.slug])
            # redirect current request to the course_detail view
            url = '{}://{}{}'.format(request.scheme,
                                     '.'.join(host_parts[1:]),
                                     course_url)
            return redirect(url)
        response = get_response(request)
        return response
    return middleware
```

When an HTTP request is received, you perform the following tasks:

1. You get the hostname that is being used in the request and divide it into parts. For example, if the user is accessing `mycourse.educaproject.com`, you generate the list `['mycourse', 'educaproject', 'com']`.

2. You check whether the hostname includes a subdomain by checking whether the split gener-ated more than two elements. If the hostname includes a subdomain, and this is not www, you try to get the course with the slug provided in the subdomain.

3. If a course is not found, you raise an HTTP 404 exception. Otherwise, you redirect the browser to the course detail URL.

Edit the settings/base.py file of the project and add 'courses.middleware.SubdomainCourseMiddleware' at the bottom of the MIDDLEWARE list, as follows:

```
MIDDLEWARE = [
    # ...
    'courses.middleware.subdomain_course_middleware',
]
```

The middleware will now be executed in every request.

Remember that the hostnames allowed to serve your Django project are specified in the ALLOWED_HOSTS setting. Let's change this setting so that any possible subdomain of educaproject.com is allowed to serve your application.

Edit the educa/settings/prod.py file and modify the ALLOWED_HOSTS setting, as follows:

```
ALLOWED_HOSTS = ['.educaproject.com']
```

A value that begins with a period is used as a subdomain wildcard; '.educaproject.com' will match educaproject.com and any subdomain for this domain, for example, course.educaproject.com and django.educaproject.com.

Serving multiple subdomains with NGINX

You need NGINX to be able to serve your site with any possible subdomain. Edit the config/nginx/default.conf.template file and replace the two occurrences of the following line:

```
server_name  www.educaproject.com educaproject.com;
```

with the following one:

```
server_name  *.educaproject.com educaproject.com;
```

By using the asterisk, this rule applies to all subdomains of educaproject.com. In order to test your middleware locally, you need to add any subdomains you want to test to /etc/hosts. For testing the middleware with a Course object with the slug django, add the following line to your /etc/hosts file:

```
127.0.0.1  django.educaproject.com
```

Stop the Docker application from the shell by pressing the keys *Ctrl* + *C* or using the stop button in the Docker Desktop app. Then start Compose again with the command:

```
docker compose up
```

Then, open `https://django.educaproject.com/` in your browser. The middleware will find the course by the subdomain and redirect your browser to `https://educaproject.com/course/django/`.

Implementing custom management commands

Django allows your applications to register custom management commands for the `manage.py` utility. For example, you used the management commands `makemessages` and `compilemessages` in *Chapter 11, Adding Internationalization to Your Shop*, to create and compile translation files.

A management command consists of a Python module containing a `Command` class that inherits from `django.core.management.base.BaseCommand` or one of its subclasses. You can create simple commands or make them take positional and optional arguments as input.

Django looks for management commands in the `management/commands/` directory for each active application in the `INSTALLED_APPS` setting. Each module found is registered as a management command named after it.

You can learn more about custom management commands at `https://docs.djangoproject.com/en/4.1/howto/custom-management-commands/`.

You are going to create a custom management command to remind students to enroll on at least one course. The command will send an email reminder to users who have been registered for longer than a specified period and who aren't enrolled on any course yet.

Create the following file structure inside the `students` application directory:

```
management/
    __init__.py
    commands/
        __init__.py
        enroll_reminder.py
```

Edit the `enroll_reminder.py` file and add the following code to it:

```python
import datetime
from django.conf import settings
from django.core.management.base import BaseCommand
from django.core.mail import send_mass_mail
from django.contrib.auth.models import User
from django.db.models import Count
from django.utils import timezone


class Command(BaseCommand):
    help = 'Sends an e-mail reminder to users registered more \
            than N days that are not enrolled into any courses yet'
```

```
    def add_arguments(self, parser):
        parser.add_argument('--days', dest='days', type=int)

    def handle(self, *args, **options):
        emails = []
        subject = 'Enroll in a course'
        date_joined = timezone.now().today() - \
                        datetime.timedelta(days=options['days'] or 0)
        users = User.objects.annotate(course_count=Count('courses_joined'))\
                        .filter(course_count=0,
                                date_joined__date__lte=date_joined)
        for user in users:
            message = """Dear {},
            We noticed that you didn't enroll in any courses yet.
            What are you waiting for?""".format(user.first_name)
            emails.append((subject,
                            message,
                            settings.DEFAULT_FROM_EMAIL,
                            [user.email]))
        send_mass_mail(emails)
        self.stdout.write('Sent {} reminders'.format(len(emails)))
```

This is your enroll_reminder command. The preceding code is as follows:

- The Command class inherits from BaseCommand.

- You include a help attribute. This attribute provides a short description of the command that is printed if you run the command python manage.py help enroll_reminder.

- You use the add_arguments() method to add the --days named argument. This argument is used to specify the minimum number of days a user has to be registered, without having enrolled on any course, in order to receive the reminder.

- The handle() command contains the actual command. You get the days attribute parsed from the command line. If this is not set, you use 0, so that a reminder is sent to all users that haven't enrolled on a course, regardless of when they registered. You use the timezone utility provided by Django to retrieve the current timezone-aware date with timezone.now(). date(). (You can set the timezone for your project with the TIME_ZONE setting.) You retrieve the users who have been registered for more than the specified days and are not enrolled on any courses yet. You achieve this by annotating the QuerySet with the total number of courses each user is enrolled on. You generate the reminder email for each user and append it to the emails list. Finally, you send the emails using the send_mass_mail() function, which is optimized to open a single SMTP connection for sending all emails, instead of opening one connection per email sent.

You have created your first management command. Open the shell and run your command:

```
docker compose exec web python /code/educa/manage.py \
   enroll_reminder --days=20 --settings=educa.settings.prod
```

If you don't have a local SMTP server running, you can look at *Chapter 2, Enhancing Your Blog with Advanced Features*, where you configured SMTP settings for your first Django project. Alternatively, you can add the following setting to the settings.py file to make Django output emails to the standard output during development:

```
EMAIL_BACKEND = 'django.core.mail.backends.console.EmailBackend'
```

Django also includes a utility to call management commands using Python. You can run management commands from your code as follows:

```
from django.core import management
management.call_command('enroll_reminder', days=20)
```

Congratulations! You can now create custom management commands for your applications.

Additional resources

The following resources provide additional information related to the topics covered in this chapter:

- Source code for this chapter – https://github.com/PacktPublishing/Django-4-by-example/tree/main/Chapter17
- Docker Compose overview – https://docs.docker.com/compose/
- Installing Docker Desktop – https://docs.docker.com/compose/install/compose-desktop/
- Official Python Docker image – https://hub.docker.com/_/python
- Dockerfile reference – https://docs.docker.com/engine/reference/builder/
- requirements.txt file for this chapter – https://github.com/PacktPublishing/Django-4-by-example/blob/main/Chapter17/requirements.txt
- YAML file example – https://yaml.org/
- Dockerfile build section – https://docs.docker.com/compose/compose-file/build/
- Docker restart policy – https://docs.docker.com/config/containers/start-containers-automatically/
- Docker volumes – https://docs.docker.com/storage/volumes/
- Docker Compose specification – https://docs.docker.com/compose/compose-file/
- Official PostgreSQL Docker image – https://hub.docker.com/_/postgres
- wait-for-it.sh Bash script for Docker – https://github.com/vishnubob/wait-for-it/blob/master/wait-for-it.sh
- Service startup order in Compose –https://docs.docker.com/compose/startup-order/
- Official Redis Docker image – https://hub.docker.com/_/redis
- WSGI documentation – https://wsgi.readthedocs.io/en/latest/

- List of uWSGI options – `https://uwsgi-docs.readthedocs.io/en/latest/Options.html`
- Official NGINX Docker image – `https://hub.docker.com/_/nginx`
- NGINX documentation – `https://nginx.org/en/docs/`
- `ALLOWED_HOSTS` setting – `https://docs.djangoproject.com/en/4.1/ref/settings/#allowed-hosts`
- Django's system check framework – `https://docs.djangoproject.com/en/4.1/topics/checks/`
- HTTP Strict Transport Security policy with Django – `https://docs.djangoproject.com/en/4.1/ref/middleware/#http-strict-transport-security`
- Django deployment checklist – `https://docs.djangoproject.com/en/4.1/howto/deployment/checklist/`
- Self-generated SSL/TLS certificate directory – `https://github.com/PacktPublishing/Django-4-by-example/blob/main/Chapter17/educa/ssl/`
- Let's Encrypt Certificate Authority – `https://letsencrypt.org/`
- Daphne source code – `https://github.com/django/daphne`
- Using Docker Compose in production – `https://docs.docker.com/compose/production/`
- Docker Swarm mode – `https://docs.docker.com/engine/swarm/`
- Kubernetes – `https://kubernetes.io/docs/home/`
- Django middleware – `https://docs.djangoproject.com/en/4.1/topics/http/middleware/`
- Creating custom management commands – `https://docs.djangoproject.com/en/4.1/howto/custom-management-commands/`

Summary

In this chapter, you created a production environment using Docker Compose. You configured NG-INX, uWSGI, and Daphne to serve your application in production. You secured your environment using SSL/TLS. You also implemented a custom middleware and you learned how to create custom management commands.

You have reached the end of this book. Congratulations! You have learned the skills required to build successful web applications with Django. This book has guided you through the process of developing real-life projects and integrating Django with other technologies. Now you are ready to create your own Django project, whether it is a simple prototype or a large-scale web application.

Good luck with your next Django adventure!

Other Books You May Enjoy

If you enjoyed this book, you may be interested in these other books by Packt:

101 UX Principles, Second Edition

Will Grant

ISBN: 9781803234885

- Work with user expectations, not against them
- Make interactive elements obvious and discoverable
- Optimize your interface for mobile
- Streamline creating and entering passwords
- Use animation with care in user interfaces
- How to handle destructive user actions

Coding Roblox Games Made Easy, Second Edition

Zander Brumbaugh

ISBN: 9781803234670

- Use Roblox Studio and other free resources
- Learn coding in Luau: basics, game systems, physics manipulation, etc
- Test, evaluate, and redesign to create bug-free and engaging games
- Use Roblox programming and rewards to make your first game
- Move from lobby to battleground, build avatars, locate weapons to fight
- Character selection, countdown timers, locate escape items, assign rewards
- Master the 3 Ms: Mechanics, Monetization, Marketing (and Metaverse)
- 50 cool things to do in Roblox

Packt is searching for authors like you

If you're interested in becoming an author for Packt, please visit authors.packtpub.com and apply today. We have worked with thousands of developers and tech professionals, just like you, to help them share their insight with the global tech community. You can make a general application, apply for a specific hot topic that we are recruiting an author for, or submit your own idea.

Share your thoughts

Now you've finished *Django 4 By Example, Fourth Edition*, we'd love to hear your thoughts! Scan the QR code below to go straight to the Amazon review page for this book and share your feedback or leave a review on the site that you purchased it from.

https://packt.link/r/1801813051

Your review is important to us and the tech community and will help us make sure we're delivering excellent quality content.

Index

Printed in Great Britain
by Amazon

11208507R00434